*Historical map of the Great Lakes region*

MAP 1.  MICHIGAN OUTLINE MAP

# MICHIGAN CENSUSES 1710-1830
## UNDER THE FRENCH, BRITISH, AND AMERICANS

Edited by Donna Valley Russell

DETROIT SOCIETY FOR GENEALOGICAL RESEARCH, INC.

Detroit • 1982

Copyright © 1982
Detroit Society for Genealogical Research, Inc.
c/o the Burton Historical Collection
Detroit Public Library
5201 Woodward Avenue
Detroit, Michigan 48202
All rights reserved

Library of Congress Card Catalogue No.: 82-70756
ISBN 0-943112-00-1

Printed in the United States of America

## CONTENTS

| | | | |
|---|---|---|---|
| Preface | vii | 1810 Census of Detroit | 87 |
| Acknowledgements | viii | 1810 Census of Michilimackinac | 100 |
| | | | 100 |
| 1710 Census of Detroit | 3 | 1820 Census of Michigan | 101 |
| | | Town of Detroit | 102 |
| 1743 Potier's Census | 13 | Wayne County | 109 |
| | | Michilimackinac County | 120 |
| 1750 Census of Detroit | 15 | Macomb County | 129 |
| | | Monroe County | 136 |
| 1762 Census | 19 | Brown County | 145 |
| | | Prairie du Chien, Crawford County | 146 |
| 1765 Census | 29 | 1827 Wayne County | 149 |
| | | Monguagon Township | 150 |
| 1768 Inhabitants of Detroit | 35 | Hamtramck Township | 150 |
| | | Brownstown Township | 152 |
| 1779 Census | 39 | Bucklin Township | 153 |
| | | Springwells Township | 154 |
| 1780 Census of Fort St. Joseph | 47 | Huron Township | 155 |
| | | Plymouth Township | 155 |
| 1782 Census | 49 | Ecorce Township | 156 |
| South Shore: Sandwich | 50 | City of Detroit | 157 |
| North Shore: Detroit | 52 | | |
| | | 1830 Census of Michigan | 161 |
| 1792 Petite Côte Census | 57 | Wayne County | 162 |
| | | City of Detroit | 170 |
| 1796 Census of Wayne County | 59 | Oakland County | 179 |
| Combined List of Detroit | 60 | Macomb County | 190 |
| Northeast and Southwest Suburbs | 62 | Clinton Township | 190 |
| West of the City | 63 | Shelby Township | 192 |
| River Rouge and Ecorce River | 64 | Washington Township | 192 |
| River Raisin | 66 | Ray Township | 194 |
| Au Sable River | 68 | St. Clair County | 194 |
| Rivière aux Loutres | 68 | Clay Township | 194 |
| Northeast of the City | 68 | Cottrellville Township | 195 |
| Grand Marais to Grosse Pointe | 70 | St. Clair Township | 195 |
| Grosse Pointe | 71 | Desmond Township | 196 |
| Huron River | 72 | Washtenaw County | 196 |
| Pointe aux Tremblés | 73 | Ypsilanti | 196 |
| | | Ann Arbor | 197 |
| 1802 Tax List of Wayne County | 75 | Ypsilanti | 197 |
| Detroit | 76 | Ann Arbor | 198 |
| Hamtramck | 78 | Dexter | 200 |
| Sargent Township | 80 | Ann Arbor | 200 |
| St. Clair Township | 82 | Panama | 210 |
| | | Saline | 202 |
| 1805 Lists | 83 | Panama | 203 |
| | | Ypsilanti | 203 |

v

1830 Census of Michigan (continued)

| | |
|---|---|
| St. Joseph County | 203 |
|   White Pigeon Township | 203 |
|   Sherman Township | 204 |
|   Green Township | 204 |
|   Flowerfield Township | 205 |
| Berrien County | 206 |
|   Niles Township | 206 |
| Cass County | 206 |
|   Dexter Township | 206 |
|   Ontwa Township | 206 |
|   Penn Township | 206 |
|   Legrange Township | 207 |
|   Pokagon Township | 208 |
| Van Buren County | 208 |
|   Penn Township | 208 |
| Michilimackinac County | 208 |
| Brown County | 210 |
| Crawford County | 212 |
| Chippewa County | 213 |
| Iowa County | 216 |

## MAPS

| | | |
|---|---|---|
| | Canada, by de l'Isle, 1703 (detail) | end papers |
| 1. | Michigan Outline Map, 1982 | frontispiece |
| 2. | Canada, by Bellin, 1755 (detail) | 8-9 |
| 3. | Detroit River, by de Léry, 1752 | 10-11 |
| 4. | Detroit River, by de Léry, 1749 | 12 |
| 5. | Detroit, by de Léry, 1752 | 18 |
| 6. | Detroit River, by Bellin, 1764, with insert of Fort Pontchartrain, 1749 | 26-27 |
| 7. | Detroit and Environs, by Montrésor, 1763 | 28 |
| 8. | Canada, by de l'Isle, 1703 (detail) | 34 |
| 9. | Artist's conception of Fort Pontchartrain in 1740 | 38 |
| 10. | Detroit in 1796, by Burton | 46 |
| 11. | Lake Erie Private Claims, by Greeley, 1810 | 92-93 |
| 12. | Detroit Private Claims, by Greeley, 1810 | 94-95 |
| 13. | Lake St. Clair Private Claims, by Greeley, 1810 | 96-97 |
| 14. | Detroit Prior to the Fire of 1805, by Burton, 1889 | 98-99 |
| 15. | Michigan Counties in 1818 | 108 |
| 16. | Michigan, by Judd, 1824 | 134-135 |
| 17. | Michigan in 1830 | 148 |
| 18. | Township Map of Wayne County, 1827 | 149 |
| 19. | Michigan and the Great Lakes, by Bradford, 1835 (detail) | 220-221 |

# PREFACE

The purpose of this book is to assemble in one place full transcriptions of all the censuses taken in Michigan before statehood in 1837. Some of the eighteen enumerations found here have been published previously, but in such disparate forms and locations that the researcher who is attempting to trace a family over the period involved in this study would have difficulty locating them all.

In the introduction to each census here, the location of the original, as well as the previous publication (if such exists), is cited. Many of these, notably those that appeared in the *Detroit Society for Genealogical Research Magazine*, were annotated. Permission to reprint has been granted by the archive or collection owning the original and the previous publisher in all cases. Other censuses have been annotated here for the first time.

The Detroit Society for Genealogical Research has also published in a separate volume an *Index to the 1840 Federal Population Census of Michigan,* edited by Estelle A. McGlynn (Detroit, 1977). *The Index to the 1850 Federal Population Census of Michigan,* compiled by the Michigan Genealogical Council and the Michigan Society of the American Daughters of the Revolution, was published in 1976 as a Bicentennial Project. Other county indices of Federal, as well as many state, censuses have been done by local genealogical societies.

## ACKNOWLEDGEMENTS

The following people were of tremendous help in the compilation of this book, and I extend my sincere appreciation to them: Mary Jane Frederickson for proofreading, Harriette Marr Wheeler for editing, George Ely Russell, C.G., F.A.S.G., F.N.G.S., for guidance, Jim Hansen of the State Historical Society of Wisconsin for help with the portions pertaining to his state, Jocelyn Koenig for indexing, Michael Knes of the Burton Historican Collection for advice and help with the maps, Janice Beebe, C.G.R.S., for typing the index, Joan Zenow for alphabetizing, and Nemo Warr, who photographed the maps.

Donna Valley Russell

# INTRODUCTION

Throughout the one hundred and thirty-five years of Michigan's history before statehood was granted on 26 January 1837, eighteen enumerations of the population were taken. They are scattered, partial, and often limited by region, but when collected in one place, present a complete picture of Michigan's residents during the one hundred and twenty years included in this study.

Many of the censuses included in this book were difficult to locate, principally because they were taken under three governments: the French from 1710 to 1760, the British to 1796, and the Americans from 1796 to the present. In nearly every instance (exceptions noted), the present editor has located a copy of the original and used that in the present compilation. Many errors in previous transcriptions have thus been corrected. The originals were found at the Archives of France in Paris, the Public Archives of Canada in Ottawa, the Federal Population Schedules in Washington, DC, and private papers in the manuscript collections of Quebec, Michigan, and Ohio. All are actual censuses; that is, enumerations of the population or a part of it, except two: the 1802 tax list of Wayne County and the 1805-6 lists of citizens at Detroit, made to determine the distribution of lots after the Great Fire. These are included because a Federal census was not taken in 1790 (since Michigan was held by the British) and the 1800 Federal census is not extant, if it was taken at all. The same is true of the Territorial Census taken in 1805. These lists show the population shortly before and after Michigan was granted territorial status in July 1805.

The only locations included here that are not in the present boundaries of the state of Michigan are the enumerations for Sandwich (now Windsor, Ontario) and Potier's 1743 census of the Huron Village at Amherstburg (Ontario), both of which were considered an integral part of Detroit until the American occupation in 1796, when the boundary between Canada and the United States, which had been established by the Treaty of Paris in 1783 following the American Revolution, was put into effect. Parts of Wisconsin were included in the Territorial Censuses of 1820 and 1830, because at that time the Territory of Michigan extended as far west as the Mississippi River.

# 1710 CENSUS OF DETROIT

The story of Antoine de la Mothe Cadillac, the founder of Detroit, has been told many times and will only be summarized here. He arrived 24 July 1701 with a small group of followers to establish a colony in the wilderness, the purpose of which was to develop the trade on the Great Lakes and defend the country against the English. He left Detroit in 1710 to serve as Governor of Louisiana, and in 1717 returned to France where he died in 1730. Of his eleven children, four were born in Detroit during his nine-year residence; his daughter Marie Therese's baptism is the first extant entry on the parish records of Ste. Anne's Church. [1]

Various and conflicting reports of the population of Detroit during those early years were reported by Cadillac himself, as well as other French officials, but no real census was made until 1710.[2] That travel in and out of the town was fluid is known, as trips to Montreal and other Great Lakes ports (notably Michilimackinac) were well recorded.[3]

The original census is at the Archives of France in Paris and is reprinted here with their permission. A copy is also available in the Burton Historical Collection of the Detroit Public Library.[4] Clarence M. Burton, Detroit's greatest historian, whose personal library was donated to the Detroit Public Library, made a copy of the census, which is now among the Cadillac Papers in both French and English[4] It also appeared in *Michigan Pioneer and Historical Collections*[5] in printed form, along with Burton's annotations, which are excellent and deferred to in the present identification of these early residents. All copies were compared by the compiler, and what follows contains only minor variations.

Burton used various manuscripts in his identifications, mainly letters and reports used by Cadillac himself, unearthed at the Archives of France, as well as the records of Ste. Anne's Church and the Montreal Notarial Records, which are primarily composed of legal contracts for the *voyageurs* and other passengers on boats coming to Detroit. Also consulted were the compilations of Canadian families by the priest Father Cyprian Tanguay.[6]

Because we now have the additional source record, *French Families of the Detroit River Region* compiled by Father Christian Denissen,[7] as well as other studies of this early period, the compiler was able to suggest further and/or alternate identifications in a very few cases. In his little book published in 1896, *Cadillac's Village*[8] 5 is a list of all the names Burton was able to find in these records, arranged alphabetically and called "Detroit's First Directory". Readers interested in tracing errant ancestors should consult this source. Remember that many of the early residents of Detroit were soldiers and had no interest in settling here, although many others did become founding fathers, and their names will be recognized by students of Detroit's history.

NOTES:

1. Ste. Anne's Church, Detroit, parish register, copy at BHC, I:5.
2. Wayne State University, *Cadillac and the Founding of Detroit* (Detroit, 1976), pp. 63-64.
3. Detroit Notarial Papers and Montreal Notarial Papers, being the records of the Royal Notaries, BHC.
4. Cadillac Papers, BHC, 6:1252 (French) and 6:1269 (English).
5. *Michigan Pioneer and Historical Collections* 33:492-5.
6. Cyprian Tanguay, *Dictionnaire des Familles Canadiennes* (Montreal, 1871).
7. Christian Denissen, *French Families of the Detroit River Region*, ed. by Harold F. Powell (Detroit, 1976).
8. Clarence M. Burton, *Cadillac's Village* (Detroit, 1896), pp. 19-35.

The census on the following page has been translated into English by the compiler; it varies only slightly from the English translation in the Cadillac Papers.

Cadillac had control of all the land in Detroit and "sold" lots to the settlers in the name of the King of France. When a parcel was transferred, a fixed rental was paid to Cadillac in lieu of taxes, in addition to a sum paid to him personally; this was called "rights relative to his trade" or privileges. If a lot was abandoned, it reverted to Cadillac, who then resold it. Most of the deeds for these original grants of land, which are French Private Claims and so-recorded, are extant. In addition, Cadillac kept a map with the numbers of the lots assigned to each settler and the consideration. A list of these appears in *Michigan Pioneer and Historical Collections* 33:373-382.

## 1710 Census

FARMERS WITH THEIR WIVES AT DETROIT:

    Delorme[1]       Des Rochers[4]
    Langlois[3]      La Jeunesse[5]
    Parent[5]        Mallet[6]

SOLDIERS WHO HAVE HOUSES ONLY, WITHIN AND WITHOUT THE FORT, AND DID NOT TAKE LAND:

    St. Aubin[7]      Delisle[9]
    La Fleur[8]

CANADIANS WHO HAVE WIVES AT DETROIT:

    La Croix[10]      Masse[12]
    Le Roy[11]        Turpin[13]

    Vin Despagne, widower[14]

FRENCHMEN WHOSE WIVES DID NOT WANT TO GO TO DETROIT:

    Chesne[15]      St. Onge[16]

CANADIANS:

    Gastineau, wife at Three Rivers[17]      Fabeau, wife at Montreal[26]
    Lesperance, bachelor[18]      the brothers Trudeaux, bachelors[27]
    Le Moyne, bachelor[19]      Rose, bachelor[28]
    Michel Campau, wife at Montreal[20]      Dardenne, bachelor[29]
    Mounier, bachelor[21]      Despre, wife at Montreal[30]
    Despens, bachelor[22]      Bisaillon, wife at Detroit[31]
    Livernois au Gaudet, bachelor[23]      Cardinal, bachelor[32]
    Roberts, wife at Detroit[24]      St. Yves, bachelor[33]
    Blondin *dit* Chevalier, bachelor[25]      Philis, wife at Detroit[34]

They are all lodged in houses built of stakes set upright, and earth, all thatched with grass; the commandant's is like the others, since the King and Company have given up bearing the cost. There are only two built of logs, one upon another; the chapel, where the missionary lives, and the warehouse of the Company. Outside the fort, at a distance of half a gunshot, there is a miserable barn and a house which serves as a stable. The mill has been struck by lightening three times this summer, which has damaged it severly, bad as it was before; it is a good gunshot from the fort, between the fort of Detroit and that of the Hurons. It is absolutely necessary to rebuild the fort entirely, from one end to another. *Hic opus, hic labor est.*

1. FRANCOIS FAFARD *dit* DELORME, farmer and interpreter, prob. b. Three Rivers ca 1660; d. Detroit 28 Jan. 1734; m. (1) Champlain 3 Nov. 1683 Magdeleine Jobin; m. (2) Detroit 30 Oct. 1713 Barbe Loisel, widow of Pierre Roussel. Lot 28 in 1707.

2. JACQUES LANGLOIS, b. 1667; d. Montreal 30 Jan. 1733; m. Marie Dusault. Lot 15.

3. JOSEPH PARENT, farmer, master toolman, and brewer; b. Que. 27 Jan. 1669; m. Beauport 31 Jan. 1690 Magdeleine Marette *dit* Lepine. Lot 37.

4. JACOB DE MARSAC DE L'OMTROU, SIEUR DESROCHERS, sgt. in Marine Dept.; b. France 1667; bur. Detroit 27 Apr. 1747; m. Montreal 12 June 1706 Thérèse David, widow of Martin Masse. To Detroit with Cadillac. Lot 30.

5. ETIENNE ESTEVE *dit* LAJEUNESSE (name often spelled STEBRE in Ste. Anne's records); in army; b. France; d. Detroit 16 July 1736; m. Que. 12 Apr. 1706 Madeleine Frappier. Lot 23 in 1707.

6. PIERRE MALLET, b. Montreal 17 Apr. 1670; m. Madeleine Thunes *dit* Dufresne, widow of François Peletier. Lot 43.

7. JEAN CASSE *dit* ST. AUBIN, corp. in garrison; b. France 1659; bur. Detroit 27 Feb. 1759, aged 100 yrs; m. Que. 7 Feb. 1707 Louisa Gaultier. Lot 46.

8. PIERRE RENE POIRIER *dit* LAFLEUR, farmer and soldier; b. 1666; bur. Montreal 5 Feb. 1744; m. Lachine 12 June 1707 Clemence Maupetit.

9. FRANCOIS BIENVENU *dit* DELISLE, b. France; bur. Detroit 29 Sept. 1751, aged 88 yrs; m. (1) Que. 1701 Genevieve Charon dit Lafrenière; m. (2) Montreal 20 Aug. 1708 Anne Lemoyne. Lot 22 in 1704.

10. JACQUES HUBERT *dit* LACROIX, b. 1654; bur. Montreal 22 Oct. 1715; m. (1) there 24 Nov. 1681 Marguerite Godet; m. (2) there 30 Sept. 1699 Romania Berthelet de Veau. In Detroit by 30 May 1705.

11. PIERRE ROY, b. Laprarie 3 Jan. 1677; m. Marguerite Ouabankikove, a Miami Indian. Came with Cadillac. Lot 51.

12. FRANCOIS MASSE, farmer; m. 1702 Marguerite Couc *dit* Lafleur, widow of Jean Fafard. A Michel Masse bought Lot 17.

13. JEAN BAPTISTE TURPIN, b. Montreal 23 Nov. 1685; m. Detroit 5 May 1710 Marguerite Fafard, dau. of Francois Fafard, above. May have returned to Montreal.

14. Poss. DESPINS or DESPEIGNES, or a variant of LEMOYNE.

15. PIERRE ST. ONGE *dit* CHENE, tailor; b. France 1654; m. (1) Montreal 29 Nov. 1676 Louise Jeanne Bailly; m. (2) there 9 Oct. 1700 Marie Moitie, widow of Jean Magnan. Lots 1 and 36.

16. CMB calls him PIERRE GAREAU *dit* ST ONGE, which suggests a relationship with Pierre above. A Pierre was b. Boucherville 1 May 1673; m. Montreal 23 Sept. 1696 Marie Guertin, widow of --- Laverge, but this man is not related to the Pierre here. Also called Xaintonge.

17. CMB calls him LOUIS GASTINEAU, SIEUR DE STE ANNE or SIEUR DU PLESSIS, b. 1674; d. 20 Feb. 1750; m. Batiscan 22 Jan. 1710 Jeanne Lemoine. Got in trouble with Cadillac and started a suit against him in Quebec. Lot 36

18. BONADVENTURE COMPIEN *dit* L'ESPERANCE, a soldier and farmer who m. Catherine Laplante. Lot 7.

19. Three LEMOYNE brothers were in Detroit at this time: Alexis, Jacques, and René. Prob. one of the latter two. René had Lot 64 and Jacques Lot 65.

## 1710 Census

20. MICHEL CAMPAU, farmer, b. Montreal 14 June 1667; bur. there 9 Sept. 1737; m. there 7 Jan. 1696 Jeanne Masse. In Detroit by 1703 when got in trouble for accusing another resident of setting the fort on fire. This is not the progenitor of the large Campau family here. Lot 18.

21. Prob. ALEXIS LEMOYNE, SIEUR DE MOUNIER. See 19.

22. DESPINS, the *voyageur* and trader who supplied the Jesuit missionaries at Detroit.

23. FRANCOIS BENOIT *dit* LIVERNOIS, b. Montreal 9 Aug. 1676; m. 1710 Angelique Chagnon. Did not stay (CMB). More likely, JACQUES GAUDE, b. Montreal 30 Oct. 1659; m. Three Rivers 4 Nov. 1696 Marguerite Duguay. Their son Jacques m. Detroit 1743 (Ed.)

24. PIERRE ROBERT *dit* LAFONTAINE, b. Boucherville 21 Sept. 1671; m. Lachine 27 Jan. 1698 Angélique Ptolomé. Had brothers Prudent, Francois, and Joseph, all in Detroit in 1708. Lot 62.

25. PIERRE BLONDIN *dit* CHEVALIER.

26. PIERRE FAVREAU *dit* LAGRANDEUR. Lot 3 in 1707.

27. CMB calls them JEAN BAPTISTE TOUTEAU, who m. Magdeleine Parent 1 Sept. 1715 and d. 1754, and his brother JOSEPH, who d. Montreal 1745. Both came in 1702. Joseph was a carpenter. Are they sons of Etienne Truteau of Montreal? (Ed.)

28. NICOLAS ROSE, a soldier, b. Que. 26 Aug. 1674; d. 1746. Bought Lot 9 from M. Argenteuil.

29. TOUISSANT DARDENNE, b. Montreal 23 Jan. 1671; to Detroit 1707. Lot 55.

30. Prob. JOSEPH GUYON DES PRES, b. Que. 22 July 1666; m. Montreal 7 Sept. 1697 Madeleine Petit-Boismorel. Lot 4.

31. PIERRE CARDINAL, to Detroit 1708. CMB claims he is the only Cardinal in Detroit who was a bachelor in 1710, but this is not consistent with Denissen, which shows him m. at Montreal 17 Sept. 1685 Marie Matou. Could also be Jacques, b. Montreal 1685, cousin of Pierre and brother-in-law of Jacques Huber dit Lacroix above.

32. MICHEL BISSAILLON, b. France; d. by 1728; m. Detroit 30 June 1710 Marguerite Fafard. Bough Lot 5 from Joseph du Vestin.

33. PIERRE ST. YVES, *voyageur*, to Detroit 1710; b. Montreal 18 Oct. 1682. He had a brother Joseph who was also in Detroit in 1710, aged 18 yrs. Tanguay says the name is St. Agne dit Hogue.

34. JACQUES DESMOULINS *dit* PHILIS, m. Charlotte Savarias who d. Detroit 1744. Of their 8 children b. in Detroit bet. 1708 and 1723, six died here, some of the smallpox in 1733. Lot 34.

MAP 2. CANADA, by Jacques Nicolas Bellin, 1755 (detail)

(Courtesy of Burton Historical Collection)

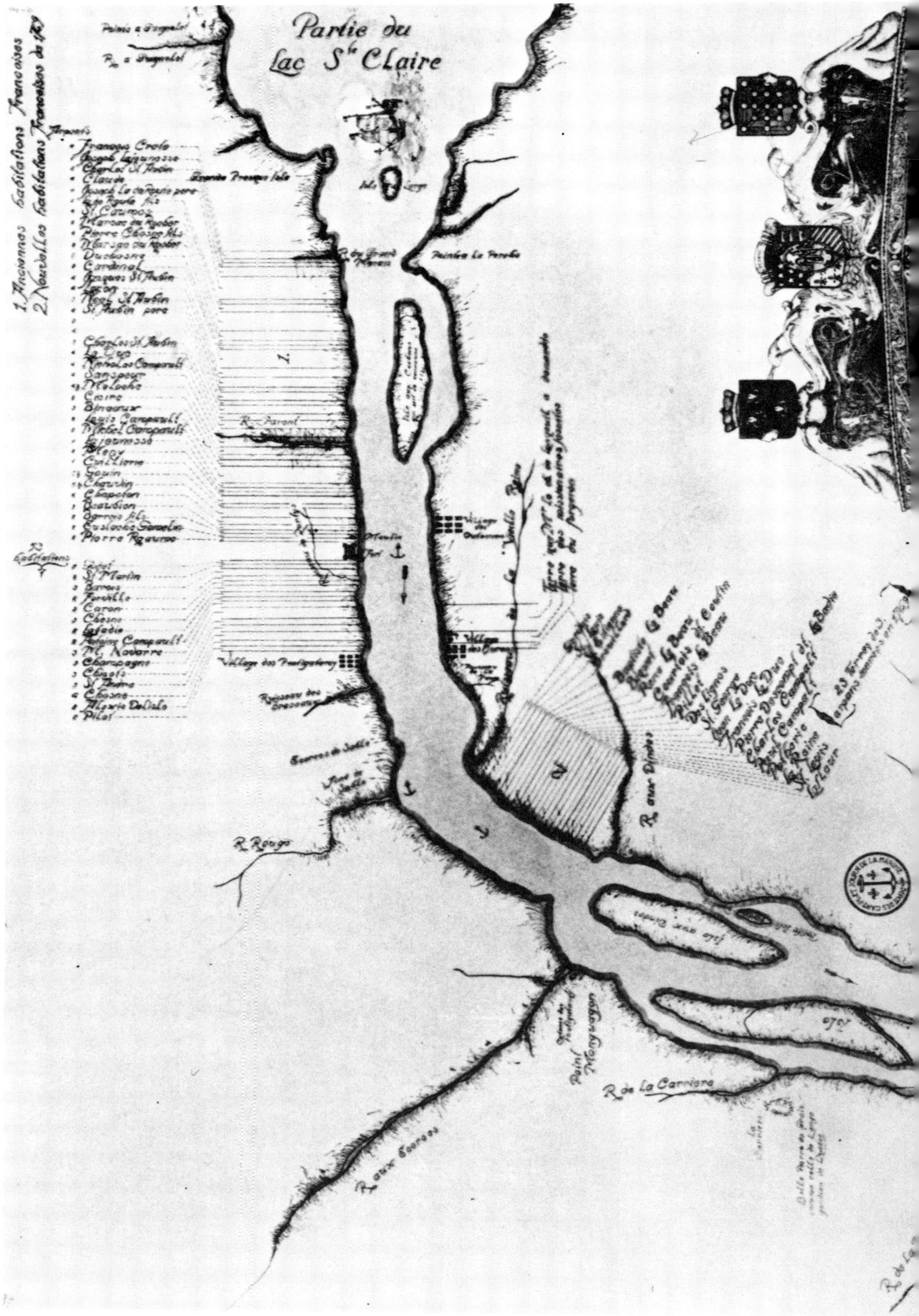

Partie du Lac Ste Claire
1. Anciennes habitations Francoises
2. Nouvelles habitations Francoises de 1749
Pointe La Peche
R. Rouge
R. aux Ecorces
R. de La Carriere
Point Monguagon
Village des Poutiyatamy

MAP 3. DETROIT RIVER, by Chaussegros de Lery, 1752  (Courtesy of Burton Historical Collection)

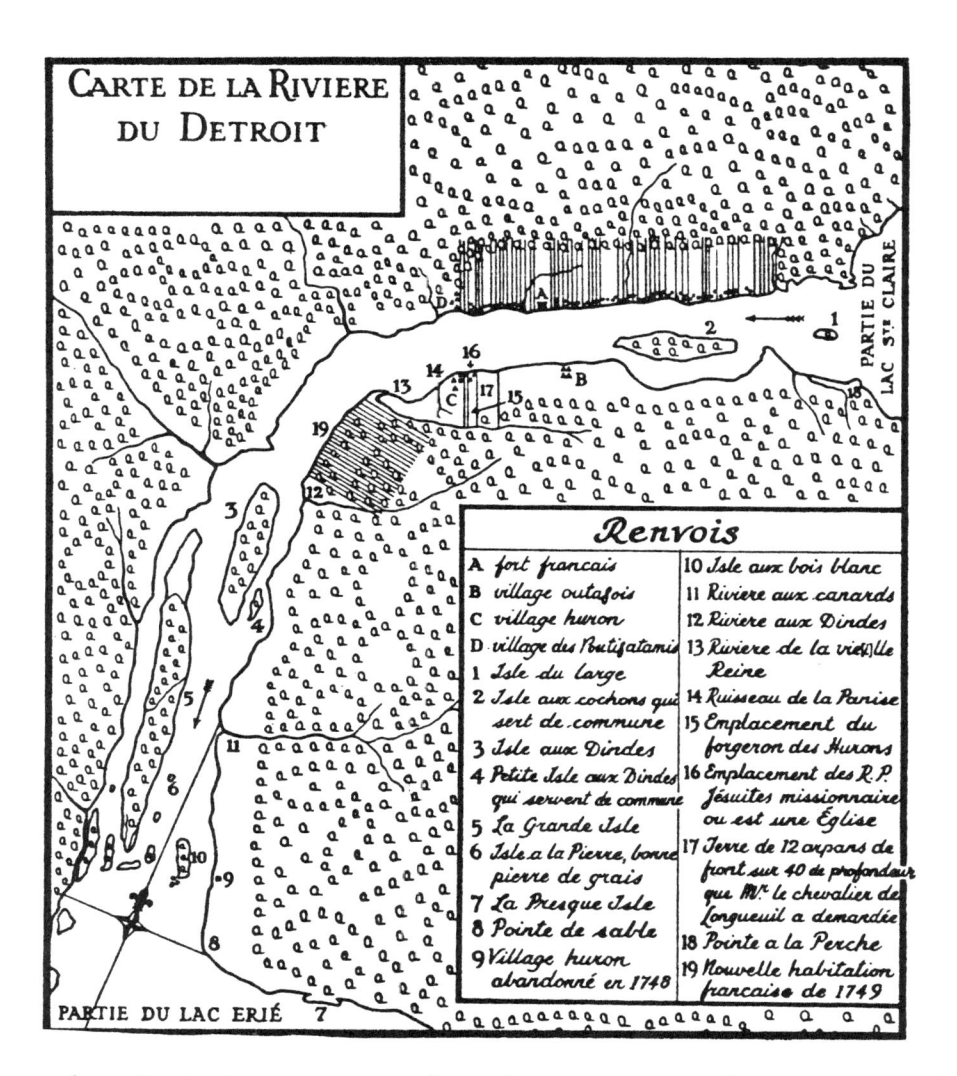

MAP 4   DETROIT RIVER, by Chaussegros de Léry, 1749
(Courtesy of Archives du Ministere des Colonies, Paris)

# POTIER'S CENSUS OF 1743

The Jesuit priest, Father Pierre Potier, pastor of the Huron Indian Mission of the Assumption on the south shore of the Detroit River, and first pastor of the Assumption Church in Sandwich, made a census of the mission at Bois Blanc Island near presentday Amherstburg, Ontario.

He published the census as part of a grammar and dictionary of the Huron language, the Indians words translated into French. This massive undertaking comprises the entire volume *Fifteenth Report of the Bureau of Archives for the Province of Ontario,* by Alexander Fraser (Toronto, 1920) and consists of photocopies of the actual pages of this *Elementa Grammaticae Huronicae.* The original is housed at the Archives de la Compagnie de Jésus in St. Jerôme, Quebec. A transcription of the census only was made by Louis Goulet. Called *Potier's Essex County Census* and printed in Amherstburg in 1925, it is not entirely accurate; interested readers are referred to the former source from which they can see the original writing. This census of 1743 should not be confused with another Potier made in 1747, which is housed at the Bibliothèque de Ville de Montreal, Salle Gagnon.

The Huron Indians who gathered here in the 18th century were located originally at Huronia on Georgian Bay, Lake Huron, scattered in an area about equal to Simcoe County today. They became the focus of the first missionary attempt in the west by the French Jesuits, because of their habit of living in fixed habitations and villages. A successful program of Christianization took place there from 1639 to 1649, but in the latter year a final brutal attack by the Iroquois wiped the community out. The Indians scattered, some to Manitoulin and other islands in Georgian Bay, as well as other northern parts of Lakes Huron and Michigan; most, however, went to Lorette, Quebec, near Montreal. The Huronia Mission has been reconstructed and is a tourist attraction near Midland, Ontario. Later, while Cadillac was at Detroit from 1701 to 1710, he encouraged Indians from several tribes to settle near the post in order to insure a continued supply of fur pelts. Included were Ottawas, Potawatomis, Ojibways (called Chippewas by the English), as well as the dissipated Hurons (also called Wyandots).

Potier's census of the Huron settlement is very specific as to the plan of the habitations; some are particularly graphic, such as this: "13th cabin - 40 under the roof of drink, gluttony, dinginess, and despair." The 413 names of the people are more descriptive than specific, often referring to relationships, such as "niece of the old man," "woman with blinky eyes," or "the one-armed Nicolas of the new house." These names will not be repeated here.

Worthy of inclusion in this compilation, however, are the lists of the French at Bois Blanc and Detroit on 22 December 1743, which appear on page 154 of the original. Each name is preceded by an Indian name given to the person and the title "Monsieur." Annotations by the editor, if such could be made, follow the name as it appeared.

FRENCH AT BOIS BLANC:

L'ESPERANCE (Jean Baptiste Billiau *dit* Lesperance, b. France, d. by 1788)
OLD REGIS
WORKER OF THE SOIL GOYAU (Jean Baptiste Gouyou *dit* Lagarde 1688-1768, soldier)
ST MARTIN (Jean Baudry *dit* Desbuttes *dit* St. Martin 1684-1755, interpreter to Hurons)

FRENCH AT DETROIT:

DE LONGEUIL (prob. a descendant of the Lemoyne de Longeuil family)
DEMUISSEAU, OFFICER (poss. Nicolas D'Aillbout DesMusseaux, Captain of Troops)
DEMUISSEAU, COM. (commissary?)
NAVARRE (Robert Navarre 1709-1791)
CHENE (Charles Chêne 1694-by 1755)
LA BUTTE (Pierre Chêne *dit* LaButte 1698-1774, brother of above)
CARON (Vital Caron 1702-1747)
BONDE, CLEAN? TONGUE (Joseph Douaire de Bondy 1700-1760)
CHAPOTON ( Jean Chapoton 1684-1760)
DE RUISSEAU, HONEST ( Alexis Trotier Sieur de Ruisseau 1688-1769)
GODET (Jean Baptiste Godet (m. 1742), father of Paul who later settled at Sandwich)
DEROCHER, GOOD MAN
BELLEPERCHE, BAD PERCH (Pierre Belleperche 1699-1767)
CHEVIN (Charles Chauvin 1702-1772)
BEAUBIEN (Antoine Cuillerier *dit* Beaubien 1697-after 1763)
CHICOT (Zacharias Cicotte 1708-1775)
BAROIL, HAND BARROW (Joseph Baril of Ste. Anne de La Perade, Quebec)
DE ST PIERRE (poss. Pierre St. Pierre *dit* Tranchemontagne or a son)
SAGUIN (François Seguin *dit* Laderoute, b. France, d. 1747)
QUEBEC MERCHANT
DOUVILLE
MAURISSEAU (poss. Pierre Morriseau, whose son Victor later came to Detroit)
LA CORN (Corneau? Pierre came later. Also a LeCorneau *dit* Sanssoucy)
BIEUS, THE HORN (poss. Bertrand de Bluche *dit* La Serre, a soldier)
BELETRE (Françcois Marie Picoté de Belêtre)

COMMANDERS AT DETROIT:

CELEREN (Jean Baptiste Celeron, associated with Belêtre)
DE NOYAU (poss. Pierre Payen de Noyon, related to DesMusseaux above)
DE BOISBERT --- MOUTH (Boisverd a large family)
PAEN (Ives-Jacques Pean, Seigneur of Lirandière, Commander of Fort Pontchartrain)
DE NOYELLES
DES CHAILLON (--- D'Eschaillons *dit* St. Ours.)
PAJOR (prob. Thomas Pageot 1707-?, son of Thomas, associated with Huron Mission)

# CENSUS OF THE INHABITANTS OF DETROIT
## ON SEPTEMBER 1st, 1750

The original of this census is at the Public Archives of Canada, Ottawa, Ontario, among the papers Archives des Colonies (Series G1, 461:28), and is reprinted here with their permission. A copy was made from microfilm (MG1, 461, reel F-765) and examined by the present editor.

The census was first published in Ernest J. Lajeunesse, *The Windsor Border Region* (Toronto, 1960), pp. 54-56. Father Lajeunesse has also given DSGR permission to reprint.

The only additions made in the present transcription are the full names for those that are partial; these appear immediately following the name as it appears on the census. The full census has additional categories, not repeated here: arpents of land under cultivation, sheaves of wheat, sheaves of oats, arpents of land in corn, horses, oxen, cows, hogs, and poultry. Figures for these categories can be found in the Lajeunesse transcription.

| Name | WOMEN | BOYS 15+ | GIRLS 15+ | BOYS -15 | GIRLS -15 | SLAVES |
|---|---|---|---|---|---|---|
| YACINTHE RÉOME (Hyacinthe Réaume) | 1 | 1 | 1 | 3 | 2 | - |
| FORVILLE (Pierre Tetard dit Fortville) | - | - | - | 1 | - | - |
| DEMOUCHELLE (Louis Joseph Dumouchel) | - | - | - | - | 1 | - |
| CECIRE (Jean) | 1 | - | 3 | 1 | 1 | 1 |
| GAUDET (poss. Jean Baptiste Godet) | 1 | - | - | 1 | 1 | - |
| MELOCHE (Pierre) | 1 | 2 | 3 | 2 | 2 | 1 |
| GAMELIN (Ignace) | 1 | 1 | - | 2 | 3 | 2 |
| JEAN PILET | - | - | - | - | 2 | - |
| LASELLE | - | - | - | - | - | - |
| L. PARENT (Laurent) | 1 | - | 1 | 3 | 4 | - |
| LE DUC (François Le Duc dit Persil) | 1 | 1 | 1 | 1 | - | - |
| CHAUVIN (Charles) | 1 | 1 | - | 4 | - | 2 |
| CHÊNE, PERE (Charles, father) | 1 | 1 | - | 2 | - | 2 |
| BEAUBIEN (Antoine Cuillerier dit Beaubien) | 1 | - | - | 2 | 2 | 1 |
| DERUISSAUX (Alexis Trottier, Sieur de Ruisseau) | 1 | - | - | - | - | 1 |
| CICOT (Zacharias Cicotte) | 1 | - | - | 1 | 1 | 1 |
| GILLES PARENT | 1 | 1 | - | 1 | 1 | 2 |
| SEGUIN (Joseph Séguin dit Laderoute) | 1 | 2 | - | 2 | 1 | - |
| CARDINAL (Jean) | 1 | 3 | 1 | - | - | - |
| I. CHENE (prob. Isidore or Léopold) | 1 | - | - | - | 1 | - |
| PELTIER (Jean Baptiste) | 1 | - | - | 2 | 3 | - |
| JAC. ST. AUBIN (Jacques) | 1 | - | - | 2 | 1 | - |
| NICOL CAMPAU | 1 | - | - | 1 | 5 | - |
| PIERRE REOME (Réaume) | 1 | - | - | 2 | 3 | - |
| BARTHE (Andrew) | 1 | - | 1 | - | - | - |
| CLAUDE CAMPAU | 1 | - | - | - | - | 1 |
| BELPERCHE (Pierre Belleperche) | 1 | 2 | 1 | - | - | - |
| JANISSE (François Nicolas Janis) | 1 | - | - | 1 | 1 | 1 |
| FRANC. ROY (François) | 1 | - | - | - | - | - |
| LABUTTE (Pierre Chêne dit La Butte) | 1 | 1 | 1 | - | 1 | 1 |
| BTE MALLET (Jean Baptiste) | 1 | 1 | 1 | - | - | - |
| BTE CAMPAU (Jean Baptiste) | 1 | - | 1 | 4 | 1 | - |
| L. CAMPAU | 1 | 1 | - | 2 | - | 3 |
| MARSAC (François) | - | 1 | 2 | 2 | 2 | 1 |
| POUPARD (Charles Poupard dit Lafleur) | - | - | - | - | - | - |
| GODEFROY (Jacques Godfroy) | 1 | 1 | 1 | - | - | 1 |
| DELISLE (Alexis Bienvenu dit Delisle) | 1 | - | - | 3 | - | - |
| DE LEMOTHE (prob. Pierre Lamothe) | 1 | - | - | - | - | 1 |
| DE QUINDRE (Louis Dagneau dit Dequindre) | 1 | - | - | 2 | 2 | 2 |
| GOUIN (Claude Jean Thomas Gouin) | 1 | - | - | 2 | - | 1 |
| CHAPOTON (Jean) | 1 | 3 | 1 | 1 | 2 | - |
| GERVAIS (Charles) | 1 | - | - | 1 | - | - |
| NAVARRE (Robert) | 1 | - | 1 | 1 | 2 | - |

## 1750 Census

|  | | | | | | |
|---|---|---|---|---|---|---|
| DESPELTEAUX | 1 | - | - | - | - | - |
| CLAUDE ANDRE | 1 | - | - | - | - | 1 |
| CUILLERIER (Jean Baptiste Cuillerier *dit* Beaubien) | 1 | 1 | 1 | - | - | 1 |
| CHAMPAGNE (Pierre Huyet *dit* Champagne) | 1 | - | - | 1 | 1 | 1 |
| LABADY (Pierre Descomps *dit* Labadie) | 1 | 1 | 1 | 2 | 2 | 2 |
| BARROIS (François Lootman *dit* Barrois) | 1 | - | 1 | - | - | - |
| ST. COSME (Pierre Laurent) | 1 | - | - | 1 | 2 | 1 |
| ANTE. ROBERT (Antoine) | 1 | - | - | 2 | 1 | - |
| JACQ. PILET | 1 | 1 | 1 | - | 2 | - |
| PAUL CAMPAU | 1 | - | - | - | 2 | - |
| CHARL. CAMPAU | - | - | - | - | - | - |
| JEAN CHAUVIN | - | - | - | 2 | 2 | 1 |
| MINY (Antoine Meny) | 1 | - | - | 1 | 2 | 1 |
| LA VE ESTEVE (Madeleine Frappier, widow Pierre) | - | 2 | - | - | - | - |
| CLAU. BINO (Claude Binau) | 1 | - | - | - | - | - |
| CHARL. CASSE | 1 | - | - | - | 2 | - |
| PIERRE BOYER | 1 | - | - | 1 | 3 | - |
| GABRIEL CASSE | 1 | 1 | - | - | - | - |
| NOEL CASSE | 1 | - | - | 2 | 1 | - |
| LOSON (Nicolas Lauson) | 1 | 1 | 1 | 1 | 1 | - |
| DUCHESNE (François Gastinon *dit* Duchêne) | 1 | - | - | 2 | 1 | - |
| JOSEPH SEGUIN (*dit* Laderoute, son) | 1 | - | - | - | - | - |
| CRÊTEL | - | - | - | - | - | - |
| COMTOIS (prob. Contois *dit* Cousin) | - | - | - | - | - | - |
| JEAN CARDINAL | 1 | 1 | - | 2 | 1 | - |
| F. DENOYER (François) | 1 | - | - | - | 1 | - |
| PATEL | 1 | - | - | - | 1 | - |
| ST. GEORGE (François Godfroy *dit* St. George) | 1 | - | - | - | 1 | - |
| BIGRAS (Joseph Amable Bigras *dit* Fauvel) | 1 | 3 | 1 | 2 | 2 | - |
| JENETTE (Jean Baptiste Le Tourneau *dit* Janette) | - | - | - | - | - | - |
| ST. GERMAIN | - | - | - | - | - | - |
| COURVILLE (poss. Joseph Cadieux *dit* Courville) | - | - | - | - | - | - |
| PIER. TREMBLAY | - | - | 1 | 3 | 1 | - |
| AMBROISE (Tremblay) | 1 | - | - | 3 | 1 | - |
| AUGUSTIN (Tremblay) | 1 | - | - | 2 | 2 | - |
| LAFOREST (Guillaume) | 1 | - | - | 1 | - | - |
| LAFEUILLADE (Joseph Davignon *dit* Lafeuillade) | 1 | 1 | - | - | - | - |
| PLICHON (Louis) | 1 | 1 | - | 1 | 2 | - |
| DINAN (Pierre) | 1 | 3 | 1 | - | - | - |
| DROUILLARD (Jean Baptiste) | 1 | 2 | 1 | 2 | 2 | - |
| MICHEL CAMPO (Campau) | 1 | - | - | 2 | 2 | - |
| LE BAU (Jean François Le Beau) | 1 | 2 | - | 1 | 1 | - |
| LOUIS BINO (Binau) | 1 | - | - | 4 | 3 | - |
| F. MALLET (François) | 1 | 1 | - | - | - | - |
| REVAU (Louis Reveau) | 1 | - | - | - | 1 | - |
| MONMIRELLE Pierre Durand *dit* Montmirel) | 1 | - | - | - | - | - |
| VILLERS (Louis) | 1 | - | - | 1 | 2 | - |
| METAYER (Joseph Meteier) | 1 | - | - | - | 1 | - |
| DUFOURD (Pierre Dufour) | 1 | - | - | 4 | 3 | - |
| JEAN GOYAU | 1 | 1 | - | 1 | - | - |
| BTE. GOYAU | 1 | - | - | 1 | 1 | - |
| ANT. CAMPAU | 1 | 1 | 4 | - | - | - |
| IGNACE BOYER | 1 | - | - | - | - | - |

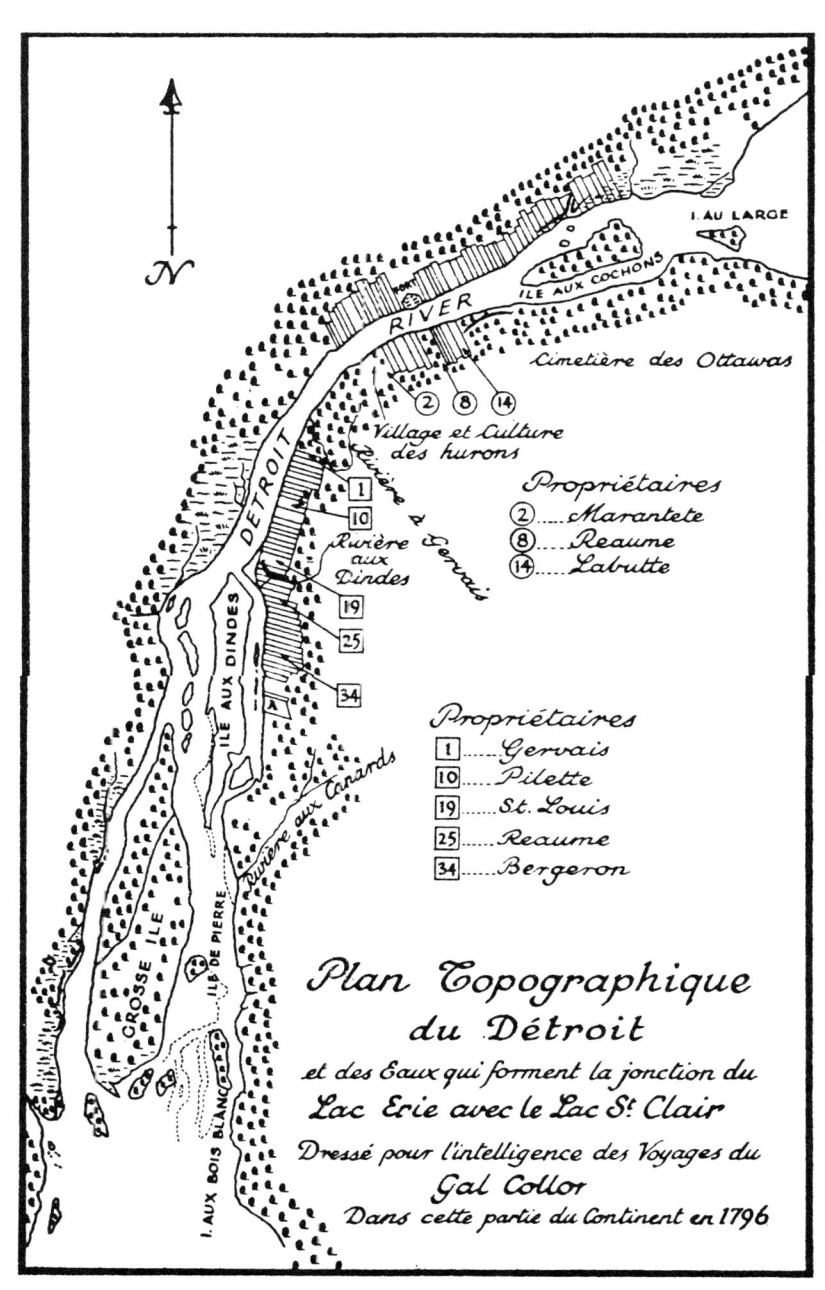

MAP 5.   DETROIT, by Chaussegros de Lery, 1752
(Courtesy of Burton Historical Collection)

# 1762 CENSUS

This census, previously undated, was found among the manuscripts of the Burton Historical Collection, variously described as of 1706 and 1796. Because the ages of the farmers are given, it is clear that the actual date was 1762, and, specifically, September or October.

Even though the British had occupied Detroit by late 1760, this census is in French, probably because it was taken by Robert Navarre, the French Notary, who was allowed to continue his duties as a liaison between the French population and the English commandant.

More data appear here than in other censuses of the period. Many French soldiers are included and place of birth is sometimes given. Note that women are not counted, but that boys, girls, slaves, and engagés (hired help) are categorized. In addition, the census is geographically arranged. Detroit was settled for about ten miles on either side of Fort Pontchartrain, as well as across the Detroit River. Arpents of land (actually 192.24 linear feet, but the term is often used interchangeably with our acre) are designated for each owner, as well as the width of each lot in the stockaded fort.

The population totals indicate 318 men, 229 boys, 187 girls, 65 slaves, and 71 hired men, although the latter may be included with their own families also. Beware of these figures, however, because many people sought the protection the fort offered and also owned land on which they farmed. The reverse is also true, that other people were living on their farms at the time of the enumeration, even though they also had lots in the fort. By comparing the entries of those enumerated twice, it is obvious which situation applies to a given individual. Often an entry shows the land occupied by hired help only. Therefore, about 85 farmers are counted twice. Attempting an estimate of the total population in 1762, we must first guess the number of women. Based on the ratio of three women to four men, as in other censuses, about 174 women would be added to the above figures. Therefore, a very rough estimate might be between 900 and 950, which is consistent with the total of 1100 in 1765.

Remember that French spelling in those days meant little or nothing; everything was phonetic. The identifications are not authoritative. Some were unidentifiable because the writing was illegible, others because the people were transients and not included in other Detroit records. Those in the fort were not asked their ages and, therefore, may be misidentified.

Data are given in the following order, except where otherwise indicated: name as shown on manuscript, identification in parentheses, birthplace if other than Canada, age, arpents of land, boys, girls, slaves, hired help. A final column gave each man's financial status (rich, comfortable, poor); because most were "comfortable," only the other two are mentioned here.

This census, originally published as "Detroit 1762 Census," by Donna Valley Stuart, appeared in the *National Genealogical Society Quarterly* 68:15-20. It is reprinted, with only minor corrections, with their permission.

## NORTH OF THE RIVER FROM THE FORT TO THE POTTAWATOMIE VILLAGE

|  | | | | | | | |
|---|---|---|---|---|---|---|---|
| St. Martin (Touissant Antoine Adhemar-St. Martin) | 26 | 2 | 0 | 1 | 1 | 2 | |
| Baroie (Jean Baptiste Lootman *dit* Barrois), b. Eng. | 72 | 3 | 1 | 1 | 0 | 0 | poor |
| Forville (Peter Tetard *dit* Forville) 2 acres | 54 | | | | | | |
| Gamelin (Laurence Eustache Gamelin) | 56 | 2 | 4 | 2 | 1 | 1 | |
| Charle Chaisne (Chêne *dit* Caossa) | 33 | 3 | 2 | 1 | 0 | 1 | |
| La Bady (Antoine Descomps *dit* Labadie), b. France | 35 | 2 | 2 | 1 | 1 | 0 | |
| L'hivernois (Etienne Benoit Livernois) | 40 | 2 | 1 | 1 | 0 | 1 | |
| Navarre (Robert Navarre), b. France | 52 | 3 | 3 | 2 | 0 | 1 | |
| Claude Campeau | 47 | 3 | 0 | 0 | 0 | 2 | |
| Cavasscie (Joseph Cabassier) | 40 | 5 | 1 | 2 | 2 | 1 | |
| Chicoste (Zacharias Cicotte) | 50 | 3 | 1 | 1 | 5 | 1 | rich |
| St. André (Claude Landry *dit* St. André), b. France | 64 | 3 | 0 | 0 | 3 | 1 | |
| Isidore Chaisne (Chêne) | 30 | 2 | 0 | 2 | 1 | 2 | |
| Widow Chaisne (Catharine Sauvage, wid. of Charles) | 30 | 2 | 1 | 0 | 1 | 0 | |
| De Lisle (Alexis Bienvenu *dit* DeLisle) | 61 | 2 | 3 | 0 | 0 | 0 | |
| Jean Pillet | 54 | 2 | 1 | 1 | 0 | 1 | |

## NORTH OF THE RIVER FROM THE FORT NORTHEAST TO GROSSE POINTE ON LAKE STE CLAIRE

|  | | | | | | | |
|---|---|---|---|---|---|---|---|
| Jean Pillet (prob. Jacques) | 62 | 2 | 0 | 0 | 0 | 1 | |
| Beaubien (Jean Baptiste Cuillerier *dit* Beaubien) | 48 | 5 | 3 | 2 | 2 | 1 | |
| Mauran (Charles Moran) 2 acres | | | | | | | |
| Godefroy (Jacques) | 42 | 2 | 3 | 1 | 0 | 1 | |
| Chovin (Charles Chauvin) | 61 | 4 | 3 | 0 | 1 | 1 | |
| Gouen (Claude Jean Gouin) | 50 | 2 | 4 | 1 | 5 | 1 | |
| Cuillerié (Antoine Cuillerier *dit* Beaubien) | 66 | 4 | 1 | 1 | 2 | 1 | |
| Miny (Antoine Meny) | 50 | 2 | 4 | 2 | 0 | 1 | |
| Noel St. Aubin | 56 | 4 | 2 | 1 | 0 | 0 | |
| Jacques Campau | 28 | 3 | 0 | 0 | 1 | 0 | |
| Louis Campeau | 60 | 3 | 1 | 0 | 3 | 0 | |
| Simon Campeau | 22 | 3 | 0 | 0 | 1 | 0 | |
| Benault (Jean Bineau *dit* Lajeunesse) | 62 | 3 | 0 | 0 | 0 | 1 | |
| Baptiste Meloche | 22 | 3 | 1 | 1 | 2 | 0 | |
| François Meloche | 30 | 1 | 1 | 2 | 2 | 0 | |
| Peltier (Jean Baptiste) | 44 | 4 | 5 | 4 | 0 | 1 | poor |
| Barthe (Andrew) 4 acres | | | | | | | |
| Le Duc (Joseph) | 76 | 4 | 2 | 1 | 0 | 0 | poor |
| Chovin son (Noel) | 32 | 3 | 1 | 1 | 1 | 0 | |
| Pierre Boyer | 53 | 4 | 1 | 4 | 0 | 0 | |
| St. Bernard (Guillaume Bernard), b. France | 46 | 4 | 1 | 1 | 0 | 2 | |
| Gabriel St. Auben | 50 | 4 | 0 | 0 | 0 | 1 | poor |
| Ignace Boyer | 41 | 2 | 0 | 3 | 0 | 0 | poor |
| Lausennette (Antoine Nicolas Lauson) | 36 | 2 | 1 | 1 | 0 | 0 | poor |
| Jacques Lauson 2 acres | 25 | | | | | | poor |
| Jacques St. Aubin | 42 | 4 | 5 | 2 | 0 | 1 | poor |
| Joseph Cardinal | 42 | 3 | 0 | 0 | 2 | 0 | |
| Cardinal father (Jacques) | 70 | 5 | 1 | 0 | 0 | 0 | |

## 1762 Census

| Name | Age | | | | | | |
|---|---|---|---|---|---|---|---|
| Baptiste Campeau | 51 | 4 | 6 | 1 | 0 | 0 | poor |
| Marsac (François) | 56 | 8 | 3 | 3 | 1 | 2 | |
| Joseph La Deroute (Séguin *dit* Laderoute) | 43 | 2 | 0 | 5 | 0 | 1 | poor |
| Marsac son (François)  2 acres | 28 | | | | | | poor |
| Gaelan? LaDeroute (Cajetan) | 40 | 4 | 0 | 1 | 0 | 0 | poor |
| Chavin *(supra cit.)*  4 acres | | | | | | | |
| Charles St. Auben | 56 | 6 | 1 | 2 | 0 | 1 | poor |
| St. George (François Godfroy *dit* St. George) b.France | 52 | 3 | 1 | 5 | 0 | 1 | poor |
| Testieau (Jean Cardinal)  3 acres | 68 | | | | | | poor |
| Joseph Cardinal  3 acres | | | | | | | |
| Paillé (Baillie?) | 64 | 3 | 1 | 0 | 0 | 0 | |
| Quintin (Quesnel?), b. France  3 acres | 40 | | | | | | poor |
| Lenguedoc (François LaCôte *dit* Languedoc) | 42 | 6 | 1 | 2 | 0 | 1 | poor |
| Louis Campault (Campau)  3 acres | | | | | | | |
| St. Bernard *(supra cit.)*  3 acres | | | | | | | |
| Pierre Tremblet, father (Pierre Tremblay) to the Illinois River  3 acres | | | | | | | |
| Gouen *(supra cit.)*  9 acres | | | | | | | |
| Tremblet son (Pierre Tremblay) | | 3 | 0 | 0 | 0 | 1 | poor |
| Tremblet son (Louis Michael Tremblay)  3 acres | 20 | | | | | | poor |
| Joregny? b. France  3 acres | | | | | | | |
| Guillaume LaForest | 41 | 3 | 3 | 2 | 0 | 1 | poor |
| LaCource (Luke Antoine Rivard *dit* LaCoursière) | 42 | 6 | 0 | 0 | 0 | 1 | |
| Gaïen (Gagnon?) | | 6 | 0 | 0 | 0 | 1 | |
| Grimard (Charles Moran *dit* Grimard) | 38 | 3 | 0 | 0 | 0 | 1 | |
| Duchaisne (François Gastinon *dit* Duchêne) | 65 | 6 | 3 | 1 | 0 | 0 | |
| Michel (Michel Yax), b. Germany | 42 | 6 | 4 | 2 | 0 | 1 | |
| Rivard *(supra cit.)*  3 acres | | | | | | | |
| Bordeleau (Charles), to the Vincennes post  3 acres | | | | | | | |
| Embroise Tremblet (Ambrose) | 50 | 3 | 2 | 2 | 0 | 0 | poor |
| Rivard *(supra cit.)*  3 acres | | | | | | | |
| Paternaude (Nicolas Patrenotre)  3 acres | 36 | | | | | | poor |
| Créquy (Jean Baptiste Aide *dit* Créqui)  3 acres | 35 | | | | | | poor |
| Nanlest (Jean Baptiste Prudhomme *dit* Nantais?) | 30 | 3 | 2 | 0 | 0 | 0 | poor |
| LaFeuillade (Joseph Davignon *dit* LaFeuillade) | 29 | 3 | 1 | 2 | 0 | 0 | poor |
| D'Estre (Pierre Estève *dit* Lajeunesse, son)  3 acres | 32 | | | | | | poor |
| Barthe *(supra cit.)*  3 acres | | | | | | | |
| Duboie (Alexis Dubois) | 36 | 3 | 1 | 1 | 0 | 0 | poor |
| Charjé  3 acres | 31 | | | | | | poor |

### SOUTH OF THE RIVER FROM THE OTTAWA VILLAGE TO THE HURON VILLAGE

| Name | Age | | | | | | |
|---|---|---|---|---|---|---|---|
| d'Estre father (Pierre Estève *dit* Lajeunesse, Sr.) | 63 | 3 | 5 | 2 | 0 | 0 | poor |
| LaBute son (Pierre Chêne *dit* LaButte) | 32 | 4 | 4 | 3 | 3 | 2 | |
| Lengloie (Nicolas Langlois) | 33 | 2 | 1 | 0 | 0 | 0 | poor |
| peren (Nicolas Langlois father or Laurence Parent) | 59 | 2 | 3 | 5 | 0 | 0 | |
| J. Lesperance (Jean Baptiste Billiau *dit* Lesperance) | | | | | | | |
| Vital Gauyeau (Goyou *dit* Lagarde) | 24 | 2 | 0 | 0 | 0 | 1 | |
| B. Gauyeau (Jean Baptiste Goyou *dit* Lagarde) | 41 | 3 | 4 | 2 | 0 | 0 | |
| G. Goyeau (Guillaume)  3 acres | 30 | | | | | | |
| L. Rhéaume (Louis? Réaume *dit* Themus) | 55 | 3 | 2 | 2 | 1 | 1 | |
| DeSault (Louis Toupin *dit* Dusault) | 40 | 3 | 2 | 4 | 0 | 1 | poor |
| Lenguedoc *(supra cit.)* | 42 | | | | | | |

| | | | | | | | |
|---|---|---|---|---|---|---|---|
| Bouron (Charles) | | 39 | 2 | 1 | 0 | 1 | 1 |
| Jacente Réaume (Hyacinthe), to the fort  2 acres | | | | | | | rich |
| Lenguedoc (supra cit.)  2 acres | | 42 | | | | | poor |
| Jannisse (Nicolas Janis) | | 45 | 3 | 1 | 3 | 0 | 1 |
| Mailloux (Joseph Maillou)  3 acres | | 34 | | | | | |
| Denoyé (François Marcheteau dit Desnoyers) | | 41 | 3 | 1 | 2 | 1 | 1 |
| Lelongeuil (Chevalier dit Longeuil), to Montreal  12 acres | | | | | | | rich |

## SOUTH OF THE RIVER FROM THE OTTAWA VILLAGE TO THE RIVER CANARD

| | | | | | | | |
|---|---|---|---|---|---|---|---|
| Gervaisse (Louis Gervais) | | 52 | 3 | 2 | 0 | 2 | 1 |
| LaBoise (Dominique Jourdain dit LaBrosse?) to the fort | | | 3 acres | | | | |
| LaMare (Charles LaMarre)  3 acres | | 35 | | | | | |
| St. Estienne (Pierre Guignard dit St. Etienne) | | | 3 | 0 | 0 | 0 | 2 |
| Michel Campau | | 50 | 3 | 5 | 2 | 0 | 1 poor |
| LeBeau (Jean Baptiste Bau dit LeBeau) | | 60 | 3 | 1 | 0 | 0 | 1 |
| Reau (Jean Baptiste Rau)  3 acres | | 35 | | | | | |
| LaRonde (François Paschal Denis LaRonde) | | 45 | 3 | 2 | 2 | 0 | 1 poor |
| Robert (Antoine) | | 50 | 3 | 3 | 4 | 0 | 0 poor |
| Pillet or Juillet (? or Antoine Juillet dit Montreuil) | | 40 | 6 | 2 | 2 | 0 | 1 |
| Meloche (Pierre) | | 38 | 6 | 2 | 3 | 0 | 1 |
| Clairmont (Louis Clermont) | | 43 | 3 | 3 | 2 | 0 | 1 poor |
| Grenon (Touissant) | | 36 | 3 | 3 | 2 | 0 | 1 poor |
| Charles Campeau | | 45 | 3 | 0 | 5 | 0 | 0 poor |
| Milhomme (François or Jean Petit dit Milhomme) | | 32 | 3 | 0 | 1 | 0 | 1 |
| Lesperance (supra cit.) b. France  3 acres | | 34 | | | | | |
| LaJeunesse (Louis Binau dit Lajeunesse son) b. France | | 45 | 3 | 3 | 6 | 0 | 1 poor |
| St. Louis (Louis Villers dit St. Louis), b. France | | 50 | 6 | 4 | 3 | 0 | 1 |
| Jiraix (Pierre Javerais dit Laderoute)  3 acres | | 32 | | | | | poor |
| Jadost (Louis Jadot), b. France | | 48 | 4 | 0 | 0 | 0 | 2 |
| LaFontaine (François Dubord dit LaFontaine), b. France | | 43 | 4 acres | | | | |
| Bordeau (Joseph)  3 acres | | 30 | | | | | poor |
| Moran, (supra cit.) to the fort  3 acres | | | | | | | poor |
| Legrand (Gabriel Christopher), to the fort, 3 acres | | | | | | | poor |
| Couture (Jean Baptiste)  3 acres | | 31 | | | | | poor |
| Susord (Louis François Susor)  3 acres | | 32 | | | | | poor |

## LOTS ON THE RIVER CANARD

| | | | | | | | |
|---|---|---|---|---|---|---|---|
| Etienne Jacob  3 acres | | 28 | | | | | poor |
| Lamisleo?, b. France  3 acres | | | | | | | poor |
| François LeBeau | | 35 | 3 | 1 | 2 | 0 | 1 |
| Lesperance (supra cit.) | | 33 | 3 | 2 | 0 | 0 | 1 |
| Veaudry (François Vaucry)  3 acres | | 34 | | | | | |
| Baptiste Drouillard | | 36 | 3 | 4 | 1 | 0 | 1 poor |
| Binault (Louis Bineau father) | | 60 | 3 | 4 | 6 | 0 | 0 poor |
| St. Rémis (Jacques Quesnel dit St. Denis dit St. Rémy) | | 46 | b. France  3 acres | | | | |
| Bergeron (Simon) | | 35 | 3 | 1 | 2 | 0 | 0 poor |
| Renau (prob. Charles Renaud)  3 acres | | 33 | | | | | poor |
| Prudhomme (François Xavier) | | 55 | 3 | 4 | 2 | 0 | 0 poor |
| St. Jean (Denis Serre dit St. Jean), b. France, 3 acres | | 40 | | | | | |
| Pageos (Thomas Joseph Pageot)  2 acres | | 32 | | | | | poor |

1762 Census

| | | | | | | |
|---|---|---|---|---|---|---|
| Peltier or Patoka (a nickname), b. France | 41 | 3 | 2 | 1 | 0 | 0 poor |
| Simon Drouillard | 32 | 4 | 1 | 1 | 0 | 0 poor |
| Cloutier (René) | 26 | 4 | 1 | 0 | 0 | 1 poor |
| Courtoie (prob. Charles Denis Courtois), to the fort | 8 acres | | | | | |

FAMILIES WHO HAVE NO KNOWN HOUSE

François Barois (Lootman *dit* Barrois), 4 boys
Soloe (Claude Solo), 1 boy, 1 girl
Badichon (Antoine Descomps *dit* Labadie), 1 girl
Jebeau (Stephen Gibaut), 2 boys
Robert (prob. Pierre Nicolas Robert), 1 boy
Widow Dumais (M. Magdelene Chevalier, widow Jacques Dumay), 5 boys, 2 girls
Temus Réaume *(supra cit.)*, 1 boy
Dubreuil (Jean Baptiste), 1 boy, 1 girl
Mélé (prob. Gabriel or Jean Baptiste Maillet), 1 boy, 1 girl
Mirten (St. Martin?), 1 boy, 1 girl
Capucien (Jean Baptiste Tiriot *dit* Capucien)
St. Mare (St. Martin?), 3 boys, 2 girls
Champagne (Pierre Huyet *dit* Champagne), 1 boy
Camparé, 2 boys
Pierre St. Auben, 3 boys, 2 girls
Bonvouloir (Joseph Amable Delières *dit* Bonvouloir), 1 boy, 1 girl

LOTS IN THE FORT (ages not given; first figure is width of lot in feet)

| | | | | | | | |
|---|---|---|---|---|---|---|---|
| Touranjeau (Jean Baptiste), outskirts | 40' | | | | | | |
| St. Rémie *(supra cit.)* | 40' | 2 | 1 | 0 | 0 | | |
| Monmirel (Durand *dit* Montmirel) | 30' | to Montreal | | | | | poor |
| Lenguedoc *(supra cit.)* | 30' | | | | | | |
| Gaudet (prob. Jean Baptiste Godet) | 67' | 1 | 1 | 1 | 0 | | |
| Cardinal father (Joseph) | 40' | to the country | | | | | |
| Lasel (Nicolas Laselle) | 40' | | | | | | poor |
| Bondy (Joseph Douaire *dit* Bondy) | 40' | 1 | 1 | 1 | 0 | | poor |
| Pougé (Joseph Gabriel Pouget) | 40' | 1 | 0 | 0 | 1 | | |
| Mauran *(supra cit.)* | 44' | 2 | 1 | 1 | 2 | | |
| Barthelmy | 55' | 1 | 0 | 0 | 0 | | poor |
| Denoyé (François Marcheteau *dit* Desnoyers) | 30' | to the country | | | | | |
| St. Auban *(supra cit.)* | 40' | to the country | | | | | |
| Seterlen (James Sterling), English | 80' | | | | | | |
| The church | 40' | | | | | | |
| Chapoton (Jean Baptiste) | 40' | | | | | | |
| Binault *(supra cit.)* | 60' | to the country | | | | | |
| Joerlico?, | 40' | to Montreal | | | | | |
| Bourgiron (Simon Bergeron) | 60' | | | | | | |
| Mag. Mesñie (Louis Jean Montmeny) | 40' | to Montreal | | | | | |
| Ramibault (Charles Nicolas), 3 boys | 40' | | | | | | poor |
| Belle Estre (François Picoté Belêtre) | 30' | Commandant | | | | | rich |
| pa---ens (Palms?) | 60' | to the country | | | | | |
| St. Cosme (Pierre), 3 boys, 3 girls | 50'? | | | | | | poor |
| Jubais (Jean Baptiste Joubert), 1 boy | 40' | | | | | | |
| Lemoin (Jean) | 18' | | | | | | |

| | | | | | | |
|---|---|---|---|---|---|---|
| Lemoin (Jean) | 18' | | | | | |
| Cardinal *(supra cit.)* | 20' | to the country | | | | |
| Legrand *(supra cit.)* | 40' | | | | | |
| Jefay? | 27' | | | | | |
| Belperche (Pierre), 1 boy | 30' | | | | | |
| Pougé *(supra cit.)* | 30' | | | | | |
| St. Bernard *(supra cit.)* | 40' | to the country | | | | |
| Cabesier *(supra cit.)* | 40' | | | | | |
| Milhomme *(supra cit.)* | 30' | | | | | |
| Belestre *(supra cit.)* | 30' | to Montreal | | | | |
| Guardhouse | | | | | | |
| Pilet (Joseph) | 30' | to the country | | | | |
| Pilet (Jean Baptiste or Jacques) | 45' | to the country | | | | |
| Langdoc *(supra cit.)* | 35' | to Montreal | | | | |
| Potdevin (Gibaut *dit* Poitevin?), 2 boys | 52' | | | | | |
| La Butte *(supra cit.)* | 40' | to the country | | | | |
| Chauvin *(supra cit.)* | 40' | to the country | | | | |
| Chicote *(supra cit.)* | 40' | to the country | | | | rich |
| DeRuisseau (Alexis Trotier *dit* DesRuisseaux) | 80' | | | | | |
| Berthe (Charles Barthe) | 90' | 3 | 2 | 1 | 1 | |
| The church | 150' | | | | | |
| Porlier/Postier? (poss. Michel Pothier *dit* Campau) | 30' | to Montreal | | | | rich |
| Belestre *(supra cit.)* | 80' | to Montreal | | | | rich |
| Réaume *(supra cit.)* | 77' | 4 | 3 | 1 | 0 | rich |
| Forville *(supra cit.)* | 60' | to the country | | | | |
| Cesire (Jean) | 50' | 1 | 1 | 1 | 0 | |
| Lasel *(supra cit.)* | 45' | 2 | 1 | 0 | 0 | poor |
| Sanschagrin (Jean Baptiste Duberger *dit* Sanschagrin) | 43' | 1 hired man | | | | |
| Campeau (Michel or Alexis) | 90' | to the country | | | | |
| The English Colonel | 30' | | | | | |
| LaButte *(supra cit.)* | 30' | 0 | 0 | 1 | 1 | rich |
| The English squire | 30' | | | | | |
| Cuillerie *(supra cit.)* | 30' | to the country | | | | |
| Chapoton *(supra cit.)* | 80' | 2 | 0 | 1 | 1 | |
| Warehouse | | | | | | |
| Cabasier *(supra cit.)* | 70' | | | | | |
| Navarre *(supra cit.)* | 80' | to the country | | | | |
| Jervais *(supra cit.)* | 40' | to the country | | | | |
| Courtois (Simon?) | 40' | 1 | 0 | 1 | 1 | |
| Gouin *(supra cit.)* | 60' | to the country | | | | |
| DeRuisseau (Julien or Alexis) | 30' | | | | | |
| DeRuisseau (one of above) | 24' | | | | | |
| Barthe *(supra cit.)* | 30' | | | | | |
| LaBroce *(supra cit.)* | 55' | 1 hired man | | | | poor |
| House of the Commandant | | | | | | |
| Dequindre (Louis Dagneau de Quindre) | 40' | 2 | 0 | 2 | 0 | |
| LaFleur (Charles Piquet *dit* Lafleur) | 60' | 0 | 1 | 0 | 1 | |
| Porlier (poss. Joseph Porlier *dit* Benalçue) | 60' | to Montreal | | | | rich |

## LOTS IN THE SUBURB STE. ROSALIE

| | | | | | | |
|---|---|---|---|---|---|---|
| LaFleur *(supra cit.)* 2 boys | 1 60' | | | | | poor |
| Versaille (Jean Vallée *dit* Versailles) | 90' | 1 | 4 | 0 | 0 | poor |
| Bigras (Joseph Bigras *dit* Fauvel) | 40' | 1 | 2 | 0 | 0 | poor |
| Tourangeaux *(supra cit.)* | 40' | 1 | 1 | 0 | 2 | |
| BeauLieux (Charles Beaulieu) | 60' | 2 | 2 | 0 | 0 | poor |
| De---leau | 40' | | | | | |
| Brisard (Jean) | 40' | | | | | |
| Dufourd (Pierre Dufour) 8 boys | 50' | | | | | poor |
| Lasueur (Michel) | 50' | | | | | poor |
| LaButte *(supra cit.)* | 50' | to the country | | | | |
| Baby (Jacques Duperon *dit* Baby) | 50' | 0 | 1 | 1 | 1 | |
| Paillé 1 hired man | 180' | | | | | |

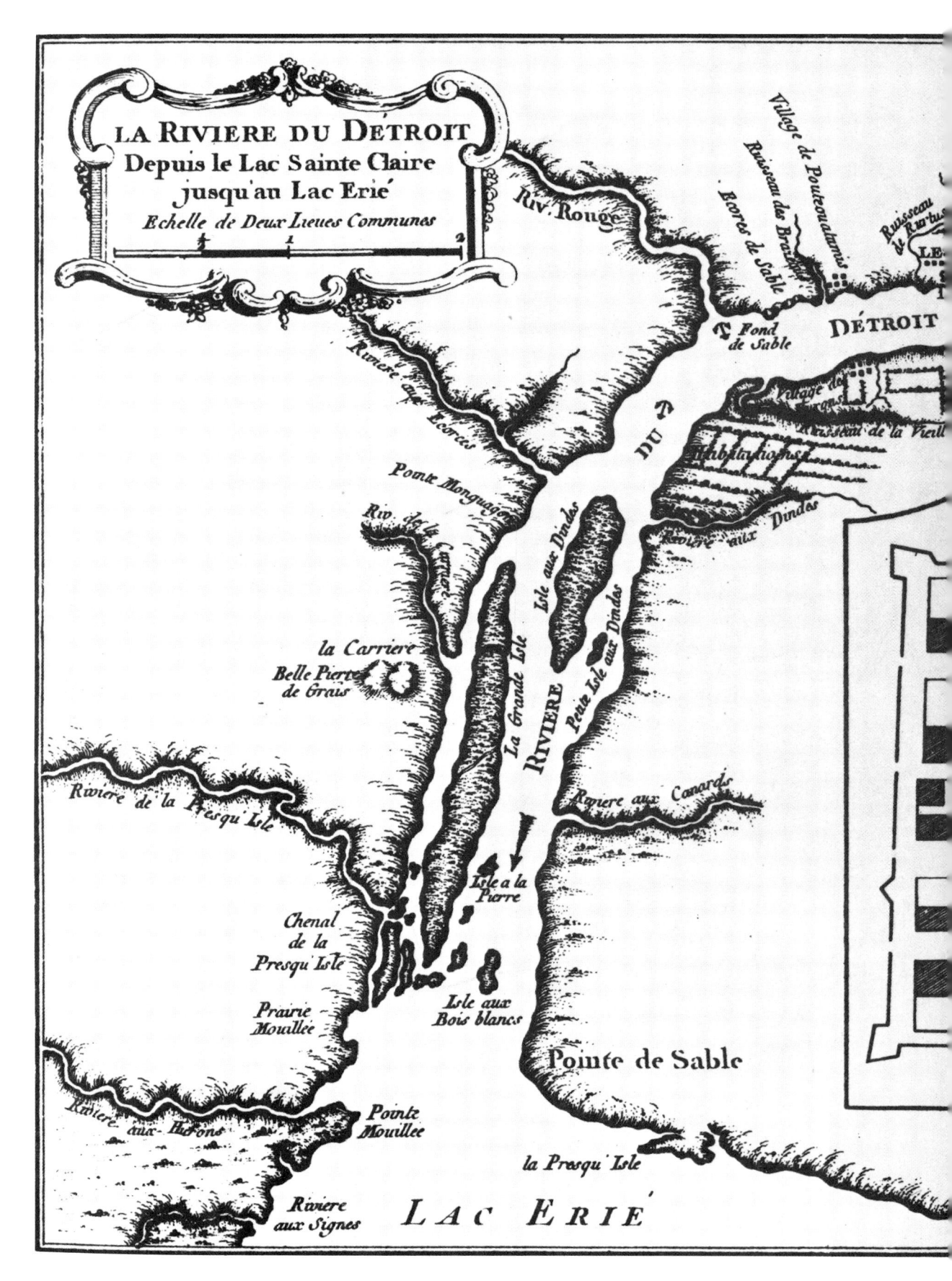

MAP 6. DETROIT RIVER, by Jacques Nicolas Bellin, 1764, with insert

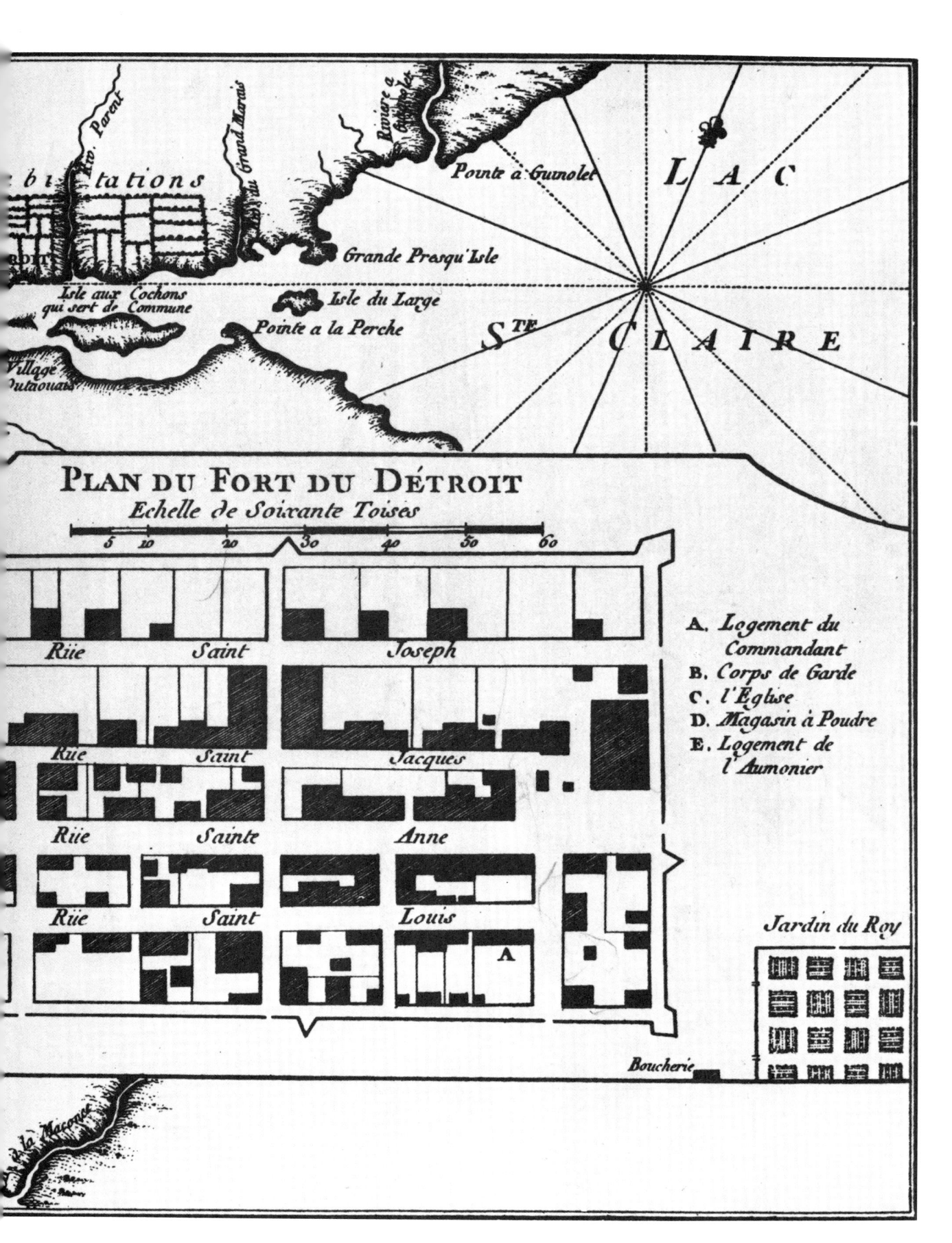

## PLAN DU FORT DU DÉTROIT
### Echelle de Soixante Toises

A. Logement du Commandant
B. Corps de Garde
C. l'Église
D. Magasin à Poudre
E. Logement de l'Aumonier

of Fort Pontchartrain, 1749

(Courtesy of Burton Historical Collection)

MAP 7. DETROIT AND ENVIRONS, by John Montresor, 1763
(Courtesy of William L. Clements Library)

## 1765 CENSUS

The British took over the government of Detroit on 29 November 1760, when Major Robert Rogers arrived with two hundred Rangers. According to the terms of the surrender, the French were allowed to keep their land. While the French government had collected property taxes from the landowners, based on the number of feet of river frontage, the English levied higher taxes in order to support the garrison, and, in addition, required the farmers to supply cordwood for the fort. The French were unreceptive to these increases and became understandably suspicious of British census takers. In fact, the enumerator of the 1765 census that follows remarked, "The inhabitants being apprehensive that I had some design upon them when I questioned them with respect to the quantity of wheat they expected this year mentioned a less quantity than they had reason to hope for."

This census was taken in August by an Englishman, which accounts for the odd spelling and lack of accent marks. People were classified as men able to bear arms, women, and children; then number of acres in front, horses, colts, bullocks, cows, calves to be reared, wheat of last year, wheat of this year, and Indian corn of this year (the last four will not be given here). The enumerator added the following remarks:

1. "The Indian corn would have been in greater abundance had proper care been taken of it; the most part has been devoured by the birds.
2. There are several farms at present uncultivated, the proprietors being partly absent and partly employed in building themselves houses.
3. The slaves are included in the numbers mentioned which in the whole may amount to 60 men, women, and children.
4. The farms are forty and some acres in depth.
5. There are besides in the fort many English merchants several of whom have bought houses."

Enumerated in this census were: 243 men, 164 women, 294 children, 484 acres under cultivation, 281 horses, 136 colts, 196 bullocks, 235 cows, and 224 calves.

The original manuscript of this census is among the William Penn Papers at the Historical Society of Pennsylvania in Philadelphia. A photocopy is at the Burton Historical Collection. It was originally published in the *Detroit Society for Genealogical Research Magazine* 43:19-26. Annotations were made by the present editor, who is always receptive to new ideas on the identification of these Frenchmen.

Michigan Censuses 1710-1830

| | MEN | WOMEN | CHILDREN | ACRES | HORSES | COLTS | BULLOCKS | COWS | CALVES |
|---|---|---|---|---|---|---|---|---|---|
| Juliet Treton[1] | 1 | 1 | 2 | 3 | 2 | 2 | 1 | 2 | 3 |
| Jean Criquis[2] | 1 | 1 | 1 | 3 | 2 | 1 | | 1 | 1 |
| Jean Rivard[3] | 1 | 1 | 2 | 6 | 1 | 2 | | 1 | 2 |
| Mich. Yacks[4] | 1 | 1 | 6 | 6 | 2 | 2 | 4 | 4 | 2 |
| Fra. DuChesne[5] | 1 | 1 | 3 | 6 | 1 | 3 | | 2 | 2 |
| Cha. Moran[6] | 2 | | | 3 | 1 | | | 1 | |
| LaCausse[7] | 1 | | | 6 | 2 | | 1 | | 1 |
| Benoit[8] | 2 | | | 3 | 2 | | | | |
| Louis Trembler[9] | 1 | | | 3 | 2 | 1 | | | |
| Champagne[10] | 1 | 1 | 2 | 3 | 1 | | | 1 | |
| Louis Janot[11] | 1 | 1 | 3 | 3 | 1 | | | | |
| Cha. St. Aubain[12] | 3 | 2 | | 4 | 2 | 2 | 2 | 3 | 3 |
| Pier St. Aubain[13] | 3 | 2 | 2 | | 1 | | | | |
| G. Laderoute[14] | 1 | 1 | 1 | 4 | 2 | 1 | | 1 | 1 |
| Fra. Marsac[15] | | | | | | | | | |
| J. Laderoute[16] | 1 | 1 | 5 | 2 | 1 | 3 | | 1 | 1 |
| Jos. Poryette[17] | 2 | 2 | 2 | | | | | 1 | 1 |
| Mar. Pilette[18] | | 1 | 3 | 2 | 2 | 1 | | 1 | 1 |
| Jean Beaubien[19] | 2 | 2 | 8 | 5 | 2 | 4 | 2 | 4 | |
| Cha. Moran[20] | 5 | 2 | 5 | 2 | 3 | 8 | 3 | 4 | 6 |
| Jac. Godefron[21] | | | | 2 | 3 | | 1 | 2 | |
| Cha. Chauvin[22] | 4 | 2 | 2 | 4 | 3 | 2 | 2 | 1 | 2 |
| Claude Goin[23] | 2 | 2 | 9 | 2 | 5 | 2 | 5 | 2 | 1 |
| Ant. Cuillerier[24] | 3 | 2 | | 4 | 3 | 1 | 3 | 1 | 1 |
| Ant. Miny[25] | 1 | 1 | 6 | 2 | 2 | 4 | 2 | 2 | 2 |
| Noel St. Aubain[26] | 4 | 2 | | 4 | 4 | | 2 | 2 | 1 |
| Jac. Campeau[27] | 2 | 2 | 1 | 3 | 2 | 1 | 4 | 3 | 2 |
| Louis Campeau[28] | 3 | 2 | 1 | 3 | 2 | 1 | 4 | 6 | 8 |
| Sim. Campeau[29] | 2 | 2 | 3 | 3 | 1 | | | 5 | 4 |
| Jean Binaut[30] | 1 | 1 | | 3 | 3 | 2 | 2 | 3 | 3 |
| Jean Cecire[31] | 3 | 3 | | 2 | 4 | 3 | 2 | 3 | 3 |
| Bapt. Melocke[32] | 2 | 1 | 2 | 3 | 2 | | 2 | 2 | 3 |
| Fra. Melocke[33] | 1 | 2 | 4 | 1 | 2 | 1 | | 2 | 2 |
| Bapt. Peltier[34] | 4 | 2 | 4 | 4 | 2 | 2 | 2 | 3 | 2 |
| Cha. Barthe[35] | 3 | 2 | | 4 | 4 | 1 | 2 | 2 | 4 |
| Phil LeDuc[36] | 2 | 1 | 1 | 2 | 2 | 1 | 2 | 2 | 1 |
| Bapt. LeDuc[37] | 1 | | | 2 | 1 | | 2 | 1 | |
| Noel Chauvin[38] | 1 | 2 | 3 | 3 | 2 | | | 1 | |
| Pierre Boyer[39] | 2 | 2 | 6 | 4 | 4 | | 4 | 2 | 4 |
| G. St. Bernard[40] | 2 | 1 | 3 | 4 | 2 | 1 | 2 | 3 | 3 |
| Gab. St. Aubain[41] | 2 | 1 | | 4 | 1 | | | 1 | |
| Ignace Voyer[42] | 2 | 1 | 3 | 2 | 1 | 1 | | 1 | 2 |
| Nicho. Loson[43] | 1 | 2 | 3 | 2 | 3 | 1 | 2 | 2 | 3 |
| Jac. Cloison[44] | 1 | 1 | 2 | 2 | 1 | 1 | | 1 | 1 |

## 1765 Census

| | | | | | | | | | |
|---|---|---|---|---|---|---|---|---|---|
| Jas. St. Aubain[45] | 2 | 1 | 8 | 4 | 4 | 2 | 2 | | |
| Jos. Cardinal[46] | 1 | | 1 | 3 | 8 | 1 | | 2 | 4 |
| Frs. Marsac[47] | 4 | 3 | 1 | 8 | 6 | 1 | 16 | 9 | 7 |
| Louis St. Abadie[48] | 1 | 1 | 2 | 3 | 2 | 1 | 2 | 3 | 5 |
| L. Martin[49] | 1 | 1 | 2 | 3 | 1 | | | 1 | 2 |
| J. Couture[50] | 1 | 1 | 1 | 3 | 1 | | | 1 | 3 |
| De Hetre[51] | 1 | 1 | 1 | 2 | 2 | 1 | 2 | 3 | 1 |
| Alex. Campau[52] | 1 | 3 | 7 | 4 | 3 | | 2 | 2 | 2 |
| A. De Lisle[53] | 2 | 1 | | 2 | 2 | 2 | 4 | 3 | 3 |
| Lio. Chesne[54] | 5 | 4 | | 2 | 2 | 4 | | 2 | 2 |
| Js. Chesne[55] | 1 | 1 | 1 | 2 | 2 | | | 1 | |
| Pierre Cardinal[56] | 1 | 1 | | 5 | 2 | 1 | 2 | 1 | 4 |
| Landery[57] | 3 | 2 | 2 | 3 | 7 | 4 | 2 | 4 | 3 |
| Cicote[58] | 4 | 4 | 2 | 3 | 3 | 1 | 2 | 5 | 4 |
| J. Cabassier[59] | 6 | 5 | 1 | 5 | 4 | 2 | 4 | 6 | 7 |
| Alex Campau[60] | 6 | 3 | 1 | 3 | 7 | 1 | 2 | 3 | 4 |
| Navarre[61] | 3 | 2 | 5 | 3 | 3 | 3 | 3 | 3 | 4 |
| Et. Varnoit[62] | 3 | | 1 | 2 | 3 | 1 | 3 | 4 | 2 |
| L'Abadie[63] | 4 | 2 | | 2 | 4 | 1 | 4 | 3 | 2 |
| Saulau[64] | 1 | | 3 | 4 | 3 | | 2 | 2 | 3 |
| Cha. Chesne[65] | 3 | 2 | 3 | 3 | 1 | | 2 | 2 | 1 |
| Gamlin[66] | 5 | 4 | 3 | 2 | 2 | 2 | 2 | 2 | 3 |
| Forville[67] | 1 | | | 2 | | | | | |
| Cha. Courtois[68] | 2 | 3 | 2 | 3 | 3 | 2 | 2 | 1 | 3 |
| St. Martin[69] | 2 | 3 | 2 | 4 | 2 | | 3 | 4 | |
| La Violette[70] | 1 | | | 4 | | | | | |
| Louis Thibaut[71] | 1 | 1 | 1 | 4 | | | | 1 | |
| Fra. L'Anglois[72] | 1 | | | 4 | | | | | |
| Montminy[73] | 1 | | | 4 | | | | | |
| Renet Cloutie[74] | 2 | 1 | 2 | 4 | 1 | | | | |
| Cha. Renaut[75] | 1 | | | 4 | 2 | | | | |
| And. Jacques[76] | 1 | 1 | 3 | 3 | 1 | 1 | | 1 | 2 |
| Pagot[77] | 1 | | | 3 | | | | | |
| Jean Lorson[78] | 1 | | | 3 | 1 | | | | |
| Fra. Prudhomme[79] | 2 | 2 | 4 | 3 | 1 | | | | |
| Tourangeau[80] | 1 | 1 | 3 | 3 | 1 | | 2 | 4 | 2 |
| S. Bergeron[81] | 1 | 1 | 4 | 3 | 4 | | | 1 | 1 |
| St. Remi[82] | 2 | 1 | 1 | 3 | 2 | 2 | 2 | 2 | 2 |
| Louis Benot[83] | 2 | 1 | 4 | 3 | 3 | 1 | 2 | 1 | 1 |
| Bapt. Rouyat[84] | 2 | 1 | 6 | 3 | 2 | | | 1 | 1 |
| Mich. Vaudrie[85] | 2 | | | 3 | 2 | | 2 | 2 | 1 |
| Fra. L'esperance[86] | 2 | 1 | 3 | 3 | 2 | 1 | 2 | 2 | 1 |
| Fra. LeBeau[87] | 2 | 1 | 3 | 3 | 2 | 1 | 2 | 3 | 2 |
| Ant. Jagob[88] | 2 | 1 | 2 | 3 | 2 | 1 | 2 | 1 | |
| Louis Lasaut[89] | 1 | | | 3 | 2 | | 2 | 1 | |
| Jean Perre[90] | 1 | | | 3 | 1 | 1 | | | |
| Moran[91] | | | | 3 | | | | | |
| L. Ronde[92] | 3 | 1 | 1 | 3 | 3 | 2 | 2 | 1 | |
| LaFontaine[93] | 1 | | | 3 | 1 | | | 2 | 3 |
| Jadot[94] | 3 | 1 | 2 | 4 | 2 | 2 | 2 | 1 | 4 |

|  | | | | | | | | |
|---|---|---|---|---|---|---|---|---|
| Gerout[95] | 1 | | 3 | 1 | 2 | | | |
| Louis Viller[96] | 2 | 1 | 1 | 6 | 5 | 2 | 2 | 4 |
| J. Lajaune[97] | 2 | 1 | 6 | 3 | 1 | | 2 | 1 |
| L'Esperance[98] | 1 | 2 | 5 | 3 | | | 2 | 3 |
| Cha. Campau[99] | 1 | 1 | 7 | 3 | 2 | 2 | 1 | 1 |
| B. Campeau[100] | 3 | 1 | 4 | 4 | 3 | 1 | 2 | |
| Grenouille[101] | 2 | | | 3 | | 2 | | |
| Trotot[102] | 2 | 1 | 1 | 3 | 3 | 1 | | |
| Sim. Rouyat[103] | 1 | 1 | 3 | 3 | 1 | 5 | 2 | 4 | 5 |
| Pierre Meloche[104] | 2 | 1 | 7 | 6 | 3 | 1 | 3 | 2 |
| Jos. Pilette[105] | 1 | 1 | 4 | 6 | 2 | 1 | 2 | 2 | 2 |
| Ant. Robert[106] | 2 | 1 | 8 | 3 | 1 | 1 | | |
| Jean Rosse[107] | 1 | 1 | 1 | 3 | 2 | 1 | 2 | 1 | 1 |
| LeBeau[108] | 1 | 1 | | 3 | 4 | 2 | 2 | 2 | 4 |
| Ravenne[109] | 3 | 1 | 5 | 3 | 1 | 1 | 2 | 1 | 1 |
| Jos. St. Etienne[110] | 2 | 2 | | 3 | 2 | 1 | 2 | 3 | 1 |
| LaMarre[111] | 1 | 1 | 1 | 3 | 1 | 1 | 2 | 2 | 2 |
| Cha. LaFleur[112] | 2 | 1 | 3 | 3 | 6 | 2 | 2 | 5 | 7 |
| Louis Jervois[113] | 3 | 1 | 5 | 3 | 9 | 2 | 2 | 4 | 4 |
| DeNoyer[114] | 2 | 1 | 3 | 3 | 2 | 1 | 2 | 1 | 3 |
| Jaunisse[115] | 2 | 2 | 5 | 3 | 1 | | 2 | 2 | 2 |
| Mayat[116] | 1 | 1 | | 3 | 2 | 1 | 2 | 1 | |
| Gaunelet[117] | 1 | 2 | 3 | 2 | 1 | | | | |
| Bauron[118] | 2 | 1 | 2 | 4 | 3 | 3 | 2 | 2 | |
| DuSaut[119] | 3 | 2 | 5 | 3 | 2 | 1 | 2 | | 2 |
| P. Reaume[120] | 2 | 1 | 4 | 3 | 4 | 3 | 8 | 5 | 8 |
| G. Goyau[121] | 1 | 2 | 7 | 6 | 4 | 2 | 4 | 3 | 5 |
| Vitel Goyau[122] | 3 | 1 | 1 | 2 | 2 | 1 | 2 | 1 | |
| Merte[123] | 2 | 1 | 3 | 2 | 3 | 1 | 4 | 1 | 3 |
| Parent[124] | 2 | 3 | 6 | 2 | 1 | 1 | 2 | 2 | |
| L'Anglois[125] | 2 | 1 | 2 | 2 | 2 | | 2 | 1 | |
| LaBute[126] | 2 | 3 | 6 | 4 | 2 | 1 | 2 | 1 | |
| DeHetre[127] | 2 | 2 | | 3 | 2 | 1 | | | |

NB. The french families in the [fort?] consist of 33 men able to bear arms, 24 women, 41 children.

---

1. Julian Fréton *dit* Nantais
2. Jean Baptiste Aide *dit* Créqui
3. Jean Baptiste Rivard
4. Michel Yax
5. Francois Gastinon *dit* DuChene
6. Charles Moran *dit* Grimard
7. Jean Baptiste LaCasse?
8. Nicolas Benoît
9. Louis Michel Tremblay
10. Pierre Huyet *dit* Champagne
11. prob. Louis Jadot
12. Charles Casse *dit* St. Aubin
13. Pierre Casse *dit* St. Aubin
14. Cajetan Séguin *dit* Laderoute
15. Francois Marsac
16. Joseph Séguin *dit* Laderoute
17. Joseph Pouget
18. Marguerite Viau, widow of James Pilet
19. Jean Baptiste Cuillerier *dit* Beaubien
20. Claude Charles Moran
21. Jacques Godefroy
22. Charles Chauvin
23. Claude Jean Thomas Gouin
24. Antoine Cuillerier *dit* Beaubien
25. Antoine Meny
26. Noel Casse *dit* St. Aubin

## 1765 Census

27. Jacques Campau
28. Jean Louis Campau
29. Simon Campau
30. Jean Binau *dit* Lajeunesse
31. Jean Cesire
32. Jean Baptiste Meloche
33. Francois Meloche
34. Jean Baptiste Peltier
35. Andrew Charles Barthe
36. Philip LeDuc
37. Jean Baptiste LeDuc
38. Noel Chauvin
39. Pierre Boyer
40. Guillaume Bernard
41. prob. Gabriel Casse *dit* St. Aubin
42. Ignace Boyer
43. prob. Antoine Nicolas Lauson
44. Jacques Lauson
45. Jacques Casse *dit* St. Aubin
46. Joseph Cardinal
47. prob. Francois Marsac
48. Antoine Louis Descomps *dit* Labadie
49. prob. Martin Levry
50. Jean Baptiste Couture
51. prob. Aloysius Deshêtres *dit* Pigeon
52. prob. Paul Campau
53. Alexis Bienvenu *dit* Delisle
54. Leopold Chêne
55. poss. Isadore Chêne
56. Pierre Cardinal
57. Claude Landry *dit* St. Andre
58. Zacharias Cicotte
59. Joseph Cabassier
60. Paul Alexandre Campau
61. Robert Navarre
62. Etienne Benoît-Livernois
63. Pierre Louis Descomps *dit* Labadie
64. Claude Solo
65. Charles Chêne *dit* Caossa
66. Laurence Eustache Gamelin
67. Pierre Tetard *dit* Fortville
68. prob. Charles Courtois
69. Touissant Antoine Adhemar-St. Martin
70. Etienne Laviolette
71. Louis Thibault
72. Francois Langlois
73. Louis Jean Montmeny
74. René Cloutier
75. Charles Renaud
76. André Jacques
77. Thomas Joseph Pageot
78. prob. Jacques Lauson
79. Francois Xavier Prudhomme
80. Jean Baptiste Guillet *dit* Tourangeau
81. Simon Bergeron
82. poss. Marguerite Morel *dit* LaDurantaye, widow of René Francois LeBeau
83. Louis Bineau father
84. Jean Baptiste Drouillard
85. Michel Vaudry
86. Francois Rochereau Lesperance
87. Francois LeBeau
88. Etienne Jacob
89. prob. Nicolas Lacelle
90. Jean Baptiste Paré
91. vacant - prob. owned by Claude Moran
92. Francois Paschal LaRonde
93. Francois Dubord *dit* LaFontaine
94. Louis Jadot
95. Pierre Geirou? Charles Girard?
96. Louis Villers *dit* St. Louis
97. prob. Charles Janson-LaPalme
98. Jean Baptiste Billiau *dit* Lesperance
99. Charles Campau
100. Jean Baptiste Campau
101. Touissant Grenon
102. Alexis Trotier *dit* Desruisseaux
103. Simon Amable Drouillard
104. Pierre Meloche
105. Joseph Pilette
106. Antoine Robert
107. Jean Baptiste Desrosier *dit* DuTremble
108. Jean Baptiste Bau *dit* LeBeau
109. Jean Louis Revau
110. Joseph Guignard *dit* St. Etienne
111. Charles LaMarre
112. Charles Poupard LaFleur
113. Louis Gervaise
114. Francois Marcheteau *dit* Desnoyers
115. Francois Nicolas Janis
116. Gabriel Maillet
117. Gagnier? Galerneau? Goulet?
118. Michel Bonhomme *dit* Beaupré
119. Louis Toupin *dit* DeSault
120. Pierre Réaume *dit* Thémus
121. Guillaume Goyou *dit* LaDouceur
122. Vital Goyou *dit* Lagarde
123. Joseph Metay *dit* LaDouceur
124. prob. Laurance Parent
125. prob. Nicolas Langlois
126. Pierre Chêne *dit* LaButte
127. prob. Hyacinthe Deshêtres

MAP 8. CANADA, by Guillaume de l'Isle, 1703 (detail) (Courtesy of Burton Historical Collection)

# THE INHABITANTS OF DETROIT IN 1768

This census, taken by Philip DeJean, the notorious notary, justice of the peace, and sometimes judge, was enclosed in a letter dated 23 February 1768 from the Commandant of the Detroit post, George Turnbull, to General Thomas Gage, Commander-in-Chief of the British forces in America. The original is among the Gage Papers at the William L. Clements Library, University of Michigan.

The portion relating to the South Shore (Canada) was reprinted in Ernest J. Lajeunesse, *The Windsor Border Region* (Toronto, 1960), pp. 63-64. An examination of the original revealed the names of the people living in Detroit, printed here for the first time, with permission of the Clements Library.

Census taking was almost an annual event under the British; we know of enumerations taken in 1773, 1778, 1779, 1780, and 1782. Those of 1779 and 1782 will be reprinted in the present collection, but the others are worth looking at also, as they show the growth of the city year by year. Philip DeJean took the census 22 September 1773, called "A General Return of all the Inhabitants of Detroit, their Possessions, Cattle, Horses, Servants, and Slaves." It counted 298 men, 225 women, 84 young men aged ten to twenty years, 284 boys, 58 young women (this number is undoubtedly low because girls married at an early age), 240 girls, 93 servants, 46 male slaves, and 39 female slaves. The agricultural portion of this census appears in Silas Farmer, *History of Detroit and Wayne County and Early Michigan* (New York, 1890), p. 334. A note added to the census states: "The Troops and Naval Department, with their Cattle etc., are not included in the above. The men servants are generally more numerous, several being now hunting and at the Indian villages."

Another census, by order of Governor Henry Hamilton, was taken 26 April 1778, and showed: 464 men, 274 women, 530 young men and boys, 438 young women and girls, 172 male servants, 39 female servants, and 127 slaves. The 1779 census follows, and another taken 1 November 1780 shows 394 heads of family, 324 young and married women, 374 young and married men, 100 absent in Indian country, 455 boys aged ten to fifteen years, 385 girls aged same, 79 male slaves, and 78 female slaves. (Farmer, *ibid.*)

This census was taken by the British, but since the notary DeJean was himself French, the manuscript is fairly easy to read. His totals show 514 1/2 acres of land under cultivation, 126 heads of family (this figure is misleading, as many farms were inhabited by the farmer and one or more of his sons; here, young men are not enumerated), 211 boys, 147 girls, 264 oxen, 336 cows, 567 hogs, 9789 bushels (or more likely *minots*; a *minot* is equal to five pecks) of wheat, 344 1/2 cords of wood. Only the first three categories will be given here. Further, annotations will not be made, as most of the people are the same as those in the 1765 census, although there are some new names. Several among them were not found in Detroit records, and their identity remains a mystery, to wit.: Pajeau, Tamizir, Manchet, Decoigne (Decouagne?), and Gravel. Note that some of the men have been given an unusual first name; these are probably names assigned by the Indians, such as Loquetoche Cardinal, Patoca Lesperance, and Papiche Meloche.

| | FARMERS | BOYS | GIRLS | | FARMERS | BOYS | GIRLS |
|---|---|---|---|---|---|---|---|
| Martel | 3 | 0 | 0 | Noël St Aubin | 4 | 2 | 1 |
| Gouin | 3 | 0 | 0 | Ant. Miny | 2 | 3 | 2 |
| Guilme St. Bernard | 3 | 0 | 0 | Cuirrier (Cuillerier) | 2 | 1 | 0 |
| Sim. Campau | 3 | 0 | 0 | Gouin | 2 | 4 | 4 |
| L St Aubin | 3 | 0 | 0 | Chauvin | 4 | 5 | 0 |
| Languedoc | 3 | 0 | 0 | Moran | 4 | 3 | 2 |
| Belestre | 3 | 0 | 0 | Beaubien | 5 | 5 | 2 |
| Pouget | 3 | 0 | 0 | Barthe | 2 | 3 | 3 |
| Jos. Cardinal | 3 | 0 | 0 | Potevin | 1 | 2 | 0 |
| L. Griffard | 3 | 1 | 0 | St Martin | 4 | 1 | 2 |
| Jc Campau | 3 | 0 | 0 | Courtois | 3 | 0 | 0 |
| Jc Loson | 2 | 2 | 1 | Caossa | 2 | 1 | 2 |
| Chs St Aubin | 3 | 1 | 2 | Gamelin | 2 | 4 | 0 |
| Pre Robert (father) | 3 | 3 | 1 | Cicote | 3 | 1 | 1 |
| Marsac | 2 | 0 | 0 | Livernois | 2 | 1 | 1 |
| Bte Chauvin | 4 | 0 | 0 | Navarre | 3 | 2 | 1 |
| Gajetan Laderoute | 4 | 0 | 1 | Campau | 3 | 0 | 0 |
| Marsac son | 2 | 0 | 0 | Cabassier | 3 | 2 | 2 |
| Jos Laderoute | 2 | 2 | 3 | Cicote | 3 | 1 | 0 |
| St Cosme | 4 | 0 | 0 | St André | 3 | 0 | 0 |
| Marsac | 12 | 3 | 3 | Isidore Chesne | 2 | 0 | 1 |
| Bte Campau | 4 | 0 | 2 | Nc Chesne | 2 | 2 | 0 |
| Loquetoche Cardinal | 3 | 0 | 0 | Cloutier | 3 | 0 | 0 |
| Jos Cardinal | 3 | 0 | 0 | Grenon | 4 | 3 | 2 |
| J C St Aubin | 4 | 6 | 3 | St. André | 3 | 1 | 2 |
| Nicolas Loson | 4 | 3 | 1 | Pajeau | 3 | 0 | 0 |
| Ignace Boyer | 2 | 1 | 3 | Tamizir | 3 | 0 | 0 |
| Gab St Aubin | 4 | 0 | 0 | Prudhomme | 3 | 4 | 5 |
| St Bernard | 4 | 3 | 2 | Tourangeau | 3 | 2 | 2 |
| Nco Boyer father | 4 | 1 | 4 | Bergeron | 3 | 2 | 2 |
| Noel Chauvin | 3 | 2 | 2 | St. Rémy | 3 | 1 | 3 |
| Phpe Leduc | 2 | 1 | 1 | Binau | 3 | 2 | 2 |
| Jos Mété (illeg.) (bracketed with next) | | | | Bte Drouillard | 3 | 5 | 1 |
| A G Barthe | 4 | 3 | 1 | Vaudry | 3 | 0 | 0 |
| Bte Peltier | 4 | 6 | 1 | Lesperance | 3 | 4 | 1 |
| Fr Meloche | 1 | 2 | 3 | Fr. Lebeau | 3 | 2 | 2 |
| Cecile | 2 | 0 | 0 | Tamizir | 3 | 0 | 0 |
| Js Binau | 3 | 0 | 0 | Estne. Jacob | 3 | 0 | 0 |
| Bte Meloche | 3 | 0 | 3 | Suzor | 3 | 0 | 0 |
| Sim. Campau | 3 | 0 | 2 | Laderoute | 3 | 1 | 2 |
| Jc Campau | 3 | 0 | 0 | Réaume | 3 | 0 | 0 |
| L. Campau | 3 | 1 | 0 | Moran | 3 | 0 | 0 |

Detroit in 1768

| | FARMERS | BOYS | GIRLS | | FARMERS | BOYS | GIRLS |
|---|---|---|---|---|---|---|---|
| Lisle Ronde | 3 | 2 | 1 | Jn Bte Estienne | 3 | 0 | 0 |
| Laffontaine | 2 | 2 | 0 | Jn Bte Paré | 3 | 0 | 0 |
| Baby | 3 | 0 | 0 | Laboise | 3 | 2 | 0 |
| Peter Pond | 2 | 0 | 0 | Rivard | 3 | 0 | 1 |
| St. Louis | 3 | 4 | 4 | Fr. Drouiliard | 3 | 0 | 1 |
| Lajeunesse | 3 | 4 | 3 | Gme Goyau | 3 | 4 | 3 |
| Patoca Lesperance | 3 | 3 | 1 | Marantet | 1 | 2 | 0 |
| Tamisir | 3 | 0 | 0 | Longueuil | 12 | 0 | 0 |
| Papiche Meloche | 3 | 0 | 0 | Dénoyer | 3 | 1 | 2 |
| Manchet | 3 | 0 | 0 | Mailloux | 3 | 1 | 1 |
| Simon Drouilard | 6 | 2 | 3 | Janis | 3 | 3 | 2 |
| Pre Meloche (father) | 6 | 5 | 3 | Oualet | 2 | 1 | 0 |
| Charron | 3 | 2 | 2 | Bouron | 4 | 1 | 0 |
| Bondy | 3 | 0 | 0 | Dussault | 3 | 1 | 1 |
| Decoigne | 3 | 0 | 0 | Réaume | 3 | 0 | 1 |
| Jn Bte Rau | 3 | 1 | 0 | Gme Grau (Goyau) | 3 | 0 | 0 |
| Jn Bte Lebeau | 3 | 0 | 0 | Vital Goyau | 2 | 0 | 0 |
| Gravel | 3 | 0 | 0 | Lesperance | 2 | 0 | 2 |
| Labadie | 2 | 0 | 1 | Parent | 2 | 3 | 5 |
| | | | | Langlois | 2 | 4 | 0 |
| | | | | Labutte | 4 | 4 | 5 |
| | | | | Dehêtre | 2 | 1 | 1 |
| | | | | Bonvouloir | 2 | 2 | 3 |

MAP 9.  ARTIST'S CONCEPTION OF FORT PONTCHARTRAIN IN 1740
(Courtesy of Burton Historical Collection)

# 1779 CENSUS

This census, called a Survey of the Settlement of Detroit, was taken 31 March 1779 in the presence of Mr. Thomas Williams, Acting Justice of the Peace; Captain John McGregor of the Town Militia; and Mr. Sampson Fleming, by Major Richard Beringer Lernoult, the Commanding Officer of the Detroit post. The original is among the Haldimand Papers at the British Museum, London.

A photocopy provided by the Public Archives of Canada revealed many errors in the previous publication of this census (*Michigan Pioneer and Historical Collections*: 10:311-327). In addition to the numbers in some categories, many of the names were misinterpreted or missed. We hope the present transcription corrects these errors.

The totals shown here are: 1,011 men, 265 women, 253 hired lodgers or young men, 100 hired lodgers or young women, 484 boys, 402 girls, 60 male slaves, and 78 female slaves. In the agricultural columns, not copied here, were: 141,517 bushels of flour, 3,273 bushels of wheat, 2,126 for seed, 3,177 bushels of Indian corn, 20 for seed, 772 bushels of peas, 71 for seed, 744 bushels of oats, 1505 for seed, 413 oxen, 779 cows, 619 steers, 1,076 hogs, 664 horses, 313 sheep, 91,790 pounds of pork, 570 pounds of beef, 17,000 pounds of oatmeal, and 7,700 pounds of butter (the last four figures represent the inventory from the fort).

In most of these censuses, the totals of soldiers and prisoners are not included in the population, but this census was taken during the Revolutionary War, which is undoubtedly a factor in their inclusion. If we subtract these categories, we find 272 men, 231 women, 454 boys, 374 girls, 60 male slaves, and 77 female slaves, a total of 1468, plus 353 hired lodgers (just who comprises this last category is not clear). This total of 1914 is more consistent with the population figure of 2107 for the following year.

The fort had been considerably enlarged just prior to this enumeration by the addition of a redoubt on the hill behind the old fort, when it was learned in August 1778 that Colonel Daniel Brodhead, Commander of the American Continental troops at Pittsburgh, was at Tuscarowas River near Sandusky with two or three thousand men. Renamed Fort Lernoult in honor of the Commanding Officer, it was also called Fort Shelby.

| Name | MEN | WOMEN | LODGERS OR YOUNG MEN | LODGERS OR YOUNG WOMEN | BOYS | GIRLS | MALE SLAVES | FEMALE SLAVES |
|---|---|---|---|---|---|---|---|---|
| Nicholas Litsenberger | 1 | | | 1 | 1 | | | |
| Antoine Goulette and wife | 1 | 1 | | | | | | |
| John McPherson | 1 | | 2 | | | | | |
| Alexr Helaire and wife | 1 | 1 | | | | 3 | 2 | |
| Nicholas Patnotte and wife | 1 | 1 | | | 1 | 5 | | |
| Antoine Miney and wife | 1 | 1 | | | 2 | 2 | | |
| François Tremblé and wife | 1 | 1 | | | | | | |
| Petite Claire | 1 | | | | 1 | | | 1 |
| Michael Yacks, Senr, and wife | 1 | 1 | 2 | | 3 | | | |
| François Duchesne and wife | 1 | 1 | 2 | 2 | 1 | 6 | | |
| Jean Bte. Crittie and wife (Crête) | 1 | 1 | | 1 | 2 | | | 1 |
| Charles Grimaure (Grimard) | 1 | | 1 | | 2 | 4 | | |
| Joseph Saucier and wife | 1 | 1 | | | | | | |
| Ambroise Tremblé | 1 | | 4 | | 3 | | | |
| Isidore Moran and wife | 1 | 1 | | | 4 | | | 1 |
| Louise Tremblé and wife | 1 | 1 | | | 2 | 2 | 1 | |
| Jacob Harsen and wife | 1 | 1 | | 1 | 2 | 2 | | |
| Louis Renau and wife | 1 | 1 | | | 4 | 2 | | |
| Ignace Thibeau and wife | 1 | 1 | | | 5 | 1 | | |
| Jacques Lauson and wife | 1 | 1 | | 1 | 1 | | | |
| Charles St. Aubin | 1 | | 1 | 1 | | 1 | | |
| Joseph Tremblé | 1 | | 1 | | 2 | | | |
| Jean Bt. Chavin and wife (Chauvin) | 1 | 1 | | | | 3 | | |
| Jean Crispé St. Jean and wife | 1 | 1 | | | 7 | 1 | | |
| Joseph Laderoute and wife | 1 | 1 | 1 | 1 | | 2 | | |
| Michael Yacks, Jun | 1 | | 2 | | 1 | | | |
| Capt. Campeau and wife | 1 | 1 | 2 | 1 | 1 | 5 | | |
| Jean Duprat and wife | 1 | 1 | 1 | | | 3 | | |
| Gajetan Laderoute and wife | 1 | 1 | 1 | 1 | 5 | | | |
| Widow Marsac | | 1 | 1 | | | 1 | | |
| J. Bt. Marsac and wife | 1 | 1 | | | | 3 | 1 | |
| Paul Marsac | 1 | | 2 | | | | 2 | 1 |
| Pierre Cardinal and wife | 1 | 1 | 1 | 1 | 4 | 1 | | |
| Joseph Cardinal | 1 | | 1 | 1 | 4 | 3 | | |
| Pierre St. Aubin and wife | 1 | 1 | 1 | | | | | |
| Bazil Campeau | 1 | 1 | 2 | | | | | |
| Jacques St. Aubin and wife | 1 | 1 | 4 | 2 | | | | |
| Louis St. Aubin and wife | 1 | 1 | 1 | 2 | 3 | 1 | | |
| James Casety and wife | 1 | 1 | 2 | | | 2 | 2 | |
| Simon Meloche and wife | 1 | 1 | | | 3 | 1 | | |
| Charles Chavin and wife | 1 | 1 | 1 | 2 | 6 | 1 | | |
| Antoine Moran and wife | 1 | 1 | | | 2 | 1 | | |
| Guillaume Bernard and wife | 1 | 1 | 1 | 1 | 4 | 3 | 1 | 3 |
| Antoine Bogert and wife (Boyer) | 1 | 1 | 1 | | | | | |

## Census of 1779

| | | | | | | | | |
|---|---|---|---|---|---|---|---|---|
| Louis Beaufait and wife | 1 | 1 | | | 1 | 3 | 1 | |
| Jean Bt Chapoton and wife | 1 | 1 | 4 | 1 | 1 | 3 | 2 | 2 |
| Jean Bt Peltier and wife | 1 | 1 | 3 | 2 | 9 | 1 | | |
| François Meloche and wife | 1 | 1 | 1 | 1 | 4 | 3 | | |
| Jean Bt Meloche and wife | 1 | 1 | 1 | 4 | 3 | | | |
| Amable Latoure and wife | 1 | 1 | 1 | | 1 | | | |
| Robert Jean and wife | 1 | 1 | | 1 | 2 | 4 | | |
| François Latoure and wife | 1 | 1 | | | 1 | | | |
| Jean Benoa and wife (Benoit) | 1 | 1 | 1 | | | | | |
| Simon Campeau and wife | 1 | 1 | | 1 | 4 | 3 | 3 | 2 |
| Antoine Robert Censé and wife | 1 | 1 | 1 | 1 | 1 | 1 | 2 | |
| Jean Bte Campau Jun, and wife | 1 | 1 | 1 | 1 | 4 | 2 | 3 | 3 |
| Jacques Campeau and wife | 1 | 1 | | 1 | 6 | | 1 | 1 |
| Hippolite Campeau and wife | 1 | 1 | 1 | 2 | | | | |
| Ignace Boyer and wife | 1 | 1 | | 1 | 1 | 1 | | |
| Noel St. Aubin and wife | 1 | 1 | 1 | 1 | | 1 | | |
| Pierre Meney and wife | 1 | 1 | 4 | | 1 | 1 | | |
| Alexis Cuillerie and wife | 1 | 1 | | | | 3 | | |
| Antoine Cuillerie and wife | 1 | 1 | 4 | 2 | | 2 | | |
| Charles Gouin and mother | 1 | 1 | 3 | 3 | | 2 | 6 | 3 |
| Jean Bte. Rivaure and wife (Rivard) | 1 | 1 | | | 7 | 2 | | 1 |
| Captain Moran and mother | 1 | 1 | 2 | 2 | 3 | 3 | | 1 |
| Pierre Durand and wife | 1 | 1 | 2 | | | | | |
| Jean Bt. Beaubien and wife | 1 | 1 | 6 | 1 | 2 | 2 | | |
| Jean Bt. Barthe and wife | 1 | 1 | 1 | | | | | |
| Joseph Reaume and wife | 1 | 1 | 2 | | 3 | 3 | | |
| James Thompson | 1 | 1 | | 4 | | | | |
| Daniel Garret and wife | 1 | 1 | | | | | | |
| Captain McGregor and wife | 1 | 1 | | | 1 | | 1 | |
| William Sterling and wife | 1 | 1 | | | 3 | | | 1 |
| Thomas Williams | 1 | | 1 | | | | 1 | |
| William Tucker and wife | 1 | 1 | | | 1 | 2 | | |
| Mr. Thorn | | 1 | | | 1 | | | |
| Thomas Cox and wife | 1 | 1 | 2 | | | | 1 | 3 |
| Mr. Cornwall, Jun., and Miller (?) | 2 | | | 1 | | | | |
| William Edgar | 1 | | 2 | | | | 1 | |
| Bernard Lafontaigne and wife | 1 | 1 | | | | | | |
| Jean Bt. Sanchagrin and wife | 1 | 1 | 1 | 1 | 2 | 2 | | |
| Greverat and Visgar | 2 | | 2 | | 2 | | | |
| John McPherson | 1 | | 1 | | | | | |
| William Forsith and wife | 1 | 1 | 3 | 1 | 6 | | | 2 |
| Thomas McCrae and wife | 1 | 1 | | | 3 | | | |
| Mrs. Fleming | | 1 | | | 1 | 1 | 1 | |
| James Cochran | 1 | | 1 | | | | | |
| Teller and Grosbeck | 2 | | 2 | | | | | |
| James Rankin | 1 | | 1 | | 1 | 2 | | |
| Thompson and Williams | 2 | | | | | | 1 | |
| Andrews and Meldram | 2 | | 2 | | 3 | | | |
| McWilliams, Martin and Trimble | 3 | | | | | | | |
| Macnamara, McLeod and wife | 2 | 1 | 4 | | | 1 | | |
| Forsith, Dyce and Macintosh | 3 | | 1 | | | 1 | | |

| | | | | | | | |
|---|---|---|---|---|---|---|---|
| Wright, White and Lyons | 3 | | | | | | |
| Mrs. Adhemar | | 1 | 1 | | 1 | 2 | 1 | 1 |
| Isaac Williams and wife | 1 | 1 | 2 | | 2 | | | |
| James Abbott and wife | 1 | 1 | 2 | | 2 | 4 | | 2 |
| Edward Riddy | 1 | | 2 | | | | | |
| Mrs. Hay and Mrs. Lamoth | | 2 | | | 3 | 3 | | 2 |
| Sarah etinnse (Ainse) | | 1 | | | | | 1 | 2 |
| Margaret Scott | | 1 | | | | 3 | | |
| Jean Bte. Rocourt and wife | 1 | 1 | | | 1 | | | |
| Thomas Smith | 1 | | | | | | | |
| Pierre Provincal | 1 | 1 | | | | | | |
| Louis Thebeau and wife | 1 | 1 | 1 | 2 | 1 | | | |
| Pierre Desnoyer and wife | 1 | 1 | | | 1 | | | |
| Pierre St. Cosme and wife | 1 | 1 | 2 | 1 | | | | |
| Mrs. Dejean | | 1 | 1 | | 2 | | 1 | 1 |
| Joseph L'Enfant and wife | 1 | 1 | 2 | 1 | 1 | 4 | 4 | |
| Philip Belanger and wife | 1 | 1 | 1 | | 1 | 1 | | |
| William Brown and wife | 1 | 1 | | | 1 | 2 | | |
| Joseph Gobielle and wife | 1 | 1 | | | 2 | | | |
| Jean Bt. Criste and wife | 1 | 1 | 2 | 2 | | 2 | | |
| Mrs. St. Martin | | 1 | | | 1 | 1 | | |
| Joseph St. Jean | 1 | | 3 | | | | | |
| Mrs. Chatlain | | 1 | | | 1 | 1 | | |
| Isaac Gagnie and wife | 1 | 1 | 1 | | | 1 | | |
| Charles and Andre Lefleur and mother | 2 | 1 | 1 | | 1 | | | |
| Prisqué Cotté and wife | 1 | 1 | | | 2 | 1 | | |
| Pierre Boamy and wife (Boemier) | 1 | 1 | 1 | | 1 | | | |
| Richard Whittle | 1 | | 1 | 1 | | 1 | | |
| William Shaw and wife | 1 | 1 | 2 | | | 1 | | |
| George Anthon and wife | 1 | 1 | | 1 | 1 | 1 | 1 | 1 |
| Antoine Cattin and wife | 1 | 1 | | | | 2 | | |
| Joseph Vallade and wife | 1 | 1 | 4 | 1 | 1 | 3 | | |
| Martin Levril and wife | 1 | 1 | 2 | | 2 | 1 | | |
| Gland Solant (Claude Solo) | 1 | | 1 | 1 | 2 | | | |
| Pierre Labady Jun., and wife | 1 | 1 | 1 | | 2 | 3 | | |
| Binac Porlier | 1 | | 2 | | | | | |
| Joseph Bourdeaux and wife | 1 | 1 | | | 2 | 6 | | |
| Louis Bellaire and wife | 1 | 1 | | | | | | |
| Alexis Campeau and wife | 1 | 1 | | | 1 | 4 | | |
| Godfroy Robert and wife | 2 | 1 | 1 | 1 | 6 | | | 1 |
| Alexis Delisle and wife | 1 | 1 | 1 | 1 | 6 | | | 1 |
| Mrs. Chesne | | 1 | 1 | 1 | | 2 | 1 | 1 |
| Jean Bt. Couture and wife | 1 | 1 | 1 | | 4 | 3 | | |
| John Edgar and wife | 1 | 1 | | | | 1 | | |
| John McErgan and wife | 1 | 1 | | | 1 | 4 | | |
| Gerard Bercelon and wife | 1 | 1 | | 1 | 2 | | | |
| Ambroise Riopel and wife | 1 | 1 | | 1 | 3 | 3 | | 1 |
| Jean Bt. Cicot, wife, and mother | 1 | 2 | | | 2 | 4 | 2 | 5 |
| Louis Visier and wife | 1 | 1 | | 1 | 2 | 3 | 1 | 2 |
| Joseph Cabasy and sister (Cabassier) | 1 | 1 | 2 | | | | 2 | 2 |

## Census of 1779

| | | | | | | | |
|---|---|---|---|---|---|---|---|
| Beaugrain and Gilbeau | 2 | 0 | 3 | 1 | 3 | | |
| Mrs. Drouillard | | 1 | | | | 1 | 1 |
| Claude Campau and wife | 1 | 1 | 1 | 3 | 3 | 1 | |
| Robert Navarre Senr. and wife | 1 | 1 | 1 | | 1 | 1 | 1 |
| Etienne Hyvernois (Livernois) | 1 | 1 | | | | 1 | 1 |
| Pierre Descompte Labady and wife | 1 | 1 | 2 | 1 | 2 | 3 | |
| Joseph Gamelin and mother | 1 | 1 | 3 | | 1 | 2 | 1 | 1 |
| St. Jean | 1 | | | | | | |
| Joseph Poupar Lefleur and wife | 1 | 1 | 1 | | | | 2 |
| François Cadoret and wife | 1 | 1 | | | 1 | | |
| Thomas Finchley and wife | 1 | 1 | 1 | | 2 | | |
| Charles Chesne and wife | 1 | 1 | 1 | 1 | 3 | 2 | |
| François Berthelet and wife | 1 | 1 | | | 1 | | 2 |
| Widow Menard | | 1 | | 1 | 4 | | |
| Louison Robedoux and wife | 1 | 1 | 2 | 2 | 4 | 2 | |
| Gerard Cochran | 1 | | 1 | | 1 | | |
| Mrs. Pike | | 1 | | 1 | 2 | 1 | |
| Mrs. Baby | | 1 | | | 3 | 5 | 1 | 3 |
| William and Alexr. Macomb and wife | 2 | 1 | 1 | 1 | 1 | 3 | 1 | 2 |
| Mrs. Laughton | | 1 | | | 1 | 1 | 1 | 1 |
| William Park | 1 | | | | | | |
| Victor Moriseau and wife | 1 | 1 | | | | | |
| Jacques Besere and wife | 1 | 1 | 1 | | 1 | 1 | |
| Josette Politte | | 1 | | 1 | 1 | | |
| Charles Bernier and wife | 1 | 1 | 1 | | 2 | 2 | |
| François Leblanc and wife | 1 | 1 | 1 | | 1 | 1 | |
| Jean Saliot and wife | 1 | 1 | | 1 | 1 | | |
| Louis Montmini and wife | 1 | 1 | | | 4 | 2 | |
| Jean Bte Reau and wife | 1 | 1 | | | 1 | 1 | |
| Antoine Meloche and wife | 1 | 1 | | | 3 | 1 | |
| Jean Bt Antiya and wife | 1 | 1 | | | 3 | 1 | |
| Jean Bt Gigniac and wife | 1 | 1 | | | 1 | | |
| Thomas Pagotte and wife | 1 | 1 | 1 | | 1 | 5 | |
| François Langlois and wife | 1 | 1 | | | 3 | 3 | |
| Louis Lajoy and wife | 1 | 1 | | | 4 | 2 | | 1 |
| Antoine Boufare and wife | 1 | 1 | 1 | | 2 | 1 | |
| Charles Reneau and wife | 1 | 1 | | | 2 | 1 | |
| Etienne Laviolette and wife | 1 | 1 | 2 | | 2 | 3 | |
| François Choisi and wife | 1 | 1 | | | 1 | 3 | |
| Charles Fontaigne and wife | 1 | 1 | | | 1 | 3 | |
| Jean Beaushomme and wife | 1 | 1 | | | 1 | | |
| Augustin Toranjeau and wife | 1 | 1 | 1 | | 1 | | |
| Pierre Proux and wife | 1 | 1 | | | 1 | 1 | |
| Pierre Charon and wife | 1 | 1 | | | 1 | 1 | |
| Pierre Campeau and wife | 1 | 1 | | | 1 | | |
| Antoine Rousseau and wife | 1 | 1 | 2 | | 1 | | |
| Etienne Jacob and wife | 1 | 1 | | | 3 | 3 | |
| Louis Ceasore and wife (Suzor) | 1 | 1 | 1 | | 2 | 4 | |
| Madame Bissonnette | | 1 | 2 | 1 | 3 | 2 | |
| René Cloutier and wife | 1 | 1 | | | 1 | | |

| | | | | | | | |
|---|---|---|---|---|---|---|---|
| Zachariah Cloutier and wife | 1 | 1 | | | 4 | 4 | |
| J. Bt Bigras | 1 | | | | | | |
| Micheal Roy and wife | 1 | 1 | 1 | | 1 | | |
| Pierre Bellaire and wife | 1 | 1 | 1 | | 3 | 3 | |
| Louis St. Louis and wife | 1 | 1 | 1 | | 1 | | |
| Jean Lajeness and wife | 1 | 1 | 4 | 1 | 1 | 3 | |
| J. Bt Toranjeau and wife | 1 | 1 | 2 | | | 1 | 1 |
| J. Bt Bertrand and wife | 1 | 1 | | 1 | 5 | 3 | |
| Joseph Drouillard and wife | 1 | 1 | 1 | | 1 | 2 | 1 |
| Joseph St. Etienne and wife | 1 | 1 | 1 | | | | |
| Simon Drouillard and wife | 1 | 1 | | | 5 | 4 | |
| Pierre Meloche and wife | 1 | 1 | 2 | 2 | 6 | 1 | |
| Joseph Bellperche and mother | 1 | 1 | 2 | 1 | 3 | 4 | |
| Jacques Peltier and wife | 1 | 1 | | | 2 | 2 | |
| J. Bt Peter and wife | 1 | 1 | | | 1 | 1 | |
| J. Bt Drouillard and wife | 1 | 1 | 4 | 1 | | | |
| Joseph Bondy and wife | 1 | 1 | 2 | | 4 | 4 | |
| Pierre Coquillard and wife | 1 | 1 | 3 | 1 | | | |
| Jean Bt Parry and wife | 1 | 1 | 3 | 2 | 2 | 1 | |
| Noel Chavin and wife | 1 | 1 | 2 | 1 | 4 | 3 | |
| Théophil Lamay and wife | 1 | 1 | 1 | | 2 | 3 | |
| J. Bt Réaume and wife | 1 | 1 | 1 | | 3 | 3 | 1 |
| Etienne Robidoux and wife | 1 | 1 | 1 | | 2 | 1 | |
| George Knaggs and wife | 1 | 1 | | | 3 | 2 | 1 |
| Pire Pothier | 1 | | 1 | 1 | | | |
| François Marentete and wife | 1 | 1 | 2 | | 5 | 1 | 1 |
| William Monforton and wife | 1 | 1 | 2 | 1 | 3 | 1 | 1 |
| Jacques Parent and wife | 1 | 1 | 1 | | 3 | | |
| Laurent Parent and wife | 1 | 1 | 1 | | 3 | 1 | |
| Mrs. Janess and son | 1 | 1 | | | 2 | 1 | |
| Claude Réaume and wife | 1 | 1 | 1 | | 5 | 1 | 1 |
| Philip Leduc and wife | 1 | 1 | | | 5 | 2 | |
| J. Bt Leduc and wife | 1 | 1 | 2 | | 1 | 2 | |
| Francis Sordellier | 1 | 1 | | | 2 | 2 | |
| Widow Malout | | 1 | 1 | 1 | 2 | | |
| Joseph Valcour and wife | 1 | 1 | | | 2 | 1 | |
| J. Bt Voilette and wife | 1 | 1 | 2 | | 3 | 1 | |
| André Benetteau and wife | 1 | 1 | 1 | 1 | 3 | 3 | |
| Charles Bourond and wife | 1 | 1 | 1 | 1 | 4 | 3 | 1 |
| Dominique Labrosse and wife | 1 | 1 | 3 | | | 1 | |
| Pierre Réaume and wife | 1 | 1 | 2 | 1 | 1 | | 1 |
| Nicolas Lenoir | 1 | 1 | | | | | |
| William Goyeau | 1 | | | | 1 | 2 | |
| Vittel Demouchelle and wife | 1 | 1 | | | 3 | 2 | |
| Louis Gauyeux and wife | 1 | 1 | 1 | | 2 | 1 | |
| Jacques Charon and wife | 1 | 1 | 1 | | | 1 | |
| Joseph Lesperance | 1 | | | 2 | 1 | | 1 | 2 |
| Julien Parent and mother | 1 | 1 | | 3 | 1 | | 1 |
| Nicolas Langlois and wife | 1 | 1 | 3 | 1 | 3 | 2 | |
| Pierre Labute and wife | 1 | 1 | 3 | 2 | | 3 | |

## Census of 1779

| | | | | | | | | |
|---|---|---|---|---|---|---|---|---|
| Hyacinth Dhetre (Deshêtres) | 1 | | 1 | 1 | 2 | 2 | | 1 |
| Micheal Cattin and wife | 1 | 1 | | | | | | |
| Charles Delisle and wife | 1 | 1 | 1 | | | | | |
| Antoine Langlois and wife | 1 | 1 | 2 | | 1 | 2 | | |
| Joseph Dechesne and wife | 1 | 1 | | | 2 | 1 | 1 | |
| Paul Campeau | 1 | | | | 1 | 1 | | |
| J. Bt Beaubien Jr. and wife | 1 | 1 | | | 1 | 1 | | |
| Joseph Beaubien and wife | 1 | 1 | 2 | 1 | 1 | | | 1 |
| Alexis Maisonville and wife | 1 | 1 | 3 | 1 | 2 | | 3 | 3 |
| Louis Labady | 1 | | | | 4 | 2 | 1 | 1 |
| Bonaventure Réaume and wife | 1 | 1 | | | 3 | 3 | | |
| Joseph Gaudet and wife | 1 | 1 | 1 | | | 3 | | |
| Joseph Bertiaume and wife | 1 | 1 | 1 | | 2 | 1 | | |
| André Peltier and wife | 1 | 1 | | | 4 | 4 | | |
| François Drouillard and wife | 1 | 1 | 1 | | 3 | 3 | | |
| Alexis Argute and wife (Arcoat?) | 1 | 1 | | | 2 | 1 | | |
| Vittal Depelteau and wife | 1 | 1 | | | | 1 | | |
| J. Bt Laperle and wife | 1 | 1 | | | 2 | | | |
| J. Bt. Parrey and wife | 1 | 1 | | | 4 | 2 | | |
| François Company | 1 | | 2 | | 2 | 1 | | |
| J. Bt Lecoursier | 1 | | | | 1 | | | |
| William Laforet and wife | 1 | 1 | | | 2 | 2 | | |
| Laurent Griffaur and wife | 1 | 1 | | | 1 | 3 | | |
| Louis Griffaur and wife | 1 | 1 | | | 3 | 3 | | |
| Basil Belanger | 1 | | | | | | | |
| Jean Thoulouse and wife | 1 | 1 | | | 1 | 2 | | |
| Nicolas Thé and wife | 1 | 1 | | | 3 | 2 | | |
| Coxes Wind Mill | | | | | | | | |
| Garrison and navy | 239 | 34 | | | 30 | 28 | | 1 |
| Extras, prisoners | 500 | | | | | | | |

Endorsed: Survey of the settlement of Detroit taken 31st March 1779 upon oath. Rcvd June 1779

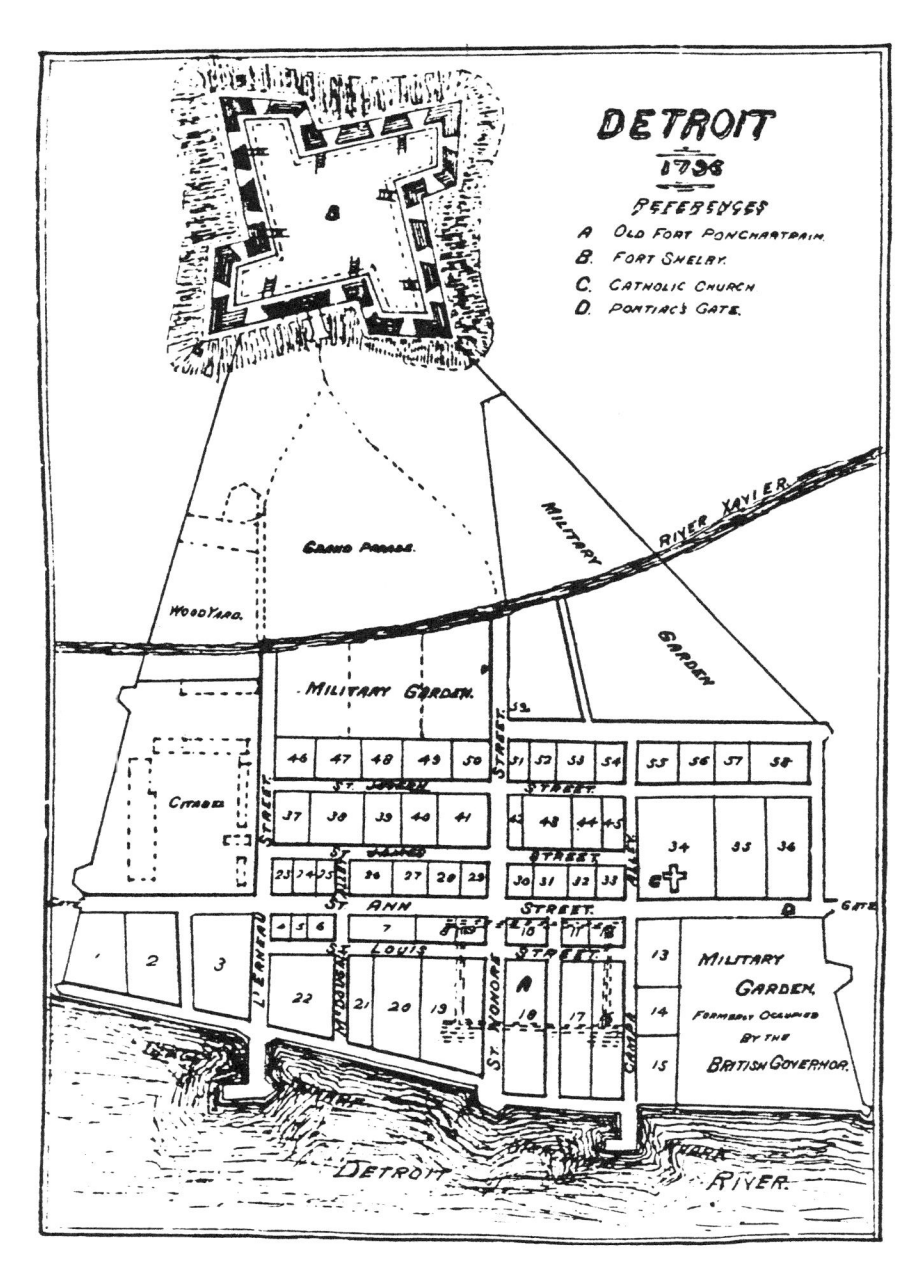

MAP 10. DETROIT IN 1796, by Clarence M. Burton
(Courtesy of Burton Historical Collection)

# 1780 CENSUS OF FORT SAINT JOSEPH

The Saint Joseph post, at present Niles, was strategically located at the junction of the principal waterways to Detroit and Fort Miami (Fort Wayne, Indiana) and near the Kankakee portage; it was the doorway to the entire Illinois country and the Mississippi River. Some historians, including Parkman and Thwaites, have placed the fort at South Bend, Indiana, probably because it is also located on the Saint Joseph River.

Established by Father Claude Allouez as a mission in 1689, it was garrisond by the French by 1700 and maintained until the spring of 1763. Chief Pontiac's plan to destroy the British by attacking all the western forts simultaneously was devasting to the fort at Saint Joseph. The commanding officer, Ensign Francis Schlosser, was taken prisoner and several soldiers were killed. The British abandoned the fort, although it was not deserted, and the residents remained. Their principal ties were with Michilimackinac rather than Detroit, and anyone doing research on these families should study those records as well.

The post continued to be the object of attack; during the Revolution, it was briefly captured and sacked by a group from Cahokia and in 1781 the Spanish raised their flag for a short time. The object was to expand their empire from west of the Mississippi River into the Great Lakes.

Throughout the period, a settlement of Frenchmen and their descendants remained, most being former soldiers or people involved in the fur trade. The Chevaliers were the most prominent family. In 1780 when this census was taken, the post had eight houses, forty-five Frenchmen, and several Pawnee slaves. Many of the Frenchmen had Indian wives.

The parish register of Saint Joseph (1720-1773) was translated, edited, and annotated by Father George Paré and Milo M. Quaife, and appears in *Mississippi Valley Historical Review* 13:201-239. See also *Wisconsin Historical Collections* 18:469-513 and 19:1-159 for the register of Ste. Ann's Church at Michilimackinac.

The original of this census is among the Haldimand Papers B97 2:370 at the Public Archives of Canada. The census had been included in a letter from Joseph Louis Ainsse, an Indian interpreter, to Lieutenant Governor Patrick Sinclair at Michilimackinac, dated 30 June 1780. A copy was provided to the present editor. Identifying these people cannot be done positively, at least by this writer. Perhaps the clues here will open the door to further records. Note particularly that several forms of the word *panise*, meaning Indian slave, appear.

This census was previously published in *Michigan Pioneer and Historical Collections* 10:406-7.

## CENSUS OF EVERY WOMAN, CHILD, AND SLAVE RESIDING AT FORT ST. JOSEPH

THE HOUSE OF M. CHEVALIER[1]
M. Chevalier
Daufinné (or Daujinné)
Gibaut
Pieriche[2]
Youtra[3]
Mme Chevalier
Mme Youtra, her daughter
Ruby, paniz
Lizette, panize
Angélique, panize, and infant son

THE HOUSE OF SR. MARCOT[4]
Marcot
Mme Marcot
four children

THE HOUSE OF MME ST. GERMAIN[5]
Mme St. Germain
her daughter and her son

THE HOUSE OF SR. MORIN[6]
Morin
Mme Morin
three infant boys

NAMES OF PRIVATE PERSONS, EACH ONE IN HIS OWN HOUSE
Joseph Hurtebize[7]      Langlois
Youtra[3]                Duchenan
Dursan                   Counol[8]
LaDouceur

THE HOUSE OF M. CARON[9]
M. and Mme Caron
Marianne, panize, and her infant son

THE HOUSE OF M. PRE[2] HURTEBIZE AND HIS EMPLOYEES
M. Pre Hurtebize      Lognon
Rolle                 Gervais

THE HOUSE OF PIERICHE[2] CHEVALIER
Pche[2] Chevalier, in war
his wife and three children

THE HOUSE OF SR. RODE[10]
M. Rode, his wife, and child

1. Louis Chevalier, b. 1730, and his wife Madeleine Réaume. He was a trader and in charge of Indian affairs after the garrison was disbanded. This was the most prominent family at Fort St. Joseph.
2. Pieriche is a diminutive of Pierre; Pre. is an abbreviation for Pieriche.
3. Jean Jutrat, b. St. Francois-du-Lac, Quebec, 14 March 1729; m. at Michilimackinac 7 July 1748 Catherine L'Archêveque.
4. A Jean Bte m. at Michilimackinac in 1758 Marie Neskech, Indian.
5. Poss. Magdeleine Chevalier, wife of Capt. Charles St. Germain, interpreter, and dau. of Louise, above. Could also be Felicité Chavignon, wife of Pierre.
6. Prob. Jean Morin, who was at St. Joseph in 1773. A Joseph Malgué Marin witnessed many marriages at Michilimackinac.
7. Prob. Pierre Heurtebize, trader, with wife Felicité Javillon, of the Montreal family.
8. More likely Coulon. Nicolas de Villiers Coulon, soldier, was first commander at St. Joseph; later went to Green Bay where he was slain by the Indians in 1733. This is probably a son or grandson from this large family.
9. A son of Claude Caron, trader at Michilimackinac by 1730; poss. Joseph.
10. A Joseph Rodde, son of Joseph of Bordeaux, France, m. at Detroit in 1787 M. Josephe Rivard. Could also be Benjamin Roche, a soldier, who witnessed a marriage at Michilimackinac in 1795. Or a Joseph Roc, whose natural daughters Louise ae 11 and Angelique ae 9 by an Indian wife were baptized at Michilimackinac in 1787.

# CENSUS OF 1782

This census was ordered by Major Arent Schuyler De Peyster, the Commanding Officer of the Detroit post, and taken between July 16th and 30th, 1782. Even though only three years had elapsed since the last enumeration, population increases were significant, showing 277 more inhabitants (exclusive of the garrison). These are due mainly to larger numbers of English, Scottish, and even Germans who had come to the community. The totals are: 321 heads of family, 254 married women, 72 widows and hired women, 336 young and hired men, 526 boys, 503 girls, 78 male slaves, and 101 female slaves. The agricultural tallies, not repeated here, include: 1,112 horses, 413 oxen, 807 cows, 452 heifers/steers, 447 sheep, 1,370 hogs, 94,250 bushels of flour, 1,804 bushels of wheat, 355 bushels of Indian corn, 4,075 bushels of wheat sown last fall, 521 arpents of Indian corn sown, 1,349 bushels of oats sown, 13,770 arpents of clear land (also described as land under cultivation).

Even though not included in the columns, a summary accompanying the census includes also 3,000 bushels of potatoes "supposed to be in the ground" and 1,000 barrels of cyder "supposed to be made." A notation at the end of the totals, made by De Peyster, states: "Exclusive of the above quantities, Hog Island will produce this harvest, one hundred bushels of wheat, and seven or eight hundred bushels of Indian corn - the small quantity of wheat owing to the late heavy rains." Hog Island is now called Belle Isle.

Like the previous census, this one was also printed in *Michigan Pioneer and Historical Collections* (10:601-611) and contains many misinterpretations of the French names. Accompanying this report were detailed inventory accounts of the Barrack Master General's Department at Detroit, pp. 614-621. The original document is among the Haldimand Papers (1782: B123:266-72) at the British Museum, London, and is reprinted here with permission. A photocopy is at the Public Archives of Canada (Haldimand Papers: Add. Mss., 21783, MG 21, Reel A-687). names found in the present list, while not the accepted spelling in many cases, are true to the way they were written and close enough to the original to be clear; when not, the usual spelling is added in parentheses.

Another transcription of the South Shore only was done by Father Ernest J. Lajeunesse, C.S.B., and appears in his book *The Windsor Border Region* (Toronto, 1960) on pp. 69-73. This one is accurate.

| (SOUTH SHORE: SANDWICH) | MARRIED WOMEN | WIDOWS/HIRED WOMEN | YOUNG/HIRED MEN | BOYS | GIRLS | MALE SLAVES | FEMALE SLAVES |
|---|---|---|---|---|---|---|---|
| François Prudhome | | | | | | | |
| Charles Fontaine | 1 | | | 4 | 2 | | |
| Jacques Bésere | 1 | | | 2 | 1 | | |
| Antoine Soumande | 1 | | | | | | |
| Pierre Meloche Jun. | 1 | | | | | | |
| Pierre Fouquerau | 1 | | 1 | 1 | 2 | | |
| Etienne Laviolette | 1 | | | 3 | 2 | | |
| Joseph Cotté | 1 | | | 5 | 1 | | |
| Louis Montmeney | 1 | | | 4 | 3 | | |
| Antoine Meloche | 1 | | | 3 | 3 | | |
| Jean Baptiste Antilliya | 1 | | | 2 | 2 | | |
| Thomas Pagotte | 1 | | 1 | 3 | 5 | | |
| Charles Renaud | 1 | | 1 | 4 | 1 | | |
| Jean Beaushomme | 1 | | | 1 | 2 | | |
| Pierre Prudhomme | | | 1 | | | | |
| Amable Gerard | 1 | | | 2 | 3 | | |
| Jean Louis Reveau | 1 | | 1 | | | | |
| François Lesperance | | | 2 | | | | |
| Pierre Proux | 1 | | 1 | 1 | 3 | | |
| Antoine Rousseau | 1 | | | | 1 | | |
| Charles Bernier | 1 | | | 2 | 1 | | |
| Antoine Boufard | 1 | | 1 | 5 | 1 | | |
| René Cloutier | 1 | | 2 | 4 | 4 | | |
| Zachary Cloutier | 1 | | | 1 | 2 | | |
| Michael Roy | 1 | | 1 | 2 | 1 | | |
| François Mouton | 1 | | | 1 | 4 | | |
| Ettienne Jacob | 1 | | 1 | 5 | 3 | | |
| Louis Sosore | 1 | | 1 | 2 | 5 | | |
| Mrs. Bissonnette | | 1 | 2 | 3 | 3 | | |
| Jean Bap. Bigras | | | | | | | |
| François Belaire | 1 | | 2 | 2 | 4 | | |
| Paul Campau | 1 | | 1 | 2 | 2 | | |
| Louis Lajeunesse | 1 | | 2 | 5 | 1 | | |
| Joseph Pouget | 1 | | 3 | 2 | 4 | | |
| Jean Bte. Touranjau | 1 | 2 | 4 | 2 | 1 | | |
| Jean Saliotte | 1 | | 1 | 1 | 2 | | |
| Guillaume Monforton | 1 | | 1 | 3 | 2 | | 1 |
| Joseph Drouillard | 1 | | 1 | | 3 | 1 | 1 |

Census of 1782

|  | | | | | | | |
|---|---|---|---|---|---|---|---|
| Pierre Meloche | 1 | | 1 | 6 | 2 | | |
| Jacques Belleperche | | 1 | | 1 | | | |
| Antoine Robert Jun. | 1 | | | 3 | 3 | | |
| Louis Robidoux | 1 | | | 3 | 3 | | |
| Joseph Bondy | 2 | | 3 | 2 | 5 | 1 | |
| Jean Bte. Drouillard | 1 | | | 1 | | | |
| Jean Bte. Drouillard Sen. | 1 | | 3 | | | | |
| Pierre Cocquillard | 1 | | 2 | | | | |
| Jean Bte. Parrey | 1 | | 3 | 2 | 3 | | |
| Augustine Toranjeau | 1 | | | | | | |
| Théophil Lemay | 1 | | 1 | 1 | 4 | | |
| Charles Réaume | 1 | | 1 | 3 | 1 | | 1 |
| Louis Lajoye | 1 | | | 5 | 2 | | |
| George Knaggs | 1 | | | 3 | 2 | | |
| James Rankin | | | | 1 | 3 | | 1 |
| François Pratt | 1 | | | 3 | 1 | 1 | 1 |
| François Marentete Gaudet | 1 | 1 | 1 | 5 | 2 | 1 | 2 |
| Charles Robidoux | 1 | | 1 | | | | |
| Jacques Parent | 1 | | 1 | 4 | | | 1 |
| Laurent Parent | 1 | | 1 | 3 | 2 | | |
| Claude Réaume | 1 | | 1 | 3 | 2 | | |
| Joseph Mathieu | | | 3 | 2 | | | |
| Philip Leduc | 1 | | 1 | 1 | 1 | | |
| Joseph Duchesne | 1 | | | 4 | 1 | | |
| Joseph Maillou | | 1 | 1 | 2 | 1 | | |
| François Janesse | | 1 | | 2 | 1 | | |
| Jean Ouillette | 1 | 2 | 2 | 3 | 2 | | |
| André Bennetau | 1 | | | 3 | 1 | | |
| Charles Bouround | 1 | | 1 | | | | 1 |
| Joseph Larente | | | | | | | |
| Jean Bte. Tourneux | 1 | | 2 | | 1 | | |
| Pierre Réaume | | | 1 | | | | 1 |
| Ignace Duvalle | 1 | 2 | 2 | 1 | 2 | | |
| Vittal Demouchelle | 1 | | 1 | 3 | 4 | | |
| Louis Goyou | 1 | | 2 | 3 | 1 | | |
| Jacques Charon | 1 | | 2 | 1 | 1 | | |
| Joseph Lesperance | | 1 | 1 | 1 | 2 | | 1 |
| Julien Parent | | | 1 | 1 | 2 | | |
| Nicholas Langlois | 1 | | 2 | 3 | 2 | | |
| Pierre Labute | 1 | 1 | 1 | 1 | 2 | 2 | 1 |
| François Gaudette | 1 | | | | | | |
| Hyacinth Dehêtre | | 1 | 2 | 1 | 1 | | |
| Charles Delisle | 1 | | | 1 | | | |
| Antoine Langlois | 1 | 1 | 1 | 5 | 2 | | |
| Jean Bte Beaubien | 1 | | | 2 | 2 | | |
| Joseph Beaubien | 1 | 1 | 1 | 4 | 2 | | 1 |
| Joseph Cecire | 1 | 1 | | | | | |
| Fontenay Dequindre | 1 | | 1 | 1 | 1 | | |
| Alexis Maisonville | 1 | | | 4 | | 2 | 2 |

|  | | | | | | | |
|---|---|---|---|---|---|---|---|
| Antoine L. Labady | | | | 3 | 3 | 1 | 1 |
| Bonaventure Réaume | 1 | | | 4 | 3 | | |
| Joseph Gaudet | 1 | | | 1 | 2 | | |
| Joseph Bertiaume | 1 | | 1 | 2 | 1 | | |
| Pierre Réaume Jun. | 1 | | | | 2 | | |
| Jean Bte Sanscrainte | 1 | | 2 | 2 | 1 | | |
| François Meloche | 1 | | 2 | 4 | 3 | | |
| Mrs. Levril | | | | 1 | 2 | 1 | |
| Pierre Geirou | | | | 1 | | | |
| Guillhaume Goyou | | | | | 2 | | |
| Nicholas Petit | 1 | | | 3 | 4 | | |
| André Peltier | 1 | | 1 | 3 | 5 | | |
| Jean Bte Lapointe | 1 | | | 2 | 3 | 1 | |
| Pierre Letrouneau | | 2 | 2 | 3 | 1 | | |
| François Drouillard | 1 | | | 4 | 3 | | |
| Louis St. Louis | 1 | | 1 | 2 | | | |
| Pierre Leverseur | 1 | | | 1 | 1 | | |
| François Sourdellet | 1 | | | 3 | 3 | | |
| Joseph Valcour | 1 | | | 2 | 2 | | |
| Jean Bte Parrey | 1 | | 2 | 4 | 3 | | |
| Joseph Beauchamp | | | | 1 | | | |
| Antoine Robert | 1 | | | 3 | | | 1 |

(NORTH SHORE: DETROIT)

|  | | | | | | | |
|---|---|---|---|---|---|---|---|
| Pierre Laperle | | | | | | | |
| A. Goulette and Litzimburger | 2 | | | 1 | | | |
| Pierre Yax | | | | | | | |
| William Forsith | 1 | | 2 | 3 | | 2 | 3 |
| John Askin | 1 | | 4 | 1 | 2 | 4 | 2 |
| Gregor McGregor | 1 | | 3 | 2 | 2 | 2 | |
| Julien Ferton | | 1 | | 2 | 2 | | |
| François Duchene | 1 | | | 1 | | | |
| Nicholas Patnotte | 1 | | | 1 | 6 | | |
| Antoine Meney | 1 | | | 2 | 4 | | |
| François Tremblay | 1 | | 1 | 4 | 2 | | |
| Michel Yax | 1 | 1 | 3 | | | | |
| Claude Duchesne | 1 | 2 | | 2 | | | |
| Pierre Duchesne | 1 | | | 2 | | | |
| Jean Bte Créqui | 1 | | | 2 | 6 | | |
| Charles Grimaur | | | | 1 | | | 1 |
| Joseph Saucier | 1 | | 1 | 2 | 5 | | |
| Jean Bte Lacoursière | | | 6 | | | | |
| Benjamin Jones | 1 | | | 4 | 1 | | |
| Laurent Griffaur | 1 | | | 2 | 4 | | |
| Isedore Maurin | 1 | | | 4 | | | |
| Augustin Tremblay | 1 | 1 | 2 | | 1 | | |
| Louis Tremblay | 1 | | | 4 | 3 | | 1 |
| Jacob Harsen | 1 | | | 3 | 3 | 1 | |

Census of 1782

| | | | | | | | |
|---|---|---|---|---|---|---|---|
| Jean Champaigne | 1 | | 3 | 1 | 6 | | |
| Mrs. Casety | | | 1 | | | 2 | 1 |
| Jacques Allard | 1 | | | 1 | 1 | | |
| André Skyanis | 1 | | 1 | 1 | | | |
| Louis Griffaur | 1 | | 1 | 4 | 3 | | |
| Jean Cripeit | 1 | 1 | 1 | | 2 | | |
| Jean Thoulouse | 1 | 1 | 2 | 1 | 3 | | |
| Louis Renaud | 1 | | | 3 | 4 | | |
| Ignace Thibeau | 1 | | | 5 | 2 | | |
| Jacques Lauson | 1 | | 2 | 3 | 2 | | |
| Joseph Tremblay | | | 1 | | | | |
| Jean Bte Chauvin | 1 | 1 | | 4 | 3 | | |
| Jean Duprau | 1 | | 1 | 2 | 3 | | |
| Gaetan Laderoute | 1 | 1 | 1 | | 1 | | |
| Mrs. Marsac | | 1 | 2 | 5 | 1 | | |
| Michel Yax Jun. | | | 1 | | | | |
| Jean Bte Marsac | 1 | | | 1 | 4 | | |
| Thomas Cox | 1 | 2 | 2 | | | 2 | 3 |
| Joseph Perinier | 1 | | | 5 | 2 | | |
| Jean Marie Dubaye | 1 | | | 3 | 2 | | |
| Joseph Laperle | 1 | | | 1 | 3 | | |
| Charles Chauvin | 1 | 3 | 2 | 6 | 3 | | |
| Jean Bte Campau Jun. | 1 | | 3 | | 6 | 1 | |
| Pierre Cardinalle | 1 | | | 4 | 2 | | |
| Joseph Cardinalle | | 1 | 1 | 3 | 4 | | |
| Jacques St. Aubin | | | 4 | | 1 | | |
| Pierre St. Aubin | 1 | 1 | 1 | | | | |
| Louis St. Aubin | 1 | | 3 | 2 | 3 | | |
| Simon Meloche | 1 | | | 2 | 1 | | |
| Robert Jean | 1 | | 1 | 1 | 3 | | |
| John Martin Franks | | | 1 | | | | |
| Antoine Moras | 1 | | 3 | 2 | 1 | | |
| Guillaume Bernard | 1 | | 1 | 5 | 5 | 2 | 5 |
| Antoine Bernard | 1 | 1 | | | 1 | | |
| Nicholas Michel dit Lorrain | 1 | 1 | 2 | | | 1 | 1 |
| Louis Beufait | 1 | 1 | 1 | 1 | 3 | 2 | 1 |
| Jean Bte Chapoton | 1 | 1 | 6 | 1 | 3 | 2 | 2 |
| Jean Bte Peltier | 1 | | 4 | 2 | | | |
| Pierre Durand | 1 | | 1 | | | | |
| Charles Lapalme | 1 | 1 | 1 | 2 | 1 | | |
| Jean Bte Meloche | 1 | | 1 | 1 | 8 | 1 | 2 |
| Philip Belangé | 1 | 1 | 4 | 1 | 3 | | 1 |
| Mrs. Benoa | | | 1 | | | | |
| Simon Campau | 1 | | | 4 | 6 | 3 | 2 |
| Jean Bte Campau | 1 | 1 | | 5 | 3 | 5 | 2 |
| Jacques Campau | | | 2 | 6 | | 1 | 1 |
| Hippolite Campau | 1 | | 3 | 1 | 1 | | |
| Ignace Boyer | 1 | | 1 | | 1 | | |
| Noel St. Aubin | | 2 | 2 | 1 | 2 | | |
| Antoine Miney | | 2 | 2 | 2 | 2 | | |

|  | | | | | | | |
|---|---|---|---|---|---|---|---|
| François Gouin | 1 | | 1 | | 1 | | |
| Alexis Cueillerie | 1 | | 1 | 1 | 4 | | |
| Nicholas Gouin | 1 | | 1 | 2 | 1 | | |
| Charles Gouin | 1 | 1 | 1 | 1 | 3 | 1 | 1 |
| Amable Latoure | 1 | | 1 | | 1 | | |
| Antoine Dequindre | 1 | | | 1 | | | |
| Robert Deninston | 1 | | | | 2 | | |
| Jean Bte Revaur | 1 | | 2 | 7 | 3 | | 1 |
| François Bellecour | 1 | | | | 1 | | 1 |
| Charles Moran | | 1 | 2 | 2 | 4 | | 1 |
| Jean Bte Beaubien | 1 | 2 | 8 | 1 | 3 | | 2 |
| John Pike | 1 | | 2 | 2 | 2 | | |
| Joseph Lusier | | | 7 | | | | |
| James Thompson | | 1 | 3 | | | | |
| Normand McLeod | 1 | | | | 1 | | 1 |
| Pere Simple | | 1 | 2 | | | | |
| Thomas Fincheley | 1 | | 1 | 3 | 1 | 1 | 1 |
| François Billiet | 1 | | 2 | | | | |
| Nathan Williams | | | 2 | | | | |
| Ridley and Hands | | | | | | | |
| John McPherson | | | | 2 | | | |
| Jean Morin | | | | 3 | | | |
| Abbott and Saunders | 1 | | 1 | 2 | 4 | | 2 |
| George Lyons | 1 | 1 | | 1 | | 1 | |
| William Groesbeck | | | 2 | | | | |
| Alexander Macomb | 1 | 2 | 4 | 3 | 4 | 3 | 4 |
| William Macomb | 2 | | | 3 | 2 | 4 | 4 |
| Duperon Baby | 2 | | 4 | 3 | 5 | 1 | 1 |
| Thomas McCrae | 1 | | 3 | 5 | | | |
| Gerret Greverat | 1 | | 6 | 3 | | 1 | |
| George Anthon | 1 | | | 1 | | | 1 |
| Jean Bte Sanchagrin | 2 | | 1 | 1 | 3 | | |
| George Cotteral | 1 | | 1 | | 1 | | |
| James May | 1 | | | | | 1 | |
| John W. Kirgan/McKirgan? | 1 | | | 3 | 5 | | |
| Daniel Garril | 1 | 1 | 1 | 2 | | | |
| William Scott | 1 | | 4 | | 3 | | |
| Pauling and Burnell | | | 2 | | | 1 | |
| Antoine Adhemar | 1 | | | 2 | 2 | 1 | 1 |
| T. Williams | 1 | | 2 | 1 | 1 | 1 | |
| Alexander Grant | 1 | | | | 4 | | 2 |
| Thomas Reynolds | 1 | | | 3 | 2 | | 1 |
| William Tucker | 1 | | | 2 | 1 | | 1 |
| Simon McTavish | | | 2 | | | | |
| William Park | | | 1 | 1 | | 1 | |
| Andrews and Trimble | | | | | | | |
| Jacob Schieffelin | 1 | | | 1 | | 1 | |
| Mrs. St. Cosme | | | 2 | | | | |
| Louis Thibeau | 1 | | 2 | | 1 | | |
| Joseph Voyer | 1 | | 2 | | | | |
| Augustine Lafoy | | | 1 | | | | |
| Patrick McGulpin | 1 | | 1 | 2 | 1 | | |

Census of 1782

|  | | | | | | | |
|---|---|---|---|---|---|---|---|
| Patrick McGulpin | 1 | | 1 | 2 | 1 | | |
| Jean Bte Roucourt | | 1 | | 1 | | | |
| Wilson and Dolsen | 1 | | | 1 | 1 | | |
| Sarah Ainnse | | | | | | | 1 |
| Isaac Gagner | 1 | | 1 | 1 | 2 | 1 | |
| Prisque Cotté | 1 | | | 2 | 1 | | |
| Jacques Peltier | 1 | | 2 | 3 | 3 | | 1 |
| Amable Maillou | 1 | | 2 | | | | |
| Isaac Williams and Son | 1 | | | 1 | 3 | | |
| Pierre Borgia | 1 | | 1 | 5 | | | |
| Joseph Ciré dit St. Jean | | 1 | 1 | 1 | | 1 | 2 |
| Jean Bte Craite | 2 | | 2 | | 3 | 1 | |
| Antoine Bernard | 1 | | 1 | | | | |
| François Gaubielle | 1 | | 1 | 3 | | | |
| Cornwall and Miller | | | 4 | | | 1 | |
| Pierre Drouillard | 1 | 1 | 1 | | 2 | 1 | 1 |
| John Carbey | 1 | | | | | | |
| Walter Goodfellow | | | | 1 | | | |
| Jean Bte Pitre | 1 | | | 3 | 2 | | |
| Trudelle and Charbonneau | | | | | | | |
| Joseph L'Enfant | 1 | | 2 | 4 | 3 | | |
| Charles Chesne | 1 | 1 | 2 | 2 | 1 | | |
| Gabriel Hunot | | | | | | | |
| Victoire Morriseaux | 1 | | | 2 | | | |
| Joseph Gamelin | | 1 | 1 | 1 | 1 | 1 | |
| Pierre Démarse | 2 | | 2 | 3 | 1 | | |
| Dominique Labrosse | 1 | | 2 | | | | |
| Joseph Baron | 1 | | | 3 | | | |
| Alexis Labady | 1 | | 2 | 2 | 3 | 1 | |
| Pierre Labady | 1 | | 1 | | | | |
| Ettienne Hyvernois and Son | 1 | | | 1 | | 1 | 1 |
| Robert Navarre and Son | 1 | | 1 | | 2 | 1 | 1 |
| Pierre Robert | 1 | | 1 | 4 | 3 | | |
| Claude Campau | 1 | 2 | 3 | | 1 | | |
| Joseph Poupar | 1 | | 1 | | 2 | 2 | |
| Registre Benoa | | 1 | 1 | | | | |
| Jean Guillebau | | | 2 | | | | |
| Jean Marie Durand | 1 | | | | | | |
| Joseph Vermette | 1 | | 2 | | 2 | | |
| Joseph Cabasy | 1 | 1 | 1 | | 2 | 1 | 1 |
| Louis Couseneau | 1 | | 1 | 1 | 1 | | |
| Louis Vissière | 1 | | | 3 | 4 | 1 | 2 |
| Jean Bte Cecot | 1 | 1 | | 2 | 4 | 4 | 4 |
| Ambroise Riopelle | 1 | 1 | | 5 | 4 | | |
| Louis Tremblay | 1 | | | | 1 | | |
| Antoine and H. Laselle | | | 2 | | | | |
| Simon Gendron | 1 | | | | | | |
| Gerard Bercelau | 1 | 1 | 1 | 3 | 2 | | |
| François Chabert § | 2 | | 3 | 2 | 2 | 1 | 1 |
| Isidore Chesne | | | | | | | |

| | | | | | | | |
|---|---|---|---|---|---|---|---|
| Alexis Delile | 1 | 1 | 2 | 6 | 2 | 1 | 1 |
| Jaques Godfroy and Son | 1 | | 2 | | 1 | | 2 |
| Charles Campau | 1 | | 1 | | | | |
| Robert Navarre Jun. | 1 | | 1 | 5 | 3 | | 2 |
| Jean Bte Couture | 1 | | | 4 | 1 | | |
| Pierre Labady Jun. | 1 | | 1 | 3 | 3 | | |
| Alexis Campau | 1 | | 1 | 3 | 4 | | |
| William Brown | 1 | | | | 1 | | 1 |
| Calude Solaut | | | | 1 | 2 | | |
| François Gamelin | | | | 1 | | 1 | |
| Antoine Revaure | 1 | | 1 | 2 | 2 | | |
| Jean Bte Réaume | 1 | 1 | 2 | 2 | 4 | | 1 |
| Joseph André | 1 | | 1 | 2 | 2 | | |
| Antoine Cattin | 1 | | 1 | 1 | 3 | | |
| Joseph Bourdeaux | 1 | | 1 | 3 | 5 | | |
| Reverend Mr. Hubert | | | | 1 | | | |
| Amable Bigras | 1 | | 1 | | 1 | | |

# PETITE COTE CENSUS OF 1792

A regional census, this enumeration covers only the part of the South Shore below the Rivière à Gervais and bisected by the Rivière aux Dindes (Turkey Creek), opposite the northern half of Ile aux Dindes (Grosse Ile) and north to the southwestern limits of the present city of Windsor, Ontario. This was called Petite Côte, and, as indicated in the Remarks, the lots were granted between 1749 and 1754. See Ernest J. Lajeunesse, *The Windsor Border Region* (Toronto, 1960) pp. lvii-lviii, for a more complete description. Father Lajeunesse also notes an error in the dates, showing certain lots were granted as late as 1756.

The census was taken by Guillaume Monforton, the Public Notary at Detroit from 1784 to 1792, and Captain of the Militia at Petite Côte. The original document is in the Monforton Register at the Public Archives of Canada, and was not examined by the compiler.

It has been reprinted twice: in *Ontario Historical Society, Papers and Records* 24:95-97, and *The Windsor Border Region*, pp. 75-76.

|  | BOYS 15+ | BOYS -15 | GIRLS | REMARKS |
|---|---|---|---|---|
| Colonel McKey (McKee) |  |  |  | All the farms from |
| Jean Bt Paré |  |  |  | River Gervais to |
| Frederick Arnold | 3 | 1 | 5 | Turkey Creek opposite |
| Isaac Dolson |  |  |  | the end of Turkey |
| Matthew Dolson |  |  |  | Island were granted |
| Judge Powell |  |  |  | by Mr. de Sabrevois |
| Philipp Fox | 3 | 4 | 2 |  |
| Thomas Smith |  | 1 | 2 | Mr. de Lajonquière |
| Joseph Bondy, Senior | 1 | 2 | 2 | Commander-in-chief |
| Thomas Smith |  |  |  | in 1751 granted |
| Major McGregor |  |  |  | provisions for three |
| Simon Drouillar | 2 | 1 |  | years to the first |
| Antoine Girardin |  |  | 1 | settlers in 1752 and |
| Guillaume Monforton | 2 | 1 | 3 | 1753, without any |
| Meldrum and Park |  |  |  | title. |
| Joseph Pouget | 2 |  | 3 |  |
| Richard Pollar |  |  |  |  |
| John Messomer |  | 2 | 4 |  |
| Meldrum and Park |  |  |  |  |
| John Snider |  |  |  |  |
| John Askin |  |  |  |  |
| Joseph Réaume | 3 |  | 4 |  |

## RIVIERE AUX DINDES (TURKEY CREEK)

| | | | | |
|---|---|---|---|---|
| Pierre Ladebauche | 1 | | | All these farms were |
| Jn B. Bigras | | | | granted in 1755-56 |
| Zacharie Cloutier | 1 | 3 | 3 | by Mr. de Celoron |
| Antoine Bouffar | 2 | 3 | 3 | who gave tickets of |
| Martin Durocher | 1 | 1 | 1 | grant to the first |
| Antoine Bouffar | | | | settlers on them. |
| Veuve (Widow) Rousseau | | | | (Date incorrect; |
| Veuve Grould | 1 | 1 | 3 | Céloron was at |
| Joseph Rochelo | 2 | | | Detroit 1751-4.) |
| | | | | |
| Benjamin Chaput | 1 | 2 | 2 | These farms were |
| Pierre Meloche | 7 | | | occupied by several |
| Joseph Pouget | | | | individuals, partly |
| Jn Louis Revau | | 2 | 2 | before and partly |
| Pierre Girard | 1 | 3 | 5 | after the Conquest of |
| Bte. Gignac | | 3 | 3 | Canada; the persons |
| Pierre Prudhomme | | 1 | 1 | herein mentioned possess |
| Charles Renau | 3 | 5 | 2 | them at present |
| | | | | by purchase or exchange |
| Thomas Pageau | 1 | 2 | 4 | and the majority of them |
| Jn Bte Antaillau | 3 | 2 | 5 | have no titles to |
| Joseph Bondy | | | | produce. . . |
| Antoine Meloche | 1 | 1 | 2 | |
| Joseph Mainville | 2 | 3 | 1 | |
| Gerv. Hodienne | | 1 | | |
| | | | | |
| François Beneteau | | 1 | 4 | |
| Louis Bourassa | | | 5 | |
| Guillaume Monforton | | | | |
| Hacques Beser | 1 | 1 | 1 | |
| Simon Bergeron | | | | |
| | | | | |
| Charles Renau | | | | These farms were |
| Joseph Rocheleau | | | | granted by the |
| Joseph Bondy, fils | | 2 | 2 | Indians about three |
| Gabriel Bondy | | 1 | 2 | years ago. The last |
| Antoine Meloche | | | | one was listed by Mr. |
| Louis Bourassa | | | | McNiff for Laurent |
| | | | | Bondy, Louis Bourassa |
| | | | | being absent. |

# THE 1796 CENSUS OF WAYNE COUNTY

The American government assumed control of the post of Detroit 15 July 1796. Three censuses were taken in the following six weeks. The first, dated 16 August, appears in the *National Genealogical Society Quarterly* 69:187-194, along with a detailed narrative of the events leading up to the capitulation and evacuation by the British, as well as biographical sketches of each man. This was composed of the merchants and other residents who lived in the fort. A second census was taken by Captains James May and George MacDougall of the Detroit Militia on 31 August, which categorizes the residents by head of family, women, white children, men slaves, women slaves, and black children. And just three weeks later, a more complete census of the entire county from Monroe to Huron River (now the Clinton River near Mount Clemens), including still another enumeration of Detroit, was taken. Frenchmen were chosen to act as enumerators this time, which fact is apparent from the spelling of the names. The two are quite similar, but both vary substantially from the 16 August census. This indicates a mobile population, not surprising, since many were fur traders.

The third census, taken by Chabert Joncaire, lists only men over fifty, men between sixteen and fifty, and women. The tabulations and totals at the end of each geograpahical area are not consistent or accurate; rather than repeat those numbers here, only the final tabulations will be given. Note, however, that the last section which deals with the area from Pointe aux Tremblés to the Great Meadow, is not included in the recapaitulations. Pointe aux Tremblés is the northern point of Anchor Bay where the St. Clair River begins, and the Great Meadow is probably near the town of St. Clair. The three censuses of Detroit have been combined, as have two taken of the immediate suburbs by the French and English. Because of the variant spellings, the more usual spelling has been used. The rest of the county was taken only once, by 21 September, and these sections, divided geographically, are self-explanatory.

The prime purpose of these frequent enumerations was two-fold: to determine the exact citizenry under the newly-formed Wayne County, of course, but also to assess the military strength of the county, in preparation for possible problems with the British. The emphasis on Militiamen is predominant, even calling them "men bearing arms" in one area. Military groups were formed and met regularly right up to the War of 1812.

The lists that follow are from the Papers of Winthrop Sargent, Secretary of the Northwest Territory under General Arthur St. Clair, and are reprinted here by permission of the Ohio Historical Society (Collection MIC 96). They have not been published previously. Two notes to the readers: some of the names are bracketed together and were apparently of men living in the same house; also, abbreviated given names should be clear, but note that Josh is Joseph, not Joshua.

## COMBINED LIST OF THE POPULATION OF DETROIT IN SEPTEMBER 1796

| Men over 50 | Men 16-50 | White Women | White Children | Men Slaves | Women Slaves | Black Children |
|---|---|---|---|---|---|---|
| | James Fraser | | | | | |
| | Baptiste Dumo | | | | | |
| | John Reed | | | | | |
| | Richard Pattinson | | | | | |
| | Hugh Pattinson | | | | | |
| | Frederick Rupart | | | | | |
| | George Leith } | | | | | |
| | William Shepherd | | | | | |
| | Alexander Duff } | | | | | |
| | James Leith | | | | | |
| | John Clark | 1 | 1 | | | |
| | James Anderson | | | | | |
| | Robert Gouie | | | | | 1 |
| | James Beird | | | | | |
| | John Cain | 1 | 2 | | | |
| | John Haughton | 1 | | | | |
| | William Andrews | 1 | | | | |
| | William Hands | 1 | 4 | | 1 | |
| | Joseph Pinard | | | | | |
| | Jacques Baby | 2 | | 1 | | 1 |
| | Angus Mackintosh | 1 | 5 | | 3 | 2 |
| | James Mackintosh | | | | | |
| | Richard Donovan | | | | | |
| | Baptiste LaBorde | | | | | |
| | John Burrell | | | | | |
| | Doctor Eberts | | | | | |
| | George MacDougal | | | | | |
| | Baptiste Dufour | | | | | |
| James Abbott, Esq. | | 2 | | 1 | 3 | 1 |
| | James Abbott, Junr. | | | | | |
| | Robert Abbott | | | | | |
| | John Dodemead | 1 | 7 | 1 | 2 | 3 |
| George Meldrum | | 1 | 7 | | 2 | 2 |
| | William Smith | | | | | |
| | William Park | 1 | 2 | | 2 | 2 |
| | Jacques Robetaille | | | | | |

1796 Census

|  |  |  |  |  |  |  |
|---|---|---|---|---|---|---|
|  | Pierre LaVigeur |  |  |  |  |  |
|  | Pierre Delorme |  |  |  |  |  |
|  | John McGregor | 1 | 1 |  |  |  |
|  | Mr. Henward |  |  |  |  |  |
| William Robertson |  |  |  |  |  |  |
|  | Robert Innis } |  |  |  |  |  |
|  | Baptiste Barthe, Junr. |  |  |  |  |  |
|  | Charles Danieau |  |  |  |  |  |
|  | Baptiste Cardinal |  |  |  |  |  |
| John Askin, Senr. |  | 1 | 6 | 3 | 1 | 3 |
|  | Jean Bte Langlois } |  |  |  |  |  |
|  | Baptiste Boist } |  |  |  |  |  |
|  | Charles Scarbeau } |  |  |  |  |  |
|  | John Deane |  |  |  |  |  |
|  | James May | 1 | 3 | 1 | 1 |  |
|  | Louis Patnotre |  |  |  |  |  |
|  | James McDonell |  |  |  |  |  |
|  | George Sharp |  |  | 1 |  |  |
|  | Robert Forsyth |  |  |  |  |  |
|  | James Vincent | 1 | 1 |  |  |  |
| Gregor McGregor |  | 1 | 5 | 1 | 1 |  |
| Rev. Mr. Lavadoux |  |  |  |  |  |  |
| Charles Gerardin, Senr. |  |  |  |  |  |  |
|  | Charles Girardin, Junr. | 1 | 2 |  |  |  |
| Pierre Drollet | Pierre Drollet |  |  |  |  |  |
| Francois Frarot | François Frarot | 1 | 3 |  |  |  |
|  | Joseph Thibault | 1 | 4 |  |  |  |
|  | Louis Decheneau |  |  |  |  |  |
| Joseph Thibault, Senr. |  | 1 |  |  |  |  |
|  | Augustin Lafoy | 1 | 2 |  |  |  |
| Joseph Voyer, Esq. |  | 1 | 1 |  |  |  |
|  | Louis Beaulieu |  |  |  |  |  |
|  | Mathew Dolson | 1 | 3 |  | 1 |  |
|  | Florence McCaulley |  |  |  |  |  |
|  | Edward Riding |  |  |  |  |  |
|  | Perish Valley |  |  |  |  |  |
|  | Pierre Valley | 1 | 3 |  |  |  |
|  | Mrs. Welch, widow | 1 | 3 |  |  |  |
|  | Prisque Cotté, Senr. | 1 | 1 |  |  |  |
|  | Prisque Cotté, Junr. } |  |  |  |  |  |
|  | Joseph Cotté |  |  |  |  |  |
|  | Joseph Nantais | 1 | 3 |  |  |  |
|  | Charles Poupard } |  |  |  |  |  |
|  | Joseph Barrieux } | 1 | 1 |  |  |  |
|  | Baptiste Bruneau } |  |  |  |  |  |
|  | Baptiste Montreuil } |  |  |  |  |  |
|  | André Duchenois } |  |  |  |  |  |
|  | Vital Bourassa } |  |  |  |  |  |
|  | François Deneau } |  |  |  |  |  |
|  | Baptiste Maconny |  |  |  |  |  |

|   |   |   |   |   |   |
|---|---|---|---|---|---|
|  | --- Jeraume |  |  |  |  |
|  | Joseph Boisdoré |  |  |  |  |
|  | --- Lafordine |  |  |  |  |
| Louis LaVictoire |  | 2 |  |  |  |
|  | Louis Lognon |  |  |  |  |
| Thomas Cox |  | 1 | 1 |  |  |
|  | Pierre Provencal | 1 | 6 |  |  |
|  | Thomas Smith | 1 | 4 |  |  |
| Patrick McNiff |  | 1 | 4 |  |  |
|  | Joseph Sere | 1 | 3 |  |  |
|  | James Donaldson | 1 | 2 | 1 | 1 |
| François Gobeil |  | 1 | 2 |  |  |
|  | François Gobeil, Junr. |  |  |  |  |
|  | Baptiste Gobeil } |  |  |  |  |
|  | Charles Gobeil |  |  |  |  |
| Jacques Peltier, Senr. |  | 1 | 7 | 2 | 1 |
|  | Jacques Peltier, Junr. } |  |  |  |  |
|  | Antoine Peltier |  |  |  |  |
|  | John Whitehead |  |  | 1 |  |
|  | Joseph Elam |  |  |  |  |
|  | Richard Monney |  |  |  |  |
|  | Louis Couteau |  |  |  |  |
| John Bonsack |  |  |  |  |  |
|  | Alexis Maisonville |  |  |  |  |

## POPULATION OF THE NORTHEAST AND SOUTHWEST SUBURBS OF THE CITY

|   |   |   |
|---|---|---|
|  | Jacob Clement/Clemens |  |
|  | François Underwood |  |
|  | Israel Hull |  |
|  | John Haines |  |
|  | Capt. Fearson (John) | 1 |
|  | Jean Bte Blache |  |
|  | Pierre Soror | 2 |
|  | Robert Kean |  |
|  | Thomas Barnet/Burnet |  |
|  | Jean Bte Bernard | 1 |
| Samuel Eddy |  | 2 |
|  | Michel Tremblay |  |
|  | Philip Bellanger | 1 |
|  | Louis Pelletier |  |
|  | Baptiste Pelletier | 1 |
|  | Isaac Gagnier | 1 |
|  | Alexis Sarah | 1 |
| Simon Drouillard |  |  |
|  | Dominique Drouillard |  |
|  | Joseph Nailson/Harrison | 1 |
|  | Samuel Edge | 1 |
|  | François Belcour | 3 |
|  | John Martin |  |

# 1796 Census

      Mathew Donovan    4
      --- Tees
      John Collins
      Philip Metay
      Michel Monet

## POPULATION TO THE WEST OF THE CITY ON THE OTHER SIDE OF THE POTTAWATOMIES (At Knaggs Creek, adjoining the Fort)

Taken by Capt. François Gamelin, Lieut. Alexander Labady, Ensign Utreau Navarre

| Men Over 50 | Men 16-50 | Women | Boys | Girls |
| --- | --- | --- | --- | --- |
|  | Simon Drouillard | 1 | 1 | 2 |
|  | Chs Lelièvre | 1 | 4 |  |
| James Howell | Jacob Visger } John Visger } | 1 | 1 | 2 |
| William Groesbeck |  | 1 | 1 |  |
|  | Jean Bte Campau } Ignatius Bouchard } Louis Barthe } |  | 1 | 4 |
| Pierre Labady |  | 1 | 1 | 5 |
|  | Amable St Combe | 1 | 2 | 2 |
| Robert Navarre, Senr. | Antne Navarre } I. Marie Navarre } Pierre Navarre } | 3 | 1 | 4 |
| Jacques André |  | 1 | 1 |  |
|  | Antoine Oudain | 1 |  | 1 |
|  | Jacques Godfrois } Bte Godfroy } | 1 | 4 | 4 |
|  | Alexis Delisle } Isidor Delisle } Bienvenu Delisle } | 2 | 2 |  |
| Lieut. Col. Chabert |  | 3 | 4 | 3 |
|  | Jacques Laselle } Etienne Dubois } | 1 | 1 | 1 |
| Simon Jandrons, Senr. | Louis Jandrons |  |  |  |
|  | Israel Ruland | 1 | 4 | 4 |
| Ambrois Riopell | Pierre Riopell } Pierre Metthez } | 2 | 4 | 4 |
| Mr. Ct (Cicot) | Joseph Cicot, Son | 2 | 6 | 4 |
| Louis Vessière, Senr. | Alexis Vesière | 1 | 3 | 3 |
|  | Chs Cabassier | 1 |  | 3 |
|  | Louis Dubois } Hypolithe Vadboncour } |  |  |  |
|  | Frans Cadoret | 1 | 2 | 3 |
|  | Bernard Campau | 3 | 2 |  |
| Ensign Navre |  | 1 | 5 |  |
|  | Josh Livernois | 1 | 3 | 5 |
| Etienne Livernois |  |  |  |  |

63

|  |  |  |  |  |
|---|---|---|---|---|
|  | Captne Gamelin | 2 | 2 | 2 |
| Chor Celeron |  |  |  |  |
| Donque Labrosse |  | 1 |  |  |
|  | Alexr Labady, Lieut. | 1 | 1 | 2 |
| Chs Chêne |  |  |  |  |
| Gabl Hunaut | Antoine Barron | 1 | 1 | 2 |
| André Vige | Pierre Chêne | 1 | 4 |  |
| Theophite Lemay | J. Bte Lemay |  | 1 | 5 |
| Joseph Baroie | Antne Trotier |  |  |  |
|  | Frans Bourassa |  |  |  |
|  | St Ours Beaudrau |  |  |  |
|  | Jn Bte Clairmont |  |  |  |
|  | Joseph Chesne |  |  |  |
|  | Frans Laurain |  |  |  |
|  | Hyacinthe Leduc |  |  |  |
|  | Baril Pepin |  |  |  |
|  | Ignace Billet |  |  |  |
|  | Jn Bte Dubord |  |  |  |
|  | Frans Lanktaw (Lanctot) |  |  |  |
|  | Frans Pepin |  |  |  |
|  | J. Bte SansCrainte, Senr. |  |  |  |
|  | Jean Baptiste SansCrainte, Jr. |  |  |  |
|  | Toussan Chesne |  |  |  |

## POPULATION OF THE COMPANY OF THE RIVER ROUGE AND ECORCE RIVER

Taken by Gabl. Godfroy, Lieut. Jn Bte Beaugrand, Ensign John Cisanney

|  |  |  |  |  |
|---|---|---|---|---|
|  | Josh Lemurains | 1 | 4 | 1 |
|  | Frans Derocher |  |  |  |
| Jacob Dixe |  | 1 | 2 | 4 |
|  | Godfroy Corbush | 1 | 1 |  |
|  | David Harkley | 1 | 1 | 2 |
| John Rainold, Senr. |  | 1 |  | 2 |
|  | George Rainold } |  |  |  |
|  | John Rainold } |  |  |  |
| Noel Chauvin |  | 1 | 1 | 2 |
|  | Jacques Chauvin |  |  |  |
| James Hobs |  | 2 |  |  |
|  | André Berthiaume | 1 |  | 2 |
|  | Josh Gaudet | 1 | 3 | 4 |
|  | Pierre Dumais | 1 | 3 | 1 |
|  | Chs Roulau |  |  |  |
| Josh Cisanney |  | 1 | 3 | 3 |
|  | Wme Cissanney } |  |  |  |
|  | James Cisanney } |  |  |  |
|  | Samuel Driverd |  |  |  |
| James Rivard | Josh Hurt } |  |  |  |
| Wm Hurt | Frans Jons } |  |  |  |
|  | Edward McCarty | 1 | 1 | 3 |
|  | Daniel Pursley |  |  |  |
|  | Jonathan Harkley |  |  |  |

## 1796 Census

|  |  |  |  |  |
|---|---|---|---|---|
|  | Daniel Pursley |  |  |  |
|  | Jonathan Harkley } |  |  |  |
|  | Thomas Boyd |  |  |  |
|  | Jesse Burbank | 1 | 1 | 2 |
|  | John Shaw | 1 |  | 1 |
| Thomas Alliz |  |  |  |  |
|  | Benjamin Jons } |  |  |  |
|  | Bte Jons } |  |  |  |
|  | Charles Baron |  |  |  |
|  | Louis Vesièrre, Junr. } |  |  |  |
|  | Touissen Riopell |  |  |  |
|  | Louis Trudel | 1 | 2 | 3 |
| Desplaine |  | 1 | 5 | 2 |
|  | Chs Chauvinet | 1 | 2 | 1 |
|  | Bte Delisle } | 1 | 1 | 2 |
|  | Josh Delisle |  |  |  |
|  | Cadorethe (Cadoret) |  |  |  |
|  | André LeClaire | 1 | 1 | 1 |
|  | Chs Labady } |  |  |  |
|  | Gabriel Chêne } | 1 |  |  |
|  | Zacary Cicot |  |  |  |
|  | divers women | 7 | 6 | 6 |
|  | Jn Bte Rousson | 1 | 1 | 1 |
|  | Josh Bondy | 1 | 4 | 3 |
|  | Josh Lemandre } |  |  |  |
|  | Pierre Campau |  |  |  |
|  | Josh Varmethe | 1 |  | 2 |
|  | Bte Salliot } |  |  |  |
|  | Chs Campaut |  |  |  |
|  | Josh Lamirande | 1 | 1 | 1 |
|  | Antoine Baron | 1 | 2 | 2 |
| Victor Morissau |  | 1 | 1 | 1 |
|  | Renez Lebeau | 1 | 2 | 5 |
|  | Baptiste Bosonme |  |  |  |
|  | Josh Parnier, Junior |  |  |  |
|  | Paul Pernier } |  |  |  |
|  | Louis Pernier |  |  |  |
| Josh Parnier, Senr. |  | 1 | 4 |  |
| Josh DuPlessé |  | 1 |  |  |
| Chs Fontaine, Senr. |  |  | 2 | 2 |
|  | Bte Drouillard | 1 |  | 1 |
|  | Louis Fontaine |  |  |  |
|  | Pierre Leblanc |  |  |  |
|  | Chs Fontaine | 1 |  |  |
|  | Chauvin | 1 |  |  |

65

## POPULATION OF THE ENTIRE RAISIN RIVER

Taken by Capt. Frans Navarre, Lieut. Joseph Menard, Ensign Jacques Navarre

| | | | | |
|---|---|---|---|---|
| | Batiste Susor | 1 | 1 | 1 |
| | Batiste Réaume, Jr. | | 1 | 1 |
| | Isidor Robert | 1 | 1 | |
| | Ignace Thuoth, Senr. | 1 | 4 | 1 |
| | Ignce Thuoth, Junr. | | | |
| | Louis Susor | 1 | 1 | 2 |
| | Josh Robert | 1 | | 1 |
| | Josh Menard | 1 | 1 | 1 |
| | Jacques Navarre | | | |
| | Frans Navarre | 1 | | 1 |
| | Isidor Navarre | 1 | | 1 |
| Josh Cecire | | 1 | | |
| | Frans Berarre | 1 | | 4 |
| Susor, Senior | | | | 3 |
| Coutheure, Senr. (Couture) | | 1 | 2 | |
| | Medard Coutheure | 1 | | |
| | Frans Leonard | 1 | 2 | 3 |
| | Jacques Desplats | 1 | 2 | 1 |
| Antne Robert | | 1 | 2 | 4 |
| | Nicholas Drouillard | 1 | | 1 |
| | Chathelleraux | 1 | 2 | 2 |
| | Dominc Drouillard | 1 | 1 | 3 |
| Paul Campeau | | 1 | | |
| | Medard Labady | | | |
| | Jacques Proult | 1 | | 1 |
| | Frans Campau | 1 | 2 | 3 |
| | Josh Drouillard | 1 | 1 | 1 |
| Deveaux | Antne Montreuil | | | |
| Dubreuil, Senr. | Josh Bissonnet | 1 | 2 | |
| Louis Labontée | Jean Bte Dussau | 1 | 2 | 4 |
| Pierre Constant | Jn Le Bellerre | 1 | 1 | |
| Laviollet | Josh Pouget } | | | |
| --- Jacob | Bte Pouget } | 1 | 3 | 4 |
| Etiene Jacob, Senr. | | 1 | 5 | |
| | Etienne Jacob, Junior | | | |
| | Wm Knaggs } | | | |
| | Wittemor Knaggs } | Mthr 1 | Sistr 2 | Brthr 2 |
| | Pierre Chaubert } | | | |
| | Antoine Rivard } | | | |
| | Etienne Robidoux } | | | |
| | Louis St Amour } | | | |
| | Jean Jacob } | | | |
| | Zacary Cloutier | 1 | 6 | 1 |
| | Mininr? Cloutier | 1 | | 1 |
| | Antne Beauregard | 1 | 1 | 1 |
| Louis Robidoux | | 1 | 1 | 1 |

# 1796 Census

| | | | | |
|---|---|---|---|---|
| Robidoux, father (Charles) | | 1 | | |
| | Pierre Demers | 1 | 1 | 3 |
| | Christome St Louis | 1 | | 3 |
| | Louis Grenons | 1 | 1 | |
| | Amable Bellere | 1 | | |
| Etienne Robidoux | | 1 | 4 | 2 |
| Joseph Carrier | | 1 | | 1 |
| | Frans Menard | 1 | 1 | 3 |
| | Bpte Roe | 1 | 2 | 1 |
| Basil Cousinaut | | 1 | 6 | 4 |
| | Jacques Martin | 1 | | 2 |
| | Bpte Laplante | 1 | | 2 |
| | Hyacinthe Bernard | 1 | 1 | 1 |
| | Louis Bernard | 1 | 1 | 1 |
| | Josh Jobbin | 1 | 2 | |
| | Michel Bourdon | 1 | | 1 |
| Bte Lapointe | | 1 | 2 | |
| | Godin (Julien Godon) | 1 | 3 | 5 |
| | Josh Ininois (Livernois) | 1 | 3 | 6 |
| | Ambroise Traversy | 1 | | 1 |
| | Frans Deleuil (Deloeil) | 1 | | 1 |
| Pierre Traversy | Jean Askin, Junr. | 1 | | |
| Rivard, Senior | | 1 | 4 | 1 |
| | Pierre Fouerau (Fournier) | 1 | | 2 |
| | Pierre Barron | | | |
| | Chs Tessiers | 1 | 2 | |
| | Frans Soudryette | | | |
| | Alexr Woillet (Ouelet) | 1 | | |
| | Bte Laselle | 1 | | 2 |
| | Alexis Solaut | 1 | 1 | 2 |
| | Jean Mrie Navarre | 1 | 1 | 1 |
| | Robert Navarre, son | | | |
| | Chs Campau | 1 | | 1 |
| | Antoine Campau | 1 | | |
| | Lenfans, son Ainée (L'Enfant) }  Josh Lanfans | | | |
| Lenfans, Senior | | 1 | 2 | |
| | André Pouparre | 1 | 4 | 1 |
| | Bte Couthure | 1 | 3 | 1 |
| | Josh Bourdeau | 1 | 2 | 1 |
| | Joseph Réaume | 1 | | 1 |
| | Antoine Nadaut | 1 | 2 | 2 |
| Josh J---- (illeg.) | | | | |

NON-RESIDENT VOLUNTEERS
Paschal Bissonnet
Josh Robidoux
Antoine Boulard
Bte Lapointe
Chs Bernard
Josh Aumais

|  |  |  |  |  |
|---|---|---|---|---|
| | Pierre Barbaut | | | |
| | Louis Laframboise | 1 | | 8 |
| | Guillaume Lapointe | | | |
| | --- Baril (prob. Jean Bte) | | | |
| | Joseph Soudryet | | | |
| | Joseph? Geniez | | | |
| | Frans Lajeunesse | | | |
| | Thibaudaut | | | |
| | Antne Riopelle | | | |
| | Dominique L'Enfant | | | |
| | Benjamin L'Enfant | | | |
| | Frans Robert | | | |
| | Jn Bte Lefebvre | | | |

## AU SABLE RIVER

|  |  |  |  |  |
|---|---|---|---|---|
| Louis Gaillard, Senr | | 1 | 2 | 7 |
| | Bte Bourdaut | 1 | | |
| | Guy (prob. Antoine Frs.) | 1 | 1 | 1 |
| | Pierre Valiquet | 1 | 1 | 1 |
| | Pierre Delaurier } | | | |
| | Pierre Beauchamp | | | |
| | Louis Bourdau | | 2 | 1 |
| | Berthiaume (Andrew) | 1 | | |

## RIVIERE AU LOUTRES (OTTER CREEK)

|  |  |  |  |  |
|---|---|---|---|---|
| Jacques Gagnier | | 1 | 4 | 5 |
| | Prospert Thibaut | 1 | 1 | 1 |
| | Baudin (Louis) | | | |
| Montminie (Louis Jean) | | 1 | 7 | 2 |
| | Vincent Couthure | 1 | 1 | |
| | Bte Taillon } | | | |
| | Bte Drouillard | | | |

## POPULATION NORTHEAST OF THE CITY: COMPANY OF CAPTNE MORANS

Taken by Captain Antoine Beaubien, Lieut. Jacques Campau, and Ensign Joseph Campau

|  |  |  |  |  |
|---|---|---|---|---|
| Pierre Cardinal | Bte Cochois | 1 | 1 | 1 |
| | Poirrier (Charles?) | 1 | 3 | 3 |
| Js Casse, Senr | Louis Casse | | 1 | 1 |
| | Gabl Casse | 1 | 1 | 1 |
| | Jacques Cass e | 1 | 1 | |
| | Constan Casse } | | | |
| | Bte Casse | | | |
| Antne Morasse | | 2 | 2 | 3 |
| | Morass, Junr. (Ignace) | | | |
| Guillaume Bernard | | 1 | 2 | 3 |
| | Bartrand (Jean Bte?) | 1 | 1 | |

## 1796 Census

|  |  |  |  |  |
|---|---|---|---|---|
|  | Hypolite Bernard } |  |  |  |
|  | Chs Bernard, brother } |  |  |  |
|  | Etienne Balard | 1 | 1 |  |
| Antoine Boyer |  | 1 | 2 | 1 |
|  | Rode, Junior (Rodier?) |  |  |  |
| Ls Beaufait, father | Louis Beufait, son | 1 |  | 1 |
| Chatotton, Senr. | L. Chapoton | 1 | 3 | 2 |
|  | Nicholas Chapoton | 1 |  |  |
| Bte Pelletier, Senr | Phili Pelletier | 1 | 1 |  |
| Bte Meloche | Jacques Metcoe? | 1 | 1 |  |
|  | Cadien } |  |  |  |
|  | Langlois } |  |  |  |
| Jean Legod | --- Meloche, obmiser? | 1 |  | 3 |
|  | Benois Chapoton | 1 |  | 2 |
|  | Robt McDougall | 1 | 2 |  |
| Simon Campau | Chs Campau } |  |  |  |
|  | Henry Campeau } | 2 | 2 | 2 |
| Barthelmi | Claude Campau | 1 | 1 | 2 |
|  | Jacques Campau |  |  |  |
|  | Antoine Campau |  |  |  |
|  | Zachari Campau } |  |  |  |
|  | Toussin Campau } |  |  |  |
|  | Joseph Campau } |  |  |  |
|  | Labbaie Campeau } |  |  |  |
|  | Augustin Malbeuf } | 1 |  |  |
|  | Amable Chtée? (Clitée?) } |  |  |  |
|  | Simon Campau Jr | 1 |  | 1 |
| Noel Casse |  |  |  |  |
| Frans Gouin |  | 1 |  |  |
| Nicolas Gouin |  | 1 | 2 | 2 |
| Josh Lauran (Lorrain) |  | 1 |  |  |
| Josh Sarasteau? (Rochereau?) |  |  |  |  |
|  | Chs Pelletier | 1 | 1 | 1 |
|  | Josh Grimar | 1 |  |  |
| Rou --- (Rochereau?) |  | 1 |  | 2 |
|  | Antoine Lesperance |  |  |  |
| Jouachim Biron | Chs Lesperance |  |  |  |
|  | Pierre Lesperance | 2 |  |  |
|  | Basil Galipau |  |  |  |
| Chs Robitaille |  |  |  |  |
|  | Basile Deloge (Desloges) |  |  |  |
| Vigare (Andrew Viger) | Bte Mont Mirelle | 1 |  |  |
|  | Antne Dequindre | 1 | 5 | 2 |
|  | Antne On--l |  |  |  |
|  | Bernard |  |  |  |
|  | Charles Gouin | 1 | 3 | 2 |
|  | Joseph Palliotte } (Pominville?) |  |  |  |
|  | Chs Rivard } } |  | 2 | 2 |
|  | Hyacinthe Dubois } |  |  |  |
|  | Louis Morans } |  |  |  |

|  |  |  |  |  |
|---|---|---|---|---|
|  | Joseph Morans } | 1 | 2 | 4 |
|  | Pierre Morans } |  |  |  |
|  | Bazile Laforge |  |  |  |
|  | Frans Bailans (Baillon) | 1 | 3 |  |
|  | Chs Morans | 1 | 1 | 1 |
|  | Josh Besau | 2 |  | 4 |
|  | Antoine Routure } |  |  |  |
|  | Fran:OIS Guy } |  |  |  |
|  | Pierre Bellaire | 1 |  |  |
|  | Laurent Maurre (Moran) | 1 |  | 2 |
|  | Moriche Morans (Maurice) |  |  |  |
|  | François Lemoine | 1 |  |  |
|  | Frans Delarier (Desloriers) | 1 | 3 |  |
|  | Antoine Baubien | 1 | 1 |  |
|  | Lambert Baubien | 1 | 2 | 2 |
|  | Jn Bte Barthe | 1 | 1 | 1 |

Total: 23 Militiamen carrying arms

## POPULATION OF GRAND MARAIS UP TO GROSSE POINTE

Taken by Frans Marsacre, Leut. Pierris Rivard, Ensign Louis Tremblai

|  |  |  |  |  |
|---|---|---|---|---|
| Bte Campau | Jean Duretthe | 2 | 4 | 5 |
|  | Jean Duretthe (Duret) | 1 | 1 |  |
| Chs Cauvin (Chauvin) |  |  |  |  |
|  | Josh Cadais | 1 | 4 | 1 |
| Jean Dubee |  |  |  |  |
| Nicolas Livierge? | Louis Chauvin | 1 |  | 2 |
|  | Antoine Chauvin } |  |  |  |
|  | Bte Chauvin | 1 | 2 |  |
|  | Jn Bte Pittre | 1 | 3 | 2 |
|  | Denis Pittre |  |  |  |
|  | Pierre Caye |  |  |  |
| Cajetan Laderoute |  | 1 | 2 |  |
| Jn Bte Dupras | Michel Dupras | 1 | 2 | 2 |
| P'ere Tremblaie |  | 1 | 1 | 1 |
| St Jean Crisst |  |  |  | 3 |
| Basile Bellange (r) |  | 1 | 1 | 3 |
| Louis Griffard |  | 1 |  | 4 |
| Layth Holdr? | Laythe | 1 |  | 2 |
|  | Andrew Snecalle | 1 |  |  |
|  | Michel Yark (Yax) | 1 | 1 | 3 |
| Jona --- (blanked out) | Michel Tremblé | 1 |  | 2 |
| Chs --- | Josh Laderoutte | 1 | 1 | 2 |
|  | Bte Laderoute | 1 | 1 | 1 |
|  | Jn Bte Dubie | 1 |  | 1 |
|  | Louis Desonier (Desnoyers) | 1 | 3 |  |
| --- (illeg.) | René Marsacre |  |  |  |
|  | Josh Robitaille | 1 |  | 1 |
|  | Michel Bauchamp } |  |  |  |

1796 Census 71

|  | | | |
|---|---|---|---|
| Chs Beauchamp } | | | |
| Bte Chauvin } | | 2 | 4 |
| Chs Chauvin | | 1 | 4 |
| Josh Campau | | | |
| Chs Campau | | | |
| Jacques Marsac } 1 | | 1 | 2 |
| Gagettans (Cajetan) Marsac } 1 | | | 3 |
| Gageth (Cajetan) Tremblé } | | | |
| Thomas Tremblé } 2 | | 3 | 3 |
| Nicholas Campau } 1 | | | 3 |
| Louis Gervais | 1 | | |
| Ignace Seniat | 1 | | 3 |
| Berthelmis | | | |
| Pierre Griffard | | | |
| Basil Thibaut | | 2 | |
| Gabriel Thibau | | | |
| Michel Tremblé | 1 | 1 | 1 |
| Josh Tremblé | 1 | 1 | 3 |
| Chs Dulack | 1 | 3 | |
| Baptis Tremblé | | | |
| Josh Bernard | | 3 | |
| Ambroise Connollieur } | | | |
| Mont Markaits } | | | |

## GENERAL CENSUS OF THE COMPANY OF GROSSE POINTE

Taken by Capt. Charles Rivard, Lt. Josh Saucier, Ensign Wm Forsyth

| | | | | |
|---|---|---|---|---|
| | Bte Rivard | 1 | 1 | 4 |
| Frans Duchaine | | 1 | 2 | 1 |
| | Michel Duchaine | | | |
| | Chs Chauvin | 1 | | |
| --Toussin Chauvin, ill | | | | |
| | Pierre Yack | 1 | 2 | 2 |
| | Jean Yack | | | |
| Josh Balise | | | | |
| | Simon Yack | | 1 | |
| | Nicholas Rivard | 1 | | |
| | Michel Rivard | 1 | | 1 |
| | Louis Bernard | 1 | | 2 |
| Nicholas Patnaude | | 1 | | 3 |
| | Nicholas Verne (t) | 1 | | |
| | Frans Meloche | 1 | 1 | |
| | Joseph Allere (Allor) | 1 | 1 | 1 |
| Louis Goulais | | 1 | | 2 |
| Jean Mcpharson | | | | |
| | Pither Luck ? | 1 | | 2 |
| Pierre Mayé | | 1 | 4 | 2 |
| Becherr (Baker) | | 1 | | |
| | Jacob Baiker } | | | |

72                          Michigan Censuses 1710-1830

|  |  |  |  |  |
|---|---|---|---|---|
|  | Batiste Labady } | 1 | 1 | 5 |
|  | Bte Yack } |  |  |  |
|  | Frans Ferton (Fréton) | 1 | 2 | 2 |
| Frans Tremblai |  | 1 | 3 | 3 |
|  | Frans Tramblai, son |  |  |  |
|  | Louis Lesperance | 1 |  | 3 |
| Laurt Griffard |  | 1 | 4 | 2 |
|  | Laurich Griffar |  |  |  |
|  | Bte Varnick | 1 |  | 2 |
|  | Josh Jarain | 1 | 1 | 1 |
| Louis Renaut |  | 1 | 3 | 8 |
|  | Lt Renaut, son } |  |  |  |
|  | Gabl Renaut } |  |  |  |
|  | Antoine Renaut } |  |  |  |
| Jacques Alard |  | 1 | 4 | 3 |
| Frans Leduc |  | 1 |  |  |
|  | Josh Leduc |  |  |  |
|  | Baptiste Donois (Denis?) |  |  |  |
|  | Julien Ferton | 1 | 3 | 3 |
|  | Louis Leduc | 1 | 2 | 1 |
|  | Ignace Thibaut | 1 | 2 |  |
| Frans Balis |  | 1 | 4 | 3 |
|  | Pierre Duchêne | 1 | 1 | 1 |
|  | Pierre Duchêne, son |  |  |  |
|  | Etienne Duchêne |  |  |  |
| Louis Maison |  | 1 | 1 | 2 |
|  | Batiste Raimond | 1 | 1 | 1 |
|  | Will Cason (Carson?) |  |  |  |
|  | Baptiste St Laron (Laurent) |  |  |  |
|  | Antne Latour |  |  |  |

## CENSUS OF THE NEW POPULATION OF THE HURON RIVER NORTHEAST OF CITY
### (THIS IS THE CLINTON RIVER AREA NEAR MOUNT CLEMENS)

Taken by Capt. William Tucker, Lt. Louis Campau, Ensign Jacques Lauson

|  |  |  |  |  |
|---|---|---|---|---|
| --- (illeg.) |  | 1 | 1 | 1 |
| --- (illeg.) |  | 1 | 2 | 4 |
|  | Joseph Robert, Sgt. | 1 | 1 | 1 |
| Pierre Drouillard |  |  |  |  |
|  | Jn Bte Nantai(s), Segt. | 1 |  |  |
| Louis St Aubin |  |  |  |  |
|  | Louis Laforge | 1 | 4 | 1 |
| Richd Canard |  |  |  |  |
|  | Seraphin Lauson | 1 |  | 2 |
|  | Alexis Pelletier | 1 | 1 | 4 |
| Sansquartier |  |  |  |  |
|  | Frans St Aubin | 1 | 1 | 1 |
|  | Jacques Canard | 1 |  |  |
| Jn Bte Comparé |  |  |  |  |

1796 Census

2

Dumays

| | | | |
|---|---|---|---|
| Wme Dawson | | | 1 |
| Jean Canard | 1 | 1 | 1 |
| William Canard | | | |
| Antoine Petit | 1 | | 2 |
| Louis Petit | 1 | | 1 |
| Jean Claire | | | |
| Henry Tucker | 2 | 4 | 3 |
| Batiste Petit | 1 | | 2 |
| Wm Tucker, Junr. | | | |
| Jn Bte Comparé | 1 | 1 | 1 |
| Robiche Robert | 1 | 1 | 1 |
| Ls Mort | 1 | 2 | 2 |
| Michel Comparé | 1 | 1 | 1 |
| Jacob Thomas | 1 | 3 | 2 |
| Nicholas Vadnais | 1 | | |
| Pierre Dupres | 1 | 2 | 2 |
| Nicholas Patnaude } | | | |
| Pierre Laperle } | | | |
| Bte Marfaere (Marsac) | 1 | 2 | 1 |
| Pierre Champagne | 1 | 4 | 1 |
| Frans Bernard | 1 | | 1 |
| Jn Bte Letournau | 1 | 1 | 1 |
| Colin Meldrum | | | |

A LIST OF INHABITANTS OF FAMILIES AGED SIXTEEN TO FIFTY FROM POINTE AUX TREMBLES TO THE GRAND MEADOW. [These names and statistics are not included in the final recapitulations. Note also that the categories are different. See Introduction to this census for further remarks.]

| | OVER 16 | | UNDER 16 | |
|---|---|---|---|---|
| | MALES | FEMALES | MALES | FEMALES |
| James Taloose (Raymond *dit* Talouse) | 1 | 1 | | 1 |
| Champain (Huyet *dit* Champagne) | 2 | 1 | | 1 |
| Swan Champain (Huyet *dit* Champagne) | 1 | 1 | | 1 |
| Sharkie (François Chartier) | 1 | 1 | 2 | 2 |
| Piro Minny (Pierre Meny) | 1 | 1 | 1 | 3 |
| Widow Denoue (Deniau? Deneau?) | 1 | 1 | 1 | 2 |
| Batist Basenee (Joseph? Basinet) | 1 | 1 | 1 | 1 |
| Jacob Hill | 1 | 1 | 1 | 3 |
| Johnson Brat (?) | 1 | | | |
| Alex Darrow | 4 | 1 | 2 | 1 |
| Tusan Shovan (Touissant Chauvin) | 1 | 1 | | |
| James Cartwrite | 2 | 1 | 1 | |
| Batist Crickey (Créqui) | 1 | 1 | | 1 |
| Wm Thorn | 3 | 1 | 1 | 4 |
| Jno Wright | 2 | 1 | 1 | 3 |
| James Robertson | 2 | 1 | 2 | 1 |
| Anthony Menny (Antoine Meny) | 3 | 1 | 2 | 5 |
| Geo Cotterell | 2 | 1 | 4 | 2 |

| | | | | |
|---|---|---|---|---|
| Widow Crickey (Créqui) | | 1 | 1 | 2 |
| Joseph Trambly | 1 | 1 | 1 | 2 |
| Jno Mary Bobian (Beaubien) | 3 | 1 | 1 | 1 |

Not including blacks or the men engaged by Messrs Meldrum and Park.
Return made by George Cotterill

## REPORT OF THE TOTAL POPULATION OF THE DIFFERENT COMPANIES AND DISTRICTS FOR DETROIT AND WAYNE COUNTY

### 21 September 1796

| | MEN OVER 50 | MEN 16-50 | WHITE WOMEN | BOYS UNDER 16 | GIRLS |
|---|---|---|---|---|---|
| The City | 15 | 91 | 39 | 40 | 55 |
| Suburbs | 2 | 26 | 19 | 15 | 25 |
| Southwest Coast | 18 | 50 | 37 | 59 | 75 |
| Rivers Rouge and Ecorse | 13 | 56 | 37 | 67 | 60 |
| Rivers Raisin, Sable, and Otter Creek | 25 | 110 | 81 | 117 | 117 |
| Northeast Coast | 23 | 69 | 48 | 55 | 53 |
| Grand Marais | 12 | 51 | 35 | 48 | 71 |
| Grosse Pointe | 15 | 40 | 35 | 45 | 65 |
| Huron River (Mt Clemens) | 6 | 32 | 27 | 32 | 35 |
| Totals | 128 | 525 | 357 | 486 | 556 |

Total of above: 2053

"There are upwards of 100 men absent whose names shall be added as they come in.

For an error in the total population of the vicinity of Detroit add 50.

Population of Sinclair (St. Clair) River not included. Add 112."

Grand total: 2215

# 1802 TAX LIST OF WAYNE COUNTY

In 1802 Michigan was part of the Northwest Territory. A proclamation was issued by William Henry Harrison, Governor and Commander-in-Chief of the Indiana Territory, that an act of Congress dated 30 April 1802 was passed "to enable the people of the Eastern Division of the Northwest Territory of the River Ohio to form a constitution and state government for admission to the United States." Further, all parts of the territory not made into states would become part of Indiana Territory (which status Michigan enjoyed from this date until 30 June 1805). Wayne County, as reorganized by Governor Harrison at Vincennes on 14 January 1803, was divided into four townships: Detroit, Hamtramck, Sargent, and St. Clair.

Apparently the tax lists of 1802 were made, or at least used, to serve as a census. Several copies were made, which, while similar, are not identical. They are not particularly difficult to read, but what is surprising is the very bad transcription printed in *Michigan Historical and Pioneer Collections* 8:530-541, in which the names are butchered almost beyond recognition. Transcriptions were found among the private papers of the Godfroy, Fraser, Walker, and Francis Navarre Papers (the last is an 1800 list of 145 residents), all at the Burton Historical Collection of the Detroit Public Library.

The categories in these lists vary somewhat, but generally include the following: name of taxpayer, bound servants (slaves), engagés (hired help), horses, cattle, houses, valuation, mills, and the amount of the tax. Often a description of the land is included; Louis Chapoton's, for example, is typical: "3 arpents in front by 40 in depth, 36 arpents in cultivation" (an arpent is slightly larger than an English acre). Because of these differences, the interested reader is advised to check one or all of the hand-written copies and to avoid the *Michigan Pioneer Collections* transcriptions.

The list that follows is the one found in the Godfroy Papers. This is a copy of the original list which was not located by this compiler. It is probably among the papers of the Northwest Territory. Nor was a map of Wayne County for 1802 showing the boundaries of these townships found. It is probably safe to say that Hamtramck comprised the area east of Detroit including Grosse Pointe, and St. Clair covered the northern settlements, mainly along the Clinton River. Short-lived Sargent Township was clearly the southwestern settlements of the Detroit River, as far south as the River Raisin (now Monroe).

DETROIT
Peter Audrain
Solo Sibley
Dr. Wm. Scott
Wm. Kelly
Thos. Mcerae (McCrae)
Richd Donovan
John Conners
Joseph Haryer (Harvey?)
Abraham Cook
Joseph Harrison
George Harrison
John Dodemead
James McDonnell
Daniel McClain (McLean)
Matthew Ernest
Charles Sweeny
Hugh Howard, Jr.
Peter Desnoyers
Joseph Campeau
Denis Campeau
St. James Wilkinson
H. Lyon
Gabriel Ricard (Richard)
James Adams
Wm. Kelly, servt
Conrad Seek
John Cameron
Robert Gouin
George Searl
Louis Lognon
James Bracken
Arch. Kournes (?)
Pierre Chartron
Antne Demarchais
John Gentle
Alex Milmine (?)
James May, Esq.
Francis Dumas
Henry Hyman
Israel Hunt
Jacob Nadeau
James Henry
Leon Gouin
Thomas Jordan
Joseph Spencer
James Williams
Chryst. Dalton
John Shaggs
Thomas Derry

John Bentley
Richard Smith
Wm. Glacken
J. Bte Rouleau
Isidore Pelletier
Joseph Thibaud
Joseph Voyez
Charles LeLièvre
David Anderson
Feophile Metté (Théophile)
Michel Ambroise
Prisque Coté, Senr
Prisque Coté, son
Joseph Coté
Chs Fs Girardin
John Burrell
Charles Bois
Ch. Poupard
Frs. Gobeye
Jos. St. Pierre
Louis Pelletier
Fran. Fréro
Widow Provençal
David McClean
Alexr McDonnell
Patrick McNiff
Augustin Lafoi
Herman Ebarts
Widow Coates
J. Bte Gobeille
Fran. Gobeye, Junr.
Samuel Hall
Robert Smart
--- Freeman
Austin (?) Longdon/Langdon
John Harvey
André Lepage
Francis Higgins
J. Bte Campeau
Antoine Pelletier
Joseph Gobeye
Antoine Campeau
Witmore Knaggs
Pierre Labadie
Robt Navarre
Gabriel Godfroy
Francis Pepin
Martin Nadeau
Benj. Chapman
Bienvenu Delisle

# 1802 Tax List

- Louis Bourguinon
- François Lafontaine
- Louis Vezière Laferté
- Chas. Cabacier
- Matth Donovan
- Wm. Russell
- Christopher Tutle
- Jacques Pelletier, Senr.
- Jacques Pelletier, Junr.
- Joseph Livernois
- Alexis Labadie
- Dominic Labrosse
- François Gamelin
- Pierre Chêne
- Chabert Joncaire
- Joseph Bobien
- Joseph Dubergé
- Paul Malcher
- Robt. + Js. Abbott
- John Nellour (?)
- Thomas Warnrone (?)
- Jno. Stanback
- Wm. Robertson
- Josiah Dulou
- T. Mahoney
- Alexis Campeau
- Pierre Labadie
- Ant. Navare
- Pierre Navare
- Josh. Charbonneau
- Fran. Desnoyers
- Jacq. + son Laselle
- Josh. Sansquartier
- Ante Medor
- Joseph Duquette
- Guillme Pitre
- Micholas Trudelle
- Joseph Hyacinte
- Pierre Roland
- Louis Gagnon
- Ignace Calvez
- Abraham Godreau
- Bonadventure Godreau
- Augustin Lagrave
- Jos. Landre
- Louis LeDuc
- Pierre Riopell
- Etienne Dupré
- Jean Lagord
- René Mellé
- Daniel Hillman
- Joseph Pinard
- Moire Angleson
- John Reburn
- Antoine Plante
- J. Bte Dirgenel
- Josh. Bourginon
- François Lepage
- Jean Henry Wilson
- Charles Chêne
- Joseph Bobien, Junr.
- Joseph André
- Louis Roi
- Wm. Andrews
- --- Abbott
- Louis Vadeboncoeur
- Jacques Bernier
- André Vigé
- J. Bte Drouillard
- Josh. Drouillard
- Joseph Bondi
- Simon Meloche
- Amable Lavictoire
- Pierre Campeau
- Antoine Baron
- Antoine Vermet
- J. Bte Dufour
- J. Bte Leblanc
- Etienne Menançon
- Pierre Leblanc
- J. Bte Saliot
- Josh. Vadebon(coeur)
- Joseph Cabanon
- Pierre Blain
- Domque Bondi
- J. Bte Lebeau
- Victoire Moriceau
- Joseph Tourangeau
- Louis René
- Pierre Fortier
- J. Bte Rouisson
- Joseph Bondi
- Louis Bourassa
- Louis LaVasseur
- Chs. M. Campeau
- Jos. Lamironte
- John Shaw
- Antne Catlin
- --- Assire(?)
- Jno. Nelson

Peter Young
Abraham Mesatte
Abraham Regalle
Charles Jones
Wm. Cissne
J. Bte Jones
James Ackins
Samuel Driver
Godfrey Corbus
Frs. Remond
Félise Metté
Aaron + Helene Thomas
John Thomas
Wm. Stroud
Henry Stroud
Frs. Chovin
Frs. Durocher
Edward McCarly
J. Beaver
Wm. Hurt
Chs. Rouleau
Pierre Dumay
Antoine Baron
Amable Riopel
Jacob Dicks
Joseph Lorain
André Pelletier
Joseph Chamberland
Isidore Delisle
Louis Boudrais
Zachary Cicot
Joseph Baron
Adrien Audlain
J. Bte Delisle
Joseph Delisle
J. Bte Cicot
Chs. Labadi, Junr.
Benaco Campeau
Bte Duplaisse (Duplessis)
François Trudelle
Toullaine Riopell
Louis Vesière, Junr.
Oliver Wisewell
Jacques Desplats
Alexn Wattell
François Lajeunesse
Joel Woodels
Charles Chovin
Antoine Lefranc
John Connelly

Wm Steers
Jno. Schrieffelin
Chas. Wallen, Esq.
Ferdinand Bates
James Wallace
Warham Strong
John Regly
Daniel Ramon
Estate of Baby (Duperon)
Jabez Stern
Batiste Pelletier, blacksmith
Henry Myers
James Fraser
Forsyth + Smith
Wm. Andrews
Jno. Askin, Junr.
Luther Bunnell
J. Bte Beaugrand
Jacob Clemens
Chs. Curry
Eliz. Callahan
Widow Delisle
Widow Théophile Lemay
George Meldrum
Jno. McGregor
Wm. Park
Northwest Company
Wm. Robertson
Gabriel Richard, priest
Wm. Smith
Estate of McCombe (Macomb)
Joseph Wilkinson
John Watson
Dr. Wm. Brown

HAMTRAMCK DISTRICT
Louis Chapoton
Antoine Boyer
--- Malcher
Isidore Morin
Antoine Moras
Col. Hamtramck
François Rivard
Julien Campau
Widow Baptist Campau
Chs. Chovin
Benj. Marsac
Michel Yack
Joseph Laderoute
J. Bte Duprat

# 1802 Tax List

- Bpe Chovin
- Baptist Chovin, son
- Latroux Marsac
- Robt Marsac
- François Marsac
- Leonard Tremblé
- Mr. Louis Tremblé*
- Gagetan Tremblé
- Nicolas Campau
- Louis Grifard
- François Blé
- Bazille Belange
- Louis Grifard
- Louis Thibaud
- Thomas Larblais
- Joseph Tremblé
- René Marsac
- Ambroise Tremblé
- Joseph Socier
- Jean Baptist Rivard
- Jean Baptist Yack
- Simon Yack
- Pierre Yack
- Nicolas Rivard
- Chas. Rivard
- Michel Rivard
- Louis St. Bernard
- Nicolas Patnotte
- Madame Allexander
- Ignace Ambroise
- Aidegé
- Alex. Grant
- Wm. Forsyth
- Jno. Kirby
- Jacob Bequier
- Pierre Maillet
- Antoine Lesperance
- François Forton
- Madame François Ambroise
- Baptist Cochois
- Laurant Grifard
- Capt. Fleming
- Baptiste Vernier
- François Bonom (Bonhomme)
- Louis Reneau
- Jacques Alard
- Baptist Celeron
- Joseph Ellair
- Julien Forton
- Ignace Thibaut
- Etienne Duchêne
- Pierre Duchêne
- M. St. Jean
- Chs. N. Gouin
- Mister Little
- Larabelle
- Louis Desaunié
- Estate of McCombe
- J. Bte Durette
- Simon Rivard
- Touissant Jassmin
- Louis Beaufait, Senr.
- Louis Beaufait, Junr.
- George Meldrum
- J. Bte Chapoton
- Felix Pelletier
- Maurice Moran
- Etienne Ballard
- Benoit Chapoton
- Robert McDougall
- Simon Campeau
- Gabriel Chêne
- Jacques Campeau
- Josh. Cadet
- François Fournier
- François Gouin
- Ant. Dequindre
- Nicolas Gouin
- Chs. Gouin
- Lubé Campeau
- Mme Rocour
- J. Bte Rivard, Senr.
- Louis Mourand
- Basil Forge
- Ante Cecil
- Chs Morand
- Batiste Daunay
- Henry Barthelet
- Bat. Pelletier
- James May, Esq.
- Jean Simare
- Gaspard Abraham
- George Meldrum
- Capt. Fearson

* Louis Tremblé was one of the wealthiest residents. Besides a slave, he owned a water mill, a saw mill, and 1 horse-power mill, plus 18 cows. He lived at the mouth of Conner Creek where it empties into the Detroit River.

Isaac Ganier
Alexis Coquillard
Simon Drouillard
Bte Lapierre
Wm. Allen
Elijah Brush, Esq.
Ante Bobien
Lambert Bobien
Josh LeDuc
François LeDuc
Charles Pelletier
J. M. Bobien, Esq.
Thomas McKee
Estate of Antoine Cosme
Jacques SaintAubin
Gabriel SaintAubin
Baptiste Laderoute
Pierre Rivard
M. St. Jean à Marrais (?)

SARGENT TOWNSHIP
Augustin Ainel
Joseph Barniou
Joseph Brisetout
Joseph Berthiaume
Lewis Bond
Ignace Bouchard
François Boismier
Gilles Bourn
Joseph Bourdeau
Amable Belaire
Louis Benneau
Joseph Bernard
Jean Louis Belaire
Joseph Blanchard
Zalmon Bedient
Joseph Bellair
J. Bte Beaugrand
Joseph Bisonette
Paschal Bisonette
Michel Baron
Pierre Baron
J. Bte Bonome (Bonhomme)
Louis Bodin
Pierre Brancho, father
Pierre Brancho, son
Antoine Beauregard
Joseph Bastonnois
Joseph Bisson
Joseph Blain

Jean Charist
Bazil Cousineau, father
Calvin Cooly
Gideon Cooly
J. Bte Couture
Joseph Chatellreau
Antoine Campeau
Zacharie Cloutier
J. Bte Carignan
Couture Medard
Claude Couture
Pierre Couture
Pierre Corneau
James Crawford
Pierre Doucet
François Delair
Pierre Demers
Nicolas Drouillard
Dominique Drouillard
Jean Dussault
J. Bte. Dubreuil, father
J. Bte Dubreuil, son
Ignace Duval, son
Ignace Duval, father
Pierre Drouillard
Joseph Duplessis
Joseph Drouillard
Samuel Egneu
J. Bte Fontaine
Gabriel Fontaine
Charles Fontaine
Jacques Ganier
Gabriel Godfroy
Alexis Gui
Louis Gaillard
William Griffith, father
Louis Grenon
William Griffith, son
Joseph Hivon (Livernois)
Joseph Jobin
Alexandre Ewing
Alexandre Ewing, father
Jean Jacob
Simon Jacob
J. Bte Jerome
Jacques Jacob
André Jourdain
Etienne Jacob, son
Joseph Jacob
John Ewing, son

# 1802 Tax List

John Jackson
Thomas Jones
Jacob ---lar (?)
Robert Irwin
George Knags
Rachell Knags
René Lebeau
Alexis Labady
J. Bte Laselle
John Loveless
J. Bte Lisleronde
Hubert Lacroix
Louis Lajoye
Ambroise Langloise
Medard Labady
Dominique Lenfant
Benjamin Lenfant
André Lafleure
Josinne Lenfant
Louis Lenfant, son
François Leonard
Etienne Laviolette, son
François Laplante
Hyacinthe Lajoye
Alexis Lauranger
J. Bte LeDuc
Guillaume Lapointe
Jean Bte Lapointe, son
Charle Lajoye
Bazil Lajoye
Augustin Lafleur
Jacques laselle
Samuel Moore
Charles Mason
Bte Monmini
Louis Monmini
Pierre Missec
Joseph Menard
François Menard
Vincent Mayeux
James Moore
Jacques Martin
François Monmini
George McDougall
Antoine Miron
Robert Navare
François Navare, father
Jean Navare, married
Jacques Navare
François Navare, son

Isadore Navare
Antoine Nadault
Joseph pouget
paul Pernier
Michel Pepin
Bazil Pepin
Jacques Prudhomme
Charles Proux
David Robb
J. Bte Réaume, father
Etienne Robidou
Louis Robidou
Joseph Robert
Isidore Robert
J. Bte Réaume, son
Joseph Réaume
Antoine Riopel
Antoine Robert
Joseph Robidou
Jean Bte Reau
Bonadventure Robidou
Louis Robidou, son
Antoine Rivard
Antoine Rivard, son
François Robert
Joseph Robidou, son
Amable Saint Cosme
Pierre Solo
Jean Bte Solo
Davis Samons
Caleb Shaw
Freeman Shaw
Louis Suzor
J. Bte Suzor, widow
Joseph Soudriette
Charles Soudriette
Benjamin Tibbett
Bte Taillon
Prosper Thibaud
Pierre Traversi
Chrysostome Villers
Eliza Wilcox
Gabriel Godfroy
François Navare, Esq.
Josh Asking, father
Bazil Cousineau
Jacques Lasselle
Jacques Gagner
Zalmon Bedient
Hutro Navare

Antoine Campeau
J. Bte Couture
George McDougall
Meldrum and Park
Jean Bte Jerome
Rachel Knaggs
Jacques Lassell

ST. CLAIR TOWNSHIP
Christ(ian) Clemens
Baptiste Comparé
Henry Tucker
Louis Campau
Louis Moore
Antoine Jubenville
Jacque Loson
Jan Clair
Antoine Petit
Louis Petit
Baptiste Petit
Joseph Bonvouloir
Antoine Prévour
Baptiste Letournau
Pierre Fenix (Phenix)
William Tucker
Louis St. Aubin
Michel Tremblé
Robert Robertjeann
Joseph Robertjean
Alexis Pelletier
Saraphin Loson
Richard Connor
Joseph Basiné, at the St. Clair River
Ignace Champan(aign)
Pierre Mini
François Chartier
Jacque Toulouse
Pierre Champagne
Jacob Hill
Alex Harris
John Cartwright
William Thorn
John Reed
James Robison
George Cottrall
Meldrum and Park
François Bonom (Bonhomme)
Antoine Rhodes
--- Brindamoor
J. M. Beaubien

Baptiste Duchêne
Nicolas Cadoret
Joseph Larivière
François Levêque
Ignace Caslet
Henry le Negre
Pierre May
Hyacinthe Dubois
antoine Leboeuf
Joseph Giare
Baptiste Créqui
Baptiste Rapitale (Rataille)
Baptiste Montreuil
Baptiste Michel
Touissant Chovin
Jean Bouquet
Baptiste Perrine
Nicolas Bonone (Bonhomme)
nicolas Patnode, at L'Anse Creuse
François Tremblé
Baptiste Tremblé
Joseph Tremblé
Louis Renau
Michel Duchêne
François Duchêne
Louis Goulet
Joseph Garoin
Louis Percy
Baptiste Marsac
Charles Chovin
Touissant Chovin
Michel Comparet
Louis Laforge
Charles Dulac
Nicolas Vagne
Pierre Lanour
Thomas Tomasse
Augustin Cabana
Frances Gray
Laban Bogard
Laurent Moore
John Wright
Joseph Campeau
Antoine Loson

# 1805 LISTS

The Great Fire occurred on 11 June 1805, the same year Michigan Territory was created and just days before William Hull, the new Governor, arrived. Accounts of the fire have been described in all the Detroit histories and will not be repeated here. Also well-documented are the plans for the new city undertaken by the Territorial Governors and Judges, the laying out and distribution of lots, and it is likely that the lists that follow were made in connection with resolving that problem. Since we have no Federal censuses for 1790 and 1800, we are printing here a compilation of those names which have been found among private papers.

Two lists of names of residents were published in Detroit newspapers years later. The first appeared in the *Detroit Free Press* 20 September 1857, submitted by J.A.G., who stated, "To the editor: Thinking that relics of olden times when disinterred are interesting, I have with some trouble taken a copy of the names of all persons who resided in the old town of Detroit on the 11 day of June 1805. The list is taken from the papers of the old Governors and Judges of the Territory, which were probably intended to determine who were entitled to draw lots under the Act of Congress for that purpose. . . "

The second list appeared in the *Detroit Post* on 9 May 1876, and is titled "Sketches of Detroit by Judge [B.H.F.] Witherell: Inhabitants of Detroit in 1806," submitted by Mrs. E.M. Sheldon Stewart. Attempts by the compiler to locate the originals were unsuccessful.

It is clear that both lists, which are similar but by no means identical, were taken from several different lists. Considering the duplication, not only between the two, but within each separate compilation as well, they have been combined into one alphabetical list. The following symbols will be used: names that appear on both lists are starred (*); those on the 1857 list only have a hyphen preceding the name (-); and those on the 1876 list only have this mark (+).

*Abbott, James
*     Mary
*     Robert
-     Sally
+Abraham, Gaspart
*Allen, William
*Anderson, David
*     David
+Attard, Baptiste
-Audrain, Peter & wife
-     Michael
-Baby, James Jr.
-Baker, ---
*Baldwin, John
-Bales, Frederick
*Ball, Polly
*Bantum, Peregrine
+Barnes, Giles
-Battle, Zacharias
+Beaubien, Antoine
-Benjamin, Mr.
*Bentley, John
+Berthelet, Henry
*Brown, William
*Brush, Elijah
*Burnet, John
*Cadorette, Miss
+Campau, Angelique
*     Dennis
*     Joseph
*     Touissant
-Chapoton, Louis
-Chartr---, Peter
+Chittenden, Chester
*Coats, Ann
-     Thomas
+Cloutier, Walter
*Comforet, Jean Bte & wife
*Conner, Jhin
*     Robert
-Conoly, Patrick
-Cook, Abraham
*Cooper, Abraham
+     Elizabeth
-Coskry, Dr. William
+Cowles, Thomas
-Creque, Horace
*Cryque, Basile
*Cote, Prisque
*     Miss

*Curry, Charles
+     Miss
+Day, Isaac & wf
*Desnoyers, Peter
+Dilhet, John
-Dillon, Frances
+Dodemead, Ann
+     James
*     John & wf
*Donovan, Matthew & wf
*     Polly
*     Sally
-Dougherty, Dauphin
+Drake, Francis
+Drouillard, Widow
+Duchenau, Louis
+Dufour, ---
-Duncan, Maria
*Durocher, Michael
*Dyson, Capt. William & wife
*Eberts, Mrs.
*     Therese
+Elliott, Capt. Matthew
-Fearson, Hannah
*     John
*Fleming, Robert
-Fouche, Charles
-Fox, Michael
+Francoeur, Augustin
*Fraro, Francois & wife
*Galerneau, Pierre
+Geel, Nancy
-Gentle, Adam
*     John
-Giffard, Joseph
-Girardin, James & wife
*Glass, Robert Jr.
*Gobeil, Baptiste
+     Charles
*     Francis & wife
+     Madeleine
*Godfroy, Gabriel
*     Miss
+Goff, John
+Gouie, Robert
*Gouin, Charles Jr.
+Greeley, Mr.
+Griswold, Stanley
*Halibut, Lydia
+Hall, Mrs. and Miss

## 1805 Lists

+Hall, Miss
-Hanford, Joseph
+Hanks, Mrs.
*Harvey, John & wife
*Hatch, Rufus & wife
*Henry, James
+     Capt. Bird
*Hoffman, George
*Horner, Archibald & wife
+Hosford, Joseph
-Hudson, Henry & wife
+Huff, George
+Hull, Abigail
*Hunt, Israel
-Jones, Ephraim & wife
*     Israel or Isaac
+     William
+Keene, William
*Kinney, John
+Knox, William
+Knaggs, George
+Labelle, ---
*Lafleur, Charles
-Lafoy, Augustin & wife
+Lane, John
*Lapage, Francis
+Lapierre, Baptiste
+Lasselier, Mrs.
+Legard, Jean
+Limare, J.
+Lognon, Augustin
-     Louis & wife
-Luptin, John
+Lyons, Archer
+McBride, Elizabeth
-McClemens, Jane
-McCloud, Francis
-McClure, Thomas
*McCroskey, James
-McDonald, James
+McDougall, George
-     James
*McIntosh, Angus
+McKee, Alexander
+McLean, David & wife
-     Polly
*McNeil, Dennis
*McNiff, Eleanor
*     Margaret
+McVay, Henry

+Mahoney, Thomas
-Mark, William
*Martin, Hugh M.
-     Hugh W.
-May, James
*Meldrum, John
-Mette, Catherine
+     Felix
*     Theophilus
-Momford, Joseph
+Monette, Marianne
-     Michel
-Morrison, Margaret
-Munroe, Robert
*Nado, Jacob
*Nowland, Sally
*Palmer, John
*Pare, George
*Pattison, Richard
+Peltier, Baptiste
+     Isidore
-Louis & wife
*Pinard, Joseph
*Piquette, Jean Baptiste
-Pottier, Antoine
+Poupard, Charles
*Provencal, Anne
*     James
*Raymond, Adam or Andrew
-Reneau, Andrew
*     Cecile
-     Garmish
*     Henriette
*Richard, Gabriel
*Robinson, John & wife
-Robertson, John
-     Mary Ann
*     William
-Rogers, Stephen
-Ross, David
-Roy, Mary
*Russell, Hiram
+St. Bernard, ---
+Saucier, Joseph
*Scott, William McDowall
*Seek, Conrad & wife
*Sibley, Solomon & wife
-Skaggs, John? (see Knaggs)
*Smart, Geroge
*     Robert

+Smith, Jacob
+    Thomas
*Smyth, Richard & wife
*Stewart, Charles
-Stone, ---
+Teere, Henry
+Ten Eyck, Conrad
+Thibault, James
+    Louis Jr.
*Town, Ephraim
*    Sarah
*Trombley, Michael
-Trumbull, Mrs.
*Tuttle, Christopher
-Vademid, Ann
+Valney, Mrs. [same?]
*Verney, Nicolas
+    Mrs.
+Villet, Johan
*Vincent, Jacques
*Voyer, Joseph & wife
-Waite, Samuel
*Watson, John
*    William
+Wayne, Antony
*Welch, George
+    Polly
*    Thomas
+Willeveny, Maurice
+    Elenne
+Wilkinson, Joseph
+Williams, Elizabeth
*    John
+    Kera
+Williamson, Joseph

COLORED RESIDENTS IN THE OLD TOWN
    [all from 1876 list]
Cato
Cooper, Elizabeth
    Joseph
Hall, Mrs. (mulatto)
    Miss (mulatto)
Harry and Hannah
Loudon and his wife Mary
Marguerite
Nell
Parker, Tom
Susan and Pompey
Voyer, Josette

# AN 1810 CENSUS OF THE DISTRICT OF DETROIT, TERRITORY OF MICHIGAN

Transcribed by Eva Murrell Harmison

Congress organized the Territory of Michigan in 1805 with Detroit as the capital. The Territory included the Lower Peninsula, present-day Chippewa County, and the eastern half of Mackinac County. General William Hull, the first governor, on 3 July 1805, issued a proclamation dividing the Territory into four districts: Erie, Detroit, Huron, and Michilimackinac. To the District of Detroit was assigned a ten-mile strip of river front, with the citadel as its center. South of the District of Detroit lay the District of Erie, and the territory north of Saginaw Bay became the District of Huron. In 1810, Governor Hull and the Supreme Court Judges Augustus B. Woodward, James Witherell, and John Griffin, constituted the legislative body of the Territory.

This transcription was taken from an original, handwritten document in the Burton Historical Collection of the Detroit Public Library and is contained in the papers of B.F.H. Witherell, son of James Witherell. The document is surely a partial transcription of the 1810 Federal census of the District of Detroit. The first pages, containing names of approximately 51 family heads, are missing; they probably contain the enumerations from at least one other area and all the "A" and some "B" surnames in Detroit. No headings for age groups are shown, but they appear to be the same as the 1810 Federal census. These are: males under 10, 10-16, 16-26, 26-45, over 45; then follows a slash mark (/) and the same categories for females. Another slash follows these numbers, and the last three categories are: free colored persons, number of slaves, and total. Abbreviated given names are: Andw-Andrew, Ane-André, Ane-Antoine, Augn-Augustin, Benjn-Benjamin, Bte-Baptiste, Dque-Dominique, Danl-Daniel, Fs and Frans-François, Gabl-Gabriel, Gaume-Guillaume (William), J. Bte - Jean Baptiste, Josh-Joseph, Ns and Nichs-Nicholas, Rt-Robert, and Wm-William.

This transcription was published in the *Detroit Society for Genealogical Research Magazine* 32:17-23. Alphabetizing was done by enumerator; note also that the figure under "total" is not accurate.

DETROIT:

Bain, Widow J. 50101/00010/109
Beard, David 00060/10100/109
Burnett, James 00100/00000/001
Bentley, John 00001/10000/002
Belcher, Bridget 01000/01010/003
Biron, Jean L 00100/10101/004
Bouate, Louis C. 10100/00100/003
Burgess, Jonathan 00000/00000/303
Brown, William 00010/00000/506
Bellanger, Bte 30201/00101/008

Barthelet, Henry 20110/20110/008
Brush, Elijah 30110/00010/61 (12)
Cadorette, Urcelle 22000/13001/009
Clark, Widow G. 00000/00001/001
Curry, Widow C. 00000/10020/104
Campeau, Joseph 10010/00100/104
Coates, Widow Ann 00000/10010/002
Conner, John 12010/21010/008
Coté, Widow M. 10020/00101/005
Cerat, Alexis 31001/01000/006

(* see below)

*Charlotte 00000/00000/202
*Campeau, Bte 10010/11010/005
Desnoyer, Peter 10010/31010/007
Desjardin, H. 01010/00000/002
Dufour, Louis 00200/00100/003
Forsyth, William 01021/41100/ 20(12)
Foster, Joel P. 00100/00000/001
Gobeye, François (Gobeil) 00201/01001/005
Fréreau, Frans 00001/10001/003
Greely, Aaron 20030/10010/108
Geel, Abraham 20110/00100/005
Dodemead Sr., J. 1121-/11010/008
Durette, J. Bte 12001/31110/00(10)
Collier, Levi 02001/00010/004
Gobeye, Charles (Gobeil) 00100/00100/002
Germain, André 10100/00100/003
Girardin, Widow J. 32100/03101/00(11)
Hunt, Henry J. 01100/00000/305
Harvey, John 01002/01010/005
Hudson, Henry 20220/10010/008
*Jones, R.H. 00101/00000/002
Joly, Pierre 00001/00001/002
Johnson, George 00110/00100/003
Jubinville, Bte 10200/00101/005
Longden, Augn (Lognon) 20011/10010/006
Lagard, Widow A. 00000/00001/001
Lalièvre, Charles 11202/10001/009
Larivière, Joseph 10010/21010/006
Lemene, François 30010/20010/007
Murphy, Thomas 00001/00010/002
Mercier, John 00011/10100/004
May, James 21021/22110/03(15)
McDonnell, J. 11013/01100/008
Miller, David 00010/01010/003
McClure, Thomas 00200/00000/002
Mahoney, Thomas 00010/00010/002
McDougall, G. 01030/00000/206
McCroskey, Wm 00002/00000/002
Mack, Stephen 00010/01010/003
Francoeur, Augn 20010/20100/006
Murray, Peter 00010/20100/004
McNeal, Danl 00001/00001/002
McNiff, Mrs 00000/00100/002
Mallette, Joseph 20200/00200/006
Meteé, Théophile 11001/30100/007
Neveu, Antoine 00010/20100/004
Lonion, Louis 00001/00000/001
Jack (Negro)00000/00000/606
Provinçal, Widow C. 00101/00301/005
Picquet, J. Bte 20010/00100/004
Jones, William 00120/01100/005
Cook, Abraham 30130/10100/009

Peltier, Louis 00110/50020/009
McClain, David 20101/12101/009
Peltier, J. Bte 10011/00010/004
Palmer, John 20001/00010/005
Parker, Thomas 00000/00000/505
Roy, Augustin 10010/10100/004
Rough, James 00610/00000/007
*Rumeau, Louis (Renaud) 30010/21010/008
Seek, Conrad 40010/20100/109
Smart, Robert 00120/10010/005
Smith, Richard 20320/32110/20(16)
Scott, William 20210/40300/10(13)
Smith, Jacob 00020/21010/006
Leclair, Joseph 10011/00100/004
Truax, A.C. 00010/00100/002
Teneyck, Conrad 00200/00000/002
Thibault, Joseph 01101/12110/008
Tremblé, Michel 20001/00001/004
Thibaudeau, J. Bte 00010/10100/003
Vanalstine, Andw 00100/00000/001
Varnay, Nicholas 30001/21100/008
Vermet, Antoine 20010/22010/008
Wendell, Josiah 00100/00000/001
Welch, Thomas 00010/00010/002
Williams, John R. 30110/00010/008
Watson, William 10010/00100/003
Watson, Joseph 00200/00000/002

COTE DU NORD-EST:

Beaubien, Antoine 22101/22110/00(12)
Boyer, Antoine 00101/10001/004
Cady, Isaac 00101/00001/003
Comparet, J. Bte 02011/00100/005
Campeau, Denis 00010/00000/001
Cécile, Antoine 00010/00100/002
Campeau, Jacques 10210/11010/007
Chêne, Gabriel 11110/41010/00(10)
Chapoton, Benoist 20111/22110/00(11)
Chapoton, Louis 01010/21111/008
Dequindre Sr., A. 01201/12101/009
Dupré, François 11001/00001/004
Dubois, Etienne 21010/30010/008
Fournier, Gaume 11110/00000/206
Gouin, Charles 00101/00002/004
Gouin, Nicholas 00001/00111/404
King, Joseph 12001/21110/009
Laperle, Joseph 03002/01101/008
Laderoute, Baptiste 11102/21010/009
Lafoy, Augustin 00001/43010/009
Sibley, Solomon 10020/11110/007

Yax, Simon 20101/00010/005

POINTE AU NICOLET:

Tremblé, Gagette 11010/40010/008

WINDMILL POINT:

Lavoye, François 10011/00100/004
Sorcier, Joseph 20011/42000/00(10)

HOG ISLAND (BELLE ISLE):

Lyons, Widow E. 11200/01001/006

COTE DE POUX:

Abbott, Robert 51020/01100/00(10)
Beaubien, Joseph 21201/00100/007
Barron, Joseph 00011/00001/003
Cabacier, Charles 20001/22110/009
Cicotte, J. Bte 02101/00001/005
Chabert, François 00101/01100/004
Campeau, Alexis 00010/00110/003
Campeau, Baptiste 22010/32010/00(11)
Dugard, John 00000/00010/102
Delonchamps, Josh 00110/30100/006
Duberger, Josh 10010/11010/005
Ducharme, Fs 00001/00100/406
Gamelin, Françs 01001/02010/005
Godfroy, Sr., Gabriel 21711/43110/00(21)
Henry, James 20410/00010/008
Knaggs, Wm 12112/00111/10(11)
Labady, Pierre D. 00121/00201/007
Lemay, A.P. 00110/10100/003
Lafontaine, Fs 00101/01100/015
Labady, Alexis 10111/40301/00(12)
Labrosse, Dque 00001/00001/002
Metté, Renné 10010/23100/008
Navarre, Robert 00111/00300/017
Parain, Joachim 01011/10010/106
Pemberton, Richd 00020/00000/002
Peltier, Jacques, 00101/00100/003
Riopel, Ambroise 00201/01200/006
Richard, Rev. Gabl 14220/2(11)201/00(25)
Shaw, John 20001/10010/005
Vessier, Louis père 10202/00110/108
Visger, Jacob 00211/02000/208
Woillet, Alexander (Ouellet) 21001/00101/006

RIVER ROUGE:

Anthony 00000/00000/505
Bellair, Joseph 20101/30100/008
Bondy, Joseph 10110/10100/005
Brevoort, Henry B. 00020/00000/103
Butler, John 20020/21100/008
Bucklin, William 00110/00001/003
Brown, Joseph 20020/11010/007
Burbank, John 10100/11010/003
Campeau, Nichs 00202/11001/007
Chauvin, François 01001/10001/004
Charbonneau, Josh 00010/00000/001
Chamberlain, Josh 30001/31010/009
Chauvin, Charles 01101/11101/007
Connelly, John 21110/01010/007
Campeau, Ante 00010/00100/002
Cattin, Antoine 20210/00100/006
Cicotte, Jacques 00200/00100/003
Cicotte, François 00100/10100/003
Clark, Andrew 00010/20010/004
Durocher, François 00001/00000/001
Delisle, Bienvenue 20030/11001/008
Delisle, Baptiste 11010/01000/004
Dumay, Pierre 11201/01010/007
Durocher, Françs 04101/10101/009
Dicks, Widow R. 01100/10101/005
Fraser, Alexander 00100/01000/002
Giles, John 21011/11011/009
Hicks, George 00000/00000/505
Hicks, Jesse 21010/00010/005
Leduc, Louis 11010/20010/006
Labady, Charles 00010/00020/003
Larose, Henry 01010/00100/003
Laferté, Louis 30010/10010/006
Lorrain, François 20010/10010/005
Larebelle, Antoine 31002/30010/00(10)
Metté, Felix 51001/10010/009
McCombs, John (Macomb) 13010/00010/006
McCarty, Edward 20101/00010/005
McVey, Hugh 10103/01000/006
Nelson, Jonathan 21011/12010/009
Price, George 20020/40020/00(10)
Patrick, Joshua 00010/10100/003
Riopel, Pierre 10010/00100/003
*Riopel, Hyacinthe 30010/00100/005
Rouleau, Charles 30010/30010/008
Rogers, Chester 11001/21010/007
Raimond, Josiah 02101/30100/005
Riopel, Toussant 00010/30010/005

Lesperance, Ané 22010/10010/007
Meem, John 00001/00010/002
Moran, Charles 12001/00110/006
Moran, Louis 01001/21001/006
Morace, Joseph (Moras) 10210/02101/008
McDougall, Rt 41001/11011/20(12)
Moran, Morice 10011/20110/029
Meldrum, George 31211/10010/16(17)
Morain, Isidore (Moran), 11021/10010/007
Morasse, Victor 00100/00201/004
Peltier, Charles 12100/12210/00(11)
Poupard, Charles 12100/00000/105
Peltier, Felix 10111/12010/008
*Rivard, François 10010/20010/005
Ryan, Edward 20001/00100/004
Russell, William 00241/01010/009
Rivard, Antoine 00010/10100/003
St. Obin, François 01110/01000/004
St. Obin, Jacques 00001/40001/006
St. Obin, Baptiste 00010/00001/002
Petit, Samuel 10010/20010/005
Tremblé, Ignace 01001/00000/002
Thibault, Lambert 00100/00000/001

GRAND MARAIS:

Blearn, James 00000/00000/707
Bellair, Etienne 11010/20100/006
Campeau, J. Bte 00010/00101/003
Chauvin, Charles 00201/00101/005
Chêne, Pierre 10001/ 00101/004
Chêne, Toussaint 30111/31010/00(10)
Chauvin, Baptiste 02110/00001/005
Campeau, Alexis 20110/31010/009
Dupra, Louis 10010/00100/003
Desaunay, Louis 00100/00101/003
Dupra, Charles 01201/00301/008
Fournier, Abraham 10010/20100/004
Fournier, François 20110/30100/008
Green, Benjamin 20010/11010/006
Griffard, Louis 01011/00001/004
Griffard, Pierre 11010/21000/006
Laderoute, Joseph 02001/42210/00(12)
Little, John 01101/01001/016
Marsac, Jacques 01010/10100/004
Marsac, Robert 10020/10000/004
Marsac, Renné 00010/30100/005
Persil, Louis 23101/11010/00(10)
Peltier, Baptiste 00100/00100/002
Pominville, Widow L. 01000/02001/004
Rivard, François 30011/20010/008

Serré, Joseph 00102/11010/006
Senné, Ignace (Senet) 12010/21010/008
Seguin, Pierre 30002/32020/008
Sorcier, Baptiste 10100/10100/004
Tremblé, Leonard 00001/00000/001
Tremblé, Louis 11201/02210/00(10)
Tremblé, Thomas 20110/10100/006
Thibault, Widow F. 01101/10001/005
Tremblé, Joseph L. 40100/02110/009

UPPER PART OF TREMBLES' CREEK:

Coulay, Oliver 00100/10100/003

GROSSE POINTE:

Ambroise, Jean L. 10010/00100/003
Ambroise, Evangile 11101/10001/006
Chovin, Baptiste 22001/02000/007
Campeau, Julien 11001/01000/007
Créque, Bazile 00010/00100/002
Duchêne, Pierre 10001/40010/007
Duchêne, Etienne 30010/20100/007
Delaunay, J. Bte 50010/10010/007
Ellair, Joseph 10010/00011/004
Flinn, John 10011/32010/009
Fortun, François (Forton) 22110/30010/00(10)
Gouin, C.N. 10011/10100/005
Grant Family of A. 20111/13221/12(17)
    (prob. Amherstburg, Ont.)
Grosbeck, William 31001/01010/007
Griffard, Laurent 11201/10101/008
Kirby, John 00200/00000/002
Marsac, Benjn 00201/20200/007
Morrain, Louis (Moran) 10010/00100/003
Patenaude, Ns 01001/21001/006
Rivard, Baptiste 32001/00200/008
Rivard, Pierre 41001/21010/00(10)
Rivard, Charles 52001/12210/00(14)
Rivard, Michel 40001/21001/009
Robison, William 00020/00000/002
Reneau, Joseph (Renaud) 00010/10010/003
Reneau, François 01100/00010/003
Robertjean, Josh 21010/20010/007
Reneau, Antoine 11010/00100/004
Senné, Jean Bte 20010/20110/007
Tremblé, Pierre 00010/10100/003
Tremblé, Widow A. 01000/12010/005
Vernier, J. Bte 32001/20010/009
Yax, Pierre 11001/10101/006

Raimon, Françs 10001/30100/006
Sargeant, Thomas 01110/01001/005
Stacey, William 00010/30010/005
Sequey 00000/00000/202
Steinbeck, John 00010/00100/002
Steers, William 11010/21100/007
St. Amour, Bte 00001/00000/001
Trudèle, François 01101/31010/008
Thomas Jr., Aaron 00200/00100/003
Thomas Sr., Aaron 00001/10001/003
Weaver, Joseph 11210/12000/008

PRAIRIE RONDE:

Bourdillon, Louis 42001/11010/00(10)
Cicotte, Joseph 10010/10010/004
Dodelin, Adrien 31010/10100/007
LeFranc, Antoine 40011/21010/00(10)
Livernois, Joseph 20100/10200/006

RIVER AUX ECORCE:

Albert, Joseph 20010/10100/005
Bourasa, Louis 11001/11200/007
Bondy, Dque 30100/21100/008
Barrieau, Joseph 11010/10010/005
Bondy, Joseph 20010/00010/004
Barron, Antoine 41110/31010/00(12)
Campeau, Pierre 22001/20010/008
Campeau, Charles 10101/00100/004
Drouillard, Dque 10010/01100/004
Despla, Jacques 10020/10000/004
Drouillard, J. Bte 31110/31010/00(11)
Dufour, J. Bte 21010/00001/005
Fraisgeau, David 00020/00010/003
Goodale, Elijah 33201/22010/00(14)
Lamironde, Joseph 40010/20110/009
Leblanc, Pierre 30010/30010/008
Labady, Pierre 00010/00100/002
Lebeau, Baptiste 00101/00100/004
Mensonon, Etienne 11010/31100/003
Morrison, Widow V. 00010/00001/002
Macgee, Henry 01010/00010/003
Monier, Louis 10011/20100/006
(Paper torn) 00010/20010/00-
(Paper torn) 02101/20101/00-
(Paper torn) 10010/30010/006
---, Baptiste 10010/41010/008
--- geau, Josh 21001/11010/007
Vermet, Joseph 00100/00100/002

Vigile, André 00101/21010/006
Vermet Sr., Joseph 11001/20001/006

MAGUAGA (MONGUAGON):

St. ---. François 20101/10000/005
Sanders, Samuel 00010/00000/001

HICKORY ISLAND:

Parker, Robert 00010/10010/002

GROSSE ISLE:

Bean, Henry 10001/00001/003
Carpenter, John 00010/01000/002
Dickson, John 00010/00100/002
Davis, John D. 21010/00100/005
Heacocks, Adna 21120/11010/009
Kemp, Jacob H. 12110/00010/005
Larabee, James 50010/00010/007
Labelle, Antoine 10001/02101/006
Myers, James 01001/00001/003
McComb, William 00101/00000/002
Mitchell, James 00100/00100/002
Thomas, John 00100/10100/003

Total amount of the inhabitants of the District of Detroit, being the division allotted to J. Watson - 2355

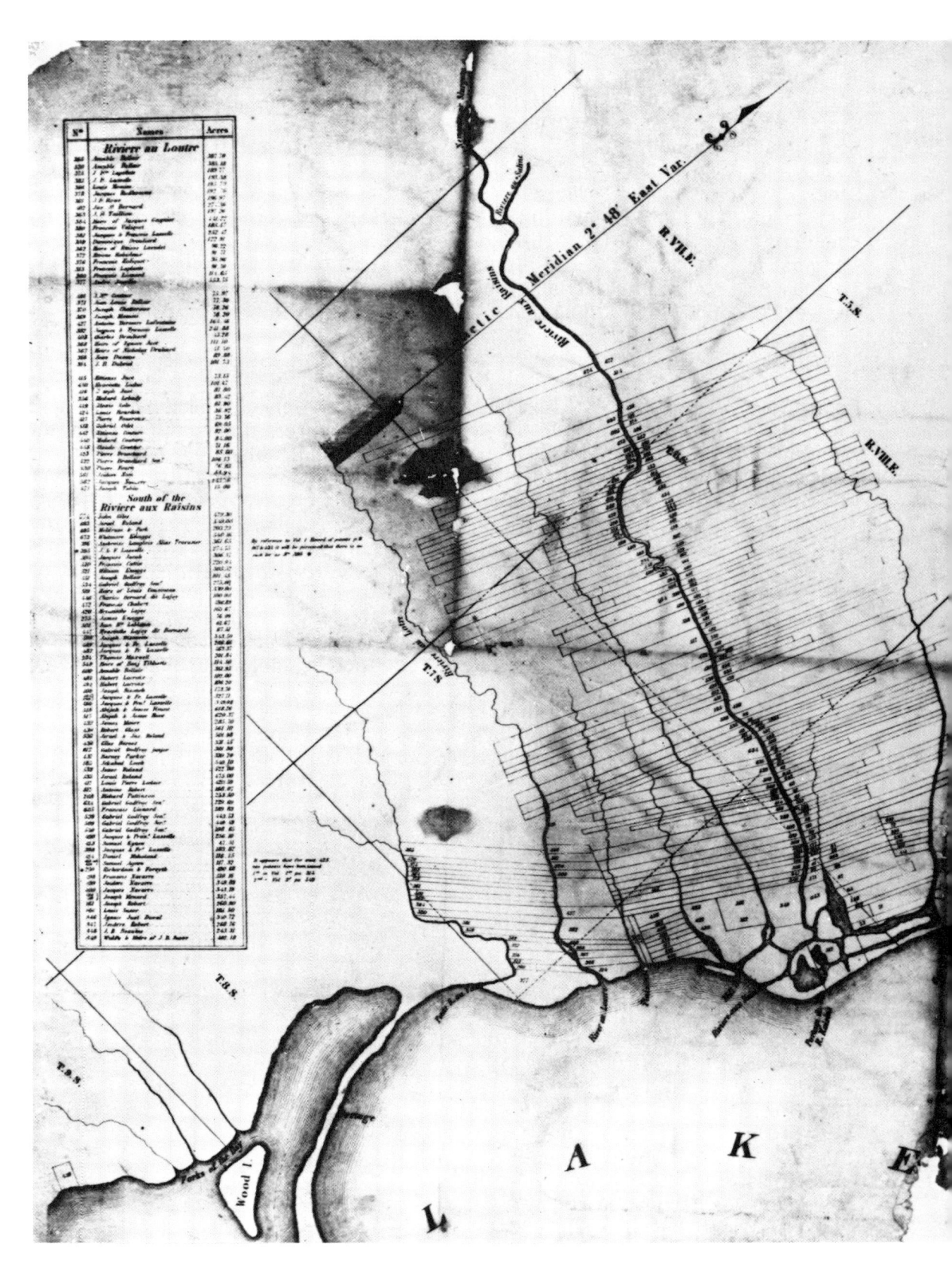

MAP 11. LAKE ERIE PRIVATE CLAIMS, by Aaron Greeley, 1810

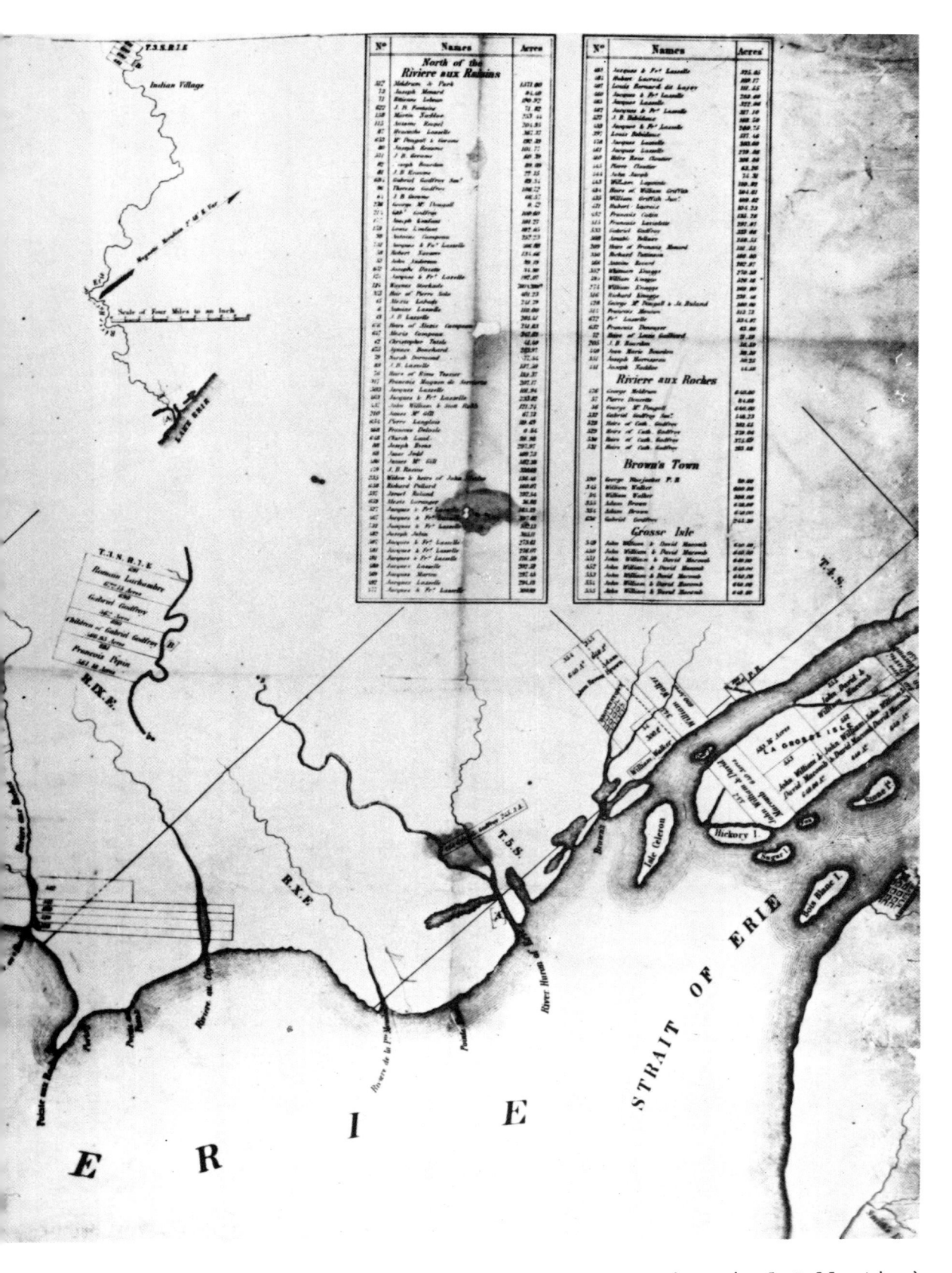

(Courtesy of Burton Historical Collection)

MAP 12. DETROIT PRIVATE CLAIMS, by Aaron Greeley, 1810

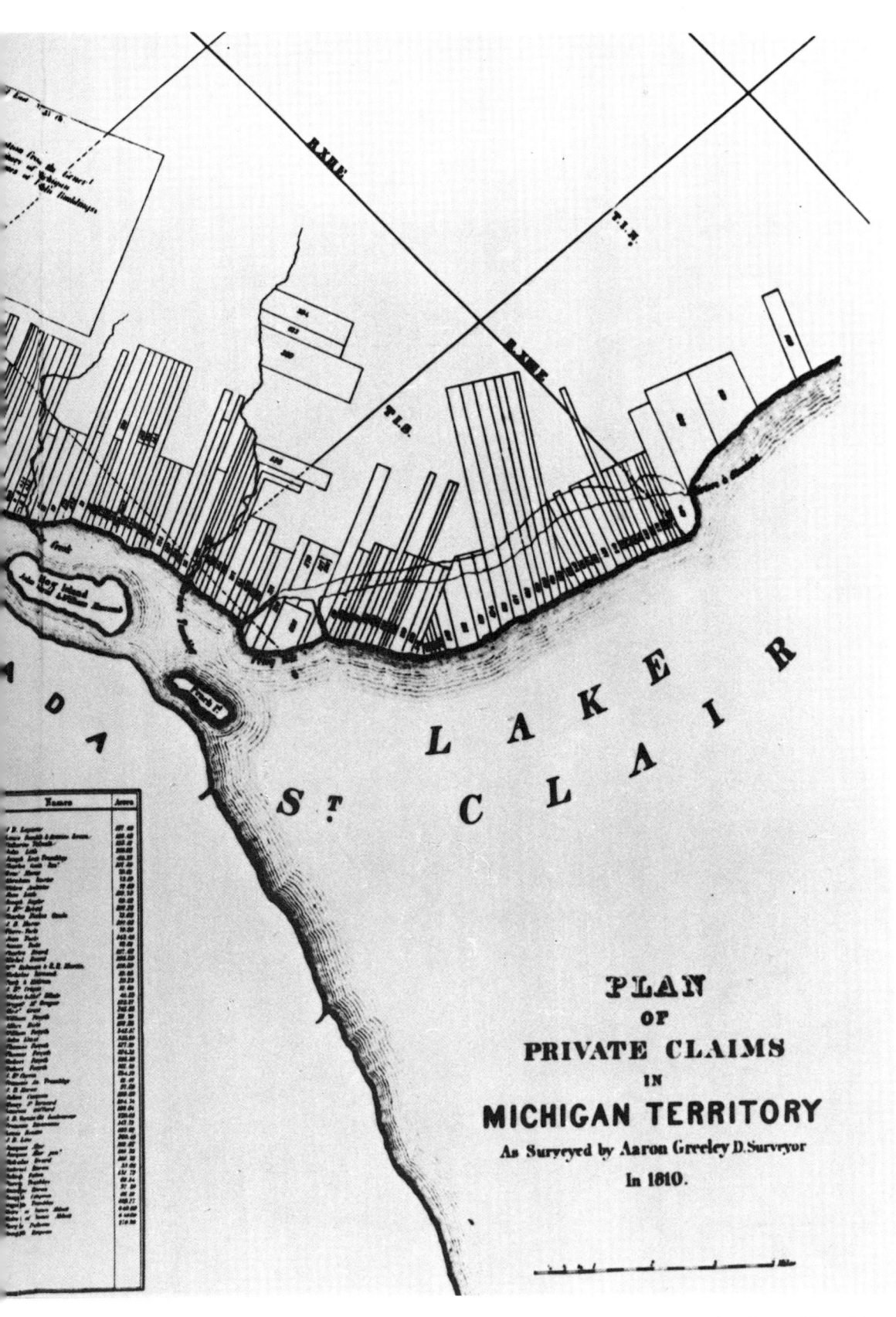

**PLAN OF PRIVATE CLAIMS IN MICHIGAN TERRITORY**
As Surveyed by Aaron Greeley D. Surveyor
In 1810.

(Courtesy of Burton Historical Collection)

| Nº | Names | Acres |
|---|---|---|
| | River Huron | |
| 630 | J. Bte Socier | 139.92 |
| 250 | Nickolus Panoad | 96.57 |
| 170 | J. B. Vernier dit Ladouceur | 114.20 |
| 199 | Francois Ambroise Tramblay | 87.83 |
| 320 | J. B. St Laurent | 58.06 |
| 566 | J. B. Tramblay | 23.00 |
| 565 | Ettienne Socier | 68.04 |
| 278 | Charles Chouin | 50.73 |
| 735 | Jean Bte Lapierre | 40.07 |
| 225 | Michel Duchesne | 67.84 |
| 505 | J. B. Petite | 91.43 |
| 220 | Pierre Griffard | 77.52 |
| 736 | Joseph Laurent | 75.29 |
| 645 | Francois Duchesne | 75.94 |
| 316 | Louis Laduc | 63.35 |
| 162 | Jean Marsac | 63.44 |
| 277 | Charles Chouin | 56.65 |
| 164 | Jas. Maitresse dit Sansfaçon | 277.87 |
| 602 | Alexis Dubai | 89.72 |
| 601 | J. B. Dubai | 127.75 |
| 513 | Louis Laforge | 101.27 |
| 149 | J. B. Parry | 88.80 |
| 165 | Joseph Dubai | 52.33 |
| 174 | Widow & Heirs of Jacob Thomas | 44.63 |
| 163 | J. Bte Noutait | 63.00 |
| 148 | Phillix Peltier | 126.90 |
| 133 | Joseph Campeau | 176.72 |
| 604 | Joseph Campeau | 372.31 |
| 238 | Louis Chappoton junior | 134.49 |
| 151 | Francois St Aubin | 139.78 |
| 319 | Joseph Campeau | 205.90 |
| 545 | Joseph Campeau | 396.73 |
| 168 | Louis Campeau | 310.31 |
| 207 | Laurent Moore | 97.35 |
| 130 | Joseph Campeau | 96.13 |
| 616 | Nicolas Campeau | 314.02 |
| 134 | Joseph Campeau | 121.94 |
| 173 | Louis Pait | 84.90 |

MAP 13. LAKE ST. CLAIR PRIVATE CLAIMS, by Aaron Greeley, 1810
(Courtesy of Burton Historical Collection)

# DETROIT

*Prior to the fire of June 11, 1805*

Issued as a Supplement to the DETROIT JOURNAL of June 11, 1889.

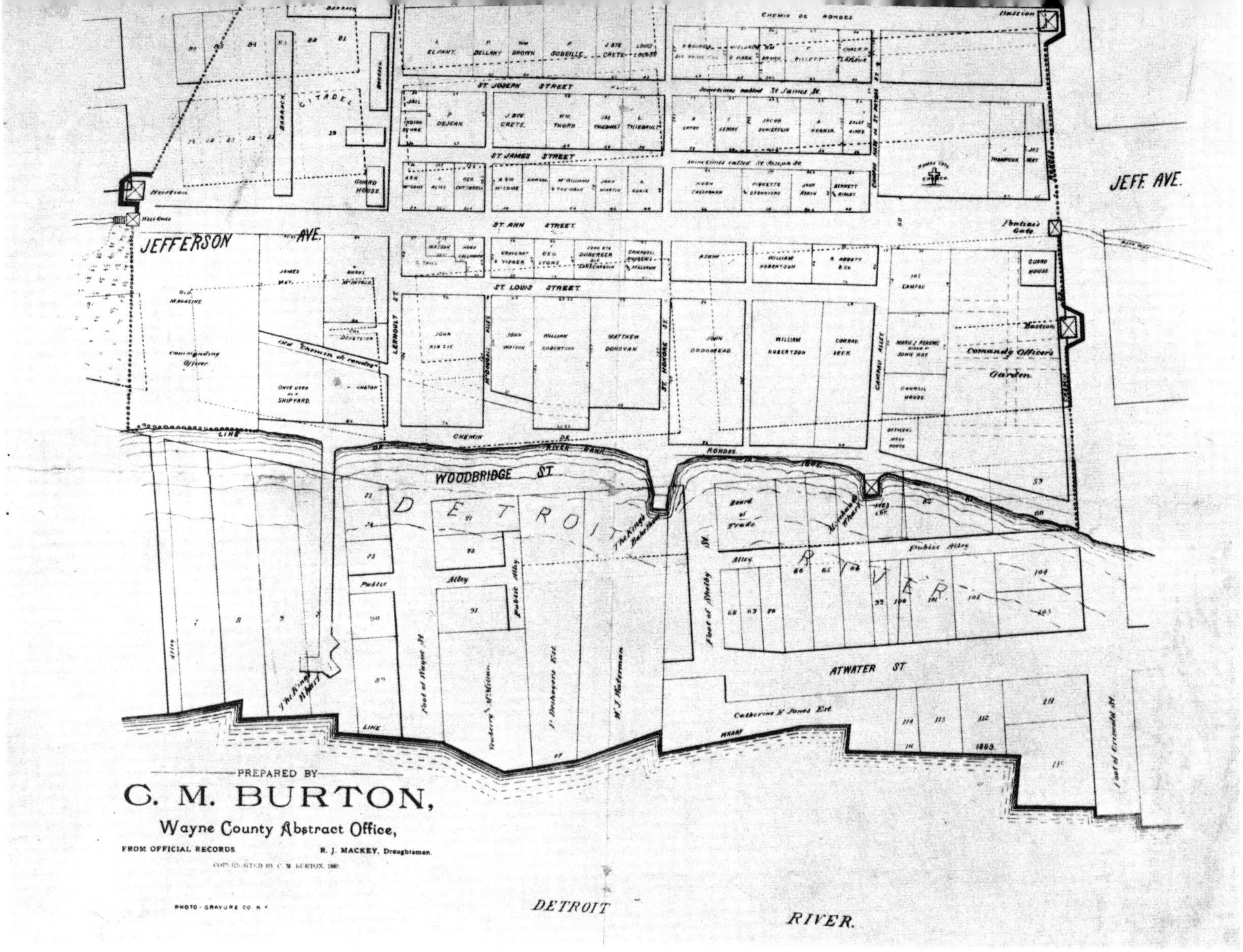

MAP 14. DETROIT PRIOR TO THE FIRE OF 1805, by Clarence M. Burton, 1889
(Courtesy of Burton Historical Collection)

# 1810 CENSUS OF MICHILIMACKINAC

Copied by Elizabeth Taft Harlan

---

This enumeration of 176 persons was copied from an 1810 census of Michilimackinac, Territory of Michigan, "within the division allotted to Samuel Abbott." It does not constitute the whole 1810 Michilimackinac census. A recapitulation, dated 9 February 1810 and signed by Reuben Attwater, Secretary of the Territory of Michigan, states that the total number of inhabitants was 512, plus 103 in the garrison, for a grand total of 615. A note adds: "Census taken at Michilimackinac, 1810, by Samuel Abbott, an Early Factor for the American Fur Company and Brother of James Abbott, a Director."

The age group headings are: males under 10, 10-16, 16-26, 26-45, and over 45. Females follow the slash (/) in the same order, and the last column is "All Other Free Persons Except Indians Not Taxed." Since the heading for slaves had no entries, it has been deleted.

The original manuscript is at the Burton Historical Collection of the Detroit Public Library. This census was published in the *Detroit Society for Genealogical Research Magazine* 34:125.

Robert Dickson 11(24)(26)2/00000/0
Jacob Franks 00440/00000/0
Harry M. Fisher 00240/00000/0
Michel Brisbois 01330/00000/0
Redford Crawford 00860/00000/0
Joseph P. Lacroix 00240/00000/0
Antoine Chemer 00530/00000/0
Lewis Grignon 00330/00000/0
James Aird 00552/00000/0
Joseph Rolette 00440/00000/0
Michel Lacroix 00560/00000/0
Charlie Marlie 20010/10100/0
Daniel O. Dunham 00431/00000/0
Louis Bensson 00330/00000/0
René Nadeau 10001/00000/0
Samuel Lashley 30220/11010/2
John B. Picard 01010/00000/1

# 1820 CENSUS OF MICHIGAN

The Territory of Michigan in 1820 extended to the Mississippi River, including the present state of Wisconsin and part of Minnesota. The population had increased to 8,765. The major concentrations were at Detroit and its contingent counties, now quickly being settled by Americans from New England and New York. The fur trade continued at Michilimackinac, and we find a large settlement of French Canadians also in Wisconsin at Green Bay and Prairie du Chien. Many of these later became United States citizens. US military posts were built at both these places; Fort Howard (also called Fort Brown) at Green Bay, on the north side of the Fox River, had a garrison of 300 men, plus another 300 infantry in cantonments at Camp Smith three miles above Fort Howard. Note than many of the heads of family here have extremely large households; these are presumably military men attached to the fort. Some of the men listed here are officers of the Third Infantry; the enlisted men were not enumerated. Fort Crawford at Prairie du Chien had 131 US troops.

The Michigan portion of this census was copied from a manuscript in the Burton Historical Collection, before the microfilm of the original was available, by members of DSGR, who carefully annotated it; it was published in the *Detroit Society for Genealogical Research Magazine* in 1949-52: City of Detroit 12:101-105, 129-131; Wayne County 12:131-32, 13:19-24, 47-50, 83-87; Oakland County 13:113-115; Macomb County 13:137-140, 14:21-23; Monroe County 14:51-54, 83-86, 109-113; Michilimackinac County 15:19-23, 47-50, 77-79. The Wisconsin counties appeared in *Wisconsin Families* in 1940: 1:17-25. The present transcription has been edited and corrected by Harriette Marr Wheeler from the microfilm for Michigan, while the Wisconsin counties were reviewed by Jim Hansen, Reference Librarian of the State Historical Society of Wisconsin, a specialist in the French families of that area, who added correct spellings (in parentheses).

Note also the following: (1) names followed by an asterisk (*) in Detroit were soldiers; presumably they were assigned to or visiting at Fort Shelby. Two lists of Detroit residents appear on the microfilm with different spellings; when in doubt, consult the film; (2) the abbreviation AFC in the Michilimackinac census refers to the American Fur Company.

The categories for the 1820 census are different for men than women, because an extra count was taken for men/boys aged sixteen to eighteen; the purpose of this was to assess the military strength of the country. The divisions are: men: under 10, 10-16, 16-26, 26-45, over 45, 16-18; after the slash the divisions are the same for women except the last. Colored persons were enumerated separately, as indicated in the transcription.

In most cases the enumerator remembered to include himself; exceptions are: Thomas Maxwell for Detroit, Charles Noble for Monroe County, William Belsher for Crawford County, and Hugh Kelly for Brown County.

## CENSUS OF THE TOWN OF DETROIT 1820

Schedule of the Whole Number of Persons in the Division allotted to Thompson Maxwell, and filed in the Office of the Clerk of the Superior Court, July 28 1821.

William Woodbridge [1] 200240/20110
Adam D. Stewart [2] 000060/00000
Mrs. Watson [3] 010210/00010
William Robertson [4] 200010/30011
James Girardin [5] 000100/00100
Thomas Chadwick [6] 000010/00000
Robert Stevinson 300010/00011
John Rowens 100010/00010
Joseph Denny 200010/02100
Evan Duchane [7] 32--1-/-1-1-
Francis Lemin [8] 111201/11001
John Durette [9] 110001/11010
Catherine Farrell [10] 200011/12010
Mary Brown [11] 200000/21010
John Lambert 000010/01100
Mary Van Tosler 000000/00100

Jos. C. LaBellaine [12] 210101/12100
Richard Bean [13] 100200/20100
Isaac W. Day [14] 010110/21010
Lizette Temblé (Tremblay) 100000/10010
Henry Sanderson [15] 010010/01110
John Bates 010411/02001
John Stoner [16] 000220/00010
John Robson [17] 000010/11010
Benj. Longe 000100/01010
Richard Baldock [18] 100010/00010
John Dewit [19] 100102/12210
Benj. Woodworth [20] 2100(13)1/31030
Nimrod Troutwine [21] 200000/00100
Oliver W. Miller [22] 100010/00010
Leonard Pike 000300/00000
Thomas Rowland [23] 100010/01111

1. B. Norwich, CT 20 Aug. 1789; d. Detroit 20 Oct 1861; son of Dudley.
2. Native of Virginia. Collector of Customs, Mackinac, 1818-1832.
3. Catherine, wife of John or widow of George E. Watson, who d. Detroit 1819.
4. M. Detroit 4 Nov. 1813 Louise Lauzon. Lived Cottrelville, St. Clair County.
5. B. Sandwich 1792; d. 1826; m. 1820 Archange Latourneau, dau. Jean Baptiste.
6. To Detroit 1821; River Rouge 7 Sept. 1824 when m. Senath Chamberlain.
7. Prob. Pierre Gastinon-Duchene, d. 1831; m. 1806 Angelique Yvon, dau. Joseph.
8. Francois Lemen-Yvon, m. 1796 Angelique Gagnier. He d. by 1854.
9. M. 1796 Anne Renaud 1774-1859, dau. Louis and Marie Anne Casse Renaud.
10. Catherine (Morris), wf. Edward Farrell, who d. Detroit 30 Oct. 1819, aet. 30.
11. Poss. widow of Henry Brown, whose estate filed for probate 16 Aug. 1819.
12. Prob. of Beneteau-LaBaleine family, though no record of Joseph.
13. Lived St. Clair County; army private; on pension 1817, voted Detroit 1820.
14. In city by 1805 fire; d. before 26 Oct. 1847; m. Mary Ann Burnett Douglass.
15. From Charlestown, MA; d. near Pontiac 18 Aug. 1834; m. Lydia Stevens.
16. Agreed with John R Williams to build wharf 1823; d. Brownstown 20 Aug. 1827.
17. Master of ships *Julie* 1815 and *Olive Branch* 1823.
18. Baker or grocer. Receipt 28 Nov. 1820 to Wm Woodbridge re Bread Account.
19. He and wf. Mary of Farmington Twp. sold land in Huron Twp. 22 Oct. 1835.
20. Hotel proprietor; b. Scituate, MA 29 Dec. 1782; d. St. Clair 10 Nov. 1874.
21. M. Margaret Price; two ch. bp. 1820. She m. (2) Pontiac 1822 Oliver Parker.
22. M. 15 Dec. 1813 Pelagie Loranger-Maisonville, b   City Treasurer 1816.
23. B. Uniontown, PA; d. Detroit 13 Aug. 1849; m. --- Springer and Catherine McNiff.

# 1820 Census

Deborah Johnson[1] 210000/01110
Austin E. Wing[2] 120010/00110
Ebenezer Hurd[3] 100010/10110
John R Williams[4] 330230/20230
Victor Roquette[5] 100010/00010
David Johnson[6] 100020/01100
William Brookfield[7] 201000/11000
Stephen Mack[8] 010140/00011
Barnabie Campau[9] 001011/20000
George McDougall[10] 001001/00001
Sylvanus Blackman[11] 100012/01001
Solomon Sibley[12] 200001/42011
John Hunt[13] 100011/20110
Paul Clapp[14] 000030/00000
Jeremiah V.R. Ten Eyck[15] 000110/00100
John P. Sheldon[16] 020210/10200
Louis Jollet[17] 100010/30010
Horatio Ball[18] 000100/00000
Sally McGonogall 000000/00010
Samuel Brittain[19] 100010/00010
W. McCoskry[20] 020001/02010
Jacob Smith[21] 100012/12000
Micheaux Trombley[22] 000001/00001
Mrs. Jane Edwards[23] 001000/00001
Orlin Barthelet[24] 200130/10110
Charette Donas 300110/00100
Antoine Nevieuz[25] 200010/30010
James McCloskey[26] 200010/10100
John Monteith[27] 010010/00100
Joseph André[28] 210101/21010

1. Widow of Royal Johnson, who d. Detroit June or July 1819.
2. B. Conway, MA 3 Feb. 1792, son Enoch Wing; d. Cleveland 27 Aug. 1849.
3. Physician, b. Sandgate, VT 28 Jan. 1779; d. Chicago 4 May 1864; bur. Elmwood.
4. B. Detroit 4 May 1782, son of Thomas; native of Albany, NY; d. 30 Oct. 1854.
5. Signed memorial in Detroit 11 Nov. 1822 as Victor Rouquette.
6. M. 16 April 1819 Abbe Hunter. Owned land in Oakland County in 1821.
7. He and wife were teachers in Detroit 1821. Later settled in Texas.
8. B. Lyme, CT 1764; d. Pontiac 11 Nov. 1826; came to Detroit from Tunbridge, VT.
9. Son Jacques and Catherine (Menard) Campau; m. --- Cicot 1808 and --- McDougall.
10. Son of Capt. George McDougall; b. Detroit 19 Oct. 1766; d. St. Clair 1842.
11. Marshall for District of Huron 1811; clerk of Woodward Ave Market 1819.
12. Son of Reuben Sibley; b. Sutton, MA 7 Oct. 1769; d. Detroit 4 April 1846.
13. B. MA; d. Hartford, NY 26 June 1827; m. Martha Larned.
14. A hatter; elected steward 13 June 1818 of Detroit Mechanics Society.
15. B. Albany, NY 1790; d. Detroit 21 July 1829; Reg. of Probate 1821; Clerk 1827.
16. B. 1792; d. Winfield, IL 19 Jan. 1871; m. 25 Oct. 1818 Eliza Whiting.
17. Luke Jollet, d. Detroit 1824; m. Antoinette Bareillos-Lajoie.
18. Bought lot 23, Sec. 8, Detroit 5 May 1821. Son of Daniel Ball of Oakland Co.
19. Sanford Brittain was Supt. of the Water Works 1837.
20. Doctor, b. PA 1764; d. Detroit 16 May 1831; m. 21 Sept. 1814 Félicité Levasseur.
21. Indian trader; lived in Detroit; d. Flint June 1825.
22. B. 1768, son Louis and Cecile (Yax); m.1795 M. Josephe Chapoton. Owned 245 acres.
23. Jean Edwards, widow of Edwin, US Army; estate filed for probate 28 June 1818.
24. Orson Bartlett a member of Detroit Lodge 337 of Masons.
25. Neveu-Francoeur, d. 1850; m. Detroit 1806 Geneviève Houde 1788-1834.
26. Native of Maryland; d. Zanesville OH 23 Dec. 1828; m. Suzanne Godfroy 1815.
27. B. Gettysburg, PA 5 Aug. 1788; d. 5 April 1868; m. Sarah Granger and --- Harris.
28. André-Clark; m. 1804 Suzanne Drouillard and 1813 Clemence Fearson.

Joseph Rowland    100010/10010
Joshua Barnard[1]  010101/00000
John Bte Peltier[2]  100130/10010
Levi Willard[3]  110110/21100
David C. McKinstry[4]  310330/11010
Gabriel Richard[5]  000020/2000
Elizabeth Waistcoat  100000/10111
David Henderson[6]  120110/11110
Harvey Williams[7]  000120/00100
Francis Furnia[8]  010110/30100
Michael Monette[9]  200010/10001
Joseph Chevallier[10]  100004/20100
Louis Thibault[11]  000010/01010
Peter J. Desnoyer[12]  210201/33010
Andrew G. Whitney[13]  000010/00100

Johsy McCarty[14]  100200/---1-
James Abbott[15]  131120/20110
Theophilus Mettez[16]  200220/10010
Richard Smyth[17]  0201(13)1/01110
Robert Irwin[18]  001001/22010
John Whipple[19]  111133/31012
Samuel Perkins[20]  000011/00001
Rufus Hatch[21]  101410/01100
Peter Audrain[22]  100121/00001
Abraham Edwards[23]  1402(12)0/31020
Henry J. Hunt[24]  010350/10300
John S. Roby[25]  110110/11010
Conrad Ten Eyck[26]  000010/00000
Levi Brown[27]  000020/00000
Polly McMillan[28]  220421/01210

1. Joshua, James, and John Barnard sold 80 A. land in Wayne County 13 Apr. 1833.
2. Son André and Catharine Meloche; 1786-1841; m. 1809 Catharine Williams.
3. Petitioner in connection with estate of Abner Willard, 21 Dec. 1827.
4. B. 1778; d. Ypsilanti 1856; son of Gen. Charles McKinstry of Berkshire, MA.
5. Priest; b. France 1767; d. 1832. Buried 1886 Ste. Anne's Church Cemetery.
6. D. Detroit 27 March 1822; signed protest to surrender to British 1 Feb. 1813.
7. Hervey, son Alpheus; b. Charlton, MA 21 July 1794; d. Saginaw 24 Dec. 1882.
8. Son of Augustin Fournier; d. 1833; m. 1800 Mary Facer; 1822 Margaret Lelièvre.
9. Son of John Bte and M. Josephe (Quévillon); m. 1788 Anne Grefard. In town 1799.
10. Son of Jos. Lionard-Chevalier and Louise Durocher; m. 1807 and 1811.
11. Appt. Adm. to estate of Joseph and Geneviève Thibault in 1833.
12. Son Jean Charles and Charlotte Mallet; b. France 1772; d. 1845; m. 1798 Louise
13. B. 1786; d. 4 Oct. 1826; m. Hudson, NY 3 April 1820 Anne E. Talman.  /Gobeil
14. Grocer and baker; Mason, m. 2 Feb. 1826 Mary St. Bernard, who d. 1827.
15. Son James Abbot; b. 1 June 1776; d. 12 March 1858; m. 1804 Sarah Whistler.
16. Son Théophile Mettez and Catherine Peltier; 1792-1844; m. 1813 Marie Gamelin.
17. From KY; in Detroit 1803; d. Grosse Ile 9 March 1836; m. Prudence Brady.
18. B. Carlisle, PA 24 Dec. 1797; d. Ft. Winnebago 9 July 1832; m. Hannah Rees.
19. B. MA 9 March 1764, son Joseph and Eunice; m. 1800 Archange Peltier. Ensign.
20. B. CT; d. 30 Dec. 1837; Capt US Army.
21. Major. Died in charge of Ft. Gratiot Lighthouse 22 Sept. 1825; m. Harriet Mack.
22. B. France; d. Oct. 1820; m. Margaret Moore; 8 ch. all b. PA.
23. Son Aaron Edwards; b. Springfield, NJ 17 Nov. 1781; d. Kalamazoo 1860.
24. Son Col. Thomas Hunt; d. 15 Sept 1826; m. 1811 Ann Mackintosh.
25. D. Detroit 25 Sept. 1823, aet. 36; wife Hannah d. Sept. 1834 of cholera.
26. From Albany 1802; b. 1782; d. 23 Aug. 1847; son of Anna and bro. of Jeremiah.
27. Silversmith; inventor gold pen; d. 1866; m. 29 May 1825 Louise Shurtliff of VT.
28. Mary Willard, wid. of Ananias McMillan; killed by Indians 29 May 1814 Detroit.

Robert Smart[1] 000141/01210
Jacob Eilert[2] 020030/00100
Mary Ann Scott[3] 021030/12010
Conrad Seek[4] 13-1-1/01110
Joseph Campau[5] 300011/20010
Stephen C. Henry[6] 000010/20300
D'Garmo Jones[7] 000110/00100
Eben Beach[8] 110310/11110
John McDonnell[9] 400021/00000
Charles Larned[10] 010020/21100
Antoine DeQuindre[11] 200210/31210
Charles Poupard[12] 001001/00000
Joseph Coté[13] 000002/00001
Alexis Bouvard[14] 000010/00001
William Brown[15] 000020/00000
Joseph Gooley[16] 103110/00020
Thomas Palmer[17] 001210/00000
Louis DeQuindre[18] 000120/10100
Levi Cook[19] 000030/10010
James Lockwood[20] 211110/30110
Eleanor Reid[21] 111200/10210
Edward White[22] 000330/00100
Ann Cotes[23] 010000/01001
Prosper Thibault[24] 000211/01101
Sarah Hubbard[25] 110520/21301
Benjamin Stead[26] 651220/21120
Samuel T. Davenport[27] 110010/20010
Thomas Johns[28] 210092/21010
Charles Gobeille[29] 100001/11000
Abraham Caniff[30] 200351/11200

1. Detroit in 1806; b. Kittle, Fifeshire, Scot.; d. 28 Oct. 1839, aet. 72.
2. Tailor; m. Grosse Pte 11 Nov. 1819 Harriet Williams, dau. of Alpheus.
3. B. Sandwich 1786, dau. of George Meldrum; d. 1825; m. Wm McDowell Scott 1801.
4. Indian captive; native KY; d. Detroit 31 Oct. 1832 aet. 62; m. Mary Morrison.
5. Son Jacques and Catherine Menard; b. 1769; d. 1863; m. 1808 Adelaide Dequindre.
6. Son John Joseph Henry; b. Harrisburg, PA 14 Jan. 1786; d. Detroit 1834 cholera.
7. Sutler 1812; b. Albany NY 11 Nov. 1787; d. 14 Nov. 1846; m. 1819 Catherine Annin.
8. In hatter business with Charles Willcox 1817; m. 27 May 1821 Elizabeth Owen.
9. B. Scotland 1780; to America 1812; member State Senate 1837; d. 1 Oct. 1846.
10. B. Pittsfield, MA 28 Dec 1791; d. 13 Aug. 1834; m. 26 March 1816 Sylvia Colt.
11. Antoine Dagneau DeQuindre, b. 1781; d. 1843; m. 1809 Catherine Chapoton.
12. Son Charles Poupard-Lafleur and Isabelle Casse; m. 1799 Felicite Campau.
13. Poss. Antoine Coté bp. 1776; confirmed Joseph 1801; buried as Joseph 1834.
14. Challenged Joseph André to a duel in 1819; case dismissed.
15. Physician; b. MA 7 Dec. 1773; d. 27 June 1838; bachelor; in Detroit 1783.
16. D. Detroit 31 Oct. 1823; m. 2 Sept. 1819 Lucy Lane; she m. (2) Stephen Bain.
17. B. CT 4 Feb. 1789; d. 3 Aug. 1868; m. Mary Amy Witherell, dau. of James.
18. B. 1786 son Antoine; d. 1829; m. 1817 Marie Desnoyers, dau Pierre Jean.
19. B. Bellingham, MA 1792, son Thaddeus Cook; d. 1866; m. Elizabeth Stevens.
20. Opened tavern in Royal Oak 1824; later in Detroit as tinsmith.
21. Eleanor Descomps-Labadie, dau. Antoine; b. Sandwich 1792; d. 1853; wid. Duncan /Reid
22. Was he in Oakland County in 1830?
23. Ann Coates, dau. James Donaldson; granted tavern license 1804; d. 1849.
24. On tax list of Sargent Twp. 1802.
25. Mother of Diodate; Edward Hubbard estate 1819 names mother, Sarah Hubbard Moony.
26. B. Leeds, Eng. 1776; d. Sept. 1821; m. Nottingham, Eng. 1798 Frances Morley.
27. Prominent lawyer from KY; d. Detroit 25 Apr. 1821; Mason.
28. Bought land 1814; d. River Rouge 24 Nov. 1822, aet. 58; m. Candis Johns.
29. Charles Gobeille m. 1810 Sarah Lagore, dau. Jean.
30. Detroit in 1819; b. Rensselaer Co., NY 26 Aug. 1791; d. 25 March 1876.

Catherine Provencelle[1] 400000/00201
Joseph Lewis   100010/21010
Joseph Belanger[2] 100100/41100
Hartwin Valance   230001/11010
Raney Mattis[3] 210010/21310
Joseph Rowe[4] 020101/01001
Levi L. Clark   000010/00100
Joseph Loveland   110010/00010
Louis Fesse[5] 200010/00100
François Gobeille[6] 210111/00010
John Barrel[7] 200000/20200
Elizabeth Noble[8] 000140/01001
Augustine Longan[9] 120102/01010
John Ramsay[10] 000010/10100
Elizabeth Lyons[11] 041310/00000

John Jinetice (Jeunesse?)   410040/02210
William C. Johnston[12] 010210/30210
William Petit[13] 110110/00120
Augustus Chapeton[14] 220210/00110
John Bapt. Savingac[15] 210011/11000
James Busher[16] 100110/11010
John Q. Tompkins[17] 200010/20010
Charles Howard[18] 100110/00010
Philip Warren[19] 02010/300130
Daniel Mack[20] 300130/11110
Warren Howard[21] 100130/10020
Charles E. Laur   011101/11001
John Biddle[22] 120010/11001
David Gwynne[23] 000010/00200
Moses Birdsall[24] 000220/00200

1. Dau. Jean Vallée and Elizabeth Drouillard; she m. 1780 Pierre Provencal.
2. None of the known Joseph Belanger families fit in this age group.
3. René Mettez, son Joseph and Catherine Dufour; m. Elizabeth Riopel 1793; d. 1825.
4. First in Detroit 1773; 1820 contracted to build schoolhouse; in Macomb County.
5. Facer; b. 1795; son Henry and Catherine Raymond; m. 1817 a Belanger.
6. Son Jean Francois and Rose Fortier; b. 1778; m. 1814 Louise Gagnier.
7. Burrell. Witnessed documents in Detroit Dec. 1796 and Jan. 1797.
8. Mrs Noble, d. 2 Sept 1827; mother of David Cooper; mbr Presbyterian Church 1825.
9. Longnon, d. 22 May 1829, aet. 63; res. River Rouge.
10. Early Methodist 1822. Perhaps estate probated 1869 in Dearborn. Widow Elizabeth.
11. Dau. George Lyons and Elizabeth Chêne; b. Detroit 7 Apr. 1787; d. 1878; teacher.
12. Contracted 1815 to bring goods on *General Jackson* from Buffalo.
13. B. Jan. 1796; d. Detroit 26 April 1826; m. Theodocia Deveaux.
14. Eustache Chapoton, b. 1792, son of Jean Bte and Thérèse Peltier; m. 1819 Judith
15. Savignac; son J. Bte and Cecile Chauvin; m. 1814 G. Lebeau.     /Coquillard.
16. In 1833 James Bushey ran ad warning *Gilmore* to redeem watch or it wd be sold.
17. Builder of engine house 1819; d. Wayne County 23 Aug. 1821.
18. Bought lot in Detroit 1818. Perhaps same as Detroit mayor 1849. To NY.
19. Sued 1819 for work done on U. of Mich.; m. Elizabeth Stacey, dau. William 1831.
20. From Rochesterville, NY; d. Detroit 20 Apr. 1821, aet. 34; wife was Hannah ---.
21. Lived River Rouge; b. 1789; d. 1834; wife was Ruth ---.  Supervisor of Spring
22. Son Charles Biddle; b. Philadelphia 2 March 1792; d. 25 Aug. 1859 in    /wells.
    White Sulfur, VA.
23. Bought land on Lake St. Clair in 1818; m. Chillicothe, OH Alice Ann Claypool.
24. M. Detroit 13 Dec. 1819 Alice Wright; moved to St. Clair County.

# 1820 Census

NOTE ON THIS PAGE FIVE FAMILIES OF FREE COLORED, FOR WHOM THE CATEGORIES ARE DIFFERENT, AS INDICATED.

J. Butler   1(-14) 2(20-25)/ 1(26-45)
Thomas Colton  1(-14) 1(45+)/3(-14) 1(26-45) 1(45+)
John Patterson [1] 1(-14) 2(14-26) 2(26-45)/ 1(-4) 1(26-45)
John L. Whiting [2] 000010/00000
Alexander Macomb [3] 300020/32322
Jer. House*  000001/00000
Francis S. Belton [4] 000010/00000
Winfield Scott*  000010/00000
Giles Porter*  000100/00000
John Anderson*[5] 000110/00021
James Monroe*  000100/00000
W. Lawrence*  000110/00100
Daniel Baker*[6] 100110/00111
Edward Brooks*[7] 000020/10010
John Garland [8] 000300/11200
J. Farley*  6103(83)0/50460
Major Stockton*[9] 300(63)(15)1/40710
Jos. L. Smith*[10] 010010/00000

J. Greene*[11] 000020/00000
C. Millen*[12] 00010/20011
Steamboat J. Rodgers [13] 000(12)50/00020
J. J. Davis*[14] 000100/00000
John H. Chunn*  000010/00000
Benjamin Delavan [15] 010103/00000
William Keith [16] 000010/00000
Thomas Wilkins [17] 000010/00000
Levi Root*  000010/00000
James Street [18] 000100/00000
John Sparks   2(-4)  1(26-45)/1(-14) 1(26-45)
Priscilla Burgess  3(-14) 1(26-45)/2(-14) 1(26-45) 1(45+)
Robert LeClair  000020/000010
Leonard Renef?  100010/100111
Louis St. George [19] 000001/00001
Anne Smith [20] 000000/20021
Mary Lette  100000/10020
John W. Hunter [21] 000301/00000

1. Listed in 1830 census of Detroit, free colored.
2. B. Columbia Co., NY 1793, son John; d. 4 Aug. 1880; m. 3 times; physician.
3. B. Detroit 3 April 1782, son Alexander; d. Washington, DC 25 June 1841. Major Gen.
   [* These names appear in either the *Army Register* or the *Biographical Register of the Officers and Graduates of West Point*. Presumably they were assigned to or visiting at Fort Shelby. It may or may not be the famous General Winfield Scott that appears on this list. His aide in 1820 was James Monroe, also on this list.]
4. M. Detroit 18 June 1818 Harriet Kirby, dau. Ephraim. At Fort Gratiot 1841.
5. Native of VT; d. 14 Sept. 1834, aet. 54.
6. B. VT; Indian captive; d. Detroit 30 Oct. 1836, aet. 61. Lt. Col. US Army.
7. B. Bordentown, NJ 1784, son William; d. 1859; m. Margaret May and Margaret Labadie.
8. B. VA 1792; d. NYC 5 June 1861; m. dau. of Jacob Smith, trader at Detroit.
9. B. Lancaster, PA 1798; d. Mt Clemens 26 Nov. 1878; m. dau. Jacob Smith.
10. B. New Britain, CT 23 May 1779; d. St Augustine, FL 27 May 1846.
11. B. Ireland; d. 21 Sept. 1840.
12. Charles Mellen b. PA; m. Detroit 3 May 1820 Eliza Scott; Captain 1828.
13. Capt. of *Walk-in-the-Water* and the *Superior*  d. Albany 28 Oct. 1820, aet. 39.
14. Artillery Lieut.; m. 17 Sept. 1821 Sarah G. Hunt.
15. Native of NY; Army surgeon; killed Natchitoches, LA 6 Nov. 1827.
16. Capt. of the first cutter on the lakes; bought land on Grosse Ile 1819.
17. Receipt for wages as mariner on the *Porcupine*  8 Aug. 1820.
18. Signed notices of Monguagon Twp. 18 Dec. 1822. Lived Nankin Twp. 1833.
19. Free colored; bought land Detroit 1816; estate in probate 13 June 1825.
20. Bought land from Richard Cornwall north of St Clair River 23 Feb. 1795.
21. Son of Elisha of Auburn, NY; voted Detroit 1825; moved to Birmingham, MI.

MAP 15. MICHIGAN COUNTIES IN 1818

# WAYNE COUNTY

Lewis Cass[1] 120230/42120
James Witherell[2] 201102/01101
John R. Leib[3] 101101/01120
Joseph Tremblé[4] 100010/00010
Pierre Dequindre[5] 000010/10010
Pierre Cedien[6] 320001/11001
John Bapt. Peltier[7] 100010/10010
Asquire Aldrich[8] 110310/20010
Abraham Fournier[9] 210010/12010
Margaret Obin[10] 000000/00010
Louis Charboneau[11] 000100/00100
John Bapt. Campau[12] 301201/10510
Jacob Visgar[13] 000001/00001
Joseph W. Visger[14] 110100/01100
Arthur Brooks 000010/00000
Peter W. Knaggs[15] 000100/10100
Whitmore Knaggs[16] 100311/10110
Joel Thomas[17] 300010/10010
Aaron Thomas[18] 300030/10010
Jesse Hicks[19] 101101/31010
Joseph Corbis[20] 100100/10100
John F. Rupley[21] 101210/10200
François Dumay[22] 200101/00110
John Sargent[23] 010010/00101
Ralph Bell[24] 210011/10010
Henry Magee[25] 101110/00010
Beckley Rowley[26] 000120/00000
John Walker[27] 000120/30100
Charles L. Canfield[28] 400011/10010
Pierre Labadie[29] 230111/10111
John M. Navarre[30] 000010/00001
Gabriel Godfroy[31] 110201/22100

1. B. Exeter, NH, son of Jonathan and Mary Gilman; d. Detroit 1866; m. E. Spencer.
2. B. Mansfield, MA 1759; d. Detroit 1859; m. Amy Hawkins 1790.
3. D. 16 April 1858, aet. 71 from St. Pauls Church; m. Margaret Conner of Philadelphia.
4. 1790-1838, son Joseph and Cecile Marsac; m. 1818 Cecile Aide-Créqui, dau. J. Bte.
5. B. 1790, son Antoine and Catherine Desrivières; m. Suzanne Robert and — Drouillard.
6. 1766-1837, son Joseph and Therese Tremblay; m. 1797 Angélique Cauchois.
7. 1771-1821, son J. Bte and Catherine Vallée; m. 1800 Suzanne Facer, dau. Henry David.
8. Contracted to build fence 1819; on tax roll 1825; census 1827. In Utica in 1837?
9. Son Augustin and Judith Touissant; bur. Greinerville 1854; m. Archange Campau.
10. B. 1780, dau. J. Bte Casse-St Aubin and Louise Deligne.
11. Son Jerome; m. 1818 Théotiste Guignier-Bourguignon and 1830 Julia Petit.
12. 1770-1834, son J. Bte and Geneviève Godet-Marentette; m. 1796 Josette Gamelin.
13. From Schenectady, NY; d. Detroit 19 Mar. 1823 aet. 53; m. 1792 Agathe Cicotte.
14. B. Sandwich 1794, son Jacob above; m. 1819 Ann Godfroy, dau. Col. Gabriel.
15. B. Detroit 1798, son Whitmore; d. Toledo 1848; m. 1819 Catherine Visger, dau. Jacob.
16. B. Maumee, OH 1763, son George Schley; d. 1827; m. 1797 Josette Labadie.
17. He and wife Phebe sold lots in Detroit 1821; estate probated 1837.
18. B. 1753, Rev. War pension; deed 1809 to wife Nancy; estate 1826.
19. Of Springwells; bought land 1809 River Rouge; estate 1826, wife Hannah.
20. Joseph C. Corbus b. River Rouge 1794. Was he in Branch County 1877?
21. B. Harrisburg, PA 1788, son John F. and Suzanne Johnson; m. 1818 Margaret Dumay.
22. B. 1794, son Pierre and Angelique Lemay; m. 1818 Thérèse Parnier-Vadeboncoeur.
23. Son Thomas and Margaret of River Rouge; wife Nancy d. 1821, aet. 24.
24. Taxpayer River Rouge 1825; a Ralh R. Bell on 1827 census roll.
25. Voter 4 Sept. 1823, A Henry Magee in Sabine Loyalists.
26. Supt. Roads Monguagon Twp 1820; Left Territory before March 1822.
27. D. Brownstown ca 1826, aet. 34; m. Elizabeth —.
28. Was he son-in-law of Lewis Cass?
29. 1742-1823, son Pierre Descomps-Labadie and Angelique Lacelle; m. 1769 Thérèse Gaillard-Lionais.
30. 1763-1836, son Robert and Marie Lootman-Barrois; m. 1787 Archange Marentette.
31. 1783-1848, Son Gabriel and Catherine Couture; m. Rose St. Cosme and Elizabeth May.

Michigan Censuses 1710-1830

John Bapt. Beaugrand [1] 410001/01010
John Armstrong (free col.)[2] 010010/01100
William Blackington [3] 200010/00100
Josette Chobere [4] 000100/00001
John B. Chamberlin [5] 411110/01010
Henry Bradley [6] 200010/00100
Alexander Odienne (free col.)[7] 010010/01100
Ezra Younglove [8] 300010/011110
Carver Gunn 000200/00000
Dominique Riopelle [9] 210010/10120
Christopher Hart 420040/21010
Joseph Laferty [10] 400001/10010
Pierre Laferty [11] 000010/00000
Thomas Reed [12] 000001/00000
Charles Cabacier 200001/11210
Joseph Du Berger [13] 001110/00001
Théotiste Bodien 010000/10002
James May [14] 220001/10310
Augustin Lefer [15] 001101/12400
Jonathan Kearsley [16] 101110/20100
John Du Garde (free col.) [17] 010010/00001
Harriet Myers [18] 210000/22011
John Garrison 220101/00101
Antoine Barreau 010002/00001
Louis LaDuke [19] 100010/12011
Henry Bertholet [20] 110011/61010
Louison Peltier 200001/42100
Thomas Noxon [21] 000001/00001
Stephen Hazel (free col.) 000011/00010
Scipio Denisen (col.) 4 persons
Louis Lognon [22] 200001/11010
Charles Wilcox [23] 110310/11110
Theophilus Mettez [24] 100101/10101
Lewis Wilson (free col.) [25] 010100/01010
Gustavus B. Rood [26] 000210/10100
Margaret Morse 200000/03210

1. Son J. Bte and Anne Alain; m. .802 Margaret, dau. Josette Chobere.
2. Was he carpenter with John Hembrow 1796? John A. Armstrong on 1827 deed.
3. Voter in Detroit 1823. Resident Oakland Co. 1825.
4. B. 1762, dau. Isidore Chêne; m. 1780 Francois Joncaire-Chabert.
5. Physician in Detroit 1817; later in St. Clair, Macomb County.
6. A Dr. Henry Bradley in Birmingham 1821; later to Royal Oak.
7. Son Antoine Hodienne; m. 1815 Elizabeth Stanbach, adopted dau. John Dugard.
8. 1798-1867; son Samuel; b. VT; m. 1820 Catherine Joncaire, dau. of #4 above.
9. 1787-1859; son Ambrose; m. 1818 Colette Guoin, dau. Nicolas.
10. Joseph Vassière-Laferté, 1780-1826; son Louis.
11. Brother; 1788-1833; m. 1823 Catherine Lafoy, dau. Augustin.
12. Voter Detroit 1825. From Richland Co., OH; to Dearborn.
13. B. Detroit 15 Jan. 1776; d. 11 Mar. 1836, son John Bte.
14. 1756-1829; b. Birmingham, Eng.; m. Rose St. Cosme.
15. prob. Augustin Lafoy, son Augustin.
16. 1786-1859; b. Dauphin Co., PA; m. Margaret Hetick, dau. George. org. Episcopal Church.
17. Witness in Circuit Court 1825.
18. Prob. widow Ignace Myers of Militia Vol; his estate probated 4 FEb. 1818.
19. B. Montreal, son René; m. 1802 Cecilia Descomps-Labadie.
20. 1776-1846; son Pierre; m. 1802 Marie Josette Duhamel, dau. J. Bte.
21. Purchased farm on River Rouge 1821. He and wife Mary deeded land Grosse Pointe 1827.
22. 1765-1823; b. Quebec, son Joseph; m. 1814 M. Louise Drouillard.
23. 1783-1827; m. Almira Rood Powers 1790-1870; vestryman St. Pauls Church 1825-27.
24. 1764-1832; b. Detroit, son Joseph; m. 1787 Catherine Peltier, dau. Andrew.
25. M. Juda Denison 20 June 1816; sailmaker in 1837 at 15 Franklin St.
26. No record found. Gilbert F. and Sidney G. Rood in Detroit later.

# 1820 Census

John McKenzie[1] 000010/01101
Levi Willard[2] 200120/00010
Henry B. Brevoort[3] 2 00001/11101
Nathaniel Champ[4] 100010/10110
Col. McAlister[5] 000002/10100
Charles Girard[6] 000001/00000
Louisan Champagn[7] 200001/10101
Abigail Gage[8] 121400/20110
Pierre Picot[9] 100110/00200
Charles Gouin[10] 000011/10002
François Champagn[11] 000010/10100
Francis Savenyac[12] 100100/10100
Louis Campau[13] 1000210/01100
Mary King 010000/30040
Robert Philamore[14] 010110/10110
François St. Aubin[15] 100201/40010

Louis Moran[16] 010102/00301
Joseph Larancell[17] 010010/10010
John Bapt. LaParle[18] 300001/11010
John Phearson[19] 000201/00010
Jean Marie Beaubien[20] 000111/02201
Benoit Chapaton[21] 120101/12011
Morris Moran[22] 210010/12011
Frances Revard[23] 111120/20000
Charles Labadie[24] 100002/20110
Gabriel Chesne[25] 110202/22210
Henry Stanton[26] 000210/10010
Samuel Sherwood[27] 100200/00110
John Hyde[28] 000010/00010
Prime Johnson (free col.) 000010/00000
Pierre Beaubien[29] 000110/02201
James Campau[30] 000101/10010

1. Signed petition 1822. A John McKenzie killed before 22 July 1829.
2. Levi and Abner Willard bought land 1825; Abner d. 1827 near Detroit.
3. B. NY 1775; d. 1858; m. 1811 Catharine Navarre, dau. Robert. Commodore.
4. 1792-1870; b. VA, son John; land in River Rouge 1820; in War of 1812.
5. B. Ireland, son Randal and Catherine (McCauley); m. dau. of John Connolly 1819.
6. M. Theoiste, an Ottawa, and dau. b. 1807.
7. 1763-1827; b. Fox Creek, son of Peter; m. Croisette-Laperle girl.
8. Estate of Henry Gage, minor, filed 1822; a bro. Alva a mariner for Customs.
9. Bought land Detroit 1809; with wife Victoire sold lot 1817. In Monroe 1825.
10. poss. Charles Francois Gouin, b. 1755, son Claude.
11. Francois Huyet-Champagne, b. 1790, son Pierre; m. 1817 Monica Campau.
12. Savignac, b. 1791, son J. Bte and Cecile; m. 1815 Genieve Campau, dau. Henry.
13. 1767-1834; son Jacques; m. .789 Catherine Menard and 1789 Therese Moran, dau. C
14. A Robert Philemon m. Mary Shackleton; son Henry b. Detroit 7 June 1819.
15. 1775-1831; son Louis; m. 1811 Basalique Campau, dau. Jean Bte.
16. 1757-1826; m. Catherine Campau, dau. Jean Bte.
17. Lorrancelle; m. Rosalie Delaunay. Children b. Detroit 1817-1820.
18. B. Montreal 1776, son Alexis Pineau-Laperle; m. Marie Landroche-Scyanis.
19. Fearson, 1753-1835; b. England; m. Amable Desaulniers-Lajomondiere. Capt. British Navy.
20. B. Canada 1763-1841 son J. Bte; m. 1789 Claire Gouin.
21. 1761-1830; son Jean Bte; m. 1788 Therese Meloche, dau. Jean Bte.
22. 1775-1863; bro. Louis and Charles; m. Felicite Meloche.
23. 1773-1841, son Jean Bte; m. 1800 Isabelle Chapoton, dau. Jean Bte.
24. B. 1771 son Pierre; m. 1810 Mary Anne Cicotte, dau. Jean Bte.
25. 1772-1830, son Charles; m. Geneviève Campau, dau. Jean Bte.
26. B. VT 1779; d. Ft. Hamilton, NY 1856; m. (2) Alexandrine Macomb; Major in 1819.
27. 1779-1862; m. Catherine ——; bought lot called the "Public Square" 1831.
28. Voter 1823. A Mr. Hyde drowned Lake St. Clair 1826. A John Hyde in 1830 census.
29. Pierre Jean Marie Cuillerier-Beaubien. Repitition of #20 above?
30. 1766-1838; son Jacques; m. 1789 Susanne Beaubien, Dau. Jean Bte.

Antoine Revard[1] 200001/11110
Joseph Spencer[2] 011220/00000
Jean Bapt. Comparit[3] 200002/11110
William Durell[4] 000011/00100
Chesley Black[5] 000010/10100
Julius Eldred[6] 100010/01010
David Nawfert (free col.) 010100/01100
Eleanor Haskin[7] 100000/00110
Henry Campau[8] 201101/22010
Robert McDougall[9] 011101/ 10202
James Gallagher[10] 100010/10010
John Meldrum[11] 120110/20100
Louis Beaufait[12] 220001/01010
Louis Chapaton[13] 200101/21101
Cecil Boyer[14] 100000/00000
George Lyons[15] 110020/00100
Lambert Thibault[16] 010010/20200

Pascal Potvin[17] 000010/02010
Isadore Moran[18] 211201/21001
Victor Morass[19] 000010/11100
William Brooks[20] 000011/30011
Beckley Thurston[21] 120010/21010
Truman Bearss[22] 011110/32010
James Spacy[23] 000010/00000
Benjamin Knapp[24] 000201/00101
Etienne Marson[25] 210010/22010
Clide Campau[26] 200010/30011
Joseph Lameron[27] 011301/11000
John Knapp[28] 000100/10100
Isaiah Tyler[29] 000010/00000
Richard Goodwin[30] 200201/11001
Elias Long[31] 100201/02110
Seth Dunham[32] 000010/00001
Jeremiah Brainard[33] 100101/00101

1. 1782-1840; b. Grosse Pointe, son J. Bte; m. Roalie Saucier.
2. Bp. Cong. Church, New Haven, CT 31 Oct. 1779, son of Nathaniel and Abigail.
3. 1738-1822; son Francois; m. 1768 Margaret Limoges.
4. May have died soon after 1820, survived by son of same name.
5. B. ME; d. Milwaukee 1849 with wife Sarah and 5 ch. surviving. Capt. of lakes steamer.
6. 1787-1851; b. Cooperstown, NY; m. 1811 Mindwell Higby at Ballston Springs, NY.
7. Widow of Henry Haskin, Sgt. 2nd Reg. US Artillery; estate prob. 8 June 1814.
8. B. 1773, son of Simon; m. 1797 Geneviève Marsac, dau. of J. Bte.
9. 1764-1846; son of Capt. George; m. 1786 Archange Campau and 1846 Geneviève Meny.
10. Perhaps same one who was a tailor in Detroit in 1837.
11. 1788-1825, son George; m. 1814 Sarah Lytle, dau. of John.
12. 1773-1851, son of Louis; m. 1804 Louise Saucier, dau. of Joseph.
    1764-1837, son of J. Bte; m. 1783 Catherine Meloche, dau. J. Bte.
    Poss. Cecilia, widow of Antoine Boyer (1748-1807); m. 1788. She d. 1849.
15. 1789-1840, son of George; m. 1817 Susanne Séguin-Laderoute, dau. of Joseph.
16. 1789-1834, son of Joseph Louis; m. 1817 Geneviève Meny, dau. Antoine.
17. Bought land in Detroit 1822-24. May have been native of Canada.
18. In Detroit 1820-29; later to Monroe County; m. Archange ——.
19. 1787-1863, son of Nicolas; m. 1817 Therese Poissant-Lasaline, dau. of Paul.
20. M. Rebecca ——; son Edward executor of estate when William Brooks d. 1833.
21. prob. Blakeley Thurston, b. Easton, NY 1782, son Joel and Miriam; d. 1858; m. Phebe
22. Bass? Resident Brownstown, constable 1820, sold land 1828. /Huttelstone.
23. Of. Huron Twp. in 1830 when bought land there.
24. D. 1823, widow Katherine, sons Daniel, Benj., Isaac, John, Walter, James, exec.
25. May refer to Etienne Mannassa or Etienne Manauson of Brownstown.
26. Poss. Claude Campau who m. 1812 Archange Saliot.
27. May be son of Benjamin Knapp who d. and estate probated in 1823.
28. No such name found. An Isaac Tyler and wife Eleanor of Sherman Twp. in 1831.
29. Voter 1823. Signed petition for raod with citizens and others of Oakland Co.
30. Resident of Brownstown in 1838. Thomas Long first fence viewer in Brownstown.
31. Voter at Monguagon 1825; JP 1828; supervisor of Brownstown 1828-30.
32. Jeremiah Gates Brainard, b. 1796; d. 1857, son of Daniel of East Haddam, CT.

## 1820 Census

William Firehaudt[1] 000010/00000
Moses Allen[2] 200010/00001
Amos Howe[3] 000020/00010
Mason Clark[4] 100010/10100
John P. Noah 000010/00000
Samuel Wing[5] 000010/00010
George Hubbard[6] 120010/11010
Joseph Allair[7] 100010/20200
Arthur Rourk[8] 200110/10100
David Smith[9] 100020/00010
Henry Dutcher[10] 000200/00000
Asa Fox[11] 200010/1000
Benjamin DeWitt[12] 100001/21010
Noah Gilbert 000010/00000
Joseph Hammond[13] 000020/10000
Nathaniel Clark[14] 000010/00000
Gardner Sherman 000010/00010
Joseph Moran[15] 211101/11000
Artemus Hosmer[16] 000020/10100
Moses Smedley 000010/00000
Zadoc Wellman[17] 000101/00001
John Clark[18] 031101/30010
Aaron Nobles[19] 130110/12110
Prince Phillips[20] (free col.) 00001/00100
Gabriel Barreau 000100/00100
John Bapt. Mexico 200001/10010
John Park (free col.) 000001/00000
John Bapt. LeBoue (Beau) 400010/00010
Izabel Drouillard 030010/20110
David Mayo[21] 000100/00000
Joseph Deslisle[22] 010001/11010
Thomas Adams[23] 000010/00000
Jacques Cicot[24] 310010/20010
Alexis Beaubien[25] 310010/20010
Daniel Goodall[26] 000100/00100
Elijah Hartshorn[27] 000010/00000

1. Finehandt. Signed petition at Detroit 1822. In St. Joseph County 1829.
2. To Detroit in War of 1812; m. Polly Barnes; to Hillsdale County 1827.
3. Taxpayer Brownstown 1825; supervisor Huron Twp. 1829; m. Anna ---.
4. Taxpayer River Huron 1825; voter Monguagon 1825; estate filed 1832; son George.
5. River Huron 1825; JP Wayne Co. 1825; in Jackson County 1833.
6. Pioneer Huron Twp. M. Ypsilanti 1836. Was he in Calhoun County 1833?
7. 1775-1842, son Alexander Blondin-Hilaire; m. Florence Girardin.
8. Ruark; lived River Huron 1825; Director Poor Brownstown in 1827.
9. Voter 1821, 1823, 1825 River Huron; of Detroit 1833; anaother in Oakland Co.
10. Estate of Henry Dutcher of Huron filed 1828; Elizabeth widow.
11. Voter Detroit 1821. Amasa Fox of Bucklin's estate filed 1829. Bro. Benj. F.
12. Of Monguagon 1825. A Benjamin DeWitt in War of 1812; Calhoun County 1859.
13. Taxpayer Hickory Island 1825; voted 1821, 1823, 1825.
14. Voter Monguagon 1825. A Nathaniel Clark aet. 64 m. Clairsa Morehouse aet. 52
15. B. St. Joseph St. 1763, son Charles; m. 1791 Catherine Boyer./Brownstown 1840.
16. B. Acton, MA 1788, son Ephraim and Mercy; d. 1844; m. Sally Lacy and Mary Dunn.
17. Voter 1821; signed petition 1827.
18. A common name in Wayne County early.
19. Detroit voter 1821, 1823; River Huron 1825; Washtenaw County 1825.
20. M. Veronica Williams; child Emily Phillips b. 1820.
21. Bought land Oakland County but on Wayne census in 1827.
22. Joseph Bienvenu-Delisle, b. 1769; m. 1801 Elizabeth Campau and 1819 Therese Chauvin.
23. Voter of name in St. Clair 1823, 1825; one in Detroit 1826-27, wife Paula Walsh.
24. 1785-1853, son J. Bte; m. 1810 Marie Anne Beaubien, dau. Lambert.
25. 1785-1832, son Joseph; m. 1812 Archange Tremblay at Detroit.
26. B. Little Falls, NY ca 1797, son Elijah; m. 1820 Susanne Baron.
27. Signed petition Oakland Co. 1823. Alfred and Pierson there in 1834.

Elijah Goodall [1] 200211 01101
George Campbell [2] 100010/20011
Joseph Bondie [3] 200001/10010
John Bapt. Rosseau [4] 010101/10101
Pierre LeBlanche [5] 200301/21011
Antoine Barreau [6] 020301/21001
Charles Roulo [7] 000100/00000
Antoine Bondie [8] 000001/
Dominique Bondie [9] 221110/20010
Joseph Barron [10] 110001/00110
Peter Perry [11] 100010/00100
Amab Bellaire [12] 000201/00010
Charles La Roche [13] 000001/00000
Charles Barron [14] 100010/00100
Joseph Barreau [15] 100100/00100
Joseph Picot [16] 000010/00000

Alexander Johndron [17] 000001/00100
Antoine Lafront [18] 020002/30101
Francis Laduke [19] 000100/00100
Charles LaVermit [20] 000200/10101
Jean Bapt. Lajeunesse 020001/00001
Louis Barasson [21] 000201/00201
John Bapt. Saliac [22] 010001/20101
Antoine Laurens [23] 200010/10100
Joseph Livernois [24] 100201/10100
Joseph Cicot [25] 110010/30110
Joseph Laurens [26] 200010/01100
Louis Bourdrian [27] 000001/10001
Louis Laurens [28] 100100/00100
Amab Laurens [29] 100100/10100
Augustin Longan [30] 111202/01010
Mary Laurens [31] 000101/01001
Francis Laurens [32] 210010/10010

1. B. England 1758; d. Ecorse 1820; m. NY 1796 Axy Picket; in Detroit 1813.
2. Bought land near Detroit 1818; estate filed 1826; widow Helen and 6 ch.
3. Joseph Bondy, b. 1781, son Joseph; m. 1806 Marie Saliot.
4. Poss. J. Bte Rousson who owned land on River Ecorse 1821.
5. Pierre Francois LeBlanc, 1773-1832, son Francois; voter Ecorse 1825.
6. Name confused with Antoine Baron, who owned land at Ecorse.
7. B. River Rouge 1797, son Charles; m. Detroit 1821 Maria Henry.
8. 1767-1821, son Joseph; m. Jane Nipiaki, a Miami Indian. Trader.
9. 1779-1858, son Joseph. m. 1799 Teresa Saliot, dau. John.
10. Bought land on River Ecorse 1825.
11. British soldier 1812; lived near Wyandotte; ch. intermarried with ch. of Daniel Goodell.
12. 1759-1821, son Jean Pierre; m. 1796 Louise Lapointe, dau. J. Bte.
13. Voter at Monroe 1823.
14. 1792-1851, son Antoine Alexis; m. Detroit 1815 Magdeleine Bariau.
15. B. 1796, son Joseph; m. Detroit 1817 Scholastique Oudin-LeFranc.
16. Joseph Picotte,; m. Detroit 26 Apr. 1810 Elizabeth Pineau.
17. Alexis Gendron-Sorel; b. Ste Anne, Quebec, son Joseph; m. Mary Louise Hamilton.
18. Antoine LeFranc of River Ecorse, taxpayer 1825.
19. M. 1819 Suzanne Drouillard, dau. Jean Bte.
20. Vermette; voted Detroit 1821 and Monroe 1823.
21. Bourassa, 1755-1834, son Rene; m. 1782 Teresa Meloche.
22. Saliot, 1776-1824, son Joseph; m. 1799 Marie Anne Bondy.
23. Lorrain, 1788-1836, son Joseph; m. 1815 Monica Metay, Dau. Rene.
24. 1760-1834, son Etienne Benoit-Livernois; m. 1780 Teresa Meloche.
25. 1777-1841, son J. Bte; m. 1804 Teresa Livernois.
26. Lorrain, 1790-1854, son Joseph; m. 1817 Jeanne Gelina; res. Springwells.
27. Boudrias, son Louis; m. Mary Jarry and 1797 Elizabeth Lemay.
28. Son of Joseph; m. 1817 Suzanne Livernois, Dau. Joseph.
29. Amable Lorrain, son Joseph; m. 1818 Archange Larabel, dau. Antoine.
30. prob. Longnon.
31. Widow of Joseph Lorrain, Sr. who d. 1805; she was Marie Louise Dagenais.
32. Son of Mary #31, m. 1804 Ann Milman, dau. Alexander.

# 1820 Census

Jacob Dicks[1] 100010/00200
Joseph Charboneau[2] 010001/11010
John Dix[3] 210010/20020
John Steinbeck[4] 000001/01100
Joseph Riopelle[5] 000010/10100
Yessiah Riopelle[6] 210010/40100
John Bapt. Riopelle[7] 310010/10110
Charles Roulo[8] 201102/41101
John Bind[9] 210001/31010
Braddock Chappell[10] 210001/31010
Benjamin Stanley[11] 211(10)(15)0/10020
Thomas Cotes[12] 200010/00010
Bazzil Thibault 400001/00010
John Bapt. Tremble[13] 510001/00010
John Bapt. Furton[14] 100000/00100
John Bapt. Chovin[15] 101101/00001

Thomas Furton 011201/21211
Evangile Tremblé[16] 000010/10001
Louison Tremblé[17] 010001/30001
Leon LaDonseur[18] 000100/11100
Thomas Willets[19] 111101/00101
Francis Thibault[20] 200011/01012
John Bapt. Vernier[21] 011201/02001
Joseph Urno[22] 200010/10100
Pierre St. George[23] 020010/22010
Louis Laferty[24] 330001/01010
Dominique Thomas[25] 000100/20100
Jacques Allard[26] 200010/20010
Jacques Allard[27] 010101/00101
Joseph DuBé[28] 110001/31010
Joseph Robertjohn[29] 200301/31010
Antoine Urno[30] 100010/00010

1. Son Jacob and Johanna; m. Suzanne Metay, dau Rene; lived Springwells.
2. Son Peter and Victoria Sarasin; m. (1) 1811 Francois Livernois; m. (2) 1828 M. Jolibois.
3. Son Jacob and Johanna; m. 1810 Archange Riopel, dau. Ambrose; probate 1835.
4. John Staimbuf in some records; m. Charlotte Campau.
5. Son Ambrose; b. 1791; m. 1817 Archange Meloche, dau. Francois.
6. Hyacinthe, son Ambrose; m. 1807 Francoise Meloche and later Angela Bondy.
7. Brother of above; m. 1808 Teresa Maillet; d. before Feb. 1844.
8. Rouleau, son Charles; 1761-1838; m. 1797 Jeanne Chauvin, dau. Noel
9. Prob. John Bird who voted 1821, 1823.
10. On census of 1827.
11. Located Oakland County 1823, 1825, and 1833.
12. Voted Detroit 1821.
13. Prob. b. Grosse Pointe 1765, son Ambrose.
14. Forton, lived Grosse Pointe.
15. Chauvin, 1768-1852, son J. Bte; m. Isabelle Campau.
16. B. 1750, son Joseph Francois; m. 1822 Félicité Alard, dau. Jacques.
17. Louis Jean Tremblay, son Ambrose or Louis.
18. LaDouceur, 1798-1849, son J. Bte; m. 1819 Archange Tremblay.
19. Bought land Detroit 1814. Witnessed deed 1825.
20. 1783-1844, son Ignace; m. 1812 Agnes Rivard, dau. Charles.
21. Vernier-LaDouceur; 1763-1834, son Laurent; m. 1790 Catherine Billiau.
22. Prob. Arnault.
23. Son Francois; m. 1815 Cecilia Greffard and 1832 Marie Duchene.
24. Laferte; 1772-1824, son Louis; m. 1800 Catherine Campau. dau. Jacques.
25. 1796-1854, son Jacob; m. 1817 Elizabeth Cloutier, dau. René.
26. b. 1782, son Jacques; m. 1811 Teresa Marsac, dau. Jean.
27. B. 1793, had ch. Detroit 1817-1822; may be reversed with above.
28. Dubay, 1777-1850, son Jean; m. 1804 Catherine Bernard.
29. Robertjeannes, son Robert; m. 1797 Catherine Petit.
30. Prob. Arnault.

John Bapt. Rivard[1] 000200/00000
Ardress Trimblé[2] 000000/20110
Nicholas Chovin[3] 010200/10100
Pierre Tremblé[4] 400010/11010
Thomas Tremblé[5] 320010/31010
Pierre Pechey[6] 300010/00010
John Bapt. St. Obin[7] 000002/00101
Pierre Griffard[8] 000101/41210
Pierre Champagne[9] 210001/10101
Louis Griffard[10] 000001/00001
Louis Griffard[11] 000001/32001
Gozette Marsac[12] 010101/00200
William Little[13] 100110/00101
John Kirby[14] 000010/00000
Joseph Tremblé[15] 320101/00201
Joseph Socie[16] 020101/12210

Jacob Purkey[17] 000110/00010
René Marsac[18] 200001/22010
John Bapt. Gouie 410001/11010
Julien Gagnier[19] 200110/10100
Bazile Courtier 100010/10010
Joseph Chovin[20] 200010/10010
Charles Gouin[21] 400002/31020
Pierre Gouin[22] 201110/30020
Abraham Cook[23] 220004/00110
Tousant Jessamine[24] 000001/00000
François Petre[25] 200001/11010
Louis Moran[26] 100001/10010
Charles Chovin[27] 000101/00101
Jean Bapt. Chovin[28] 000100/00101
Louis Dupra[29] 210010/01003
Joseph St. John[30] 000212/12011

1. Could be son J. Bte b. 1795 or son Charles b. 1801.
2. Prob. Ambroise Tremble who lived in Grosse Pointe 1825.
3. B. 1784, son J. Bte Chauvin; m. 1809 Angelique Constant.
4. B. 1780; d. 1850, son Francis; m. 1808 Susanne Greffard.
5. 1775-1849, son Louis; m. 1803 Euphrosine Thibault, dau. Augustin.
6. Pichet, son Basil; m. 1812 Monica Desaulniers, dau. Louis.
7. 1757-1845, son James; m. 1800 Angelique Brillant.
8. B. 1773, son Louis; m. 1795 Louise Dupray and later Teresa Yax.
9. 1761-1826, son Pierre; m. 1785 Margaret Greffard, dau. Louis.
10. 1739-1826, son Louis; m. 1765 Margaret Casse-St. Aubin.
11. Son Louis above; 1771-1852; m. 1804 Elizabeth Pominville and 1818 Jane Cardinal.
12. Cajetan Marsac, 1775-1848, son Francis; m. Marie Saucier.
13. In Grosse Pointe in 1827; Supervisor Hamtramck Twp. 1819; Lieut. of Militia 1826.
14. Wife Alice; in Grosse Pointe 1827; app't Captain 1818 by Lewis Cass.
15. 1770-1837, son Louis; m. 1789 Cecilia Marsac, dau. Francis.
16. Saucier; 1768-1828, son Joseph; m. 1796 Marie Josephe Thibault.
17. Voted Detroit 1823.
18. B. 1777, son Francis; m. 1806 Eulalie Gouin, dau. Charles.
19. B. 1792, son Isaac; m. 1816 Theotiste Saucier, dau. Joseph.
20. 1786-1852, son J. Bte; m. 1814 Monica Rivard, dau. J. Bte.
21. 1776-1833, son Joseph; m. 1808 Elizabeth Labadie, dau. Alexis.
22. B. 1781, son Joseph Nicolas; m. 1811 Elizabeth Rivard, dau. J. Bte.
23. 1774-1847; tailor; in Detroit by 1810; m. 1829 Elizabeth Thorn.
24. Touissant Jessamine; voted Detroit 1821 and 1823.
25. Pitre; 1783-1873, son J. Bte; m. 1814 Veronica Rivard, dau. J. Bte.
26. 1757-1826, son Charles Claude; m. 1794 Catherine Campau.
27. 1737-1821, son Charles; m. 1761 Louise Boyer, dau. Pierre.
28. 1794-1868, son J. Bte; m. 1823 Sarah Groesbeck, dau. William.
29. Duprat; b. 1783, son J. Bte; m. 1807 Julia Pominville, dau. Joseph.
30. Prob. Joseph Cerre-St. John; voted Detroit 1820; appp't. Capt. 1805.

# 1820 Census

Louis Desanier[1] 100010/01001
Touisant Chêne[2] 020001/01210
Alexander Campau[3] 210102/22110
Peter Van Avery[4] 201201/10100
Henry Campau[5] 000010/00100
Joseph Campau[6] 120201/10010
Robert P. Lewis[7] 000140/02010
John Ladarout[8] 110201/22110
John Streite[9] 000010/00000
Charles Poureia[10] 101201/12100
Robert Marsac[11] 100101/02000
William P. Fraser[12] 200010/00001
John Armstrong[13] 000020/00000
Henry Conner[14] 200051/30111
William Tucker[15] 200010/10010
Edward Ryon[16] 220001/00110
Catherine Beaubien[17] 200000/20310
Théophile Dumay[18] 200010/00020
James Abbott[19] 000100/00100
John Palmer[20] 220012/02000
Elizabeth Weaver[21] 000100/01001
Seth Poppino[22] 300010/11010
David McCarthy[23] 000100/00000
Mrs. Burbank[24] 00000/00100
Thomas Anderson[25] 100100/00100
Prosper Lawrence[26] 000010/00100
Francis Chovin[27] 100101/10100
Joshua Chappell[28] 100022/11100
Paul D. Anderson[29] 100010/00010
John Burbank[30] 000110/00000
William Stacy[31] 000001/21010
Aaron Thomas[32] 000001/00001

1. Desaulniers, 1785-1847, son Louis; m. 1809 Teresa Seguin-Laderoute.
2. 1768-1834, son Charles; m. 1798 Teresa Campau, dau. J. Bte.
3. Alexis, b. 1771, son J. Bte; m. 1795 Agathe Chene, dau. Charles.
4. 1795-1859; b. nr. Hamilton, ON; War of 1812; member Legislature 1835.
5. 1787-1822, son Francis; m. 1820 Monique Seguin-Laderoute, dau. Pierre.
6. Several of this name in the county.
7. Voted Detroit 1820, 1821, 1823, 1825; taxpayer 1825; in Hamtramck 1827.
8. J. Bte. Seguin-Laderoute, b. 1774, son Joseph; m. 1801 Archange Cardinal.
9. In 1827 census.
10. Prob. Charles Paul Poirier, son Charles; m. 1798 Jeanne Laperle.
11. 1774-1840, son Francois; taxpayer Grand Marais 1825.
12. Several of this name. One b. Ecorse 1820, d. 1855.
13. Name found on several documents 1826, 1827, 1834.
14. 1780-1840, son Richard and Margaret Bower; m. 1808 Teresa Tremblay, dau. Louis.
15. Prob. son of William who was b. NJ and d. Macomb Co.; settled on Clinton R. 1805.
16. M. Abigail Johnson; ch. b. Detroit 1806-1811 and bp. Ste Anne's Church.
17. Dau. Antoine Vernet; m. 1815 Antoine Beaubien, who d. 1820.
18. 1788-1826, son Pierre; m. 1815 Josette Bourassa, dau. Louis.
19. Prob. James Whistler Abbott, 1805-1860, son James and Sarah ---.
20. D. 1826; innkeeper; m. Archange Tremblay; she m. (2) William Simmons.
21. Poss. widow of William Weaver who lived River Rouge in 1811.
22. Papineau; one of first trustees of the Methodist Church, Detroit, 1822.
23. Adm. and poss. son of Edward McCarty, whose estate filed 3 April 1826.
24. Sally Burbank, widow of Jesse who d. ca. 1814. She was Sarah Hickley, m. 1803.
25. Voted 1823. A Thomas and Anna of St. Lawrence Co., NY sold lots Detroit 1836.
26. Voted 1821 to 1825. First Supervisor and JP in Huron Twp. 1827.
27. 1766-1824, son Noel; m. Abigail King; lived Greenfield 1824.
28. Voted Detroit 1821.
29. Estate probated 1839, Arminda Anderson adm'x; lived River Rouge.
30. Lived River Rouge 1825; m. Hannah (Dicks), widow of William Cissne.
31. A founder Methodist Church River Rouge 1810; m. Elizabeth Thomas; d. 1823.
32. Rev. War pensioner CT; b. ca. 1747, estate filed 1826, widow was Eleanor.

Alanson Thomas [1] 410010/10010
John Macomb [2] 010121/10001
Ezekiel Chamberlin [3] 100010/22010
Josiah Raymond [4] 000101 /10001
Henry Presson [5] 000010/00100
John Cramer [6] 000100/00100
William Bucklin [7] 000201/01110
Daniel Tuttle [8] 120001/12011
Joseph Hicock [9] 100010/10100
William McCarty [10] 100011/21010
Nicholas Brewer [11] 200001/01110
Edward McCarty [12] 000100/10010
George Johnson [13] 000100/00100
Elial Crompton [14] 010010/00000
Daniel Bucklin [15] 000110/00000
Amasa Fox [16] 100010/00100
Benjamin Williams [17] 100010/10010
Alexander Lucket [18] 000001/10001
John Starks [19] 000100/10100
Andrew Bell [20] 000010/00001
John Cramer [21] 101101/11100
James Welch [22] 000010/ 10001
Francis Ruff [23] 000010/20100
Marenus Harrison [24] 100100/00100
Josiah Beckley [25] 100010/10100
Francis Reynom [26] 400001/11121
Hugh McVay [27] 100210/11100
Mehetable Kilbourn [28] 110200/01101
Andrew Nichols [29] 100121/00001
Joseph Fowler [30] 000100/10100
Abraham Kilbourn [31] 000100/00000
Joseph Hanchet [32] 220210/01010

1. Bought land on River Rouge 1817; sold land with wf. Margaret in Dearborn 1843.
2. John Navarre Macomb; d. 1889, son Jean and Christina Livingston; m. Caroline Macomb.
3. M. Mary Schrandel; had son George b. York (Toronto) 1796, bp. Detroit 1821.
4. Not found in records; poss. brother of #26.
5. Preston; m. Mary Ann McVay, prob. dau. Henry; a son Wm. Henry bp. 1821.
6. Poss. son of #21 below; lived Bucklin Twp. 1828-29.
7. Bought 400 acres on River Rouge 1809; m. Margaret Tompkins; estate prob. 1829.
8. M. Jane ---;of Plymouth Twp. 1836 and 1840; of Jefferson Co., WI when sold 1847.
9. 1788-1867; M. E. minister Detroit 1815; m. 1816; taxed River Rouge 1825.
10. 1788-1844; poss. son Edward; m. Maria C. (Audrain) Hoffman, dau. Pierre.
11. Taxed River Rouge 1825.
12. Poss. son Edward and bro. of William. A McCarty on Grosse Ile by 1789.
13. Several of name. One Sheriff of Brown County before 1823.
14. He and William Crompton in Detroit 1807; voted Detroit 1821 and Oakland 1825.
15. Lieut. of Mich. Terr. Militia 1819; estate filed 3 March 1823.
16. Of Bucklin Twp.; estate prob. 1829, widow living, five children.
17. Poss. son of John and Nancy. One Benjamin Williams m. Mary Ponchat.
18. John Lucket appears in several early records but no Alexander.
19. Lived River Rouge 1825, or one of same name.
20. Witness at trial of Stephen Simmons 1830 Detroit. Voted Pontiac 1821.
21. Poss. the Mr. Cramer who d. at River Rouge by 28 March 1826.
22. A James Welch of Camden Twp., Kent Co., ON sold land Detroit 1837.
23. Of Bucklin 1828, Pekin 1831, Dearborn 1834; b. Detroit 1795; wife Mary/Polly.
24. Of Nankin Twp., estate prob. 14 April 1849; widow Hannah, 8 sons, 6 daughters.
25. Wife d. River Rouge 16 Feb. 1819; voted Detroit 1825.
26. Poss. Francis Raymond, son Michel; m. Detroit 1802 Rosalie Lemay.
27. Voted 1823; may be he who m. Elizabeth Burbank instead of Henry (who d. 1807).
28. Widow of Anthony of River Rouge, whose estate filed 3 Oct. 1815.
29. Rev. War pensioner, NH service; from St. Lawrence Co., NY; b. ca. 1751.
30. Of US Army 1818 when sold land in IL; lived River Rouge 1825.
31. Voted 1823; may be son Anthony or Joseph of River Rouge.
32. M. Nancy ---; taxed River Rouge 1825; founder of ME Church Detroit 1822; d. 1849.

Hiram Johns[1] 100100/00100
Elijah Downer[2] 110122/10101
Gilman Smith[3] 000010/00010
Robert Abbott[4] 231101/30010
Louis Roula[5] 000100/00000
John Bapt. Dumay[6] 010210/00101
Joel Thomas[7] 010001/00001
James Desplat[8] 110001/00001
George Hix (free col.) 000000/01101
Joseph Beaubien[9] 100010/31100
--- Frasher 110010/12001
Bienvenue Deslisle[10] 200002/10010
Louis Cicot[11] 200010/00100
Francis Cicot[12] 110011/30110
John Peltier[13] 000100/00000
James Chittenden[14] 110010/01010
Jane Keith[15] 200100/10010
Terence Smith 100310/00100

Gideon Leet[16] 120201/01111
Manoah Hubbard[17] 200220/21010
Sylvester Bates[18] 100020/22010
Patrick Daniels 000010/00001
William Macomb[19] 100010/20110
John A. Rucker[20] 200020/30100
Johnathan Hicock 000010/20000
Adna Hicock[21] 120101/11000
Ashbel Wilcox 200010/21010
Augustus Coan[22] 101211/01010
Frederick Campbell 000010/00000
Joseph Bates[23] 000001/00000
Abraham Truax[24] 100140/11200
Joseph Ellis[25] 000100/00000
Jonathan Cole 000100/00000
John Sturgess[26] 100010/20100
Jason Thurston[27] 100001/02001
Pierre Yax[28] 010001/00000

1. M. Jeanne Cissne, dau. William; constable 1821; founder of Methodist Church.
2. B. Shaftsbury, VT ca. 1774; d. River Rouge 1824, son Cyprian and Hannah Wil-
3. Voted 1821; signed petition 1822.    /loughby
4. 1771-1853, son James and Mary Barkle; m. 1798 Elizabeth Audrain, dau. Pierre.
5. Rouleau; 1799-1853, son Charles; m. 1823 Victoire Vermet, dau. Antoine.
6. 1792-1829, son Pierre; m. 1819 Veronique Baron, dau. Antoine.
7. Of River Rouge 1824, wife Sophia; of Bucklin 1829; wife Catherine in 1831.
8. Desplas; 1765-1820, son J. Bte; m. Francoise Lajeunesse.
9. B. 1779, d. by 1835, son Joseph; m. 1810 Marie Tremblay, dau. Louis.
10. B. 1776, son Alexis; m. 1817 Monica Livernois, dau. Joseph.
11. B. 1789, d. by 1842, son J. Bte.; m. 1815 Veronique Beaubien.
12. 1787-1859, son J. Bte; m. 1809 Felicity Peltier, dau. Jacques.
13. Several of name. One b. 1801, son J. Bte.
14. Trader in Detroit; d. by 18 April 1835; to Grosse Ile ca. 1818; wife Elizabeth.
15. Prob. Jane (Dick) Keith, wife of William, ship captain; dau Jane m. John Rucker.
16. 1765-1826; of Grosse Ile 1817; wife in 1818 was Lucinda.
17. Wife Betsey; taxed Grosse Ile 1825; there 1827.
18. Taxed Grosse Ile 1825; voted Detroit 1821 and Monguagon 1825.
19. D. 1826, won William and Sarah Dring; m. Monica Navarre, dau. Robert.
20. 1788-1845, son John Peter Rucker and Jane (Marshall); m. 1809 Sarah Macomb, dau.
21. 1767-1829, son James and Ruth (Orvis); m. Hudson, NY Polly Andress./ William.
22. Augustus and Peter Coan subscribed to a memorial 20 April 1826.
23. Rev. War pensioner, CT. service; b. ca. 1749; a Mr. Bates d. Grosse Ile by 1826.
24. 1778-1844, son Caleb and Fytje (Van Patten); m. 1817 Lucy Melinda Brigham.
25. Voted Detroit 1825.
26. Taxed River Huron 1825; a John and Ardiloury (Sturgis) of Brownstown sold land 1828.
27. 1760-1835, son Joel and Miriam Blakely; m. 1815 Betsey Paine, dau. Gen. Edward.
28. 1763-1826, son Michael and Catherine (Herbinne); m. 1783 Archange Seguin, dau.
    /Julian.

Pierre Rivard[1] 021301/21201
Charles Rivard[2] 220101/10111
Michael Rivard[3] 421301/11101
Henry Harton 030010/11110
William McKonkey[4] 000001/00000
Philip Ternier[5] 000100/00000
John A. Grant[6] 301110/30110

Francis Griffard[7] 200001/31100
Francis Furton[8] 000010/00100
John Kirby[9] 010001/00001
Isaiah Walton[10] 200001/20010
Enoch Tuttle[11] 000110/00000
Benjamin F. H. Witherell[12] 000100/00000

1. 1766-1847, son J. Bte; m. 1795 Archange Séguin, dau. Joseph.
2. 1764-1825, son J. Bte; m. 1788 Archange Saucier, dau. Joseph.
3. 1770-1846?, son J. Bte; m. 1794 Agnes Saucier, dau. Joseph.
4. William McKonkins vote rejected 1823.
5. Poss. Philip Tarrier; voted Detroit 1821, 1823, 1825.
6. Adopted son of Alexander Grant, ca. 1778-1854; m. 1803 Judith Campau, dau. J. Bte.
7. Prob. son of Laurence Greffard; m. 1808 Cecilia Renaud.
8. Fréton, b. 1792, son Francois; m. 1820 Soulange Senet, dau. Ignatius.
9. Sold land on River Rouge 1817; JP Wayne Co. 1832; Supervisor Hamtramck 1841.
10. Estate prob. 21 Sept. 1835, widow Hannah, who bought land River Rouge 1835.
11. Bought land Pekin Twp. 1832; estate prob. 1863 Dearborn; son Harvey aet. 16.
12. Benjamin Franklin Hawkins Witherell, 1797-1867, son James and Amy Hawkins; m. (1) 1824 Mary Ann Sprague of Poultney, VT; (2) 1837 Delia Ingersol; (3) 1848 Casandra Brady.

## MICHILIMACKINAC COUNTY

Joseph Valencourt[1] 000101/01001
George Ermatinger[2] 110110/30010
Theodore G. Wallace 000100/00000
Almon Green[3] 000010/00000
William Gorton 000100/00000
Tunis Hagerman[4] 000010/00000
Benjamin Rusette 000001/00000
Lewis S. Johnson[5] 100200/11000
Barnard Stone 100010/00100
John B. Deloupe 000100/00000

Joseph Picar[6] 000100/00000
Joseph Martin[7] 000100/00000
David B. Gor an[8] 000100/00000
Louis Gurnon[9] 000010/00000
Jean M. Deroche(r) 00000100000
Antoine Leroncette 000010/00000
Pollet Brisboy[10] 100000/01010
William Aikin[11] 000010/00000
Bela Chapman[12] 000010/00000
Alexis Bodwin[13] 000010/00000

1. D. 13 June 1845, aet. 94. Name in American Fur Co. ledger 1830.
2. Coroner of Mackinac Co. 1818; signed in Chippewa Co. 1831 and 1833.
3. Taxed in Mackinac County 1825.
4. In American Fur Co. Journal (1821-1829). Tucius Hagerman voted 1821.
5. Poss. b. Sault Ste Marie 1793; d. Malden, ON 1825; British soldier War of 1812.
6. Picard; account with American Fur Co. July 1830.
7. Vote rejected at Prarie du Chien, Crawford Co., 1825.
8. M. Madeleine Laplante 4 Sept. 1822. American Fur Co. Journal.
9. Lewis Gurno, voted at Sault Ste Marie 1825.
10. Brisbois; signed at Prarie du Chien 1824; did he m. 1825 Antoine Saloncette?
11. Aitken, chief trader of American Fur Co; bur Aitkinsville (Swan River) on
12. Probate Judge Mackinac County 1840.      /Mississippi River 1851.
13. Poss. Baudoin, "a man without a fault," in Perrault's narrative.

# 1820 Census

Joseph Bodwin[1] 000010/00000
Charles Churette[2] 000001/00000
Francis Decarraux[3] 000010/00000
Jean Halt 000010/00000
Joseph Lecuyer[4] 000010/00000
John B. Lamiraud 000010/00000
Joseph Lemars[5] 000010/00000
Antoine Mossaie[6] 000010/00000
Michael Pitit[7] 000010/00000
Antoine Picard[8] 000010/00000
Paul Revit[9] 000010/00000
Antoine Archambau 000100/00000
Louis Dubruil[10] 000010/00000
Hipolite Recheil 000010/00000
Alexis Boudrie 000010/00000
Edward Lebuffe 000010/00000
Ambrose Davenport, Jr.[11] 001100/00000
Henry A. Levake[12] 000100/00000
Etienne Jolieau[13] 000100/00000
Alexis Cadotte[14] 000100/00000
Benjamin Vincent[15] 000100/00000
Joseph Neveo[16] 000100/00000
Joseph Frotocheau[17] 000100/00000
Lyman Warren[18] 000100/00000
Truman A. Warren[19] 000100/00000
John B. Bazanais[20] 000001/00000
Michael Bazanais[21] 000100/00000
Louis Bailey[22] 000100/00000
Joseph Fontaine[23] 000100/00000
Joseph A. Fontaine[24] 000100/00000
John Bt. Guillot[25] 000100/00000
Benjamin Morrin[26] 000010/00000
Louis Poison[27] 000100/00000
Michael Brisset[28] 000100/00000
Berthume Gauthier[29] 000100/00000
Andrew Morin 000100/00000

1. A Bodwine signed a petition in Crawford Co. 1821; at Sault 1831.
2. Charrett purchased mdse 1827-28.
3. Poss. an Indian Chief Daykauray - not likely, however.
4. Mar. by the Rev. Samuel Mazzuchelli to Lozette LaRonde 24 July 1831.
5. Poss. Joseph Lemmery who voted Prarie du Chien 1823 and 1825; Green Bay 1831.
6. Antoine Mace and stepson boatmen with American Fur Co. 1821-29.
7. Petit signed as Inhabitant of Chippewa County 1833.
8. Signed as Inhabitant Mackinac County 1829, Chippewa 1833.
9. Rivet; American Fur Co. Ledger 1828-30.
10. In American Fur Co. Ledger 1827-30. Did he settle Monroe Co in 1825?
11. Prob. son of Ambrose Davenport who came to Mackinac 1796 and stayed.
12. Constable of Mackinac Co. 1824; JP 1829; member House of Rep. 1835.
13. Etienne Jolineaux signed petition at Sault 1822.
14. American Fur Co. Journal 1821. Poss. son of Michael there earlier.
15. B.K. Vinces signed petition Mackinac 1821. Was he m. Detroit 1827 or 1830?
16. Joseph Neveaux signer Detroit 1822. Vote rejected Monroe Co. 1821.
17. Jean Bte Frotochaud in American Fur Co. Ledger July 1830.
18. 1795-1847; m. 1827 Mary Cadotte, dau. Michel; agent American Fur Co. 1824.
19. Brother of above; from VT 1818; also m. a dau. of Michel Cadotte.
20. Jean Bte Bazinet in American Fur Co. Ledger 1828, bought children's shoes.
21. Credited with 264 muskrats and 93 kittens 7 July 1823 by American Fur Co.
22. Signed petition at Sault 1822. Did he live Monroe Co. 1825, 1826, 1831?
23. American Fur Co. Ledger July 1827.
24. American Fur Co. Ledger July 1828 and 1830.
25. Member Lac du Flambeau Outfit 1822 (AFC Journal).
26. M. Margaret Bazinet 19 Feb. 1830.
27. Lived St. Mary's, Chippewa Co.; signed 1831 for road from Saginaw to Sault.
28. American Fur Co. Ledger 1829, bought blanket, licorice, shaving box, soap, flannel.
29. American Fur Co. Ledger 1827; also a Guillaume in 1828.

Laurent Danie   000100/00000
Baptist Derosier [1]  000100/00000
Charles Marcebois   000100/00000
Solomon Martin   000100/00000
Francis St. John [2]  000010/00000
John B. Chrostier [3]  000010/00000
Baptist Dubois [4]  000001/00000
John Agnew [5]  000010/00000
George Chanler   010111/65010
Joseph Bailey [6]  100001/11000
John Campbell [7]  300110/00101
William McGulpin [8]  000210/30010
Patrick McGulpin [9]  100201/10111
Cecilia McCullough [10] 100000/10010
Lorin Hodge [11] 000310/21100
Rix Robinson [12] 000130/00000
William Farnsworth [13] 000010/00000
Michael Dousman [14] 202706/21110

David Stone [15] 000001/00000
Chauncey Bush [16] 000100/00000
Eliakim Fields [17] 000100/00000
Charles Willcox [18] 000010/00000
Edward Biddle [19] 000130/10000
Alfred Hodge [20] 000100/01000
John Graham [21] 000020/00000
John W. Mason [22] 000010/00000
Elijah Warner [23] 000010/00000
Macue [24] 000010/00000
Mateva [25] 000010/00000
Dona   000010/00000
Narcis Vincent [26] 000100/00000
Constant Relle   000110/00000
Constant Mechant   000100,
George Mitchell [27] 020123/10101
Orge [28] 001100/00000
Lewis Crawford   001100/00000

1. In American Fur Co. Ledger 1827-29.
2. Voted at Sault 1825; signer Crawford Co. 1829, Chippewa Co. 1833.
3. Chortier; appears as Crochier in AFC Ledger 1827, 29, 30.
4. Signer at Sault 1831-32.
5. At Sault 1823 as Clerk of elections; clothing and trunk purchased NY 1822.
6. Fur trader; his step-dau. m. Edward Biddle.
7. Voted Mackinac Co. 1820, 21, 23, 25. One of name in Prarie du Chien 1821.
8. Son of Patrick; m. 1811 Magdeleine Bourassa; warden Ste Ann's, Mackinac.
9. Tailor; in Detroit 1782; accounts with Askin 1785-95; m. Madeleine Créqui.
10. Name appears in American Fur Co. retail accounts.
11. 1789-1870, son Benjamin & Sarah Churchill; m. 1812 Phebe Baker; 1824 Amanda Mallory.
12. 1798-1875, son Edward & Eunice; m. 1821 dau. Indian chief; trader; State Senator.
13. Independent trader at mouth of Menominee River; at Sheboygan 1859.
14. B. PA; to Mackinac after 1796; land owner, Probate Judge 1833-40.
15. From Walpole, NH; in fur trade Detroit before 1812; partner of Conant.
16. Grand Juror Wayne Co. 1820; Of NYC when he and wife Amelia bought land Wayne Co.
17. Voted 1821, taxed Mackinac 1825; in AFC Journal as E. E. Fields.
18. Voted 1820-21; firm name Wilcox and Beach; prob. father Gen. O.B. Wilcox, Detroit.
19. Son of Charles and bro. of Nicholas of Philadelphia; to Mackinac 1808; m. Indian.
20. 1795-1832, son Benjamin and Sarah Churchill; m. 1820 Sophia English, dau. Abel.
21. Voted 1821 and 1825; signed 1829-30.                    and Anna Caulkins.
22. Indian agent; Register of Probate 1821; Clerk of Court 1821; Postmaster 1822-25.
23. Taxed Detroit 1812; Signed Mackinac 1821, 1825; Constable 1824.
24. John McCue and Mary Lawles to W. C. Hulbert, Deeds:K; AFC Ledger.
25. Medard Metivier Deeds:D, AFC Ledger.
26. Son J. Bte Vincent; m. Detroit 1826 Clotilde Bourgeat, dau. Pierre.
27. Son of Dr. David Mitchel, b. Scot., and Chippewa; in AFC Ledger 1821.
28. Prob. Louis St. Onge, in AFC Ledger 1829-31.

Daniel Dingley[1] 000100/00000
Thomas Conner[2] 000001/00000
Jesse Muncey[3] 000230/10100
Louis Chevalier[4] 012201/11100
François Petermaulx 000010/00000
Michel Lecroix[5] 000010/00000
Charles Marlet[6] 020001/00100
François Bodwin[7] 300010/00100
François Pajae[8] 10010/00100
Louis Bennette[9] 000100/00000
Derushe[10] 000010/00000
Amor Lebui 000100/00000
Cuttoe[11] 000010/00000
Jacques 000100/00000
Louis Curba[12] 000100/00000
Rami Neddo[13] 000001/00100
Duba[14] 000010/00000
Bourtiyi 00200/00000
Michael 000100/00000

Pierre Lefleur 000100/00000
Thomas P. James[15] 110140/10110
Henry G. Graveraet[16] 100010/30100
Bournevint Gadupée[17] 000100/00000
Richard Pendergrass[18] 000100/00000
Alexis Griguire[19] 000100/00000
John B. Rhele 000010/00000
Baptist Vincent[20] 000100/00000
Peter Labouche 000010/00000
John Wheton[21] 100110/00100
Louis Beresaw[22] 300010/10000
Augustine Cadotte[23] 200020/00000
Charles Beautien[24] 000010/30000
Morrice Metta[25] 100100/30000
François Louisenois[26] 410001/10000
Pierre Louisnois 000100/00000
Pierre Asselliea 000001/02000
John B. Testroe[27] 000001/01000
Joseph Quezeno[28] 000010/00000

1. M. 25 July 1827 Isabelle Duchêne; had interest in Folleavoine Outfit, AFC 1822.
2. M. 27 July 1830 Susanne Duchêne; blacksmith.
3. Voted Mackinac 1821, 23, 25   Large account with AFC 1827-28.
4. Of the prominent Mackinac and Fort St. Joseph family.
5. Merchant at Mackinac 1815.
6. 1778-1856; m. 1804 M. Josephe Vaillancourt, dau. Joseph.
7. Children of Francis Baudoin and Catherine bp. 1818-21 Ste. Ann, Mackinac.
8. Francois Parge voted Mackinac 1821.  Francis Page in AFC Journal.
9. Voted Mackinac 1823.
10. Amable Derocher voted Green Bay 30 June 1825.
11. Jacques Coteau's vote rejected Mackinac 1821.
12. Louis Curbat voted Sault 1825.
13. Voted Mackinac 1820-25.  René Nadeau signed 1829.
14. Louis Dubé voted Green Bay 1823 and 1825.
15. Name in AFC Journal 1821; voted Mackinac 1820, 21, 23, 25.

16. Indian agent, Chippewa interpreter; voted Mackinac 1821-25.
17. Bonadventure Gardpies vote rejected Green Bay 1823.
18. Signed petition Mackinac 1825.
19. Alexis Gregoire and Josette Paul married 23 Feb. 1828.

20. M. Teresa Rivet.  A son Narcisse to Detroit 1824, m. Clotilde Bourget.
21. Wheaton, voted Mackinac 1820-21.  Treasurer Mackinac Co. 1824.
22. Bourassa, carpenter employed by AFC; Ensign in militia 1824.
23. Interpreter Lac du Flambeau Outfit; Augustus Cadotte m. Madeline, Indian, 1822.
24. Beaubien voted 1821-23; m. Teresa , Indian, 14 Dec. 1822.
25. In AFC Ledger 1821.  Also called Maurice Matta.
26. Louisinac or Louisignan; voted Mackinac 1821-25.
27. Tesseraux signed petition 1825; voted 1821-23.
28. Joseph Cousineau voted Green Bay 6 Sept. 1821.

Bombier   000100/00000
Joseph Petit   000001/00000
Labay[1]   000010/00000
John B. Paro[2]   000010/00000
Calaway   000010/00000
Elijah E. Robinson[3]   100010/00001
Paul McGinness[4]   201101/00001
Ambrose Davenport[5]   110001/31010
L. Rolette[6]   000100/00000
Joseph Rolette[7]   000010/00000
John B. Berthelott[8]   000010/00000
Thomas Laguthry[9]   000110/00000

THE FOLLOWING MEN ARE ALL AGED 26-45 AND LIVING ALONE:
Crepo[10]
P. Gremare[11]
Baptist Marchand[12]
Antoine Faubert[13]
Alexander Berthiaume[14]
Michael Fabre
Baptist Durenseau
Louis Gagne[15]
Joseph Boursier[16]
Pierre Welsh
Simeon Lemay
Joachim Pominville[17]
Bastien Pominville[18]
Pierre Grenier
Joseph Potvin[19]
Joseph Lemay
Louis Cardinal
John B. Credit[20]
Melish Secard
François Lerivière
Luc Larivière
Pion
François Bouthilier[21]
Antoine Leduc[22]
Charles Toin[23]
Joseph Potvin
Julien Viette[24]
Louis Provensalle[25]
Etienne Dubois

1. Charles Labay, boatman 1822-23 with Iroquois Outfit; voted Mackinac 1823.
2. Poss. son J. Bte Perrault, who m. an Indian and lived at the Sault.
3. M. Marian F. Calvi 22 Nov. 1824. Capt. of Militia 1824.
4. Voted Mackinac 1820-21.
5. Resident of Mackinac from 1796 to death; War of 1812 under Croghan and Gen.   /Harrison.
6. Laurent Rollette; in AFC Journal.
7. Merchant at Mackinac 1815; Chief Justice; at Prarie du Chien 1828-31.
8. Berthelet, signed 1821; owed AFC for postage pd in NY on 3 letters.
9. Thomas LaGuthrie m. Mary, an Indian, 16 July 1823. Voted 1821-12.
10. AFC Journal for 1 bbl. pork, 1 bbl. flour, 1 tin kettle 1822.
11. Pierre Grimard, signed at Prarie du Chien 21 Jan. 1830.
12. Boatman with Upper Mississippi Outfit 1821; in AFC Journal.
13. In AFC Journal 1821-29.
14. With Illinois Outfit 1821. Paid $16.67 by AFC for trip to Montreal.
15. Gagnier, boatman with Upper Mississippi Outfit. Wintered at Green Bay 1821.
16. Joseph Nourcier a boatman with Upper Mississippi Outfit 1821.
17. Boatman with Upper Mississippi River Outfit 1821.
18. Boatman with Upper Mississippi Outfit 1821.
19. A Joseph Poitevein m. Catherine Girard Detroit 1822 and settled Macomb County.
20. Crede, Credet, Crady, Creedie. Voted at Mackinac 1823-25.
21. One of this name at Prarie du Chien. Assoc. Justice Crawford Co. 1819.
22. In AFC Journal 1822. Joseph Rolette paid his order for Antoine Leduc.
23. With Upper Mississippi Outfit 1821. Paid $75 by Russell Farnham 1822.
24. Julien Villiotee signed at Prarie du Chien Jan. 1830.
25. In AFC Journal 1822 for 2 ga. whiskey furnished him at Green Bay.

# 1820 Census

Joseph Brisbois [1] 000010/00000
Alexis Bailey [2] 000010/00000
Mary Hogan [3] 100000/21010
William Sylvester [4] 000100/00100
James Finch [5] 000010/00000
Sarrell    000010/00000
Jacques Parisian [6] 000010/00000
George Boyd [7] 410010/10020
Louis Bonnier    000100/00000
Moses (no entries)
S. Burr [8] 100000/01010
Timothy Worthington [9] 000010/00000
James Orr [10] 000010/00000
Benjamin Clapp [11] 000200/00000
Josiah Willard [12] 001110/00100
Wilson Dart    000010/00000
John McCarty [13] 000010/00000
Richard H. Blinn [14] 000010/00000
David (no entries)
George Gordon    100010/00000

Benjamin K. Pierce [15] 100010/20100
John S. Pierce [16] 000100/00000
Francis Joy [17] 000010/00000
Isaac Blanchard [18] 000010/00000
Louis Collame [19] 000010/00000
William Graham [20] 000100/00000
Jonas Stone [21] 000010/00000
James Homer [22] 000100/00000
Charles Collins [23] 000100/00000
William Suts [24] 000001/00100
Morris Blakesley [25] 000100/00000
James O. Whitty [26] 000010/00000
Samuel Dunlap [27] 000010/00000
Jesse Fenton [28] 000010/00000
Elias Willegus    001100/00000
Francis Thompson    000100/00000
Daniel Finnemore    000100/00000
Ebenezer Ayres    000100/00000
Benjamin Allen    000010/00000
Daniel Brown [29] 000100/00000

1. Ensign Michigan Terr. Militia 1822; voted Crawford Co. 1823.
2. Bailly, clerk of Crawford Co. Court 1824; voted Prarie du Chien 1825.
3. Name in AFC Journal 1821-29. Caroline Hogan m. Robert White 1824.
4. In AFC Journal, when charged $50 for medicine, advice for self and wife.
5. Constable Mackinac Co. 1821; Ensign 1822; voted 1822.
6. Boatman with Lac du Flambeau Outfit 1821. Owed AFT $5 for one NY trunk.
7. 1779-1846, son of George of Maryland; m. dau. Joshua Johnson, Indian agent.
8. Widow? Andrew Burr voted Mackinac 1821 and 1825.
9. In AFC Journal; voted 1821.
10. A Col. Orr mentioned by Solomon Sibley to Adam Stewart, collector at Mackinac.
11. Notary Public 1821; printer; expenses paid to NYC and Washington by AFC.
12. Voted 1820,1821. Certified election 1820 and 1825.
13. Voted Green Bay 1821-24; signed memorial 1833.
14. AFC received from him 1821 6000 gal. whiskey, 85 bbl. flour, pork, beef.
15. 1790-1850, son Benjamin & Ann Kendrick; Capt at Mackinac 1815; m. --- Laframboise.
16. 1796-1824, bro. of above and Pres. Pierce; m. Marietta O. Puthuff, dau. William.
17. Sergeant under Capt. Pierce's Company, US Army, April 1820.
18. Sgt. in Capt. Pierce's Co. 1820; m. Mary Babcup 1824; voted 1823-25; signed 1829.
19. Sgt. Colame in Capt. Pierce's Company.
20. Mentioned in Capt. Pierce's Orderly Book; m. Lucy Garlick 21 May 1822.
21. Corp. in Capt. Pierce's Co. 1820. Voted 1821-25.
22. Private in Capt. Pierce's Company.
23. Private in Capt. Pierce's Company.
24. Sgt. Suts in Capt. Pierce's Company; in AFC Journal 1821.
25. Corp. in Capt. Pierce's Company.
26. Corporal, soldier between 1818-20. AFC Journal 1821.
27. Mentioned in Capt. Pierce's Orderly Book 1818-20.
28. Private in Orderly Book 21 July 1819; voted 1825.
29. Private in Capt. Pierce's Company.

John Brown[1] 000100/00000
John Biles[2] 000010/00000
John Bennette 000010/00000
Isaac Brady[3] 000100/00000
George Plume[4] 000100/00000
Samuel Barker[5] 000100/00000
John Berryman 000010/00000
Andrew Clark[6] 000010/00000
George Callahan[7] 000100/00000
John Campbell[8] 000010/00010
Benjamin J. Cuff[9] 000010/00000
William Devost[10] 000100/00000
William L. Davis[11] 000100/00000
John Dilsaver[12] 000010/00000
Charles Decker[13] 000010/00000
John Fry 000100/00000
Jabez Fales[14] 000010/00000
John Ferron[15] 000010/00000
Charles Gordon 000010/00000

John Griffen[16] 000001/00000
Joshua R. Gedney 000010/00000
John Goriske[17] 000010/00000
John Giddens 000001/00000
Robertson Gibson[18] 000100/00000
Louis Gandy 000100/00000
Nathan Herring[19] 000100/00000
Adam Hemple[20] 000010/00000
Joshua Huffman 000010/00000
John Hugg[21] 000010/00000
James Johnson[22] 000010/00000
Samuel Jones[23] 000010/00000
Henry Kiefer[24] 000100/00000
George Knox[25] 000010/00000
David Kid[26] 000010/00000
George W. Kinsey 000100/00000
Barnard McKinney[27] 000010/00000
Hugh Morrell[28] 000010/00000
Henry Miller[29] 000010/00000

1. Private in Capt. Benjamin Pierce's Company 1820.
2. Voted Mackinac 1823.
3. Signed petition 1829.
4. George Bloom, private Capt. Pierce's Company 1820.
5. Private Capt. Pierce's Company 1818-20.
6. Private Capt. Pierce's Company 1818-20.
7. Paid by AFC Sept. and Oct. 1821 for 22 days building wall for store, $22.
8. Paid for blacksmith work for AFC.
9. Cuffe a private in US Army, 1818-20.
10. Private US Army 1818-20.
11. Mentioned in Capt. Pierce's Orderly Book 1818-20.
12. Private in Pierce's Company 1819-20.
13. Private in Capt. Pierce's Orderly Book 1818-20.
14. Private in Capt. Pierce's Orderly Book 1818-20.
15. John Farrel private in Capt. Pierce's Orderly Book 1818-20.
16. D. Philadelphia ca. 1840, son Cyrus; Assoc. Justice Mich. Terr. Supreme Court.
17. Private Gorisky in Pierce's Company 1818-20; voted 1823.
18. Roter T. Gibson voted Mackinac 1823.
19. Capt. Pierce's Company 1818-20.
20. Capt. Pierce's Company 1818-20; voted 1823-1825; signed 1829.
21. Capt. Pierce's Company Orderly Book 1818-20; see Mathew Shaw next page.
22. One of name b. NY, enlisted Sacketts Harbor; disch. 24 Apr. 1824 Mackinac.
23. Capt. Pierce's Orderly Book 1818-20.
24. Capt. Pierce's Company; voted 1823; m. 28 Jan. 1822 Mary Malone.
25. Private 21 Apr. 1820 in Capt. Pierce's Company.
26. Mentioned in AFC Journal Oct.-Nov. 1822; taxed at Sault 1823.
27. Private Capt. Pierce's Company 1820.
28. Capt. Pierce's Orderly Book 1819.
29. Private Capt. Pierce's Company 1818-20.

# 1820 Census

Richardson May[1] 000100/00000
William Miles 000010/00000
William Nichols[2] 000010/00000
Bryan O. Conner[3] 000010/00000
Samuel Parker 000010/00000
Joseph Pierce 000100/00000
John Plumley[4] 000010/00000
Nathan Puffer[5] 000001/00000
Henry Rogers[6] 000010/00000
Josiah Readlion[7] 000010/00000
Samuel Rickmon 000100/00000
James Randall 000100/00000
Joseph Robertson 000010/00000
John Swinfin 000001/00000
Alpheus Simpkins[8] 000010/00000
Mathew Shaw[9] 000100/00000
Peter Scarret[10] 000010/00000
William Thompson[11] 000100/00000
William White[12] 000001/00000
Robert T. Gibson[13] 000010/00000
Jabez Waldon[14] 000010/00000
Phillemon Blake[15] 000010/00000
Francis Rogers[16] 000100/00000
Andrew Austin[17] 000100/00000
Paul Labatt[18] 000100/00000
Pierre Cheaton[19] 000100/00000
William Thomas[20] 000100/00000
Henry McGraw[21] 000010/00000
David Boileau 000100/00000
James White[22] 000010/00000
Jeremiah Scanlon [10] 00010/00010
George Douts 000100/00000
John A. Chew 000010/00000
William Story 000100/00000
Archibald Alexander 000010/00000
John Brown[23] 000010/00000
Michael Bayton 000010/00000
Lewis Beck[24] 000010/00000
Thomas W. Bowen 000010/00000
John Conway 000100/00000

1. Name in AFC Journal 1821; voted Sault 1825; signed there 1831 and 1833.
2. Private, US Army, at Mackinac 1818-20; voted 6 Sept. 1821.
3. A Bryant Conner's vote was rejected Detroit Sept. 1823.
4. Private, US Army, at Mackinac 12 July 1819.
5. 1771-1851, son Nathan and Caty Clapp; m. 23 Aug. 1795 Abigail Joslin, dau. Samuel and Abigail Wilder; in US Army 1812-1822; Pensioner War of 1812.
6. Private, at Mackinac 1818-20.
7. Private Redline, US Army, 1818-1820; voted Brown County 1823-25.
8. Private, Capt. Benjamin Pierce's Company 1818-1820.
9. Private, at Mackinac 1818-20; On 15 Dec. 1820, Hugg (previous page) made a deposition about an attack on Shaw that resulted in his death.
10. Private in Pierce's Company; in Orderly Book; voted 1823.
11. William Tomason or Thomerson in AFC Journal 1821.
12. Private in Lt. Daniel Curtis' command at Mackinac 1818; voted at Sault 1825.
13. Voted at Mackinac 1824; signed 1831.
14. Private, US Army, under Capt. Pierce, 1818-1820.
15. Private under Capt. Pierce 1818-20; voted 1825.
16. In Capt. Pierce's Orderly Book 1818-20.
17. Private, US Army, in AFC Journal 1821.
18. In Capt. Pierce's Orderly Book 1818-20.
19. A musician mentioned in Capt. Pierce's Orderly Book 1818-20.
20. Private, Capt. Pierce's Company; tried for desertion Detroit 30 June 1818.
21. Charged with desertion in NY 1818, sentenced to Mackinac to serve out term, / with no pay.
22. Private under Lt. Daniel Curtis Mackinac 1818.
23. Private at Mackinac 1818-20.
24. Private, at Mackinac 1818 under Lt. Daniel Curtis.

Miles Carlson   000010/00100
James Espey   000010/00000
Patrick Esmond   000010/00000
Alexander McDonelld[1]   000100/00000
Felix McDonelld[2]   000010/00000
Phillemon W. Norwood   000100/00000
Edward Orry   000010/00000
Lepton Percelle   000010/00000
John A. Southerland   000100/00000
John Stephens   000010/00000
George Steine   000010/00000
William Wallace[3]   000010/00000
Henry Whiteman   000010/00000
Thomas Williams   000010/00000
Philip Labatt   000010/00000
William Beaumont[4]   000010/00000
Peter Mulleur[5]   120010/20000
Pierre Montrax   /00000
Souchong Lagissie[6]   0000001/00000

Joseph Paul[7]   000001/00000
John Antoine Cuquier   000001/00000
Pierre Lipine   000001/00000
Micael Vaundren   000101/00000
Joseph Gagnior   100011/1000
Joseph Delvair[8]   000001/00000
Ramsey Crooks[9]   10(10)(112)(63)(16)/54140
Antoine Martin[10]   000001/00000
Daniel Beresaw[11]   010232/01221
Francois Truckey[12]   410100/20100
Louis Berbier   001110/00000
William Henry Puthuff[13]   010010/01010
Joseph Dousman[14]   100132/30100
Joseph Watson[15]   210020/10010
Robert Garratt[16]   000100/00000
Samuel Abbott[17]   000010/00000
Alvah Cable[18]   000010/00000
Samuel La[19]   311201/31110
Perish Lorin   000001/00000

1. Called McDona in Capt. Pierce's Orderly Book 1818-20.
2. Same.
3. Clerk of the Lower Wabash Outfit, AFC 1821.
4. Famous surgeon with US Army who made intestinal experiments on Alexis St. Martin; b. Lebanon, CT 1796; d. St. Louis, MO 1853.
5. AFC Journal shows he was paid in 1822 for hauling timber for new buildings in Pointe au Sable. Pierre Mullar voted 1823; Peter Muller voted 1825.
6. Names of Joachim and Josette Lagassy in AFC Journal 1821.
7. Debtor to AFC Retail store account.
8. Mentioned in Mackinac Co. deeds 1824.
9. B. Greenock, Scotland ca 1786; d. NYC 6 June 1859. Made overland trip to Astoria in 1810; Head of American Fur Co. at Mackinac. John J. Astor transferred his interest in AFC to Crooks in 1834.
10. Boatman with Fond du Lac Outfit 1821-22; son Antoine and Indian mother; b. 1794.
11. Bourassa; b. Mackinac 8 Oct. 1752, son Rene; m. Marguerite Bernard.
12. Voted Mackinac 1823.
13. 1769-1814; Virginian; m. Mary Smith, dau. Thomas, surveyor in Detroit. Capt.
14. From PA, son Michael; Assoc. Judge County Court 1818-19; m. Rosalie Labarde.
15. Poss. Secretary to Governors and Judges; m. Sally Mira Witherell, dau. James.
16. Auctioneer of Mackinac County 1820; voted 1821; census taker 1820.
17. 1778-1851, son James and Mary Barker Abbott, bro. of Judge James; m. Detroit 1827 Teresa Beaufait, dau Louis.
18. Owner of Schooner *Farmer* 1823; voted Mackinac 1821 and 1825; inspector Sault 1825.
19. Poss. Samuel Lasley, tavernkeeper at Mackinac.

## 1820 Census

## MACOMB COUNTY: TOWN OF MOUNT CLEMENS

Christian Clemons [1]  000102/31110
John Stockton [2]  100100/10100
Andrew Westbrook [3]  141251/50010
James Robertson [4]  001110/00101
John B. Desnoyer [5]  000010/30100
Peter Yax, Jun. [6]  000010/00100
Simeon Cadot [7]  100010/30100
Ignace Morass [8]  100301/32101
Enoch Huntley [9]  002010/10010
William Johnson [10]  000010/00100
Joseph Stead [11]  340010/10010
Nathl Squires [12]  311101/40101
Asa Partridge [13]  000010/00100
Eleasor Scott [14]  100211/20201
Ira Andrews [15]  100010/10100

Charles Beteau [16]  000010/50010
Job Hoxsie [16]  200121/01010
Joseph Leister [17]  101110/10100
Mitchell Tremblé [18]  210101/00201
William Andrews [19]  000010/00000
Levi Blaucet [20]  000010/00000
Ezekiel Allen [20]  000010/30010
Elisha Harrington [21]  010010/30010
Ezra Prescott [22]  000010/00000
Leo Tremblé [23]  200010/102 00
Charles Tucker [24]  201011/31111
Julia Forton [25]  310201/11010
John B. Doud [26]  041001/21000
Nan Moe [27]  310001/12010
Charles Peltier [28]  020101/00101

1. 1768-1844; to Detroit 1795; to Clinton 1798; laid out town of Mt. Clemens.
2. 1791-1878; m. Mary Allen, step-dau. Christian Clemens; War of 1812,Civil War.
3. Capt. Terr. Militia 1818; Superintendant of Roads 1819; voted 1825.
4. Voter St. Clair Co. 1825.
5. B. 1788, son Gregoire; m. 1812 Rosalie Peltier, b. 1796, dau. Alexis.
6. B. 1784, son Pierre; m. 1815 Monique Huyet-Champagne.
7. B. 1789, son Joseph; m. 1812 Bridget Yax, dau. Peter.
8. 1776-1850, son Nicholas; m. 1798 Frances Chauvin, dau. Pierre.
9. Voted Macomb 1821-25. Poss. at St. Joseph River 1835.
10. Voted Macomb 1823-25.
11. 1784-1842; m. Mary A. ---, 1777-1840; bur. Utica.
12. 1752-1832; m. Jemima Dilno who d. 1811; Rev. Soldier; in Macomb by 1817.
13. Constable Detroit 1818; voted Macomb 1825, Oakland 1821; d. ca. 1830.
14. JP Macomb County 1819; Sterling Twp. 1821; voted 1825.
15. Voted Macomb 1821; Oakland 1823; Detroit 1825; d. Birmingham 1855, aet. 68.
16. From Canada, lumberman; d. 1827, bur. Romeo; his son Job to Lapeer County.
17. 1779-1844; m. Sally --- who d. 1883; bur. Utica; JP Macomb Co. 1822.
18. Michael, b. 1768, son Louis; m. 1790 Marie Lauzon; m. 1795 Marie Chapoton.
19. Poss. m. Angelique Duberger, dau. J. Bte; son b. Detroit 1797.
20. Bro. of Orison Allen; m. --- Russell 2 Dec. 1821; county comm. 1825.
21. 1776-1848; m. Susanne Conner, first white child b. in county; bp. 1783 Moravian
22. From NH; first Pros. Attorney of Macomb Co. 1819; JP 1821.     /Mission.
23. B. 1794, son Louis; m. 1815 Catherine Campau, dau. Alexis.
24. Son William and Catherine Heyl; he rcvd Private Claim #147; bro.Joseph next page.
25. Julian Freton, b. 1760, son Julian; m. 1783 Teresa Billiau.
26. An Edward Doud d. 1867, bur. Catholic Cemetery Clinton Twp.
27. Nun Moe, voted Macomb 1821-24; Treasurer 1829; m. C. Higgins 7 Sept. 1836.
28. B. 1767, son Andrew; m. 1789 Archange Casse-St. Aubin, dau. J. Bte.

Jacob Tucker[1] 100020/10010
Benoit Tremble[2] 110010/10010
John Tucker[3] 400120/00010
Louis Nickla 000101/33210
Felix Peltier[4] 400002/10110
Coleman Funston[5] 100100/00010
Antoine Dequindre[6] 20002 /11010
END OF TOWN

Henry Chapaton[7] 100010/11100
Joe Miller[8] 000010/10010
Joseph Robertoy[9] 301001/11010
Baptist Thomas[10] 320010/21010
Rafle Lafleur[11] 000010/10010
Laurence Moore[12] 311101/00110
Ignace Thebe[13] 011101/00101
Robert Bellont[14] 200010/20010

Jno. B. Bourbien[15] 000010/10100
Louis Chapoton[16] 100011/10100
Fran. Habady[17] 211001/43010
Felix Thomas[18] 000010/10100
George Thomas[19] 001100/01001
Robert Thomas[20] 220010/10010
Louis Laforge[21] 001201/01001
John B. Duba[22] 300001/00000
Francis Duba[23] 3000010/20010
Alexis Duba[24] 100010/10010
Madam Conash 220000/20200
George Sear[25] 400001/02101
Baptist Blay[26] 000010/10010
Etienne Rattail[27] 100010/00010
Etienne Bellor 310001/22011
Joseph Sofacor[28] 000010/40100
Pierre Chovin[29] 3100001/01010

1. Son William & Catherine Heyl ;Detroit 1807; in first Constitutional Congress 1835.
2. Supervisor Roads & Highways, Harrison Twp. 1818.
3. Poss. son William above or Henry and Nancy (Edwards); prob. m. Josette Chapoton.
4. 1769-1830, son J. Bte; m. 1792 Catherine St. Aubin; m. 1808 M. Pominville.
5. Irishman; signer Macomb 1822; voter 1825 tho' not naturalized; d. 1836.
6. Son Francis Dagneau Dequindre; m. 1808 Jeanne Pilet, dau. J. Bte.
7. 1790-1859, son J. Bte; m. 1817 Magdeleine Drouillard; m. 1829 Angelique Lafoy.
8. 1786-1852; voted Macomb 1825. A Joseph and Daniel Miller from Genesee, NY.
9. Voted Macomb 1821.
10. 1784-1851, son Jacob; m. 1805 Mary Blay, dau. Francis.
11. Son Raphael; m. 1810 Theotiste Laforge, dau. Louis.
12. Son Francis; m. 1786 Ursule Belanger; m. 1794 Susanne Pineau.
13. Thibault; b. 1769, son Ignace; m. 1794 Magdeleine Laforest.
14. Belan, b. 1794, son Francis; m. 1815 Monique Moras, dau. Nicolas.
15. Beaubien, 1789-1833, son Lambert; m. 1818 Cecilia Boyer, dau. Antoine.
16. 1782-1851, son J. Bte; m. 1818 Susanne Tucker, dau. Henry; m. 2nd Sophia Robitaille, dau. Joseph.
17. Prob. Labadie; d. 1834; m. Apollonia Girardin and 1817 Mary Ann Greffard, dau.
18. 1795-ca. 1856, son Jacob; m. 1816 Elizabeth McDonald, dau. Aquila.     /Louis.
19. Bro. of above, b. 1798; m. 1823 Susanne Deshetres, dau. Aloysius.
20. Bro. of above, 1780-1859; m. 1804 Cecilia Dubay, dau. Jean M.
21. 1753-1839, son John Simon Pradet-Laforge; m. 1783 Margaret Campau.
22. Dubay, b. 1773, son John Marie; m. 1805 Teresa Dulac.
23. Bro. of above, b. 1789; m. 1815 Angelique Goulet, dau. Louis.
24. Bro. of above, 1779-1866; m. 1821 Cecilia Blay, dau. Francis.
25. Prob. Sire.
26. B. 1782, son Francis; m. 1806 Archange Dulac, dau. Charles.
27. Ratel, son Antoine; m. 1818 Archange Laperle, dau. Jospeh.
28. 1771-1852, son Andrew Sansfacon; m. 1804 Catherine Chauvin.
29. B. 1767, son Charles; m. 1812 Rosalie Robertjeanne.

# 1820 Census

Paul Rattail[1] 200011/01011
John B. Rattail[2] 410101/11010
Baptist Nicla[3] 110210/22201
Pere Elloir[4] 200010/20010
Baptist Coshway[5] 100100/10100
Nicholas Mason[6] 100010/10100
Baptist Dulac[7] 000010/20100
John B. Vernier, Jun.[8] 000010/20100
Francis O. Tremblé 300010/20110
Joseph Elloir[9] 100010/00100
Joseph Vannatten[10] 000101/00101
Hugh McKay[11] 200010/00010
Charles Peltier[12] 000010/10010
Francis Chortie[13] 101101/01001
Madam Mena[14] 411100/20101
Louis Sambernor[15] 320101/01101

John Cartwright[16] 200100/00110
William Hill[17] 000010/12100
Archibald McDonell[18] 000010/20100
John K. Smith[19] 100010/00010
Nicla Frederick 100100/00100
Francis Fleury[20] 300010/22200
William Thorn[21] 000101/00011
Ira Marks[22] 200110/10010
George Cottrell[23] 200011/10100
Joseph Chortie[24] 200010/10100
Joseph Basena[25] 000010/00000
Joco Iouro[26] 000100/00110
Joseph Mena[27] 210010/11010
Joseph Mye[28] 100111/21101
Margaret Mye 300000/00100
Lambert Yax[29] 000010/00000

1. Son Charles Ratel; m. 1814 Pelagia Duchene, dau. Francis.
2. Bro. of above; m. 1806 Mary Valley, dau. Charles.
3. Grand Juror 1819 Macomb County.
4. Peter Alard; 1787-1856, son James; m. 1812 Agatha Laperle, dau. Joseph.
5. Cochois, an Indian trader at Flint & Saginaw 1819; at Treaty of Saginaw.
6. Voter Macomb 1825.
7. 1795-1848, son Charles; m. 1817 Julia Chauvin, dau. J. Bte.
8. 1795-1830, son J. Bte; m. 1819 Monique Lauson.
9. Alard, b. 1795; son Jacques; m. 1818 Magdeleine Tremblay, dau. Francis.
10. Voted Macomb 1825.
11. Grand Juror Macomb Co. 1819; voter Oakland 1821.
12. Prob. d. Mt. Clemens 27 June 1872, aet 78; there by 1814.
13. Chartier, b. 1751; m. 1786 Amable Raymond-Toulouse, dau. J. Bte.
14. Prob. Mary Ann Petit, b. 1778, dau. Nicolas; m. 1795 Pierre Meny as 2nd wife.
15. St. Bernard, voted St. Clair Co. 1825.
16. M. Theotiste Bazinet, b. 1792, dau Joseph.
17. Son of Jacob and Dorothea Seck; m. Elizabeth Robinson.
18. M. Nancy Carter, son b. 1817 and daughter 1819.
19. 1786-1855; m. 1818 Catherine McDonald, native of Westchester Co., NY.
20. M. Mary Maillet. Children b. Detroit m. in St. Clair after 1820.
21. M. Elizabeth Cottrell, b. 1785, dau. George.
22. Voter St. Clair 1825; signed petition there 1834.
23. B. 1782; bur. Marine City, son George; m. 1817 Archange Meny, dau. Pierre.
24. Chartier, b. 1789, son Francis; m. 1813 Nancy Hill, dau. Jacob.
25. Basinet, b. 1789, son Joseph; m. 1823 Jane Hill, dau. Jacob.
26. James Lareau?
27. B. 1781, son Antoine; m. 1809 Genevieve Laperle, dau. Joseph.
28. A family of Nyes in Macomb, but none with these given names.
29. B. 1798, son J. Bte; m. Ann Hathaway, b. 1804, dau. Abner.

Joseph Yax[1] 000010/00000
Henry Cottrell[2] 100010/10100
Loren Blanchard[3] 000100/00000
David Cottrell[4] 000100/01200
William Brown[5] 210010/31010
Peter Dupré[6] 000010/00110
Baptist Medo 100010/10100
Jacob Baker[7] 000020/21100
Michell Dechien[8] 200301/21010
Madam Pettee(Peltier?) 000000/50010
Francis Chartie[9] 200010/40010
Joseph Bodeno[10] 210001/52010
Joseph Year 200001/21200
Baptist Yax[11] 020001/11010
Baptist Yax, Jr.[12] 100010/00100
Sam Ward[13] 000030/10200
Louis Tebo[14] 200001/12020
Oliver Record[15] 220001/10110

Mrs. Knapp 321000/11010
Alexander Harrow[16] 000010/00000
James B. Woolverton[17] 200110/20010
Louis Chortie[18] 100010/00010
Mrs. Harrow 010000/00210
Antoine Boudrin/rie 000010/00000
Francis Yax[19] 000010/01010
Joseph Cottrell[20] 000010/20100
William Meldrum[21] 000110/21100
Nicholas Boyer[22] 010001/01201
Joseph Labla[23] 010100/00010
Edward Tucker[24] 000120/01201
Joseph Hays[25] 010001/11010
James A. Clark[26] 100010/00000
Ebenezar Kittridge[27] 100021/10010
Isaac Russ[28] 010001/00001
Henry Doyle[29] 000010/00100
James Conner[30] 110011/11010

1. B. 1796, son J. Bte; m. 1821 Victoria Labadie-Badichon, dau. Antoine; m/2 1834.
2. B. 1790, son George; m. 1819 Mary Ann Campau, dau. Louis.
3. Voter St. Clair 1821-23.
4. 1797-1869, son George; m. 1820 Catherine Lauzon, Dau. Seraphin.
5. One of name m. Eliza Jacox 23 Feb. 1837; voter St. Clair 1825.
6. Son of Louis; m. 1809 Magdeleine Crete, dau. J. Bte.
7. 1772-1853, son N. Baker; m. Cecilia Laforest, dau. J. Bte.
8. B. 1776, son Francis; m. 1797 Jeanne Petit, dau. Nicolas.
9. 1786-1874, son Francis; m. 1809 Monique Meny, dau. Antoine.
10. A Louis Boudinas voted Detroit 1823.
11. B. 1761, son Michael; m. 1781 Regina Christina Huyet-Champagne.
12. 1785-1834, son of above; m. 1817 Teresa Meny, dau. Antoine.
13. 1784-1854; m. Syracuse, NY Elizabeth Lambertson of Manlius; Capt. on Great Lakes.
14. Thibault, 1771-1847, son Ignace; m. 1816 Archange Bertrand.
15. Ricard, b. 1774, son Alexis; m. 1805 Catherine Boyer.
16. On St. Clair River 1796; Capt. Marine Dept., Detroit 1789; d. by 1823.
17. Nephew of Mrs. Sam Ward?
18. B. 1795, son Francis; m. 1820 Archange Cottrell, dau. George.
19. B. 1785, son Pierre; m. 1805 Archange Thomas, dau. Jacob.
20. B. 1793, son George; m. 1818 Mary Soulange Rivard, dau. Charles.
21. 1794-186-?, son George; m. 1816 Genevieve Rivard, dau. Michael.
22. B. 1763, son Ignace; m. 1797 Julia Tremblay.
23. Leblanc, son Jacques; m. 1826 Mary Louisa Pilet, dau. Jacques.
24. Grand Juror 1819; voter 1825; trustee ME Church Mt. Clemens 1841.
25. Came from Canada ca. 1800; settled Clinton Twp; d. 1845, wife d.1856 ae. 70.
26. Scotchman; vote rejected 1823; not naturalized by 1825.
27. Cattle mark recorded 1822; voter 1825; estate probated 1835 Bruce Twp.
28. Built first lake boat for Christian Clemens 1820-22 at Mt. Clemens.
29. Petitioner 1829. A James Doyle d. Detroit 1821.
30. B. 1771, son Richard and Margaret Bower; m. 1803 Mary Welch, dau. John.

# 1820 Census

Ezra Burgess[1] 100010/10100
James Fulton[2] 000430/01100
John Conner[3] 210101/11110
Peter Rice[4] 110010/10010
William Marshall[5] 010010/00010
Peter Snay[6] 210110/11110
Antoine Grifor[7] 100010/10100
Joseph Peltier[8] 101110/01001
Julia Labau (Lebeau) 200010/20110
Francis Labau 200110/10100
Madam Dopheny 100011/21110
Joseph Pomereille[9] 100101/00001
Joco Laturna[10] 100010/00010
Gazette Tremblé[11] 010001/22010
Baptist Marsac 000201/11000
Henry Tremblé[12] 000010/00000
Harvey Cook[13] 010010/41010
Jonathan Bennett[14] 200010/00100
Thomas Fowler[15] 000010/00000
Madam Moor 010000/10010
Henry Halsey[16] 000110/00000
Monsieur Junette 000110/00000
Pierre Brandamour[17] 220001/12011
Philip Jarvis 000010/51010
Baptist Dechien 010001/02120
Martin Peckins[18] 000220/00110
Richard Sansberry 110010/10010
Samuel Wilson[19] 100030/00100
Aaron Wheeler 100020/00100
Harry Saunders
Hector Sanford

1. Bought 250 A. land in Utica 1821; d. 1853 or 1858; bur. Curtis Cemetery.
2. Sheriff 1818-1822; bought land at St. Clair hoping to make it county seat.
3. 1765-1857, son Richard and Margaret Bower; m. Alice Thorn; in Harrison by 1810.
4. Voter St. Clair 1823-25.
5. Widower of Sarah Heath; m. Detroit 1825 Cecilia Patrenotre, dau. Nicolas.
6. Prob. a descendant of Pierre Senet.
7. Antoine Greffard, 1794-1873, son Laurence; m. 1815 Teresa Freton.
8. B. 1788, son Alexis; m. Margaret Patrenotre, dau. Nicolas.
9. Prob. Joseph Pominville who lived near Mt. Clemens, though family does not fit.
10. James Letourneau, b. 1793, son of J. Bte; m. 1818 Mary Ann Duchene.
11. Cajetan in Detroit 1795; bought land on Lake St. Clair 1801.
12. Taxpayer Milk River Point 1825.
13. Coroner of Macomb County 1825; signer 1829.
14. John Bennett recorded cattle mark 1827; first blacksmith in Washington.
15. M. 11 Feb. 1822 Mahaly Mou?; voter 1825.
16. Voter 1821; Lt. of Militia 1821; first burial in old cemetery on Gratiot Tpke.
17. Son Jean Philip; m. 1802 Judith Desnoyers; m/2 1823 Judith Tremblay, dau. Augustin.
18. Voted Detroit 1821 and St. Clair 1825.
19. Poss. m. Elizabeth Meloche and dau. b. near St. Clair River 1819.

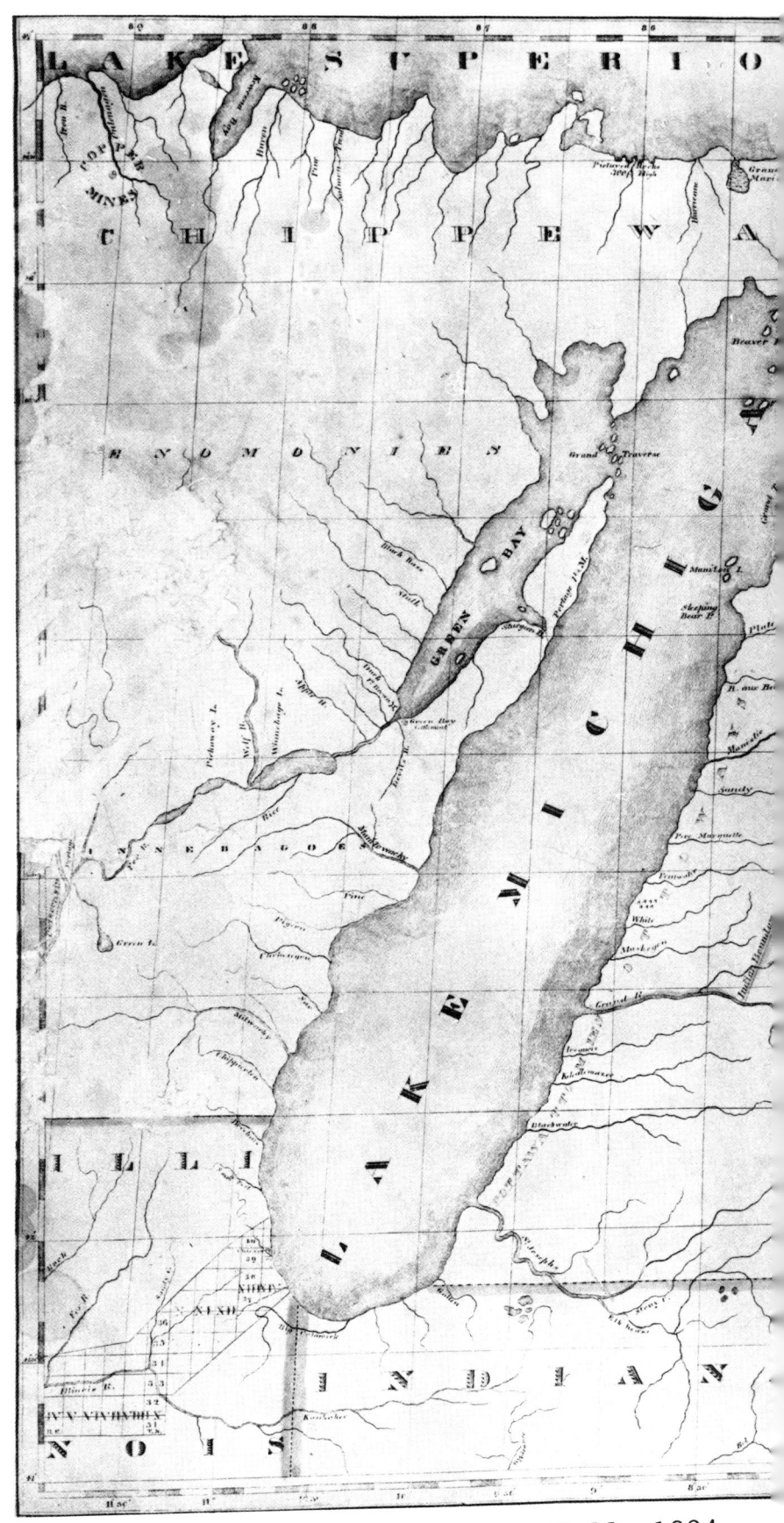

MAP 16.   MICHIGAN, by Philu E. Judd, 1824

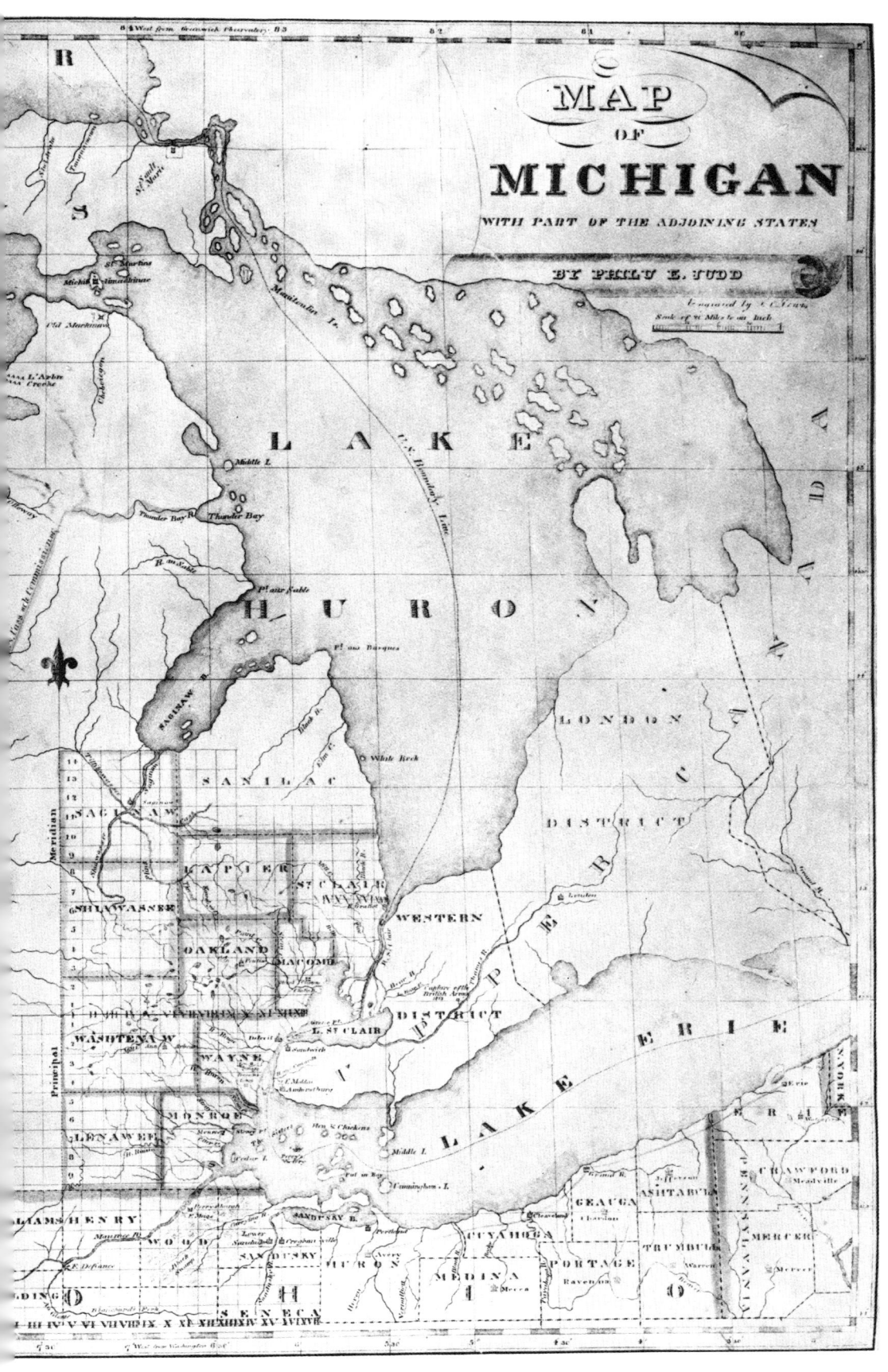

(Courtesy of Burton Historical Collection)

Michigan Censuses 1710-1830

## MONROE COUNTY

Wolcott Laurence[1] 000010/20100
Charles J. Lauman[2] 100100/00200
John Anderson[3] 100301/01201
Oliver Johnson[4] 010010/00100
Laurent Durocher[5] 300110/21011
Elijah West 000200/01100
Moses Preston[6] 000101/10101
James Bentley[7] 100110/11100
Charles Neddo[8] 010100/01000
Reuben Cooley[9] 000100/00100
Harvey Bliss[10] 100010/20010
Joseph Bradish[11] 100011/10101
Louis Couture[12] 010111/01110
Callah Leonard[13] 000100/00110
Andrew Calhoun[14] 000001/01101
Andrew Calhoun, Jr.[15] 001(12)(21)1/00100
Randall S. Rice[16] 000010/00010
William G. Taylor[17] 020010/01010
Daniel Mulholland[18] 200001/11001
Antoine Neddo[19] 210010/01100
John A. Jeffers[20] 100001/01101
Jonas Clark[21] 200111/01101
Henry Disbrow[22] 000101/01010
Benjamin F. Stickney[23] 011211/11001
Joseph Prentiss[24] 020020/01010
William Willson[25] 000100/10101
Ambrois Trembley[26] 001220/00001
John L. Bellair[27] 001220/10010
Colman J. Keeler[28] 120001/11200
Eli Hubbard[29] 310010/10100

1. In county by 1817; County Comm. 1818; Legislative Council 1823.
2. 1795-1870, son James and Marion Griswold; m. 1819 Mary Guy, b. 1798, dau. Anthony.
3. 1771-1840; Scotch; m. Elizabeth Knaggs (1772-1854), dau. George and Rachel Schley.
4. 1784-1868, son Robert & Sarah Blake, Harrington, CT; m. Elizabeth Disbrow, dau.
5. B. 1786, son Laurent; m. 1811 Monique Cosme, dau. Amable; m/2 Agathe /Henry.
6. Voted 1820 Monroe; vote rejected 1823. /Navarre.
7. 1784-1864; Englishman; m. 1816 Amanda Barker; at River Raisin by 1816.
8. B. 1802, son Antoine; m. 1820 Mary Duclos, dau. Anthony.
9. Son Gideon and Elizabeth Mauger; m. 1820 Susanne Cicotte.
10. Hervey, b. 1789, son Israel & Lucinda Kingsley, Royalton, VT; m.1815 Nancy Woodbury.
11. Voter 1821; petitioner 1834.
12. B. ca. 1774, son J. Bte; m. 1795 Teresa Revau-Lajeunesse, dau. Louis.
13. Prob. Nicolas, b. 1797, son Francois; m. 1818 Catherine Valiquet.
14. Signed petition River Raisin 1816; voter 1820.
15. Signed petition River Raisin 1816; voter 1820.
16. Surgeon of the Militia, 2nd Regiment, Monroe Co., 1818.
17. Voter 1820; Col. of Militia 1820, resigned 1823.
18. From Ireland; m. Isabella Egnew at Painted Post, NY 1794; Supervisor Roads 1818.
19. B. 1792, son Antoine; m. 1816 Archange Couture, dau. J. Bte.
20. B. CT 1775; m/1 Susanne Robertson; m/2 Regina Boemier, dau. Francis & Ursula.
21. Vote rejected 1820.
22. 1773-1855; from Trenton, NJ where he m. Sarah Anderson in 1794. She d. 1855.
23. Agent to Pottawatomi and Miami Indians Ft. Wayne 1815-16; voted Detroit 1820;
24. Petitioner 1822; voter 1823. /Monroe 1821.
25. Constable 1821; voter 1823.
26. Petitioner 1807; voted Detroit 1823.
27. B. 1797, son Louis.
28. Petitioner 1822; voter Detroit 1823.
29. Voter 1821-25; JP 1825.

## 1820 Census

Noah Hubbard [1] 300004/32010
William Sibley [2] 000010/10010
Jacques Navarre, 2nd [3] 000110/00010
Robert Navarre, 2nd [4] 300010/00000
Francis Navarre, 2nd [5] 000010/00000
Utro Navarre [6] 000201/01001
Francois Lavoie [7] 210002/10010
Leon Guoin [8] 200010/00010
John King 000100/00100
Joseph Ambrois 000101/00000
Thomas Willson [9] 000110/00000
Alcott C. Chapman [10] 000010/10100
John M. Alford [11] 100100/00100
Luther Harvey [12] 010160/10200
Augustus Thorp [13] 001101/00010
James Sutcliff [14] 110010/20010
Joseph Nephew [15] 300010/10010

Anthony L. Briggs [16] 200010/00010
Abraham Speers [17] 400110/11010
George Alfred [18] 000101/01001
John Bte Cicott, Jr. [19] 000010/01100
Antoine Lasselle [20] 000011/00100
Hemon Alfred [21] 200010/00100
Lewis Bond [22] 220001/21020
Samuel H. Gale/Gate 100110/10100
Louis C. Buotte [23] 200010/20100
Henry Potter 020010/21000
John Bte. Lasselle [24] 110100/00201
Reuben Kelsey [25] 000020/00010
Giles Chapin [26] 000010/10010
Gideon Badger [27] 100001/10001
Luther Parker [28] 210020/00010
Oren Rhodes [29] 000020/20011
Reuben H. Aylsworth [30] 100010/10010

1. Prob. Manoah Hubbard who was in Wayne Co. by 1823; candidate for Legislature 1825.
2. Petitioner 1822; voted 1823-5.
3. B. 1788, son Francois; m. 1814 Catherine Couture.
4. B. 1785, son Francois; m. 1815 Susan Moore.
5. B. 1784, son Francois.
6. Francois Navarre-Utrau, b. 1759; m. 1781 Marie Louise Godet.
7. Son Etienne Lavou; m. 1808 Marie Gouin, dau. Charles.
8. B. 1781, son Charles; m. 1813 Esther Tremblay, dau. Joseph.
9. First Lt. of Militia 1819.
10. Voted 1820-25; petitioner 1826.
11. From NY in 1818; voter 1821; petitioner 1828; to Trenton 1865.
12. B. Burlington, VT 1789; Lt. of Militia 1819; voted 1821; in Detroit 1823.
13. Voted 1820-23; made statement on election fraud 1825.
14. Voter 1821-23; petitioner 1822.
15. Neveu-Francoeur, son Michel; m. 1810 Louise Boemier.
16. Voted 1820-25; Adjutant of Militia 1829; Lt. Col. 1826.
17. Voted 1821; in Wayne Co. 1825.
18. Prob. Alford; Revolutionary War soldier under Gen. Putnam.
19. B. 1783, son J. Bte; m. 1818 Marianne Navarre, dau. Isidore.
20. 1781-1832, son Jacques; m. 1810 Catherine Navarre, dau. Isidore.
21. Voter 1820-21.
22. From NJ; m. Ann Smith, b. 1779; Major of 2nd Regiment 1805.
23. Voted 1823-25; app't Constable but later dismissed in election controversy.
24. 1761-1820, son Nicolas; m. 1787 Margaret Meloche; m. 1790 Catherine Rivard.
25. M. Archange Navarre, b. 1792, dau. Francois.
26. Ensign of Militia 1819.
27. Voted 1821-25.
28. Voted 1821-25.
29. Signed petition 1816 at River Raisin. Voted 1820-25.
30. Voter 1820-21.

Ambrois Charland[1]  000010/30010
Joseph Tunnicliff[2]  200010/00110
Ambrose Stewart  110140/00210
Francis West  100001/01101
James Owen[3]  010010/00010
Samuel Egnew[4]  000014/10100
Isaac P. Skinner[5]  100110/00200
Dominique Pouchette[6]  000010/10100
Isaac Lee[7]  010010/20100
Joseph Farrington[8]  100020/00010
William Stebbins[9]  100100/00100
James Cornell[10]  001200/10100
Charles Martin[11]  000010/10100
David Frary[12]  200020/20010
Samuel Felt[13]  100301/01010
Jean Mary?  000001/00000
Antoine Bougard, Jr.[14]  100010/30100
Joseph Loranger[15]  211230/20110
Gabriel Godfroy, Jr.[16]  801241/10222
John Bte Valiquette[17]  100100/01010
Francis Moton[18]  200001/12010
Wiliam Root  100010/10100
John Robb[19]  310110/12010
John Diver[20]  000010/21001
Elizabeth Tacier  200210/00101
Edward Schofield (col.)  000010/00000
Joseph Jobin[21]  020001/21001
Antoine Mero[22]  000010/11010
Stephen Downing[23]  120101/02001
Francis St. Crant[24]  200010/20010
Nathan Wilcox  300020/20020
Pierre Borrow[25]  320101/20101
Francis Deli[26]  320101/10201
Silas Lewis[27]  200010/10010
Luther Dorriel[28]  200010/10010
Allen Tibbits[29]  100110/00100

1. Son of Alexis; m. 1810 Angelica Martin, b. 1793, dau. James.
2. B. Richfield, NY; m. 1816 Pauline Drouillard, dau. Dominique; went to Detroit.
3. Voter 1823-25.
4. B. Ireland; petitioner in Monroe 1816; coroner 1817.
5. Constable Monroe 1819; voter 1820-25.
6. B. 1793, son Joseph; m. 1819 Mary Ann Bernard-Lajoie.
7. Wife Abigail; son b. Buffalo, NY 1810; JP 1816; Register Monroe 1817.
8. Voter 1820-25; election inspector 1825.
9. Capt. of Militia 1819; voter 1821.
10. Voter 1820, 1825.
11. Voter 1820-25.
12. M. Becket, MA Esther Kingsley; to Ohio 1804; to MI 1817; d. 1820.
13. Voter 1820-21; Sheriff 1821; d. before 11 Dec. 1821.
14. B. 1793, son Antoine; m. 1815 Justine Deloeil.
15. Son of Claude; m. 1809 Rosalie Chabert, dau. Francois.
16. 1783-1848, son Gabriel; m. 1808 Elizabeth May, dau. James.
17. B. 1794, son Francois; m. 1815 Louise Meny, dau. Joseph.
18. Son Francis; m. 1809 Catherine Navarre, dau. John Francis.
19. Petitioner 1816; voter 1820-25.
20. A Mr. Diver was an early mail carrier bet. Cleveland, Erie, and Ft. Meigs(Monroe).
21. 1763-1829, son Louis; m. 1884 Margaret Levry-Martin, dau. Martin.
22. 1776-1837, son Joseph Miron; m. 1810 Felicity Lacelle, dau. J. Bte.
23. Signed petition 1816 at River Raisin; Supervisor of Roads Frenchtown 1818.
24. B. 1786, son J. Bte Sanscrainte; m. 1814 Marie Bourdeau, dau. Joseph.
25. 1772-1835, son Jacques Antoine Baron; m. 1797 Marie Anne Cousineau.
26. Son Francois Michel Deloeil; m. 1793 Anne Ursule Sordelier, dau. Francis.
27. In War of 1812 under Gen. Hull; m. Lydia Chilson; killed by tree 1 Dec. 1853.
28. Voter 1821-25.
29. Voter 1820-25; signer 1823-26.

## 1820 Census

Hubert Lacroix[1] 110040/11110
John Paxton[2] 200010/00010
François Dubois[3] 200010/20010
Joseph Chattelroi[4] 001301/01101
James Robb 011210/10001
John Bobean[5] 110010/00100
Peter Compeau[6] 101300/00100
Richard Goodwin 201401/11001
John Cornish 100110/21100
Levi Collier[7] 210201/00010
James Hazard[8] 010200/11210
John Bte. Rosseau[9] 100100/00100
Alexis St. Crant[10] 200110/00100
John Welsh[11] 100011/00000
André Boudré[12] 300001/10100
Joseph Neddo[13] 310010/01001
Gabriel Lafontain 210010/10010
Louis Gieau 010010/20001
Charles Lafleur 200100/00100
John Bte Laduc[14] 100001/20010
Joseph Greaves/Gieau 300011/21100
Francis Bourdeaux[15] 200110/30110
Stephen Willamy 000001/00000
Etienne Dubois[16] 220001/01001
John Bte Bowoodlan 200001/01010
Christome Velaire[17] 101201/00101
Basile Cousineau[18] 230010/20010
Louis Mominy[19] 110001/21001
Jacque Mominy[20] 000100/00100
John Bte Roe, 2nd[21] 200110/01100
Dominique Roe[22] 000200/20100
Jacques Clothier[23] 000001/00000
Joseph Morass[24] 320210/00010
Daniel Duvalle[25] 200110/10010
Louis Drouillard[26] 100110/00200
Charles Drouillard[27] 000101/01001

1. 1779-1827, son Dominique; m. 1810 Archange Jerome, dau. J. Bte.
2. B. 1788, son Thomas and Geneviève Levitre; m. 1818 Théotiste Lacelle, dau. James.
3. Son Stephen; m. 1792 Margaret Labadie; m. 1823 Susanne Facer.
4. 1762-1831, son Joseph; m. 1794 Archange Dusault.
5. B. 1787, son Joseph; m. 1817 Regina Meny; m. 1820 Louise Nadeau.
6. B. 1796, son Francois; m. 1817 Josette Parnier, dau. Joseph.
7. Voted 1823-25.
8. 1825 election of Monroe Co. held in his house.
9. Rousson, b. 1795, son J. Bte; m. 1817 Margaret Réaume, dau. Joseph.
10. Romain-Sanscrainte, b. 1788, son J. Bte; m. Monique Réaume, dau. Joseph.
11. Vote rejected 1821.
12. Boisdoré, son J. Bte; m. 1816 Mary Saliot, Dau. J. Bte.
13. Son Joseph; m. 1810 Louise Menard; m. 1815 Ursule Gaillard.
14. 1775-1834, son J. Bte; m. 1804 Louise Gaillard, dau. Louis.
15. 1786-1828, son Joseph; m. Geneviève Menard; m. 1822 Agathe Reaume.
16. Son Stephen; m. 1792 Margaret Descomps-Labadie, dau. Alexis.
17. 1762-1822, son Louis Villers-St. Louis; m. 1785 Josette Suzor, dau. Louis.
18. Son Basil; m. 1805 Louise Toupin-Dusault, dau. Francis.
19. Montmeny, b. 1768, son Louis Jean; m. 1798 Margaret Gagnier, dau. James.
20. Montmeny, son Louis; bro. of above; m. 1820 Terese Couture, dau. Louis.
21. Rau, b. 1793, son J. Bte; m. 1816 Geneviève Jacob, dau. John.
22. Rau, b. 1797, son J. Bte; bro. of above; m. 1817 Geneviève Bernard-Soulange, /dau. Joseph.
23. B. 25 Nov. 1781, son René.
24. B. 1781, son Nicolas; m. 1807 Monique Gouin, dau. Francis.
25. B. 1788, son Ignace; m. 1811 Josette Drouillard, dau. Francis.
26. Son Charles; m. 1815 Catherine Bernard, dau. James.
27. B. 1786, son J. Bte; m. 1778 Louise Quesnel, dau. James.

Louis Laforge[1] 020010/30010
Joseph Laforge[2] 110010/22010
John Bte Drouillard[3] 000001/00000
John Mary Robideau[4] 000020/10010
Alexander Rudd 300010/10010
Antoine Guie, Jr.[5] 100100/20100
John Dusa[6] 000100/00100
Pierre Jacob 100010/10100
Nicholas Lapoint[7] 100010/21100
François Navarre[8] 311111/01301
Issadore Navarre[9] 221101/02201
Jaque Navarre[10] 121101/21000
Pierre Bonaventure[11] 100001/10100
Joseph Robert[12] 311101/12010
Francis Menard[13] 110000/12201
Eneas Tuott-Duval[14] 000201/00001

Agat Robert[15] 230200/01201
François Robert[16] 230001/11101
Charles Chovarre, 1st[17] 010101/00101
Ambroise Langlois[18] 010101/01201
Alexis Labadie[19] 010002/00000
Antoine Bougard[20] 020001/00000
John M. Menard[21] 100010/00100
John Dazett[22] 000001/00101
Thomas S. Jones[23] 000110/10200
Robert Navarre[24] 020001/00000
John Bte Major[25] 010011/10010
François Lasselle[26] 110001/30000
Antoine Compeau 000011/00001
Louis Petit[27] 100001/00010
François Fraro[28] 000001/00001
Benjamin Lenfant[29] 000001/00000

1. B. 1784, son Louis; m. 1805 Térèse Tremblay, dau. Joseph.
2. B. 1786, son Louis; bro. of above; m. 1806 Angelique Pare.
3. B. 1755, son J. Bte; m. 1780 Charlotte Drouin; m. 1809 Elizabeth Gagnier.
4. Son Louis, m. 1815 Josette Lebeau, dau. J. Bte.
5. B. 1796, son Antoine; m. 1818 Mary Poulin, dau. Francis.
6. B. 1798, son John Francois; m. 1820 Margaret Montmeny.
7. B. 1791, son J. Bte; m. 1815 Clara Cousineau, dau. Louis.
8. 1763-1826, son Robert; m. 1790 Marie Suzor, dau. Louis Francois.
9. 1768-1835, son Robert; bro. of above; m. 1795 Francoise Labadie, dau. Alexis.
10. B. 1766, son Robert; bro. of above; m. 1800 Basile Lapointe; m. 1823 Marie Laferte.
11. Signed petition 1822.
12. 1766-1834, son Pierre; m. Marie Godet; m. 1798 Louise Duval.
13. B. 1773, son Pierre; m. 1791 Angelique Jacob, dau. Etienne.
14. Ignace Thuot-Duval, 1751-1826, son Thomas; m. 1776 Louise Lebeau.
15. Agathe, widow; dau. J. Bte Réaume; m. 1795 Isadore Robert, son Pierre.
16. 1781-1834, son Pierre; m. 1803 Julia Bourdeau, dau. Joseph.
17. Chauvin, 1737-1821, son Charles; m. Louise Boyer, dau. Joseph.
18. 1761-1826, son Andrew; m. 1794 Susanne Sordelier.
19. 1774-1843, son Pierre.
20. 1762-1828, son Alexis; m. 1792 Térèse Cloutier.
21. B. 1793, son Jean Marie; m. 1818 Monique Beauregard, dau. Antoine.
22. 1746-1836, son Jean; m. 1804 Catherine Roitel, dau. Joseph.
23. B. Montreal 1788, son Robert; m. 1818 Geneviève Cosme, dau. Amable.
24. B. 1765, son Robert; m. 1809 Geneviève Bourdeau, dau. Joseph.
25. To River Raisin 1806, son Etienne; m. 1807 Rose Boemier.
26. Son Jacques; m. 1807 Angelique Godfroy; m. 1810 Clara Cosme.
27. Son Solomon; m. 1810 Susanne Lafontaine, dau. Antoine.
28. Frérot; voted 1825.
29. B. 1778, son Joseph.

# 1820 Census

John Bte Jerome[1] 000012/10101
Catharine L. Couture[2] 001110/10201
Etienne Labeau[3] 110010/20100
Charles Chovarre, 2nd[4] 110001/12010
Joseph Rheume[5] 020201/22211
Francis Tuotte (Thuot) 010001/21101
Mary Lafleur 010100/10001
Thomas Caldwell[6] 100110/00300
Charles Prue, Jr[7] 000110/00100
Thomas Knaggs[8] 100010/21010
Joseph Reuland[9] 120010/10010
Thomas Knowlton[10] 000010/10010
James Moore[11] 000001/00001
John Lawrence[12] 000110/00000
Joseph Bissonnette[13] 201211/02010
John Bte St. Grant[14] 200001/10010
Basile Lajoie[15] 100010/00100
Jeremiah Laurence[16] 010101/00100
John Bronson 000010/11010
John Brown[17] 000010/30100
Stephen Downing, Jr[18] 000200/00100
Rufus Downing[19] 100010/10200
James Knaggs[20] 120002/40010
Felix Mettie[21] 400001/10010
William Brown[22] 110101/11110
George Giles[23] 110111/30010
Elijah Martin[24] 000011/11001
Levi Dexter[25] 010001/00000
Francis Mettie[26] 320010/00010
Samuel Getty[27] 130010/00010
Seth Wells[28] 100101/11110
Lewis Wells[29] 000100/00100
Marque Bobean[30] 110201/10200
Erastus Ferguson[31] 300020/10010

1. 1762-1832; m. Mary Delienes-Belanger (1758-1832).
2. Prob. Catherine Lenfant, dau. Joseph, who m. J. Bte Couture.
3. B. 1792, son Rene; m. 1815 Mary Judith Chauvin, dau. Charles.
4. 1761-1834, son Noel; m. 1790 Susanne Godet, dau. Rene.
5. B. 1772, son J. Bte; m. 1795 Genevieve Suzor, dau. Louis.
6. B. 1788, son William; m. 1817 Mary Anne Lacelle, dau. James.
7. Prou, b. 1798, son Charles; m. 1819 Mary Kickson, dau. John and Sarah Peck.
8. 1782-1831; m. Catherine Pouget, dau. Joseph; Indian interpreter.
9. Voted 1820-23.
10. Voted Monroe 1820-21; in Detroit 1823-25.
11. To River Raisin 1809; petitioner 1816; died 1826.
12. Lieutenant of Militia 1818.
13. B. 1764, son Stephen; m. 1793 Agnes Robert, dau. Anthony.
14. B. 1779, son J. Bte Sanscrainte; m. 1814 Coleta Robert.
15. B. 1777, son Louis; m. 1817 Catherine Bissonett, dau. Joseph.
16. JP 1818; voted 1820-25.
17. Voted 1820-25.
18. Voted 1823-25.
19. Signed petition 1816; voted 1820-25.
20. 1780-1860, son George & Rachel Schley; m. 1805 Jemima Griffen; m/2 Pelagie Robert.
21. Metay, b. 1766, son Joseph; m. 1793 Catherine Lemay, dau. Theophile.
22. M. Angelique Bissonet, b. 1806, dau. Joseph.
23. Voted 1825; Lieut. 1820.
24. Ensign 1820; Lieut. 1821; voted 1820-21.
25. Voted 1821-1823.
26. Metay, b. 1773, son Joseph; m. 1799 Cecile Labadie, dau. Antoine.
27. Voted 1820.
28. Supervisor of Raisinville 1818; voted 1820-23.
29. Captain of Militia 1819; voted 1820-25.
30. Beaubien, son Joseph; m. 1817 Monique Nadeau, dau. Antoine.
31. Voted Detroit 1821; voted Oakland 1823.

Augustus Delore   000001/10010
James McManus[1]   210001/30111
Augustus Lacourse[2]   000001/11010
John Adams   211101/12110
Charles Prue, Sr[3]   020101/10001
Charles Laroch   000001/00000
August C. Lafleur   300020/00020
Louis Bernard[4]   020101/10010
John Bte Revard[5]   000001/00000
John Bte Conjer[6]   200001/12010
Eneas Bouchard[7]   100101/01011
Sarah Dormand[8]   000000/00001
Pierre Robideau   010101/21002
William Preston[9]   000210/00100
Louis Laduc[10]   111201/01101
Louis Laduc, Jr[11]   100020/00200
Augustus Revarrd[12]   200010/10010
Joseph Evon[13]   000212/01010
Antoine Brisette   000001/00000

Alexis Loranger[14]   000111/00000
Barnaby Parker   100011/20010
Edmond S. Rhodes   230010/20010
Samuel Choats[15]   020201/41010
Antoine Robert[16]   000011/00010
Joseph Chamberland[17]   020011/11001
Isaac Robert[18]   100010/10100
Robert Albain   210001/11110
Louis Robideau[19]   110110/40010
Alexis Navarre[20]   200020/20010
Joseph St. Bernard[21]   000011/10201
Francis Cousineau[22]   110010/00101
Joseph Robideau[23]   200101/12110
Joseph Roe[24]   000010/10100
Glote Predom[25]   000010/10101
Tusa Martin[26]   000100/00100
François Reno   110010/30100
Laurent Reno[27]   000100/00100
John Bte Baumée[28]   200010/10100

1. 1776-1829, b. Ireland; m. Honora O'Rorke, dau. Patrick and Bridget.
2. Augustin Rivard-Lacoursiere, b. 1787, son Francis; m. 1811 Susanne Deloeil.
3. Prou, b. 1760, son Francis; m. 1808 Teresa Goyou, dau. William.
4. Son Louis Bernard-Lajoie; m. 1797 Louisa Jacob, m/2 1817 Margaret Robideau.
5. Son Antoine; b. 1785; m. 1830 Eleanor Daudelin.
6. Son Joseph Hus-Cournoyer; m. 1806 Archange Huyet-Champagne.
7. Ignace, son Louis; m. 1797 Magdeleine Campau, dau. Alexis.
8. B. 1776, son Louis; m. 1815 Agnes Chauvin, dau. J. Bte.
9. In MI by 1816; voted 1821-25; signed memorial 1822.
10. B. 1759, son Francis; m. 1788 Cecilia Champagne, dau. Pierre.
11. B. 1789, son of above; m. 1815 Margaret Trudel, dau. Francis.
12. Rivard, b. 1787, son Antoine; m. 1811 Archange Yvon; m/2 1829.
13. Yvon, b. 1754, son Joseph; m. 1783 Margaret Sordelier.
14. Son Augustin; m. 1818 Catherine Tessier, dau. Pierre.
15. JP 1817 for district of Erie; voted 1821-25.
16. 1747-1829, son Antoine; m. 1777 Teresa Drouillard, dau. J. Bte.
17. 1747-1832; m/1 Josephine Moret; m/2 1798 Josephine Larose.
18. 1786-1847, son Antoine; m. 1817 Monique Chamberland, dau. Joseph.
19. B. 1780, son Etienne; m. 1807 Archange Bernard, dau. Joseph.
20. B. 1791, son Jean Marie; m. 1812 Monique Dusault, dau. J. Francois.
21. B. 1759, son William; m. 1816 Genevieve Saucier.
22. B. 1795, son Basil; m. 1816 Mary Robidou, dau. Joseph.
23. B. 1767, son Etienne; m. Catherine Lapointe, b. 1782, dau. J. Bte.
24. Rau, b. 1797, son J. Bte; m. 1819 Genevieve Cousineau, dau. Louis.
25. Claude Prudhomme, b. 1793, son Pierre; m. 1818 Teresa Martin.
26. B. 1797, son Jacques; m. Sophia Auban-Lagarde.
27. B. 1797, son Louis; m. 1819 Adelaide Comparet, dau. Michel.
28. Baumier, son Francois; m. 1814 Colette Drouillard, dau. Nicolas.

# 1820 Census

Pierre Corneau[1] 110001/02010
John Bte Lapoint[2] 100020/22020
John L. Monette[3] 210010/11010
Guililme Lapoint[4] 010210/02100
Pierre Jacob 200010/22010
Louis Bono[5] 010001/11001
Pierre Clothier[6] 010010/31100
Joseph Jacob[7] 110110/11110
Joseph Clothier[8] 110020/01000
Louis Jacob[9] 220010/21010
Dominique Drouillard[10] 010101/00000
Hyacynth Lajoice[11] 210101/22100
Alexis Arcourte[12] 000001/20100
Jacob Martin[13] 010001/01101
Basile Martin[14] 000100/00010
Urna Derouser[15] 020001/01010
Francis Derega-Plant[16] 010201/03110

Newel Valiquette[17] 000100/00100
John Bte Lacourse 110001/21000
Lewis Gagnier[18] 100200/10100
Lewis Gania 000010/31010
Alexis Cousineau[19] 200010/00100
Antoine Lagard[20] 200001/11010
Alexis Gineau 000010/00100
François Lajuiness[21] 200100/00100
John Bte Couture[22] 200010/20100
Joseph Varmet[23] 200010/20100
John Bte Roe, 1st[24] 200101/02101
Israel St. Bernard[25] 000110/00000
Benjamin Cooley[26] 000100/00100
Antoine Lafontaine[27] 100301/01101
Pierre Gagnier[28] 100110/10001
Usta Gagnier[29] 200010/10100
Francis Leonard[30] 020101/10100

1. Son Louis; m. 1801 Catherine Belair; m. 1820 Archange Cousineau.
2. B. 1776, son J. Bte; m. 1808 Margaret Cousineau, dau. Basil.
3. B. 1790, son Michel; m. 1813 Margaret Sanscrainte, dau. J. Bte.
4. B. 1778, son J. Bte; m. 1802 Marie J. Villers-St Louis.
5. Bonneau, b. 1761, son Dominique; m. Ursula and T. Cousineau.
6. B. 1775, son René; m. 1810 Jeanne Villers-St. Louis, dau. Chrysostum.
7. B. 1782, son Etienne; m. 1805 Margaret Bernard-Lajoie, dau. Louis.
8. B. 1783, son René; m. 1818 Catherine Jacob, dau. Jean.
9. B. 1784, son Etienne; m. 1805 Martha Pouget, dau. Joseph.
10. 1764-1824, son J. Bte; m. 1790 Marie J. Laviolette, dau. Etienne.
11. B. 1773, son Louis; m. 1800 Amable Sanscrainte; m. 1806 M. St. Louis.
12. B. 1773, son Alexis Arcouet; m. 1800 Cecile Valcour; m. M. Lagarde.
13. Prob. James 1769-1824; m. 1792 Louise Bernard-Lajoie, dau. Louis.
14. B. 1799, son James; m. 1819 Marie Desanges-Gouin, dau. Francis.
15. Prob. René Theodore Duroseau, son René; m. 1800 Angélique Meloche.
16. Son Pierre Louis Leriger-Laplante; m. 1797 Louise Malet, dau. Louis.
17. Noel, son Francois; m. 1815 Monique Gagnier, dau. James.
18. B. 1793, son James; m. 1816 Clara Menard, dau. Francis.
19. B. 1793, son Louis Basil; m. 1816 Victoire Rau, dau. J. Bte.
20. 1752-1823, son Francis; m. Marie Langevin-Lacroix.
21. B. 1795, son Louis; m. 1816 Louise Leonard, dau. Francis.
22. B. 1787, son J. Bte; m. 1813 Angélique Menard; m. 1830 Angélique Reaume.
23. 1784-1830, son Joseph; m. 1810 Marie Pineau, dau. Joseph.
24. B. 1766, son J. Bte; m. 1790 Margaret Lapointe, dau. J. Bte.
25. B. 1795, son Joseph; m. 1825 Catherine Lafontaine, dau. Antoine.
26. Coulay, b. England 18 Dec. 1793, son Gideon & Elizabeth Mauger.
27. B. 1781; m. 1814 Archange Suzor, dau. Louis.
28. Son James and Mary J. Larchêveque; d. 1834; m. 1815 Veronique Martin, dau. James.
29. Augustus, b. 1788; bro. of above; m. 1810 Angélique Leonard, dau. Francis.
30. B. 1765, son J. Bte; m. 1787 Angelique Couture; m. 1804 Angélique Robidou.

Bateme Gagnier[1] 000010/30100
Joseph Valiquette[2] 110110/00100
Jacques Chovar 000001/00001
John Bte Favero[3] 120010/10010
Joseph Dusa[4] 110010/10100
Louis L. Brisbo 220001/11001
Etienne Duso[5] 000100/00100
Joseph Shattelroe[6] 100111/02001
Antoine Guie, Sr.[7] 200001/10001
Peter St. Grant[8] 2000001/10100
John Bte Bourdeau[9] 001111/03001
Dominique Shattelreau 100101/00100
Medu Labadie[10] 201201/02110
Joseph Duval[11] 110010/32010
Hicynth Laduc[12] 000001/00000
John Bte Suzor[13] 000100/00100
Etienne Duval[14] 101120/10200
Francis Pullah[15] 321202/00010

Andrew J. Diver[16] 000100/00100
Francis Menard[17] 000100/00100
Dominique Suzor[18] 000010/00100
Charles Duvalle 100100/00100
Pierre Bruso[19] 210001/52010
Francis Luso[20] 300010/00100
Pierre Fonier[21] 000001/11001
Antoine Sezeau 100010/00100
Pierre Bourdeau[22] 410010/11110
Michael Compau[23] 000101/10001
François Compau 000100/00100
Ignace Champaigne[24] 020012/00011
Oliver Cooley[25] 210010/00100
Joseph Poupard[26] 000010/01000
André Poupard[27] 000010/01000
Joseph Blanchard 000001/00000
Francis Gondeau[28] 000101/11001
John Bte Rulo[29] 110001/21010

1. Bartholomew, bro. of Pierre; 1782-1828; m. 1810 Archange Leonard, dau. Francis.
2. B. 1790, son Francis; m. 1815 Monique Gagnier, Dau. James.
3. Favreau, son J. Bte; m. 1815 Mary Leonard, dau. Francis.
4. B. 1785, son John Francis Dusualt; m. 1815 Mary Beaudrais, dau. Louis.
5. Son John and bro. of above; m. 1820 Monique Thuot-Duval, dau. Ignace.
6. 1762-1831, son Joseph Chattelereau; m. 1794 Archange Dusault.
7. Guy, son Francis; m. 1793 Angelique Bourdeau.
8. B. 1782, son J. Bte; m. 1812 Veronique Larabel.
9. 1766-1828, son Joseph; m. 1800 Louisa Bousom, dau. Jean Bousom-Gascon.
10. Medard, 1776-1846, son Pierre; m. 1799 Teresa Robert, dau. Antoine.
11. 1784-1840, son Ignace; m. 1804 Catherine Lafontaine, dau. Antoine.
12. Petitioner 1816; voted 1820-25.
13. B. 1796, son J. Bte; m. 1820 Teresa Labadie, dau. Michel.
14. B. 1782, son Ignace, bro. of Joseph above; m. 1811 Louise Bissonnet, dau. Gabriel.
15. Son Francois Poulin; m. 1803 Marie Lavergne, dau. Louis.
16. Poss. mail carrier bet. Cleveland, Erie, and Fort Meigs (Monroe).
17. B. 1799, son Joseph; m. 1820 Basille Suzor, dau. Louis.
18. B. 1792, son Louis; m. 1820 Monique Duval, dau. Ignace.
19. 1772-1832, son Pierre Brancheau; m. 1808 Margaret Rau, dau. J. Bte.
20. Loson, signed petition 1816; voted 1821.
21. 1778-1838, son Pierre Fournier; m. 1803 Margaret Bousom, dau. John.
22. 1781-1834, son Joseph; m. 1803 Genevieve Sordelier, dau. Francois.
23. Prob. son of Paul Alexander, b. 1753.
24. B. 1774 in Grosse Pointe, son Pierre.
25. Son Gideon; m. 1809 Archange Yax, dau. J. Bte.
26. B. 1789, son andrew; m. 1820 Angelique Nadeua, dau. Martin.
27. B. 1787, bro. of above; m. 1819 Theotiste Nadeau, dau. Martin.
28. Gondon, son Julien; m. 1805 Catherine Langlois; m. 1811 Elizabeth Fontaine.
29. Son Joseph Rouleau; m. 1806 Monique Senecal, dau. Antoine.

1820 Census

Alexis Solo[1]  110300/13001
Tusa Solo[2]  100100/00010
Joseph Neddo[3]  000100/10010
Dominique Sauture  000010/10100
James Bourke[4]  100101/22101
David Simmons[5]  411301/21210
Joseph Montour[6]  200010/10100
Joseph Beauzum[7]  110010/30010
Martin Neddo[8]  110201/02001
Alexis Neddo[9]  000010/00100
John Bte Lature[10]  000010/21010
Joseph Soudriette[11]  100001/00010

François Laviolette[12]  000001/00000
Charles Blanchard[13]  000110/00010
Pierre DeChien[14]  120010/00010
Platt Navarre[15]  30010/30100
Etienne Couteur[16]  100010/30100
Claude Couteure[17]  200010/30010
Louis Couture[18]  010100/10100
Joseph Phelps  200010/10100
John Clock[19]  000010/00100
David Clock  200100/00100
Paul Navarre[20]  000010/11010

1. 1763-1818, son Claude; m. 1791 Marie Payet, dau. Joseph.
2. B. 1794, son Alexis; m. 1818 Genevieve Bourg/ke, dau. James.
3. B. 1794, son Antoine; m. 1816 Angelique Vermet; m. 1819 Marie Solo.
4. James Bourg m. Margaret Coron.
5. Voted 1821-25; m. Margaret Robb or Rapp; son J. Bte b. 1802.
6. Petitioner 1822.
7. Poss. Joseph Amable Bousom-Gascon, b. 1788, son Jean; m. Marie Nadeau.
8. Nadeau, son J. Bte; m. Marie Reaume, dau. J. Bte.
9. B. 1789, son Martin; m. 1820 Pelagie Bissonet, dau. Joseph.
10. 1780-1833, son Francois; m. 1811 Agathe Bourdeau, dau. Joseph.
11. B. 1788, son Francois; m. 1803 Ursule Boemier, dau. Francois.
12. 1775-1828, son Etienne.
13. Voted 1821-23.
14. 1774-1831, son Pierre; m. 1806 Angelique Yvon.
15. Alexis Platt Navarre, son J. M.; m. 1814 Teresa Beauregard.
16. B. 1787, son J. Bte; m. 1811 Margaret Lebeau; m. 1825 Julia Baril.
17. B. 1777, bro. of above; m. 1805 Susanne Robert; m. 1814 Catherine Chamberlan.
18. B. 1796, son Louis; m. 1819 Julia Reaume, dau. J. Bte.
19. Signed petition 1823; voted 1825.
20. B. 1798, son Francois; m. 1818 Teresa Beaubien, dau. Joseph.

BROWN COUNTY

John Law  220433/41120
Lewis Rouse  100011/10100
Louis Grignon  310131/13110
Piere Grignon  011012/00101
Joseph Jordan/ain  100010/31110
John Jacobs  100010/01000
Bazzel Larock  000001/31010
John Ambroziene  000010/00100
Amab Duroshee(er)  110100/00100
John B. Labord  120101/10100
Joseph Dusharm (Ducharme)  310001/
Charles Rider  000110/00000
John McCarty  000210/00000
Robert Irwin  000320.00100

George Johnston  310010/11010
Louis Bordone (Bourdon)  000010/01010
Pierre Province  211111/11010 (Provençal)
Joseph Owle  100012/20100 (Houll)
Piere Province  000100/00100 (Provençal)
Augustin Bonter  000101/22100
Lewis Dubey  310011/41000
Battell Mee  010000/00100 (Barthelmy ---)
Pierre Grignon, Jr.  100311/02100
Richard Pricket  111001/30000
Battes (Bte) Brodder  110001/30000
Battes (Bte) Jovin  000010/10100
Peter Holrock  000011/00000
Benjamin Lecuyer  110200/11000

Battes Perrygore (Bte Pellegore) 400001/10000
Augustine Tebo (Thibault) 200020/00200
James Brisk/h 000301/11110
Gabriel Robbe (Rabbi) 100001/22010
Perish Bruno 100010/30000
Betsy Sanders 000001/10100
James Porlier 101211/10000
Alex Garlopee (Gardipier) 320020/22000
Augustine Leboff 000010/10000
Charles Reome 000001/00000
Louis Gravitte (Gravelle) 100012/00310
Daniel Heydorn 000110/00010
Benjamin Smith 000100/00000
Robert Clark 000001/00000
P. Mushow - no data
George Forkee (Fortier) 010001/00000
Battes (Bte) Saintrock 000001/20100
Francis Meldrum 000001/20000
Chas. Bovair 000001/00000
Battes (Bte) Longwere 000001/00000
Matthew Erwin 100001/10200
Chas. L. Cass 000(23)(50)0/11000
Wm Toulson 000110/00100
Hillery Bruno 000010/00010
James Leonard 000010/00000
John Culberson 000(16)(53)0/00010
Ming Villon 000190/00000
Spencer Monday 000010/10110
Wm. Liscomb 100000/00110

Jas. Vanvotenburg 200000/00010
Daniel Murphy 000000/00010
Jas. Hancock 100000/00010
Philip Boyle 200000/20010
Wm. Martin 00000/00010
Wm. Purvis 00000/00010
John Coleman - no data
Mrs. Littleton 00000/00001
Britton Evans 202(25)(46)3/20110
Daniel McNeal 300000/10010
Francis Wheeler 00000/00100
Jas. Williams 00000/00100
Wm. McLaughlin 00000/00100
Elijah Shockley 00000/00010
Walter Furlong 00000/00110
B. Parks 10000/10110
S. W. Hunt 100(30)(43)0/00110
George H. Grovenor 003(51)(26)0/00000
John B. Williamson 110000/00100
E. B. Roach 00000/00100
Andr. Lewis - no data
Dan'l Curtis 220(23)(36)16/10010
Ezekiel Harris 00000/10010
Joseph Glass 00000/20001
Wm. Beasley 100000/30001
Jas. Lafitte 00000/00010
Wm. Whistler 310(32)(45)0/50151
Augustine Grignon 310140/11010
COMPANY 122(36)(31)0/00012

## VILLAGE OF PRAIRIE DU CHIEN, CRAWFORD COUNTY

Peter Sharifoo (Chalifoux) 100030/21000
John L. Finley 210032/10100
Peter Lassoe (Lessard) 100220/00100
John W. Johnson 000021/20000
Charles Lappoint 001111/11200
Francis Bouthillier 000101/00000
Francis Gallarnow 000010/21101
Jacynth St. Cier 100111/300000
Robert Cooke 000081/00000
Joseph Crealy (Crelie) 001121/00100
Oliver Sharia (Cherrier) 300110/00100
Joseph Sney (Sent) 000001/00100
Peter Coviel (Courville) 010010/22010
Joseph Borette (Barette) 101110/01000
Thomas McNeir 100110/01100
Joseph Rolette 100(41)11/01100
Michael Brisbois 211513/40301
Benjamin Cadot 000010/10100

Benjamin Roy 000100/10100
Scott Campbell 010111/20000
Augustine Rock 120010/11000
John Akane 200100/00000
Theodore Loupian (Lupien) 100020/10100
Antwain Lashepell(Lachapelle) 200011/21110
J. H. Lockwood 000183/00000
Louis Jollie 000010/20000
Nicholas Bolvine 000212/00100
Fort Crawford: 131 Troops US Army
Wilfred Owens 000321/00000
Jacob Barthomy 100001/20010
John Simpson 010111/01010
Francis Lappoint 221201/01010
John Marriequarrie (Quéret) 01000/01010
Peter Larivier 121301/100010
Francis Provow (Provost) 000010/31010
Strange Powers 000020/20100

Peter Lappoint 101410/20010
Francis Periaw 210010/00110
John Marie Cardinel 320001/00110
Baptiste Talbaier 000100/00100
Francis Vurtify (Vertefeuille) 010010/20010
Joseph Revor (Rivard) 200100/00100
Francis Shenvair 430110/00010 (Chenevert)
Alexander Devrie 100010/10000
Denis Courtway (Courtois) 001201/12001

Charles Menor (Menard) 000011/00000
Mary Laffontisey 101300/00101
John Limery 000020/00100 (Lemery)
John Johnson 000001/00001
Augustine A. Blier 010221/20100
Lewis Devotion 000030/00000
Jessie Shull 000020/00000
Tunis Bell 000010/00000

Note: a slip on microfilm within Wayne County lists Pierre and Augustin Grignon; these are almost certainly in Brown County (Hansen).

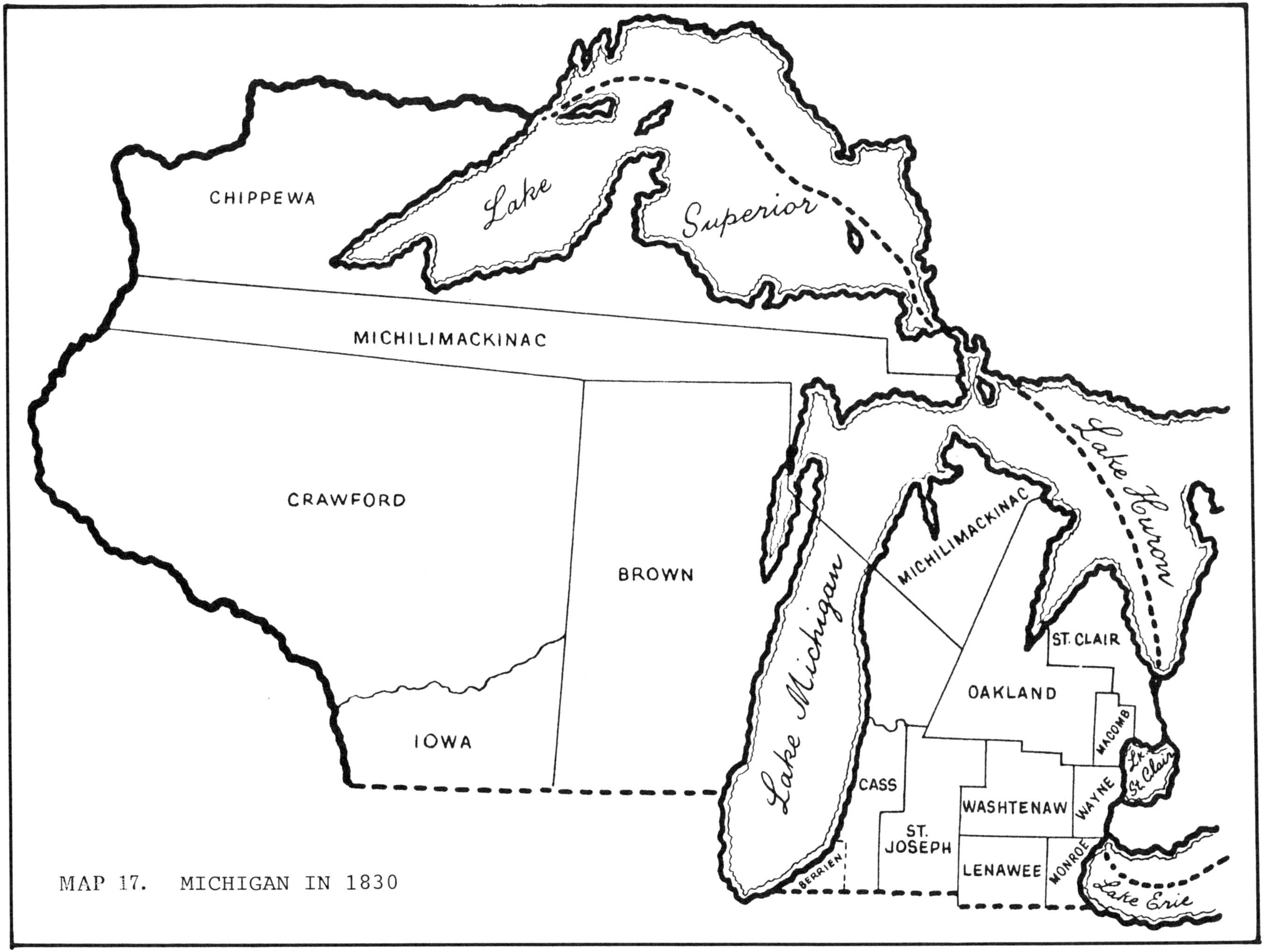

MAP 17. MICHIGAN IN 1830

## 1827 WAYNE COUNTY: MICHIGAN TERRITORIAL CENSUS

In 1827 Wayne County, which occupied the same area which it has today, was subdivided into the City of Detroit and eight townships, whose limits are indicated in the map below. A Territorial census taken that year counted all the county's population into five categories: head of family, white males under 21 years, white males over 21 years, white females, and colored persons. Returns from the City of Detroit, within the District allotted to B. H. F. Witherell, were published as a special folding chart in *Michigan Pioneer and Historical Collections* 12:461 (1887). Returns for the rest of the county were published in the *Detroit Society for Genealogical Research Magazine* 19:51-57. They were copied by Mrs. Edgar M. Montgomery and Mrs. Raymond Millbrook, who also prepared the map. If enumerations were also made in other areas of Michigan in 1827, these are not extant.

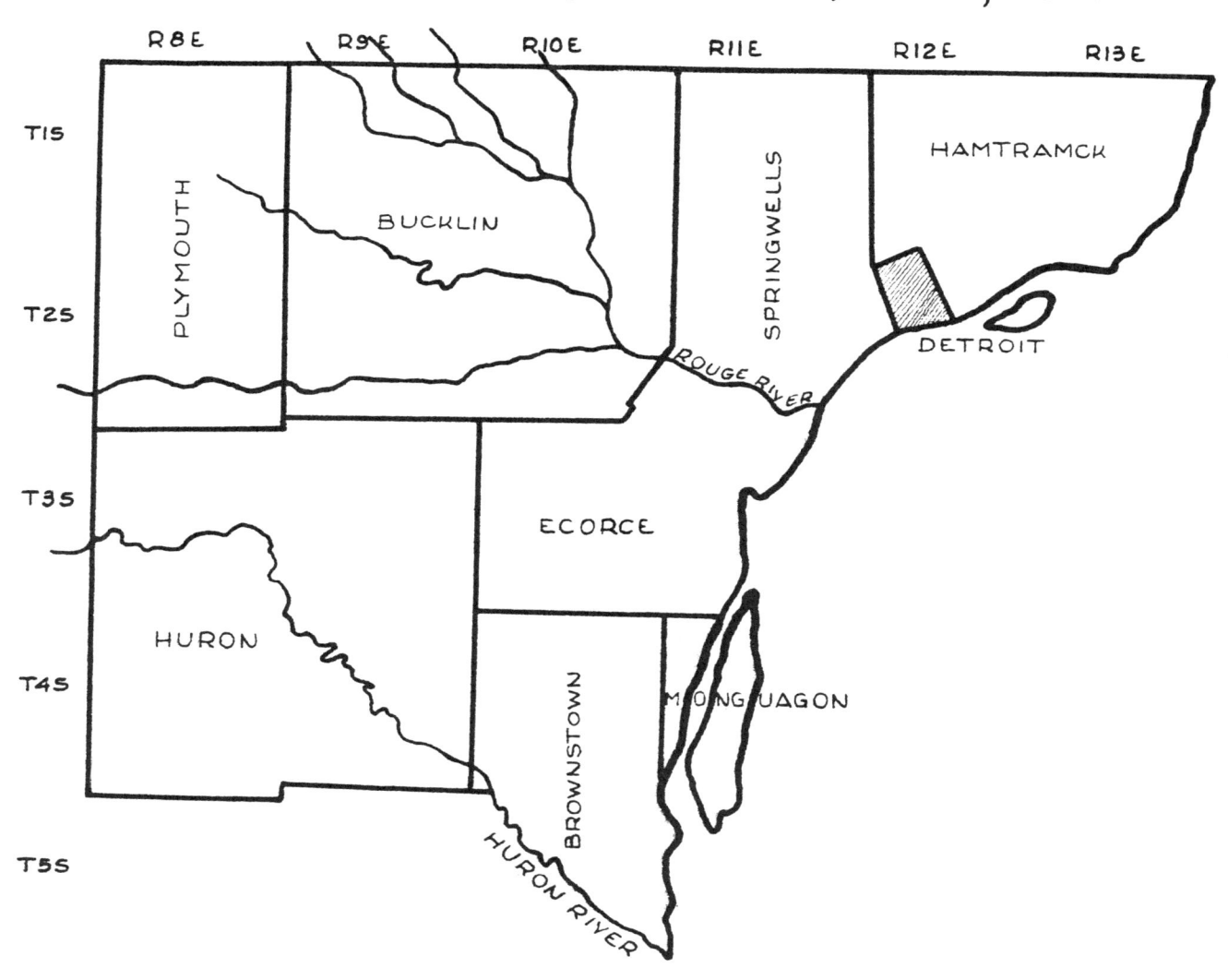

MAP 18.   TOWNSHIP MAP OF WAYNE COUNTY, 1827

## WAYNE COUNTY

Categories are: Heads of Family, White males -25, White males 25+, and Colored

### MONGUAGON TOWNSHIP
Assessors: Manoah Hubbard, Gardner Brown, Artemus Hosmer

|  | | | | |  | | | | |
|---|---|---|---|---|---|---|---|---|---|
| James Chittendon | 1 | 3 | 1 | 0 | Robert Harris | 0 | 0 | 1 | 0 |
| William Keith | 4 | 4 | 2 | 0 | David Lull | 1 | 4 | 4 | 1 |
| Richard Smith | 2 | 1 | 2 | 4 | Aaron Budd | 3 | 0 | 3 | 0 |
| Joseph Simpson | 1 | 2 | 3 | 0 | Andrew Crawford | 2 | 0 | 4 | 0 |
| Manoah Hubbard | 2 | 12 | 4 | 0 | Hannah Bates | 3 | 0 | 5 | 0 |
| Joseph B. Leet | 1 | 2 | 3 | 0 | David Davis | 1 | 0 | 3 | 0 |
| Hart Warren | 0 | 1 | 0 | 0 | Martin Dunning | 0 | 4 | 0 | 0 |
| J. Rusto | 0 | 0 | 2 | 0 | Samuel Hall | 0 | 2 | 0 | 0 |
| William McCombs | 2 | 0 | 4 | 0 | Benj. Dewitt | 1 | 0 | 5 | 0 |
| Samuel Smith | 3 | 0 | 2 | 0 | Francis Hicks | 0 | 0 | 1 | 0 |
| John A. Rucker | 2 | 0 | 6 | 0 | Daniel N. Smith | 1 | 0 | 1 | 0 |
| Christopher Hastarett | 5 | 0 | 4 | 0 | Artimus Hosmer | 3 | 4 | 4 | 0 |
| Abram Speer | 2 | 0 | 1 | 0 | Alvin Chase | 0 | 0 | 2 | 0 |
| Polly Northrop | 2 | 0 | 4 | 0 | Henry Lawlitz | 1 | 0 | 2 | 0 |
| Richard Goodwin | 2 | 0 | 0 | 0 | Elihu Ward | 1 | 0 | 2 | 0 |
| Joseph Hammond | 1 | 1 | 2 | 0 | Abram C. Truax | 2 | 5 | 8 | 1 |
| Gardner Brown | 1 | 0 | 5 | 0 | | | | | |

### HAMTRAMCK TOWNSHIP
Assessors: Louis Beaufait, John Grant, William Little

|  | | | | |  | | | | |
|---|---|---|---|---|---|---|---|---|---|
| Antoine Reneau | 2 | 2 | 2 | 0 | Lambert Chauvin | 0 | 1 | 2 | 0 |
| Joseph John, Sr. | 2 | 1 | 7 | 0 | George Washington | 0 | 1 | 0 | 2 |
| Joseph John, Jr. | 1 | 1 | 2 | 0 | --- Chatterdon | 1 | 1 | 2 | 0 |
| James Allard, Sr. | 3 | 1 | 2 | 0 | Antone Boye(r) | 0 | 1 | 2 | 0 |
| Louis Allard | 2 | 2 | 3 | 0 | Louis St. Lorent | 0 | 1 | 0 | 0 |
| Joseph Furton | 2 | 1 | 2 | 0 | John Grant | 4 | 2 | 6 | 0 |
| James Allard, Jr. | 4 | 1 | 4 | 0 | Louis Duprat | 1 | 1 | 1 | 0 |
| Thomas Noxon | 0 | 2 | 1 | 0 | John Kerby | 2 | 1 | 2 | 0 |
| Pierre St. George | 2 | 2 | 6 | 0 | John Tramblé | 5 | 1 | 3 | 0 |
| Joseph Reneau | 4 | 1 | 3 | 0 | William Little | 2 | 1 | 4 | 0 |
| Leon Varnier | 3 | 1 | 2 | 0 | John B. Chauvin | 1 | 1 | 1 | 0 |
| Charles Varnier | 0 | 1 | 1 | 0 | Joseph Lafauret(fôret) | 2 | 1 | 2 | 0 |
| Mary Duchine | 0 | 0 | 1 | 0 | Pierre Tremblé | 6 | 1 | 4 | 0 |
| Robert Varnier | 2 | 1 | 2 | 0 | Louis Griffarre | 2 | 2 | 6 | 0 |
| François Thibaut | 2 | 2 | 5 | 0 | Pierre Chauvin | 2 | 1 | 2 | 0 |
| Thomas Willet | 1 | 2 | 1 | 0 | Baptiste Dupré | 0 | 1 | 3 | 0 |
| John B. Tramblé | 2 | 1 | 4 | 0 | Baptiste St. Aubin | 0 | 1 | 0 | 0 |
| Henry Tramblé | 1 | 1 | 3 | 0 | Pierre Pichet | 4 | 1 | 2 | 0 |
| Louis Tramblé | 2 | 1 | 6 | 0 | Vangille Tramblé | 2 | 1 | 2 | 0 |
| Magdelaine Tramblé | 0 | 0 | 1 | 0 | François Allard | 1 | 1 | 1 | 0 |
| François Forton | 0 | 3 | 6 | 0 | Charles Laferté | 4 | 0 | 2 | 0 |
| Charles Griffard | 0 | 2 | 1 | 0 | Thomas Tramblé | 6 | 1 | 7 | 0 |

## 1827 Wayne County

|  | | | | |  | | | | |
|---|---|---|---|---|---|---|---|---|---|
| Simon Chauvin | 2 | 1 | 5 | 0 | Joseph B. Campau | 1 | 1 | 3 | 0 |
| John B. Garrand | 0 | 1 | 3 | 0 | Whitmore Knaggs | 1 | 1 | 1 | 0 |
| Esquire Aldridge | 3 | 1 | 3 | 0 | Louis Beaufait | 3 | 1 | 4 | 0 |
| Joseph Dubé | 3 | 1 | 5 | 0 | Fanny Parry | 2 | 1 | 2 | 0 |
| Abraham Fournier | 5 | 1 | 3 | 0 | John Meldrum | 3 | 1 | 5 | 0 |
| John B. Séguin | 1 | 1 | 1 | 0 | François Mettiz | 1 | 1 | 2 | 0 |
| Ignase Séguin | 0 | 1 | 1 | 0 | John L. Leib | 3 | 2 | 3 | 0 |
| Pierre Séguin | 2 | 1 | 3 | 0 | Alexander Deyarmand | 3 | 2 | 3 | 0 |
| Louis Maurin | 2 | 1 | 2 | 0 | Maurise Moran | 2 | 2 | 8 | 0 |
| Leon F. Rivard | 0 | 1 | 1 | 0 | Benoît Cappotton (Chapoton) | 1 | 2 | 6 | 0 |
| Robert Tramblé | 2 | 1 | 1 | 0 | Robert Stead, Sr. | 1 | 4 | 0 | 0 |
| Joseph Tramblé, Jr. | 3 | 2 | 4 | 0 | Daniel LeRoy | 3 | 1 | 5 | 0 |
| John B. Peltier | 1 | 1 | 2 | 0 | Joseph Renau | 0 | 1 | 2 | 0 |
| Henry Conner | 4 | 3 | 4 | 0 | Gabriel Chene | 2 | 5 | 8 | 0 |
| Robert Marsac | 1 | 1 | 0 | 0 | James Campau, Sr. | 0 | 2 | 2 | 0 |
| Gagetan Marsac, Sr. | 1 | 1 | 1 | 0 | James Campau, Jr. | 3 | 1 | 2 | 0 |
| Gagetan Marsac, Jr. | 1 | 1 | 2 | 0 | Antoine LaLansette | 0 | 2 | 1 | 0 |
| Nicola Chauvin | 0 | 1 | 2 | 0 | Edward LaLansette | 3 | 2 | 1 | 0 |
| William Forsith | 0 | 1 | 0 | 0 | François St. Aubin | 3 | 3 | 8 | 0 |
| Sol L. Bignal | 0 | 1 | 2 | 0 | Obery Hokins | 3 | 2 | 4 | 0 |
| George Moran | 0 | 1 | 3 | 0 | James Witherald | 3 | 1 | 3 | 1 |
| Baptiste Dulac | 1 | 1 | 3 | 0 | Louis Perau | 1 | 1 | 2 | 0 |
| Joseph Ellard | 2 | 2 | 6 | 0 | Michel Monette | 1 | 1 | 1 | 0 |
| Phillip Tenior | 0 | 1 | 0 | 1 | John Cahoon | 0 | 1 | 1 | 0 |
| Henry Hudson | 3 | 7 | 4 | 1 | Joseph Thibeau | 0 | 1 | 3 | 0 |
| Michel Rivard | 3 | 2 | 3 | 0 | Abraham Wendle | 2 | 1 | 2 | 0 |
| Leon Rivard | 3 | 4 | 4 | 0 | Gabriel St. Aubin | 0 | 1 | 2 | 0 |
| Pierre Rivard | 1 | 5 | 6 | 0 | William Baity | 0 | 1 | 0 | 0 |
| Louis Goulette | 1 | 1 | 6 | 0 | François Petre | 5 | 2 | 4 | 0 |
| Ambroize Tramblé | 0 | 1 | 0 | 0 | Leon Chauvin | 0 | 1 | 2 | 0 |
| Pierre N. Gouin | 3 | 1 | 5 | 0 | Baptiste Chauvin, Jr. | 1 | 1 | 2 | 0 |
| Charles N. Gouin | 4 | 2 | 5 | 0 | Michel Duprax | 2 | 1 | 5 | 0 |
| Bazile Courtier | 0 | 1 | 3 | 0 | Charles Chauvin | 0 | 1 | 1 | 0 |
| Pierre Bonhomme | 0 | 1 | 0 | 0 | Louis Dupray | 4 | 3 | 2 | 0 |
| Joseph Socier | 0 | 1 | 0 | 0 | Elizabeth St. John | 2 | 1 | 4 | 0 |
| François Marsac | 0 | 1 | 1 | 0 | Louis Desaulniers | 1 | 1 | 3 | 0 |
| William Hattin | 0 | 1 | 1 | 0 | Pierre Delorme | 1 | 2 | 3 | 0 |
| Joseph Tremblé, Sr. | 2 | 3 | 2 | 0 | François Rivard | 1 | 3 | 3 | 0 |
| George Laforge | 0 | 1 | 1 | 0 | Leon F. Rivard | 0 | 1 | 1 | 0 |
| Dominique Griffarre | 0 | 1 | 2 | 0 | Touissant Chêne | 4 | 2 | 3 | 0 |
| John B. Durette | 0 | 3 | 4 | 0 | Pierre Chêne | 0 | 1 | 0 | 0 |
| Isidore Maurin | 2 | 3 | 5 | 0 | Antoine Denduren | 1 | 1 | 2 | 0 |
| Victor Morrass | 2 | 4 | 3 | 0 | Peter Vanevery | 4 | 3 | 3 | 0 |
| Abraham Edwards | 4 | 4 | 7 | 0 | Pierre Séguin | 1 | 1 | 2 | 0 |
| John Lawson | 4 | 5 | 8 | 0 | Louis Chapotton | 1 | 2 | 4 | 0 |
| William Cook | 4 | 3 | 4 | 1 | John B. Campau | 1 | 1 | 1 | 0 |
| John B. Séguin | 4 | 1 | 4 | 0 | Widow Boye(r) | 2 | 2 | 1 | 1 |
| Charles White | 0 | 1 | 1 | 0 | Henry St. Bernard | 0 | 1 | 0 | 0 |
| George Nelson | 0 | 1 | 7 | 0 | Charles Gouin | 0 | 2 | 1 | 0 |
| John Martin | 3 | 1 | 4 | 0 | René Marsac | 2 | 1 | 8 | 0 |

|  | | | | |  | | | | |
|---|---|---|---|---|---|---|---|---|---|
| Louis Campau | 2 | 1 | 2 | 0 | Ignase Bourdignon | 1 | 3 | 3 | 0 |
| Henry Chappoton | 4 | 2 | 2 | 0 | James O. Lewis | 2 | 1 | 3 | 0 |
| François Griffard | 5 | 1 | 4 | 0 | Pierre Dequindre | 0 | 1 | 3 | 0 |
| Coleman Funston | 2 | 1 | 1 | 0 | Charles Moran | 1 | 2 | 2 | 0 |
| Thomas Knapp | 2 | 1 | 2 | 0 | Richard Jones | 1 | 1 | 2 | 0 |
| Pascal Potvain | 0 | 1 | 4 | 0 | Joseph Spencer | 0 | 1 | 0 | 0 |
| Ellis Doty | 4 | 1 | 2 | 0 | Henry Dean | 3 | 4 | 2 | 0 |
| Louis LeDuc | 1 | 2 | 1 | 0 | George Dunks | 1 | 5 | 1 | 0 |
| Julien Gagnier | 4 | 1 | 1 | 0 | Thimothy Dequindre | 0 | 1 | 2 | 0 |
| Dominique Thomas | 3 | 1 | 3 | 0 | Lambert Thibaudau | 1 | 2 | 6 | 0 |
| Antoine Rivard | 4 | 1 | 6 | 0 | Pierre Condelle | 0 | 1 | 1 | 0 |
| Antone Neveux | 1 | 0 | 4 | 0 | Baptiste Baubien | 1 | 1 | 5 | 0 |
| Charles Delisle | 3 | 1 | 2 | 0 | Antoine Baubien | 4 | 1 | 4 | 0 |
| Conrad Seek | 2 | 2 | 2 | 0 | Charles Trowbridge | 2 | 2 | 3 | 0 |
| Beriah Wm. Mirl | 3 | 1 | 2 | 0 | John Hunt | 3 | 1 | 3 | 0 |
| Mary Comparet | 0 | 0 | 3 | 0 | B. F. Larned | 2 | 1 | 3 | 0 |
| Louis Moran | 0 | 2 | 4 | 0 | | | | | |

## BROWNSTOWN TOWNSHIP
Assessors: Jacob Knox, David Smith, William Hazard

|  | | | | |  | | | | |
|---|---|---|---|---|---|---|---|---|---|
| John Sturgis | 3 | 1 | 4 | 0 | Garrett Combs | 1 | 2 | 2 | 0 |
| John Hilhouse | 0 | 1 | 0 | 0 | Ahil Aspinwall | 4 | 1 | 3 | 0 |
| Moses Roberts | 1 | 1 | 4 | 0 | Arthur Rourk | 3 | 1 | 3 | 0 |
| Truman Bears | 3 | 3 | 4 | 0 | Stephen Hilbert | 0 | 1 | 0 | 0 |
| Seth Dunham | 2 | 3 | 2 | 0 | James Witt | 1 | 1 | 2 | 0 |
| Elizabeth Walker | 1 | 2 | 4 | 0 | Rupard Long | 1 | 1 | 3 | 0 |
| John Canton | 0 | 1 | 0 | 0 | Hyram A. Truax | 2 | 1 | 3 | 0 |
| David Clark | 3 | 1 | 1 | 0 | Benjamin Finch | 2 | 1 | 1 | 0 |
| John Meloche | 4 | 1 | 2 | 0 | John Conrad | 0 | 1 | 2 | 0 |
| Martha Wells | 7 | 0 | 5 | 0 | Aelna Climax | 3 | 2 | 2 | 0 |
| Joseph Pulsopher | 6 | 4 | 2 | 0 | Geo. Clark | 5 | 2 | 5 | 0 |
| Hugh Bingham | 1 | 1 | 1 | 0 | Elias Vruland | 1 | 2 | 2 | 0 |
| Ephram Bears | 0 | 1 | 2 | 0 | Samuel Vruland | 2 | 3 | 1 | 0 |
| Jason Whirlslin | 2 | 1 | 2 | 0 | Jacob Knox | 1 | 2 | 3 | 0 |
| Stephen Mauansau | 6 | 7 | 4 | 0 | David Smith | 2 | 1 | 4 | 0 |
| Glacid Campau | 3 | 2 | 5 | 0 | William Hazard | 2 | 1 | 1 | 0 |
| Joseph Tamisant | 2 | 2 | 1 | 0 | Benjamin Riggle | 0 | 1 | 1 | 0 |
| Bazul Bondy | 1 | 1 | 3 | 0 | James Vruland | 0 | 1 | 3 | 0 |
| Joseph Bondy | 2 | 7 | 0 | 0 | Jacob Vruland | 0 | 4 | 0 | 0 |
| James Knap | 0 | 2 | 1 | 0 | William Fletcher | 2 | 2 | 3 | 0 |
| --- Tyler | 2 | 1 | 3 | 0 | Elias Long | 0 | 1 | 1 | 0 |
| William Williams | 0 | 1 | 1 | 0 | Garret Vruland | 2 | 1 | 4 | 0 |
| Moses J. Hill | 4 | 1 | 4 | 0 | Stephen Alazell | 0 | 0 | 0 | 4 |
| Blakley Thirsten | 3 | 1 | 3 | 0 | George Ludson | 0 | 0 | 0 | 3 |
| Jason Thirsten | 1 | 2 | 2 | 0 | Garrit Vruland | 2 | 1 | 4 | 0 |
| John Haydin | 3 | 2 | 6 | 0 | | | | | |

## BUCKLIN TOWNSHIP
Assessors: Joseph Hanchett, Henry Wells, William McCarty, Leon G. Harrison

|  | | | | |  | | | | |
|---|---|---|---|---|---|---|---|---|---|
| Elisha Mudg | 1 | 1 | 2 | 0 | William McCarty | 4 | 2 | 4 | 0 |
| Hanson Thomas | 5 | 1 | 4 | 0 | Robert H. Abbott | 1 | 1 | 1 | 0 |
| Aaron Thomas | 4 | 2 | 3 | 0 | David Rider | 3 | 1 | 4 | 0 |
| Francis Lanon | 4 | 1 | 2 | 0 | James Dunn | 5 | 1 | 2 | 0 |
| Francis Dumay | 2 | 1 | 4 | 0 | John Rodenbough | 0 | 1 | 2 | 0 |
| John Buckley | 1 | 1 | 4 | 0 | Peter Rodenbough | 0 | 1 | 2 | 0 |
| Henry Cramer | 3 | 1 | 4 | 0 | William Smyth | 0 | 1 | 2 | 0 |
| Thomas Chadwick | 1 | 1 | 1 | 0 | Ruben Stark | 0 | 1 | 0 | 0 |
| John Cramer | 2 | 2 | 1 | 0 | George Durfee | 2 | 1 | 5 | 0 |
| George Brown | 2 | 2 | 3 | 0 | John J. Andrews | 7 | 2 | 3 | 0 |
| Elijah Mudg, Jr. | 2 | 1 | 3 | 0 | John Griswold | 1 | 1 | 1 | 0 |
| Elijah Mudg | 1 | 1 | 3 | 0 | Richard Joslin | 4 | 1 | 1 | 0 |
| Margaret Bucklin | 4 | 3 | 3 | 0 | Thomas Harper | 1 | 2 | 1 | 0 |
| Daniel Tuttle | 2 | 1 | 2 | 0 | Dexter Briggs | 0 | 1 | 1 | 0 |
| Daniel Tuttle, Jr. | 0 | 1 | 2 | 0 | Zebrina Lemmons | 0 | 1 | 1 | 0 |
| James Bucklin | 1 | 3 | 4 | 0 | Joshua Lemmons | 0 | 1 | 1 | 0 |
| Joel Thomas | 1 | 1 | 2 | 0 | John G. Welsh | 2 | 1 | 2 | 0 |
| Conrad Teneyck | 2 | 7 | 5 | 0 | Ebenezer Jones | 0 | 1 | 0 | 0 |
| Joseph Hanchett | 2 | 1 | 1 | 0 | Mica Adams | 4 | 1 | 2 | 0 |
| Elisha Warren | 1 | 2 | 2 | 0 | Henry Wells | 1 | 1 | 1 | 0 |
| Martin Frazer | 1 | 1 | 5 | 0 | Joseph Keller | 1 | 1 | 4 | 0 |
| Joseph Kingsley | 2 | 1 | 5 | 0 | Amos Gordon | 1 | 2 | 3 | 0 |
| Salmon Kingsley | 0 | 1 | 1 | 0 | Gideon Gooding | 0 | 1 | 1 | 0 |
| Alvin Coleman | 0 | 1 | 1 | 0 | Glade Cobb | 1 | 1 | 0 | 0 |
| Harvey Tuttle | 1 | 1 | 2 | 0 | Frisby Chubb | 0 | 1 | 1 | 0 |
| John Williams | 4 | 1 | 1 | 0 | William A. Osband | 3 | 1 | 2 | 0 |
| Bartum Durfey | 0 | 1 | 1 | 0 | Marcus Swift | 3 | 1 | 2 | 0 |
| John Lazer | 2 | 1 | 3 | 0 | George M. Johnson | 3 | 1 | 3 | 0 |
| John Mudg | 1 | 1 | 3 | 0 | James Woods | 1 | 1 | 2 | 0 |
| Abraham Crispell | 1 | 1 | 3 | 0 | Benjamin Williams | 1 | 1 | 2 | 0 |
| Thomas Ricca | 2 | 1 | 3 | 0 | James Abbott | 3 | 2 | 1 | 0 |
| Richard McCurdy | 1 | 2 | 2 | 0 | Thomas Maxwell | 0 | 1 | 2 | 0 |
| William Clay | 2 | 1 | 3 | 0 | James Maxwell | 0 | 1 | 2 | 0 |
| Francis Ruff | 3 | 1 | 3 | 0 | Joseph Hickcox | 3 | 2 | 2 | 0 |
| Francis Newbury | 0 | 1 | 0 | 0 | Philemon Blake | 1 | 1 | 1 | 0 |
| Ezekiel Chamberlin | 0 | 1 | 0 | 0 | Thomas Johns | 1 | 1 | 1 | 0 |
| Joshua Chamberlin | 3 | 1 | 2 | 0 | Asa Edgecomb | 1 | 2 | 1 | 0 |
| Marrinus Harrison | 3 | 1 | 2 | 0 | Joseph Young | 0 | 1 | 1 | 0 |
| Leon G. Harrison | 2 | 1 | 3 | 0 | William Hickcox, Jr. | 0 | 1 | 0 | 0 |
| Charles Harrison | 2 | 1 | 1 | 0 | William Hickcox | 3 | 1 | 1 | 0 |
| Hiram Wightman | 0 | 1 | 3 | 0 | Amasa Fox | 2 | 2 | 2 | 0 |
| James Wightman | 5 | 1 | 3 | 0 | Joshua Davis | 1 | 1 | 5 | 0 |
| Abraham Wightman | 5 | 1 | 3 | 0 | Joseph H. Fowler | 0 | 1 | 3 | 0 |
| Stephen G. Simmons | 2 | 0 | 4 | 0 | Moses Bruce | 4 | 1 | 2 | 0 |
| William Clute | 0 | 1 | 1 | 0 | Ebenezer Pate | 6 | 1 | 2 | 0 |
| Carson McCurdy | 0 | 1 | 0 | 0 | Benjamin Bell | 1 | 2 | 1 | 0 |
| Volney Wightman | 0 | 1 | 0 | 0 | Ralph B. Bell | 2 | 2 | 2 | 0 |
| Madison Wightman | 1 | 0 | 0 | 0 | Thomas Gildard | 1 | 1 | 1 | 0 |
| Garret Houghtailing | 1 | 1 | 1 | 0 | James Griswold | 0 | 1 | 3 | 0 |

| | | | | | | | | | |
|---|---|---|---|---|---|---|---|---|---|
| George Bois | 2 | 1 | 4 | 0 | Joseph Green | 0 | 1 | 0 | 0 |
| Benjamin Green | 0 | 1 | 0 | 0 | | | | | |

## SPRINGWELLS TOWNSHIP
Assessors: James May, G. Godfroy

| | | | | | | | | | |
|---|---|---|---|---|---|---|---|---|---|
| Samuel Smith | 4 | 2 | 5 | 4 | François Cicot | 1 | 2 | 6 | 0 |
| Thomas Flinn | 3 | 1 | 0 | 0 | Levy Willards | 4 | 4 | 2 | 0 |
| Peter Cox | 6 | 1 | 0 | 0 | Benj. B. Kirckerviles | 2 | 2 | 6 | 1 |
| Wm. Chartton | 0 | 0 | 0 | 5 | Leonard Lenox | 0 | 0 | 0 | 6 |
| Old Jack | 0 | 0 | 0 | 2 | Michael Carey | 2 | 6 | 2 | 0 |
| Last two entries living at back of | | | | | Antoine Lesperance | 2 | 1 | 3 | 0 |
| Joseph Visgar's house | | | | | Antoine Lesperance | 3 | 1 | 2 | 0 |
| George Hicks | 0 | 0 | 0 | 3 | Elan Macdonnell | 0 | 3 | 2 | 0 |
| John Valantine | 2 | 1 | 4 | 0 | Augustin Berthillet | 0 | 3 | 1 | 0 |
| Henry Yeager | 0 | 1 | 1 | 0 | Robert Abbott | 3 | 4 | 6 | 0 |
| John Hide | 0 | 1 | 1 | 0 | John Knaggs | 1 | 2 | 3 | 0 |
| Alexis Odien | 0 | 0 | 0 | 6 | Jacob Dix | 2 | 2 | 5 | 0 |
| Harry Pollock | 0 | 0 | 0 | 2 | John Dix | 3 | 1 | 2 | 0 |
| Joseph Beaubian | 3 | 1 | 4 | 0 | Joseph Charboneau | 2 | 1 | 2 | 0 |
| Joseph Livernois | 4 | 2 | 5 | 0 | Alexis Deslisle | 0 | 1 | 1 | 0 |
| Francis Livernois | 0 | 1 | 0 | 0 | John Stainback | 1 | 4 | 4 | 5 |
| Antoine Laurent | 4 | 1 | 3 | 0 | Joseph Riopell | 0 | 1 | 3 | 0 |
| Samuel W. Lapham | 1 | 1 | 1 | 0 | Hycinth Riopell | 3 | 1 | 9 | 0 |
| Joseph P. Campeau | 3 | 1 | 3 | 0 | William Stevis | 0 | 1 | 2 | 0 |
| *Joseph Cicot | 3 | 1 | 6 | 0 | John Laurent | 3 | 1 | 2 | 0 |
| Toutsaint Laurent | 2 | 1 | 3 | 0 | Charles Rouleaux | 3 | 2 | 6 | 0 |
| John Langdon | 1 | 1 | 3 | 0 | Ezra Younglove | 1 | 1 | 3 | 0 |
| Richard McDonnell | 1 | 3 | 2 | 0 | Daniel Dwight | 0 | 1 | 1 | 0 |
| John Strong | 0 | 3 | 0 | 0 | Daniel Thompson | 4 | 10 | 6 | 0 |
| George Campbell | 3 | 2 | 5 | 0 | Selden Champion | 2 | 1 | 3 | 0 |
| Louis Tebeau | 0 | 1 | 2 | 0 | Ignace Rouleau | 3 | 7 | 1 | 0 |
| John Stark | 2 | 1 | 5 | 0 | Philip Chabert | 1 | 1 | 4 | 0 |
| Baptist Varvet | 1 | 1 | 4 | 0 | Jean Navarre | 1 | 1 | 1 | 0 |
| William Crompton | 1 | 2 | 2 | 0 | P. D. Labadie | 4 | 1 | 4 | 0 |
| Widow Stacey | 0 | 0 | 4 | 0 | Antoine Mettez | 0 | 2 | 2 | 0 |
| David Burbank | 0 | 1 | 4 | 0 | James Knaggs | 1 | 3 | 0 | 2 |
| Isaac Woodcock | 1 | 1 | 1 | 0 | John Brown | 2 | 4 | 5 | 0 |
| John Burbank | 1 | 1 | 2 | 0 | Jacob Gilbert | 1 | 3 | 2 | 0 |
| Travis Adams | 1 | 1 | 1 | 0 | Ebenezer Mattocks | 3 | 4 | 3 | 0 |
| Hugh McVay | 6 | 2 | 4 | 0 | James May | 3 | 1 | 6 | 1 |
| E. Farnsworth | 0 | 3 | 2 | 0 | George Combs | 0 | 2 | 3 | 0 |
| Henry Gallaspie | 0 | 2 | 3 | 1 | Augustine Lafoy | 0 | 2 | 6 | 0 |
| Abram Salsbury | 3 | 3 | 5 | 0 | Joseph Socier | 2 | 1 | 4 | 0 |
| Joset Dumay (widow) | 3 | 0 | 2 | 1 | Louis C. Boitte | 6 | 1 | 3 | 0 |
| Alexis Vermet | 0 | 1 | 1 | 0 | Charles Cabacier | 0 | 3 | 5 | 0 |
| Peter Barthiume | 1 | 1 | 3 | 0 | John Andrews | 0 | 3 | 2 | 0 |
| John Bapt. Dumais | 5 | 4 | 3 | 0 | Widow Laferty | 5 | 0 | 4 | 0 |
| Therase Deslisle | 1 | 1 | 7 | 0 | Peter Godfroy | 3 | 2 | 4 | 1 |
| William Burbank | 0 | 1 | 3 | 0 | Dominick Riopell | 2 | 1 | 4 | 0 |
| Louis Laurent | 2 | 1 | 3 | 0 | Baptiste Riopell | 6 | 1 | 3 | 0 |

1827 Wayne County

|  | | | | |  | | | | |
|---|---|---|---|---|---|---|---|---|---|
| Baptiste Campeau | 4 | 1 | 4 | 0 | John Dugard | 0 | 1 | 0 | 3 |
| Charles Campeau | 1 | 1 | 1 | 0 | Alexis P. Campeau | 2 | 3 | 5 | 0 |
| Joseph Visgar | 3 | 1 | 5 | 0 | Alexis Campeau | 2 | 1 | 2 | 0 |
| Peter W. Knaggs | 1 | 1 | 4 | 0 | Gabriel Godfroy | 4 | 3 | 5 | 0 |

## HURON TOWNSHIP
Assessors: Warrinner Corkins, George Jewett, Chauncey Morgan

|  | | | | |  | | | | |
|---|---|---|---|---|---|---|---|---|---|
| Joseph Teny | 2 | 1 | 1 | 0 | Lucius Corkins | 2 | 1 | 2 | 0 |
| Amos How | 2 | 1 | 3 | 0 | James Johnson | 1 | 1 | 1 | 0 |
| Samuel Wing | 3 | 2 | 1 | 0 | Warriner Corkins | 3 | 1 | 3 | 0 |
| David Landner | 3 | 1 | 3 | 0 | Nathan Wilcoxen | 3 | 1 | 3 | 0 |
| John F. Smith | 2 | 1 | 1 | 0 | Matthew Woods | 2 | 2 | 6 | 0 |
| Minor Mallet | 2 | 2 | 2 | 0 | George Jewett | 2 | 2 | 2 | 0 |
| Mason Clark | 2 | 1 | 2 | 0 | Parker Lawrence | 2 | 2 | 2 | 0 |
| John J. Richaven | 1 | 2 | 3 | 0 | Clement Louden | 0 | 1 | 1 | 0 |
| Henry Duchin | 1 | 1 | 2 | 0 | Rocky McMath | 4 | 1 | 5 | 0 |
| Austin Walles | 2 | 2 | 2 | 0 | Samuel Toligne | 0 | 1 | 1 | 0 |
| Abner Johnson | 3 | 1 | 6 | 0 | Samuel Toligne, Jr. | 0 | 1 | 6 | 0 |

## PLYMOUTH TOWNSHIP
Assessors: Roswell Root, Erastus W. Markweather, Henry Lyons

|  | | | | |  | | | | |
|---|---|---|---|---|---|---|---|---|---|
| Henry Lyons | 3 | 2 | 3 | 0 | Henry Erskine | 2 | 1 | 4 | 0 |
| John Tibbits | 4 | 2 | 5 | 0 | Luther Lincoln | 0 | 2 | 1 | 0 |
| James T. Taft | 1 | 1 | 1 | 0 | Clark Griswold | 0 | 2 | 1 | 0 |
| Job M. Taft | 1 | 2 | 1 | 0 | Caleb Fuhinor | 2 | 1 | 5 | 0 |
| Hiram Larabea | 0 | 1 | 3 | 0 | Earl D. Hoisington | 2 | 1 | 2 | 0 |
| Johathan D. Davis | 0 | 2 | 4 | 0 | Gardner Simmons | 2 | 1 | 1 | 0 |
| Henry Ward | 1 | 2 | 2 | 0 | Ira Stuart | 1 | 1 | 1 | 0 |
| Roswell Root | 5 | 3 | 4 | 0 | Richard Barton | 0 | 2 | 4 | 0 |
| Orra Clarry | 2 | 1 | 4 | 0 | William Basto | 1 | 1 | 3 | 0 |
| Dexter Carlton | 5 | 1 | 5 | 0 | William Hazen | 0 | 1 | 3 | 0 |
| William Teipel | 4 | 2 | 3 | 0 | Richard Joslin | 4 | 1 | 1 | 0 |
| Peter Teipel | 0 | 1 | 2 | 0 | Warren Stone | 3 | 1 | 2 | 0 |
| Allan Tibbits | 0 | 1 | 1 | 0 | Justus Andrews | 1 | 1 | 4 | 0 |
| Justies Gilkey | 3 | 1 | 2 | 0 | Morris Andrews | 2 | 2 | 1 | 0 |
| Erastus W. Starkweather | 4 | 1 | 4 | 0 | Wm. Tibbits | 1 | 1 | 2 | 0 |
| Benjamin Slocum, Jr. | 3 | 1 | 5 | 0 | Joseph Yerkes | 1 | 2 | 4 | 0 |
| Dirl Ramsdell | 1 | 1 | 1 | 0 | Daniel L. Cady | 4 | 1 | 1 | 0 |
| George W. Dun | 0 | 1 | 1 | 0 | Ira Rice | 3 | 1 | 4 | 0 |
| Reuben Wood | 0 | 1 | 2 | 0 | John Miller | 3 | 1 | 4 | 0 |
| Walter McFoslin | 5 | 1 | 2 | 0 | Benjamin Welsh | 0 | 1 | 0 | 0 |
| Wm. Starkweather | 2 | 1 | 1 | 0 | Amos Sands | 2 | 1 | 3 | 0 |
| David Phillips | 1 | 1 | 1 | 0 | Leonard Fellows | 0 | 1 | 1 | 0 |
| John Van Luwen | 3 | 1 | 2 | 0 | Albert G. Fellows | 0 | 1 | 1 | 0 |
| Samuel Sterline | 0 | 2 | 0 | 0 | moses Bradford | 2 | 1 | 1 | 0 |
| Rufus Thayer | 0 | 1 | 1 | 0 | Jared Faisman | 2 | 1 | 5 | 0 |
| A. B. Markham | 1 | 1 | 2 | 0 | Areunah Bradford | 2 | 2 | 6 | 0 |
| Almeron Allen | 1 | 2 | 0 | 0 | Samuel Burd | 5 | 2 | 2 | 0 |

|  | | | | |  | | | | |
|---|---|---|---|---|---|---|---|---|---|
| Stephen Andrews | 0 | 1 | 0 | 0 | Philander Burd | 1 | 2 | 1 | 0 |
| Jacob Folsom | 0 | 1 | 0 | 0 | Lucretia Downer | 1 | 2 | 4 | 0 |
| Archibald Y. Mussy | 1 | 1 | 3 | 0 | Ira M. Hough | 0 | 1 | 1 | 0 |
| Lemuel Cole | 1 | 1 | 2 | 0 | Isaac Cummings | 0 | 1 | 2 | 0 |
| Alfred More | 1 | 1 | 2 | 0 | Timothy J. Sheldon | 0 | 2 | 3 | 0 |
| Fisher A. Fellows | 0 | 1 | 1 | 0 | Philo Pailes | 0 | 1 | 0 | 0 |

ECORSE TOWNSHIP
Assessors: Daniel Goodell, Nathaniel Clark, James Jacox

|  | | | | |  | | | | |
|---|---|---|---|---|---|---|---|---|---|
| Dominique Bouche | 4 | 3 | 6 | 0 | Bonaventure Delise | 4 | 2 | 3 | 0 |
| Peter Lafferty | 1 | 2 | 3 | 0 | Antoin Nenect | 3 | 1 | 3 | 0 |
| Peter Lablance | 4 | 2 | 5 | 7 | Lewis Duce | 3 | 1 | 3 | 0 |
| Peter Lablance, Jr. | 1 | 1 | 1 | 0 | Jean Bt. Raveno | 0 | 1 | 0 | 0 |
| Lewis Lablance | 1 | 1 | 2 | 0 | Nathaniel Clark | 0 | 1 | 0 | 0 |
| Simon Nuson | 1 | 1 | 2 | 0 | William Hill | 0 | 1 | 1 | 0 |
| Jean Bt. Nuson | 0 | 1 | 1 | 0 | Abigail Jaicox | 5 | 1 | 1 | 0 |
| Alexander Labadie | 2 | 1 | 2 | 0 | James Jaicox | 0 | 1 | 0 | 0 |
| Archey Goodell | 0 | 1 | 2 | 0 | Isiah Jaicox | 0 | 1 | 0 | 0 |
| Jonas Goodell | 0 | 1 | 2 | 0 | Nathan Case | 3 | 2 | 4 | 0 |
| Lewis Burrassau, Jr. | 1 | 1 | 1 | 0 | Joseph Morrah | 2 | 2 | 3 | 0 |
| Charley Rulo | 0 | 1 | 0 | 0 | Joseph Barron | 0 | 1 | 1 | 0 |
| Jean Bt. Ceciott | 0 | 1 | 3 | 0 | Joseph Barron, Jr. | 2 | 1 | 4 | 0 |
| Lewis Burrassau | 0 | 1 | 1 | 0 | Solomon Barron | 0 | 1 | 1 | 0 |
| Andra Bourdrais | 3 | 1 | 3 | 0 | Michel Compo | 1 | 1 | 1 | 0 |
| Ira Kellogg | 2 | 1 | 2 | 0 | Jean Bt. Compo | 0 | 1 | 0 | 0 |
| Hannah Hick (widow) | 2 | 1 | 5 | 0 | Jean Bt. Nassico | 3 | 2 | 4 | 0 |
| James Bryant | 2 | 1 | 3 | 0 | Tusaint Drullard | 0 | 1 | 0 | 0 |
| Joseph Corbus | 4 | 1 | 4 | 0 | Joseph Dubo | 2 | 1 | 1 | 0 |
| Wm. McMurphy | 1 | 1 | 4 | 0 | Daniel Goodell | 1 | 1 | 2 | 0 |
| Wm. McVay | 2 | 1 | 1 | 0 | Elizabeth Drouillard (widow) | 2 | 0 | 3 | 0 |
| Francis Nemsica | 2 | 1 | 2 | 0 | Lewis Caskennett | 2 | 1 | 3 | 0 |
| John Corbus | 1 | 1 | 3 | 0 | Peter Perrier | 2 | 1 | 3 | 0 |
| Jacob Orr | 1 | 1 | 3 | 0 | Jean Bt. Labé | 6 | 1 | 1 | 0 |
| Lewis Rouloe | 0 | 1 | 3 | 0 | Joseph Payett | 2 | 1 | 3 | 0 |
| Joseph Pelkey | 1 | 1 | 2 | 0 | Charles Barron | 3 | 1 | 3 | |
| John Cook | 1 | 4 | 5 | 0 | Joseph Barron | 2 | 1 | 2 | 0 |
| John Bondy | 2 | 1 | 2 | 0 | Lewis Larno | 2 | 1 | 3 | 0 |
| Harry Displain | 3 | 1 | 4 | 0 | Antoin Lafray | 1 | 1 | 4 | 0 |
| Alexander Frazier | 2 | 1 | 3 | 0 | Charles Banway | 2 | 1 | 4 | 0 |
| Charles Labidu/y | 3 | 1 | 3 | 0 | Antoine Lapage | 1 | 2 | 2 | 0 |
| Jaques Cicott | 3 | 1 | 4 | 0 | | | | | |

# 1827 Wayne County

CITY OF DETROIT, within the district allotted to B. F. H. Witherell
Note that the categories are not the same as the rest of Wayne County. Those here are the same as the 1820 census: Males: -10, 10-16, 16-18, 16-26, 26-45, 45+. Females: -10. 10-16, 16-26, 26-45, 45+. Each head of family was asked if he were naturalized. If the answer was negative, an asterisk (*) follows the name.

Lewis Cass* 120120/4210
James Witherell 201102/01101
John R. Leib 101101/01120
Joseph Tremblé 100001/00010;
   Colored (hereafter FC) male 16-26.
Pere Dequendre 000010/10010
Pierre Cedien 320001/11001
John Bt. Peltier 100010/10010
Asquire Aldridge 110310/20010
Abr'm Fournier 10010/12010
Margaret Obin 000000/00010
Ls Charbonneau 000100/00100
Jn. Bt. Campeau 301201/1 (torn)
Dominique Riopel 210010/10120
Christopher Hart 420040/21010
Joseph Laporte 400001/10010
Pierre Laffarty 000010/00000
Thomas Reed 000001/00000
Chas Cabatier 200001/11210
Joseph du Berger 001110/00001
Théotiste Badien 010000/10001
James May 220001/10310
Augustin Lefoy 001101/12400
Jonathan Krisley 101110/20100
John du Garde (no data)
Haritte Myers 210101/00101
John Garrison 220101/00101
Antoine Barriou 010002/00001
Louis LaDuke 100010/12011
Henry Bertholet 110011/61010
Loison Peltier 200001/42100
Thomas Knoxon 000001/00001
Stephen Hazzel 1 FC female 45+
Lefio Dennison (FC) males: -14, 26-40
   females: - 14, 14-26 (1 in ea. category)
Louis Lagnion 200001/11010
Chas. Wilcox 110310/11110
Théophile Metter 100101/10101
Lewis Wilson (no data)
Gustavus B. Rood 000210/10100
Margaret de Morth 200000/32100
John Makensie 000010/11010
Levi Willard 200120/10510
Jacob Visger 000001/01100

Joseph W. Visger 000001/01100
Arthur Brook 000010/00000
Peter W. Knaggs 000100/10100
Whitmore Knaggs 100311/10110
Joel Thomas 300010/10010
Aron Thomas 300030/20010
Jesse Wise 101101/31010
Joseph Corlies 100100/10100
John F. Ripley 101210/10200 FC female 45+
François duDemois 200101/00110
John Sargeant 010010/00101 FC male -14,
   FC female 14-26
Ralph Bell 210011/10010 FC male 14-26,
   female 14-26, and 45+
Henry Magee 101110/00010
Berkley Rowley 000201/00000
John Walker 000120/30100
Charles L. Canfield 400011/10000
Pierre Labadie 230111/10110
John M. Navarre 000010/00110
Gabriel Godfroy 110201/22101 FC male -26,
   and 45+. FC femal
J. Beaugrand* 410001/01000 FC male - 14,
   and to 45. FC female -14 and to 26/
John Armstrong 000001/00010
William Blackington 200010/00100
Josette Cholière 000100/00001
J. B. Chamberlain 411110/10100
Henry Bradley 200010/00100 FC male - 14,
   and to 45. FC females same categories.
Alexr. Younglove 300010/11110
Carver Gunn 000200/00010
Henry B. Brevoort 200001/11010
Nathl Champ 100010/10110
Col. McCollister * 000002/10100
Chas. Girard 000001/00000
Louison Champagne 200001/10101
Abigail Gage 121400/20110
Pierre Picot 100110/00200
Chas Gavin 000011/10002
François Champagne 000020/00200
François Lavigne 100100/10100
Louis Campeau 100021/01100
Mary King 010000/30000

Robert Fillamore  010110/10140
Frs. St. Aubin * 100201/40010
Louis Moran  010102/00311
Joseph Lorancell  010010/10010
John Bt. Leporte  300000/11010
John Pherson  000201/00010
Jean Marie Babion  000111/02201
Benoît Chappeton  120101/12011
Morris Moron  210010/21111
Frs. Rivored  111120/20000
Chas. Labadie  100002/20110
Gabriel Chêne  110202/22210
Henry Stanton  000210/10010
Samuel Sherwood  100200/00110
John Hyde  000010/00010
Prime Johnson  (no data)
Pierre Beaubien  000110/02201
John Knapp  000100/10111
Isaih Tyler  000010/00001
Richard Goodwin  200201/11001
Elias Long  100201/02100
Seth Dunham  000010/00001
Jeremiah G. Brainard  100101/00100
Wm. Firehaudt  000010/00000
Moses Allan  200010/00000
Amos Houle  000020/00101
Mason Clarke  10010/10101
John P. Noah  000010/00000
Samuel Wing  000010/00000
George Hubbard  120100/11010
Joseph Allaird  100010/20200
Arthur Ruark  200110/10100
David Smith  100020/00001
Henry Dutcher  000200/00000
Asa Fox  200001/21000
Benj. Dewit  100001/21000
Noah Gilbert  000010/00000
Joseph Hammon  000020/10000
Nathl Clarke  000010/00000
Gardner Sherman  000010/00010
Jos. Mason  211101/11011
Artemas Hosmer  000020/10110
Moses Smedley  000010/00000
Zadik Wellman  000101/00000
John Clarke  031101/30010
Aron Nobles  130110/12100
James Campeau  000101/10010
Antoine Rivard  200001/10100
Joseph Spencer  011220/00000
John Bt. Camperet  200001/11110

William Durrell  000011/00100
Chester Blake  000010/10110
Julius Eldred  100010/01000
David Newfart  000000/00010
Eleanor Haskin  100000/01010
Henry Campeau  201101/22001
Robert C. McDougall  011101/10210
James Gailagher  100010/10000
John Meldrum  120112/00110
Louis Beaufait  220001/01001
Louis Chappatan  200101/21100
Cecil Boyer  100000/00000
George Lyions  110010/00100
Lambert Thebault  010010/20210
Paschall Patchvin  000010/02001
Isadore Marian  211201/21000
Victor Morass  000010/11111
William Brooks  000011/30010
Beckley Thurston  120010/21010
Truman Bass  011110/32000
James Sperry  000010/00010
Benj. Knapp  000201/00010
Etienne Marsan  210010/22111
Claud Campeau  200010/30000
Joseph Lamereau  011302/11000
  FC male -25; female -14.
Prince Phillip  000000/00010
Gabriel Barreau  000100/00100
John Bt. Mexico  200001/10010
John Park  FC male 26-45
John Bt. Lebon  400010/00010
Isabel Druilliard  030010/20100
David Mayo  000100/00000
Joseph Delyle  010001/11000
Thomas H. Adams  000010/00000
Jacqui Cicot  310010/20010
Alexis Beaubien  310010/20010
Daniel Goodale  000100/00100
Elijah Hartshorn  000001/00000
Elijah Goodale  220211/01101
George Campbell  100010/20011
Jos. Bondie  200001/10010
Jean Batille Rousseau  010101/10101
Pierre LaBlanche  200301/21011
Antoine Barreau  020301/21001
Charles Rulou  000010/00000
Antoine Bondie  000001/10000
Jos. Barreau  110001/00110
Peter Perry  1000010/00100
Amab Bellairre  000201/00010

1827 Wayne County

Charles Larosche 000001/00000
Charles Barreau 100010/00100
Joe Piatt 000010/00000
Alexander Jooderan 000001/00100
Antoinelet Fron 020002/30101
Francis Laduc 000100/00100
Charles L. Vermet 000200/10101
Jean Btste le Jeunesse 020001/00001
Louis Bourasson 000201/00201
John Bt. Laliat 010001/20101
Antoine Lorens 200010/10100
Jos. Livernois 100201/00100
Jos. Cicot 110010/30110
Jos. Lorens 100100/00100
Louis Boudrion 000001/10000
Louis Lorens 100100/00100
Amab Lorens 100100/10110
Augustin Longon 111202/01010
Francis Lorens 210010/10000
Mary Lorens 0000101/01000
Jacob Dix 100010/00210
Jos. Charbeno 010001/11020
John Dix 210010/20000
John Steinback 000001/01100
Jos. Riopel 000010/10100
Yessich Riopel 210010/40100
John Bt. Riopel 310010/10110
John Bt. Riopel 310010/10110
Chas. Roulo 201102/11101
John Bird 210001/31010
Broddac Chappel 210001/11010
Benjn Stanley 211(10)(15)0/10020
Thomas Cotes 200010/00010
Basil Thebault 400001/10001
John Bt. Tremblé 510001/00010
John Bt. Shovin 101101/00001
Thomas Forton 011201/21211
Evangele Tramblé 000010/10000
Louison Tremblé 010001/30000
Leon Ladouseur 000100/11100
Thomas Willitts 111101/00101
Francis Thebault 200011/01012
John Bt. Vernier 011201/02001
Jos. Urno 200010/10100
Pierre St. George 020010/22210
Louis LaForte 330001/10010
Dominique Thomas 000100/20100
Jacquis Allors 200102/00010
Jacquis Allors 010101/00101
Jos. DuBé 1100013/10100

Jos. Rabergon 200301/31010
Antoine Urino 100010/00010
John Bt. Rivard 00020/00000
Andress Tremblé 000002/00110
Jos. Lacie 020101/12210
Nicholas Chovin 010200/10100
Pierre Tremblé 400010/11010
Thomas Tremblé 320010/00010
Pierre Piechey 300010/00010
Jean Bte St. Aubin 000002/00101
Pierre Griffard 010101/41210
Pierre Champagne 210001/10101
Louis Grifard 000001/00001
Louis Grifard 000001/32001
Goyette Marsac 010101/00200
William Little 100110/00101
John Kirby 000001/00000
Joseph Tremblé 320101/00201
Jacob Purky 000110/00010
René Marsac 200001/22000
John Bt. Lacie 410001/11010
Julien Gagnier 200110/10110
Bassille Cotien 100010/10000
Joseph Chovin 200010/10010
Cherres Gavin 400002/31010
Pierre Gavin 201110/30020
Abraham Cooke 20004/00120
Touissant Jessamine 000001/00010
François Petre 200001/11000
Louis Moran 100001/10010
Charles Chovin 000101/00110
John Bt. Chovin 000100/00101
Louis de Pra 210010/01001
Joseph St. John 000212/12003
Louis Dessenier 100010/01011
Touissant Chêne 020001/01201
Alex. Campeau 210102/22110
Peter Van Avery 201201/10110
Henry Campeau 000010/00100
Jos. Campeau 120201/10000
Robert P. Lewis 000140/02010
John Ladaroot 110201/22110
John Streite 000010/00010
Chas Poineniea 101201/12100
Robert Marsac 100101/02000
Wm. P. Frasher 200010/00000
John Armstrong 000020/00000
Henry Conner 200512/01100
Wm. Tucker 200010/10000
Edward Ryn * 220001/00111

Catherine Beaubien   200000/20310
Théophile Dumais   200010/00010
Jas. Abbott   000100/00110
John Palmer   220012/02020
Elizabeth Weaver   000100/01000
Seth L. Popino   300010/11000
Mrs. Burbank   00000000101
Thos. Anderson   100100/00110
Prosper Lawrence   000010/00100
Francis Chovin   100101/10100
Joshua Chappell   100022/11100
Paul D. Anderson   100010/00010
John Burbank   000110/00000
Wm. Stacey   000001/21010
Aron Thomas   000001/00001
Alanson Thomas   410010/10010
John Macomb   010120/10001
Ezek. Chamberlain   1000102/20100
Josia Raymond   000101/10000
Henry Presson   000010/00100
John Cramer   000100/00100
Robert Abbott   231101/30001
Louis Roulo   000100/00001
John Bt. Dumais   010210/00101
Joel Thomas   010001/00000
Jas. Desplat   110001/00000
George Hix FC mlae 14-26, 26-45.
    FC female -14, 14-26; 1 other person
Jos. Beaubien   100010/31110
--- Frasher   110010/12000
Benvenue Delyle   200002/00110
Louis Cicot   200010/00100
Francis Cicot   110011/30110
John Peltier   000100/00010
James Chittendon *   110010/01000
John Keith   200100/10011   FC male
    FC male 26-45, 45+
Terrence Smyth   120201/01111
Monoah Hubbard   200220/21010
Sylvenster Bates *   100020/22001
Patrick Daniels   000010/00010
William Macomb   100010/20100
John K. Rucker   200020/30100
    FC male 14-26
Jno. Hickock   000010/20000
Adna Hickock   120101/11010
Ashhell Wilcox   200010/21000
Augustus Coan   101211/01010
Fredrk Campbel   000010/00000
Joseph Bates *   000001/00000

Wm. Bucklen   000201/01111
Daniel Tuttle   120001/12011
Joseph Hickock   100010/10100
Wm. McCarthy   100011/21010
Nicholas Brewer   200001/01110
Edw. McCarthy   000100/10010
George Johnson   000100/00100
Eli L. Crompton   010010/00000
Daniel Bucklen   000110/00000
Amasa Fox   100010/00100
Benj. N. Williams   100010/10010
Alexdr Lucket   000001/00000
John Starks 000100/10101
Andrew Bell 000001/00000
John Kremer   101101/11101
James Welch   000010/10000
Francis Ruff   000010/20100
Marenus Harrison 100100/00100
Josiah Bookley 100010/10121
Francis REgnon   400001/11100
Hugh McVay   100210/11101
Mehitabel Kilbourn   110200/01101
Andrew Nichols   100121/00000
    FC male 40+
Joseph Fowler   000100/11001
Abr. Kilbourn   000100/00000
Jos. Hanchett *   220210/10010
Hiram Johns   1000100/00110
Elijah Downer   110122/10110
Gilman Smith   000010/00000
Abraham Truax   100141/01210
Joseph Ellis   000100/00000
Jonathan Cole   00010/00000
John Sturgiss*   100010/20101
Jason Thurston   100001/02000
Pierre Yax   010001/00000
Pierre Rivard   021301/21201
Charles Rivard   220101/10111
Michael Rivard   421301/11101
Henry Hudson   030010/11110
Wm. McKonker   000001/00000
John A. Grant   301110/30110
François Grifard   200001/31100
Francis Furton   000010/00100
John Curry 010001/00000
Isaih Walton   200001/20010
Enoch Tuttle   000001/10000
B.F.H. Witherell   000100/00000

# 1830 CENSUS OF MICHIGAN

The Territory of Michigan in 1830 included the entire state as well as the present states of Wisconsin and Minnesota, or as far west as the Mississippi River. However, county lines were quite different from today's, as indicated on the map. The population had increased threefold since 1820 (from 8,896 to 27,378) and was to accelerate in the years before statehood was granted in 1836. The completion of the Erie Canal in 1825 opened this western land to New Englanders and New Yorkers, who streamed in, attracted by the cheap and fertile land, mainly in the southern counties. The population for the entire Territory was 31,346 free whites, 32 slaves, and 261 free colored.

The makeup of the citizenry of Michigan was quite varied. While the southern part of the state was mainly agricultural, the northern counties included many people at Michilimackinac and Sault Ste Marie who were involved in the fur trade. Note the large number of single men; many of these were French Canadians who did not remain to become American citizens. Note also the soldiers at the two military posts in Wisconsin and at Michilimackinac.

In 1961, this census was published as a separate volume by DSGR, *1830 Federal Census: Territory of Michigan*; the present publication includes many corrections to that transcription. Parts of Wisconsin had also been previously published: an index to Brown County appeared in *Wisconsin Historical Collections* 13:468-72; Chippewa and Crawford Counties in *Wi consin Families* 1:89-93, 129-135, 223-234.

The following transcription gives the ages in years of free white males before the slash and free white females after the slash, using these categories: to 5, 5-10, 10-15, 15-20, 20-30, 30-40, 40-50, 50-60, 60-70, 70-80, 80-90, 90-100, over 100. Zeros were not added after the last male or female; therefore, a reading of 01/00001 would indicate a family composed of one male 5-10 and one female 20-30. The age divisions for free colored (FC) are different and are given specifically, such as "1 male 36-55, 1 female 24-36." Note also the asterisk following the names of over ninety heads of household: these men owned slaves. Since no names were given, these statistics were not copied here, but the interested reader will find the schedules "Additional Slaves and Free Colored" pages 114 and 115 of the DSGR publication mentioned above or on the National Archives microfilm. While the names of all the heads listed in this earlier publication were re-examined for the present volume, the enumeration of males and females was not, but was copied from that transcription. This allows two chances for error, and the reader is therefore urged to consult the original microfilm.

## WAYNE COUNTY ( NOT INCLUDING DETROIT)

James Chittenden 00000002/00000001
William H. St. Clair 1000001/11001
Thomas Shadwick 110001/00001
William Clute 100001/11001
Stephen G. Simmons 11000001/1012101
Audrain Abbott 10001/10001
Gilbert Bagnel 0120111/2001001
Leonard Hopkins 110001/100001
James Sillay 0030011/10010011
Charles Cabateer 00002010l/00012101
Nancy Thompson 13/00100101
John Andrus 0000201/20002
Mary Lafferty 01031/010101
Ezra Younglove 0111001/1101101
Peter Godfrey 102011/11001
David C. Lewis 0100001/000001
Dominique Riopel 0010001/111000101
William McCarty 020201/0120101
Joseph H. Fouter 000001/12101
Joseph Hicken 1110001/001001
Alansen Thomas 2223001/00101
Mary Weaver 0000101/00001
William Burbank 10012/01101
George Trisket 20001/00001
Abraham Sansbroy 00103001/00110001
John Cook 10200101/112101
Richard McDowell 1000010001/10101
John Dix 1002001/0010101
Samuel Smith 3102001/010001
Rodman Stodard 010001/00001
William Sterrs 00001/0002001
John Strong 100011/0001
Aaron Thomas 0202101/00001
John Reid 100004/00002
Peter W. Knaggs 200001/010001
John Dugard free col. male 36-55;
    10-24, 36-55
John Tyler Free col. male 24-36, 36-55
    females 24-36
Benjamin Lee 0010001/001100
Juba Barrows 00201/0001
William Little 011011/12000100001
Joel Thomas 0001001/101001
Manoah Hubbards 0020503/0002001
Daniel Corby 000002/20001
Michael Dotton 100001/0001
Robert D. Smith 00012/1002
Henry Campeau 011000001/00000001
Henry Conner 02320001/0210201

Thomas Welch 1100211/1100001
Henry Clark 320001/01101
Patrick Mahoney 10001/10001
Gabriel Godfroy Sr. 0012100001/021002
John M. Navarre 00000101/00000001
Joseph Livernois 1013011001/11111
Louis Roulough 000001/001
Martha Cronenworth 001001/311001
Jacob Dix 111001/11001
Antoine Lorrow 1120001/111001
Joseph Charbonneau 00200001/010001
Hannah Kelly 00001001/0000001
Jacob Mountinger 0000001/0000001
Joseph Riopell 1002001/10200001
Tousant Riopell 0012101/133101
John Bte Riopell 0302101/101001
Peter Bareume (Barriau) 001001/001
Joseph Bareume(Barriau) 000031/001
Vimic Dumais 11/01001
Ignais Coté 10001001/001
Joseph Cicott 11101001/022101
Antoine Campeau 110011/20001
Henry Hudson 00111011/00010001
Elizabeth Stacy ---/0011101
John Baptist Laderout 11011001/011001
John Martin 1111201/121001
Margaret Knaggs 01/000101
Joseph Campeau 11100101/0001001
Peter Laderout 110001/010101
Robert Marsac 20000201/00001
John Bte Chovin 001020001/00001
Peter Wm. Avery 02310101/211001
George Lyon 221001/01001
Francis Rivard 01013001/00002001
Peter Delorum 10000101/020001
Lewis Desony (Desaulniers) 0000101/
    00010100001
Lewis Grossbeck 10011/0002
Louis Dupré Sr. 00001/00001
Louis Dupré Jr. 0102002/01
John Bte Garraut 00001/02001
John Bte Chovin 000101/011001
John Bte Durett 0000110001/10012101
Abba Snelling 121001/01001101
Charles Bigalow 000422/00001001
Victor Morass 1100001/021101
Isadore Morrow 00001101/01020001
Joseph Lemerine 101110011/110001
Antoine Habaré 10001/00001

# 1830 Census

Antoine Lapousée 100011/11001
Antoine Boyois 010101/010010001
Francis Cicott 00100011/0121001
John Brown 020030001/103001
Alexander P. Campeau 1010200101/01200001
Gabriel Godfroy Jr. 1132001/0120101
Thomas Knoxon 000010101/000100001
Antoine Reynor 00011001/1000001
Evangelist Tremblé 2100001/110011
Peter St. George 0000001/1103
Joseph Robertjohn 100001/20001
Francis Allair 200001/10001
Louis Allair 22 0000000001/110010001
Jock Allair 11020001/0010001
Paul Marsac 000001/20001
Joseph Forto 100001/10001
Joseph Renno 2120001/020001
Charles Saucer 10001/00001
Robert Saucer 30001/01001
Francis Thibeault 1011001/00100100001
Thomas Willett 0000001/00001
Leon Laducer 011001/20001
John Bte Tromblée 0020001/0210001
Henry Tromblée 200001/01001
Lewis Tromblée 1101001/022101
Francis Forté 0102201/000010001
Lambert Chovin 100001/20001
Bazile Sperry 01102001/001
Bazile Craky (Créqui) 000000001/011000001
James Ousterout 100011/00001
John Grant 01021101/2111001
Henry Tibits 0001/0001
Joseph Shaw 00000001/000000001
Leonard Shaw 20001/00001
Royal Huisington 00001/21001
Gilbert Cropper 110001/11001
John Willson 00001/0001
Jonathan F. Chubb 21001/00001
Benjamin Slocum 1110101/011201
Francis Rotnour 00001/02001
Darius C. Arnold 00001/10001
Stephen S. Blanchard 00000001/0002001
Philo Burd 10002/10001
Michael Rotnour 01010001/00001001
Peter Hendricks 10001/10001
James T. Tafft 210111/01001
Henry Ward 0001011/000101
Daniel Tibits 10001/00001
John Vn Loovin 22001/00101
Roswell Root 1111101/011001
Jonathan Davis 000022/111011

William Davis 0202101/0001001
Thomas Beadell 110001 /001001
Elizabeth Coleman 00001/00000001
Joseph Kingsley 00110002/1210001
Warren Tuttle 00102001/0001
Christopher Gour 0002001/0000001
Nathaniel Eldridge 000001/120001
James Dunn 112011/001001
William Smith 001013/30001
John I. Anders 0131001/0110001
Henry Erskine 010103/202001
Daniel Anders 000001/10001
Timothy Lyon 00103001/010111
John Beaton 120011
Daniel L. Cady 1211102/000001
Samuel Stanburgh 10011/0001
Nancy Fralick 02111/101001
Ira Bronson 1000101/011002
Morris Andrews 21001/01001
Thomas Pinkney 00001/10001
John Tibbitts 0200001/0030001
Joziah Stanburgh 1012/010001
Jacob Stanburgh 000001/120001
Minna Bradford 0001101/0000001
William H. Simmons 1220011/000101
James Palmer 10001/00001
James Abbott 220001/00001
Charles G. Abbott 00001/00001
Erastus Hensza 00001/10001
Walter McFarland 01202001/00001001
Dexter Carlton 0011101/0121101
Samuel Blackmore 00001/001
George M. Johnson 102011/220101
Marcus Swifft 111101/000101
William Osburn 220011/00001
Benijah Holbrook 00011/00001
James Kile 00001/10001
Elias Davenport 000001/20221
Elijah Barton 00001/10001
Micah Adams 030001/20101
Henry Wells 00001/10001
John Cahoon 001001/000001
Alva Dolson 0001/---
Ebenezer Smith 120001/00001
Isaac Wilkinson 00222001/00011001
Joseph Keller 02011001/0120001
Robert A. Forsyth 010001/00022
Luther Rawson 0000001/000001
Benjamin Vincint 010001/02001
John Hide 0001001/0110001

James Dufoe 001121/00001
Henry B. Brevort 0130001/0011001
Daniel Baker 0000001/0001001
George Henderson 00001/10003
Elisha Warren 210011/10102
Isaac W. Day 00001021/0003001
Alexander O'dian 221001/00101
Ephraim Farnsworth 100002/10001
Joseph H. Smith 12002/11001
James Welch 01020001/0021
Thomas L. Knapp 12001/10101
Charles C. Trowbridge 10011/101111
Joel Finch 01221001/1110001
Edins Rood 100001/12001
Abner Johnson 1200011/12001
John Mullet 210001/113001
John A. Rucker 1011002/022202
Samuel Todd 00001/00001
John Hyde 0000001/0000001
Theodore G. Holding 100001/00001
William Johnson 0110001/0000001
Isaac D. Miller 101011/210001
Luther Scovill 0001001/000001
Ann Dickman 0111/0100001
William Loucks 00003/21001
Joseph Obien 000001/20001001
Asa H. Otis 001001/220001
Carpenter Chaffee 30001/00001
Ora Otis 000011/10001
Hiram Snider 02000001/0010001
Elisha Stephens 00001/01001
John Starks 100002/011001001
Zial Wakefield 00002/00001
John Longdon 00001/10001
Beverly Longdon 11001/00001
James Randle 010002/0000001
Joseph Beaubien 02100001/0012001
Amable Lorrow 101001/121001
Samuel Lapham 110102/10001
Joseph P. Campeau 0201001/0010001
Charles Roulough Jr. 010001/0101
Charles Roulough Sr. 0200000001/00220001
John Bte Vermit 110001/121001
Joseph Lorrow 012001/10001
Conrad Ten Eyck 0010202/220002
Jacob Hammel 11001/0001
Elizabeth Cady 0000001/0000000001
John F. Rupely 0010002/111001
Francis Dumais 111001/11011
Warren Fenton 100001/00001

Elias Woodruff 00002/10001
George M. Martin 00001/0001
Rufus Wells 01211001/1101101
James Bucklin 100101/100001
Amos Gordon 110001/21001
Catherine Cramer 02000001/000001
Timothy Bucklin 11001101/111001
Margaret Bucklin 122/0002001
Hezekiah Gridley 000001/10001
Thompson Maxwell 001000000001/0000000001
Daniel Tuttle 000001001/000100001
Benjamin F. Fox 10002/00001
John Persall 0100001/0000001
George Herington 000001/04001
Clark Persall 000100001/00000001
Phineas Fullerton 01101001/0110101
Samuel Danes 110001/10001
Almond Fullerton 1001000001/10001
Simon Canfield 210101/00101
Jonathan Davis 0000011/ 000100101
Moses Bruse 13000001/100001
Thomas Gilderd 0000001/000001
Ralph R. Bell 11012101/00010001
George Norris 000001/20001
John Harris 020001/100001
Dines Sackett 10002/20011
Robert Lyon 0100101/1121001
Benjamin Bell 0010001/11
Benjamin Green 1110001/121001
Joseph Green 0111001/210001
George Boyce 110002/011011
William Weston 232001/002001
Alanson Fairfield 00001/00000001
Peter Keater 100001/000001
David Lapham 20001/00001
Simon Downer 0123101/010001
Alva Smith 10001/10001
Dexter Briggs 00001/20001
Joshua Simmons 20213/0001101
Zebina Simmons 10001/00001
Mashal Everest 00112001/1101101
John C. Griswold 010001/00001
John Welch 111011/010001
William Bartow 0001001/01010001
Benjamin Welch 00001/10001
Joseph Yerkus 000100001/00001
Clark Griswold 00001/0001
John Miller 221001/001201
William Hickcox 01101001/12001
Able Lamonion 10001/00001

Hiram S. Fuller 00001/10001
Rosecrance Holmes 002011/230101
John Briggs 00001/0001
Chancy Reynolds 00004/00001
Israel Fuller 00000001/00000001
Moris Newman 110001/01001
Nathaniel Newman 0001101/1101
Joseph Dickason 11001/01001
Israel Whipple 012001/100001
William D. Robinson 20001/00011
Arnold Whipple 00001/10001
William Utley 110002/212001
Ephraim H. Utley 10002/00001
G. D. Chubb 000101/00001
Rufus Haire Jr. 000111/10001
Lyman Terrill 0000100001/00000001
Philo Taylor 201011/002001
Levi Phelps 112001/120001
Isaac Peck 0130101/00111
Alfred Burris 20020001/011001
Peter Teple 000002/20001001
William Teple 00103001/00111
Hiram Larriwell 10001/11001
William Tibbits 01001/20001
Justice Gilkey 13001/00001
Lovel Aldrich 1001001/1222001
Henry Lyons 021001/20101
Asa Parkerd 10001/12001
Samuel Sterling 00001/10001
Silas Sly 200001/00001
A. B. Markham 001101/001001
Austin Perrin 100001/020001
David Phillips 200001/00001
Gennet Ramsdell 21101/001001
Gideon P. Benton 10002/100011
William Packerd 00001/20002
Pardon Briggs 0111001/0010001001
Sylvanus Tafft 0000100001/0001
Dyer Ramsdell 010001/00001
Israel Nash 301101/01001
Anthony Danderaut 100001/30001
John Bapt. Lapiere 20001/00001
Jennie Beaubien 020121/202101001
Antoine Beaubien 000000101/0000001
Lambert Thibault 2000101/031101
Timothy Dequindre 000001/20001
Julien Gagnier 120301/011001
Gilbert Dolson 10011001/0201
Griffith Roberts 000001/10101
Lewis Morrain 000001/10001

Henry Chapaton 021001/001001
Peter Dequindre 100001/01101
Francis Griffard 1221001/0021001
Clemons Louison 00001/00100001
Augustus Bourdeno 00001/1001
Lambair Beaubien 110001/100001
Pierre Beaubien 000001/20001
Antoine Rivard 0011001/1102001
Louis Grossbick 100001/0000101
Charles Grossbick 100001/0000101
Joseph Tiberdo 1000001 /0100001
Mary Comparil 0011/001101
Charles Morrain 100001/11001
Jean Tromblée 00101/0001001
Byram Guren 000001/201010001
Darius Lampson 001001/0101
Paul Verbrinkien 00001001/000001
Théophilus Mettez 001101/010001
Almina Willcox 02/010101
John Leib 00100201/00100001
John Meek 02010001/0021001
Abraham Furnier 1112001/1110001
Joseph Tromblée 102100001/221001
Augustus Tromblée 0000101/300001
John Laderoot 10001/10001
Peter Laderoot 00011001/0011001
Ebenezer A. Mason 1001001/1000300
Ignas Laderoot 30001/00001
John Bte Peltier 0001001/0010001
Peter Rivard 100001/00001
Leon Rivard 00001/00001
Gazel Marsac 20001/11001
James Boutton 000011/10001
Joseph Dubois 10101001/0030101
Francis Petre 1230011/0100001
Eustach Rivard 20001/00001
Tousaint Chesne 201020001/0110001
Leon Rivard 00001/10001
Lewis Chapoton 00200101/00002011
Sarah Meldrum 0011/10003
Abraham Cook 01010002/0101001
Artemus Hosmer 2000241/20111
James Stanton 001021/---
Timothy F. Sheldon 000011/000211
Cyprian S. Hooker 000102/00001
Ira Towle 000101/000001
Bradford Campbell 00001/11001
William Smith 1110001/001101
John Langs 00001/---
Israel Osburn 000001/---

Francis Ramo 0013000001/2010001
Francis Lorrow (Darrow?)0111101/0001001
John Palmer  10001/0001
William C. Maples 211001/013001
Hannah Hicks 01011001/00010001
Randolph Croude 100011/001011
Jacob Willheilm 000001/00010001
Joseph Philett 00001/---
Antoine Vermet 00001/00010001
Joseph Vermet 00001/00001
Lewis Peltier 01001/00001
John Bondy 210001/00101
Lewis Cicott 2030001/021001
Charles Larwill 00001/---
John Bte Campeau 00102001/00101001
Julien Campeau 00001/000001
James W. Knaggs 00101/1001101
Alexander Campeau 0000001/00011
Antoine Mettez 110101/100001
Piere Laberdy 22020001/00001
John Knaggs 100011/000000001
John Lawson 0011401/1311001
Stephen Hill 100021/1200011
George Young 1110001/0111100001
Hannah Akins 000001/000000001
Peter Cox 2202001/1020001
Thomas Flinn 0010001/020101001
George Washington free col: male 24-36; female 24-36.
John Hayes 000001/120001
William Lappin 0002101/0100001
Michel Dupra 01000001/011000001
Joseph Chovin 1000001/00001
William Hudson 20001/10001
Philip Tirrier 000001/10001
Chales Chartrain 100001/0002
Jubare Champaine 200101/000110001
Moris Morain 00201001/0211101
Terrais Champain 00012/01012101
George Campbell 0110001/210001
Elijah G. Downer 0001/10101
Gashet Marsac 10000001/---
Piere Gouin 20110001/102101
Louis Forté 10011/20011
Piere Rivard 000020001/00020101
Archange Rivard 00112/000101001
Michel Rivard 000220001/0012
Peter Broset 000000001/000001001
Andrew Brot 000001/20101
Joseph Allair 11101001/111111
Lucretia Downer 0001/00100001

John L. Trombley 00221001/2100001
John Kerby 0101001/200001
Denison R. Rose 00100101/201001
Thomas C. Brown 121001/100001
Warren Leet 0121001/2101001
Charles Grifford 10001/0001
Ambrose Trombleé 0000001/10001
Asquire Aldrich 11112111/0010001
Daniel Thompson* 3110(11)442/0022001
Robert Abbott 01200001/0120001
Mary Whiteman 12201/010101
Volney Wightman 01001/00001
Titus Dort 000011/00001
Samuel Tabine 000001/112001
Elijah Quick 100001/20001
Zina H. Hastings 211120001/2010201
Leonard Harrison 002001/211001
William Pangburn 0000000001/000000001
Merenus Harrison 311001/010001
Charles Harrison 110001/10001
Hiram Wightman 010011/12
Joshua Chamberlin 030001/20001
Miriby Chamberlin 001/0011001
Francis Ruff 120001001/10201
Richard McCurdy 00001001/000101
William Clay 20101/011001
John Flinn 0010001/0001
James Donells 320001/000010001
James Woods 00000001/00100001
William B. Hunt 10001/20002
Henry Clark 340001/01001
John Midges 000100001/00110001
John Sager 1100001/11101
Mich Mudge 10001/0001
Jacob Orr 0010011/000001
John Burbank 1100101/11101
Abraham Crispwell 00002001/00110001
Hart Warren 01002/10001
Thomas Tromblée 12121001/302001
Catherine Lafferty 01121/0000101
Piere Chovin 020001/1100101
Piere Pecha 1121001/010001
Simon Chovin 120001/01112
Nicholas Chovin 1000001/001001
Peter Grifford 02010101/1031001
Elias Jewell 111101/011001
Peter Tromblée 1113001/1111001
Louis Griffard 100001/20001
Elijah Emmerson 00100001/120001
William Hatton 011001/000001
Joseph Tromblée 0001301/0010001

# 1830 Census

Louis Goulett 001001/23001
Louis Griffard 00000001/0010001
Peter Bonholm 10000001/20001
Charles Gouin 00121001/00301001
George Laforge 100001/000001
William Starkweather 110001/100001
Warren Stone 230001/00001
Hannah Critchet 10001/0110001
Thomas Critchet 10001/00001
Esther Sands 0011/0000101
George Vickery 01100001/0011001
George W. Dunn 20002/00001
Luther Lincoln 100011/10002
Edward Vickery 21001/020001
David Vincent 210001/00001
Samuel Parlow 202101/020001
James Purdy 01010001/1121001
Elisha Kelly 20001/10001
William S. Gregory 0100001/0111001
Ichiel Davis 100001/00001
Allen Tibbitts 10001/10001
John Vn Sickle 113011/020001
Benjamin Williams 0101001/0200001
Caleb Tichener 0101101/002
David Hathaway 00001/0001
David D. Cady 3111001/012001
Zenus Bird 11001/00001
Samuel Bird 01210001/00001001
Henry Fairman 010011/21101
Daniel Tuttle 101001/10001
Rise L. Fellows 100001/10001
Festus A. Fellows 00001/10001
Jerry Fairman 0110001/112001
Joseph Willson 000001/000001
Alfred Moore 10101/200001
Archabald Murry 101011/200001
Jacob Combs 11004/200001
Noah Ramsdell Jr. 110001/001001
Noah Ramsdell Sr. 101021/110001
Ameriah Thare 00000001/00001001
Henry Bradley 100001/1110001
Isaac Goodwin 00210001/ 1110001
Justice Andrews 20002/00001
Paul W. Hasin 000001/011001
Erastus Starkweather 2022001/1110001
William Crampton 10011/11001
Ebenezer Jones 10001/0001
Ephraim Francis 12010001/0010001
Ira Steward 20001/00001
Samuel Bouton 00002/00010001

John Yerkus 000011/00001
Harvey Bradley 112001/110001
Gardner Simmons 20001/00001
Samuel Gates 00002/00001
John Durrin 000110001/000100001
Jerrard Griswold 000000001/00000001
John Parkinson 0021001/1001001
William Harper 000011001/00001
Lewis Lablain 01001/11001
David Cudworth 100001/00001
Garret Houghtaling 101001/000001
John Thare 10001/00001
Benjamin Harper 12001/100001
Adolphus Brigham 10001/11001
Richard Jostling 112001/000001
Barton Durfee 00001/20001
Allen Durfee 10001/10001
John Barlow 0111101/1110101
Mabel Stephens 1220001/00001
Judah Lewis 0101001/0100001
Hamilton Andrews 00001/---
Martin Fraser 1100001/102001
David Rider 0102001/1000001
George Durfee 001101/1111001
Peter Rodebough 10001/10001
John Rodebough 112001/010001
John Bouts 000001/120001
Welcome Bird 00001/---
Lemuel Cole 100001/21002
George McKeen 001001/22
William Houston 00102101/00100001
Hugh R. Clide 100001/10001
Albert G. Fellows 200021/00001
James Fellows 00000001/00020001
Moses Bradford 1100101/10101
Arony Bradford 0001101/0000001
Stephen M. Aldrich 110101/11001
Morton Linden 00001/10001
Darius C. Arnold 00001/10001
Nathan Johnson 01211001/00011001
John Westfall 00001/00001
Peter Berdan 20002/01001
James Cahoon 10001/11001
Reuben Wood 00001/30001
Ira M. Huff 20001/00001
Isaac Cummings 100002/01001
Elihu Drury 102111/1100001
Able Pachin 100001/10001
Lois Morris 2010021/00022001
Reubin Stark 000000001/01000001

Carlisle Wilkinson 000001/00001
James Maxwell 000000001/0001001
Robert Abbott, Jr 101001/10001
Joseph Visgar 101001/12002001
Mary Ann Chapple ---/0010000001
David Tull 0000111/001101
Noah M. Wells* 0100001/000101
George Morain* 20001/000010001
Henry Harris ---
Francis Campeau 110001/200001
Thomas B. Clark 1010001/00001
James Clark 00001/00001
Hannah Stead 121/000001
Isaac A. Combs 0100001/11001
Miranda Aspinwall 02201001/010001
James Vreland 100101/01101
Stephen Minawsaw 01111/1011201
Joseph Bondy 00111001/---
John Melosh 011101/200001
Joseph Lemerin 001011/---
Adna Willcox 01001/00002
Close Campeau 0110001001/012001
James Sutcliff 0000201/0101
Tarraise Delisle 00001/0211001
Charles Laberdy 13100001/0002001
Mary Laberdy 00100001/000001
John Bte Rivard 00001/00001
Achsah Goodell 01002/00001001
Jonas Gooddell 100001/01001
Alexander Laberdy 02010001/200001
Solomon Rousaw 00000101/200001
John Bte Rousaw 0000000001/00000001
Tarrais Lablain 10121/0113101
Peter Lafferty 0110001/200001
Dominique Bondy 00211001/0102001
Louis Berrisaw 1001010001/000011
Peter Lafayette 20001/00001
Alexander Aubin 00001001/---
Peter Lablain 110011/00101
John Bte Sallier 11001/10002
Archange Sallier 10021/020001
John Bte Drulliard 00101001/12100001
Antoine Odin 100010001/001100001
John Bte Porose 00000001/00011
John Bte Campeau 00011/001
Joseph Borrow 002002/22001
John Bte Labow 00210001/---
John Bte Lapage 0010101/00011
Charles Borrow 1020001/011001
Vernick Labow 00002/000101

Lewis Amon 101001/02001
Jack Borrow 00002/00010001
Peter Perry 101001/120001
Joseph Morrow 00010001/0020011
Joseph Piatt 2100001/01101
Seth Jones 101031/01001
Submit Duitt 00010000001/011101001
Francis Hicks 20002/10002
Abijah Jacox 01201011/001
Richard Long 100001/11001
Josiah Chase 000011/0001
Peter Bordow 00001/---
Garret A. Vreland 21000001/101001
Abraham Truax 0110001/011301
William Keith 1211001/101001
Joseph Hammon 010001/000001
Richard Smyth 00000101/00000001
Lucindy Leet 000001/000020001
Ara Sprage 100111/00011
Joseph Simpson 2000341/01102
Joseph Lesperance 00001/00011
Thomas Lewis 00012/111001001
Augustus Stone 110001/01001
Benjamin Lappin 0001/---
John Crider 000011/00001
Mary Norfolk 00013/001201
John Bartley 00001/00001
Samuel Richardson 202021/010021
Aaron Budd 011001/201001
Gardner Brown 10010001/0011
Asahel L. Bird 10001/00001
Philip Persons ---
Robert P. Harris 10000001/000001
Dominique Bondy 10001/0001
Peter Sancraint 0201001/20101
Bazile Bondy 200001/01101
James D. Fett 201001/10001
Darius C. Vreland 2001100001/00001
Jacob William 1110101/101101
Cornelius Springsteen 0000001/100101
Jonathan Wells 0000001/---
Elias Vreland 110011/10001
John Pattee 023101/00001
Martha Wells 022101/---
Henry Ducher 100001/10001
John Crofoot 0000111/0111101
James Johnson 20001/00001
Warriner Corkins 110001/10001
Nathan Willcox 0020101/01020001
John T. Smith 200101/00001

# 1830 Census

John Haden 1011101/0321001
David Gardner 121001/0101001
Lucius Corkins 210001/01001
Clement Lowder/Lovider 0010001/00001
Mary McMath 01022/0021101
Stephen Mory 10001/00001
Thomas Combs* 010101001/20001
William H. Cannon 00001/00010001
Hully St. George 00121/0010001
George Jewitt 01002/10001
Simeon A. Dunn 01001/0001
Mathew Woods 00101012/01130001
Nathaniel Case 100211/0110001
Lewis Northrop 10001/00110001
Jonathan Fay 120001/00001
Garret Vreland 0020011/0101001
John Phorbs(Forbes?) 10001/100001
Reuben Griswold 00001/00001
Lydia Hickcox 00002/0000001
Jacob Knox 00011001/00110001
David Smith 0020101/0101001
Simon Bronson 111001/000001
Benjamin Knapp 00101/20001
Thomas Long 10002/00101
John Conrad 200001/01001
Elias Long 010000001/---
Sarah Clark 11003/0220001
William Button 00001/00001
John Bte Mexico 11020101/111001
Tousant Druilliard 01102/00111001
Joseph Borrow 00001001/00000001
Benjamin F. Larned* 201011/000001
Joseph Pulsiver 120151/10002
David Clark 012001/000001
E. P. Hastings 200202/001101
Vincent Dufort 000000001/0000001
Paskile Poudrain 0000001/0010001001
Charles Gouin 0011000101/1311101001
John Potrain 01001/00001
Antoine Lesperance 11011001/00001001
Michael Monett 00010000001/00000001
Louis Laduck 200030001/10000001
James Witherell 0010100001/000100001
Francis St. Obin 10100001/1222001
Jacques Campeau 120001001/110011
Gabriel Chesne 31101101/0110201
Thomas Stead 000102/0100001
Louis Charbenaw 010001/01001
Louis Thibault 0000001/0010001
Daniel Gooddell 100001/01001

Leonard Lenox (free col.) 2 males 10-24, 1 36-55, 1 55-100. 2 females 10-24, 1 24-36
William McCormac 010001/0100001
Hugh McVey 32020001/0020001
Francis Laterno 21100011/11001
Daniel Grason (free col.) 1 male 55-100.
Spencer French (free col.) 1 male 24-36. 1 female 10-24, 1 24-36
George Washington (free col.) 1 male 24-36, 1 female under 10, 1 10-15.
Prime Johnson (free col.)1 male 55-100
William Charlton (free col.) 2 males under 10; 1 36-55; 1 female under 10; 1 24-36
Louis Lorrow 111001/110001
Tousaint Lorrow 110001/31001
Alexander Fraser 0200001/100111
Welcome Delisle 022000101/00101001
Antoine Chiguin 1100001/010101
Alexander Vermit 000001/10001
Ebenezer Pate? 1402101/0011001
Alexander Belisle 0000001/000001
William Woodbridge 01101001001/0102101001

Enumerator: Nathaniel Champ, who states in part:. . . the aforesaid is correct and true according to the best of my knowledge and belief, Excepting the family of David Clark, who resides on an Iseland at the mouth of the Detroit River. On being informed there was no opportunity or chance of conveyance on the Iseland to his house, I took the account of his family from his next neighbor who said he knew the family well and could give them in as correct as I could get them from him or the family. Their number consist of five whites." Detroit 27 November 1830

CITY OF DETROIT
Cullen Brown 00015/00101
James T. Penny 001091/30021
Gerry Spencer 301311/10001
John Brown (free col.) 2 males 10-24
William Dusel 320312/00012
John W. Woolsey 100011/10002
John Hale* 100111/211001
Francis P. Browning* 30013/31012001
Alexander Grant 00001/00001
Benjamin F. H. Witherell 100011/11011
Alexander D. Frazier 00001/00011
Randal S. Rice 100001/010001
John Justice 121005/21
Patrick Sheyney(Chene) 100001/00001
Stephen Wells 00011/00101
Henry Raymond 00001/00001
Barnabas Campeau 02010001/0002
Henry Chipman* 2001001/112101
Benjamin Woodworth* 0210321/ 0001101
James Conden 000001/---
John R. Williams 0122201/01010101
Oliver W. Miller* 00010001/0000001
William Hart 110061/000010001
Walter B. Hewett 100021/00011
Daniel B. Cole 01110001/0100101
Jonathan Keeney 0122101/0001101
John E. Schwarts 110101/10211
Eben Beach 1110121/00022001
John Cook (free col.) 1 male 10-24, 2 24-36
   3 females under 10, 1 10-24, 1 24-36
Gabriel Louisignon 10011/00001001
James McDonald 1211001/1001001
Jesse Osburn* 01111011/111101
Alanson M. Hurd* 001121/10012
Josiah R. Dorr 000011/00021
John J. Deming 111011/10022
Charles F. Reed 00001/---
Thomas Rowland 0011001/000101
Catherine McNiff ---/000110001
Alexander McArthur 00012/2001
John Manuel 100000001/000011
Thomas Knowlton 11000001/010001
James Cicot 0002001/131001
John Collins 112013/21001
Joseph Garrow 00002/0001
James Woodward 000001/010001
Daniel O'Dell 011001/010001
Benjamin Carnes 000001/01001
Hiram Cadnell 01001/10001

Joseph Mosley (free col.) 1 male under 10,
   1 36-55. 2 females under 10, 1 10-24,
   1 24-36
William Brewster* 100111/11011
Knowles Hall 000211/11101
John Batist Vernier 0000000001/00000001
Michael Hale 00023/20011
Lenis C. Boit 1130001/001001
John Haley 010001/001001
Joseph Bour 110001/002001
Charles Delisle 120001/00001
George Beardsley 0100101/1102101
Michael Kerley 000001/00001
William Russel 01000001/00000001
John Smyth 00101/00001
John Weese 10001/100011
Harriet Myres 0001/0010001
Tousant Lesperance 10001/10001
Batist Lesperance 10011/0001
Charles Duchene 20001/0001
Phleben (Fabian) Jubenvill 100001/1001
Francois Degeridan (Desjardins?) 000001/001
Henry Howard 10011/00011101
Charles Carter 000001/00001
Gustavus B. Rood 010001/111101
John Wilson 1200001/000001
Antoine Greenwood 00001/00011
Joseph Bush 10001/00001
Henry Sanderson 00002001/01001001
John Roberts 000111/11002
Marshal Chapin* 101111/1100011
Samuel Phelps 0001114/00001
James O. Lewis 01001/3100101
Hugh Brady* 02010001/00210102
David French 001002/001011
Otis G. Eels 10001/01001
Lucine Lyon 000001/---
George Cooms 00000001/10023001
William McCroskey 000100001/001011
August Kunse 000001/0001
Julius Eldred* 2021111/0101011
John Howard 2000(10)5/1010201
Theophilis Mettez 001101/001001
Mathias Blotner 1001011/010011
John Beach 110001/10001
John Lebott 0310001/100001
James Hammon 000001/---
Briah Merrit 011001/001011
John Passage 20001/000010001
Henry Berthlett 010100011/0101001
Ruel W. Robinson 10001/01001

# 1830 Census

John Patteson (free col.) 1 male 10-24, 1 24-36, 1 36-55. 1 female under 10, 2 10-24, 1 36-55.
Augustin Berthlett 1/0001
Francis VanAntwerp 00005/0001
Susanna Duchene 10012001/0000101
Sip Forth (free col.) 1 male 36-55 1 female 36-55
Morris Miller (free col.) 2 males 10-24, 1 24-36. 1 female 36-55.
Baptist St. Amour 010100001/0012201
Peter Conden 100101/00001
Joseph Laflure 020000001/0010001
Samuel Parra 000001/00001
John Cook* 000101/00001
Michael Doran/Dosan 00001/---
James Williams 0101001/120101
Henry V. Disbrow 000011/00011
Peter Denoyer 01110101/1211101
Peter Desnoyer 01001/10011
Henry M. Campbell* 0200011/1030012
John Dumark 1000001/210001
Jonathan Kearsley 000021/001101
Abram Noyce 000001/10101
Lewis B. Sturgis 000010001/00001001
Martha TenEyck* 00000001/000011
George A. Okeef 000011/---
Solomon Sibley* 101020001/002110101
John K. McDongle 000000001/00001
Victor Watson 0101100001/0010001
George Fearson 00001/20011
Cyprian Stevens 001001/000001
Francis Lemon 101020001/01000001
James Slaughter (free col.) 2 males under 10, 1 24-36. 1 female under 10, 2 10-24
Mary Brown 0011/0011102
Pierre Landrosh 220001/01
Charles Leaned 000010001/0000100001
Francis Fournier Jr. 210001/00001
Mary McMillen 0001(15)02/0010201
Israel Noble 200001/000001
Robert Smart 010010001/0110001
William Wattles 0101681/0011101
Owen Aldrich 00105641/10211
Martha Wheaton ---/000001
Narcisse Vincent 20001/00000100001
David Cooper 1200101/110012
Elias Doty* 0102201/0000101
Matthew A. Stewart* 10002/02101
David C. McKinstry* 0205731/0011101

Samuel Perkins* 000010001/00001001
Nicholas Goutrie 100031/102101
Joseph Andre-Clark 11201001/121112
Nancey Bates 002001/000001
Mary Raymon 001011/00000001
Dominique Thomas 120001/002001
John Griffard 00001/30001
Mark Brown 00002/10011
Susan Dubois 00101/000000101
Saripha Shank 102001/010001
Elizabeth Lyond ---/00112
Gabriel Richard 000001001/---
James Whipple 00002/11001
Antoine Nephew (Neveu) 0011001/0001101
Charles Wismett? 01002/00001
Horace Tereawen* 1211201/1000001
Joseph Chadnin 0000001/00001
John O'Conner 0100211/100001
Samuel B. Picket 0011101/002
Martin Story 00002/20001
Mary Stoner 00001/00100001
Margaret Packard 01/111010011
Louis Pelkey 02200001/0010101
Benjamin Morris (free col.) 1 male 36-55 1 female 10-24, 1 36-55
Joseph Amlin 010011/11001
Isac Trottier 010001/20001
Patrick Dunevan 00000201/00001
Levi Willard 121001/010001
John Farrod 111111/11000101
Jeremiah Moors 110001/00011
Robert Henderson 1001/00001
Paul D. Anderson 001001/000001
Shelemeth S. Hall 0000001/002001
Frederick Dean 01001/20101
William Partlow 120001/100011
Philip Warren 1000001/001101001
Medan (Medard) Tremble 00001/000100001
Josiah Goddard 201011/ 021101
Abigail Ryon 01/0000001
Thomas Scott 000002/0000001
Horace Wilson 100011/01001
Thomas Coquilliard 000101/200001
Richard Bury 310001/0110011
Leonard Loomis 000001/111001
Tousant Founier 00001001/00001
Antoine Jubenvill 123001/100101
Joseph Chevalier 011000001/2200001
Jacob Barton 000001/0000011
Nathan B. Carpenter 000102/110001

Phineas Davis Jr 0010301/201021
Tunis S. Wendall* 00011/00002
Justin Rice* 10000101/1200101
Edward Bingham 00011/00002
Elliot Gray 000111/00001
Josh Tucker 010003/00002
John Bronson* 0000021/20112
Francis Clockmire 000001/---
James Abbott 00003001/0011001
Thomas Daily 100001/0100001
Justus Wood 1200001/110001
Louis Reneau 000001/10001
John B. Laparte 00121001/1200001
Peter Lafroy 1021001/1102001
Antoine Dequinder 0111002/122001
Henry Newberry 100041111/01
Emmod Hanley/Hawley? 2112222/010001
Benjamin B. Kercheval* 100001/12001
John Palmer 001012/110002
Joseph Campeau 22112001/210101
Conrad Seek 00102001/---
Philanda Holland* ---/001311
George Bowman 00023/10001
William Sloss 01000001/100111
Charles Jackson* 000012/101001
James W. Hinchman 100001/00002
Abram C. Canniff 0011031/0210001
Eleasur Kay 01131101/00111
Hannah Roby 0210010001/000131
John Hendree* 100001/10012
Francis Sugar 00000001/01022
Warren Dingley* 000141/---
A. B. Hinkley 0001402/----
Joseph Mallett 002001/001101
Thomas Henton (free col.) 1 male under 10,
    1 10-24, 2 36-55. 3 females under 10,
    2 24-36, 1 36-55
Paschal Lasell (free col.) 1 male 24-36
    1 female 36-55
Alva H. Ewers/Evers? 100031/00101
Guy H. Leonard 00001/---
Harvey Williams 000243/101021
John Mettez 10001/10001
Catherine Phalan 01002/000020001
DeGarmo Jones 100011/101211
Simon Poupard 00001/20001
Jairus Baldwin 110001/10001
Peter Clark 02336012/0001001
Alexander Gage 0011001/00001
Stewart Johnson 00001/00011

William Sims 0000001/---
Alexander Campbell 1110442/00003
William Larkins 12000001/110001
Frederick Bird 20022/00001
John Roseter 0101001/0011
Samuel Reid 011001/210001
Robert McLaren 000006/10121
James Harner* 100004/20002
John Sweet 000001/000001
Edward Brooks 000000101/222011001
Bela Knapp 00013/---
Elias S. Swan 000001/00101
Thomas Palmer 1200211/210011
Thomas J. Owen 000011/000001
John Truax 0001101/10001
Stephen Bane 22206/11011
Jeremiah Dean 010121/10013
Arza Brown 000001/---
Margaret Moon 100011/00021101
Henry S. Cole 201012/10112
Levi Brown 100001/010101
Cyril Cook 100001/101011
Levi Cook 00001101/001001
Asa Madison 110321/00001
John McDonald 01200002/111001
Reynold Gillett 100001/00101
Thomas C. Sheldon 001001/200201
Ann Coats ---/00000001
John Waring 100011/00001
Jacques Geridan 030001/00001
Jane Thibault 000001/00003001
Andrew Mack* 01100222/01011221
John Burtis 000002/000001
Charles Chapman 00001/0001
John Canan 100011/00001
John Splan 100001/00001
Henry Whitney 020001/0000101
William Robinson 011111/01101001
John Barrack 01001/1001
John Scot 000101/00001
Harvy Griswold 000152/210101
John Garrison 000110001/0010001
Maria King 01/1110001
Samuel D. Johnson (free col.) 1 male 10-24,
    1 24-36, 1 36-55. 2 females under 10,
    1 10-24, 1 24-36
Benjamin Clarke 211001/11001
Charles Howard 000001/10001
Nathaniel Champ 201002/010001
Ira Andrus 2010001/111001

Elenor Harris 00002/0001001
Henry Lafray 21000111/000001
George Perkins (free col.) 1 male 10-24, 1 24-36, 3 36-55. 1 female 24-36
Abram Sykes (free col.) 1 male under 10, 1 24-36. 1 female under 10, 1 24-36
Patrick W. Heley 10001/1001
Etienne Crate 21000001/0200001
Jacques Pelkey 0001001/1120001
Francois Matenna 0000101/00010001
Nancy Torrey (free col.) 3 males under 10, 1 10-24. 1 female 36-55
Antoine Rabbay 0010001/221001
Samuel Sherwood 100001/120001
Elijah Convers/Conners 2100002/011001
Peter N. Geridan 00101/1001
Joseph Fursio 2000001/1010001
Samuel Todd 00001/0001
Augustin Chapaton 1020002/2210001
Theophilus Mettez 000000001/000100001
Joseph Cota 00000002/00000001
Linus Davenport 001011/10102
Shadrach Gillett 11101/2010211
Adna Merritt 200011/00001
Ebenezer Hurd 1010001/202101
Eustace Chapiton 121111/200001
Elizabeth Gagnier 0111/001201
Philip Morin 200001/110001
John B. Jubenvill 0000101/00000001
Joseph Slumb 1000001/000010001
Timothy Fales 0101321/30011
John Scott 300001/001001
John White 2000001/011111
Matthew Moon 100012/10001
Titus Adams 0100001/001001
Thomas Dorothy 000001/000001
Silas Smith 100001/210001
Joseph Kid 00001/000110001
Colman Funston 220021/000001
Henry Wheaton 0110001/011001
Robert Bata 121001/121001
John Burdino 00001/00001
Francois Laturno 210011/011001
Silas Allen 0200111/1000001
Charles Gladue 10001/0001
Charles Larned* 001002/212001
Joseph W. Torry 000001/100001
Lewis Rice 000011/11011
John Henley 002001/1000101
Cornelius Scanlon 110003/000101

Lewis Cass 0002101/003202
Peter Savina 1000001/000011
Henry Wool 2101001/00201
Antoine Dunor 2000001/020001
Stephen Hasle (free col.) 1 male 10-24, 1 30-55. 1 female 5-10, 1 36-55
Henry D. Sired 00001/---
Sheldon McKnight 00001/---
George W. Dunks 10001/20001

Enumerator: Samuel Sherwood
17 September 1830

MONROE COUNTY
Harry Conant 0010101/21011
Oliver Johnson 0110001/011001
Thomas G. Cole 00001/10001
Lambert Cauchois 000101/00001
Dan B. Metler 110110001/10011
Robert G. Clark 01100011/002002
Luther Parker 010120101/010001
John J. Wendell 010011/10001
Joseph Wood 101001/010201
Ethel Birch 300001/01011
Alcott C. Chapman 2000332/11111
Peter P. Ferry 110100001/011101
John Kromer 200001/10001
John Brown 0001011/300001
Edward D. Ellis 00101/00001
Jasper B. Lane 100001/12001
Norman D. Curtis 00002/10001
Noble D. Curtis 00211001/0000001
George Alford 000000001/020000001
Thomas McDowell 0000101/10011
Seneca Allen 0110002/101101
Ezekiel A. Peltier 00011/20002
Wolcott Lawrence 220000101/011001
Nathan Noble 20002/10101
Lewis Rose 00101/00001
Isaac P. Skinner 111011/011001
Sylvester Remington 00001/0011
Albert K. Heacock 1010111/01001
N. W. Wadsworth 001012/0002
Paschal Mallet 001011/10001
Jonathan Vickers 00011/0020101
Henry Disbrow 00000001/01000001
P. W. Warriner 000001/00101
Francis Fairchild 00001/30001
Lester P. Clark 00011/10001
Augustin Detaillein 01000001/000001

Miles Thorp 000001/00001001
Augustin LeCoursier 0110001/200101
Joseph Mahewe 1010001/0100001
Joseph Kilbourn 10101/10001
Mrs. Brown 100001/111101
Joseph Nephew 1111001/000101
Louis Bernard 211000001/001001
Laurent Reneau 210001/010011
Josephus Rose 200001/00001
Joseph Loranger 3211301/102101
Philander M. Jeffries 00001/0001
Hiram Brown 220201101/100101
Joseph C. Garwood 10011/00001
Wyman A. Town 000001/31001
John Gilmore 000000001/000000001
William Gates 200001/010001
Robert Clark 01011001/0110101
James Fowler 00001/00001
Michael Gregory 00001/10001
Hiram Vinel 10101/00001
Jean Bt. Roseau 010000101/0000001
Alexis Labadie 00000002/---
Jean Marie Navarre 000000001/00000001
Peter Benson 20001/10001
Charles Noble 100011/10001
John Anderson 00010001/10021001
A. E. Wing 001001/020021
Wm. L. Riggs 000001/001011
Joseph Dazet 0000000001/001000001
William Page 1000001/1010001
James Mattocks 1100001/011001
Winslow Duncan (Dunton) 1100001/10101
Ralph Bailey 0021101/1100001
Charles J. Lanman* 010001/31001
James Shew 000011/00001
Anthony L. Briggs 2120101/300102
James Hale 120101/202101001
Alanson Fox 021011/001001
William Bancroft 10001/0001
Luther Stoddard 0010001/011
William Ruland 00001/0001
William Bicie 0010001/111001
John Mulhollen 00001/10001
Felix Hinchman 001001/101001
Daniel Parker 00000001/---
François Robert 0011101/00010001
François Robert Jr. 00001/0001
Mrs. Navarre 00121/00001101
Levi P. Humphrey 000012/---
François Bordeau 0022101/01000001
David Stoddard 0011001/021001

Hyacynthe Duval 200020001/00011
Joseph Stuart 00112001/0101101
John Paxton 002001/3100011
Jacques Navarre 001021001/00200001
James J. Godfroy 30011/10001
Laurent Durocher 0111001/221201
Joseph Genereux 0000001/11001
Mrs. Poupard 00002/00010001
Jean B. Letour 1100001/101101
Augustin Lefleur 11200001/100001
Louis Leduc 01020001/00010001
Medard Couture 000001/00000001
Daniel Cornwell 1110001/011201
Mrs. Lacrois 0101/010001
Antoine Robert 00001/001
Charles Nadeau 22001/00001
Antoine Ducleau 00010001/---
Alexis Soudriette 10101/00001
Charles Lafleur 102001/01001
Joseph Nadeau 220001/110001
Antoine Nadeau 1110001/021001
Benjamin L'Enfant 00000001/---
Louis Petit 00010001/1000001
Mrs. Campeau 00000001/000000001
Louis Couture 00001001/000000001
François Lasselle 00010001/0012
Louis Proux 10001/00001
Earl Sexton 011001/100001
Antoine Bougard 010001/21111
Mrs. Proux 00002/00010001
Antoine St. Comb 2000011/01001
John Whipple 011010001/3112001
David M. Jacobs 11001/10001
Luther Harvey 220120101/012101001
Warren Bartlet 0200001/21001
Jacob B. Parker 211000001/1011001
Reuben Stoddard 0011001/010201
John Ramsey 1200001/021001
Anthony McNulty 110001/100001
John Diver 000000001/00000001
Michael Chronenwidt 00001/0001
Simon Knapp 1010001/110001
Kraft Deniger 000001/11001
Charles Ogiley 00000001/00000001
Lodowick Knapp 101001/00001
Samuel Stone 00220021/120001
William Shew 000030001/10001
Betsy Williams ---/10001
William Dunlop 111001/010001
Enos Jackson 1010101/211111
Isadore Navarre 001200001/100200011

James Isbel 100011/100001
Joseph Farrington 0100001/1001001
Jacob Shew 00001/1001
John Alford 111001/11001
Ambroise Charland 1100001/112101000001
William Ryan 00002/---
Robert Navarre 00011/0001
Truman Bernard 0000011/---
William Preston 100001/00001
Joseph Ruland 00001001/001
William Frost* 0010001/0210001
Robert Albain 00021001/0010011
Jean Marie Menard 0110001/20001
Platt Navarre 223001/001001
Edmund Littlefield 2020001/0001001
Amos Root 0220001/100001
William Walker 00001/00001
Minor Downing 110001/10001
Asa Adams 10001/0001
Joseph Nadeau 0211101/200001
Jean Bt. LeDuc 10100001/0011001
Jean Bt. Smith 220001/001001
Leander Béseau 11001/100001
Tousaint Soleau 121001/21001
Peter LaCroix 000001/10001
James Robb 0000001/10011
Dominique LaCroix 3200001/000001
Dominique Couture 100001/111001
Alexis Navarre 112001/101001
Edward Loranger 10001/0001
John B. Hitchcock 111001/01101
Gabriel Fontaine 1220101/100101
Justin Bennet 00000001/---
David Simmons 10001/10001
François Sanscrainte 012011/100001
Jean B. Lamourande 10001/00011
Pierre Bordeaux 01100001/1110001
Jean B. Nadeau 00001/11001
Joseph Poupard 0200001/21001
André Poupard 0200001/---
Augustin Navarre 1011001/00001
François Gaudon 00000001/00020001
Madam Soleau 001011/00011001
Joseph Gaillard 2311001/011101
Alexis LeBeau 10002/20101
Lewis E. Bond 001120001/02200011
Jean Bt. LaCass 000110001/0010001
Joseph Giguerre 00101/0001
Joseph Beauhomme 1011001/11111
Jean Bt. Robert 000001/10001

Mrs. Fix 112001/0201001
Joseph Menard 022001/210001
Antoine Nadeau 1100001/101001
Martin Nadeau 000110001/000000001
Alexis Nadeau 0110001/31001
Joseph Robert 00001/1001
Joseph Bordeaux 210001/01101
Dominique Coutoure 10001/200011
Joseph Nadeau 101001/200001
Nehemiah Lovewell 100011/100001
Joseph Clark 100001/0001
Joseph Bissenet 000101/---
Alexis Bissnet 11001/21001
Samuel Atkinson 5240001/0100012001
Elihu Ward 00012011/0000101
Horace Hart 1131001001/012001
Joshua Parker 00100001/0011001
Luther Dorrell 111101/101001
Walter Comstock 1010001/002101
William Mills 00011001/10000001
William W. Jones 00001/0001
George Darrow 21000002/1011001
Charles Charter 10001/00001
Timothy Sprague 00001/0001
James Smith 002001/320001
Richard Peters 220012/010001
Morris Wells 300001/00001
Mrs. Wells 0001/10010001
Martin Smith 0001102/0110001
Jonathan Fisher 00010001/0000001
John Pitts 1200001/100001
Lewis Wells 010002/0101
James Squires 300011/01001
Riley Ingersol 100001/10001
William Burch 001100001/---
George Sorter 11200001/110001
Isaac Sorter 0000001/120001
Elijah Martin 0000001/---
Calvin Lamkins 00101/1001
William W. Brown 11001/20001
Francis Farwell 021101/211101
Samuel C. Heacock 01001101/03001
Jacques Bissenet 00001/20011
Joseph Dufour 1000001/110001
Joseph Bissenet Sr. 001100002/00000001
Samuel H. Gale 0210001/2010010001
Alvin Powers 1301001/1201001
Mrs. McManus 00111/120110101
John Baldwin* 100011/0011
Leon Gouin 1110001/010011
Isaac Burch 100001/00001

Pierre Navarre 000001/10011
Jacques Navarre 0010001/000001
Jean Bt. Bouvier 10001/10001
François Navarre 0100111001/0001000001
Claude Couture 31101001/121001
Robert Navarre 1011001/120001
Mrs. Cadorette 00001001/0000001
Bazil Deschartlet 100001/0001
Louis Robidoux 0200111/011111
François Lavoie 12210001/0000001
Louis More 0000001/1000100001
John T. Baldwin 00100001/00000001
Tibbal Baldwin 100001/00001
Benjamin F. Stickney 00003001/001
Joseph Tremblé 110110001/10001
William Wilson 200011/10001
Isaac B. Worden 000000001/0000001
Budd Martin 0200001/101001
Mrs. Merrit 01001/0100001
William D. Corbett 00000012/10111001
Ebenezer Ward 100011/10001
Joseph Prentice 0100101/0000001
Luther Whitmore 00110001/0101101
Leonard Whitmore 00001/00001
Hiram Bartlet 000001001/111001
Noah Whitney* 100100001/0011001
Colman J. Keeler 00102001/00012
Samuel F. Keeler 0000101/001
Amara Bishop 000002/---
Alvin Evans 000021/---
Joseph Titsworth 000001/000001
Joseph Roop 00001/00011
Eli Hubbard 2111001/101001
John Roop 20001/00001
Roswell Ruby 1010001/00100011
John Phillips 001010001/000210001
Phillip Phillips 00001/00002
John Lewis 0000201/0000001
Andrew Jacobs 0110001/1010001
Moody Mills 020001/21001
John Laborn 11001/10001
Robert Martin 0000000001/000000001
Levi Thomas 0111001/1310001
Joseph Martin 210001/011011
Caleb Horton 00101/00001001
John Holmes 221001/10101
William Sibley 00111001/00001001
Augustin Prentice 00001/00001
Samuel Horton 10001/1001
Cyrus Fisher 00011/01001

William Wilkinson 231001/000001
Jesse Mills 00001/20001
Pierre Corneau 00100001/1000101
Louis Garneau 00001/00001
Louis Bernard 20011/10101
Joseph Douquette 20001/00001
Jean Bt. Descharlet 20001/10001
François Villere 100011/12001
William Lapointe 11020001/000001
Bartholomew Momonie 20001/10001
Benjamin Soliere 10001/00001
Claude Soleau 20001/10001
Pierre Clouthier 01010001/1121001
Antoine Bernard 10001/0001
François Momone 200001/000001
Alexis Labadie 01011/10001
Antoine Gee 210011/01101
Joseph Poulin 10001/10001
Isadore Morin 000110001/---
Louis Morin 000000001/0001001
François Poulin 001110001/00000001
Charles Drouillard 0100000001/000000001
Louis Bodin 10112001/112001
Alexis Knaggs 20001/30001
Henry St. Bernard 10000001/201001
Bazil Martin 10001/110001
Joseph Faubert 0100001/002001
Pierre Robert 100001/20001
Jean Bt. Sanscrainte 20200101/011001
Joseph Robert 00012/10011
Jean Bt. Riopel 100001/10001
Leon Souliere 010101/11001
Antoine Lasselle* 0000001/010001
Jean Bt. Lasselle 200001/10001
Jacques Bernard 20001/00001
Madam Lasselle 00101/000010001
Jean Bt. Courneille 21010001/121101
Hyacythe Bourgard 00002/20001
Pierre Robideau 00000001/00200001
Leon Chovin 1000021/00011
Stephen Downing 000110001/00200101
Ephraim Adams 200001/10001
Henry Doyle 2100001/01001
Claude Chovin 000101/00000001
Alexis Belmar*000000001
François Centure 00001/000000001
Alexis Loranger 212001/02001
Jean Bt. Cicotte 2100001/120011
Mrs. Knaggs 0011001/1111001
Mrs. Langlois 00001/0000101

Joseph Langlois 000001/00001
Samuel M. Smith 000001/---
Joseph Ivan 0020110001/000000001
Alexis Loranger 00001001/---
Joseph Ivan Jr. 2000001/10001
François Delaille* 000130001/00010101
Louis LeDuc-Percie 012001/01001
Pierre Valiquette 201002/10001
Pierre Nadeau 10001/00001
Alexis Beaubien 0102001/002
Antoine Delaille 00001/10001
Leon Mettez 100001/10001
Hubert Duchesne 10001/00001
Pierre Duchesne 00011001/0000001
Thomas Caldwell* 31200011/010201
Jean Marie Beaubien 1310001/100001
Lambert LeDuc 11001/20001
Stephen Smith (free col.) 1 male under 10, 1 10-24, 2 24-36. 1 female under 10, 1 24-36
Charles Proux* 000001/---
Alvin Chase 00002/20001
James Setford 101001/101001
Stephen Downing Jr. 000001/210001
Joseph Bourdignon 01110001/1212001
Charles Vermet 100001/00001
James Knaggs 0101101/0112001
Richard Mettez 10001/00001
George Knaggs 00001/0001
François Mouton 11200001/010101
Benjamin Lamkins 0120001/0011001
James Stewart 000101/00001
William Brown 00012001/01100001001
Abraham Maston 211001/101001
Oziel Lamkins 00001/0001
Antoine Coate 00000001/---
Truman Curtis 0022001/110011
Rufus Downing 220001/00101
Hubert Mettez 00001/0001
William Willard 1101101/2111001
John Mulks 00121001/01002001
Warner Peirce 200001/210001
James Cornell 110021/210011
Robert G. Hayward 200101/00001
Joseph Robideau 01101001/0110101
Joseph Jacob 1010001/00000101
Daniel Duval 0111001/211011
Daniel Newkirk 00002001/10123001
Daniel Mulhollen 00020001/20020101
Regis Racicote 00110001/00000001
Felix Mettez 010010011/00100001

Antoine Drouillard 100001/21001
Joseph Campeau 100000001/00000001
Joseph Roe 100011/11001
Julien Prairie 00001001/---
Nicholas LaPointe 1110001/120001
Dominique Drouillard 00001/00001
Joseph Duceau 1110001/121001
Gabriel Duceau 02001/30001
Jean Bt. LeBrash 0010001/0001
Felix Paré 1200001/11001
Jean Bt. Cloutier 200001/02001
Bazil Couzineau 0221101/001101
Lewis Jacob 00001/0001
Job Bodette 020001/210001
Jean Bt. Roe 000001/212001
Antoine Roe 10001/00001
Peter Jacob 2100001/01101
John Jacob 0011/1120101
Pierre Picotte 0122101/000101
Dominique Pougé 1100001/101001
Claude Prudhomme 100001/11011
Madam Martin 00001/00101001
Jean Marie Menard 000001/21001
Paul Lucier 10001/00001
François Menard 010001/00001
Louis Momonie 0001000001/00100001
Lent Martin 00101001/00001
James Mulhollen 00001/1001101
François Couzineau 02101100001/0100110011
Theodore Dorézeau 001111/12001
Louis Jacob 0111101/00111
Joseph Morass 1120201/10001
Antoine Lamorie 010001/21001
George Hall 1012001/010101
Salmon Keeney 0020001/021001
Louis Montreville 1211001/101001
Etienne Ratelle 1210001/110001
Hyacynthe Bernard 01120001/2020001
Samuel Willard 00001/0001
Eli Bodette 210001/111001
John Bt. Borneau 201001/01001
Fones Green 0110000001/000001
Richard Hayward 10001/10001
Joseph Barron 000001/30001
Antoine Barron 00001/10001
François Lajeunesse 121001/11001
Alexis Couzineau 221001/11101
Louis Gagnier 020001/21001
Alexis Ganard 110001/110001
Antoine Larabell 10001/00001
Dominique Roe 2200001/102001

Bazil Baron 00001C001/10001
Antoine Lafontaine 1210001/20001
Ettiene Duceau 200001/11001
Jean Bt. Ganard 00001/11001
Louis Lavoie 00111001/01101001
Pierre Baron 021000001/0101001
Pierre Gagnier 1100001/11001
Joseph Valliquette 221001/000001
Agustin Gagnier 1111001/110001
Joseph Derval 020001/010211
Pierre Jourdan 00001/00001
Nicholas Ganard 001001/1201
Joseph St. Bernard 110001/01001
Hiram Collier 100001/00001
Levi Collier 20001/01001
Madame Roe 10101/10001001
Andrew Diver 010001/1300001
Mrs. Jobin 00001/011100001
Toussaint Martin 000001/21001
Antoine Chovin 00002/000100001
Joseph Goodrich 00111001/0000001
Waterbury Gray 22120001/0101101
Daniel Clarke 10300001/000101
Joseph Robert Sr. 001110001/0120001
Amos Taylor 000001/00001
Jacob Leonard 20001/10101
Hiland Beach 0200001/102001
John Corson 100001/110001
Noel Valiquette 100001/00001
Antoine Mersau 000000010001/0001001
Mrs. Josette Gagnier ---/00000001
Francis Charter 1020001/00001
Ettiene LeBeau 220011/112001
Antoine Cozivent 200001/00001
Avery Plummer 0112101/02
James H. Miller 1000001/120001
Mrs. Mary Vermette 1111/122001
Antoine Chartelot 00002000001/100010001
Pierre Campau 111001/101001
Antoine Gie 001000001/00000001
Jean Bt. Belcour 111001/010001
Mrs. Archange Laviolet 11/10011
Toussaint Valiquette 00001/0001
Isaac Robert 2010001/11001
Jean Bt. Drouillard 10001/10001
Jean Bt. Fevereau 01111001/01100001
Jean Bt. Duceau 10001/12001
Joachim Gireux 0000001/1020001
Augustin Antailleur 202002/01001001
Alexis Arquoette 11000001/10001

Pierre Aubin 0000001/10001
Medard Labadie 01201001/00011001
Joseph Drouillard 000000001/000011001
François Lozon 01210001/2100001
Joseph Duval 0210001/1011001
Hyacynthe LeDuc 00010001/---
Jean Bt. Suzar 120001/110001
Henry Fournier 10001/0001
Pierre Brancheau 11110001/2212201
Joseph Brancheau 00001/10001
Michael Duval 111011/02001
Ettiene Duval 021000201/21101101
Ignace Robert 1000011/20001
Samuel Agnew 01000001/221001
Dominique Suzor 110001/100001
François Navarre 20001/00001
Robert F. Navarre 100011/11002
Dennis Drouillard 200001/12001
Frederick Rowe 00001/---
Frederick Baker 00001/---
Addison Burch 00001/31001
Antoine Sargeant 0100001/100002
Pierre Duval 000011/20001
François Menard 1000101/12001
François Champagne 0110001/21001
Paul Navarre 120011/011001
Oliver Cooley 0021001/222001
Joseph Cadé 000001/20001
William Austin 001001/110001
Andrew Murry 1100001/00001
Joseph Chamberlin 000020001/0001
James Bently 1200013/20211
Benjamin Cooley 000001/20002
Louis Chamberlin 10001/11001
Jean Bt. Dubrais 10001/20002
James Ellison 01001/00001
Henry F. Cisco 00001/0000000001
Michael McDonell 10001/10001
David Wellman 1110001/020001
Ethel Choate 00001/10001
Hiram Miller 000001/31001
Joshua Miller 00002001/0001001
Peter D. Labadie 00001/---
Andrew Monteure 00001/---
Antoine Navarre 00001/---
Joseph Comtois 00001/---
John Clock 0000001/000001
John Bemis 000000001/---
Theodore E. Phelps 000001/---
Charles Martin 000001/0000010001

Jean Bt. Baumiere 0310001/011001
Ettiene Réaume 310001/10002
Joseph Réaume 00001101/00011
John McClung 0000010001/000001
Alex Sanscrainte 100101/01001
Peter Sanscrainte 1101001/201001
Augustin Duceau 20001/01001
Jean Bt. Charboneau 121001/000001
Thomas Bondie 101001/11001
Louis Marie 000001/222001
Eustace Bondie 00011/0010001
Laurent Bondie 00001/00001
Jean Bt. Rousson 010011/210001
Peter Coan 00001/10001
Augustus Coan 01100001/01000001
Edmund Coan 10001/00001
Joseph Johnson 001001/00101
Nelson Smith 100001/10001
David Davis 2000001/003001
Peter Lafleur 100001/00001

Enumerator: Felix Hinchman
    22 November 1830

OAKLAND COUNTY
Amos Mead 00011001/0111201
Warham Lee 000001/00001
George W. Collins 010011/220001
Seymour Newton 000021/00101
David Wilson 0000001/101001
James V. Newman 000001/---
Wardwell Green 3011001/02001
Hezekiah B. Smith 000011/00001
Lealand Green 00122/00002
Rufus Thayer 000010001/00111001
Ethan Lapham 0011201/00002
David Simmons 10002/10001
Walker Kent 00101/10001
Thomas Pinkerton 00001/10001
John Gould 010001/20101
James Gunning 11001/10001
Nathaniel Tallmadge 00001/---
John Dewitt 000001/000001
Henry Bartow 00001/00001
William Yerkes 311001/010001
Abel Chase 00110001/00000001
Peter Chase 000001/10001
Bela Chase 13102/101001
Samuel Lemmon 021001/010001
Henry/Sterry? Lyon 10001/10011

Penfield Johnson 00001/1001
Pitts Taft 0001001/1000001
Hiram Wilmarth 101102/11001001
James Wilkinson 100021/00001
Lyman W. Andrews 00102/00001
Samuel Hungerford 110021/00001
Abigail Simmons 0011/0101001
Cyrenus Simmons 00102/00001
Jacob Carlisle 00001/10001
Randal Chapman 0110001/002001
Joseph Eddy 000030011/000020001
Isaac Phillips 1201001/0112001
Sarah Thornton 0004/00000001
John Hiles 20002/10001
Ross Phillips 10001/00001
Isaac VanDuyn 00102/1001
James VanDuyn 00001/0001
David Guile 010100001/00100001
David Guile Jr. 00001/00001
Reuel Sherman 001001/000001
Henry VanAmburgh 010200001/00100001
Willis Pardee 00001/00001
Orange K. VanAmburgh 00001/0001
Stanton Hazard 100021/10001
Mary Macumber---/0001001
Charles Andrews 00001/00001
Samuel B. Mulford 001001/12001
Erastus Ingersoll 1231101/2002001
Ansel Hiles 100001/10001
Howland Mason 110001/200001
Solomon Walker 10203001/0101001
Jacob Wood 010001/10001
Merit Randolph 10001/10001
Asa Randolph 0100001/0120001
John Blanchard 00002/00001
Matthew VanAmburgh 010001/10001
Arthur Power 00023101/0201101
Ezekiel Webb 2201101/111211
Lucy Wood 0000001/01001
Miles Mansfield 00004/00001
Benjamin Monroe 00101/00001
Samuel Mansfield 00000001/0010001
Ebenezer Stuart 00012/00001
Isaac Scudder 1200001/20001
William Dailey 00211001/02020001
Solomon Rogers 0101101/0120201
James Power 10011/00001
Benjamin Andrews 01113001/01000001
Joseph Andrews 020001/100001
Orin Weston 00021/20001

David Marden 00001/0001
Daniel M. Baker 2100001/012001
Hiram O. C. Harris 10001/0001
Harry Bronson 0000001/0200001
Ebenezer Sage 000001/00001
Nathan Power 30011/10011
Thomas Ingersoll 1121101/0101101
William Howell 11001/10001
Nathaniel Tallman 00001/10001
William Dilling 00002/10001
Samuel P. Shearman 10021/10001
Jonathan Lewis 00200001/00011001
George Tibbits 20101/20001
Timothy Tolman 0201101/101
Barney R. Pease 10001/00001
John Handy 00001/---
Ebenezer G. Stevens 00001/---
Joel Seeley 311101/002001
Willard Porter 10001/11011
Elisha Doty 00011001/0210101
Pillip Marlatt 100001/010001
Chauncey D. Wolcott 021001/20100101
Charles Grant 0011121/1110201
George Brownell 20001/00001
Elihu Cooley 0000101/0000001
Benjamin P. Wixom 20001/00001
Isaac Wixom 10011/10101
Edward Steele 100001/00001
Elias Brant 1100001/001101
Horace Brant 10003/00001
William Garfield 110001/00001
Cornelius Austin 1111001/130001
William Tenny 012101/0101
Abraham Eddy 00001/30001
Thomas Johns 1011001/111001001
Benjamin A. Horner 10001/00011
Henry Harrington 110001/11001
Grafton Simmons 000002/---
Lewis Norton 000001/---
Gilbert W. Prentis 00001/---
Warren Jarvis 201111/21001
Samuel Power 00002/10001
Solomon Woodford 1000001/0010001
Edward White 000001/00001
Reuben Murray 00001001/00200001
Samuel Mead 000001/0011001
George Lee 00001/0001
Lyman Boughton 00001/10001
George Case 10001/00001
Eric Prince 100001/00001

Roswell Pettibone 101001/120001
James Brown 000001/000001
Samuel Gage 0223201/1001001
Lyman Giddings 0130001/010001
Myra Garfield 0110111/1322101
Robert Crawford 0110001/0312101
Frederick Monroe 000011/---
Harmon Pettibone 10001/00001
Jeremiah Sessions 00001/00001
John Crawford 1000001/00001
Nelson Wolcott 0211/1011001
Samuel D. Nichols 100001/11001
Orange Culver 00001/21001
Walter Sprague 00001/0001
William McMichael 100001/0001
Ira Crawford 10001/00001
David Coomer 0000002/001
Jonathan Case 01001001/0001001
Samuel T. Bryan 00001/10001
John R. Robinson 100001/21001
Joseph M. Irish 00001/00001
James Stoughton 010001/31001
Morgan L. Wismer 10001/10001
Thomas Battis 101001/111001
John W. Turner 01100001/212101
Harry Brownson 01101/10002
Lewis Smith 120102/100001
Abell Bigelow 01100001/10210001
Ezekiel H. Sabin 00101/01001
James J. Hunter* 0121101/1100001
Oliver Torry 000101/00001
Peter Richardson 010001/000001
Hamilton Kyle 0200001/1020001
Samuel Colby 00001/00001
Thomas Irish 00001/0001
Rial Irish 00001/10001
David Kyle 000001/10001
Enos Parker 01011001/01010001
Ebenezer F. Smith 30002/00101
William Annett 000101/10001
Stephen Smith 110101/100010001
John Runyen 00001001/001
Henry Kyser 100001/20001
Elijah Case 00100001/00000001
Laban Smith 110101/021001
Isaiah G. Turner 101101/000001
Nathan Herrick Jr. 201020001/00001
William Durkee 20003001/10001001
John Ellinwood 20012101/1000111
Erastus Durkee 000002/10001

Zadock Allen 000001/10001
Sylvester Stodard 00102101/00021001
Henry W. LeRoye 00002/00101
Isaac W. Ruggles 1000001/1000001
Solomon Close 000172/000101
Elisha Beach 200122/00012
Thomas J. Drake 000001/001001
John M. Mack 00001/1001
Alphonso Newcomb 00001/00001
Levi Burlingham 000011/10001
Orson Bartlett 0020001/100001001
alfred Judson 10011/0001
Gideon O. Whittemore 11003/00103001
Solomon Frost 012021/011011
Olmstead Chamberlain 0110011/211001
Oragin D. Richardson 000011/00001
Thomas Simpson 0101011/0001001
Horatio H. Howard 10002/0011
Sewell Wesson 0011001/000001
Daniel LeRoye 01015002/0112001
Roswell T. Merril 10001/1001
William Thompson 0121101/0101101
Asher Bucklin 0001202/001001
David Paddock 110041/00011
David Perin 110001/100101
Daniel Hunter 00102/11011
Orison Allen 1010022/111001
Samuel Cellinson 200011001/010101
Alexander Ostrander 000002/10001
Asa Sawtell 00000101/---
Amasa Andrews 000032/00011
Elkanah Comstock 000011/00110001
Elias Comstock 000011/20002
Joshua S. Terry* 1100102/010101
Scipio Denison (free col.) 1 male under 10, 1 10-24, 1 24-36. 1 female 24-36
Benjamin C. Stanley 0101001/002001
John Miller 100001/210001
Harvey Seeley 200011/011011
Joshua Terry 121011/102001
Oliver Parker 112001/200001
David Parker 2100001/100101
Ephraim Monk 1000001/01101
John Rockwell 00013101/1210101
Amaza Bagley 01113011/0010001
Harvey Parke 0100101/101011
Joseph J. Todd 10003/20001
Joseph Todd 000020001/00000001
William Chamberlin 00011001/00201
Asa B. Hadsell 020011/000101

John Chamberlin 010111/100001
George Hornell 001101/020001
Alexander M. Morais 100101/10001
Ezra Rood 0122101/1200101
Ogden Clark 101001/210001
David Leake 22001/00001
Nathaniel Pearshall 100001/20001
Ezekiel Cook 010001/10001
Hiram Hartwell 000001/211001
Linus Jacox 01002/0011
Charley Blake 200001/011001
John B. Chamberlin 000000001/---
Apollis Dewey Jr. 011011/100001
Joel Saxton 100122/101001
George Morris 0100011/01001
John Vaugn 002101/312001
John Diamond 01001001/0000001
Samuel Middaugh 0000001/223101
James McHenry 100001/10001
Caleb A. Lamb 100001/20001
Joseph Gilbert 01300011/010101
Barney Jones 0111001/0000001
Elijah Bull 10001/00001
Joseph McLaughlin 010001/010001
Job Smith 102001/001001
David Lano 00002/00001
John Crawford 0010001/000101
John C. Smith 001000001/00011001
Daniel Powell 000001/---
Isaac P. Webster 110101/101001
Andrew Simpson 00001/000
Robert Wallace 101100001/2021001
Daniel Grinell 010001/000001
John Stringer 10001/00002
Jacob Sly 11110001/101101
Jacob Baker 2101201/012011
Daniel Wood 0110001/0121001
Doras Morton 411002/000001
George Gage 010011/00001
Horatio Lee 00101/20001
Henry S. Smith 11001/21001
Elijah Bullock 00121101/00000001
Dillacene Stoughton 201101/120001
Richard Bignal 101001/110001
Samuel Babcock 1100001/101001
Asahel Heath 000001/00001
Scriba Blakeslee 011001/20001
Harvey Lee 210001/00001
Robert Gordon 00120001/0111000101
Joseph Barkley 103101/200001

Thomas Barkley 121001/100001
Seth A. L. Warner 0120101/000001
Robert Wixom 00002/0001
George Culver 12010101/211011
Moses Pick 10002/0001
Robert McCracken 13000001/000001
Abraham Piasley 00000001/---
Nathan S. Philbrick 0101001/0000001
Sanford Utley 000000001/000
Jared Conner 10101/01001
William Lemmon 110001/10001
John North 11001/20001
John Wilcox 0110011/200011
Amaziah Stoughton 001010001/00110001
Samuel T. Cooley 00002/0001
Andrew S. Cooley 10001/20001
Isaac Heath 0110001/0110001
David Brown 100001/001001
Edmond Cook 000001/000001
Lorenzo Warren 10002/20001
Martin Lee 11001/10001
Briant Bartlett 00001/---
George White 212001/101001
James Gould 10001/10001
Benjamin Fuller 001100001/00102001
Asa Fuller 00110001/00000001
Benjamin Fuller Jr. 00001/0001
Samuel C. Barton 10001/100001
Clement P. Rust 10001/00001
Hiram Rust 00011/0000001
Joseph Blindbery 10010001/0121001
Seymour Gray 2200001/002101
Thomas Rouse 010001/11001
Martin Shepherd 100001/000001
Simon Bottsford 000200001/00000101
Morris Jenks 10011/00001
Amasa Ives 00001/0001
Henry S. Babcock 010001/220001
Abraham Crawford 0000111/0001001
Asa Parker 0211101/0020001
William Ives 0000101/000301
Thadeus Griswold 00001/0000001
Joseph Dodd 0211101/0100101
Joseph Wilcox 00011/20001
William Hall 1111001/010001
Adolphas Gould 000101/11001
Mason R. James 01002/10001
George Beardslee 01001001/20021001
Milton Crawford 00001/220001
John Fall 220001/001001

Nathaniel Armstrong 011001/20001
Alexander McClung 00002001/0111001
James McClung 010001/001001
Peter Louw 0011101001/001001001
Henry Dunham 110001/101101
Janitt Stuart 31/01010001
Henry Serviss 000202/112001
Josiah Nichols 010001/001001
James Lockwood 1201001/011201
Samuel Torbert 1020001/101001
Wakeman Bradley 10001/0001
Daniel Burrows 111001/110001
Franklin B. Sanders 000001/330001
Benjamin Norris 10001/00001
Rufus Beach 120001/101001
John F. Keyes 110001/10001
Joseph Chase 000010001/000000001
Samuel Addis 122000001/011101
Erastus Burt 10001101/11102
David Chase 10001/00001
Cromwell Badding 0021011/1100101
Socrates Hopkins 010001/00101
Josiah Alger 0222101/0000101
David Crawford 00010101/00012001
Alanson Park 200001/01001
Robert Crawford 101001/121001
Calvin Marvin 0012001/2101
Isaac Bailey 10001/0001
Harvey Perkins 110001/10001
James Hall 1001?/1012001
Osha Hall 100001/11001
Ira Toms 120101/00001
Orin Sprague 110001/10011
William Stanley 010201/102001
William Poppleton 001011/101001
David Crooks 01001/00000001
John Jones 00011001/00000001
Ramah Cole 100001/10001
Alvah Butler 011001/200001
Elias Daniels 00001/00001
Samuel W. Harding 000001/00001
Robert Park 11210001/0012001
Israel Curtis 0111001/0101001001
Thomas Curtis 10001/10001
Harvey Parker 1010011/11101
John Waldrom 100001/11001
Matthias Fuller 01000001/00100001
Leonard Sprague 01001/00001
Benjamin Chambers 0111001/0011001
Linus Cone 20001/00001

# 1830 Census

Avery Jones 1101101/012001
Northrup Jones 2000001/012101
Deborah Gibbs 1012/0201001
Humphrey Adams 1210001/201001
Guy Phelps 1120001/011001
Thadeus Thompson 120001/010001
John Booth 110001/210001
David B. Ford 2000101/00001
John Miller 100101/10001
Johnson Niles 0011111/002001
John Coon 10001/00001
Ira Jennings 200011/10001
Joel Welman 1100001/000001
Willard Daniels 000101/21001
Silas Sprague 0110101/221101
Edmond Downer 00001/00011
Andrew Downer 000000001/000000001
William Chapman 0010001/2112001
Joel Potter 0022001/102201
Esick Brown 211101/0101001
Orin Jenks 122001/000001
Henry Hutchinson 001011/20011
Prudence Jenks 0011/00011001
William Cammins 0000001/100001
Joseph Park 1000001/100101
Daniel Ball 002110001/00210101
John Kennedy 01102/02002
Elijah Willits 020001/01001
David Harmon* 00111001/00000001
Jeremiah Hunt 00011/20001
John Hamilton 111041/11101
James Day 1020002/011001
John W. Hunter 101003/012111
Seymour Hunt 00001001/1110001
Major Curtis 1120001/1120001
Austen Wakeman 00001/0001
William Curtis 10001/0001
Michael Bloomburg 212002/011001
Diadate Hubbard 110002/101011
John Evans 000001/00001
Henry Lilys 000111/20001
Frederick Cline 11000011/110001
Abraham Hoagland 100101/10001
Denis Quick 10001/00001
Willard Johnson 110001/010001
Jacob Phillips 1100911/20001
Thomas Hall 100010001/00001
Calvin Pirin 0101001/1020001
Phineas Pirin 010001/21101
Cornelius Valentine 00001/10001

John Valentine 001000001/000100001
Abner Robinson 0121001/0101101
Abraham Burns 213101/101001
Washington Stanley 00001/10001
William Hurd 00001/0001
Levi Hunt 10001/00001
Michael Pearsall 01201001/00011001
Clark Beardslee 10001/10001
Salmon J. Matthews 110021/000001
Joshua Davis 210120001/001021001
Jesse Perin 020101/201001
George Taylor 1211101/0010001
William Patrick 00011001/01100001
Ezra Baldwin 00011001/00110001
Isaac L. Smith 010011/001001
Henry Tuttle 0001001/0000001
John Doty 1010001/111001
John Valentine Jr. 11000101/11001
Solomon Caswell 210001/10001
Ralph J. Chittenden 000021/10001
Eli Willits 1110001/001001
Asa Castle 00100001/00000001
Henry Almy 00001/0000001
Zeba Rice 100001/20001
Robert Grimby 10000101/00001
Samuel Satterlee 101101/010011
Stephen V. R. Trowbridge 211011/012001001
Peter D. Merrill 0000101/20000101
Erastus Cripsy/Crissy 001001/210001
Edward Martin 21001001/02001001
John Ackerman 200001/110001
George Postle Jr. 00001/0001
Thomas Sturgess 22211001/0000001
James Coleman 00110001/0010001
John Vannater 300000101/000010001
Peter Schoonover 10201/10002
John Young 10012/000110001
Johnathan Perin 111111/121001
Daniel Vanatter 11022/20101
Cyrus A. Chipman 11001/00001
Champlin Green 010001/20001
Cyrus A. Clark 30002/00001
Hope Green 0001/00010001
Aaron Willman 1000010001/01001
Major Evins 00000001/00001
Cornelius Derkin 020001/201101
Samuel Rhodes 00001001/00110001
Elisha Glazier 010011/21001
Elijah Sanburn 122001/10011
Ethan Coomar 0000001/---

James Kemp 00000001/00000001
Hiram M. Rhodes 30002/00002
Henry Blount 100001001/210001
Norton N. Frost 10001/10001
Allen Anscomb 0020120001/110001
Alpheus Colton 111001/011101
William Martin Jr. 10001/00001
Christopher Barnhart 00001/2001
Hinman Wooster 200011/00001
Ira Smith 10001/00001
William Martin 01010001/1120001
Benjamin W. West 10001/00001
Stephen Wilson 10001/10001
Moses Wilson 00001/0001
Moses Goodall 000001/00001
David Williams 200001/01001
Zenas Fox 000001/10001
Isaiah Wheeler 0110101/0010001
Henry Larraway 00001/0001
David Carlisle 00001/100001
William VanAntwerp 010100001/00101001
Michael Marry 00001/00001
Erastus Ferguson 1212001/0001001
John Wood 000001/000000001
John Warner 0200001/101001
James G. Johnson 000001/10001
Joshua Fay 000001/00001
VanRensellear Harper 00001/1001
Myron Park 00001/00001
Calvin Park 20001/00001
George P. Morse 000001/00001
Jacob Brown 021001/102001
Clement Pearsoll 11001/10001
Samuel Gibbs 011001/101001
James Bailey 00101/10001
Hiram Smith 110011/000001
Jehial Smith 000001/10001
Jesse Gregory 000011/200011
Sylvester Francis 00011/00001
Alfred Phelps 00001/10001
Cyrus Watkins 100011/10001
Henry Gibson 10122001/0010001
Nathan Douglas 411001/101011
Samuel F. Chipman 10002/00001
Cyrus Chipman 000210001/00100101
John Frank 100111/11001
Hawley Brownson 00001/---
Horace Barber 121102/1010101
David Young 20001/0001
Benjamin G. Loomis 000001001/00000001

Asa Underwood 10001/10001
Daniel Bronson 001000001/00001101
John Sheldon 000100001/000100001
John P. Sheldon 110001/112101
Lewis Tibbals 020101/002001
William Bronson 101001/0001
David Dort 010001/110001
Horace Lathrop 00102/20001
Jabez T. Pember 110002/20001
Ebenezer Knight 022001/100201
William Phillips 111001/100001
Josiah Dewry 1002001001/121000101
Lewis B. Johnson 10002/00001
Orville Morrison 011001/201001
Joseph Jackson 0212001/1001001
George M. Shaw 000023/21001
Ethel T. Benedict 1112001/101001
Henry Bradley 210001/020001
James Trimmer 200001/020001
John Lamb 0110001/310001
Jacob VanWagoner 01220001/0100001
Sidney S. Campbell 00003001/000201
John F. Hamlin 000022/---
John Curtis 10000101/22001
Jesse Thorp 00003001/00010001
Lyman G. Wilcox 00001/00011
John S. Livermore 10001/01001
Uri Adams 00001/10001
William Burbank 001001001/110001
Lemuel Taylor 01111001/021011
Elisha Taylor 111021/110001001
William T. Snow 00001/00001
Stillman Bates 200001/10001
Morris Perry 00001/0000101
Joshua B. Taylor 111001/100001
Truman Cook 0002001/000001001
Craig Palmerton 1120001/100001
Nathaniel Millard 00212001/0111001
Eleazer Millard 00220001/020101
James Steele 01110001/200111
William Price 01001/20001
Ezra Bellows 11100001/021001
Michael VanWagoner 21200001/010001
John Henry 11221001/00011
Phineas Hill 0200001/20001
Levi W. Cole 00001/10001
John Horton 242101/101001
Peter Rice 00010001/---
James Dineen 021001/2100001
Sherman Hopkins 10001/0001

# 1830 Census

Gilbert Parrish 1210011/110001
Nathan Scott 110011/02001
Benedict Baldwin 2110011/101201
Needham Hemmingway 011011/3110010001
Liman Bemis 121001/101001
Jeremiah Hunt 210001/102001
Alanson Dukes 1001/0001
William Crawford 022001/200101
John W. Kilroy 1111001/111001
Almon Giddings 0211001/100101
Russel Thurston 10011/10001
Jesse Dukes 011100201/1120001
Philip Biglar 122021/000101
Jacob Biglar 00001/20001
Hiram Hatsid 010101/11101
Ezra Brewster 0121001/0000001
William Kyle 20001/00001
Ira Harmon 000001/2300001
David Harmon 000001/10001
Solomon Dukes 110001001/10001
Ezra Newman 10001/10001
Joseph Davis 21110001/0102001
Samuel Hilton 000001/20001
Samuel S. Tower 00011/00001
Otis C. Thompson 10001/00001
George Balow 000020001/00001001
Cyrus Bliss 012001/210001
William Snell 020001/110001
Peter Grosbeck 00001/0001
David Lawrence 00001/000001
Ludlow Shadbolt 010001/211001
Samuel Smith 00001/20001
David G. Winslow 1000001/213101
John Miller 110001/20002
John Wilber 010001/01001
Isaac Willits 210001/010001
William Utley 10001/00001
John Miller 00000001/---
Harry VanWagoner 00001/10001
Mark Adams 0012102/0110001
John Sargeant 110001/11001
John M. Biglar 00001/0001
John Biglar 00100001/00000001
Joseph Dunbar 000001/121001
Levi LeRoye 00212001/0201101
Horace Hovey 00001/10001
Abner Morrill 000001/00001
George Postle 00210101/0102101
Edmund Jewett 0102101/0020001
Nathan Knight 01100101/01001

Alexander Graham 020000101/10101
Stephen Shippey Jr. 000001/20001
William S. Adams 10001/00001
Gurdon Chapel 201001/021001
Obediah Murray 0000001/01001
John Wilson 1 white female 40-50. FC males: 4 under 10, 2 10-24, 1 36-55. 1 female 10-24
Daniel Fowler 100001/00001
Hugh W. Kay 0020001/0000001
James Graham 0011100001/000000001
Ira Roberts 100101/122001001
Nathaniel A. Baldwin 000010001/00002
Benjamin Horton 012100101/210101
Roger Sprague 001130001/0001
Henry Vannatter 110001/12001
Nathan Lawrence 11110001/110001
Luther H. Webster 211001/010011
William Purdy 110001/10001
Johnson Green 000001/10001
Jonathan Burgess 0101101/0111001
Emanuel M. Young 30001/00001
Robert Thomas FC: 2 males 24-36
Orin Bates 10001/11001
Joel Loomis 00001/00001
Martin Ames 130101/00001
Edmond Lampson 10001/1000101
Jeremiah Riggs 02004001/101101
Leonard Weed 0001101/001101
Henry Dean 200001/00001
Aaron Smith 0020001/0102001
Ebenezer Smith 101101/0010101
Milton Hyde 210111/110002
Roswell Matthews 00012/0001
Benjamin Phelps 0100011/000001
Sylvester Smith 1001101/0000201
Truman Fox 011001/00100101
Charles C. Hascall 10013/10011
Jared Storken 110001/12001
Aaron W. Dean 00001/0001
Charles Cahoon 110001/121001
David Lyon 210001/01001
Moses Villendine 00001/10001
Josiah Smith 0122001/201001
Judah Church 0021001/01010101
Zachariah Olmsted 2010010001/0200001
David Douglas 2311001/0001001
William Morris 021031/11011
William Blackington 0020001/00101
Ezra S. Parke 210001/01111
Stephen Shippey 20012001/1020001

Elijah S. Fish 112011/100001
Ziba Swan, Jr. 200001/001001
Ziba Swan* 020000001/011001001
Orange Ferguson 00001/10001
Pierce Patrick 10001/10001
William Barton 01011101/0001
Joseph Patten 001001/110001
Horace Hopkins 000001/000001
John Brownell 00011001/00000001
Thadeus Martin 1100001/1010001
William Lee 100001/01001
Andrew West 002001/100001
John Daniels 100001/10001
Ebenezer Wilson, Jr. 00001/00001
Elisha Hunter 010000001/00001001
Amaziah Stoughton, Jr. 00001/0001
Marvin Henry 311001/011001
Denison Smith 001200001/00100001
Simeon Burt 02000001/0112101
Michael Beach 320002/01001
Benjamin Tingly 00011/0001
Eli Curtis 011001/010011
David Johnson 111001/120001
Thomas McGraw 0001001/00010001
Ebenezer Wilson 0010001/0001001
Lyman Case 000001/211001
Joseph Green 310001/00001
Nathaniel Case 121001/10001
Rober Beaty* 00001/10001
William R. Kidd 0111001/1110001
Thomas Johnson 112001/1100001
Andrew Miller 0001101/00010001
Wilkes Durkee 110100001/101001
Timothy Pierce 000001/---
Mathew Tiers 1010001/111101
Daniel Ferguson 000120001/221101
Luther Phillips 1101001/0102001
Asahel Fuller 121101/010011
Archibald Phillips 100011/00001
Roswell Root 00001/---
William Roberts 200021/120001
Martin W. Richards 000001/---
Edwin Fairchild 000001/---
Washington Thompson 01011001/0101001
Jeremiah Smith 200121/00002
Jacob Stevens 00001001/00201001
Robert Perry 0223001/1100001
George Perry 110011/130001
Rufus Stevens 30003/01001
Jonathan Dayton 010011/100001

John Todd 101022/10001
Ephraim S. Williams 1101322/30001
Gardiner Williams 00001/00001
Lewis Major 1000101/1221
Peter Allard 000001/10001
Charles McLean 1110101/002001
Nathaniel Foster 000001/121001
Douglas Thompson 0110001/2002001
Lewis M. Moran 00105/---
Daniel Stanard 000011/000101
John Brown 000021/00101
Abraham Whitney 00003/00011
Artimus W. Bacon 00001/---
Lauren P. Riggs 2001311/10001
Eleazer Jewett 00001/---
Nathaniel Ladd 000022/01001
Robert F. Winchill 11001/00001
Ezekiel R. Ervings 10001/00001
Edward H. Spencer 00002/10001
Joseph McFarlin 10001/10101
Simeon Perry 00002/10001
Edmond Perry 10111001/120111
Ferdinand Williams 00001/10001
James Marshal 00001/21001
Ezra I. Perrin 020001/101101
George W. Burrows 01001/001001
Harvey Durfee 12001/00001
Austin Durfee 10001/02001
Oliver Williams 00121001/00010001
Schuyler Hodges 100001/00001
Edwin Edwards 200001/00001
Charles Parker 100001/200001
James Cornell 0001/0001
Nahum Curtis 2121001/0100101
Ezekiel Kellogg 020101/120001
Saville Harris 100001/000001
Jeremiah Curtis 1110002/101001
Charles Terry 10001/0001
Nathan Terry 0011100001/00010001
Daniel S. Judd 00111001/0100001
James Valentine 100101/00001
Lucius H. Fuller 000101/20101
Jesse Chapman 22101/00101
James Allen 11100001/0011001
Joseph Hawks 010001/10001
Charles Johnson 010001/12001
Isaac J. Voorhies 001001/00001
Ira Donaldson 112001/000001
Jacob Carman 0010110⅓/00100001
Peter Leonard 00001/20001

Isaac Voorh    00001/10001
Isaac Tucker 1012101/0100101
Allen Briggs 0110001/110001
Alexander Galloway 00112001/0111001
Thadeus Alvord 0000001/01101001
Joseph L. Griffing 000001/000001
Joseph Harris 000020001/0011
Asahil Murray 00100001/0001001
Orlando Murray 00001/0001
Herman Harris 100011/0000101
Elisha Harris 010001/20001
Samuel Lyon 100001/20001
Joseph Bancroft 11200011/110001
John Southard 100001/000001
Jacob N. Voorhies 102001/120002
George Rhinehart 000001/0200001
Parley Rogers 2020001/000001
Joseph Morrison 1111001/0011001
John Morrison 00001/0001
Chester Webster 300001/010001
Malon Hubbel 11001/11001
Nathaniel B. Hathaway 021101/102001
Henry W. McDonald 000001001/01200101
Henry L. Teeple 100011/10101001
George B. Teeple 00001/1001
Christopher Logan 10001/0001
Ira Stowell 0110001/0010001
Roswell Hilton 10001/10001
Abner Knapp 110101/02001
Samuel Hubbel 200001/01101
John Drake 11001/11001
Henry Thomas 0020201/00020001
Chester Phillips 01002/00000001
Ephraim Colby 00001/2001
Abraham Butts 100001/10001
John S. Tucker 00001/0001
John Galloway 2231001/010101
Steven Reeves 010001/21001
John Clark 0000101/010001
Calvin Hotchkiss 200000101/010010001
Abner Davis 010001/10001
Polly Gates 0001/0001001
Samuel Murlin 2010001/0011001
Thomas Merlin 000000001/000000001
George Butson 010000001/00000001
William Thomas 00101/100001
Chester Goodrich 00001/0001
Salmon Matthews 000000001/00000001
Reuben C. Beach 100001/11001
Alanson Goodrich 20001/10001

Zenas Goodrich 00001/ 0001
A. Nelson Hitchcock 00001/10001
James Ackerman 002010001/00000001
Avery Swan 00001/0001
Lewis Mann 00001/21001
Joseph Lee 00101001/00000001
Samuel L. Millis 130001/00101
Winthrop Worthing 0000101/0000001
David Hollenbeck 000001/21001
Horace Johnson 00001/20001
James H. Ackerman 11001/100011
Orestes Taylor 0010001/0320001
Freeman Waugh 0001201/0011001
Sheldon Waugh 10001/0001
Charles Kelley 000001/130001
Harmon A. Payne 00003/20001
George Smith 0000011/20001
Edward Swan 01011001/01100101
Lewis Grieves 0001001/101001
Elizer Goodrich 11011001/1000001
Calvin P. Webster 10001/10001
James Skidmore 100001/11011
Luke Lawson 00001001/00000001
Richard Hathorn 100001/220001
Daniel Millard 1110001/111001
Daniel Kelley 00001/10001
Lemuel Castle 010102/211001

Enumerator: Amos Mead
  20 November 1830

LENAWEE COUNTY
Thomas Reed 1111101/1010001
Mary Allen 10012/32001
Samuel Craig 300010001/10001
Joseph Corbus 21101/11101
Richard Corbus 0001/0010001
John Allen 00001/21
Benaniah Jones 2311111/00101
Thadeus Wight 201001/21201
Silas Benson 10001/0011
Cornelius Millspaw 01001/11201
Henry Upton 00001/10001
Charles Blackman 02211/01111
Uriah Fletcher 000001/---
Abner Rice 1001/1001
Isaac Powers 10201/2101
Henry VanBuskerk 01021/2101
Peter Low 211211/1211
Peter Benson 0010001/002001

Daniel Mangas 00001/1001
John Mangas 00001/1001
James Eaton 00111001/00010001
William Eaton 20001/00001
Conrad Lambertson 0000001/---
Jonothan Hall 00001/---
Appolus Drouin 10001/20001
Calvin Brown 00000001/---
George Brown 00003/00001
Sheldon Murwine 00001/10001
John Harrison 0000001/0001001
A. Tuller 0122201/110001
Willis Merritt 0311101/001001
E. P. Champlain 100001/02001
Seneca Hale 210001/01001
James Patchen 0000011/003001
William McNair 000001/---
David Robinson 00112001/00001001
Christopher Barrett 000101/002001
John Huych 0111001/211001
Peter Jones 0210101/122000101
Samuel Clay 10001/00001
Theodore Bissell 01002/11001
Anson Hall 000001/---
Jonothan Clark 000011/10001
Henry Beck 00001/---
John Pennington 2001101/1010001
Horace Kidder 100111/12110101
Levi Salsbury 0101001/1011101
Robert Aylesworth 000001/110001
Darius Comstock 100250001/0100201
William Jackson 0001101/011101
Catherine Tye 1/000001
John Arnold 0001201/131101
Aphius Hill 100011/00001
Nathan Comstock 00011/20001
Cornelius A. Stout 1100011/1101
Betsy Maples ---/0010001
George Scott 00001/20001
Allan Chaffee 00001/00001
Abram West 110001/202001
Jonothan Ha (blurred) 011001/000001
Thomas Sackrider 0000001/000001
Elijah Browning 10001/0001
Daniel Odell 000011/1001
Anson Howell 011111/210101
Wm. H. Rowe 00001/0001
Samuel Todd 01020101/0000001
Moses Bugby 0421001/000001
Cary Rogers 100011/012001

Samuel Weldon 010001/21101
James Whitney 0212001/0110001
Jeremiah Stone 002001/000001
John Wood 110001/110001
David Wiley 1000001/110001
Pliny Field 001111/0021101
D. Torry 00002/00001
John Chapman 1110101/0110001
David D. Bennet 00001/00001
Jacob Brown 0212101/200001
John Powers 001001/10001
Jacob Jackson 0001001/---
Anson Jackson 000001/10001
Job Comstock 111001/121001
Lymon Peas 101001/10001
Elijah Johnson 100011/1001
Silas Simmons 00001/---
Samuel Carpenter 02013001/1220001
Lewis Nickerson 102002/000001
Cassander Peters 210001/000001
Nelson Bradish 10001/00001
William Brooks 00001/1001
William Edmond 23102001/1012001
Josiah Baker 00002/10001
Currin Bradish 00101/00001
Seth Lammon 00001/000001
Levi Shumway 2110101001/111001
N. W. Cole 12001/01001
Daniel Gleason 01010001/00001001
Rubin Davis 10001/10001
Samuel Davis 101001/130001
John Fitch 00001001/0000101
Stephen Fitch 00001001/00110001
Daniel Walsworth 1100001/1112001
Aron S. Baker 10001/00001
Nehemia Bassett 1211001/0100101
William Foster 1010001/210201
Ephrim Dunbar 101001/110001
Elias Dennis 11012001/21001
I(s)aac Dean 01022001/2001201
Nathan Pelton 000001/120001
C. N. Ormsby 00002/000001
Turner Stetson 000012/00001
Noah Norton 010001/211001
Addison Comstock 00002/10002
Asher Stephens 00102/00002
Charles Morris 200011/01001
Samuel Burton 1100101/2120001
Hannah Gifford 12/10001001
John Comstock 21210001/0101001

Edward Pooley 010111/00001
John Brears 00011/00001
John Smith 00001/00001
John Moffat 00011/---
Giles Hubbard 121011/00011
Samuel Cook 00001/---
Horace Case 20001/00011
Stephen Pope 010111/0101
Elias Underwood 0001/0001
A. Underwood 00001/0010001
Job Cox 011101/0111
Timothy Nash 001101/00211
Noah Emmons 0001/1001
Jacob Woodward 011111/10101
Clark Wood 020001/2
Curtis Page 00002/00001
Peter M. Collins 1110101/2121001
George Taylor 100110001/11101
Gersham Reed 0012001/002001
Robert Cross 00002/00000001
Howel B. Norton 20001/00001
Thomas Goodrich 0001101/1021101
Ira Goodrich 10001/02011
John Gregg 1110001/1101110001
Hugh Gregg 1110001/101101
Mathew Frost 002001/---
Josiah Wheeler 211001/0121001
Joseph Wheaton 3200001/010001
Ebenezer Stone 00000001/000001
John J. Schnall 01001/20002
John Oharrow 00002/---
Almon Sperry 00000001/---
Phillip Hottenstein 00002/---
William Clayton 00000001/---
Elijah Wright 000011/001001
Horrace Goodrich 1210101/000001
James W. Cole 00022/---
Alpheus Kies 1010221/011001
Thomas Lazell 000012/20001
Benjamin B. Fisk 212001/000001
High Hillich 100001/11011
Thomas Griswold 0210001/101001
William Nisbet 011001/01001
William Smith 10001/10001
Jeremiah Arnold 1210001/02011
Joseph Bangs 0121101/0000011
Don A. Reed 10001/11001
Ebenezer Anderson 00112/---
S. Blackmar 000110101/000010001
Hiram Ensign 0001/0001
Joseph Pratt 0000101/0000001

Solomon Ostrander 021101/02001
C. Derbyshire 111012/0012001
Joseph Farrington 00003/0001
Jacob Schock 100002/00001
Henry Mangus 00001/20001
Joseph John 20001/01001
Isaac Bangs 1001/00001
Warren Perry 000021/00001
John M. Clark 00001/10001
Eliphalet Clark 0012001/0100001
John O'Conner 110011/110001
Jos. T. Borland 011022/11002
S. A. Holbrook 00004/00001
Simmeon Dewey 1100201/1100001
D. B. Reed 100011/010001
Stilman Blanchard* 010013/10011
Ashiel Finch 00102/00002
James Young 000111/000010001
Musgrove Evans 1112201/001111
Daniel Pittman 110021/11011
Jacob Hall 00101001/0011001
George Corkner 00001/00001
Amos Stocking 20005/10001001
William Avery 000001/000001
Charles Stephens 000012/10011
Jesse Osburn 0121001/211101
Joseph Camburn 011011/21001
Jacob Ketchum 01011001/00200001
Moses Smith 0112101/1101001
Joseph Gray 00001/10001
Asa Gillmore 00001/0001
Thomas Sisson 1222001/122001
Holder Sisson 000001/130001
Alanson Bangs 10002/10101
Jos. B. McRay 100011/12112001
George Metcalf 110001/000001
Reuben Saterthweight 00001/00001
Alanson Donvan 1100001/011001
William H. Hoy 01120001/111001
Timothy Mitchel 010001/---
E. F. Blood 0000011/0001
Jasper Hawood 00001/---
Ezra Blanden 000001/---
Daniel Waring 00002/---
Abram VanOrsdal 000001/120001
Abner Spofford 00112001/0110001
William Tilton 00001/---
Thomas Nelson, Jr. 0012001/221001
Jacob Mangas 02020001/1001
Love Moyer 10001/10001

Robert Smith 221001/101001
Joseph Beals 0010101/0212101
Josiah Huminway 020001/020001
John Murphy 10001/10001
Patrick Hamilton 200001/000001
David L. A. Maples 1000100001/02001
John Walsworth 00110001/00110001
David Biseby 0010001/011201
Daniel Smith 1112011/0010001
Charles Heveland 20001/1001
Milo Comstock 101001/020001
Benjamin Mather 10002/01002
Harvey Bliss 1111001/0110001
George Stout 20001/0001
Caleb Wheeler 1110001/210001
Morris Birch 110001/002001
Sam'l Randall 020001/301001
Stilman Goff 0001/1001
Gideon West 00201001/00100001
John Preston 00101001/000000001
Ebenezer Gilbert 00001/20001
John Preston Jr. 00001/0001
Margret Kidzie 11121/101001
Samuel A. Stewart 221001/000001
James Fowle 00001/00001
Anthony McKey 000001/00001
Isabella Clark 000131/00120001
Jonas Ray 1100001/100001
Isaac Randall 1110201/1000001
Almon Harrison 00002/10001
George Gile 2111001/001001
Solomon Harrison 00001/0001
Jacob Lane 200011/00001
Moses Vallentine 000011/30001
John Barker 000001/000000001
Willard Goff 010001/100010001
Timothy B. Goff 212001/0110001
William Naper 100001/110001
Joseph Arna 01001/20001

Enumerator: Musgrove Evans
    27 September 1830

MACOMB COUNTY

CLINTON TOWNSHIP
Christian Clemens 00102001/11002
John Stockton 101011/110111
Silas Halsey 100021/10001
Chancy G. Cady 00102/00010001
Harvey Cook 0000101/0111001
Charles Marther 000021/00001
Etiene Blay 301/01001
John B. Blay 1000001/00001
Lucy Wilcox 1001/00001
Ezekiel Allen 010121/12011
Joseph Potvin 100111/21001
Henery Tayler 00001/200001
Gazeton Tremblé 010010001/00020001
Ignace Seney Senior 01201001/00100001
Baptist Dulac 111001/20001
Antoine Griffard 220001/101001
Alfred Ashley 11023101/101210001
Horace H. Cady 10001/10001
Lewis Denoyer 0100001/310001
Peter Tremblé 10001/200010001
Job C. Smith 2211001/011101
Joseph Hayes 010010011/0001001
Richard Butler 000001/00001
Benoitt Tremblé 1010101/111001
William McDonel 121002/110001
Daniel Niffin 10001/0001
Asel Haskins 00010000101/000000001
John Crawford 0002000001/00100001
Jedediah Millard 00001/1001
Elias McCall 1021101/0000001
Parsons Craft 111001/012001
Elisha Harrinton 00001001/1120001
James Conner 101000011/0100001
Horatio Haskins 1012/0200101
Sylvester Atwood 00001/00001
Laucious Haskins 00001/000101
Hiram Atwood 10001/10001
Christopher Douglas 1012001/2121
Charles Crittenden 010001/001101
David Merrit 1011001/2112001
Samuel Stroup 10001/00001
Aron Conklin 311001/112001
Zephemiah Cambell 1100011/00001
Patrick H. Chase 10001/1001
Patrick Martin 0001/---
John Daly 00001/---
Edmund Daly 00120001/002

## 1830 Census

John Brock 00001/---
Antoine Varnier 100011/10001
Peter Blay 00001/00001
Hubert Forton 110001/10101
Julian Forton Jun. 220001/022001
Francis Forton 101101/101001
James C. Edgerly 101001/011001
Abner Rice 00001/---
George Thomas 100001/30001
Peter Alard 0011001/0101001
Paul Rattel 0310011/100001
Francis St. Aubin 10001/1001
Etienne Ballard 130000001/1000001
Peter Croix 00002/0001
John Cottreal 300001/011001
Lewis Tremblé 00021/0010001
Joseph Allard 110001/021001
John B. Lorier 0231101/0101001
Ignace Jones Jr. 210021/211001
Simon Cady 0001001/002001
Peter Champign 210001/10001
John B. Rivard 000001001/---
John B. Varnier 100001/20002
John B. Rattel 121100001/0100101
Rosele Chovin 1012/01000001
Oliver Dehaitre* 10001/0001
Joseph Metnor 0000001/013001
Jaque Thebo 0100001/100001
John B. Marsach 00000001/1011
Nicholas Maison 111001/011001
Charles Rivard 11001/00001
John Tingley 100011/11001001
Antoine Morass 10001001/10001
William Owls 00000001/0221001
Gorman Burges 00000101/000100001
Denis Forton 20001/10001
Charles Peltier Jr. 110001001/111001
Francis Dubay 1121011/0101
Robert Thomas Jr. 00001/00001
Francis Forton 110001/020001
Felix Thomas 020001/101001001
Simon Dubay 100001/20001
Alexis Dubay 1110101/1110001
John M. Dubay 000011/1002
Pierre Leno 00001/10001
Lewis Dehaitre 21001/00001
Baptist Thomas 00001/20111
Jaque Miller 0100001/300001
Robert Thomas Sr. 0110001/0310001
David Meldrum 210011/10001

Mitchel Rivard Jr. 000001/10001
Hiram Rivard 00001/---
Paul Ceire 001011/1000101
Fabien John 00001/00001
Felix Peltier 03120000101/2000001
William Meldrum 120021/111101
Jacob Baker 0010001/00010001
Peter Barnier 000001/10001
John B. Forton 001002/21001
Paul More 00001/10001
Joseph Robataile 01011001/0101
William Tucker 10001/10001
Charles Tucker 211001/112001
Francis Dequinder 00100011/0011001
Edward Tucker 22100011/100011
John Tucker 2211001/2000001
Bazile Laforge 10001/100001
Lewis Petis 00000001/00123001
Baptist Peltier 10001/10001
John Conner 00201001/00010001
Joseph Pennock 0100001/0010001
Sewel Kyes 10001/10001
Robert P. Lewis 00000011/00001001
Hubert Yax 110001/20001
Joseph Lafore 210101/00001
Alexis Goulette 110001/11101
Gilbert Yax 00001/00001
Moses John 10001/11001
Lewis Laforge 2010101/0121001
Francis Yax 0001101/1100001
Felix Laforge 10001/00001
Jacob Tucker 1010012/100001
Ignace Thebo 200020001/000010001
John B. More 102101/30101
Tousainth More 10001/0001
Lewis Chapoton 0110001001/01
Jaque Latournau 120001/11002
Joseph Peltier 0110101/000020001
Ignace Morass 00200001/01020001
Joseph Dupuis 010001/000101
Julien Forton Sr. 0030000001/01010001
Seraphine Delona 00003/0002001
Charles Peltier Sr. 000010001/001100001
Francis Labady 12300001/1001001
John B. Campau 10000101/10001
John B. Dubay 20111001/01001
Antoine Rivard 100001/10001
William Little 110001/00001
Antoine Dequinder 0011001/112001
Leon Peltier 021001/200001

James Meldrum 020011/20001
John B. Maranda 00010001/001001
Joseph Pomanville 310011/010001
John B. Thomas Sr. 1301211/1112001

SHELBY TOWNSHIP
William Smith 200001/21001
Harly Rice 0010001/0000001
Eleazer Scott 000010001/00100001
Sully Torrington 222001/110001
Almon Mack 00001/00001
Jedediah Messenger 0000001/100001
William N. Davis 200001/00001
Benjamin Kittridge 10001/0001
Elisha Batchelor 000021/000010001
Amasa Messenger 200001/001001
Jonothan T. Allen 1112001/20201
Luman Squires 00001/00001
Nun Moe 02131001/1000101
Noel Buck 000001/---
Samuel Sacket 000011/10001
William McCalister 00001/---
Joseph Lester 0010001/221001
Job Hoxie 00110001/00000001
Joseph Head 0020101/0000001
Nathaniel Squires 101100001/0121001
David H. Brown 110001/112001
Ethan Squires 1000101/1101
Samuel Beeman 0300001/121001
Elisha M. Porter 10001/00001
Alvin J. Dunbar 100011/12001
Adam Price 10011001/0211001
Louisa Price 0112/010001
Ebenezer Fish 0010001/01110001
Asa Huntly 10001/20001
Charles Batchelor 0000001/21001
Samuel Fowler 200001/01101
Andrew Brown 00001/00001
Moses Hempstead 0022001/1100001
Ethan McCollam 00010001/0000101
Daniel W. Phillips 00102011/---
Joshua Price 00001/00002
Tobias Price 00002/000110001
Mathias Graves 001011/00100001
Alay Arnold 00002001/01120001
Harvey Lewis 120001/010101
Sylvester Darling 11100011/001201
Josiah Lockwood 10001/10001
George Handscom 211101/020001
Brotten Adams 00001/00001

Collin Vands 00001/10001
Marcus Nye 200001/00001
Elias Wilcox 01001/01001
John Adams 00010001/000001
Anden Adams 000001/21001
George Adams 1001/0001
Russell Goff 1001101/112001
Ira Preston 1101001/110001
Samuel Axford 3023101/0110001
John Chapman 1100001/001001001
Freeman Blakey 211001/11001
Samuel Sumner 100001/10001
Abel Warren 101000101/122101
Orison Withy 10001/20001
Solomon Wales 1101001/0021101
Hiram Miller 000001/010001
Elon Dudley 000001/11001
Elisha Nichols 00001001/00010001
Daniel B. Nichols 20001/00001
Russell Andrews 200001/01001
Calvin Davis 211001/111001
Alijah Owens 122011/100001
James Lawson 1021001/0101011
William Arnold 002000001/011101001
Cyrenes Arnold 000001/10001
Orestus Millerd 00001/10001
Ezra Burges 2010001/231101
Samuel N. Wells 3122101/0102001
Anthony King 00021/2221001
Lanson Arnold 00001/10001

WASHINGTON TOWNSHIP
Edward Hoard 2121001/1001001
Daniel Thurston 0300201/10001
Ezra B. Throop 000001/1
Lazarus Green 00220001/00000001001
Otis Lamb 1111001/111001
Wilks L. Stuard 2000201/00021
John Bennett 121101/200001
Amos Parks 00001/---
Freedom Monroe 000001/10001
John Finch 11011/00001

Jonas Cutler 000001/01001
Hiram Benjamin 00002/0001
Sylvester Finch 20101/0001
Adison Chamberlin 10001/0001
Major Webster 20001/00001
N. T. Taylor 100131/02011
Liman T. Ginney 001001/10001

# 1830 Census

Leander Tremblé 200101/00001
Rhominah Bancroft 01001/010001
Daniel Alverson 110001/01001
James Starkweather 00011/00001
Nathan Roger 0111101/01000001
Gad Chamberlain 012020001/01110001
Ezra Finch 011001/20001
John B. Craft 200001/021001
Gideon Gates 111001/111001
Horatio Nye 310001/01001
William Edget 11001/30001
Charles Webster 000002/20001
George Gideons 2200001/100001
Josiah Hamblin 00011/0001
Archibald Powel 010011001/000000001
William Nichols 000111/00001
Eben Kimble 01100001/300001
William Richards 100002/10001
Cadle Wilbur 1221001/101101
Zephina Davison 10001/20001
Ezra Hamblin 00101001/01100001
Ezra Prentice 00001/00001
Hiram Wilcox 00002/0001
Asel Bazley 1110001/120001
Roswell Webster 3121100101/1100000101
Horace Foot 1010001/010001
Gideon Flory 00121001/01100001
Alexander Tacles 111101/010001
Silas Scott 000001/---
Edward Arnold 1111001/110001
David Brotton 00001/0001
Henry Price 111001/111201
Christopher Arnold 1201001/221001
Isaac Shilman 202001/020001
Jefferson Nye 10001/20001
Milton H. Webster 00001/00001
Moses Freeman 00011/00001
George T. Powel 10001/10001
Milo S. Curtis 000001/20001
Phillip Price 00211/00010001
Henry Myers 2220011/101001
Andrew Stit 2110001/223001
Alexander McGregor 00122001/0010101
Vinus Wood 00001001/10010001
Daniel Dickison 010000001/00000001
Sanford Wood 21002/10001
Adon Taft 210001/00001
Silas Haden 01001/00001
John H. Perry 1/000001
Elisha Stone 10001/00001

Zelotus Stone 010001/310001
Orsel Dudley 100001001/010010001
Ely Webster 00001/0001
Henry Jersy (?) 230001/011001
William Scott 00100001/001001
Josiah W. Bowls 100001/10001
Aron Stone 121001/210001
Rufus Carpenter Sr. 000100001/00110001
Rufus Carpenter Jr. 310001/00001
Nathan Fay 110001/100001
Zebulon Haden 001001/000001
Nathan Nye 12001/10101
Price B. Webster 00011/10001
Levi Hoard 00001/10001
Justien H. Butler 10001/11001
Rowland Hall 00001/---
John B. Hollister 010001/100001
Alvin Nye 200012/00001
Albert Edget 00001/10001
Peter Edget 00110001/02000001
John O. Arander 00001/---
George Gideons 311001/00001
William Abbott 0021001/020001
Isaac Thompson 2000001/0223001
Lesstin Gideons 112001/111001
John Axford 01120011/1110001
Francis Roby 12012001/10021
Alfonso Smith 10001/00001
William A. Burt 112101/00001
John Allen 000111/010001
George Wilson 1120001/010001
Benjamin Tubs 00221001/2020101
Daniel Miller 100001/110001
Charles Beagle 110001/202101
John Kesler 10003/00001
Thomas Roby 20001/10101
Elon Andrews 0220101/120301
Jacob Harris 00010001/000001
Joseph Miller 0111001/0020001001
Civil Burlingham 0011/110001
Nathan B. Miller 0130001/210001
Jeremiah Lockwood 1011001/1201001
Arby Smith 1211101/1000201
Joel Dudley 110001/12001
Townsend Lockwood 201001/021001
Wills Wearing 10001/10001
Ira Miller 000001/23001
Nearmyna Thompson 220001/210001
Hiram Corkins 011011/011101
Robert Townsend 00000001/0002001
Samuel Haden 0100001/00001

Aron Haines 1100001/121001
Lebeous Lockwood 101011/121101
Seemour Arnold 00001/00001
Envis Townsend 00001/20001
William Allen 0102101/122001
James Torrington 00002001/00000001
William Souls 00001/---
Hiram Hopkins 00101/---
Peter Price 00001/00002
Peter Aldrich 122211/1100001
Job Howl 021001/010001
James Lessley Jr. 000002/---
James Lessley Sr. 00000001/001000001
Erastus Day 00123001/0010001
Stevin P. Chamberlain 20001/00001
Joseph Chartier 1011001/121001
Hubbard Hall 10003/10001
Charles Wells 0301001/0021001
Alexander Handford 00001/20001
David Hill 010001/20001
Lewis Tremblé 10001/00001
Rufus Hall 1000001/10001
James Hinks 000110001/00100001
James C. Hinks 00001/11001
Ebenezer Kettredge 20010010001/031001
Josiah Sleeper 00111001/10000001
Benjamin Gould 2110001/001001
Link Fisher 000001/220001
Andrew Matoon 100001/11001
Mark Winchal 00001/10001
George Throop 00001/11001
Sewel Hovy 2110001/010001
Mitchell L. Tremblé 000110001/00100001

RAY TOWNSHIP
James Thompson 221001/110001
Benona Knap 100002/10001
Benjamin Procter 110001/01001001
William H. Baker 100001/030101
Aron Howard 00000001/---
William Hall 00001/00011
Joseph Chub 14010101/21102001
William Stephens 00001/0001
Joseph Freeman 000000001/000000001
Chancy Bailey 200001/01011
Israel Belknap 00001/100001
Eds Warner 010001/001001
Darius Finch 223001/011001
Edmund Steward 1101301/112001
Hiram Woolman 20001/0010010001

John Proctor 100001/10001
Reuben R. Smith 320001/00001
Charles Tuper 10001/00001
Dunius Sessions 00001/00001
Norman Perry 100001/10001
Hosea Northrup 210001/02001
John A. Warren 100001/00002
Appolis Fuller 000011/---
Roswell Green 000001/21001
Asel King 1001001/0100001
Dennis (?) Fowler 000001/0001
Noah Webster 010011/00001
Carpus Redway 010001/100001
Nathaniel Thompson 111101/111001
Benjamin Freeman 3030001/010001

Enumerator: William Meldrum
27 November 1830

ST. CLAIR COUNTY

CLAY TOWNSHIP
John Cartright 122001/100001
Charles Charter 100001/11100101
Dominique Meny 00001/10001
Azil Able 110001/10001
John Bayney 10001/10001
Jean B. Coshany 110000001/00000001
Lambert Mini 20002/10101
Joseph Basney 1000101/21002
Louis Crotin 000001/00101
William Honsin 1330001/001
Joseph Brown 01001001/00000001
George Allan 00001/20001
Joel Carington 0110001/13001
Johnson L. Frost 101001/011001
Mrs. John Staffance 001/022101
William Hill 0201001/211101
William Austin Senr. 10001101/1012101
Isaac Case 020001/100001
Jonathan Austen 10001/10001
William Austen Jr. 200001/1001
Sarah Hartford 0111/0111001
Phineas L. Wright 00001/1001
Jacob Horson 0010011/1000101
Merit Spencer 00001001/01000001
Francis Horsan 2110101/120201
Harvey Steward 1200211/0020001
Benjamin Newhall 20011001/00001
Silas Miller 121001/1000100001

Ebenezer Nubach 0100101/10001
Ira Marks 1111001/020001
Jacob G. Striet 0000001/---
John K. Smith 0110001/120101
Robert Little Jr. 10101/00001001
James Dunlop 20001/00001
Jacob Dur 00220001/00110001
Louis I. Brakemor 00110001/100022
Seth Taft 000001/10002
Samuel B. Gruning 011001/110101
John Hanon 000001/---
George Arnow 00001/00000001

COTTRELLVILLE TOWNSHIP
Nicholas Hofmaster 1100001/302001
Samuel Hayward 0000011/01001
Francis Flurie 0110001/1110001
James Fulton 2200021001/110101
John B. Yax Jr. 000001/10001
William Williams 000002/001001
Thomas Robertson 000001/101020001
Joseph Miney 0111001/2110001
Henry Robertson 00001/20001
Henry Cotrell 1110001/110001
Gilbert Yax 00001/00001
Nicholas Buie 000010001/20001001
Stephen Chortier 11001/11001
Francis Shortier 1011101/1111001
Jonass Clark 00110001/00000001
David Cottrell 110001/110011
William Brown 1002001/0111001
George Cottrell 3020001/010001
Francis Buvia 10001/1001
John B. Petit 00001001/000201
Peter Dupray 0000001/00000001
George Mayeye 100001/10001
John Flin 0000000001/00000001
Francis Duchesne 001001/100001
Michael Duchêne Sr. 01010001/00001001
Louis Coshrais 000000001/0112001
Mrs. Catherine Jenaw 1/01011
Louis Chartier 300001/300001
Eaton Roussell 00000001/010001
David Robertson 211001/00001
Jacques Lozon 400001/10001
John B. Yax Sr. 1010200001/000010001
David Lockwood 1000010001/20001
Samuel Ward 0011411/0111001
George P. Hankledrak 010001/110001
Bela Knapp 00002/00011

Amsa Heminger 100001/00101
James Robertson 100002/110011

ST. CLAIR TOWNSHIP
Aimy Sanders FC: 1 male 36-55
Andrew Wisbrook 10003001/02201
James Reed 120001/11001
James Baird 00000001/00011001
John Baird 00001/210001
West Barney 010001/11001
Oliver Record 01201001/0001001
Clark Warden 201111/001101
Bazilla Whalen 000001/000001
Andrew A. Wisbrook 210012/00001
Edward A. Rose 100001/00001
Timothy Halpin 210001/00001
Robert Alexander 1110001/1110001
Thomas Furgo 0010000001/001000001
Daniel McIvor 1011201/20101
William Galliger 2201001/001001
James B. Wolverton 1120001/210001
James Ogden 001001/10001
Daniel Stewart 110001/010001
Almon Able 000001/010001
Martin Pickens 0010001/010001
George Palmer 001011/10001
Charles Phillips 0112201/101001
John F. Basset 0100101/100001
Daniel Ferguson 220011/00001
Horace R. Gerome 000014/10001
John Robertson 100001/1001
Leroy Barker 0010111/0001001
Jerad Miller 100101001/10101
Horatio James 0220112/3011001
Thomas C. Fay 0101002/011010101
John Cox 00012/0011
Harman Chamberlin 01101/01001
Mrs. Tacy L. Hopkins 01111/0010011
Bazil Thibalt 100001/00001
Louis St. Bernard 0000010001/00110001
Ernest Berdsley 0101101/101001
Robert Love 10001/00001
William Baird 00011001/00101
Michael Duchêne Jr. 10102/1001
Eliphalet Webster 0000001/---
Jonothan Burnom 000001/121011
Edward Carlton 0020201/1210001
Stephen Sterling 010101/101001
Thomas Dart 1000011/11001
Joseph Buckley 00010001/---

## DESMOND TOWNSHIP

Joseph P. Bunce 020001/001111
William Perkins 001012/010001
Z. W. Bunce 101032/00001
Reuben Hambleton 121011001/010001
Samuel Petiet 011110001/01001001
Reuben Dodge 10001/0001
Richard Simsbury* 01100011/00200101
Richard Bean 101021/110001
William Jackson 00005/---
John Hinley, Esquire 1100111/11101
Peter H. Whiting 00016/20011
David Cleaveland 00001/00001
William Osmer 00001/10001
Wheaton Osmer 10001/00001
Ralph Mahoney 110001/000001
William R. Goodwin 10101/01001
William McClure 00001/0001
Asa Hagecum 10001/10001
Morass McGavry 210001/010001
Jean B. Beavan/Beaubien? 10001000001/
James Hall 310011/10001    20001
Richard Goodwin 01000001/---
Robert Chambers 00002/0001
Lydia McColum 1/1110001
Jeremiah Harington 02012101/111001
Louis Thibolt 21101001/1100001
Asa Gilbert 230006/101/001011
Gilbert Elliot 0000011/---
Samuel Wilson 011005/111001
John Yale 100011/00001
Isaac Davis 210001/00001
Jean B. Desnoyers 0100201/20001
Peter Coshwais 20001/00001
Isaac Lemon/Simon? 00001/00001
John Doran 0010211/---
Felix Peltier 000001/10001
John L. Biron 0112101/0011
Jonathan Burch 000012/---
John Ryley 000001/000
Ephraim Sumerfie(l)d 011001/010001
Louis Trombley 000001/00001
Edward Sails 101001/001001
Joseph Desnoyer 10100001/000101
Secial Garinez? 001/2111001
John H. Wisbrook 00001001/01001
Louis Faser 202021/01001
James Gill 00005801/---
Joseph Metivia 00002/1001
L. P. Brady 00001/---

Major A.R. Thompson 001001/000001
Capt. W.F. Cobbs 010001/02002
Thomas James (soldier) 11/200001
Corp. Jim Thomas---/000001 (sic)
Weston Stevens 1/100001
Wm. Lamb 1/100001
James Young 01/00001
Lt. P. Hentzlman 00001/---
Doctr. P. Barker 000001/---
U.S. Garrison (Fort Gratiot soldiers)
    000029)(35)2/---
James W. Cook 00101/---
Lt. Simbton 00001/---

Enumerator: James H. Cook
  26 October 1830

## WASHTENAW COUNTY

### YPSILANTI

Neron Sisson 011001/220201
Erastus Priest 000011/0001
Eli Bradshaw 11110001/1020001
Amariah Rawson 01000001/0031011
Adolphus Dalrymple 00001/20001
Stephen Randolph 20002/00001
Carnahan McCord 001002/1001
Isaac Howe 100011001/12001001
Horatio Howe 00001/00001
Christopher Hartsough 01022001/0011101
Orante Grant 000000011/00010001
Letetia Hubbard 01012/1001001
James Fleming 0112101/---
Fleming McMath 10001/120111
Erastus Coy 22001/00001
Ezra Derby 00101/200001
Zolva Bowen 100001/10011
Daniel Richards 010001/121201
John Dickinson 000020001/00010001
John Bryan 220111/013001
Abraham Clawson 0002001/0000001
Liba Easton 00001/01001
Matthias W. Clawson 00001/00001
Jason Cross 100020001/00001001
William P. Frazier 0110001/1100001
Josiah Rosencrants 00300001/01000001
Philander Ballou 11001/00001
Salmon Champion 1100030001/011101
Joseph Mcloy 10015/0000201
James Stewart 0000401/0000001
Eleazer Smith 0112501/0010001

Benjamin Woodruff 2120011/002011
Samuel Stackhouse 021201/101101
Arden H. Ballard 000113/1011
Chester Perry 0101221/0001201
Oliver Wetmore 00013001/01002001
James Farsythe 100001/11001
Ransom Todd 00001/10001
Joseph Burt 0101411/11111
Orrin Derby 00002/00101
Mark Norris 010031/010011
Beverly Davenport 12200001/0001001
Webber Gee 00002/10001
James Jacobs 010001/11101
Eldvidge Gee 110201/100001
Levi J. Hull 000111/12002
William Lockwood 00001/00001
Sewell Blackmer 00001/00002
William Sperry 00011/1001
David H. Orsen 0010101/0011201
Joel H. Sanford 100001/210001
Anson Sperry 00002/0001
Thomas Reid 00001/00001
Benjamin H. Smith 000101/11001
John Stewart 11120001/110001
Thomas R. Brown 100001/110001
Henry Massacan 12003/010001
William C. Tibman 10002/00001
Lewis Freeman 000021/00011
J. L. Rose 10013/10011
Abel Millington 0011001/0011001
Martin Barnheart 00001/00001
Elias Norton 0100101/001001
Daniel Bostwick 00001/0001
David Stiles 01102001/000101

ANN ARBOR
Allen B. Thomas 120011/01001
David B. Downer 000001/---
Ira Wood 00001/10001
James Wood 01200001/1201101
Levi Bunt 00001/0001
Martin Campbell 100001/10001
Lewis Campbell Sr. 10001/11001
George C. Lathrop 00001/00001
Lewis Campbell 00002001/00001001
Nathaniel Gott 0010101/0000001
Bethuel Farrand 0202001/111001
John Bird 01100001/2011001
Gideon Olmstead 001000001/010000001
Tilly Nichols 100011/210001

Josiah Birkley 21002/00001
James Welch 01100001/002010001

YPSILANTI
Seth Ballou 00100001/00020001
Jose Phillips 00102001/00100001
John Wilson 10000001/11111
Abel Crane 00000001/0000001
Samuel Pierson 010001/21001
Hiram Tuttle 120001/00102
Benoni Brown 10311001/0000101
Loyal Tuttle 10001/00001
Isaac Miller 3010001/111101
Rudd Stiles 00001/0001
William Rose 121101/21101
Benjamin J. Olmsted 2011001/0111001
Israel H. Olmsted 10001/00001001
John Youngs 010001/100001
David Huff 00001001/10010001
Jonathan Train 010001/202001
Orson Underwood 010001/21001
Samuel Sterns 000001/00001
Asa N. Ballard 1111001/0110001
William Kittridge 100101/010001
William Wilson 10000101/0001
Cyrus Churchell 2010001/0101001
Lyman Graves 201011/01001
Charles Jocelin 10001/10001
James Ash 20201001/00010001
Joseph Sears 1000001/00001
Daniel Gorton 00011/000011
Job Gorton 00021002/0111101
William L. Earle 1020111/20101001
Judson Durkee 00002/---
Henry Wright 211001/101001
William Densmore 0100001/11120001
Alexander McIntire 1001/10001
Ebenezer Williams 0111201/1111101
Elizabeth Thompson 2/02001
George McDouble 00001/10001
Andrew Muir 00001001/00000001
Daniel W. Russell 000001/000001
Timothy McIntire 000021/00001
Cary Stark 230001/000001
James Miller 01001/100001
John N. Russell 30001/00001
John G. Thayer 200001/021001
Alanson Snow 111001/110001
Daniel French 0000001/0000001
Taylor Stewart 110001/10001

Dennis Cole 100001/00101
Fanny Welch 0012/1201201
Willard Hall 1001001/0101001
William T. Stevens 01111001/0110101
James Martin 221001/100001
John Terhune ---/00001
Joseph Crane 00001/001
Joseph H. Peck 020111/110001
Isaac Otis 011101/10101
John Phillips 001011/00001
Andrew Parker 2100001/100101
Abraham Dickinson 031001/202001
Andrus McKinstry 000001/10001
David W. Owen 1201001/1021001
David Hardy 0001101/012101
Selden Champion 10100001/0100001
John Trotter 00001/---
Asa H. Reading 00001/0001
Joseph Brown 000010001/000000001
David Stewart 110001/100001
Josiah P. Turner 011001/12101
Asa Rice 100011/10001
Nehemiah P. Parsons 00001/20101
Jonothan G. Morton 00011/10001
Alexander Dryamond 001210001/00011
John Hinkley 100011001/000001
William Day 1010001/10011
Curry Doyle 2111001/0101001
James Ackerson 00101001/01100001
James Smith 1010001/0011001
George R. Albee 1000001/0000001
Rebecca Cramer 021/110001
Minard Miller 122101/010001

ANN ARBOR
John Hudson 01100001/1011001
Eno Oakley 00001/20001
Robert Geddes 0100111/00001
Jacob Hardy FC: 1 male under ten, 1 10-24, 1 24-36, 1 55-100. 1 female 36-55
James Scofield 10001/10001
Harry Hardy 0000001/---
George Prusia 1200101/10011
Henry Mauer 0001001/0110001
Joseph P. Riggs 2110001/010101
Harvey Austin 00002/10001
Lorin Mills 10012/001
Joseph Parsons 000001/---
Samuel T. Topping 120001/01011
William Bott 4000001/001001

Cyrus Beckwith 10001/10101
Edward Gee 00001/20011
Benjamin H. Packard 0010001/002001
Hezekiah Riggs 121101/101201
Castle Southerland 32010011/002001
Irvin Bains 100011/01001
Ezekiel Page 20001/10001
Zenas Nash 0000101/0000001
Charles Thayer 000060001/10021
Gideon Wilcoxson 0011001/0010001
Thomas Tyler 010021/10001
Thomas T. Crandall 010001/11001
Samuel VanFossen 011107/211003
John Sargent 000011/00002
Elijah Canniff 00004/000101
Asa L. Smith 000012/210001
Edward Clark 1010001/00001
William Hunt 110111/210101
Henry Welch 1310001/100101
John Allen 010101/000001
Martin Davis 1010012/111001
Edward Torrey 000001/20001
Alanson Randall 11001/10001
Joseph Sperry 10113/00011
David Page 000210001/000100001
Colbin Cornwell 0010112/020201
David E. Lord 110101/110001
Daniel True 01100001/00010001
Benjamin Gee 10001/1001
Thomas Chambers 000001/21001
Ezra Platt 010001/10102
George Klinedob 00001/10001
Joseph Harrington 00001/20001
James Weeks 000001/10001
Asa Gunn 00000001/100001
Elisha Belcher 000001/00001
James Kingsley 00001/00001
Sylvester Mills 10001/00001
Samuel Camp 021002/1001001
Ira W. Bird 00000001/1001
Arthur Nowland 23111101/01110001
Marcus B. Hannson 110001/001001
Israel Branch 00000001/00011001
William T. Branch 000001/10001
Robert Bolton 0011001/001001
Daniel Brown 00016/10005
James T. Allen 10001/10011
Alanson Gunn 00001/---
Jonathan Case 21000001/002101001
Joseph Harrison 10001/10001

Isaac Smith 001031/01111
Alba P. Smith 200021/10001
Frederick Smith 00001/0001
Clive Carpenter 1020001/110001
Israel Esty 12211001/0011001
Matthias Arnold 11001/10001
Hugh Vreeland 1001/10101
Obadiah Weller 1200101/000001
Thomas Weller 200001/121001
Benjamin Webber 100012/110001001
John Cobb 00001/1001
Sidney Dewey 00001/00001
John Lowry 010001/200001
Alanson R. Holcomb 100001/00001
Horace Booth 00001/00001
Virgil Booth 00001/10001
Stephen Beckwith 000020001/00101001
Joel B. Strickland 10001/00001
Rufus Wright 100011/10001
Richard Lord* 000010011/001000001
Daniel B. Brown 02202001/00012001
Ruth Stratton 00102/00011201
Christian Zuck 120001/10111
Isaac Markham 10001/11101
John Richey 11001/00001
Daniel Walker 2100001/003001
Henry Babcock 11001/10001
Isaac Sterling 00100001/00000001
Daniel Backer 00001/0001
Perses Mills 001/00000011
Calvin Fargo 100001/10001
Amos Wait 20001/00001
Alva Blodgett 000001/10001
Porter Lathrope 00011/00001
William Hurlbert 000011/30001
Ralph Updike 0110211/200001
John G. Morse 0021201/00000010001
John McCollum 00001001/01001001
David Scott 00201001/000100001
Roswell Britton 120000101/110001
Asa Bushnall 2110001/011001
George Allen 1000011/20001
Lumace Gee 00022/101001
Christopher Gee 0021401/310001
--- Conklin 310001/200001
Levi Hiscock 000001001/12000100101
John Anderson 10001/10001
Simon Mills 111001/012101
Ezra Maynard 00011001/00110001
Joseph W. Stuart 10001/00001

Ephraim B. Cornish 00001/01001
Andrew Cornish 0103001/0010001
Arlinda Stoddard 01/200001
Ezra Carpenter 00111001/00021001

Horace Carpenter 01001/00001
Roswell Parsons 01001001/0001001
Josiah Norris 20011/0001
Luke Wetmore 11301001/0110101
Samuel McDowell 200011/01002
Oliver W. Wetmore 100111/01101
Andrew Coryell 21001/01001
Aaron Barney 2110101/1001001
Charles Anderson 100001/010001
Lewis Barr 311011/01101
Jason Clark 102122/230001
Augustus Mills 121001/001001
Elihue Mills 010001/002001
Erastus Root 011101/---
Henry Rumsey 0120001/001101
Ebenezer Morton 0010201/1101001
James Hiscock 231001/130001
Elisha W. Brockway 130001/00001
John Strickland 0210001/0011101
Harvey Chubb 00002/10001
John Chandler 10210001/0310001
Eli Chandler 00001/0001
John A. Ensworth 11001/01001
William Stubbs 100001/10001
Phillip McKeenan 00001/0001
Michael Stubbs 00101/32001
William Pringle 110001/100001
John Moe 0000400101/00120001
Elam Moe 00001/20001
Aaron Rosengrants 000021/42011
Hugh McCall 2202001/0000001
John Renwick 21011/00001
Isaac Secord 1220001/1001001
Avis Brundage 01101/0011001
George McGoundes 00001/10001
Moses Allen 001101/101101
Eli Conklin 100001/12001
William Allen 110001/01001
David Botsford 000011/10001
David Hurd 100001/001010001
Joseph Lorce 210001/01001
Benjamin Sutton 121101/200001
James Noyes 101011/111001
John C. Carpenter 00001/000001
John Nixen 000001/011001

Isaac Sutton 00001/10001

DEXTER
Alexander Laverty 010102/102001
John G. Shaffer 0121001/0101

ANN ARBOR
Zenas Leland 11311001/20102001
Nathan Leland 10001/10001
Charles Kingsley 00001/---
Larkin Ball 10031/01001
John Gorman 1101101/012101
William Curtis 00110001/---
John Cromon 00002001/0122001
Abraham Cromon 1111001/2120001
Eber White 000001/20001
Eli Higby 00002/00001
Grant Perry 20011/10001
Joseph Perry 00010001/0021
John Gardiner 00000001/10000001
Norman Burgess 10003/01001
Geo. Parker 00001/00001
Seth Robinson 00001/0001
Thomas Brownell 00002/12001
Orrin White 011011/110001
Tillotson Ewens 01110011/01100001
Amos Hicks 12120001/301001
Moses Clark 00010001/0002101
Elnathan Botsford 100101/00001
Cephas Hawks* 01112001/0100101
Geo. Rash 1201001/1010001
James Love 110001/00001

DEXTER
Samuel W. Dexter 001001/10012
Samuel Roberts 0111101/0110101
John Durand 000010001/---
Josepheus Case 20011/00001
Major D. Mills 00001/0001
I. W. Bennett 00018/---
Samuel Blackman 02114111/00004001
William R. Deland 100001/01001
Linus Gillet 100001/01001
Joseph Spinnings 00001001/---
Samuel Clement 11120001/1011001
Peter Shilling 00010101/00100001
Jacob Paul 0110001/002001
James Butterfield 3002101/0110001
William Hatt 1100101/013001
Zadock Randall 210001/013001

Thomas Vanscoter 110001/1001
Jefferson Smith 00001/00001
Robert M'Cartney 100011/10001
Jacob Stuffy 100101/10001
Martin Warfle 00001/0001
William VanFossen 20001/00001
Charles D. Topping 21001/10001
John K. Bingham 20003/10001
David Geddes 10001/00002
Samuel Wrath 10001/11001
Elias Smith 11200002/1001201
Henry Smith 10001/10001
David Stoat 10011001/02101001
Jesse C. Smith 000101/00001
James C. Cleland 00011/00101
Lucy Huxford 00002/00010001
Amie Putnam 000011/00000001
Cornelius W. Brink 020001/00101
Chauncey S. Goodridge 0222401/111101
John Comisay 01001001/20102
Samuel W. Foster 00011/00011
Alexander D. Crane 00001/00001
Cyril Nichols 010011/2001
Nathaniel Noble 111001/010001
William Boucher 000001/00001
Adrian Quackenbush 10011001/0200001
Sally Noble 0121/0011001
Thomas Noble 00001/0001
Rufus Crossman 100101/20001
Joseph Arnold 02007/10001
William Harford 200002/100001
Charles B. Taylor 100001/021
Levi Whitcomb 100001/000001
Thomas Lee 02110001/0001101
John Browning 2121001/0101001
Rogers Carr 00003001/00010001
Girardus Noble 000001/010011
Isaiah Phelps 0202001/1010101
Henry Warner 000122/00002001
William Lemon 310001/11001
Sidney S. Derby 00001/10001
Richard Brown 00002/10101
Rufus Nichols 001001/120001
David Dudley 1200101/101101
Daniel Lason 000001/000001
Richard Peterson 001200001/00100001
Cornelius Ousterhout 112011/0110001
Palmer Force/Loree 00001/00001
Solomon Peterson 00002/---
Benjamin Pettengill 00001/21001

George Hurd 01001/11001
Buford Thompson 00001/1001
Samuel Newton 1100001/0111001
George Sherman 000001/00001
William H. Sherman 00002/00001
John G. Peterson 10001/00001
William Nichols 0010002001/0000000001
Josiah Nichols 0112001/1110001
Daniel Bryant 010001/10101
Samuel Gorton 20001/00001
Henry Rowley 200001/10001
George Roberts 1011001/121001
Silas W. Gorton 200011/01001
Ira Seymour 11010001/1011301
Salmon H. Matthews 101121/00002001
Conrad Epley 1111001/011001
Spencer Williams 10001/00001
Henry Cascadin 110001/120001
John Williams 0122111/0100200101
Marines Kinney 0101101/202001
Tillison Wheeler 0100001/100001
Elisha Cranston 0120201/0011101
Charles Stark 010001/20001
Israel Sims 10002/20001
Daniel Morrell 000001/10001
Thomas Alexander 2220001/200101
Luther Boyden 1011101/0101001
Morris Richmond 200001/01001
Simeon Richardson 120010001/10001
Peter Sears 2211011/0001101
Frederick Goodenow 200011/011001
James Crampton 2211211/200111
Daniel Hixon 10001/10001
Daniel S. Brooks 000001/01001
Daniel Porter 010001/101001
Richard C. Dillon 001002/11011
James Popkins 0320001/001001
Hiram Arnold 101001/10001
George W. Peters 2010001/211001
Horace Leek 101021/0000101
Ira D. Mosher 11002/10001
Hiland Dillon 100101/10002
Peter Goodenow 000000001/000000001

ANN ARBOR
Horace Ball 110001/020001
Squire Rice 20001/10001

PANAMA
Peter Michael 10100001/0001001001
John Dix 100111/1002201
Isaac Thomas 00111001/11001001
Nathan Thomas 01001/10001
Mary Peterson 211/000101
Joseph Wicoff 1010211/121001
Harvey Green 00001/0001
George Green 2200001/0012001
John Simons 11110001/012001
Jonathan Thomas 10101/00001
Jarvis Titus 000001/0000001
Joseph Wood 311001/000001
Daniel S. Birch 10001/00001
Daniel Thomas 01110001/00010001
George Renwick 1100001/001001
Samuel McCormick 10001/20001
Joseph Stevens 110001/022001
Frederick Christley 200001/010001
Welcome J. Parleton 111001/00001
Wheaton Bullock 000012001/010000001
Samuel McCormick 100001/20001
Silas Wheelock 0002111/10001
Hannah Hawkins 002011/00010001001
Burden Hix 012001/20011
John Everett 111001/000001
John McCormick 2211301/1002001
James Mulholland 10001/00001
Esak Pray 110101/111001
Justin Phelps 0121001/000101
Rufus Page 0111001/10100001
Augustus Root 100001/10002
Henry Delong 32001/100101
William Packer 1000001/120001
Robert Patterson 1111201/0102001
David Larawa 000120001/000010001
Jonas Larawa 110001/20011
Aaron Blood 00011001/21111
Lewis Cook 10001/10001
Reuben Davis 00000001/00000001
Elisha B. Parker 021001/100001
William Bennitt 110011/00001
Elizabeth Wood 0001/00002001
Jason Cook 00001/2001
Samuel Mapes 2220201/011001
Joseph Lapham 10001/10001
Elkhanna Pratt 10120001/0000001
Edmund Pratt 00001/0001
Sidney Puzo 100001/00001
Washington Harrington 02001/11001

Enoch Shippey 00001001/02100001
Robinson Bennett 001010001/110010001
Levi Jones 1001001/1210001
Eli H. Evans 1002001/000101
John Dutcher 000001/10001
Jesse Peters 10001/0001
Austin Packard 00001/10001
Joseph Peters 00001/10001
James H. Mundy 00002/0001
Constant Woodworth 0113001/000001
Samuel Carpenter 00001/10001
John Dickinson 000011/0001
Osman Smith 00001/10001
Charles Lewis 20002/01001
Joseph Sterling 00101/00001
Waldron Norris 0121001/100101
Adam Bouk 10012001/10201001
Jacob Larawa 000001/210001
Daniel Tobias 200001/110001
Thomas Blackwood 10001/00001
John Brewer 000101001/200001001
Elias Brewer 01000001/00100001
John Smith 00001/0001
Daniel T. Norton 0201001/1001001
Ira Rice 220001/11101
Harvey Brew 10001/00001
Ransetta Beers 10001/0001
Abel P. Parkhurst 20101/00001
James Jackson 101201/0101001
William Jayne 020001/11001

SALINE
Silas Lewis 220001/010001
Arba Lambson 000001/0001
Joseph Gillet 000002/0001
Leander Lebaron 10003/00001
Alba Williams 020010001/0211001
Orson Howe 01111101/111001
Adolphus Spoor 100001/10001
John Thompson 0000211/0001
Luther Hatch 00002/---
Jesse Meacham 001101/000001
Hannah Gilbert 11111/0100101
Elias Jennings 01100001/100001001
Aaron B. Goodwin 010001/001001
Timothy Hunt 100011/20001
Jared A. Stillman 210001/010001
Smith Lapham 10102/100001
Henry Rouse 201001/030001
Aaron Swain 020001/210001

Thomas Wood 00002/00001
Amos Edson 00001/1001
Orange Risdon 1220311/011001
Jason Gillet 00001/010001
Porter VanValkenbergh 00001/---
John Joslin 222001/00010001
Benjamin Kellogg 000001/020032
Orrin Parsons 020032/210101
Chester Parsons 000011/20001
VanRanselear Tyler 200011/01101
Daniel Cross 001001/030001
Matthias Valentine 00011001/00200001
Levi B. Pratt 021001/002101
George Foster 101001/200001
Jeremiah Post 1121001/110101
Rachel Miller 01011/1020101
John Howard 002001/011001
Isaac C. Holmes 2110011/010101
Thirza Amsbury 01/10001
Jacob Whitney 120011/002001
Thomas Wood 10002/21001
Aretus Belden 00021/00001
Eli Gray 2100001/013011
Silas Fraser 11101001/0111101
John Walworth 00001/010001
William M. Walworth 10001/00001
Mary Walworth 00011/00110001
Isaac Brown 0101001/0010001
John Child Jr. 10001/12001
Elijah W. Craig 000001/10001
David W. Craig ---/000001
Elisha Knight 120001/020001
Boaz Lambson 02100001/211001
Ira Bonner 210111/010101
James Mabee 1220001/000001
Benjamin Walworth 021001/00001
Noah Holcomb 000001/10001
Danford M. Stone 000001/1001
Russell Briggs 10001/00001
Nicholas Vendstine 121101/110101
Rue Wheelock 0210001/0010001
George Dowels 130001/002001
John Smith 210001/012011
Evelyn Scranton 000101/10002
Lewis Lebarron 00001/---
Seth Tripp 000001/01001
Ansel Ford 001001/---
Miner Mallot 100001/10101
Anthony Doolittle 0111001/010101
Thomas Pool 010001/210001

Noah Stevens 1121001/010101
Jesse Stevens 112101/101001
Nathan Meeker 00101/0001
Henry A. Francisco 011011/110001
--- Overocher 00001/00001
Peter Lawry 000020001/000100001

PANAMA
Hiram Tooker 00011/110001
Moore Speer 21135001/0001101
John Curtis 20000001/010001
Charles H. Kellogg 10001/00001
Henry Kimmell 1112001/1001001
Robert Barr 01221001/0120101
James Patterson 0010001/001111
Daniel B. Fust 20001/10001
Gershom Seeley 121001/001
Mary Pine 00002/00000001
Mary Fowler ---/000000001
Jonathan Goodell 200001/00001
Joseph Fowler 012001/000001
David Fowler 110001/01001
James Trumbull 221001/221001
Alan Pine 10001/02001
ohn S. Worden 2200101/001101
D. K. Wisner 220101/00101
Thomas N. Andrews 11111001/0100001
James Karr 00100001/00202
Nathan Andrews 10001/10001
Almond Sweeting 2100001/00001
Betsy Morton 01/010001
Henry Wansey 100001/22001
Jared Wansey 210001/102001
Sylvania Newcome 001/001001
Benjamin Robbins 200001/01001
John Tyler 0040001/0100001
Jasper Eddy 10001/00001
Wm. Eddy 002001/01001
Lyman Mayo 11001/12001
Michael Letson 20001/00001
Anthony Case 1200001/1020001
Seeley Neale 000010011/11101001
Ira Camp 110001/20011
Joseph Ames 100001/11101
Isaac Sims 100001/10001001
Phillip Sims 300001/01001
Joseph Mayo 00011001/00000001
Elias Baker 01000001/20001
John Pettibone 2111011/1110001
Phineas Silsby 110011/0111

Thomas Booth 2000001/111001
James N. Voorhies 2120011/010001
Anthony R. Swartout 101001/031001
Alanson Hiscock 310001/01001
Isaac Hiscock 000020001/00110001
Jacob Bacon 110101/220001
Olive Pettibone 000011/000010001
Daniel Crippin 111022/111001
Shubael Goodspeed 03001001/000001
David Goodspeed 00001/10001
Edward L. Rogers 10001/00001
James Pullen 0012201/0101001
Theron Wilcox 0110001/0012101
Peter Wooden 00001/0001
Lydia Crandall ---/1100001
Phillip Saule 00101001/00010001
David Heron 00001/00001
Charlotte Bramble 1/010001

YPSILANTI
David Brooks 00301001/0210001

SALINE
James Wheaton 00001/---

Enumerator: Geo. W. Jewett
   6 October 1830

ST. JOSEPH COUNTY

WHITE PIGEON TOWNSHIP
Abraham Rickert 112101/1011001
John Baum 001210001/01000001
Thomas Odell 212001/120001
Peter Klinger 000011/20001
Daniel Shehamer 2121001/1111001
John Bass 000001/20001
Daniel Bass 00001/---
Robert Cummins 0001001/0000001
Jacob Bonesmasher 3110001/020001
David Frederick 00001/---
Benjamin Pinters 00001/---
Nathaniel Lyas 220011/01201
William Meek 1220301/0112001
Waston W. Bliss 100101/110001
Samuel Pratt 0013/---
Joel Levinch 12001/10001
Jacob Coleman 01001011/0022001
John Baliss 310001/01001
Simon Drouiler 111001/11001

Edward Baliss 010001/21001
Christopher Grant 110001/22001
Thomas Napp 0000101/1111001
John Fidler 100001/10001
Solomon Hartman 1212101/00001
Valentine Shultz 00001/0001
Hart L. Stewart 00217/1021101001
Lewis Stephenson 0000211/11001
Elias Taylor 000101/00111
Alonzo Castle 00001/---
Peter Cook 0001101/---
Nathan Levinch 101101/100001
Levi Beckwith 11011001/0121001
Henry Payne 000002/00001
William Plewin 101101/013001
Arza Newell 00001/---
George Hall 00001/---
John Coats 1001201/0021001
Jonathan Nichols 111011/020001
Jesse Baum 00001/0001
Frederick Littois 011001/002
Samuel Holmes 000000001/00000001
John Winchell 00112001/00200001
Benlding Reid 1010102/0001201
Benjamin Reed 0000001/---
David Winchell 00002/0001
James Luper 1000001/01311
A. C. Stewart 10001/010011
James Walace 0001/---
James Napp 100101/0001000001
Henry Carpender 000001/1001
Ezra Olds 110001/1000001
Joseph Olds 1000001/233001
Almond Laurence 21001/01001
Daniel Linn Jr. 00001/0001
Daniel Linn Sr. 0010001/0011001
John Lyons 00001/---
William G. Riggs 100001/00001
E. H. Brown 200001/21101
William Stephens 2210001/101001
Simon Ward 000000001/0100001
Thomas Hall 000001/100001
A. J. Smith 000001/0001
Asahel Levery* 0010(10)2/010021
Lewis Judson 00002/---
Anderson Clark* 10003/10021
Neal McGuffy 110042/10002
Leonard Cutter 0012001/200001
Arla Heald 110101/111011
Martha Waterman 11/002001

Obadiah Laurence 10001/10001
Laben Keys 11001/210101
Joshua Gale 00101201/00001001
Jeremiah Laurence 301001/00001
Alvin Calkon 00001/10001
David Crawford 001001/20001
Anderson Martin 00113001/0000101
Isaac Hardin 10004/10001
Jacob Croy 1110001/0122
John Croy 20002/10001
Daniel Murry 10100011/00001
Benjamin Drake 11000011/020001
Lent Martin 00101001/00001
Reed Page 00002/---
Hubble Loomis 000001/20001
Amariah Phelps 01002001/00000001
Reuben Wilder 0000001/---
Lawson Bancroft 000001/---
Binajah Wilkinson 200001/00001
John Robbe 01200001/0000001
Oren Rudes 1100001/022001
Leonard Stetsts 2000001/10001
Solomon Hichcock 00002/2001
Luther Newton 0001301/000101
Charles Richards 10005/11001
Amos Barr 1100001/1112001
John Miller 00001/00001
Hugh Fuller 12100010001/201101
William Thompson 0212201/0111001
Jacob McEnterfer 0021001/2301001
Solomon McEnterfer 00001/00001
Jacob Shinnabarger 200011/01001
Louis Cashawe 01001/00003

SHERMAN TOWNSHIP
John Sturgiss 3110001/011001
John and William Powers? 00101/---
L. Fullman 101001/1101
Mary Buck 10211/1110001
Taman Bass 1100001/0021001
Richard Hopkins 112101/021001
Samuel M. Stewart 00003101/200111
Thomas Carter 101011/10001
Thomas Hall 00001/000001
John B. Clark 10002/00001
Ephraim Bass 00002/20001
Obd. Olds 00001/00001
Moses Roberts 310001/120001
Blakly Thirston 0020001/0000001
Sabin Thirston 200001/01001

John D. Filkins 10001/00001
William Hunter 230101/ 100001
Isaac Tayler 120111/10001
Roswell Shelhouse 000011/30001
Henry Powers 010112/102001
John Foreman 3200201/3200201
Horace Kenney 0221101/0011101
Joseph D. Lauer 0010001/021001
Samuel McKey 00002/10011
Jonathan Engle 000110001/---
Amos Howe 001011/10101
Alexander McMillan 011231001/01011001
John Cady 000003/---
Abijah C. Luby 010001/110001
William Fletcher 000011001/00110001
William Hazzard 220011/00011
William Conners 00001/---
George W. Dille 10001/0001

GREEN TOWNSHIP
John Morse 200001/00001
William F. Bolton 0011311/20001
Fineas Bonner 210002/11001
John Corbes 100001/01001
John Kysne 000210001/00001
Joseph Hanchet 0010101/1000101
Jonathan Kirk 103031/00001
Jeremiah --- 301013/210111
Elijah Spurgin 000001/---
Jobe Brunson 001030101/0211001
Isaiah Hulbert 00001/---
Seth Dunham 0001101/001001
John D. Richardson 100001/10001
Samuel Smith 00201001/0010001
Lewis Denison/Generow? 101032/1001
Matthew McGilpin 00001/---

BRADY TOWNSHIP
John Chandler 100011/11001
Sellick Longwell 21110001/1100001
Elisha Done 110011/11001
Abiel Fellows 020300001/1130001
Jonathan Wood 10001/10101
Erastus Guilford 01101/10021001
William Duncan 00100001/00010001
Delman Duncan 00002/1001
John Wilds 110001/100001
Daniel Willmarth 000001/10001
Godfrey Knight 1001200001/1000100001
David Beadle 000110001/000000001

FLOWERFIELD TOWNSHIP
Misall Beadle 1201001/1102001
Henry Denver 00001/00001

John Insly 00100101/010001
Enoch Horn 1210001/201001
David M. Hanson 1101102/112001
Andrew Fitzgerald 00001/1001
Christopher Barr 00010001/01200001
Stephen Hoit 003010001/0010001
Joseph Bair 10001/11001001
Peter Wigert 00002/01001
Isaac Gemmer? 2100211/211011
Andrew Calhoun 2200001/010001
Abner Calhoun 22001/00001
Titus Bronson 0001101/1000001
John M. Jones 10001/10011
Thos. Stillwell 020001/111101
Abraham J. Shafer 100011/20001
John Kelly 120001/100001
Thomas Barber 00123001/01001001
John Nesbit 0012/---
Noble McKinstry 0002001/001101
Towner Savage 10100101/11001000
Abner Wood 00001/00001
Ephraim Harisen 10001/00101
Bazzle Harrison 00112101/01200001
Henry Whiple 100001/10101
James Fellows 00001/0001
William Bishops 200011/020001
James Smith 1020001/1200001
John McConpsey 000001/200001
Jeremiah McElvein 221001/012001
John McElvein 000210011/0011
Greer McElvein 100011/20001
Joseph Frakes 10011/20001
Robert Frakes 111300001/0001001
William Hunt 00001/00001
Harry Smith 2120001/1101001
William Harris 200001/01001
Nathan Harrison 110001/22001
Jno. B. Barns 010011/11101
Selden Norton 0000001/11101
David L. Dille 100001/00001
William Giddings 1023101/0101201
Isaac Barns 200101/00001
N. E. Mathews 0000101/00001
Ralph Tuttle 110001/10001
Isaac Barns 0001211/0110001
Lewis Campau 100432/10001
Leonard Stalen* 11107/100002
Elois Robear 10001/00001

Enumerator: Elias Taylor
12 November 1830

## BERRIEN COUNTY

### NILES TOWNSHIP
Lawrence Kavenaugh 11010001/0011201
William Huff 20011/02001
Timothy L. Smith 2011312/21011
Augustus B. Newell 000062/00002
Benjamin Chandler* 0010001/0110001
Julius Brown 011011/000001
Amos Fairley 010210001/00100001
Antoine Obian 010001/20001
Lewis Couture 00001/---
John Pike 0012001/111001
John Johnson 0013001/0010001
Stephen Dalie 010001/10001
Ephraim Lacy 000100001/00011
Elijah Lacy 100043/10001
Samuel B. Walling 00002/00002
Daniel Burisso 100010001/10002
Joseph Bertrand Sen. 10004001/01000001
Antoine Burisso 100002/10001
Joseph Bertrand Jun. 10001/00001
Alexander Huston 110031/10011
Robert Pininwell 121142002/100111
Abraham Colvin 000031/---
Lemuel Johnson 000001/000001
Frances pagee 2012701/11001
David Willson 0010201/1010101
Eli Ford 221031/10101
Pitt Brown 01002/002
John Boon 10001/0001
William Emmons 101001/221001
Thomas K. Green 000001001/---
Moses Finch 010001/21011
Benona Finch 200001/00001
Isaac Gray 2200001/001011
Morgan Wilson 210041/011001
Samuel Sales 111211/21101
Jacob Hickman 120001/110001
Peter Hickman 100001/220001
John Johnson Junr. 10001/00001
George H. Claypool 00001/00001
Sherick Ford 100001/00001
William C. Webster 0011001/0232001
Cornelius Sparks 2121001/021001
James Burnett 0000111/---
Garret Shuart 1211321/10011
William Justice 010021/110001

## CASS COUNTY

### DEXTER TOWNSHIP
Sterling Adams* 0000201/01001
Lathrop Johnson 00012/10001
John Melville 00020001/0010001
Abraham Edwards 0120611/212101
William A. Davis 2010011/110001000001
John Hudson 100011/00001
William Blackmarr 0120202/102001
Sylvester Meacham 100011/0111001
Jacob Smith 0111001/022101
Ezra Beardsley 1020201/0011001
William Bogart 001002/10100000001
John Bogart 0010001/120101
Frederick Garver 01021001/02010001
Thomas A. H. Edwards 10011/00001
John Silsbee 0000201/001101
Isaac Hulse 0022101/00010001
George Meacham 00011/00001
Adam Miller 11022011/2102001
Russel Bogart 0100001/211001
Othne Beardsley 10002/00001
William Tibbets 300101/00001
John Corkins 1210001/1001101
John Baldwin 1001101/111
John Mayville 000001/10001
Thomas Parget 100001/00001
Armstrong Davidson 1111201/0111201
Mathew G. Odell 10001/00001
Aaron Brooks 000001/21001

### ONTWA TOWNSHIP
Joseph Quinbee 000001/0000001
James Odell 0110111/210001
Canada Smith 0210201/0023001
Thomas Sullivan 100001/10002

### PENN TOWNSHIP
John Rhinehart 00113001/011100001
John Price 0010201/011001
Frederick Harrisson 0010001/2101001
Abram Davidson 0010102/010001
Russel Peck 01210001/2121001
Rodney Hinkley 000101/21001
Henry Whitehead 30001/000011
John Townsend 20001/00001
George Jones Sen. 0001201/00010001
George Jones Jun. 31002/110001
William M. Philips 10011/21001

William McCleary 00023001/00010001
Samuel Boyles 10002/00001
Martin Shields 2221001/0010001
Daniel McIntosh 001020001/00120001
Charles Jones 1112001/112001
William H. Brice 00002/00002
John Agard 1000101/011001
Thomas Vanderhoof 110001/122001
John Currey 0002/1001
Alexander Fulton 0002/---
Joseph Guard 00001001/00021001
Samuel Rich 20001/00001
Thomas Muncey 21001/010001
Russel Babcock 000101/01001
Jacob Mourland 200001/00001
William Griffis 20002/10001
Samuel Morris Jun. 10001/00001
Jacob Charles 00001/10001
Samuel Morris Sen. 00011001/00000001
David Carpenter 110101/00001
Jonathan Guard 31011/000001
John Knight 00000001/00000001

LEGRANGE TOWNSHIP
John Simpson 200001/112001
Thomas Simpson 020001/21001
Elias Simpson 20001/10001
Yoakley Griffin 02100001/00121001
Jonathan Prater 010002/1110001
Martin C. Whitman 0010001/1121001
James Dixson 120001/00011
Makus Louks 00011/00010001
Abraham Townsend 01002001/01001111
Gamael Townsend 00001/000002
Thomas McKinney 0010101/00111001
Joseph R. Barnard 00001001/0011001
Iry H. Putman 210011/000001
William B. Wright 01011001/00101001
Eli Bunnil 00001/10001
Samuel Shuart 200001/10001
Isaac Shuart 100011/11001
Jobe Davis 022011/21101
Jobe Wright Jun. 00001/00001
William W. Welch 2121001/010101
Stephen Marmon 110001/010101
Moses Reames 111001/01001
Nathan Norton 1001001/000001
Maxwell Zanes 0001/010001
John Pettigrew 010001/212001
Nathan Reed 10001/10001

Isaac Williams 00001/---
Benajah Williams 11002/10101
Andrew Grubb 20110001/032001
John Reed 00021001/00011001
Abner Thorp 12101/100101
Giles Norton 020001/201001
William Reams 00001/20001
Enoch Lundy 1011001/221001
Abram Titsworth Sen. 10011/10001
Abram Titsworth Jun. 01210001/0000001
Henry Lybrook 0001100001/0001300101
Sarah Ritter 12/001001
Robert Willson 00122001/00020001
David Brady 1010002/00001
Abram Louks 02011/100001

POKAGON TOWNSHIP
John Kenzie 0212201/101001
William Morris 100001/20001
John Ray 000011/00001
Lewis Edwards 10002/20001
William Garwood 010111/011101
Jacob Kenzie 311001/010001
Huzziel Putnam 100001/010001
Joseph L. Jacks 00001/1001
Nathan Haynes 2000001/11201
Isaac W. Ducket 000001/210001
Hugh Marrs 210001/00002
Joseph Garwood 021002/211001
Israel Markham Sen. 0100000001/00001001
Samuel Markham 020011/10001
Israel Markham Jun. 0100001/10001
Baldwin Jenkins 1211101/0111001
Henry Sefford 10001/00001
Archibald Clyburn 0002001/00101001
John Burk 020011001/000031
George McCoy 200201/0210001
Daniel Fisher 00001/0001
Samuel Morton 110101/201101
Jacob Landros 300001/10001
William Mourton 0000001/2000001
Joseph Gardner 100001/1001
Lane Markham 0001/00001
Esquire Thompson 1210101/201001
Adam Solida 1003/1120101
Ashbill B. McCullom 10001/00001
Emery Brown 110001/01001
Chapel Brown 010001/10001
Jonathan Jones 10001/10101
Jesse Touey 12112001/0002001

Alexander Rodgers 1102101/0020101
Thomas Buck 201011/000001
Samuel Landis 10001/00001
William Kirk 00001/22001
Samuel Witter 10001/11001

VAN BUREN COUNTY

PENN TOWNSHIP
Dolphin Morris 110001/10001

Enumerator for Berrien, Cass, and Van Buren Counties: Alexander H. Edwards 10 November 1830

MICHILIMACKINAC COUNTY

Whitman Taylor 00001/---
Robert M. Taylor 00001/---
Peter White 00001/---
James Wheeler 00001/---
William Lasley 00001/---
Louis Bonart 200001/---
Jean Bt. Picard 00001/---
Antoine Allard 000001/00001
François Louisignant 11010001/1001101
Charles Marley 01001001/0111001
Jesse Muncey 1100101/111001
Jane Cramer 00101211/00010001
René Nadeau 00001000001/---
Thomas A. B. Boyd 00001/---
John A. Drew 1100101/11111
Abraham Wendell 020001/10001
Jeremie LaDuc 0100001/210001
Edward Boisvert 210001/00001
Thomas Guthry 0100001/001
William Mitchell 00011011/10211
Mary Hogan ---/011101
Joseph Robillard 00001/0001
Ambrose R. Davenport 010111001/0132001
Eloi Bouchard 100101/0001
Simon Champagne 000000001/---
John Whelan 001002/---
Pierre Duvernay 211011/1
Jean B. Thesserault 0000000001/---
Théophile Fontaine 200001/10001
Henry G. Graveradt 1011001/222001
Samuel C. Lasley 01210011/0112011
Joseph Gooley 00010001/---
Alolphe L. St. Germain 0001/---

Ignace Lapierre 000001/---
François Lapierre 0001/---
Joseph Hobbs 00000012/---
Augustin Pond 4000101/031001
Charles André 0100010101/1000001
François Trottier 01111001/222001
Antoine Martin 1101110001/---
Jonas A. Stone 1120001/1000011
Isaac Blanchard 10001012/20001
Joseph Delvair 0000000001/000
Pierre Sellier 000000001/00001
Jose Laverdu 00000000001/---
Michel Donne 02110101/11001
Augustin Hamelin 211000001/11
Michael Jeandron 010000001/10001
John Graham 0000003/1
Jean B. Perrault 0000001/110001
Louis Grondin 10100001/00001
James Phalen 000001/---
Francis Robinson 210001/---
George McGulpin 110021/0011
Chauncey Warner 000001/---
Julius Perris 00001/---
George Yarns 10000001/10001
Cecil McCulloch 001/1111001
Thomas Wm. Drew 0000001/0000001
Joseph Namenville 0000300101/0012
Louis Charboneau Jr. 001001/---
Samuel Lasley 20001/01001
Charles Beaubin 000001/0211
Antoine Descoteaux 0001/---
Thomas Vasdebonier 00001/---
Joseph Gautier 00001/---
Paul Germain 00001/---
Moyse Girardin 0001/---
Augustin Girardin 00001/---
Joachim Trudelle 00001/---
Charles A. Provost 00001/---
Edward St. Arnaud 000001/---
Joseph Veau 00001/---
Charles Moncell 000001/---
Jean Bt. Bisaillon 00001/---
Frs. H. Paquette 00001/---
Paul Caye 0001/---
Frs. H. Bertrand 00001/---
Joseph Vaillancour 00001/---
François Bertrand 0001/---
Joachim Desrivières 00001/---
Charles Monsseau 00001/---
Edward Blanchard 00001/---
Joseph Gervais 00001/---

Jean Bt. Marchand 00001/---
Joseph Gauvreau 00001/---
Jules Lachance 00001/---
Isidore Vanier 00001/---
Louis Loreiau 000001/---
François Levigne 00001/---
John Kittson 00001/---
Norman W. Kittson 0001/---
Jean Bt. Durocher 00001/---
David Holmes 0001/---
Eaneas McDonell 0001/---
François Lavigne 000001/000
Julien Cau--- 00001/---
Théophile Cayotte 00001/---
Joseph Trudille 00001/---
Charles Lorain 00000001/---
Jean Bt. Tabeau 00000001/---
Toussaint Payant 00001/---
Toussaint Homier 0001/---
David McGulpin 01001/10001
Joseph Lozon 201101/1101
Adam D. Steuart 000001/---
Antoine Dequiear 00000000001/---
Henry B. Hoffman 00001/---
William McGulpin 1211101/0120001
Simon Allard 100001/010001
Madelaine Laframboise 001/00211001
Thérèse Schindler 10011/1202322
Leon Chenier 001000001/01
William Sylvester 121021/20011001
Joseph Renville 200001/00001
 ugustin Rousseau 110011/11111
Henry Welcome 010001/---
Samuel Abbott 0000101/00001
Peter J. Therien 120001/111
Michael Donsman 0011433/0112201
Robert Stuart 21000011/111002
Jacques Hubert 100001/11001
Claude Charboneau 00001/0001
Jean Peltier 1010001/11
George Boyd* 1111311/0100001
Thérèse Caune 0101/0121001
Lizette Pilotte 00111/0000001
Madelaine Cadotte 101/000001
Eber Ward 0001001/---
Rix Robinson 100182/02001
Joseph LaPine 100001/00001
Margaret Andrews 0001/110001
Louis Charboneau Sr. 02010001/002001
Edward Biddle 01001121/121001
Pierre Tiberre 00001/---

James Stevens 000002/---
John Campbell 1310001/100001
Andrew Cruse 000001/---
Joseph Paul 000000000001/---
Enos Cutler* 0000001/00001001
Robert A. McCabe* 0000001/---
William Alexander 000001/---
Moses E. Merrill 00001/---
Ephraim K. Smith 00001/---
Isaac Lynde* 10001/00001
Richard S. Satterlee 101001/02002
David Jones 0000101/---
Caleo Sibley 00001/---
Thomas I. Titus 00023/---
Jonathan P. King 000001/---
Charles H. Oakes 10081102/21
Andrew Burr 000001/---
Paul Seneschel 0000001/1
Charles Wm. Wulff Borup 00001/---
Bazel Beaubien 1011001/101201
Charles Cloutier 00000001/---
François Rochambeau 00001/---
William M. Ferry* 2(19)(18)(20)453/5(10)(16)
  (13)563
John S. Hudson 100001/0100001
Louis Bourassa 1200002/1010001
Edward Lasseur 000001/0001
Louis St.Ange 000001/00001
Benjamin Morin 00001/000001
John Dixon 000001/---
Thomas Doughaly 000001/---
Louis Bonet 00001/3
François Dufinais 000001/ 00001
John McClure 000001/---
Peter Kellar 00001/---
James Shearer 00001/---
Peter I. Dejion 000011/0002011
Samuel W. Caldwell 000001/---
Jean Bt. Lebeau 00000001/---
Benjamin Lonche 00001/---
Macaine Bourk 00001/---
George Sayers 00001/---
Gordon T. Brownell 00001/---
Michael Griffin 000001/00001
Obadiah Taylor 000001/---
William Ryan 000001/---
William Moore 000001/---
Simpson Vorn 000001/---
Samuel Dorrell 000001/---
James Nugent 000001/---
Alexis Gregoire 0000001/---

John Plackett 000001/---
William Goddard 000001/---
John W. King 00001/---
Jacob Trimbley 00001/---
George Rex 00001/---
Bowman Bishop 000001/---
Charles Eddo 00001/1
David Chamberlain 00001/---
Isaac Miller 00001/---
Levi Stevens 00001/---
Christopher Genung 00001/---
Samuel S. Hollenback 00001/---
Henry Gretzler 00001/---
William Stone 00001/---
Stephen Murphy 10001/10001
John Wilcox 00001/---
Thomas Jewett 00001/---
Ethan Topping 0000001/---
William O. Brownell 00001/---
George Lesley 00001/---
Elias Rose 00001/---
Thomas Andrew 000001/---
Chester Kimball 00001/---
Peter Guillet 000001/---
John Mershon 00001/---
James L. Murphy 00001/---
Cadwallader Evans 011001/00001
James Lawrence 110001/110001
Francis Higgins 000001/---
William Miers 00001/---
William Thompson 000001/---
James Fisher 00001/---
Daniel Finnemore 000001/---
William Alger 000001/---
Joseph Anthony 00001/00001
Nelson P. Burnet 00001/---
Samuel Bunting 000001/---
Alvin Bates 000001/---
James Brazier 00001/---
Edwin Baker 00001/---
Henry H. Sibley 00001/---
William Brown Jr. 0001(12)2/---
Hercules L. Donsman 00001/---
John Connor 0000001/---
John Dunfan 000001/---
Henry French 000001/---
Joel Condon 00001/---
Ephraim V. Francis 000001/---
Daniel Gillis 000001/---
William Garrison 000001/---

Holly Green 000001/---
Jacob Harrison 000001/---
Thomas D. Hart 000001/---
Horatio N. Hastings 000001/---
Thomas W. Irvine 00001/---

Robert Lingart 0000001/---
John Lansing 00001/---
John McCamon 000001/---
Charles McIntyre 000001/---
Robert Macklin 000001/---
William Magee 011001/10001
John Myerly 00001/---
Ezekiel Napton 000001/---
John F. Neiman 000001/---
John Reed 00001/---
Joseph Stroopsinsky 0000001/---
Lewis Shores 000001/---

Enumerator: Jonathan P. King
    30 August 1830

BROWN COUNTY

Oliver W. Phelps 00001/0001
Nathaniel Perry 100001/01001
James Clark 000201/10002
Samuel Ryan 210001/000011
Gabriel Bailey 00001/00001
John Horndorf 00001/---
Ezekiel W. Solomon 0101000101/0000001
Nathan Gooddell 001011/20001
Morgan L. Martin 00002/---
George Johnston 4111211/011012
Stephen H. Walker 100001/00001
Robert Irwin Jr. 101112/12022
John T. Reed 10001/00001
Robert Irwin Sr. 00000001/0011001
Elijah Murray 000001/---
Alexander J. Irwin 01000101/10001
James Riley 00000001/2200001
William Dickinson 000005/2100201
William Wilson 000001/---
Samuel Irwin 00003/---
John Bevins 110000/020001
Alexander Labord 00001/1001
Chester Mills 000001/---
John C. Smith 000001/---
Boneventure Gardipier 00001/---
Rensalear Marshall 200003/11001

John Nichols 110001/10001
Robert M. Eberts 00001/---
Louis Courbielle 000111/10001
François Martan (Martin) 010001/01001
François Boidoin (Baudoin) 0110001/120001
Jean B. Fauvel 001021/---
Joseph Jourdain 1100101/0022001
Alexander DeGerdin (Desjardin) 1100011/00002
Rosalie Dousman 01101/0221011
Louis Rouse 022002011001/211001
Jean B. Genor 200001/200001
Adeline Gorman 20001/11011
Elijah E. Robinson 31001201/01101
John Lawe 00129313/3221422
Samuel W. Beall 00001/00001
James D. Doty 111101/100001001
Pierre Carbonno 011020001/00101001
Antoine Carbonno 00001/20011
Albert G. Ellis 20101/10001
Linus Thompson 1000301/0001
David McClary 0000001/---
Benjamin Smith 000001/---
Clifford Belden 000001/---
Louis Bopre (Beaupré) 00313001/001100100001
John McCarty 101002/01101
Pierre Carbonno Jr. 200001/00001
Richard F. Cadle 010001/000001
Simon Gammon 000001/10202
François Dashna Sr. 0000001/---
Amos Ames 000001/00001
Richard Pricket 110100001/011101
William T. Gilbert 000001/00001
Daniel Whitney 200(10)2/00011
John Ingram 000001/---
Joseph Hould(Houll) 1010001/321001
John Roe 000001/---
Luke Bisson (Buisson) 00001/1001
John Smith 00001/---
Joseph Lemeur (Lemieux) 11001/11001
Henry B. Kelso 000001/21001
Alexander Gardipier 1111101/10111
Levi Warrington 300001/00001
Increase Claflin 20052/12001
John Gunn 0000001/11001
Amable Jervais (Gervais) 11000100001/00001
Jesse Saunders 000002/001101
Isaac Jacques 000001/11
J. B. Montcrève 0000011/---
Augustus Grignon 0013(11)11031/221102001031

Charles Miller 0000001/---
Daniel Olds 0121211/1110001
Charles Chapman 000001/---
Hiram Hurd 010001/110001
Moses Hardwick 20001/11001
John P. Arndt* 0111(12)31/0102001
Luther Leonard* 0000101/---
Frederick Blue 00000001/00001
William Farnsworth 2000241/100021
Joseph Ducharm 001120001/0000010001
Henry S. Baird 010101/20021
Jean B. St. Vincent 020001/10001
Augustus Thibault 1120001/---
Luther Gleason 000021/10001
Ebenezer Childs 000001/00001
John Hogarthy(Hagarty?) 1110011/210011
Amable Dorocher 21011/---
John Whistler 00001/---
John H. Kinzie 200031/20002
Dominique Brunet 30021001/132300100001
Perish Grignon 00002201/1000201
Jean B. Grignon 1001301/210111
Paul and Amable Grignon 301093111/110201
Augustus Bisson (Buisson) 100001/0001
Ira Ladd 000011/---
Jean B. Jomvine 10001010101/12200101
Jean B. Laborde 010002/3000011
François Dashna Jr. 100001/10001
Pierre Chalifout 010001/3400100001
Joseph Pellegore 001210001/0010001
Jacques Vieaux 434322101/220020001
Cutting Marsh 000002/10101
--- Sherman 000001/00001
Pierre Paquette 1000401/101001
George Fisher 10001/01001
Colonel William Lawrence of the 5th Regiment US Infantry, Commanding Fort Howard at Green Bay, M. Ty (Michigan Territory) 7324 (171)(55)4/44348211
Major D.E. Twiggs* of US Infantry, Commanding Fort Winnebago, Portage, Wisconsin, M. Ty. 4320(118)(44)1/520265
Lewis Grignon 1102201/011122
Peter Gerard 000001/20001
Daniel W. Hubbard 210002/101001
John Marston 100002/00001
John White 0000111/---
M. Powers 000002/000 (name was originally Pozé)

François Laventure 400020001/000110001
Joseph Couvrette 0000101/001001
James Porlier 402140001/1102201
Joseph Paquette 10001/11001
Louis Gravelle 00100000001/000021
Bazil Larock (Laroque) 100000001/2111001
Pascal Larock 11001000001/11000001
Simeon Lecuyer ---/00001
Jean B. Dupré 200001/001001
Louis Bordeaux 100001/121001
Joseph Courvalle 11000001/112001
Louis Dubé 00110001/0111001
Louis Fizette 000001/---
James Neville 000001/0001
Mad Lavigne 002/001101
Jean B. Lemerie 10001/0001
Perish Brunet 1100001/001001
Peter Powell 01100002/001
Charles Tuller 00001/---
Joseph Boisvert 00100001/00000001
Eleazer Williams 010011/10111
Laurent Fortier 0000001/---

Enumerator: Henry S. Baird
  3 August 1830

CRAWFORD COUNTY

Joseph Rolette* 0300(65)(18)50001/0123
Pierre Lessard 1010011/011001
Michael Brisbois 012221001/0011003
Hyacinth St. Cire 0100012/21201
Paggy (Pelagie) Pizanne ---/00001
Maria Fashnatch 00001001/001
James Reed* 100001/11101
Julien Larivière 10111/210011
Joseph Deschampt 10002101/01001
Michel Larivière 10011/00001
Pierre Larivière 000210001/0001001
Tunis Bell 0000001/000001
Marie Lapointe 000111/101101
Louis Chattelle 0000001/---
Charles Lapointe 100052/00101
James H. Lockwood 000106/---
John C. Hayes 020002/21001
Etienne Dyonne 001011/11001
Joseph Brisbois 100001/0001
William M. Read* 0100001/01011
Antoine Lachapelle 022011/0011001
François Gallarneaux 02011003/211101

François Labatte 200001/00001
Amable Grignon 11001/01001
Oliver Cherrier 1120001/01001
Jean Bt. Pion 110002/01011
Augustin Rock Sr. (Laroque) 1002001/001
  001001
Patrick Brenan* 0000042/---
John Marsh 00002/---
Jean Brunet* 0001231/001001
John Simpson 00100021/001001
Pierre Barette 21101/00101
Louis Arriandeaux 010001/10001
Strange Powers (Étrange Pozé) 00001/111001
Hubert Lapansé 00001/0001
Charles Tranche 01001/21001
Louison Montvaille 00001/10001
Gilliaume Gauthier 01011001/11121
John Lemery 1100101/00001
François Chenevert 0022201/020001
Jn Bte Loyer 0001001/21001
Pierre Lembert(Lambert)000011/---
Joseph Rivard 1100011/020001
Andrew Bazin 000301/---
Joseph Prince 0000001/00001
Benoni Carré (Queret) 00003/---
Antoine Reed 0000201/---
Charles St. Antoine 201001/00011
Joseph T. Booth 100002/10001
François Provost 0001011/0022001
John Miller 100011/00001
Charles Menard Jr. 10001/0001
Bazel Gagnier 00001 /000101
Louis Stram 101200001/0010001
Charles Menard Sr. 1201101/00001001
Lewis Grenards 000001/11001
Denis Courtois 00001001/0001
Jos. M. Street* 1223001/102001
Samuel Gilbert 330011/000001
Samuel Griffen 00001/---
George Colicoeur 122001/000001
Col. W. Morgan* 2602(96)(96)3/460083

Enumerator: Joseph Brisbois
  1 October 1830

# 1830 Census

## CHIPPEWA COUNTY

These men all aged 30-40, living alone:
Geo. Bary
Wm. Cole
Hamson Hyler
John Dauson
Luke Brennan
Joseph Sellers
John Dutton
Sam'l Houlton
Dudley Johnson 000011/---
These men all aged 20-30, living alone:
James McMackimon
Peter Moore
James Bicknell
Benjamin Love
William Bell
Nicholas Patterson
William Johnson
George Ballard
George Riley
Corlenias Sirve
John Boylen
Benj. Chapman
John Trimble
Francis Grady
Hart Pelten
Benj. Busco
William Dougherty
Isaac Ingraim
Geo. Bungo FC: 1 male 24-36
Antoin LaLonde 0000001/---
Pierre Lapipein 00001/---
Francis St. Johns 0100001/02
Ax Carpenter 00001/---
Frances L'mur 0000001/---
Benj. Cadotte 2100001/0101
Daniel Dingley 000001/02001
John B. Corbin 0000001/---
Alex Corbin 10001/---
Louis Corbin 10001/01
Michael Cadotte Sr. 000000001/000000001
Michael Cadotte Jr. 0000201/000021
Alex Nephew 20001/00001
J. B. Rowbedo 0100001/001
Jas. Mershaw 000101/---
Frances L'mue 1200001/---
Jas. Gothier 10001/---
Seymour January 100001/---

Thomas Conner 3001001/010201
Souvreigh Daié 0010001/0001
B. F. Baker 000001/---
William Stitt 00001/---
J. B. Privonlille 00001/---
Joseph Pekoin 100001/---
J. B. Trolensho 10001/1
Bazile DuGenna 00001/---
John Hulbert 010001/00001
Robt. E. Clary 10101/00111
Louis T. Jameson 00001/---
James Allen 00001/---
Lafayette Wilcox 000001/000
Edwin James 110001/00001
Abel Bingham 0250001/242011
Isaac Butterfield 000001/---
William Roy 00001/---
John Agnew 000001/---
Elijah O'Brien 00001/000
Joel Spense 011001/00001
Joseph Adams 00001/2001
William C. Cole 21001/00001
James Parkinson 010001/000101
Thomas Cooper 000001/200001
Jacob Morosh 0000001/---
Pierre LaPorte 00010001/---
Francis Audrain 1100010001/00001
George Ermatinger 10000001/000001
Thomas Thompson 00000001/---
Charles Failes 00001/---
Richardson May 000001/---
Margaret Richio 01/00001
Joseph Rice 000001/---
Ephraim Johnston 0000001/212001
Joseph Dollard 000001/10001
Robert Morren 00001/---
Louis Poipin 00001/0001
Hippolite Berlangate 00001/---
Francis L'Branche 0001/---
James Ermatinger 00001/10001
Peter Howl 00001/---
Joseph Bersho 00001/---
Joseph Boisiart 0001/---
Plymouth Bolio 0001/---
Dennis Felix 00001/1001
Louis LaDebouche 10000001/11001
Marthe Bession 200001/0001
Alexia Boudwine 1000001/0102
Peter Bouchea 0001/---
J. B. Turelle 00000001/---

Leonard Loomis 000001/01
Jacob Little 001/---
John Tanner 0110001/0101
Michel Noline 110001/002001
Pierre LaNut 00001/---
Frs. LaMura 10001/100001
J. B. DeNunma 00001/---
T. Rohaville 0001/---
A. DeRagoue 0001/---
Francis Gothier 00001/---
J. B. Gothier 00001/---
Lyman Warren 150001/00201
Geo. Ritchy 00001/---
Jno. Goodale 00001/---
Wm. R. Elsworth 00001/---
Anias Lovejoy 00001/---
Thomas Cooper 00001/---
F. Rynd 00001/---
Jno. Davison 2nd 00001/---
Martin Ploof 000001/---
Adam Holcraft 000001/000
David Frederick 000001/---
J. Parkerson 00001/---
J. Spence 000001/000
T. Handy 000001/---
Wm. Guthrie 000001/---
Thomas Morton 000001/---
G. S. Cooper 0000001/---
S. Thomas 0000001/---
T. Neill 0000001/---
Chas. Luntz 0000001/---
John Guy 000001/---
Mathew Feilden 000001/---
John Sargents 000001/---
James Stevens 000001/---
Jos. Adams 000001/---
William Sinvine 000001/000
John Garrison 000001/---
Jacob Shuster 000001/---
James Filson 00001/---
Augustine Lavine 00001/---
Amiable Kadian 0000001/---
Charles Gittwood 00001/---
John Brown 0000001/---
Joseph Grimour 00001/---
Pierre Borbour 00001/---
Joseph Fontain 0000001/---
Joseph C dotte 00001/---
Joseph Fontain 0000001/---
Tousaint Piquette 0001/---

Antoin Laloucette 000000001/---
John Holiday 0000101/001
Francis Beonoin 100001/1
Gabriel L'Trois 0000001/---
These men all aged 20-30, living alone:
D. White
A. McVaughton
J. A. C. Deming
R. Hull
John Wade
Wm. R. Green
M. Vanbuskirk
W. T. Bidwell
John Davison 1st
Nelson Segur
R. Kinshallow
R. Cotton
James Rickman
Josiah Wade
Mansfield Wallace 000001/---
Thomas Ermatinger 10001/10001
John Battise Piquette 01001/0001101
Antoine Gingrass 0000001/101001
Francis Piquette 00000001/00111
Joseph Sunderland 1111001/---
Francis Dufault 001001/---
Daniel Keith 0001/---
Thomas Edwards 00001/1
Rufus Hunter 00001/---
H. A. Levake 100001/1
Jas. Laplante 020210001/0002001
Aitken Cointoura 0011111/1
John Holley 01000001/20001
Susan Johnston 00111/0120001
John Crossman 00001/---
Francis Disome 301001/000001
John B. Lalonde 1/0001
George Johnston 200001/01001
Joseph Miniclier 20001/301101
Michael Bouskay 000001/---
Francis Piquette 2nd 00001/---
Hyhaeh Coone 00001/---
J. A. Margin 00001/---
Sam'l Ashman 020001/1
Louis Noline 2010001/011001
William Aitken 222001/---
Eustace Roussain 22100001/---
Paul Bolio 0111001/10001
Bela Chapman 200001/11001
Jas. LaPointe 00001/1

Eneas LaBede 10001/---
Androw Godfroy 00001/---
Charles Carloe 00001/000
Paul Bowvia 00001/---
Paul Proha 00001/000
Batice Bario 000001/---
Joseph Chorrell 00001/1
Andrus Godfroy 2nd 00001/---
Charles Chirrette 010000001/---
J. B. Mershaw 0000001/001
Jas. Anshelia 00001/---
Pierre Toussaint 00001/---
J. LaBelle 00001/---
Charles Piquette 11001/00001
Frs. Bouskay 00021/---
Henry Wynecore 000010001/---
Pierre San Piqued 00001/---
Donnald McDonald 000001/---
Toussaint Bouskay 011001/01001
J. B. Campbell 00001/---
Antoin Chorrette 000001/---
Pier Terdeiff 00001/---
Oliver Fangain 001001/000001
Genevieve DuGray ---/10001
Francis L'Londe 010111/01111
Francis L'Equea 00001/---
Joseph Sutrarro 001001/110001
Antwoine Manassaw 010000001/00101
Pierre Jarvais 00001/---
Francis Borbonno 0110001/---
Thomas Shaw 100001/---
John Battise Bonno 1200001/1101
Joseph Jonevine 00001/---
Jacob Coreire 00001/---
Louis DuBraye 00001/---
Louis Brounelle 0000001/---
Charles Jassaint 000001/---
Issabelle McFarlane 1/20001
Marian Miniclen 001/0000001
Joseph Brisbois 0010000001/---
Antoin Canton 2000001/0000
Joseph Busha 000001/30001
Antoine Joisbainé 000001/---
Christain Wachter 01000001/---
Ambrose Davenporte 00001/20001
Nicholas Decotoe 22001/---
Antoin Cornie 00001/0001
Leslie Duncan 11001/110001
Sheldon Ball 000001/---
Jas. LaPorte 0001/---

Jas. DuRushea 00001/---
J. B. Brula 001/---
Saple Blevoir 0001/---
William Ross 00001/---
Jas. Depier 00001/---
Charles Chorbollais 00001/---
M. LaTour 00001/---
M. Champaigne 0001/---
Jas. Jivray 00001/---
Jas. L'quier 00001/---
Daniel Willione 00001/---
H. R. Schoolcraft* 101011/100011
These men all aged 20-30 and living alone:
D. Potter
T. Williams
James Young
Charles Falrey
Elijah Dimrock
Martin Fulmer
Isaac Tallmage
D. Ross
M. Riley
J. Dunlova
W. Stevens
D. Mosses 100001/0201


These men all aged 20-30 and living alone:
A. Mowery
J. M. Romer
James Convase
Isaac Sutfins
Arnold Rennold
Sam'l Spaulding
Daniel Stevens
Aaron Whitcomb
Geo. C. Clarke
Jno. W. Stevens
David Copp
Reuben Bemis
Barret Ward 10001/11001
John Keehe 10001/00001
These men all aged 20-30 and living alone:
Thomas Garaside
Wm. A. Sheer
Wm. Wybrough
Robert Nally
Benj. Sullivan
D. Southter
William Thompson
G. R. Rutter
Edward Burke

Richard Burtiss
Wm. McCornisten
William C. Andrys
James Woherty
Wm. Stevens
M. A. St. John 000001/---
J. Leary 000001/---
James Schoolcraft 00001/---

Enumerator: James S. Schoolcraft
  29 August 1830

IOWA COUNTY

James B. Estes* 000211001/010111
Jacob Hamilton 00001001/---
John G. Fennimore 00001/10001
Arthur Asher 00002/---
William Baker 000021/---
John Denning 0000101/---
McVey Armstrong 00012/---
John O'Mara 00002/---
Michael Kenwick 00001/---
Levi Parrish 01201001/01000001
Thomas Simpson 00002200001/100001
Joseph B. Hunter 000001/01001
Thomas Brazier 101001/110001
Bird Millsap 310011/00001
Daniel Moore 100001/001
Samuel Charles 000001/---
John Sherman 000001/---
James Hamilton 00002/---
Morgan Kehore 0000001/---
Elijah Mayfield 001201/110001
Paul M. Gratiot* 200001/00101
James H. Kirkpatrick 120001/20001
John B. Terry 0000241/00101
Robert Ropes 00003/---
Daniel Young 00001/---
Morton McMahon 0000001/11001
Joel Walmsley 00003/---
Nicholas Walsh 000021/000
John C. Thomas 120001/10001
John Rodgers 010001/10001
William T. Bush 0002601/000
Guyon Kenneday 000011/000
Armistead Floyd 00111/0202001
William Fleharty 01013/210001
Richard H. Kirkpatrick 00003/---
James Melvin 200001/11001

Peter A. Lorimer 0001411/00001
Stephen Thrasher 100005/01001
Allen R. Daugherty 100002/01001
Henry Redmond 000001/0000001
Luke Smith 10001/10001
James Brady 100011/00001
Patrick Moneghan 120001/10001
Elisha E. Brock 100011/01001
Nicholas Shay 0000011/000001
Edward Tracey 000001/---
Wallace Rowan 100001/12001
Abner Nicholls 000022/030001
Nelson Bird 000001/00001
James Masden 121011/1010001
Nicholas Wells 00001/---
Lewis Kinney 00000001/1000001
John L. Chastain 00001/---
John Sublet 00011/20101
Jefferson Smith 00002/---
Richard Wilson 00001/---
Patrick McKinney 0000001/---
Henry Blaney 0000101/---
James Scantling 0000001/---
Otis Mastic 0000001/---
Joseph Bailley 000011/---
John Hood 20002/00001
William F. Manegan 000001/---
Noble F. Dean 000011/00001
George B. Cole 00001001/---
John Campbell 000001/---
Robert R. Read 0010011/000001
Asa Duncan 000021/---
Matthew Fitch 100001/1001
Abram Miller 1111001/0011101
David Matlock 000001/---
George Carroll 1101001/0002001
John Woods 00001/---
Henry Dodge* 0001101/1121001
Alexander Buttersworth 0000001/---
Robert Henry 0021101/0100001
Elijah Wentworth 001010001/0020001
James P. Cox 00001/---
Felix McBride 0000101/200001
Charles Gaines 100001/00001
Jordan P. Cockrum 00001/10001
Robert N. Chatsey 00002/---
Herbert Fluellin 0000011/---
Elisha Hyde 000001/---
Emerson Green 100001/10001
Francis Baldwin 00000001/---

William A. Phelps 000112/---
Thomas Jenkins 000012/---
Richard Highton 00001/---
Patrick Horan 00001/---
William Garretson 00001/---
Alexander McKinley 0000001/---
Peter Fitzgerald 00001/---
Isaac Martin 00001/---
Claibourne Davis 00002/---
James H. Lay 00004/10001
John Messersmith 0012101/220001
Lewis Vanmatre 00003/---
William Hopson 00001/00001
Garret D. Farris 000011/121001
William J. Madden* 2100301/10001
Elanson Miller 00001/0001
Richard Murphy 0000011/---
James Hayes 000003/---
Robert Daugherty 00000001/---
Henry Bowers 0000001/---
Philip McDade 0000011/---
David Dixon 00001/---
George Robinson 00001/---
James Robinson 00005/---
James Nugent 00001/---
John Fullarton 000001/00001
James H. Gentry* 0000011/000001
Charles B. Tomlinson 000002/---
William Guillim 010001/0000001
Absalom Louder 100001/10001
George Scott 000011/---
Andrew P. Vanmatre* 000044/---
John Thomas 0000001/---
John B. Primer 00113001/000001
John Daugherty 000042/---
James Hanley 000001/---
John Moore 1000201/110001
Harris Alexander 30001/00001
John Ray 10002/00001
Daniel M. Parkinson 001001/010001
Joseph Fanning 00001/---
Thomas Lacey 0000101/00001
Thomas H. Price 000101/---
John Parkinson* 0000321/---
Robert C. Hoard 0100211/000001
Robert Hickland 00000001/---
Robert P. Guyard 000012/---
James Kendall 01112001/0100001
Adam Heimer 100001/001
John Dillon 0000011/---

Hiram Currant 00002/---
James Knox 00000011/---
Jesse M. Harrison 000021/---
George Medaira 00002/0001
Francis Gehon 000101/000001
Aaron Westerfield 00001/---
Daniel Creighton 0000001/---
Jonathan Ferrill 01001/10001
John Daniels 00000001/---
John Rankin 000021/---
James Morrison* 11004/11001
Samuel Woodsworth 00005/---
Thomas McCraney 112011/001001
Jacob Leas 000012/---
Elisha Fish 0000001/32101
George Force 000001/---
Esau Johnson 00003/00001
Andrew Orr 0000011/---
John C. Kellog 00001001/0000001
Ebenezer Brigham 0000401/---
William Wallace 0000001/011001
William Deveisse 000052/---
John B. Skinner 001204/121101
Omri Spafford 00003/---
Samuel Paxton 00003/---
William Hale 002100001/01010001
Elias Shook 00001/10001
Alfred McConnell 000001/---
William McCloskey 000001/---
Elisha Hartour 00001/---
Crawford Million 00001/---
Abraham Searles 00001/---
Henry Lee 000012/---
William S. Hamilton 00004/---
Alexander Cox 00001/10001
Warner Lewis 00002/---
Benjamin Million 20010001/1011001
George W. Lott 2001001/010001
Stephen G. Hale 100002/20002
Aaron Hawley 211012/001001
Benjamin C. Stephenson 00001/---
Asa Lamb 0010001/0211001
Verni Lovett 1000011/000001
Moses Hallet 120001/1000001
Thomas Phalen 00001/---
Reuben S. Ware 20001/01001
John R. Shultz 000001/00001
Christopher Plank 00010001/0111001
Joseph Paine 00101/1001
Martin Nort 1000001/020001

John B. Vairin 0100101/0101001
Roderick Lamount 00001/---
Terrance Kyle 00100001/0010001
Samuel Stebbins 100001/10001001
Henry J. Mosley 00002/---
Hughes W. Birch 00002/---
John M. Curtis 100021/00111
William Bowles 000000001/---
Jonathan Olmstead 1010001/101001
Lewis Osterstag 100001/1001
Joseph Hebert 000001/10001
Louis Chatalin 110001/10001
Antoine Bé 0100001/100001
John P. Gratiot 020001/20001
John B. Lognier 000001/---
Paul Lognier 0000001/---
Joseph Minet 0000001/---
Louis Wood dit Bois 000001/---
Pierre Bodin 000001/---
Michael St. Cyr 00001/---
Julius Gibson 00001/---
Augustin Hebert 00001/---
Bernard Smith 0000001/---
Joseph Polander 0000001/---
Louis Marchand 00001/---
Eugene Fournier 00001/---
Thomas Ward 000001/---
Michael Gales 00001/10001
Robert Kirkendall 00001/---
Joseph Vairin 0000001/---
Joseph Morrell 0100001/---
Nicholas Hebert 0000001/---
John Vicent 000000001/---
Joseph Gagnier 00000001/---
James O'Brien 00000001/---
John R. Coons 100001/00001
Louis Bussis 0100101/01001
Henry Gratiot* 202000101/121001
Robert B. Powell 100001/20001
Robert Campbell 10001/00001
Antoine Bricklin 000001/210001
Michael Shelby FC: 2 males -10, 2 24-36.
 1 female -10, 1 24-36
Antoine Pauquette 1000001/12001
John B. Guyon 111001/010001
Joseph Greenwood 000001/001001
Benjamin King 110001/10101
Jock B. Montplaisir 000001/301001
Joseph Eno 210001/00001
Amherst C. Ransom 0100101/10001

John R. Armstrong 000004/---
John McNulty 000021/---
Michael Finlay 1001001/111001
George W. Ames 01001/10001
James Hawthorn 000001/---
Jameson Hamilton 2110012/12001
Paul Gerbo 1100001/1000001
Joseph Ailer 000001/21001
Catherine Mayott ---/010001
Benjamin Glover 000001/---
John Codle 0000001/---
Patrick Doyle 000001/---
Patrick Sullivan 220001/01001
Patrick Cleary 00001/---
Dennis O'Neil 0000001/---
Peter Carr 00003/---
William Hewlings 0003201/0000001
William C. Overstreet 00001/---
Harvey Caverner 00001/---
Peter Kinney 00201001/00010001
Isaac B. Cowan 220001/00001
Benjamin Carr 00002/---
Nathan Perkins 00001/---
James Nagle 00001/---
Joseph Clegg 0000001/---
Ahab Bean 2021001/011101
Abram Looney 00001/---
Peter Sharer 100001/10001
John Wilson 000001/---
Lewis Curtis 0021201/000101
John Paul 1000301/0001
Nicholas Hoffman 00100001/---
James Murphy* 010001/100010001
Dennis Murphy 20001/00001
Michael Murphy 100001/00001
Francis Doulin 000001/10001
Daniel Shannon 00001/---
John Tharp 00001/---
Patrick Murphy 00001/---
Andrew Murphy 0000000001/---
Laurence Ryan 011001/100001
François DeLisle 000000001/---
George Rollins 000000001/000000001
Peter O'Leary 1010001/111001
Whiting Johnson 00003/---
Samuel Carlton 000001/21001
Alexander Willard 01112001/2111001
Justus DeSelhurst 0000011/00001
Michael Fouche 0000011/000001
George G. Shattuck 2100232/012101

George W. Ferguson 0000001/---
Thomas Potter 000001/---
Robert Collet* 1100001/100001
James C. Wright 10002/210001
James Wisswell 010001/010012
William T. Richards 00003/10001
Abner Westrope 200011/12001
Robert Terry 000011/---
Thomas Welsh 0100001/020101
Jesse Bond 0010001/0000001
Jesse Looney 00011/10001
Dawson E. Parrish* 10001/10001
Lewis Nealey 10001/00001
Moses Eastman 1221001/011101
Patrick Devine 000001/---
Francis Roy 0110001/122001
Amable Gregnon 100001/010001
Michael Lepiere 0010001/00000001
Louis Menage 1000001/011001
Pierre Pauquette 11003101/101001
George Fisher 100001/10101
Joseph Plant 00001/2001
Augustin Fillion 20001/0001
Thomas G. Hanely 0010001/000001
William Wayman 000011/---
John Armstrong 000021/10101
Ira Morrell 0000011/---
Moses Hickland* 200001/10001
John Clews 000001/---
Aaron Boyce 210011/01001
Jesse Haldeman 000011/---
Andrew McWilliams 10002/00001
Richard Ray 111001/010001
Rebecca Clark FC: 1 female 55-100
Orris McCartney 110003/10002
Solomon Arthur 00001101/0000001
Henry C. Bushnell 00012/10001
Nahum Dudley 000011/---
William M. Morrison 00001/00001
Henry W. Hodges 00001/---
Oliver P. Sherman 010001/11001
William D. Adney 010002/10101
Robert Hatwell 100002/10011
Joseph Hardy 000032/---
Martial Detantaboratz 0000631001/---
François Nicholas 000001/11011
William Anderson 000021/---
Loring Wheeler 00016/---
Thomas Hore 10001/001
Elizabeth Davis 0101/0100001

Richard H. Bell 000001/---
George W. Jones 00002/20001
William Gates 210001/20001
John Morgan 000001/20001
Dennis Quinby 000002/---
Richard H. Palmer 10012/00001
Absalom McCormack 0000101/---
Etienne Dubois 0000011/---
Silas Brook 000031/---
Thomas Jourdan 0112201/1020001
Benjamin Forman 00004/---
Robert Waller* 000044/---
William Gilham 110001/10001
William Bowmer 100101/31001
Joseph Lupton 000011/---
Thomas Good 1100021/11001
John McCormack 00002/---
Thomas W. Floyd 010011/100001
Francis Jarrot 00003/---
James H. Langworthy 000021/---
Ebenezer Orn 231113/101101
Pierre Teller 100001/10001
Thomas Fitzpatrick 00002/---
Robert Saucer 00003/---
Roland R. Holmes 000001/000001
Thomas Moss 20002/0001
Jonathan Meeker 000102/---
Thomas Cunningham 2030001/111001
Jacob Houzer 20011/00001
Elijah Turner 00003/---
William Davidson 000002/---
James McHenry 000011/---
John Shipley 000011/00001
Frederick Holman 020012/20001
Joseph Dixon 00002/000001
Trueman Hibberts 010021/000001
Ambrose Kenneday 000001/20001
John H. Roundtree 0000(21)(15)/00001
James R. Vinyard 00001/00001
Burchett B. Lawless 00002/01001
John Carpenter 0001001/---
William P. Preston 000001/---
Ashford Rollins 00001/00001
Samuel Cole 0000001/---
Andrew Murphy 000011/---
Francis Kirkpatrick 21004/10001
Joseph Hawks 10210001/120001
Page Blake 000011/100001
James Moody 10001/02001
Thomas Parrish 100011/00001

Continued on page 222

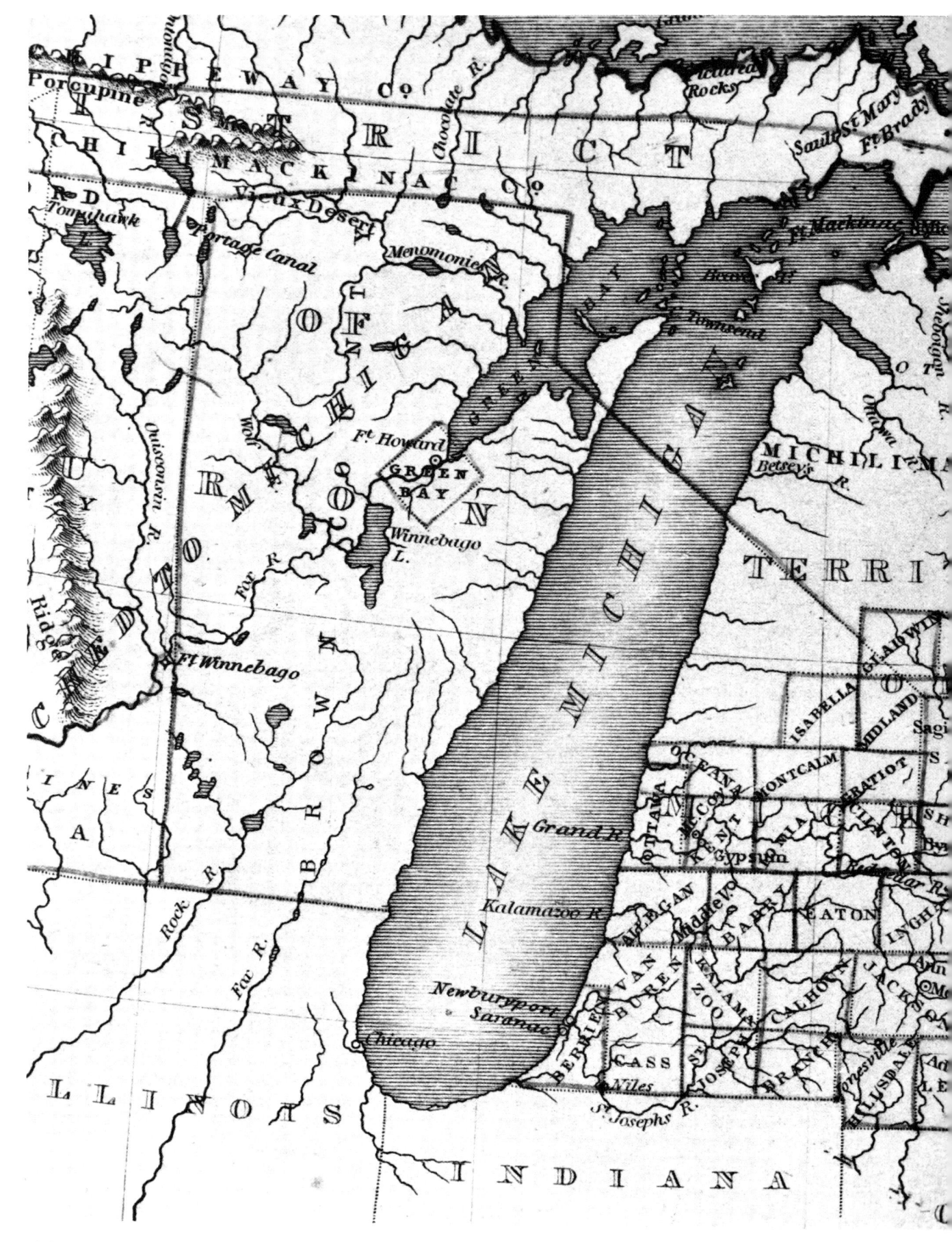

MAP 19. MICHIGAN AND THE GREAT LAKES, by Thomas G. Bradford, 1835 (detail)

(Courtesy of Burton Historical Collection)

Frederick Dixon 0000111/---
Peter Warfield 00110001/02100001
John Loofborough 0000001/---
Robert W. Grey 00002/---
James Woods 100002/20001
Levi Gilbert 00000001/00000001
Samuel Fretwell 00003/---
Henry Nicholls 300011/210001

Enumerator: James B. Dallam
  8 October 1830

# INDEX

ABBOTT, ... 54, 77
  Audrain 160
  Charles G. 161
  Elizabeth (Audrain) 119
  James 42, 60, 84, 103, 117, 119, 128, 153, 160, 161, 172
  James Whistler 117
  Mary 84
  Mary (Barger) 128
  Mary (Barkle) 119
  Robert 60, 77, 89, 84, 119, 154, 160, 164, 166
  Robert H. 153
  Sally 84
  Samuel 92, 128, 209
  Sarah (...) 117
  Sarah (Whistler) 103
  Teresa (Beaufait) 128
  William 193
ABLE, Almon 195
  Azil 194
ABRAHAM, Gaspard 79, 84
ACKERMAN, James 187
  James H. 187
  John 183
ACKERSON, James 198
ACKINS, James 78
ADAMS, Anden 192
  Asa 175
  Brotten 192
  Ephraim 176
  George 192
  Humphrey 183
  James 76
  John 142, 192
  Jos. 214
  Joseph 213
  Mark 185
  Mica 153
  Micah 161
  Paula (Walsh) 113
  Sterling 206
  Thomas 113
  Thomas H. 158
  Titus 173
  Travis 154
  Uri 184
  William S. 185
ADDIS, Samuel 182
ADHEMAR, ... (...) 42
  Antoine 54
  St. Martin (see St.Martin)
  Touissant Antoine 33
ADNEY, William D. 219
AGARD, John 207
AGNEW, John 122, 213
  Samuel 178
AIDE, Jean Baptiste 32
  Crequi, Cecile 109
  Crequi, J. Bte 109

  dit Crequi, Jean Baptiste 21, 32
AIDEGE, ... 79
AIKIN, William 120, 214
AILER, Joseph 218
AINEL, Augustin 80
AINNSE, Sarah 55
  see Etinnse
AIRD, James 92
AITKEN, see Aikin
AKANE, John 146
AKINS, Hannah 164
ALAIN, Anne 110
ALARD, see Elloir
  Felicite 115
  Jacques 72, 79, 115, 131
  James 131
  Peter 191
ALAZELL, Stephen 152
ALBAIN, Robert 142, 175
ALBEE, George R. 198
ALBERT, Joseph 91
ALDRICH, Asquire 109
  Lovel 163
  Owen 171
  Peter 194
  Stephen M. 165
ALDRICK, Asquire 164
ALDRIDGE, Asquire 157
  Esquire 151
ALEXANDER, ... (...) 79
  Archibald 127
  Harris 217
  Robert 195
  Thomas 201
  William 209
ALFRED, George 137, 173
  Hemon 137
**ALFORD, see** Alfred
  John 175
  John M. 137
ALGER, Josiah 182
  William 210
ALLAIR, Florence (Girardin) 113
  Francis 161
  Jock 161
  Joseph 113, 164
  Louis 161
ALLAIRD, Joseph 158
ALLAN, George 194
  Moses 158
ALLARD, Antoine 208
  Francois 150
  Jacques 53, 115
  James 150
  Joseph 191
  Louis 150
  Peter 186
  Simon 209
  Teresa (Marsac) 115

ALLEN, ... (Russell) 129
  Almeron 155
  Benjamin 125
  Ezekiel 129, 190
  George 199
  James 186, 213
  James T. 198
  John 187, 193, 198
  Jonothan T. 192
  Mary 129, 187
  Moses 113, 199
  Orison 129, 181
  Polly (Barnes) 113
  Seneca 173
  Silas 173
  William 80, 84, 194, 199
  Zadock 181
ALLERE, Joseph 71
ALLIZ, Thomas 65
ALLOR, see Allere 71
ALLORS, Jacquis 159
ALMY, Henry 183
ALVERSON, Daniel 193
ALVORD, Thadeus 187
AMBROIS, Joseph 137
AMBROISE, ... 17
  Evangile 90
  Francois (...) 79
  Jean L. 90
  Ignace 79
  Michel 76
AMBROZIENE, John 145
AMES, Amos 211
  George W. 218
  Joseph 203
  Martin 185
AMLIN, Joseph 171
AMON, Lewis 166
AMSBURY, Thirza 202
ANDERS, Daniel 161
  John T. 161
ANDERSON, Anna 117
  Arminda 117
  Charles 199
  David 76, 84
  Ebenezer 189
  Elizabeth (Knaggs) 136
  James 60
  John 106, 136, 174, 199
  Paul D. 117, 160, 171
  Sarah 136
  Thomas 117, 160
  William 219
ANDRE, Charles 208
  Claude 17
  Clemence (Fearson) 102
  Jacques 63
  Joseph 56, 77, 102, 104
  Suzanne (Drouillard) 102
ANDRE-CLARK, see Andre, Joseph 102, 171

ANDRESS, Polly 119
ANDREW, Thomas 210
ANDREWS, ... 41, 54
  Amasa 181
  Angelique (Duberger) 129
  Benjamin 179
  Charles 179
  Elon 193
  Hamilton 165
  Ira 129
  John 154
  John J. 153
  Joseph 179
  Justice 165
  Justus 155
  Lyman W. 179
  Margaret 209
  Morris 155, 161
  Nathan 203
  Russell 192
  Stephen 156
  Thomas N. 203
  William 60, 77, 78, 129
ANDRUS, Ira 172
  John 160
ANDRYS, William C. 216
ANGLESON, Moire 77
ANNETT, William 180
ANNIN, Catherine 104
ANSCOMB, Allen 184
ANSHELIA, Jas. 215
ANTAIL'LEUR, Augustin 178
ANTHON, George 42, 54
ANTHONY, ... 89
  Joseph 210
ANTILLIYA, Jean Baptiste 50
ANTIYA, Jean Bt. 43
ARANDER, John O. 193
ARCHABALD, Murry 165
ARCHAMBALL, Antoine 121
ARCOAT, see Argute 48
ARCOUET, Alexis 143
  Cecile (Valcour) 143
  M. (Lagarde) 143
ARGENTEUIL, M. 7
ARGUTE, see Arcoat 48
  Alexis 48
ARMSTRONG, John 110, 117, 157, 159, 219
  John A. 110
  John R. 218

  Nathaniel 182
ARNA, Joseph 190
ARNAULT, see Urno 115
ARNDT, John P. 211
ARNOLD, Alay 192
  Christopher 193
  Cyrenes 192
  Darius C. 161, 165
  Edward 193
  Hiram 201

ARNOLD, Jeremiah 189
  John 188
  Joseph 200
  Lanson 192
  Matthias 199
  Seemour 194
  William 192
ARNOW, George 195
ARCUOETTE, Alexis 178
ARRIANDEAUX, Louis 212
ARTHUR, Solomon 219
ASE, James 197
ASHER, Arthur 216
ASHLEY, Alfred 190
ASHMAN, Sam'l 214
ASKIN, Jean 67
  Jno. 78
  John 52, 61
ASKING, Josh 81
ASPINWALL, Ahil 152
  Miranda 166
ASSELLIEA, Pierre 123
ASSIRE(?), ... 77
ASTOR, John J. 128
ATKINSON, Samuel 175
ATTARD, Baptiste 84
ATTWATER, Reuben 92
ATWOOD, Hiram 190
  Sylvester 190
AUBAN-LAGARDE, Sophia 142
AUBIN, Alexander 166
  Pierre 178
AUDLAIN, Adrien 78
AUDRAIN, ... (...) 92
  Elizabeth 119
  Francis 213
  Margaret (Moore) 103
  Maria C. 117
  Michael 84
  Peter 76, 84, 103
  Pierre 117, 119
AUGUSTIN, see Tremblay 17
AUMAIS, Josh 67
AUSTEN, Jonathan 194
  William 194
AUSTIN, Andrew 127
  Cornelius 180
  Harvey 198
  William 178, 194
AVERY, Peter Wm. 160
  William 189
AXFORD, John 193
  Samuel 192
AYLESWORTH, Robert 188
  Reuben H. 137
AYRES, Ebenezer 125

BABCOCK, Henry 199
  Henry S. 182
  Russel 207
  Samuel 181
BABCUP, Mary 125

BABION, Jean Marie 158
BABY, ... 36
  ... (...) 43
  (Duperon), ... 78
  see Duperon dit Baby 25
  Duperon 54
  Jacques 60
  James 84
BACKER, Daniel 199
BACON, Artimus W. 186
  Jacob 203
BADDING, Cromwell 182
BADGER, Gideon 137
BADICHON, see Descomps 23
  Victoria 132
BADIEN, Theotiste 157
BAGLEY, Amaza 181
BAGNEL, Gilbert 160
BAIKER, Jacob 71
BAILANS, Frans 70
BAILEY, Alexis 125
  Chancy 194
  Gabriel 210
  Isaac 182
  James 184
  Joseph 122
  Louis 121
  Ralph 174
BAILLEY, Joseph 216
BAILLIE?, see Paille 21
BAILLON, see Bailans 70
BAILLY, see Bailey 125
  Louise Jeanne 6
BAIN, J. (...) 87
  Lucy (Lane) Gooley 104
  Stephen 104
BAINS, Irvin 198
BAIR, Joseph 205
BAIRD, Henry S. 211, 212
  James 195
  John 195
  William 195
BAITY, William 151
BATTELL MEE, 145
BAKER, ... 84
  Aron S. 188
  B. F. 213
  Becherr 71
  Cecilia (LaForest) 132
  Daniel 106, 162
  Daniel M. 180
  Edwin 210
  Elias 203
  Frederick 178
  Jacob 132, 181, 191
  Josiah 188
  N. 132
  Phebe 122
  William 216
  William H. 194
BALARD, Etienne 69
BALDCOCK, Richard 101

BALDWIN, ... 185
  Ezra 183
  Francis 216
  Jarius 172
  John 84, 175, 206
  John T. 176
  Nathaniel A. 185
  Tibbal 176
BALES, Frederick 84
BALIS, Frans 72
BALISE, Josh 71
BALISS, Edward 204
  John 203
BALL, Daniel 102, 183
  Horace 201
  Horatio 102
  Larkin 200
  Polly 84
  Sheldon 215
BALLARD, Arden H. 197
  Asa N. 197
  Etienne 79, 191
  George 213
BALLOU, Philander 196
  Seth 197
BALOW, George 185
BANCROFT, Joseph 187
  Lawson 204
  Rhominah 193
  William 174
BANE, Stephen 172
BANGS, Alanson 189
  Isaac 189
  Joseph 189
BANTUM, Peregine 84
BANWAY, Charles 156
BARASSON, Louis 114
  Rene 114
  Teresa (Meloche) 114
BARBAUT, Pierre 68
BARBER, Horace 184
  Thomas 205
BAREILLOS, Antoinette 102
  -Lajoie, Antoinette 102
BARETTE, Joseph 146
  Pierre 212
BAREUME/BARRIAU, Joseph 160
  Peter 160
BARGER, James 128
  Mary 128
BARIAU, Magdeleine 114
BARIL, Jean Bte. 68
  Joseph 14
  Julia 145
BARKER, Amanda 136
  John 190
  Leroy 195
  P. 196
  Samuel 126
BARKLE, Mary 119
BARKLEY, Joseph 181

BARKLEY, Thomas 182
BARLOW, John 165
BARNARD, James 103
  John 103
  Joseph R. 207
  Joshua 103
BARNES, Giles 84
  Polly 113
BARNET/BURNET, Thomas 62
BARNEY, Aaron 199
  West 195
BARNHART, Christopher 184
BARNHEART, Martin 197
BARNIER, Peter 191
BARNIOU, Joseph 80
BARNS, Isaac 205
  Jno. B. 205
BAROIE, see Barrois 20
  Joseph 64
BAROIL, see Baril 14
BAROIS, Francois, see Lootman
  dit Barrois 23
BARON, Antoine 65, 77, 78, 119
  Antoine, see Barreau 114
  Bazil 178
  Charles 65
  Jacques Antoine 138
  Joseph 55, 78
  Michel 80
  Pierre 80, 178
  Susanne 113
  Veronique 119
BARR, Amos 204
  Christopher 205
  Lewis 199
  Robert 203
BARRACK, John 172
BARREAU, Antoine 110, 114, 158
  Charles 159
  Gabriel 113, 158
  Joseph 114, 158
BARREL, John 105
BARRETT, Christopher 188
BARRIEAU, Joseph 91
BARRIEUX, Joseph 61
BARRIOU, Antoine 157
BARROIS, see Barois 23
  see Lootman 17, 23
  Jean Baptiste Lootman dit
    see Baroie 20
BARRON, Antoine 64, 91, 177
  Antoine Alexis 114
  Charles 114, 156
  Joseph 89, 114, 156, 177
  Magdeleine (Bariau) 114
  Pierre 67
  Solomon 156
BARROWS, Juba 160
BARTHE, ... 21, 24, 36
  A. G. 36

BARTHE, Andrew 16, 20
  Andrew Charles 33
  Baptiste 61
  Charles 24, 30
  Jean Bt. 41
  Jn. Bte 70
  Louis 63
BARTHELET, Henry 79, 87
  Orlin 102
BARTHELMI, ... 69
BARTHELMY, ... 23
BARTHIUME, Peter 154
BARTHOLOMY, Jacob 146
BARTLER, Hiram 176
BARTLET, Warren 174
BARTLETT, Brian 182
  Orson, see Barthelet, Orlin 102
  Orson 181
BARTLEY, John 166
BARTON, Elijah 161
  Jacob 171
  Richard 155
  Samuel C. 182
  William 186
BARTOW, Henry 179
  William 162
BARIO, Batice 215
BARTRAND, Jean Bte? 68
BARY, Geo. 213
BASENA, Jane (Hill) 131
  Joseph 131
BASENNEE, Batist/BASINET,
  Joseph 73
BASINE, Joseph 82
BASINET, see Basena 131
  see Basenee, Batist 73
  Joseph 131
BASNEY, Joseph 194
BASS, see Bearss 112
  Daniel 203
  Ephraim 204
  John 203
  Taman 204
  Truman 158
BASSET, John F. 195
BASSETT, Nehemia 188
BASTO, William
BATA, Robert 173
BATCHELOR, Charles 192
  Elisha 192
BATES, Alvin 210
  Ferdinand 78
  Hannah 150
  John 101
  Joseph 119, 160
  Nancey 171
  Orin 185
  Stillman 184
  Sylvester 119, 160
BATTIS, Thomas 180

BATTLE, Zacharias 84
BAU, see LeBeau 22
  Jean Baptiste 33
  dit LeBeau, Jean Baptiste 22, 33
BAUBIEN, Antoine 70, 152
  Baptiste 152
  Lambert 70
BAUCHAMP, Michel 70
BAUDIN, Louis 68
BAUDOIN, see Bodwin 120
  see Doidon 211
  Catherine (...) 123
  Franics 123
DAUDRY, Jean 12
  dit Desbuttes dit St. Martin, Jean 12
BAUM, Jesse 204
  John 203
BAUMEE, Colette (Drouillard) 142  John Bte. 142
BAUMIER, see Baumee 142
  Francois 142
BAUMIERE, Jean Bt. 179
BAURON, ... 32
BAYNEY, John 194
  Michael 127
BAZANAIS, John B. 121
BAZIN, Andrew 313
BAZINET, Jean Bte. 121
  Joseph 131
  Margaret 121
  Theotiste 131
BAZLEY, Asel 193
BE, Antoine 218
BEACH, ... 122
  Eben 104, 170
  Elisha 181
  Elizabeth (Owen) 104
  Hiland 178
  John 170
  Michael 186
  Reuben C. 187
  Rufus 182
BEADELL /BEADLE 161, 205
DEADLE, David 205
BEAGLE, Charles 193
BEALL, Samuel W. 211
BEALS, Joseph 190
BEAN, Ahab 218
  Henry 91
  Richard 101, 196
BEARD, David 87
BEARDSLEE, Clark 183
  George 182
BEARDSLEY, Ezra 206
  George 170
  Othne 206
BEARD, Ephram 152
BEARS, Truman 152
BEARSS, Truman 112

BEASLEY, Wm. 146
BEATON, ... 161
BEATY, Rober 186
BEAUBIAN, Joseph 154
BEAUBIEN, ... 36
  see Beautien 123
  see Beavan 196
  see Bobian 74
  see Bobean 141
  see Bourbien 130
  see Cuillerie 20
  see Cuillerier 16, 17, 20
  Alexis 113, 158, 177
  Antoine 14, 32, 68, 88, 84, 117, 163
  Archange (Tremblay) 113
  Bazel 209
  Catherine 117, 160
  Catherine (Vernet) 117
  Claire (Gouin) 111
  J. M. 82
  Jean 30
  Jean Baptiste 32, 41, 48, 51, 54, 111
  Jean Marie 111, 177
  Jennie 163
  Joseph 48, 51, 89, 113, 119, 141, 160, 162
  Lambair 163
  Lambert 113, 130
  Marie (Tremblay) 119
  Marie Anne 113
  Pierre 111, 158, 163
  Susanne 111
  Teresa 145
  Veronique 119
BEAUBIN, Charles 208
  Chs. 71
BEAUCHAMP, Joseph 52
  Pierre 68
BEAUDRAIS, Louis 144
  Mary 144
BEAUDRAU, St Ours 64
BEAUFAIT, Louis 41
  Ls 69
  Louis 79, 112, 128, 150, 151, 158
  Louise (Saucier) 112
  Teresa 128
BEAUGRAIN, ... 43
BEAUGRAND, Anne (Alain) 110
  J. 157
  Jn Bte 64
  J. Bte 78, 80, 110
  John Bapt. 110
  Margaret (Chobere) 110
BEAUHOMME, Joseph 175
BEAULIEU, Charles 25
  Louis 61
BEAU LIEUX, see Beaulieu 25
BEAUMONT, William 128

BEAUPRE, see Bopre 211
  Michel 33
BEAUREGARD, Antne 66
  Antoine 80, 140
  Monique 140
  Teresa 145
BEAUSHOMME, Jean 43, 50
BEAUTIEN, Charles 123
  Teresa (...) 123
BEAUZUM, Joseph 145
BEAVER, J. 78
BEAVAN/BEAUBIEN, Jean B. 196
BECK, Henry 188
  Lewis 127
BECKET, M. 138
BECKLEY, Josiah 118
BECKWITH, Cyrus 198
  Levi 204
  Stephen 199
BEDIENT, Zalmon 80, 81
BEDNOIN, Francis 214
BEEMAN, Samuel 192
BEERS, Ransetta 202
BEIRD, James 60
BELAIRE, Francois 50
BELAN, see Bellont 130
  Francis 130
BELAIR, Catherine 143
BELAIRE, Amable 80
  Jean Louis 80
BELANGE, Bazille 79
  Philip 53
BELANGER, Basil 48
  Joseph 105
  Philip 42
  Ursule 130
BELCHER, Eusha 198
BELCOUR, Francois 62
  Jean Bt. 178
BELDEN, Aretus 202
  Clifford 211
BELESTRE, ... 24, 36
  Francois Marie 14
  Francois Picote 23
BELISLE, Alexander 167
  Welcome 167
BELKNAP, Israel 194
BELL, Andrew 118, 160
  Benjamin 153, 162
  Ralph R. 109
  Ralph 109, 157
  Ralph B. 153
  Ralph R. 162
  Richard H. 219
  Tunis 147, 212
  William 213
BELLAIR, Etienne 90
  John L. 136
  Joseph 80, 89
  Louis 136
BELLAIRE, Amab 114, 158

BELLAIRE, Jean Pierre 114
   Louis 42
   Louise (Lapointe) 114
   Pierre 44, 70
BELLANGE(R), Basile 70
   Bte. 87
   Philip 62
BELLECOUR, Francois 54
BELLEPERCHE, Jacques 51
   Pierre 14, 16
BELLERE, Amable 67
BELLONT, Monique (Moras) 130
   Robert 130
BELLOR, Etienne 130
BELLOWS, Ezra 184
BELLPERCHE, ... (...) 44
   Joseph 44
BELMAR, Alexis 176
BELPERCHE, see Belleperche 16
   Pierre 24
BELSHER, William 101
BELTON, Francis S. 106
   Harriet (Kirby) 106
BEMIS, John 178
   Liman 185
   Reuben 215
BENAULT, see Bineau 20
BENEDICT, Ethel T. 184
BENETEAU-LaBALEINE, ... 101
BENETTEAU, Andre 44
BENJAMIN, ... 84
   Hiram 192
BENLY, James 178
BENNEAU, Louis 80
BENNET, David D. 188
   Justin 175
BENNETAU, Andre 51
BENNETT, I. W. 200
   Jonathan 133
   John 133, 192
   Robinson 202
BENNETTE, John 126
   Louis 123
BENNITT, William 201
BENOA, ... (...) 53
   see Benoit 41
   Jean 41
   Registre 55
BENOIT, ... 30
   see Benoa 41
   Angelique 7
   dit Livernois, Angelique
     (Chagnon) 7
   Francois 7
   dit Livernois, Francois 7
   Nicolas 32
BENOIT-LIVERNOIS, Etienne 33, 114
BENOT, Louis 31
BENSON, Peter 174, 187
   Silas 187
BENSSON, Louis 92

BENTLEY, Amanda (Barker) 136
   James 136
   John 76, 84, 87
BENTON, Gideon P. 163
BEQUIER, Jacob 79
BERARRE, Frans 66
BERBIER, Louis 128
BERCELAU, Gerard 55
BERCELON, Gerard 42
BERDAN, Peter 165
BERDSLEY, Ernest 195
BERESAW, Daniel 128
   Louis 123
   Marguerite (Bernard) 128
BERGERON, ... 36
   S. 31
   Simon 22, 23, 33
BERLANGATE, Hippolite 213
BERNARD, ... 69
   Antoine 53, 55, 176
   Archange 142
   Catherine 115, 139
   Chs. 67, 69
   Frans 73
   Genevieve (Saucier) 142
   Guillaume 20, 33, 40, 53
   Hyacinthe 67, 177
   Hypolite 69
   Jacques 176
   James 139
   Jean Bpt 62
   Josh 71
   Joseph 80, 142
   Louis 67, 71, 142, 174, 176
   Louisa (Jacob) 142
   Margaret (Robideau) 142
   Marguerite 128
   Truman 175
   William 142
BERNARD-LAJOIE, Louis 142, 143
   Margaret 143
   Mary Ann 138
BERNIER, Charles 43, 50
   Jacques 77
BERRISAW, Louis 166
BERRYMAN, Joel 126
BERSHO, Joseph 213
BERTHE, see Barthe 24
BERTHELET, Francois 43
   Henry 84
BERTHELET de VEAU, Romania 6
BERTHELMIS, ... 71
BERTHIAUME, Alexander 124
   Andre 64
   Andrew 68
   Joseph 80
BERTHILLET, Augustin 154, 171
   Henry 170
BERTHOLET, Henry 110, 157
   Marie Josette (Duhamel) 110

BERTHOLET, Pierre 110
BERTIAUME, Joseph 48, 52
BERTRAND, Archange 132
   Francois 208
   (Frs.) H. 208
   J. Bt 44
   Joseph 206
BESAU, Josh 70
BESEAU, Leander 175
BESERE, Jacques 43, 50
BESSION, Marthe 213
BETEAU, Charles 129
   Jcb 129
BEUFAIT, Louis 53, 69
BEVINS, John 210
BICKNELL, James 213
BICIE, William 174
BIDDLE, Charles 105, 122
   Edward 122, 209
   John 105
   Nicholas 122
BIDWELL, W. T. 214
BIENVENU, Alexis 33
   dit DeLisle, Alexis 16, 20, 33
   Anne (Lemoyne) 6
   dit Delisle, Anne (Lemoyne) 6
   Francois 6
   dit Delisle, Francois 6
   Genevieve (Charon dit
     LaFreniere) 6
   dit Delisle, Genevieve
     (Charon dit Lafreniere) 6
BIENVENU-DELISLE, Joseph 113
BIEUS, see Bluche dit La Serre 14
BIGALOW, Charles 160
BIGELOW, Abell 180
BIGLAR, Jacob 185
   John 185
   John M. 185
   Philip 185
BIGNAL, Richard 181
   Sol L. 151
BIGRAS, see Fauvel 17
   Amable 56
   J. Bt 44
   Jean Bap. 50
BIGRAS dit FAUVEL, Joseph 25
   Joseph Amable 17
BILES, John 126
BILLET, Ignace 64
BILLIAU, Catherine 115
   Jean Baptiste 12, 33
   Teresa 129
BILLIAU dit LESPERANCE, Jean
   Baptiste 12, 21, 33
BILLIET, Francois 54
BINAU, ... 36
   see Bino 17
   Claude 17
   Js 36
   Jean 33

BINAU dit LAJEUNESSE, Jean 33
  Louis 22
BINAULT, ... 23
  see Bineau 22
BINAUT, Jean 30
BIND, John 115
BINEAU, Louis 22, 33
BINEAU dit LAJEUNESSE, Jean 20
BINGHAM, Abel 213
  Edward 172
  Hugh 152
  John K. 200
BINO, Clau., see Binau 17
  Louis, see Binau 17
BIRCH, Daniel S. 201
  Ethel 173
  Hughes W. 218
  Morris 190
BIRD, Asahel L. 166
  Frederick 172
  Ira W. 198
  John 159, 197
  John, see Bind 115
  Nelson 216
  Samuel 165
  Welcome 165
  Zenus 165
BIRDSALL, Alice (Wright) 105
  Moses 105
BIRKLEY, Josiah 197
BRION, Jean L. 87
  John L. 196
  Jouachim 69
BISAILLON, ... 5
  Jean Bt. 208
BISEBY, David 190
BISHOP, Amara 176
  Bowman 210
BISHOPS, William 205
BISONETTE, Joseph 80
  Paschal 80
BASSAILLON, Marguerite (Fafard) 7
  Michel 7
BISSELL, Theodore 188
BISSENET, Jacques 175
  Joseph 175
BISSNET, Alexis 175
BISSON/BUISSON, Augustus 211
  Luke 211
BISSONET, Angelique 141
  Joseph 141
  Pelagie 145
BISSONETT, Catherine 141
  Joseph 141
BISSONNET, Gabriel 144
  Josh 66
  Louise 144
  Paschal 67
BISSONNETTE, ... (...) 43, 50

BISSONNETTE, Agnes (Robert) 141
  Joseph 141
  Stephen 141
BLACHE, Jean Bte 62
BLACK, Chesley 112
  Sarah (...) 112
BLACKINGTON, William 110, 157, 185
BLACKMAN, Charles 187
  Samuel 200
  Sylvanus 102
BLACKMAR, S. 189
BLACKMARR, William 206
BLACKMER, Sewell 197
BLACKMORE, Samuel 161
BLACKWOOD, Thomas 202
BLAIN, Pierre 77
BLAKE, Charley 181
  Chester 158
  Page 219
  Philemon 153
  Phillemon 127
  Sarah 136
BLAKELY, Miriam 119
BLAKESLEE, Scriba 181
BLAKESLEY, Morris 125
BLAKEY, Freeman 192
BLANCHARD, Charles 145
  Edward 208
  Isaac 125, 208
  John 179
  Joseph 80, 144
  Loren 132
  Mary (Babcup) 125
  Stephen S. 161
  Stilman 189
BLANDEN, Ezra 189
BLANEY, Henry 216
BLAUCET, Levi 129
BLAY, Archange (Dulac) 130
  Baptist 130
  Cecilia 130
  Etiene 190
  Francis 130
  John B. 190
  Mary 130
  Peter 191
BLE, Francois 79
BLEARN, James 90
BLEVOIR, Saple 215
BLIER, Augustine A. 147
BLINDBERY, Joseph 182
BLINN, Ricard H. 125
BLISS, Cyrus 185
  Harvey 190
  Harvey/Hervey 136
  Israel 136
  Lucinda (Kingsley) 136
  Nancy (Woodbury) 136
  Waston W. 203
BLODGETT, Alva 199

BLONDIN, ... 5
  Pierre 7
BLONDIN dit CHEVALIER, ... 5
  Pierre 7
BLONDIN-HILAIRE, Alexander 113
BLOOD, Aaron 201
  E. F. 189
BLOOM, George 126
BLOOMBURG, Michael 183
BLOTNER, Mathias 170
BLOUNT, Henry 184
BLUE, Frederick 211
BOAMY, see Boemier 42
  Pierre 42
BOBEAN, John 139
  Joseph 139
  Louise (Nadeau) 139
  Marque 141
  Monique (Nadeau) 141
  Regina (Meny) 139
BOBIAN/BEAUBIEN, Jno. Mary 74
BOBIEN, Ante 80
  J. M. 80
  Joseph 77
  Lambert 80
BODENO, Joseph 132
BODETTE, Eli 177
  Job 177
BODIEN, Theotiste 110
BODIN, Louis 80, 176
  Pierre 218
BODWIN, Alexis 120
  Francois 123
  Joseph 121
BODWINE, see Bodwin 121
BOEMIER, see Boamy 42
  Francis 136
  Louise 137
  Regina 136
  Rose 140
  Ursula (...) 136, 145
BOGARD, Laban 82
BOGART, John 206
  Russel 206
  William 206
BOGERT, see Boyer 40
  Antoine 40
BOHOMME, Michel 33
BOHOMME dit BEAUPRE, Michel 33
BOIDOIN/BAUDOIN, Francois 211
BOILEAU, David 127
BOIS, see Wood dit Bois 218
  Charles 76
  George 154
BOISDORE, see Boudre 139
  J. Bte. 139
  Joseph 62
BOISIART, Joseph 213
BOISMIER, Francois 80
BOIST, Baptiste 61
BOISVERD, ... 12
BOISVERT, Edward 208

# Index

BOISVERT, Joseph 212
BOIT, Lenis C. 170
BOITTE, Louis C. 154
BOLIO, Paul 214
    Plymouth 213
BOLTON, Robert 198
    William F. 205
BOLVINE, Nicholas 146
BOMBIER, ... 124
BONARD, Louis 208
BONAVENTURE, Pierre 140
BOND, Ann (Smith) 137
    Jesse 219
    Lewis 80, 137
    Lewis E. 175
BONDI, Domque 77
    Joseph 77
BONDIE, Antoine 114, 158
    Dominique 114
    Eustace 179
    Jane (Nipiaki) 114
    Joseph 114, 158
    Laurent 179
    Marie (Saliot) 114
    Teresa (Saliot) 114
    Thomas 179
BONDY 36
    see Douaire 23
    Angela 115
    Bazile 166
    Bazul 152
    Dominique 166
    Dque 91
    John 156, 164
    Joseph 44, 51, 89, 91, 152, 166
    Joseph, see Bondie 114
    Josh 65
    Marie Anne 114
BONESMASHER, Jacob 203
BONET, Louis 209
BONHOLM, Peter 165
BONHOMME, Pierre 151
BONNEAU, see Bono, Louis 143
    Dominique 143
BONNER, Fineas 205
    Ira 202
BONNIER, Louis 125
BONNO, John Battise 215
BONO, Louis 143
    T. (Cousineau) 143
    Ursula (...) 143
BONOM/BONHOMME, Francois 79, 82
    J. Bte 80
    Nicolas 82
BONSACK, John 62
BONTER, Augustin 145
BONVOULOIR 37
    see Delieres 23
    Joseph 82

BOOKLEY, Josiah 160
BOON, John 206
BOOTH, Horace 199
    John 183
    Joseph T. 212
    Thomas 203
    Virgil 199
BOPRE/BEAUPRE, Louis 211
BORBONNO, Francis 215
BORBOUR, Pierre 214
BORDEAU, Francoise 174
    Joseph 22
BORDEAUX, Joseph 175
    Louis 212
    Pierre 175
BORDONE, Louis 145
BORDOW, Peter 166
BORETTE, Joseph 146
BORGIA, Pierre 55
BORLAND, Jos. T. 189
BORNEAU, John Bt. 177
BORROW, Charles 166
    Jack 166
    Joseph 166, 167
    Marie Ann (Cousineau) 138
    Pierre 138
BORUP, Charles Wm. Wuff 209
BOSONME, Batpiste 65
BOSTWICK, Daniel 197
BOTSFORD, David 199
    Elnathan 200
BOTT, William 198
BOTTSFORD, Simon 182
BOUATE, Louis C. 87
BOUCHARD, Eloi 208
    Eneas 142

    Ignace, see Eneas 142
    Ignatius 63
    Louis 142
    Magdeleine (Campau) 142
BOUCHE, Dominique 156
BOURCHEA, Peter 213
    William 200
BOURDEAU, Joseph 80
BOUDINAS, Louis 132
BOUDRE, Andre 139
    Mary (Saliot) 139
BOUDRIN/RIE, Antoine 132
BOUDRION, Louis 159
BOUDWINE, Alexia 213
BOUFARE, Antoine 43, 50
BOUGARD, Alexis 138, 140, 174
    Justine (Deloeil) 138
    Terese (Cloutier) 140
BOUGHTON, Lyman 180
BOUK, Adam 202
BOULARD, Antoine 67
BOUQUET, Jean 82
BOUR, Joseph 170
BOURASA, Louis 91

BOURASSA, see Barasson 114
    see Beresaw 123, 128
BOURASSA, Frans 64
    Josette 117
    Louis 77, 117, 209
    Magdeleine 122
    Rene 128
    Vital 61
BOURASSON, Louis 159
BOURBIEN, Cecilia (Boyer) 130
    Jno. B. 130
BOURDAU, Louis 68
BOURDAUT, Bte 68
BOURDEAU, Agathe 145
    Angelique 144
    Genevieve 140
    Genevieve (Sordelier) 144
    John Bte. 144
    Josh 67
    Joseph 138, 140, 144
    Julia 140
    Louisa (Bousom) 144
    Marie 138
    Pierre 144
BOURDEAUX, Agathe (Reaume) 139
    Francis 139
    Genevieve (Menard) 139
    Joseph 42, 56, 139
BOURDENO, Augustus 163
BOURDIGNON, Ignase 152
    Joseph 177
BOURDILLON, Louis 91
BOURDON, Louis 145
    Michel 67
BOURDRIAN, Joseph 114
    Louis 114
BOURDRAIS, Andra 156
BOURDRIE, Alexis 121
BOURGARD, Hyacythe 176
BOURGEAT, Clotilde 122
    Pierre 122
BOURGET, Clotilde 123
BOURGINON, Josh. 77
BOURGIRON, see Bergeron 23
BOURGLKE, Genevieve 145
BOURGUINON, Louis 77
BOURK, Macaine 209
BOURKE, James 145

BOURON 37
    Charles 22, 44
BOUROUND, Chales 51
BOURRIAN, Jeanne (Gelina) 114
BOURSIER, Joseph 124
BOURTIYI 123
BOURKAY, (Frs.) ... 215
    Michael 214
    Toussaint 215
BOUSOM, John 144
    Louisa 144
    Margaret 144

BOUSOM-GASCON, Jean  144
  Joseph Amable  145
BOUTHILIER, Francois  124, 146
BOUTON, Samuel  165
BOUTS, John  165
BOUTTON, James  163
BOUVAIR, Charles  146
BOUVARD, Alexis  104
BOVER, Ignace  33
  Pierre  30
BOUVIER, Jean Bt.  176
BOWEN, Thomas W.  127
  Zolva  196
BOWER, Margaret  117, 132, 133
BOWERS, Henry  217
BOWLES, William  218
BOWLS, Josiah W.  193
BOWMAN, George  172
BOWMER, William  219
BOWOODLAN, John Bte.  139
BOWVIA, Paul  215
BOYCE, Aaron  219
  George  162
BOYD, George  125, 209
  Joshua (Johnson)  125
  Thomas  65
  Thomas A. B.  208
BOYDEN, Luther  201
BOYE(R), ... (...)  151
  Antone  150
BOYER, see Bogert  40
  Antoine  69, 78, 88, 112, 130
  Catherine  113, 132
  Cecil  112, 158
  Cecilia  112, 130
  Ignace  17, 20, 36, 41, 53, 132
  Joseph  140
  Julia (Tremblay)  132
  Louise  116, 140
  Nco  36
  Nicholas  132
  Pierre  17, 20, 33, 116
BOYLE, Philip  146
BOYLEN, John  213
BOYLES, Samuel  207
BOYOIS, Antoine  161
BRACKEN, James  76
BRADFORD, Areunah  155
  Arony  165
  Minna  161
  Moses  155, 165
BRADISH, Currin  188
  Joseph  136
  Nelson  188
BRADLEY, Harvey  165
  Henry  110, 157, 165, 184
  Wakeman  182
BRADSHAW, Eli  196
BRADY, Casandra  120

BRADY, David  207
  Hugh  170
  Isaac  126
  James  216
  L. P.  196
  Prudence  103
BRAINARD, Daniel  112
  Jeremiah  112
  Jeremiah G.  158
  Jeremiah Gates  112
BRAKEMOR, Louis I.  195
BRAMBLE, Charlotte  203
BRANCH, Israel  198
  William T.  198
BRANCHEAU, Joseph  178
  Pierre  144, 178
BRANCHO, Pierre  80
BRANDAMOUR, Jean Philip  133
  Judith (Desnoyers)  133
  Judith (Tremblay)  133
  Pierre  133
BRANT, Elias  180
  Horace  180
BRAT, Johnson  73
BRAZIER, James  210
BREARS, John  189
BRENAN, Patrick  212
BRENNAN, Luke  213
BREVOORT, Catharine (Navarre)  111
  Henry B.  89, 111, 157, 162
BREW, Harvey  202
BREWER, Elias  202
  John  202
  Nicholas  118, 160
BREWSTER, Exra  185
  William  170
BRICE, William H.  207
BRICKLIN, Antoine  218
BRIDGET, Belcher  87
BRIGGS, Allen  187
  Anthony L.  137, 174
  Dexter  153, 162
  John  163
  Pardon  163
  Russell  202
BRIGHAM, Adolphus  165
  Ebenezer  217
  Lucy Melinda  119
BRILLANT, Angelique  116
BRINDAMOOR, ...  82
BRINK, Cornelius W.  200
BRISARD, Jean  25
BRISBO, Louis L.  144
BRISBOIS, see Brisboy  120
  Joseph  125, 212, 215
  Michael  146, 212
  Michel  92
BRISBOY, antoine (Saloncette)  120
  Pollet  120

BRISETOUT, Joseph  80
BRISETTE, Antoine  142
BRISK/H, James  146
BRISSET, Michael  121
BRITTAIN, Samuel  102
  Sanford  102
BRITTON, Roswell  199
BROCK, Elisha E.  216
  John  191
BROCKWAY, Elisha W.  199
BRODDER, Battes  145
BRONSON, Daniel  184
  Harry  180
  Ira  161
  John  141, 172
  Simon  167
  Titus  205
  William  184
BROOK, Arthur  157
BROOKFIELD, William  102
BROOKS, Aaron  206
  Arthur  109
  Daniel S.  201
  David  203
  Edward  106, 112, 172
  Margaret (Labadie)  106
  Margaret (May)  106
  Rebecca (...)  112
  William  106, 112, 153, 188
BROSET, Peter  164
BROT, Andrew  164
BROTTON, David  193
BROUNELLE, Louis  215
BROWN, ... (...)
  Andrew  192
  Angelique (Bissonet)  141
  Arza  172
  Benoni  197
  Calvin  188
  Chapel  207
  Cullen  170
  Daniel  125, 198
  Daniel B.  199
  David  182
  David H.  192
  E. H.  204
  Eliza (Jacox)  132
  Emery  207
  Esick  183
  Gardner  150, 166
  George  153, 188
  Henry  101
  Hiram  174
  Isaac  202
  Jacob  184, 188
  James  180
  John  126, 127, 141, 154, 161, 170, 173, 186, 214
  Joseph  89, 194, 198
  Julius  206

BROWN, Levi 103, 172
   Louise (Shurtliff) 103
   Mark 171
   Mary 101, 171
   Pitt 206
   Richard 200
   Thomas C. 164
   Thomas R. 197
   William 42, 56, 78, 84, 87, 104, 132, 141, 177, 195, 210
   William W. 175
BROWNELL, George 180
   Gordon T. 209
   John 186
   Thomas 200
   William O. 210
BROWNING, Elijah 188
   Francis P. 170
   John 200
BROWNSON, Harry 180
   Hawley 184
BRUCE, Moses 153
BRULA, J. B. 215
BRUNDAGE, Avis 199
BRUNEAU, Baptiste 61
BURNET, Dominique 211
   Jean 212
   Perish 212
BRUNO, Hillary 146
   Perrish 146
BRUNSON, Jobe 205
BRURTIS, John 172
BRUSE, Moses 162
BRUSH, Elijah 80, 84, 87
BRUSO, Margaret (Rau) 144
   Pierre 144
BRYAN, John 196
   Samuel T. 180
BRYANT, Daniel 201
   James 156
BUBANK, Hannah (Dicks) Cissne 117
BUCK, Mary 204
   Noel 192
   Thomas 208
BUCKLEN, Daniel 160
   Wm. 160
BUCKLEY, 153, 195
BUCKLIN, Asher 181
   Daniel
   James 153, 162
   Margaret 153, 162
   Margaret (Tompkins) 117
   Timothy 162
   William 89, 118
BUDD, Aaron 150, 166
BUGBY, Moses 188
BUIE, Nicholas 195
BUISSON, see Bisson 211
BULL, Elijah 181

BULLOCK, Elijah 181
BUNCE, Joseph P. 196
   Z. W. 196
BUNNELL, Luther 78
BUNNIL, Eli 207
BUNGO, Geo. 213
BUNT, Levi 197
BUNTING, Samuel 210
BOUTTE, Louis C. 137
BURBANK, ... (...) 117, 160
   David 154
   Elizabeth 117
   Jesse 65, 117
   John 89, 117, 154, 160, 164
   Sally/Sarah (Hickley) 117
   William 154, 160, 184
BRUCH, Addison 178
   Jonathan 196
   William 175
BURD, Philo 161
   Philander 156
   Samuel 155
BURDINO, John 173
BURGES, Ezra 192
   Gorman 191
BURGESS, Ezra 133
   Jonathan 87, 185
   Norman 200
   Priscilla 106
BURISSO, Antoine 206
   Daniel 206
BURK, John 207
BURKE, Edward 215
BURLINGHAM, Civil 193
   Levi 181
BURNELL, ... 54
BURNET, John 84
   Nelson P. 210
BURNETT, James 87, 206
BURNOM, Jonothan 195
BURNS, Abraham 183
BURR, Andrew 125, 209
   S. 125
BURRASSAU, Lewis 156
BURRELL, see Barrel 105
   John 76, 60
BURRIS, Alfred 163
BURROUGHS, Daniel 182
BURROWS, George W. 186
BURT, Erastus 182
   Joseph 197
   Simeon 186
   William A. 193
BURTISS, Richard 216
BURTON, Samuel 188
BURY, Richard 171
BUSCO, Benj. 213
BUSH, Amelia (...) 122
   Chauncey 122
   Joseph 170

BUSH, William T. 216
BUSHA, Joseph 215
BUSHER, James 105
BUSHEY, James, see Busher, James 105
BUSHNALL, Asa 199
   Henry C. 219
BUSSIS, Louis 218
BUTLER, Alvah 182
   J. 106
   John 89
   Justien H. 193
   Richard 190
BUTSON, George 187
BUTTERFIELD, Isaac 213
   James 200
BUTTERSWORTH, Alexander 216
BUTTON, William 167
BUTTS, Abraham 187
BUVIA, Francis 195

CABACIER, Charles 77, 89, 110, 154
CABANA, Augustin 82
CABANON, Joseph 77
CABASIER, ... 24
CABASSIER 36
   see Cabasy 42
   Chs. 63
   J. 31
   Joseph 20, 33
CABASY, see Cabassier 42
   Joseph 42, 55
CABATEER, Charles 160
CABATIER, Chas. 157
CABESIER, ... 24
CABLE, Alvah 128
CADAIS, Josh 70
CADE, Joseph 178
CADET, Josh. 79
CADIEN, ... 69
CADIEUX dit COURVILLE, Joseph 17
CADILLAC, ... 6
CADLE, Richard F. 211
CADNELL, Hiram 170
CADORET, see Cadorethe 65
   Francois 43
   Frans 63
   Nicholas 82
CADORETHE, ... 65
CADORETTE, ... 84
   ... (...) 176
   Urcelle 87
CADOT, Benjamin 146
   Bridget (Yax) 129
   Joseph 129
   Simeon 129
CADOTTE, Alexis 121
   Augustine 123
   Augustus 123

CADOTTE, Benj. 231
   Madelaine 209
   Madeline (...) 123
   Mary 121
   Michael 121, 213
CADY, Chancy G. 190
   Daniel L. 155, 161
   David D. 165
   Elizabeth 162
   Horace H. 190
   Isaac 88
   John 205
   Simon 191
CAHOON, Charles 185
   James 165
   John 151, 161
CAIN, John 60
CAJETAN, see Tremble, Gazette 133
CALAWAY, ... 124
CALDWELL, Mary Anne (Lacelle) 141
   Samuel W. 209
   Thomas 141, 177
   William 141
CALHOUN, Abner 205
   Andrew 136, 205
CALKON, Alvin 204
CALLAHAN, Eliz. 78
   George 126
CALVEZ, Ignace 77
CALVI, Marian F. 124
CAMBELL, Zephemiah 190
CAMBURN, Joseph 189
CAMERON, John 76
CAMMINS, William 183
CAMP, Ira 203
   Samuel 198
CAMPARE, ... 23
CAMPAU 36
   see Campault 21
   see Pothier 24
   ... (Cicot) 102
   ... (McDougall) 102
   Adelaide (Dequindre) 104
   Agathe (Chene) 117
   Alex. 31
   Alexander 117
   Alexis 56, 129, 142
   Alexis, see Alexander 117
   Angelique 84
   Ant. 17
   Antoine 67, 69
   Archange 109, 112
   Archange (Saliot) 112
   Bapt. 78
   Baptist (Mrs.) 78
   Barnabie 102
   Basalique 111
   Bernard 63
   Bte 36, 70

CAMPAU, Bte/Jean Baptiste 16
   Catherine 111, 115, 116, 129
   Catherine (Menard) 102, 104, 111
   Cha. 32
   Charl. 17
   Charles 33, 46
   Chs 67, 69, 71
   Claude 16, 43, 55, 69, 112
   Clide 112
   Dennis 84
   Elizabeth 113
   Felicite 104
   Francis 117
   Frans 66
   Genevieve 111
   Genevieve (Godet-Marentette) 109
   Genevieve (Marsac) 112
   Genieve 111
   Glacid 152
   Henry 111, 112, 117
   Hippolite 53
   Isabelle 115
   Jacques 20, 33, 53, 68, 69, 102, 104, 111, 115
   James 111, 151
   Jc 36
   Je 36
   Jean Baptiste 33
   Jean Bte 41, 53, 63, 109, 111, 117, 120
   Jean Louis 33
   Jeanne (Masse) 7
   John B. 151, 191
   John Bapt. 109
   Joseph 68, 69, 84, 104, 117
   Joseph B. 151
   Josette (Gamelin) 109
   Josh 71
   Judith 120
   Julien 78
   L. 16, 36
   Lewis 205
   Louis 72, 82, 111, 132, 152
   Magdeleine 142
   Margaret 130
   Mary Ann 132
   Michel 5, 7, 22
   Monica 111
   Monique (Seguin-Laderoute) 117
   Nicol 16
   Nicholas 71
   Nicolas 79
   Paul 17, 33, 50
   Paul Alexandre 33
   Pierre 178
   Sim. 36

CAMPAU, Simon 33, 53, 69, 112
   Susanne (Beaubien) 111
   Teresa 117
   Therese (Moran) 111
   Touissant 84
   Toussin 69
   Zachari 69
CAMPAULT, Louis 21
CAMPAUT, Chs 65
CAMPBEL, Fredrk 160
CAMPBELL, Alexander 172
   Bradford 163
   Frederick 119
   George 114, 154, 158, 164
   Helen (...) 114
   Henry M. 171
   J. B. 215
   John 122, 126, 209, 216
   Lewis 197
   Martin 197
   Robert 218
   Scott 146
   Sidney S. 184
CAMPEAU, ... (...) 174
   Alex. 159
   Alexander 164
   Alexander P. 161
   Alexis 42, 77, 89, 90, 155
   Alexis P. 155
   Ante 89
   Antoine 76, 80, 82, 160
   B. 32
   Baptiste 21, 89, 155
   Barnabas 170
   Bazil 40
   Benaco 78
   Bte. 88
   Capt. 40
   Charles 22, 91, 155
   Chs. M. 77
   Claud 158
   Claude 20
   Close 166
   Denis 76, 88
   Francis 166
   Henry 69, 158, 159, 160
   Hippolite 41
   J. Bte 76, 90
   Jac. 30
   Jacques 41, 79, 88, 167
   James 158
   John Bte. 164, 165, 157
   Joseph 76, 82, 87, 159, 160, 172, 177
   Joseph P. 154, 162
   Julien 90, 164
   Labbaie 69
   Louis 20, 30, 157
   Lube 79
   Michel/Alexis 24
   Nichs 89

CAMPEAU, Paul 48, 66
  Pierre 43, 77, 91
  Sim. 30
  Simon 20, 41, 79
CAMPERET, John Bt. 158
CAMPO, see Campau 17
  Michel 17
CANAN, John 172
CANARD, Jacques 72
  Jean 73
  Richd 72
  William 73
CANFIELD, Charles L. 109, 157
  Simon 162
CANIFF, Abraham 104
CANNIFF, Abram C. 172
  Elijah 198
CANNON, William H. 167
CANTON, Antoin 125
  John 152
CAOSSA, see Chaisne/Chene 20
CAOSSA 36
  Charles 33
CAPUCIEN, see Tiriot 23
CAPPOTTON/CHAPOTON, Benoit 151
CARBEY, John 55
CARBONNO, Antoine 211
  Pierre 211
CARDINAL, ... 5, 24
  Archange 117
  Baptiste 61
  Jacques 7, 20
  Jane 116
  Jean 16, 17
  Joseph 20, 21, 23, 31, 33, 36, 40
  Loquetoche 36
  Louis 124
  Marie (Matou) 7
  Pierre 7, 31, 33, 40, 68
CARDINALLE, Joseph 53
  Pierre 53
CARDINEL, John Marie 147
CAREY, Michael 154
CARIGNAN, J. Bte 80
CARINGTON, Joel 194
CARLISLE, David 184
  Jacob 179
CARLOE, Charles 215
CARLSON, Miles 128
CARLTON, Dexter 161
  Edward 195
  Samuel 218
CARMAN, Jacob 186
CARNES, Benjamin 170
CARON, ... (...) 48
  Claude 48
  Joseph 48
  Vital 14
CARPENDER, Henry 204
CARPENTER, Ax 213
  David 207

CARPENTER, Ezra 199
  John 91, 219
  John C. 199
  Nathan B. 171
  Olive 199
  Rufus 193
  Samuel 188, 202
CARR, Benjamin 218
  Peter 218
  Rogers 200
CARRE/QUERET, Benoni 212
CARRIER, Joseph 67
CARROLL, George 216
CARSON, see Cason 72
CARTER, Charles 170
  Nancy 131
  Thomas 204
CARTRIGHT, John 194
CARTWRIGHT, John 82, 131
  Theotiste (Bazinet) 131
CARTWRITE, James 73
CASCADIN, Henry 201
CASE, Anthony 203
  Elijah 180
  George 180
  Horace 189
  Isaac 194
  Jonathan 180, 198
  Josepheus 200
  Lyman 186
  Nathan 156
  Nathaniel 167, 186
CASETY, ... (...) 53
  James 40
CASHAWA, Louis 204
CASKENNETT, Lewis 156
CASLET, Ignace 82
CASON, Will 72
CASS, Chas. L. 146
  E. (Spencer) 109
  Jonathan 109
  Lewis 109, 116, 157, 173
  Mary (Gilman) 109
CASSE, Bte 68
  Charl. 17
  Charles 32
  Constan 68
  Gabl 68
  Gabriel 17, 33
  Isabelle 104
  Jacques 33, 68
  Jean 6
  Js 68
  Louis 68
  Louisa (Gaultier) 6
  Noel 17, 32, 69
  Pierre 32
CASSE dit ST. AUBIN, Charles 32
  Gabriel 33
  Jacques 33

CASSE dit ST. AUBIN, Jean 6
  Louisa (Gaultier) 6
  Noel 32
  Pierre 32
CASSE-ST. AUBIN, Archange 129
  J. Bte 109, 129
  Louise (Deligne) 109
  Margaret 109, 116
CASTLE, Alonzo 204
  Asa 183
  Lemuel 187
CASWELL, Solomon 183
CATLIN, Antke 77
CATO (colored) **86**
CATTIN, Antoine 42, 56, 89
  Micheal 48
CAU---, Julien 209
CAUCHOIS, Angelique 109
  Lambert 173
CAULKINS, Anna 122
CAUNE, Therese 209
CAUVIN, Chs 70
CAVASSEIE, see Cabassier 20
CAVERNER, Harvey 218
CAYE, Paul 208
  Pierre 70
CAYOTTE, Theophile 209
CEASORE, see Suzor 43
  Louis 43
CECIL, Ante 79
CECILE, Antoine 88
CECIOTT, Jean Bt. 156
CECIRE 36
  Jean 16, 30
  Joseph 51
  Josh 66
CECOT, Jean Bte 55
CEDIEN, Angelique (Cauchois) 109
  Joseph 109
  Pierre 109, 157
  Therese (Tremblay) 109
CEIRE, Paul 191
CELEREN, see Celeron 12
CELERON, Baptist 79
  Chor 64
  Jean Baptiste **14**
CELLINSON, Samuel 181
CENSE, Antoine Robert 41
CENTURE, Francois 176
CERAT, Alexis 87
CERRER-ST. JOHN, Joseph, see St. John 116
CESIRE, Jean 24, 33
CHABERT, ... 63
  Francois 55, 89, 138
  Philip 154
  Rosalie 138
CHADNIN, Joseph 171
CHADWICH, Senath (Chamberlain) 101
  Thomas 101, 153

CHAFFEE, Allan 188
  Carpenter 162
CHAGNON, Angelique 7
CHAISNE, Catharine (Sauvage) 20
  Charles 20
  Charles, see Chene dit Caossa 20
  Isidore, see Chene 20
CHALIFOUT, Pierre 211
CHALIFOUX, Peter 146
CHAMBERLAIN, David 210
  Ezek. 160
  Gad 193
  J. B. 157
  Josh 89
  Olmstead 181
  Senath 101
  Stevin P. 194
CHAMBERLAN, Catherine 145
CHAMBERLAND, Joseph 78, 142
  Josephine (Larose) 142
  Josephine (Moret) 142
  Monique 142
CHAMBERLIN, Adison 192
  Ezekiel 118, 153
  George 118
  Harman 195
  John 181
  John B. 110, 181
  Joseph 178
  Joshua 153, 164
  Louis 178
  Mary (Schrandel) 118
  Miriby 164
  William 181
CHAMBERS, Benjamin 182
  Robert 196
  Thomas 198
CHAMP, John 111
  Nathaniel 111, 167, 172
  Nathl 157
CHAMPAGN, ... (Croisette-Laperle) 111
  Francois 111
  Louisan 111
  Monica (Campau) 111
  Peter 111
CHAMPAGNE, see Huyet 17, 23
  see Huyet-Champagne 132
  ... 30
  Cecilia 142
  Francois 157, 178
  Louison 157
  Margaret (Grehard) 116
  Monique 129
  Pierre 32, 73, 82, 116, 142, 159
  Simon 208
CHAMPAIGNE, Ignace 144
  Jean 53

CHAMPAIGNE, M. 215
  Pierre 144
CHAMPAIN, Swan 73
  Terrais 164
CHAMPAINE, Jubare 164
CHAMPAN(AIGN), Ignace 82
CHAMPIGN, Peter 191
CHAMPION, Salmon 196
  Selden 154, 198
CHAMPLAIN, E. P. 188
CHANDLER, Benjamin 206
  Eli 199
  John 199, 205
CHANLER, George 122
CHAPATON, Angelique (Lafoy) 130
  Augustin 173
  Benoit 111
  Catherine (Meloche) 112
  Henry 130, 163
  J. Bte. 112, 130
  Jean Bte. 111
  Louis 112
  Magdeleine (Drouillard) 130
  Therese (Meloche) 111
CHAPEL, Gurdon 185
CHAPETON, Augustus 105
  Judith (Coquillard) 105
CHAPIN, Giles 137
  Marshal 170
CHAPITON, Eustace 173
CHAPMAN, Alcott C. 137, 173
  Bela 120, 214
  Benj. 76, 213
  Charles 172, 211
  Jesse 186
  John 188, 192
  Randal 179
  William 182
CHAPOTON, ... 24
  Benois 69
  Benoist 88
  Benoit 79
  Catherine 104
  Eustache, see Chapeton, Augustus 105
  Isabelle 111
  J. Bte 79, 130
  Jean 14, 16
  Jean Baptiste 23
  Jean Bt 41
  Jean Bte 53, 105, 111
  Josephe 102
  Josette 130
  L. 69
  Lewis 163, 191
  Louis 78, 88, 84, 130
  Marie 129
  Nicholas 69
  Sophia (Robitaille) 130
  Susanne (Tucker) 130

CHAPOTON, Therese (Peltier) 105
CHAPOTTON, Louis 151
CHAPPATAN, Louis 158
CHAPPEL, Broddac 159
CHAPPELL, Braddock 115
  Joshua 117, 160
CHAPPETON, Benoit 158
CHAPPLE, Mary Ann 166
CHAPPOTON, Henry 152
CHARBENAW, Louis 167
CHARBENO, Jos. 159
CHARBONEAU, Claude 209
  Jacob 115
  Jean Bt 179
  Jerome 109
  Johanna (...) 115
  Joseph 115, 154
  Julia (Petit) 109
  Louis 109, 208, 209
  Susanne (Metay) 115
  Theotiste (Guignier-Bourguignon) 109
CHARBONNEAU, ... 55
  Joseph 160
  Josh. 77, 89
  Ls 157
CHARIST, Jean 80
CHARJE 21
CHARLAND, Alexis 138
  Ambrois 138
  Ambroise 175
  Angelica (Martin) 138
CHARLES, Jacob 207
  Samuel 216
CHARLOTTE, ... 88
CHARON, Genevieve 6
  Jacques 44, 51
  Pierre 43
CHARON dit LAFRENIER, Genevieve 6
CHARRETT, see Churette 121
CHARRON 36
CHART---, Peter 84
CHARTELOT, Antoine 178
CHARTER, Charles 175, 194
  Frances 178
CHARTIE, Francis 132
  Monique (Meny) 132
CHARTIER, see Chortie 131
  Francois 82, 131
  Francois, see Sharkie 73
  Joseph 194
  Louis 195
CHARTRAIN, Charles 164
CHARTRON, Pierre 76
CHARTTON, Wm. 154
CHASE, Abel 179
  Alvin 150, 177
  Bela 179
  David 182

# Index

CHASE, Joseph 182
   Josiah 166
   Patrick H. 190
   Peter 179
CHASTAIN, John L. 216
CHATALIN, Louis 218
CHATELLREAU, Joseph 80
CHATHELLERAUX 66
CHATLAIN, ... 69
   ... (...) 42
CHATSEY, Robert N. 216
CHATTELEREAU, Joseph 144
CHATTELLE, Louis 212
CHATTELROI, Archange
   (Dusault) 139
   Joseph 139
CHATTERDON, ... 150
CHAUBERT, Pierre 66
CHAUVIN 36
   ... 65
   see Chavin 40, 70
   see Chovarre 140
   see Chovin 115
   Antoine 70
   Baptiste 90, 151
   Bte 36, 70, 71
   Catherine 130
   Cecile 105
   Cha. 30
   Charles 12, 16, 20, 32,
     53, 89, 90, 141, 151
   Chs 71
   Frances 129
   Francois 89
   J. Bte 115, 116, 131,
     142
   Jacques 64
   Jean 17
   Jean Bte 53
   Jeanne 115
   John B. 150
   Julia 131
   Lambert 150
   Leon 151
   Louis 70
   Mary Judith 141
   Nicola 151
   Noel 30, 33, 36, 65, 115
   Pierre 129, 150
   Simon 151
   Therese 113
   Touissant, see Shovan,
     Tusan 73
   --Toussin 71
CHAUVINET, Chs 65
CHAVALIER, Pieriche/Pierre
   48
CHAVIGON, Felicite 48
CHAVIN, ... 21
   see Chauvin 40
   Charles 40

CHAVIN, Jean Bt. 40
   Noel 44
CHEATON, Pierre 127
CHEMER, Antoine 92
CHENE, see Chaisne 20
   see Sheyney 170
   Agathe 117
   Charles 14, 33, 77, 117
   Chs 65
   Elizabeth 105
   Gabriel 65, 79, 88, 151, 158
   Isadore 33
   Isidore 110
   Isidore/Leopold 16
   Leopole 33
   Louise Jeanne (Bailly) 6
   Marie (Moitie) Magnan 6
   Pierre 6, 12, 33, 65, 90, 151
   Teresa (Campau) 117
   Touisant 117
   Toussaint 90, 151, 159
CHENE dit CAOSSA, see Chaisne 20
   Charles 33
CHENE dit LaBUTTE, Pierre 12,
   16, 21, 33
CHENEE, Pierre 77
CHENEVERT, Francois 212
CHENIER, Leon 209
CHERRIER, Oliver 146, 212
CHESNE, ... 5
   ... (...) 42
   Cha. 31
   Charles 43, 55, 111
   Gabriel 111, 167
   Genevieve (Campau) 111
   Isidore 36, 55
   Joseph 64
   Js. 31
   Lio. 31
   Ne 36
   Tousaint 163
   Toussan 64
CHEVALIER, ... 5
   ... (...) 48
   Daufinne/Daujinne 48
   Gibaut 48
   Jos. 103
   Joseph 171
   Louis 123
   Louise (Durocher) 103
   M./Louis 48
   Madeleine (Reume) 48
   Magdeleine 48
   Pieriche/Pierre 48
   Pierre 7
CHEVALIER dit LONGEUIL, see
   LeLongeuil 22
CHEVALLIER, Joseph 103
CHEW, John A. 127
CHICOSTE, see Cicotte 20
CHICOT, see Cicotte 14

CHICOTE, ... 24
CHITTENDEN, Chester 92
CHIGUIN, Antoine 167
CHILD, John 202
CHILDS, Ebenezer 211
CHILSON, Lydia 138
CHIPMAN, Cyrus 184
   Cyrus A. 183
   Henry 170
   Samuel F. 184
CHIRRETTE, Charles 215
CHITTENDEN, Elizabeth (...) 119
   James 119, 160
   Ralph J. 183
CHITTENDON, **84**, 160
CHITTENENDON, James 150
CHOATE, Ethel 178
CHOATS, Samuel 142
CHOBERE, Isidore (Chene) 110
   Josette 110
   Josette (...) 110
   Margaret 110
CHOISI, Francois 43
CHOLIERE, Josette 157
CHORBOLLAIS, Charles 215
CHORRELL, Joseph 215
CHORRETTE, Antoin 215
CHORTIE, Amable (Raymond-
   Toulouse) 131
   Archange (Cottrell) 132
   Francis 131, 132
   Joseph 131
   Louis 132
   Nancy (Hill) 131
CHOTIER, see Chrostier 122
   Stephen 195
CHOVAR, Jacques 144
CHOVARRE, Charles 140, 141
   Louise (Boyer) 140
   Noel 141
   Susanne (Godet) 141
CHOVIN, (Frs) ... 78
   see Chauvin 20
   Abigail (King) 117
   Angelique (Constant) 116
   Antoine 178
   Baptist 79
   Baptiste 90
   Bpe 79
   Charles 78, 82, 116, 130,
     159
   Chs. 78
   Claude 176
   Francis 117, 160
   Isabelle (Campau) 115
   J. Bte 116
   Jean Bapt. 116
   John Bapt. 115
   John Bt. 159
   John Bte. 160
   Joseph 116, 159, 164

CHOVIN, Lambert 161
  Leon 176
  Louise (Boyer) 116
  Monica (Rivard) 116
  Nicholas 116, 159, 164
  Noel 20, 117
  Piere 164
  Pierre 130
  Rosalie (Robertjeanne) 130
  Rosele 191
  Sarah (Groesbeck) 116
  Simon 164
  Touissant 82
CHRISTLEY, Frederick 201
CHRONENWIDT, Michael 174
CHROSTIER, John B. 122
CHTEE?, Amable 69
CHUB, Joseph 194
CHUBB, Frisby 153
  G. D. 163
  Harvey 199
  Jonathan F. 161
CHUNN, John H. 106
CHURCH, Judah 185
CHURCHELL, Cyrus 197
CHURCHILL, Sarah 122
CHURETTE, Charles 121
CICOT, ... (...) 42
  see Cicotte 16
  Felicity (Peltier) 119
  Francis 119, 160
  Francois 154
  Jacques 113
  Jacqui 158
  J. Bte 78, 113, 114, 119
  James 170
  Jean Bt. 42
  Jos. 159
  Joseph 63, 114, 154
  Louis 119, 160
  Marie Ann (Beaubien) 113
  Teresa (Livernois) 114
  Veronique (Beaubien) 119
  Zacary 65
  Zachary 78
CICOTE 36
  ... 31
CICOTT, Catherine (Navarre) 137
  Francis 161
  Jacques 156
  J. Bte 137
  John Bte 137
  Joseph 160
  Lewis 164
CICOTTE, Agathe 109
  Francois 89
  Jacques 89
  J. Bte 89
  Jean Bte. 111, 176

CICOTTE, Joseph 91
  Mary Anne 111
  Susanne 136
  Zacharias 12, 20, 33
  Zacharias, see Cicot 16
CIRE dit ST. JEAN, Joseph 55
CISANNEY, James 64
  John 64
  Josh 64
CISCO, Henry F. 178
CISSANNEY, Wme 64
CISSNE, Hannah (Dicks) 117
  Jeanne 119
  William 117, 119
  Wm. 78
CLAFLIN, Increase 211
CLAIR, Jan 82
CLAIRE, Jean 73
  Petite 40
CLAIRMONT, see Clermont 22
  Jn Bte 64
CLAPP, Benjamin 125
  Caty 127
  Paul 102
CLARK, see Andre-Clark 102
  Anderson 204
  Andrew 89, 126
  Clairsa (Morehouse) 113
  Cyrus A. 183
  David 152, 167
  Edward 198
  Eliphalet 189
  G. (...) 87
  Geo. 152
  George 113
  Henry 160, 164
  Isabella 190
  James 166, 210
  James A. 132
  Jason 199
  John 60, 113, 187
  John B. 204
  John M. 189
  Jonas 136
  Jonass 195
  Jonothan 188
  Joseph 175
  Lester P. 173
  Levi L. 105
  Mason 113, 155
  Moses 200
  Nathaniel 113, 156
  Ogden 181
  Peter 172
  Rebecca 219
  Robert 146, 174
  Robert G. 173
  Sarah 167
  Thomas B. 166
CLARKE, Benjamin 172
  Daniel 178

CLARKE, Geo. C. 215
  John 158
  Mason 158
  Nathl 158
CLARRY, Orra 155
CLARY, Robt E. 213
CLAWSON, Abraham 196
  Matthias W. 196
CLAY, Samuel 188
  William 153, 164
CLAYPOOL, Alice Ann 105
  George H. 206
CLAYTON, William 189
CLEARY, Patrick 218
CLEAVELAND, David 196
CLEGG, Joseph 218
CLELAND, James C. 200
CLEMENS, Christ(ian) 82
  Christian 129, 190
  Jacob 78
CLEMENT, Samuel 200
CLEMENT/CLEMENS, Jacob 62
CLEMONS, Christian 129
CLERMONT, Louis 22
CLEWS, John 219
CLIDE, Hugh R. 165
CLIMAX, Aelna 152
CLINE, Frederick 183
CLITEE?, see Chtee? 69
CLOCK, David 145
  John 145, 178
CLOCKMIRE, Francis 172
CLOISON, Jac. 30
CLOSE, Solomon 181
CLOTHIER, Catherine (Jacob) 143
  Jacques 139
  Jeanne (Villers-St. Louis) 143
  Joseph 143
  Pierre 143,
  Rene 139, 143
CLOUTHIER, Pierre 176
CLOUTIE, Renet 31
CLOUTIER 36
  Charles 209
  Elizabeth 115
  Jean Bt. 177
  Mininr? 66
  Rene 23, 33, 43, 50, 115
  Terese 140
  Walter 84
  Zacary 66
  Zachariah 44
  Zacharie 80
  Zachary 50
CLUTE, William 153, 160
CLYBURN, Archibald 207
COAN, Augustus 119, 160, 179
  Edmund 179
  Peter 119, 179

## Index

COATE, Antoine 177
COATES, ... (...) 76
  Ann (...) 87
  Ann (Donaldson), see
    Cotes, Ann 104
  COATS, Ann 84, 172
  John 204
  Thomas 84
COBB, Glade 153
  John 199
COBBS, W. F. 196
COCHOIS, see Coshway 131
  Baptist 79
  Bte 68
COCHRAN, Gerard 43
  James 41
COCKRUM, Jordan P. 216
COCQUILLARD, Pierre 51
CODLE, John 218
COINTOURA, Aitken 214
COLAME, see Collame 125
COLBY, Ephraim 187
  Samuel 180
COLE, Daniel B. 170
  Dennis 198
  George B. 216
  Henry S. 172
  James W. 189
  Jonathan 119, 160
  Lemuel 156, 165
  Levi W. 184
  N. W. 188
  Ramah 182
  Samuel 219
  Thomas G. 173
  William C. 213
  Wm. 213
COLEMAN, Alvin 153
  Elizabeth 161
  Jacob 203
  James 183
  John 146
COLICOEUR, George 212
COLLAME, Louis 125
COLLET, Robert 219
COLLIER, Hiram 178
  Levi 88, 139, 178
COLLINS, Charles 125
  George W. 179
  John 63, 170
  Peter M. 189
COLT, Sylvia 104
COLTON, Alpheau 184
  Thomas 106
COLVIN, Abraham 206
COMBS, Garrett 152
  George 154
  Isaac A. 166
  Jacob 165
  Thomas 167
COMFORET, ... (...) 92

COMFORET, Jean Bte 84
COMISAY, John 200
COMPARE, Baptiste 82
  Jn Bte 72, 73
  Michel 73
COMPARET, Adelaide 142
  J. Bte 88
  Mary 152
  Michel 82, 142
COMPARIL, Mary 163
COMPARIT, Francois 112
  Jean Bapt. 112
  Margaret (Limoges) 112
COMPARY, Francois 48
COMPAU, Francois 144
  Michael 144
  Paul Alexander 144
COMPEAU, Antoine 140
  Francois 139
  Josette (Parnier) 139
  Peter 139
COMPIEN, Bonadventure 6
COMPIEN dit L'ESPERANCE,
  Bonadventure 6
  Catherine (Laplante) 6
COMPO, Jean Bt. 156
  Michel 156
COMSTOCK, Addison 188
  Darius 188
  Elias 181
  Elkanah 181
  Job 188
  John 188
  Milo 190
  Nathan 188
  Walter 175
COMTOIS, see Cousin 17
  Joseph 178
CONANT, ... 122
  Harry 173
CONASH, Madam 130
CONDELLE, Pierre 152
CONDEN, James 170
  Peter 171
CONDON, Joel 210
CONE, Linus 182
CONJER, Archange (Huyet-
  Champagn) 142
  John Bte 142
CONKLIN, ... 199
  Aron 190
  Eli 199
CONNELLY, John 78, 89
CONNER, Alice (Thorn) 133
  Bryan O. 127
  Bryant 127
  Henry 117, 151, 159, 160
  James 132, 190
  Jared 182
  John 87, 84, 133, 191
  Margaret (Bower) 117, 132, 133

CONNER, Mary (Welch) 132
  Richard 117, 132, 133
  Robert 84
  Susanne 129
  Susanne (Duchene) 123
  Teresa (Tremblay) 117
  Thomas 123, 213
CONNERS, see Convers 173
  John 76
  William 205
CONNOLLIEUR, Ambroise 71
CONNOLLY, John 111
CONNOR, John 210
  Margaret 109
  Richard 82
CONOLY, Patrick 84
CONRAD, John 152, 167
CONSTANT, Angelique 116
  Pierre 66
CONTOIS dit COUSIN 17
CONVASE, James 215
CONVERS/CONNERS, Elijah 173
CONWAY, John 127
COOK, Abraham 76, 84, 116, 163
  Cyril 172
  Edmond 182
  Elizabeth (Stevens) 104
  Elizabeth (Thorn) 116
  Ezekiel 181
  Harvey 133, 190
  James H. 196
  James W. 196
  Jason 201
  John , 156, 170, 171
  Levi 104, 172
  Lewis 201
  Peter 204
  Samuel 189
  Thaddeus 104
  Truman 184
  William 151
COOKE, Abraham 159
  Robert 146
COOLEY, Andrew S. 182
  Archange (Yax) 144
  Benjamin 143, 178
  Elihu 180
  Elizabeth (Mauger) 136
  Gideon 136, 144
  Oliver 144, 178
  Reuben 136
  Samuel T. 182
  Susanne (Cicotte) 136
COOLY, Calvin 80
  Gideon 80
COOMAR, Ethan 183
COMMER, David 180
COOMS, George 170
COON, John 183
COONE, Hyhaah 214

COONS, John R. 218
COOPER, Joseph 86, 105
  Abraham 84
  David 105, 171
  Elizabeth 84
  Elizabeth (colored) 86
  Thomas 213, 124
COPP, David 215
COQUILLARD, Alex 80
  Judith 105
  Pierre 44
  Thomas 171
CORBETT, William D. 176
CORBES, John 205
CORBIN, Alex 213
  John B. 213
  Louis 213
CORBIS, Joseph 109
CORBUS, see Corbis 109
  Godfrey 78
  John 156
  Joseph 156, 187
  Richard 187
CORBY, Daniel 160
COREIRE, Jacob 215
CORIEL, Peter 146
CORKINS, Hiram 193
  John 206
  Lucius 155, 167
  Warriner 166
  Warrinner 155
CORKNER, George 189
CORLIES, Joseph 157
CORNEAU, ... 12
  Archange (Cousineau) 143
  Catherine (Belair) 143
  Louis 143
  Pierre 80, 143, 176
CORNELL, James 138, 177, 186
CORNIE, Antoin 215
CORNISH, Andrew 199
  Ephraim B. 199
  John 139
CORNWALL, ... 41, 55
  Richard 106
CORNWELL, Colbin 198
  Daniel 174
CORON, Margaret 145
CORSON, John 178
CORYELL, Andrew 199
COSHANY, Jean B. 194
COSHRAIS, Louis 195
COSHWAIS, Peter 196
COSHWAY, Baptist 131
COSKRY, William 84
COSME, Amable 136, 140
  Antoine 80
  Clara 140
  Genevieve 140

COSME, Monique 136
COTA, Joseph 173
COTE, ... 84
  Antoine, see Joseph 104
  Ignais 160
  Joseph 76, 104
  M. (...) 87
  Prisque 76, 84
COTEAU, Jacques 123
COTES, Ann 104
  Thomas 115, 159
COTIEN, Bassille 159
COTRELL, Henry 195
  Joseph 50, 61
  Prisque 42, 55, 61
COTTERAL, George 54
COTTERELL, Geo. 73
COTTERILL, George 74
COTTON, R. 214
COTTRALL, George 82
COTTREAL, John 191
COTTRELL, Archange 132
  Archange (Meny) 131
  Catherine (Lauzon) 132
  David 132, 195
  Elizabeth 131
  George 131, 132, 195
  Henry 132
  Joseph 132
  Mary Ann (Campau) 132
  Mary Soulange Rivard 132
COUC, Marguerite 6
COUC dit LAFLEUR, Marguerite 6
COULAY, see Cooley 143
  Elizabeth (Mauger) 143
  Gideon 143
  Oliver 90
COULTURE, Teresa (Revau-Lajeunesse) 136
COUNOL, see Coulon 48
COURBIELLE, Louis 211
COURNEILLE, Jean Bt. 176
COURTIER, Bazile 116, 151
COURTOIE, see Courtois 23
COURTOIS 36
  Cha. 31
  Charles 33
  Charles Denis 23
  Denis 147, 212
  Simon? 24
COURTWAY, Denis 147
COURVALLE, Joseph 212
COURVILLE, see Cadieux 17
  Peter 146
COUSENEAU, Louis 55
COUSINAUT, Basil 67
COUSINEAU, Alexis 143
  Archange 143
  Basil 139, 143, 143
  Basile 139
  Bazil 80, 81

COUSINEAU, Clara 140
  Francis 142
  Genevieve 142
  Joseph 123
  Louis 140, 142
  Louis Basil 143
  Louise (Toupin-Dusault) 139
  Margaret 143
  Marie Anne 138
  Mary (Robidou) 142
  T. 143
  Victoire (Rau) 143
COUTEAU, Louis 62
COUTEUR, Etienne 145
COUTEURE, Claude 145
COUTHEURE, ... 66
  Medard 66
  Bte 67
  Vincent 68
COUTOURE, Dominique 175
COUTURE, see Coutheure 66
  Angelique 143
  Angelique (Menard) 143
  Angelique (Reaume) 143
  Archange 136
  Catherine 109, 137
  Catharine L. (Lenfant) 141
  Claude 80, 176
  Dominique 175
  J. 31
  J. Bte , 82, 136, 141, 143
  Jean Baptiste 22, 33
  Jean Bt. 42
  Jean Bte 56, 143
  Lewis 206
  Louis 136, 139, 145, 174
  Medard 174
  Pierre 80
  Terese 139
COUVRETTE, Joseph 212
COUZINEAU, Alexis 177
  Bazil 177
  Francois 177
COWAN, Isaac B. 218
COWLES, Thomas 84
COX, Alexander 217
  James P. 216
  Job 189
  John 195
  Peter 154, 164
  Thomas 41, 53, 62
COY, Erastus 196
COZIVENT, Antoine 178
CRAFT, John B. 193
  Parsons 190
CRAIG, David W. 202
  Elijah W. 202
  Samuel 187
CRAITE, Jean Bte 55
CRAKY?CREQUI, Bazile 161

CARMER, Catherine 162
  Henry 153
  Jane 208
  John 118, 153, 190
  Rebecca 198
CRAMPTON, James 201
  William 165
CRANDALL, Lydia 203
CRANDELL, Thomas T. 198
CRANE, Abel 197
  Alexander D. 200
  Joseph 198
CRANSTON, Elisha 201
CRATE, Etienne 172
CRAWFORD, Abraham 182
  David 182, 204
  Ira 180
  James 80
  John 180, 181, 189
  Lewis 122
  Milton 182
  Redford 92
  Robert 180, 182
  William 185
CREALY, Joseph 146
CREDIT, John B. 124
CREIGHTON, Daniel 217
CRELIE, Joseph 146
CREPO, ... 124
CREQUE, Bazile 90
  Horace 84
CREQUI, Baptiste 82
  Jean Baptiste 32
  Jean Bte 52
  Madeleine 122
CREQUIL, see Creckey 74
  see Crickey, Batist 73
CREQUY, see AIDE dit
    CREQUI 21
CRETE, see Crittie 40
  J. Bte. 132
  Magdeleine 132
CRETEL 17
CRICKEY, ... (...) 74
  Batist 73
CRIDER, John 166
CRIPEIT, Jean 53
CRIPSY/CRISSY, Erastus
  183
CRIQUIS, Jean 30
CRISPELL, Abraham 153
CRISPWELL, Abraham 164
CRISST, St. Jean 70
CRISTE, Jean Bt. 42
CRITCHET 165
  Thomas 165
CRITTENDEN, Charles 190
CRITTIE, see Crete 40
  Jean Bte 40
CROFOOT, John 166
CROIX, Peter 191

CROMON, Abraham 200
  John 200
CROMPTON, Eli L. 160
  Elial 118
  William 117, 154
CRONENWORTH, Marhta 160
CROOKS, David 182
  Ramsey 128
CROPPER, Gilbert 161
CROSS, Daniel 202
  Jason 196
  Robert 189
CROSSMAN, John 214
  Rufus 200
CROTIN, Louis 194
CROUDE, Randolph 164
CROY, Jacob 204
  John 204
CRUSE, Andrew 209
CRYQUE, Basile 84
CT/CICOT, ... 63
CUDWORTH, David 165
CUEILLERIE, Alexis 54
CUFF, Benjamin J. 126
CUFFE, see Cuff 126
CUILLERIE, ... 24
CUILLIERIER, see Beaubien 16
  see Cuirrier 36
  see Cuillerier dit Beaubien 17
  Ant. 30
  Antoine 12, 32
  Jean Baptiste 32
CUILLERIER-BEAUBIEN, Pierre Jean
  Marie 111
CUILLIERIER dit BEAUBIEN, Antoine
  12, 16, 20, 32
  Jean Baptiste 17, 20, 32
CUIRRIER, see Cuillerier 36
CULBERSON, John 146
CULLERIE, Alexis 41
  Antoine 41
CULVER, George 182
  Orange 180
CUMMINGS, Isaac 156, 165
CUMMINS, Robert 203
CUNNINGHAM, Thomas 219
CUQUIER, John Antoine 128
CURBA, Louis 123
CURBAT, Louis 123
CURRANT, Hiram 217
CURREY, John 207
CURRY, ... 84
  C. (...) 87
  Charles 84
  Chs. 78
  John 160
CURTIS, Daniel 127
  Dan'l 146
  Eli 186
  Israel 182
  Jeremiah 186

CURTIS, John 184, 203
  John M. 218
  Lewis 218
  Major 183
  Milo S. 193
  Nahum 186
  Noble D. 173
  Norman D. 173
  Thomas 182
  Truman 177
  William 183, 200
CUTLER, Enos 209
  Jonas 192
  Leonard 204
CUTTOE 123

DAGNEAU de QUINDRE, Louis 24
DAGNEAU dit DEQUINDRE, Louis
  16
DAIE, Souvreigh 213
DAILE, Stephen 206
DAILEY, William 179
D'AILLBOUT DesMUSSEAUX,
  Nicholas 12
DAILY, Thomas 172
DALLAM, James B. 222
DALRYMPLE, Adolphus 196
DALTON, Chryst. 76
DALY, Edmund 190
  John 190
DANDERAUT, Anthony 163
DANES, Samuel 162
DANIE, Laurent 122
DANIEAU, Charles 61
DANIELS, Elias 182
  John 186, 217
  Patrick 119, 160
  Willard 183
DARDENNE, ... 5
  Touissant 7
DARE, Angelique 140
DARLING, Sylvester 192
DARROW, Alex 73
  George 175
DART, Thomas 195
  William 125
DASHNA, Francois 211
DAUDELIN, Eleanor 142
DAUGHERTY, Allen R. 216
  John 217
  Robert 217
DAUNAY, Batiste 79
DAUSON, John 213
DAVENPORT, Ambrose 121, 124
  Ambrose R. 208
  Beverly 197
  Elias 161
  Linus 173
  Samuel T. 104
DAVENPORTE, Ambrose 215
DAVID, ... 125

DAVID, Therese 6
DAVIDSON, Abram 206
  Armstrong 206
  William 219
DAVIGNON dit LAFEUILLADE,
  Joseph 17, 21
DAVIS, Abner 187
  Calvin 192
  Claibourne 217
  David 150, 179
  Elizabeth 219
  Ichiel 165
  Isaac 196
  J. J. 106
  Jobe 207
  John D. 91
  Jonathan D. 155, 163
  Joseph 185
  Joshua 153, 183
  Martin 198
  Phineas 172
  Reuben 201
  Rubin 188
  Samuel 188
  Sarah G. (Hunt) 106
  William 161
  William A. 206
  William L. 126
  William N. 192
DAVISON, John 214
  Jno. 214
  Zephina 193
DAWSON, Wme 73
DAY, ... (...) 84
  Erastus 194
  Isaac
  Isaac W. 101, 162
  James 183
  Mary Ann Burnett (Douglass) 101
  William 198
DAYKAURAY, ... 121
DAYTON, Jonathan 186
DAZET, Joseph 174
DAZETT, Catherine (Roitel) 140
  Jean 140
  John 140
DE---LEAU, ... 25
DEAN, Aaron W. 185
  Frederick 171
  Henry 152
  I(s)aac 188
  Jeremiah 172
  Henry 185
  Noble F. 216
DEANE, John 61
DeBLUCHE, Bertrand 14
de BLUCHE dit LaSERRE, 14
  Bertrand
De BOISBERT, see Boisverd 14

De BONDY, Joseph 12
DECARRAUX, Francis 121
DECHENEAU, Louis 61
DECHIEN, Baptist 133
  Francis 132
  Jeanne (Petit) 132
  Michell 132
  Pierre 145
DECKER, Charles 126
DECOIGNE 36
DECOTOE, Nicholas 215
DeGERDIN/DESJARDIN, Alexander 211
  Francois 170
DEHAITRE, Lewis 191
  Oliver 191
DEHETRE 37
  ... 31, 32
  see Deshetres 48
  Hyacinth 48, 51
DEJEAN, ... (...) 42
DEJION, Peter I. 209
DELAILLE, Antoine 177
  Francois 177
DELAIR, Francois 80
DELAND, William R. 200
DELARIER, Frans 70
DELAUNAY, J. Bte 90
  Rosalie 111
DELAURIER, Pierre 68
DELAVAN, Benjamin 106
De LEMOTHE, see Lamothe 16
DELEUIL, Frans 67
DELI, Francis 138
DELIENES-BELANGER, Mary 141
DELIERES dit BONVOULOIR, Joseph Amable 23
DELIGNE, Louise 109
DELILE, Alexis 56
DELISE, Bonaventure 156
DELISLE, ... 5
  ... (...) 78
  see Bienvenu 16
  see Bienvenu dit DeLisle 20
  A. 31
  Alexis 33, 42, 63
  Anne (Lemoyne) 6
  Baptiste 89
  Bienvenu 63, 76
  Bienvenue 89
  Bte 65
  Charles 48, 51, 152, 170
  Elizabeth (Campau) 113
  Francois 6, 218
  Genevieve (Charon dit Lafrenier) 6
  Isidor 63
  Isidore 78
  J. Bte 78
  Joseph 78
  Josh 65
  Tarraise 166

DELISLE, Therese (Chauvin) 113
DELOEIL, see Deleuil 67
  Justine 138
  Susanne 142
DELOGE, Basile 69
DELONA, Seraphine 191
DELONG, Henry 201
DELONGHAMPS, Josh 89
De LONGEUIL, ... 14
DELORE, Augustus 142
DELORME, ... 5
  Magdeleine (Jobin) 6
  Pierre 61, 151
DELORMS, Francois 6
DELORUM, Peter 160
DELOUPE, John B. 120
DELVAIR, Joseph 128, 208
DELYLE, Benvenue 160
  Joseph 158
DEMARCHAIS, Ntne 76
De MARSAC de L'OMTROU, Sieur DESROCHERS, Jacob 6
  Therese (David) Masse 6
DEMARSE, Pierre 55, 67
DEMERS, Pierre 80
DEMING, J. A. C. 214
  John J. 170
de MORTH, Margaret 157
DEMOUCHELLE, see Dumoucheu 16
  Vittal 51
  Vittel 44
DE MOUNIER, Alexis 7
DEMUISSEAU, ...
DENDUREN, Antoine 151
DENEAU, see Denoue/Deniau 73
  Francois 61
DENIAU, see Denoue/Deneau 73
DENIGER, Kraft 174
DENINSTON, Robert 54
DENIS, see Donois 72
DENISEN, Scipio 110
DENISON, Juda 110
  Scipio 181
DENISON/GENEROW, Lewis 205
DENISSEN, ... 7
DENNING, John 216
DENNIS, Elias 188
DENNISON, Lefio 157
DENNY, Joseph 101
DENOUE/DENIAU/DENEAU, ... (...) 73
DENOVER, Peter 171
DE NOYAU, see Noyon 14
DENOYE, see Marcheteau dit Desnoyers 22, 23
DE NOYELLES, ... 14
DENOYER 37
  ... 32
  F./Francois 17
  Lewis 190
DENSMORE, William 197
DeNUNMA, J. B. 214
DENVER, Henry 205

DEPELTEAU, Vittal 48
DEPIER, Jas. 215
de PRA, Louis 159
DEQUIEAR, Antoine 209
DE QUINDRE/DEQUINDRE 16
... (Drouillard) 109
see Dagneau 16
see Dagneau de Quindre 24
A. 88
Adelaide 104
Ant. 79
Antne 69
Antoine 54, 104, 109, 130, 172, 191
Antoine Dagneau 104
Catherine (Chapoton) 104
Catherine (Desrivieres) 109
Fontenay 51
Francis 191
Francis Dagneau 130
J. Bte 130
Jeanne (Pilet) 130
Louis 104
Marie (Desnoyers) 104
Pere 157
Peter 163
Pierre 109, 152
Suzanne (Robert) 109
Thimothy 152
Timothy 163
DeRAGOUE, A. 214
DERBY, Ezra 196
Orrin 197
Sidney S. 200
DERBYSHIRE, C. 189
DEREGA-PLANT, Francis 143
Louise (Malet) 143
DERKIN, Cornelius 183
DEROCH(R), Jean M. 120
DEROCHER, Amable 123
Frans 64
"Good Man" 14
DEROSIER, Baptist 122
DEROUSER, Angelique (Meloche) 143
Urna 143
DERRY, Thomas 76
DERUSHE, ... 123
DERUISSAUX, see Trottier 16
DeRUISSEAU, see Trotier dit DesRusseaux 24
Julien/Alexis 24
DERVAL, Joseph 178
De St PIERRE, see St. Pierre dit Tranchemontagne
DESANGES-COUIN, Francis 143

DESANGES-COUIN, Marie 143
DESANIER, Louis 117
Teresa (Seguin-Laderoute) 117
DESAULNIERS, see Desanier 117
Louis 116, 117, 151
Monica 116
DESAULNIERS-LAJOMONDIERE, Amable 111
DeSAULT, see Toupin dit Dusault 21
Louis 33
DESAUNAY, Louis 90
DESAUNIE, Louis 79
DESBUTTES, Jean 14
DES CHAILLON, see D'Eschaillons dit St. Ours 14
D'ESCHAILLONS dit ST. OURS, ... 14
DESCHAMPT, Joseph 212
DESCHARTLET, Bazil 176
Jean Bt. 176
DESCHESNE, Joseph 48
DESCOMPS, Antoine Louis 33
Pierre Louis 33
DESCOMPS dit LABADIE, Antoine 20, 23, 33
Pierre 17
Pierre Louis 33
DESCOMPS-LABADIE, Alexis 139
Angelique (Lacelle) 109
Antoine 104
Cecilia 110
Margaret 139
Pierre 109
DE SELHURST, Justus 218
DESHETRES, see Dhetre 48
Aloysius 33, 130
Hyacinthe 33
Susanne 130
DESHETRES dit PIGEON, Aloysius 33
DESJARDIN, see DeGerdin 211
H. 88
DESLISLE, Alexis 119, 154
Bienvenue 119
Joseph 113
Monica (Livernois) 119
Therase 154
DESLOGES, see Deloge 69
DESLORIERS, see Delarier 70
DESMOULINS, Charlotte (Savarias) 7
Jacques 7
DESMOULINS dit PHILIS, Charlotte (Savarias) 7
Jacques 7
DESNOVER, Pierre 42
DESNOYER, Alexis 129
Charlotte (Mallet) 103
Gregoire 129
Jean Charles 103

DESNOYER, John B. 129
Joseph 196
Louise (Gobeil) 103
Peter 88
Peter J. 103
Rosalie (Peltier) 129
DESNOYERS, see Desonier 70
Fran. 77
Francois 33
Jean B. 196
Judith 133
Marie 104
Peter 76, 84
Pierre Jean 104
DESONIER, Louis 70
DESONY/DESAULNIERS, Lewis 160
DESPAGNE, Vin 5
DESPEIGNES/DESPINS/LeMOYNE 6
DESPENS, ... 5
DESPINS/DESPEIGNES/LeMOYNE 6
DESPINS, ... 7
DESPELTEAUX 17
DESPLA, Jacques 91
DESPLAINE, ... 65
DESPLAS, see Desplat 119
J. Bte 119
DESPLAT, Francoise (Lajeunesse) 119
James 119
Jas. 160
DESPLATS, Jacques 66, 78
DESPRE, ... 5
DESRIVIERES, Catherine 109
Joachim 208
DES ROCHERS, ... 5
DESROSIER, Jean Baptiste 33
DESROSIER dit DuTREMBLE, Jean Baptiste 33
DesRUISSEAUX, see Trotier 24
Alexis 33
DESSENIER, Louis 159
D'ESTRE, see Esteve dit Lajeunesse 21
DETAILLEIN, Augustin 173
DETANTABORATZ, Martial 219
DEVEAUX, ... 66
Theodocia 105
DEVEISSE, William 217
DEVINE, Patrick 219
DEVOST, William 126
DEVOTION, Lewis 147
DEVRIE, Alexander 147
deVILLIERS COULON, Nicholas 48
DEWEY, Apollis 181
Sidney 199
Simmeon 189
DEWIT, Benj. 158
John 101
Mary 101
DEWITT, Benj. 150
Benjamin 113

DEWITT, John 179
DEWRY, Josiah 184
DEXTER, Levi 141
  Samuel W. 200
DEYARMAND, Alexander 151
DIAMOND, John 181
DICK, Jane 119
DICKASON, Joseph 163
DICKINSON, Abraham 198
  John 196, 202
  William 210
DICKISON, Daniel 193
DICKMAN, Ann 162
DICKS, Ann (Milman) 115
  Hannah 117
  Jacob 78, 115
  Mary 115
  R. (...) 89
DICKSON, John 91
  Robert 92
DILHET, John 84
DILLE, David L. 205
  George W. 205
DILLING, William 180
DILLON, Frances 84
  Hiland 201
  John 217
  Richard C. 201
DILNO, Jemima 129
DILSAVER, John 126
DIMROCK, Elijah 215
DINAN, Pierre 17
DINEEN, James 184
DINGLEY, Daniel 123, 213
  Isabelle (Duchene) 123
  Warren 171
DIRGENEL, J. Bte 77
DISBROW, Elizabeth 136
  Henry 136, 173

  Sarah Anderson 136
DISOME, James 214
DISPLAIN, Harry 156
DIVER, Andrew 178
  Andrew J. 144
  John 138, 174
DIX, Francoise (Livernois) 115
  Jacob 154, 159, 160
  John 115, 154, 159, 160, 201
  Margaret (Jolibois) 115
  Peter 115
  Victoria (...) 115
DIXE, Jacob 64
DIXON, David 217
  Frederick 222
  John 209
  Joseph 219
DIXSON, James 207
DODD, Joseph 182

DODELIN, Adrien 91
DODEMEAD, ... (...) 84
  Ann 92
  J. 88
  James 84
  John 60, 76, 84
DODGE, Henry 216
  Reuben 196
DOLLARD, Joseph 213
DOLSEN, ... 55
DOLSON, Alva 161
  Gilbert 163
  Mathew 61
DONA, ... 122
DONALSON, Ira 186
  James 62
DONAS, Charette 102
DONE, Elisha 205
DONELLS, James 164
DONNE, Michel 208
DONOIS, Baptiste 72
DONOVAN, ... (...) 92
  Mathew 63
  Matth 77
  Matthew 84
  Polly 84
  Richard 60
  Richd 76
  Sally 84
DONSMAN, Hercules L. 210
  Michael 209
DONVAN, Alanson 189
DOOLITTEL, Anthony 202
DOPHENY, Madam ... 133
DORAN, John 196
DORAN/DOSAN, Michael 171
DOREZEAU, Theodore 177
DORMAND, Sarah 142
DOROCHER, Amable 211
DOROTHY, Thomas 173
DORR, Josiah R. 170
DORREL, Luther 175
  Samuel 209
DORRIEL, Luther 138
DORT, David 184
  Titus 164
DOTTE, Joseph C. 214
DOTTON, Michael 160
DOTY, Elias 171
  Elisha 180
  Ellis 152
  John 183
  James D. 211
DCUAIRE, Joseph 12
DCUAIRE de BONDY, Joseph 12
DCUAIRE dit BONDY, Joseph 23
DCUCET, Pierre 80
DCUD, Edward 129
  John B. 129
DOUGHALY, Thomas 209
DOUGHERTY, Dauphin 84

DOUGHERTY, William 213
DOUGLAS, Christopher 190
  David 185
  Nathan 184
DOUGLASS, Mary Ann Burnett 101
DOULIN, Francis 218
DOUSMAN, Joseph 128
  Michael 122, 128
  Rosalie 211
  Rosalie (Labarde) 128
DOUQUETTE, Joseph 176
DOUTS, George 127
DOUVILLE, ... 14
DOWELS, George 202
DOWNER, Andrew 183
  Cyprian 119
  David B. 197
  Edmond 183
  Elijah 119, 160
  Elijah G. 164
  Hannah (Willoughby) 119
  Lucretia 156
  Simon 162
DOWNING, Minor 175
  Rufus 141, 177
  Stephen 138, 141, 176, 177
DOYLE, Curry 198
  Henry 132, 176
  James 132
  Patrick 218
DRAKE, Benjamin 204
  Francis 84
  John 187
  Thomas J. 181
DREW, John A. 208
  Thomas Wm. 208
DRING, Sarah 119
DRIVER, Samuel 78
DRIVERD, Samuel 64
DROLLET, Pierre 61
DROUILARD, Simon 36, 203
DROUILLARD, ... 109
  ... (...) 43, 84
  Antoine 177
  Baptiste 22
  Bte 36, 65, 68
  Catherine (Bernard) 139
  Charles 139, 176
  Charlotte (Drouin) 140
  Colette 142
  Dennis 178
  Domine 66
  Dominique 62, 80, 138, 143, 177
  Dque 91
  Elizabeth 105
  Elizabeth (...) 156
  Elizabeth (Gagnier) 140
  Francis 139
  Francois 48, 52

## Index

DROUILLARD, Fr. 37
  Isabel 158
  Izabel 113
  J. Bt. 44
  J. Bte 77, 91, 139, 140, 142, 143
  Jean Baptiste 17, 33
  Jean Bt. 178
  Jean Bte. 51, 114, 140
  Joseph 44, 50, 80, 178
  Josette 130
  Josette (LeBeau) 140
  Josh 66, 77
  Louis 139
  Louise 110
  Louise (Quesnel) 139
  Magdeleine 130
  Marie J. (Laviolette) 143
  Nicholas 66
  Nicolas 80, 142
  Pauline 138
  Pierre 55, 72, 80
  Simon 23, 44, 62, 63, 80
  Simon Amable 33
  Suzanne 102, 114
  Teresa 142
  Tousant 167
DROUIN, Appolus 188
  Charlotte 140
DRULLARD, Tusaint 156
DRULLIARD, John Bte 166
DRURY, Elihu 165
DRYAMOND, Alexander 198
DUBA 123
  Alexis 130
  Angelique (Goulet) 130
  Cecilia (Blay) 130
  Francis 130
  John B. 130
  Teresa (Dulac) 130
DUBAY, see Duba 130
  see Dube 115
  Alexis 191
  Cecilia 130
  Francis 191
  Jean M. 130
  John B. 191
  John M. 191
  John Marie 130
  Simon 191
DUBAYE, Jean Marie 53
DUBE, Catherine (Bernard) 115
  Jean 115
  Joseph 115, 151
  Louis 123, 212
DUBEE, Jean 70
DUBERGE, Joseph 77
DUBERGER, Angelique 129
  J. Bte. 129
  John Bte. 110

DUBERGER, Joseph 110, 157
  Josh 89
DUBERGER dit SANSCHAGRIN, Jean Baptiste 24
DUBEY, Lewis 145
DUBIE, Jn Bte 70
DUBO, Joseph 156
DUBOIE, see Dubois 21
DUBOIS, Alexis 21
  Baptist 122
  Etienne 68, 88, 124, 139, 219
  Francois 139
  Hyancinthe 69, 82
  Joseph 163
  Louis 63
  Margaret (Descomps-Labadie) 139
  Margaret (Labadie) 139
  Stephen 139
  Susan 171
  Susanne (Facer) 139
DUBORD, Francois 33
  Jn Bte 64
DUBORD dit LaFONTAINE, Francois 22, 33
DUBRAIS, Jean Bt. 178
DUBRAYE, Louis 215
DUBREUIL, ... 66
  J. Bte. 80
  Jean Baptiste 23
DUBRUIL, Louis 121
DUCE, Lewis 156
DUCEAU, Augustin 179
  Ettiene 178
  Gabriel 177
  Jean Bt. 178
  Joseph 177
DUCHAINE, Frans 71
  Michel 71
DUCHAISNE, see Gastinon dit Duchene 21
DUCHANE, Angelique (Yvon) 101
  Evan 101
DUCHARM, Joseph 211
DUCHARME, Fs. 89
  Joseph 145
DUCHENAN, ... 48
DUCHENAU, Louis 84
DUCHENE, see Duchesne 17
  Baptiste 82
  Charles 170
  Etienne 72, 79, 90
  Francis 131
  Francois 32, 52, 82
  Isabelle 123
  Marie 115
  Mary Ann 133
  Michael 195
  Michel 82
  Pelagia 131

DUCHENE, Pierre 72, 79, 90
  Susanna 171
  Susanne 123
DUCHENOIS, Andre 61
DUCHER, Henry 166
DUCHESNE, see Duchene 17
  see Gastinon 17
  Claude 52
  Fra. 30
  Francis 195
  Francois 40
  Hubert 177
  Joseph 51
  Pierre 52, 177
DUCHIN, Henry 155
HUCHINE, Mary 150
DUCKET, Isaac W. 207
DUCLEAU, Antoine 174
DUCLOS, Anthony 136
  Mary 136
duDEMOIS, Francois 157
DUDLEY, David 200
  Elon 192
  Joel 193
  Nahum 219
  Orsel 193
DUFAULT, Francis 214
DUFF, Alexander 60
DUFINAIS, Francois 209
DUFOE, James 162
DUFORT, Vincent 167
DUFOUR, ... 84
  Baptiste 60
  Catherine 105
  J. Bte 77, 91
  Joseph 175
  Louis 88
  Pierre 17, 25
DUFOURD, see Dufor 17, 25
DUFRESNE, Madeleine 6
DUGARD, John 89, 110, 155, 160
DU GARDE, John 110, 157
DU GENNA, Bazile 213
DU GRAY, Genevieve 215
DUGUAY, Marguerite 7
DUHAMEL, J. Bte. 110
  Marie Josette 110
DUITT, Submit 166
DUKES, Alanson 185
  Jesse 185
  Solomon 185
DULAC, Archange 130
  Baptist 131, 190
  Baptiste 151
  Charles 82, 130, 131
  Julia (Chauvin) 131
  Teresa 130
DULACK, Chs 71
DULOU, Josiah 77
DUMAIS, see Dumay 23

DUMAIS, Francis
　　John Bapt. 154
　　John Bt. 160
　　Magdelene (Chevalier) 23
　　Pierre 64
　　Theophile 160
　　Vimic 160
DUMARK, John 171
DUMAS, Francis 76
DUMAY, Angelique (Lemay) 109
　　Francis 153
　　Francois 109
　　Jacques 23
　　John Bapt. 119
　　Joset (...) 154
　　Josette (Bourassa) 117
　　Magdelene (Chevalier) 23
　　Margaret 109
　　Pierre 78, 89, 109, 117, 119
　　Theophile 117
　　Therese (Parnier-Vacebon-coeur) 109
　　Veronique (Baron) 119
DUMAYS, ... 73
DUMO, Baptiste 60
DUMOUCHELL, Louis Joseph 16
DUN, George W. 155
DUNBAR, Alvin J. 192
　　Ephrim 188
　　Joseph 185
DUNCAN, Asa 216
　　Delman 205
　　Leslie 215
　　Maria 84
　　William 209
　　/Dunton, Winslow 170
DUNEVAN, Patrick 171
DUNFAN, John 210
DUNHAM, Daniel O. 92
　　Henry 182
　　Seth 112, 152, 158, 205
DUNKS, George 152
　　George W. 173
DUNLAP, Samuel 125
DUNLOP, James 195
　　William 174
DUNLOVA, J. 215
DUNN, George W. 165
　　James 153, 161
　　Mary 113
　　Simeon A. 167
DUNNING, Martin 150
DUNOR, Antoine 173
DUNTON, see Duncan 174
DUPERON dit BABY, Jacques 25
DUPLAISSE/DUPLESSIS, Bte. 78
DUPLESSE, Josh 65
DU PLESSIS, Jeanne (Lemoine) 6
　　Joseph 80

DU PLESSIS, Louis 6
DUPRA, Charles 90
　　Julia (Pominville) 116
　　Louis 90, 116
　　Michel 164
DUPRAS, Jn Bte 70
　　Michel 70
DUPRAT, see Dupra 116
　　J. Bte 78, 116
　　Jean 40
　　Louis 150
DUPRAU, Jean 53
DUPRAX, Michel 151
DUPRAY, Louis 116, 151
　　Peter 195
DUPRE, Battiste 150
　　Etienne 77
　　Francoise 88
　　Jean B. 212
　　Louis 132, 160
　　Magdeleine (Crete) 132
　　Peter 132
DURPES, Pierre 73
DUPUIS, Joseph 191
DUQUETTE, Joseph 77
DUR, Jacob 195
DURAND, see Montmirel 17
　　Jean Marie 55
　　John 200
　　Pierre 41, 53
DURAND dit MONTMIREL 23
　　Pierre 17
DURELL, William 112
DURENSEAU, Baptist 124
DURET, see Duretthe 70
DURETT, John Bte 160
DURETTE, Ann (Renaud) 101
　　J. Bte 79, 88
　　John 101
　　John B. 151
DURETTHE, Jean 70
DURFEE, Allen 165
　　Austin 186
　　Barton 165
　　George 153, 165
　　Harvey 186
DURFEY, Bartum 153
DURKEE, Erastus 180
　　Judson 197
　　Wilkes 186
　　William 180
DUROCHER, (Frs) ... 78
　　Francois 89
　　Francs 89
　　Jean Bt 209
　　Laurent 136, 174
　　Louise 103
　　Michael 84
　　Monique (Cosme) 136
DUROSEAU, Rene 143
　　Rene Theodore, see Derouser, Urna 143

DUROSHEELER, Amab 145
DURRELL, William 158
DURRIN, John 165

DURSAN, ... 48
DUSA, John 140
　　John Francois 140
　　Joseph 144
　　Margaret (Montmeny) 140
　　Mary (Beaudrais) 144
DUSALT, Archange 139
DUSAULT, Archange 144
　　J. Francois 142
　　Marie 6
　　Monique 142
DuSAUT, ... 32
DUSEL, William 170
DUSHARM, Joseph 145
DUSO, Etienne 144
　　Monique (Thuot-Duval) 144
DUSSAU, Jean Bte 66
DUSSAULT 37
　　Jean 80
DUSUALT, John Francis 144
DUTCHER, Elizabeth (...) 113
　　Henry 113, 158
　　John 202
DUTHUFF, William Henry 128
DuTREMBLE, Jean Baptiste 33
DUTTON, John 213
DUVAL, Catherine (LaFontaine) 144
　　Daniel 177
　　Etienne 144, 178
　　Hyacynthe 174
　　Ignace 80, 144
　　Joseph 144, 178
　　Louise 140
　　Louise (Bissonnet) 144
　　Michael 178
　　Monique 144
　　Pierre 178
DUVALLE, Charles 144
　　Daniel 139
　　Ignace 51, 139
　　Josette (Drouillard) 139
DUVERNAY, Pierre 208
du VESTIN, Joseph 7
DWIGHT, Daniel 154
DYCE, ... 41
DYONNE, Etienne 212
DYSON, ... (...) 84
　　William 84

EARLE, William L. 197
EASTMAN, Moses 219
EASTON, Liba 196
EATON, James 188
　　William 188
EBARTS, Herman 76
EBERTS, ... 60

## Index

EBERTS, ... (...) 84
   Robert M. 211
   Therese 84
EDDO, Charles 210
EDDY, Abraham 180
   Jasper 203
   Joseph 179
   Samuel 62
   William 203
EDGAR, John 42
   William 41
EDGE, Samuel 62
EDGECOMB, Asa 153
EDGERLY, James C. 191
EDGET, Albert 193
   Peter 193
   William 193
EDMOND, William 188
EDSON, Amso 202
EDWARDS, Aaron 103
   Abraham 103, 151, 206
   Alexander H. 208
   Edwin 102, 186
   Jane (...) 102
   Jean, see Jane 102
   Lewis 207
   Nancy 130
   Thomas 214
   Thomas A. H. 206
EELS, Otis G. 170
EGNEU, Samuel 80
EGNEW, Isabella 136
   Samuel 138
EILERT, Harriet (Williams) 104
   Jacob 104
ELAM, Joseph 62
ELDRED, Julius 112, 158, 170
   Mindwell (Higby) 113
ELDRIDGE, Nathaniel 161
ELLAIR, Joseph 79, 90
ELLARD, Joseph 151
ELLINWOOD, John 180
ELLIOT, Gilbert 196
ELLIOTT, Matthew 84
ELLIS, Albert G. 211
   Edward D. 173
   Joseph 119, 160
ELLISON, James 178
ELLOIR, Agatha (Laperle) 131
   Joseph 131
   Magdeleine (Tramblay) 131
ELSWORTH, Wm. R. 214
EMMERSON, Elijah 164
EMMONS, Noah 189
   William 206
ENGLE, Jonathan 205
ENGLISH, Abel 122
   Anna (Caulkins) 122
   Sophia 122
ENO, Joseph 218

ENSIGN, Hiram 189
ENSWORTH, John A. 199
EPLEY, Conrad 201
ERMATINGER, George 120, 213
   James 213
   Thomas 213
ERNEST, Matthew 76
ERSKINE, Henry 155, 161
ERVINGS, Ezekiel R. 186
ERWIN, Matthew 146
ESMOND, Patrick 128
ESPEY, James 128

ESTEVE/STEBRE, Etienne 6
   Madeleine (Frappier) 6
ESTEVE dit LAJEUNESSE/STEBRE,
   Etinne 6
   Madeleine (Frappier) 6
   Pierre 21
ESTINNE, Jn Bte 37
etinnse, see Ainse 42
   Sarah 42
ESTRE, Belle, see Beletre 23
ESTY, Israel 199
EVANS, Alvin 176
   Britton 146
   Cadwallader 210

   John 183
   Musgrove 189, 190
EVEREST, Mashal 162
EVERETT, John 201
EVERS, see Ewers 172
EVINS, Major 183
EVON, Joseph 142
EWENS, Tillotson 200
EWERS, Alva H. 172
EWING, Alexandre 80
   John 80

ABRE, Michael 124
FACER, Catherine (Raymond) 105
   Henry 105
   Henry David 109
   see Fesse, Louis 105
   Mary 103
   Susanne 139
   Suzanne 109
FAFARD, Francois 6
   Jean 6
   Magdeleine (Jobin) 6
   Marguerite 6, 7
   Marguerite (Couc dit Lafleur) 6
FAFARD dit DELORME, Francois 6
   Magdeleine (Jobin) 6
FAILES, Charles 213
FAIRCHILD, Edwin 186
   Francis 173

FAIRFIELD, Alanson 162
FAIRLEY, Amos 206
FAIRMAN, Henry 165
   Jerry 165
FAISMAN, Jared 155
FALES, Jabez 126
   Timothy 173
FANGAIN, Oliver 215
FANNING, Joseph 217
FARGO, Calvin 199
FARLEY, Charles 215
   J. 106
FARNHAM, Russell 124
FARNSWORTH, E. 154
   Ephraim 162
   William 122, 211
FARRAND, Bethuel 197
FARREL, John 126
FARRELL, Catherine 101
   Catherine (Morris) 101
   Edward 101
FARRINGTON, Joseph 138, 175, 189
FARRIS, Garret D. 217
FARROD, John 171
FARWELL, Francis 175
FARSYTHE, James 197
FASER, Louis 196
FASHNATCH, Maria 212
FAU, John 182
FAUBERT, Antoine 124
   Joseph 176
FAUVEL, Jean B. 211
FAVERO, John Bte. 144
   Mary (Leonard) 144
FAVREAU, see Favero 144
   J. Bte. 144
   Pierre 7
FAVREAU dit LEGRANDEUR, Pierre 7
FAY, Jonathan 167
   Joshua 184
   Nathan 193
   Thomas C. 195
FEARSON, see Phearson 111
   (Capt.) ... 79
   Clemence 102
   George 171
   Hannah 84
   John 62, 84
FEBEAU, ... 5
FEILDEN, Mathew 214
FELIX, Dennis 213
FELLOWS, Abiel 205
   Albert G. 155, 165
   Festus A. 165
   Fisher A. 156
   James 165, 205
   Leonard 155
   Rise L. 165
FELT, Samuel 138

FENIX/PHENIX, Pierre  82
FENNIMORE, John G.  216
FENTON, Jesse  125
    Warren  162
FERGUSON, Daniel  186, 195
    Erastus  141, 184
    George W.  219
    Orange  186
FERRILL, Jonathan  217
FERRON, John  126
FERRY, Peter P.  173
    William M.  209
FERTON, Frans  72
    Julien  52, 72
FESSE, ... (Belanger)  105
    Louis  105
FETT, James D.  166
FEVEREAU, Jean Bt.  178
FIDLER, John  204
FIELD, Pliny  188
FIELDS, E. E.  122
    Eliakim  122
**FILSON, James  214**
FILKINS, John D.  205
FILLAMORE, Robert  158
FILLION, Augustin  219
FINCH, Ashiel  189
    Benjamin  152
    Benona  206
    Darius  194
    Ezra  193
    James  125
    Joel  162
    John  192
    Jonas  192
    Moses  206
    Sylvester  192
FINCHELEY, Thomas  54
FINCHLEY, Thomas  43
FINLAY, Michael  218
FINLEY, John L.  146
FINNEMORE, Daniel  125, 210
FIREHAUDT, William  113
    Wm.  158
FISH, Ebenezer  192
    Elijah S.  186
    Elisha  217
FISHER, Cyrus  176
    Daniel  207
    George  211, 219
    Harry M.  92
    James  210
    Jonathan  175
    Link  194
FISK, Benjamin B.  189
FITCH, John  188
    Matthew  216
    Stephen  188
FITZGERALD, Peter  217
FITZPATRICK, Thomas  219
FIX, ... (...)  175

FIZETTE, Louis  212
FLEHARTY, William  216
FLEMING, (Capt) ...  41
    James  196
    Robert  84
FLETCHER, Uriah  187
    William  152, 205
FLEURY, Francis  131
    Mary (Maillet)  131
FLIN, John  195
FLINN, John  90, 164
    Thomas  154, 164
FLOYD, Armistead  216
    Thomas W.  219
FLORY, Gideon  193
FLUELLIN, Herbert  216
FLURIE, Francis  195
FOLSOM, Jacob  156
FOND du LAC, ...  128
FONIER, Margaret (Bousom)  144
    Pierre  144
FONTAIGNE, Charles  43
FONTAIN, Joseph  214
FONTAINE, Charles  50, 80
    Chs  65
    Elizabeth  144
    Gabriel  80, 175
    J. Bte  80
    Joseph  121
    Joseph A.  121
    Louis  65
    Theophile  208
FOOT, Horace  193
FORCE/LOREE, Palmer  200
FORCE, George  217
FORD, Ansel  202
    David B.  183
    Eli  206
    Sherick  206
FOREMAN, John  205
FORGE, Basil  79
FORKEE, George  146
FORMAN, Benjamin  219
FORSITH, ...  41
    William  41, 52, 151
FORSYTH, ...  78
    Robert  61
    Robert A.  161
    William  88
    Wm.  71, 79
FORTE, Francis  161
    Louis  164
FORTH, Sip  171
FORTIER, George  146
    Laurent  212
    Pierre  77
    Rose  105
FORTO, Joseph  161
FORTON, see Fortun  90
    see Furton  115

FORTON, Denis  191
    Francis  191
    Francois  79, 150
    Hubert  191
    John B.  191
    Julia  129
    Julian  191
    Julien  79, 191
    Teresa (Billiau)  129
    Thomas  159
FORTUN, Francois  90
FORTVILLE, see Forville, see
    Tetard  16
    Pierre  33
FORVILLE, ...  24, 31
    see Tetard dit Fortville  16
    Peter Tetard dit  20
FOSTER, George  202
    Joel P.  88
    Nathaniel  186
    Samuel W.  200
    William  188
FOUCHE, Charles  84
    Michael  218
FOUERAU, Pierre  67
FOURNIER, see Fouerau  67
    Abraham  90, 109, 151
    Abr'm  157
    Archange (Campau)  109
    Augustin  103, 109
    Eugene  218
    Francis  171
    Francois  79, 90
    Gaume  88
    Henry  178
    Judith (Touissant)  109
    Pierre  144
    Tousant  171
FOURQUERAU, Pierre  50
FOUTER, Joseph H.  160
FOWLE, James  190
FOWLER, David  185, 203
    Denis  194
    James  174
    Joseph  118, 160, 203
    Joseph H.  153
    Mahaly (Mou?)  133
    Mary  203
    Samuel  192
    Thomas  133
FOX, Alanson  174
    Amasa  113, 118, 153, 160
    Asa  113, 158
    Benj. F.  113
    Benjamin F.  162
    Michael  84
    Truman  185
    Zenas  184
FRAISGEAU, David  91
FRAKES, Joseph  205
    Robert  205

FRALICK, Nancy 161
FRANCIS, Ephraim 165, 210
   Sylvester 184
FRANCISCO, Henry A. 203
FRANCOEUR, Augn 88
   Augustin 84
FRANK, John 184
FRANKS, Jacob 92
   John Martin 53
FRAPPIER, Madeleine 6
FRARO, ... (...) 84
   Francois 84, 140
FRAROT, Francois 61
FRARY, David 138
   Esther (Kingsley) 138
FRASER, Alexander 89, 167
   James 60, 78
   Martin 165
   Silas 202
   William P. 117
FRASHER, ... 119, 160
   Wm. P. 159
FRAZER, Martin 153
FRAZIER, Alexander 156
   Alexander D. 170
   William P. 196
FREDERICK, David 203, 214
   Nicla 131
FREEMAN, ... 76
   Benjamin 194
   Joseph 194
   Lewis 197
   Moses 193
FRENCH, Daniel 197
   David 170
   Henry 210
   Spencer 167
FREREAU, Frans 88
FREDO, Fran. 76
FREROT, see Frado 140
FRETON, see Ferton 72
   see Furton 120
   Julian 32, 129
   Teresa 133
FRETON dit NANTAIS, Julian 32
FRETWELL, Samuel 222
FRON, Antoinelet 159
FROST, Johnson L. 194
   Mathew 189
   Norton N. 184
   Solomon 181
   William 175
FROTOCHAUD, Jean Bte 121
FROTOCHEAU, Joseph 121
FRY, John 126
FUHINOR, Caleb 155
FULLARTON, John 217
FULLER, Appolis 194
   Asa 182
   Asahel 186

FULLER, Benjamin 182
   Benjamin Jr. 182
   Hiram S. 163
   Hugh 204
   Israel 163
   Lucius H. 186
   Matthias 182
FULLERTON, Almond 162
   Phineas 162
FULLMAN, L. 204
FULMER, Martin 215
FULTON, Alexander 207
   James 133, 195
FUNSTON, Coleman 130, 152
   Colman 173
FURGO, Thomas 195
FURLONG, Walter 146
FURNIA, Facer 103
   Francis 103
   Margaret (Leuevre) 103
FURNIER, Abraham 163
FURSIO, Joseph 173
FURTON, Francis 120, 160
   Francois 120
   John Bapt. 115
   Joseph 150
   Soulange (Senet) 120
   Thomas 115
FUST, Daniel B. 203

GADUPEE, Bournevint 123
GAGE, Abigail 111, 157
   Alexander 172
   Alva 111
   George 181
   Henry 111
   Samuel 180
GAGNE, Louis 124
GAGNER, Isaac 55
   Jacques 81
GAGNIE, Isaac 42
GAGNIER, ... 33
   Agustin 178
   Angelique 101
   Angelique (Leonard) 143
   Archange (Leonard) 144
   Augustus, see Usta 143
   Bartholomew, see Batema 144
   Bateme 144
   Bazel 212
   Clara (Menard) 143
   Elizabeth 140, 173
   Isaac 62, 116
   Jacques 68
   James 139, 143, 144
   Joseph 178, 218
   Joseph, Mrs. 178
   Julien 116, 159, 163
   Lewis 143
   Louis 177
   Louise 105

GAGNIER, Mary J. (Larcheveque) 143
   Monique 143, 144
   Pierre 143, 144, 178
   Theotiste (Saucier) 116
   Usta 143
   Veronique (Martin) 143
GAGNIOR, Joseph 128
GAGNON, see Gaien 21
   Louis 77
GAIEN, see Gagnon 21
GAILAGHER, James 158
GAILLARD, Joseph 157
   Louis 68, 80, 139
   Louise 139
   Ursule 139
GAILLARD-LIONAIS, Therese 109
CAINES, Charles 216
GALE, Joshua 204
   Samuel H. 175
   /Gate, Samuel H. 137
GALLARNEAUX, Francois 212
GALERNEAU, ... 33
   Pierre 84
GALES, Michael 218
GALIPAU, Gasil 69
GALLAGHER, James 112
GALLARNOW, Francis 146
GALLASPIE, Henry 154
GALLIGER, William 195
GALLOWAY, Alexander 187
   John 187
GAMELIN 36
   ... 31, 64
   ... (...) 43
   Francois 56, 63, 77
   Francs 89
   Ignace 16
   Joseph 43, 55
   Laurence Eustache 20, 33
   Marie 103
GAMMON, Simon 211
GANARD, Alexis 177
   Jean Bt. 178
   Nicholas 178
GANIA, Lewis 143
GANIER, Isaac 80
   Jacques 80
GANDY, Louis 126
GARDINER, John 200
GARASIDE, Thomas 215
GARDIPIER, Alex 146
   Alexander 211
   Boneventure 210
GARDNER, David 167
   Joseph 207
GARDPIES, Bonadventure 123
GAREAU, Marie (Guertin)
   Laverge 6
   Pierre 6

GAREAU dit St. ONGE, Marie
    (Guertin) Laverge  6
  Pierre  6
GARFIELD, Myra  180
  William  180
GARINEZ, Secial  196
GARLAND, ... (Smith)  106
  John  106
GARLICK, Lucy  125
GARLOPEE, Alex  146
GARNEAU, Louis  176
GAROIN, Joseph  82
GARRAND, John B.  151
GARRATT, Robert  128
GARRAUT, John Bte.  160
GARRET, Daniel  41
GARRETSON, William  217
GARRIL, Daniel  54
GARRISON, John  110, 157, 172, 214
  William  210
GARROW, Joseph  170
GARVER, Frederick  206
GARWOOD, Joseph  207
  Joseph C.  174
  William  207
GASTINEAU, ...  5
  Jeanne (Lemoine)  6
  Louis  6
GASTINEAU, SIEUR DE STE ANNE/
    SIEUR DU PLESSIS, Louis  6
GASTINON, Francois  32
GASTINON dit DUCHENE,
    Francois  17, 21, 32
GASTINON-DUCHENE, Pierre  101
  see Duchane  101
GATE, Samuel, see GALE  137
GATES, Gideon  193
  Polly  187
  Samuel  165
  Willaim  174, 219
GAUBIELLE, Francois  55
GAUDE, Jacques  7
  Marguerite (Duguay)  7
GAUDET, see Godet  16, 23
  Francois Marentete  51
  Joseph  48, 52
  Josh  64
GAUDETTE, Francois  51
GAUDON, Francois  175
GAUTHIER, Berthume  121
  Gilliaume  212
GAUTIER, Joseph  208
  Louisa  6
  GAUNELET, ...  32
GAUVREAU, Joseph  209
GAUYEAU, B. see Goyou dit
    Lagarde  21
  Vital, see Goyou dit
    Lagarde  21
GAUYEAUZ, Louis  44

GAVIN, Chas  157
  Cherres  159
  Pierre  159
GEDDES, David  200
  Robert  198
GEDNEY, Joshua R.  125
GEE, Antoine  176
  Benjamin  198
  Christopher  199
  Edvidge  197
  Edward  198
  Lumace  199
  Webber  197
GEEL, Abraham  88
  Nancy  84
GEHON, Francis  217
GEIROU, Pierre  33, 52
GELINA, Jeanne  114
GEMMER, Isaac  205
GENDRON, Simon  55
GENDRON-SOREL, Alexis  114
  Joseph  114
GENEREAU, Joseph  174
GENEROW, see Denison  205
GENIEZ, Joseph  68
GENOR, Jean B.  211
GENTLE, Adam  84
  John  76, 84
GENTRY, James H.  217
GENUNG, Christopher  210
GERARD, Amable  50
  Peter  211
GERADRIN, Charles  61
GERBO, Paul  218
GERIDAN, Jacques  172
  Peter N.  173
GERMAIN, Andre  88
  Paul  208
GEROME, Horace R.  195
GEROUT, ...  32
GERVAIS, see Jervais  21
  ...  48
  Charles  16
  Joseph  208
  Louis  22, 71
GERVAISE, Louis  33
GERVAISSE, see Gervais  22
GETTY, Samuel  141
GLARE, Joseph  82
GIBAUT dit POITEVIN, ...  24
GIBBS, Deborah  183
  Samuel  184
GIBSON, Henry  184
  Julius  218
  Robert T.  127
  Robertson  216
  Roter T.  126
GIDDENS, John  126
GIDDINGS, Almon  185
  Lyman  180
  William  205

GIDEONS, George  193
  Lesstin  193
GIE, Antoine  178
GIEAU, Louis  139
GIFFORD,  84,  188
GIGNIAC, Jean Bt.  43
GIGUERRE, Joseph  175
GILBEAU  43
GILBERT, Asa  196
  Ebenezer  190
  Hannah  202
  Jacob  154
  Joseph  181
  Levi  222
  Noah  113, 158
  Samuel  212
  William T.  211
GILDARD, Thomas  153
GILDERD, Thomas  162
GILE, George  190
GILES, George  141
  John  89
GILHAM, William  219
GILKEY, Justice  163
  Justies  155
GILL, James  196
GILLET, Jason  202
  Joseph  202
  Linus  200
GILLETT, Reynold  172
  Shadrach  173
GILLIS, Daniel  210
GILLMORE, Asa  189
GILMAN, Mary  109
GILMORE, John  174
GINEAU, Alexis  143
GINGRASS, Antoine  214
GINNEY, Liman T.  192
GIRARD, Catherine  124
  Charles  33, 111
  Chas  157
  Theoiste (...)  111
GIRARDIN, ... (...)  84
  Apohlonia  130
  Archange (Latourneau)  101
  Augustin  208
  Charles  61
  Chs Fs  76
  Florence  113
  J.  88
  James  84, 101
  Moyse  208
GIREUX, Joachim  178
GIRFFARD, Pierre  90
GITTWOOD, Charles  214
GLACKEN, Wm.  76
GLADUE, Charles  173
GLASS, Joseph  146
  Robert  84
GLAZIER, Daniel  188
GLEASON, Luther  211

GLOVER, Benjamin 218
GOBEIL, see Gobeye 88
... (...)
  Baptiste 62,
  Charles 62,
  Francis
  Francois 62
  Louise 103
  Madeleine 84
GOBEILLE, Charles 104
  Francois 105
  J. Bte 76
  Jean 104
  Jean Francois 105
  Louise (Gagnier) 105
  Rose (Fortier) 105
  Sarah (Lagore) 104
GOBEYE, Charles 88
  Fran. 76
  Francois 88
  Frs. 76
  Joseph 76
GOBIELLE, Joseph 42
GODDARD, Josiah 171
  William 210
GODEFRON, Jac. 30
GODEFROY, see Godfroy 16
  Jacques 20, 32
GODET, Ejan Baptiste 14, 23
  Jean Baptiste, see Gaudet 16
  Marguerite 6
  Marie 140
  Marie Godet 137
  Paul 12
  Rene 141
  Susanne 141
GODET-MARENTETTE, Genevive 109
GODFREY, Peter 160
GODFROIS, Jacques 63
GODFROY, see St. George 17
  ... 84
  Androw 215
  Andrus 215
  Angelique 140
  Ann 109
  Bte 63
  Catherine (Couture) 109
  Corbush 64
  Elizabeth (May) 109, 138
  G. 154
  Gabl. 64
  Gabriel 76, 80, 81, 89, 84, 109, 138, 155, 157, 160, 161
  Jacques 16, 56
  James J. 174
  Peter 154
  Rose (St. Cosme) 109
  Robert 42

GODFROY, Suzanne 102
GODFROY dit ST. GEORGE, Francois 17, 21
GODIN, Julien 67
GODON, see Godin 67
GODREAU, Abraham 77
  Bonadventure 77
GOFF, John
  Rusell 192
  Stilman 190
  Timothy B. 190
  Willard 190
GOIN, Claude 30
GOOD, Thomas 219
GOODALE, Daniel 158
  Elijah 91, 158
  Jno. 124
GOODALL 184
  Axy (Picket) 114
  Daniel 113
  Elijah 113, 114
  Susanne (Baron) 113
GOODDELL, Jonas 166
GOODELL, Achsah 166
  Archey 156
  Daniel 114, 156
  Jonas 156
  Jonathan 203
  Nathan 210
GOODENOW, Frederick 201
  Peter 201
GOODFELLOW, Walter 55
GOODING, Gideon 153
GOODRICH, Alanson 187
  Chester 187
  Elizer 187
  Horrace 189
  Ira 189
  Joseph 178
  Thomas 189
  Zenas 187
GOODRIDGE, Chauncey S. 200
GOODSPEED, David 203
  Shubael 203
GOODWIN, Aaron B. 202
  Isaac 165
  Richard 112, 139, 150, 158, 196
  William R. 196
GOOLEY, Joseph 104, 208
  Lucy (Lane) 140
GONDEAU, Cahtrine (Langlois) 144
  Elizabeth (Fontaine) 144
  Francis 144
GONDON, see Gondeau 144
  Julien 144
GORDON, Amos 153, 162
  Charles 126
  George 125
  Robert 181

GORISKE, John 126
GORHAM, David B. 120
GORISKY, see Goriske 126
GORMAN, Adeline 211
  John 200
  Madeleine (Laplante) 120
GORTON, Daniel 197
  Job 197
  Samuel 201
  Silas W. 201
  William 120
GOTHIER, Francis 214
  J. B. 214
  Jas. 213
GOTT, Nathaniel 197
GOUEN, see Gouin 20
  ... 21
GOUIE, John Bapt. 116
  Robert 60, 84
GOUIN 36
  ... 24
  C. N. 90
  Charles 41, 54, 69, 88, 84, 111, 116, 137, 151, 165, 167
  Charles Francois 111
  Charles N. 151
  Chs. 79
  Chs. N. 79
  Claire 111
  Claude 111
  Claude Jean 20
  Claude Jean Thomas 16, 32
  Elizabeth (Rivard) 116
  Elizabeth Labadie 111
  Eulalie 116
  Francis 139
  Francois 54, 79
  Frans 69
  Joseph 116
  Joseph Nicolas 116
  Leon 76, 175
  Marie 137
  Monique 139
  Nicholas 54, 88
  Nicolas 69, 79
  Piere 164
  Pierre 116
  Pierre N. 151
  Robert 76
GOULAIS, Louis 71
GOULD Adolphas 182
  Benjamin 194
  Jeams 182
  John 179
GOULET, ... 33
  Angelique 130
  Louis 82, 130, 165
GOULETTE, A. 52
  Alexis 191
  Antoine 40

COULETTE, Louis 151
GOUR, Christopher 161
COUTRIE, Nicholas 171
GOUYOU, Jean Baptiste 14
GOUYOU dit LAGARDE, Jean
    Baptiste 12
GOVEAU, William 44
GOYAU, see Grau 37
    Bte. 17
    G. 32
    Gme 37
    Jean 17
    Vital 37
    Vitel 32
GOYEAU, G., see Guillaume 21
    Guillaume 33
    Guillhaume 52
    Louis 51
    Teresa 142
    Vital 33
    William 142
GOYOU dit LaDOUCEUR, Gillaume 33
GOYOU dit LAGARDE 21
    Jean Baptiste 21

GRADY, Francis 213
GRAHAM, Alexander 185
    John 185
    John 122, 208
    Lucy (Garlick) 125
    William 125
GRANGER, Sarah 102
GRANT, A. 90
    Alex. 79
    Alexander 54, 120, 170
    Charles 180
    Christopher 204
    John 150, 161
    John A. 120, 160
    Judith (Campau) 120
    Orante 196
GRASON, Daniel 167
GRATIOT, Henry 218
    John P. 218
    Paul M. 216
GRAU, Gme, see Goyau 37
GRAVEL 36
GRAVELLE, Louis 146, 212
GRAVERADT, Henry G. 208
GRAVERAET, Henry G. 123
GRAVES, Lyman 197
    Mathias 192
GRAVITTE, Louis 146
GRAY, Eli 202
    Elliot 172
    Frances 82
    Isaac 206
    Joseph 189
    Seymour 182
    Waterbury 178

GREAVES/GIEAU, Joseph 139
GREELEY, ... 84
    Aaron 88
GREEN, Almon 120
    Benjamin 90, 154
    Champlin 183
    Emerson 216
    Fones 177
    George 201
    Harvey 201
    Holly 210
    Hope 183
    Johnson 185
    Joseph 154, 162, 186
    Lazarus 192
    Lealand 179
    Roswell 194
    Thomas K. 206
    Wardwell 179
    Wm. R. 214
GREENE, J. 106
GREENWOOD, Antoine 170
    Joseph 218
GREFARD, Anne 103
GREFFARD, Antoine, see Grifor, Antoine 133
    Cecilia 115
    Laurence 79, 133
    Louis 116, 130
    Mary Ann 130
    Susanne 116
GREGG, Hugh 189
    John 189
GREGNON, Amable 219
GREGOIRE, Alexis 123, 209
    Josette (Paul) 123
GREGORY, Jesse 184
    Michael 174
    William S. 165
GREMARE, P. 124
GRENARDS, Lewis 212
GRENIER, Pierre 124
GRENON 36
    Louis 80
    Touissant 22, 33
GRENONS, Louis 67
GRENOUILLE, ... 32
GRETTARD, Margaret 116
GRETZLER, Henry 210
GREVERAT 41
    Gerret 54
GREY, Robert W. 222
GRIDLEY, Hezekiah 162
GRIEVES, Lewis 187
GRIFARD, Francois 160
    Laurant 79
    Louis 79, 159
    Laurich 72
GRIFFARD, Antoine 190
    Cecilia (Renaud) 120
    Elizabeth (Pominville) 116

GRIFFARD, Francis 120, 163
    Francois 152
    Jane (Cardinal) 116
    John 171
    L. 36
    Laurent 90
    Laurt 72
    Louis 70, 90, 116, 164, 165
    Louis (Dupray) 116
    Margaret (Casse-St. Aubin) 116
    Pierre 71, 116, 159
    Teresa Yax 116
GRIFFARRE, Dominique 151
    Louis 150
    Laurent 48, 52
    Louis 48, 53
GRIFFEN, Cyrus 125
    Jemima 141
    John 126
    Samuel 212
GRIFFIN, Michael 209
    Yoakley 207
GRIFFING, Joseph L. 187
GRIFFIS, William 207
GRIFFITH, William 80
GRIFFORD, Charles 164
    Peter 164
GRIFOR, Antoine 133
    Teresa (Freton) 133
GRIGNON 211
    Amable 211, 212
    Augustine 146
    Augustus 211
    Jean B. 211
    Lewis 92
    Louis 145
    Paul 211
    Perish 211
    Piere 145
    Pierre, Jr. 145
GRIGUIRE, Alexis 123
GRIMAR, Josh 69
GRIMARD, see Grimaure 40
    see Moran dit Grimard 21
    Charles 32, 52
GRIMAURE, see Grimard 40
    Charles 40
GRIMBY, Robert 183
GRIMOUR, Joseph 214
GRINELL, Daniel 181
GRISWOLD, Clark 155, 162
    Harvy 172
    Jerrard 165
    John 153
    John C. 162
    Marion 136
    Reuben 167
    Stanley 84
    Thadeus 182
    Thomas 189

GROESBECK, Sarah 116
   William 54, 63, 116
GRONDIN, Louis 208
GROSBECK, ... 41
   Peter 185
   William 90
GROSSBECK, Lewis 160
GROSSBICK, Charles 163
   Louis 163
GOVENOR, George H. 146
GRUBB, Andrew 207
GRUNNING, Samuel B. 195
GUARD, Jonathan 207
   Joseph 207
GUERTIN, Marie 6
GUI, Alexis 80
GUIE, Angelique (Bourdeau) 144
   Antoine 140, 144
   Mary (Poulin) 140
GUIGNARD, Joseph 33
GUIGNARD dit St. ETIENNE,
   Joseph 33
   Pierre 22
GUIGNIER-BOURGUIGON,
   Theotiste 109
GUILE, David 179
GUILFORD, Erastus 205
GUILLAUME, see Goyeau 21
   ... 121
   Bernard 68
GUILLEBAU, Jean 55
GUILLET, Jean Baptiste 33
   Peter 210
GUILLET dit TOURANGEAU, Jean
   Baptiste 33
GUILLIM, William 217
GUILLOT, John Bt. 121
GUNN, Alanson 198
   Asa 198
   Carver 110, 157
   John 211
GUNNING, James 179
GUOIN, Charles 137
   Colette 110
   Esther (Tremblay) 137
   Leon 137
   Nicolas 110
GUREN, Byram 163
GURNO, Lewis 120
GURNON, Louis 120
GUTHRIE, Wm. 214
GUTHRY, Thomas 208
GUY, see Guie 144
   Anthony 136
   Antoine Frs. 68
   Francis 144
   Franois 70
   John 214
   Mary 136
GUYARD, Robert P. 217
GUYON, John B. 218

GUYON DES PRES, Joseph 7
   Madeleine (Petit-Boismorel) 7
GWYNNE, Alice Ann (Claypool) 105
   David 105

HA(blurred), Jonothan 188
HABADY, Felix 130
HABARE, Antoine 160
HADEN, John 167
   Samuel 193
   Silas 193
   Zebulon 193
HADSELL, Asa B. 181
HAGARTY, see Hogarty 211
HAGECUM, Asa 196
HAGERMAN, Tucius 120
   Tunis 120
HAINES, Aron 194
   John 63
HAIRE, Rufus 163
HALDEMAN, Jesse 219
HALE, James 174
   John 170
   Michael 170
   Seneca 188
   Stephen G. 217
   William 217
HALEY, John 170
HALIBUT, Lydia 84
HALL, Miss... 84
   Miss ... (colored) 86
   ... (...) 85
   ... (...) (colored) 86
   Anson 188
   George 177, 204
   Hubbard 194
   Jacob 189
   James 182, 196
   Jonothan 188
   Knowles 170
   Osha 182
   Rowland 193
   Rufus 194
   Samuel 76, 150
   Shelemeth S. 171
   Thomas 183, 204
   William 182, 194
   Willard 198
HALLET, Moses 217
HALPIN, Timothy 195
HALSEY, Henry 133
   Silas 190
HALT, Jean 121
HAMBLETON, Reuben 196
HAMBLIN, Ezra 193
   Josiah 193
HAMELIN, Augustin 208
HAMILTON, Jacob 216
   James 216
   Jameson 218
   John 183

HAMILTON, Mary Louise 114
   Patrick 190
   William S. 217
HAMLIN, John F. 184
HAMMEL, Jacob 162
HAMMON, James 170
   Joseph 158, 166
HAMMOND, Joseph 113, 150
HAMTRAMCK, (Col.) ... 78
HANCHET, Joseph 118, 205
   Nancy 117
HANCHETT, Jos. 160
   Joseph 153
HANCOCK, Jas. 146
HANDFORD, Alexander 194
HANDS, William 60
HANDSCOM, George 192
HANDY, John 180
   T. 214
HANELY, Thomas G. 219
HANFORD, Joseph 85
HANKLEDRAK, George P. 195
HANKS, ... (...) 85
HANLEY, James 217
   ?Hawley, Emmond 172
HANNAH (colored) 86
HANNSON, Marcus B. 198
HANON, John 195
HANSON, David M. 205
HARDIN, Isaac 204
HARDING, Samuel W. 182
HARDWICK, Moses 211
HARDY, David 198
   Harry 198
   Jacob 198
   Joseph 219
HARFORD, William 200
HARINGTON, Jeremiah 196
HARISEN, Ephraim 205
HARKLEY, David 64
   Jonathan 64, 65
HARLAN, Elizabeth Taft 92
HARMON, David 183, 185
   Ira 185
HARNER, James 172
HARPER, Benjamin 165
   David 165
   Thomas 153
   Van Rensellear 184
   William 165
HARRINGTON, Elisha 129
   Henry 180
   Joseph 198
   Susanne (Conner) 129
   Washington 201
HARRINTON, Elisha 190
HARRIS, ... 102
   Alex 82
   Elenor 173
   Elisha 187
   Ezekiel 146
   Henry 166

HARRIS, Herman 187
  Hiram O. C. 180
  Jacob 193
  John 162
  Joseph 187
  Robert 150
  Robert P. 166
  Saville 186
  William 205
HARRISON, Almon 190
  Bazzle 205
  Charles 153, 164
  George 76
  Hannah (...) 117
  Jacob 210
  Jesse M. 217
  John 188
  Joseph 76, 198
  Leon G. 153
  Leonard 164
  Marenus 118, 160
  Marrinus 153
  Merenus 164
  Nathan 205
  Solomon 190
HARRISSON, Frederick 206
HARROW, ... (...) 132
  Alexander 132
HARRY (colored) 86
HARSEN, Jacob 40, 52
HART, Christopher 110, 157
  Horace 175
  Thomas D. 210
  William 170
HARTFORD, Sarah 194
HARTMAN, Solomon 204
HARTON, Henry 120
HARTOUR, Elisha 217
HARTSHORN, Alfred 113
  Elijah 113, 158
  Pierson 113
HARTSOUGH, Christopher 196
HARTWELL, Hiram 181
HARYER/HARVEY, Joseph 76
HARVEY, ... (...) 85
  John 76, 88, 85
  Luther 137, 174
HASCALL, Charles C. 185
HASIN, Paul W. 165
HASKIN, Eleanor 112, 158
  Henry 112
HASKINS, Asel 190
  Horatio 190
  Laucious 190
HASLE, Stephen 173
HASTARETT, Christopher 150
HASTINGS, E. P. 167
  Horatio N. 210
  Zina H. 164
HATCH, ... (...) 85
  Harriet (Mack) 103

HATCH, Luther 202
  Rufus 85, 103
HATHAWAY, Abner 131
  Ann 131
  David 165
  Nathaniel B. 187
HATHORN, Richard 187
HATSID, Hiram 185
HATT, William 200
HATTIN, William 151
HATTON, William 165
HATWELL, Robert 219
HAUGHTON, John 60
HAWKINS, Amy 109
  Hannah 201
HAWKS, Cephas 200
  Joseph 186, 219
HAWLEY, see Hanley 172
  Aaron 217
HAWOOD, Jasper 189
HAWTHORN, James 218
HAY, ... (...) 42
HAYDIN, John 152
HAYES, James 217
  John 164
  John C. 212
  Joseph 190
HAYNES, Nathan 207
HAYS, Joseph 132
HAYWARD, Richard 177
  Robert G. 177
  Samuel 195
HAZARD, James 139
  Stanton 179
  William 152
HAZEL, Stephen 110
HAZEN, William 155
HAZZARD, William 205
HAZZEL, Stephen 157
HEACOCK, Albert K. 173
  Samuel C. 175
HEACOCKS, Adna 91
HEAD, Joseph 192
HEALD, Arla 204
HEATH, Asahel 181
  Isaac 182
  Sarah 133
HEBERT, Augustin 218
  Joseph 218
  Nicholas 218
HEIMER, Adam 217
HELAIRE, Alexr 40
HELEY, Patrick 172
HEMBROW, John 110
HEMINGER, Amsa 195
HEMMINGWAY, Needham 185
HEMPLE, Adam 126
HEMPSTEAD, Moses 192
HENDERSON, David 103
  George 162
  Robert 171

HENDREE, John 172
HENDRICKS, Peter 161
HENLEY, John 173
HENRY, Bird 85
  James 76, 85
  John 184
  John Joseph 104
  Maria 114
  Marvin 186
  Robert 216
  Stephen C. 104
HENSZA, Erastus 161
HENTON, Thomas 172
HENTZLMAN, P. 196
HENWARD, ... 61
HERBINNE, Catherine 119
HERINGTON, George 162
HERON, David 203
HERRICK, Nathan 180
HERRING, Nathan 126
HETICK, George 110
  Margaret 110
HEURTEBIZE, Felicite (Javillon) 48
  Pierre 48
HEVELAND, Charles 190
HEWETT, Walter B. 170
HEWLINGS, William 218
HEYDORN, Daniel 146
HEYL, Catherine 129, 130
HIBBERTS, Trueman 219
HICHCOCK, Solomon 204
HICK, Hannah (...) 156
HICKCOX, Joseph 153
  Lydia 167
  William , 162
HICKEN, Joseph 160
HICKLAND, Robert 217
HICKLEY, Sarah 117
HICKOCK, Adna 160
  Joseph 160
  Jno. 160
HICKLAND, Moses 219
HICKMAN, Jacob 206
  Peter 206
HICKS, Amos 200
  Francis 150, 166
  George 89, 154
  Hannah 164
  Hannah (...) 109
  Jesse 89, 109
HICOCK, Adna 119
  James 119
  Johnathan 119
  Joseph -18
  Polly (Andress) William 119
  Ruth (Orvis) 119
HIDE, John 154, 161
HIGBY, Eli 200
  Mindwell 112
HIGGINS, C. 129

HIGGINS, Francis  76, 210
HIGHTON, Richard  217
HILBERT, Stephen  152
HILES, Ansel  179
    John  179
HILHOUSE, John  152
HILL, Aphius  188
    David  194
    Dorothea (Seck)  131
    Elizabeth (Robinson)  131
    Jacob  73, 82, 131
    Jane  131
    Moses J.  152
    Nancy  131
    Phineas  184
    Stephen  164
    William  131, 156, 194
HILLICH, High  189
HILLMAN, Daniel  77
HILTON, Roswell  187
    Samuel  185
HINCHMAN, Felix  174, 179
    James W.  172
HINKLEY, A. B.  172
    John  198
    Rodney  206
HINKS, James  194
    James C.  194
HINLEY, John  196
HISCOCK, Alanson  203
    Isaac  203
    James  199
    Levi  199
HITCHCOCK, A. Nelson  187
    John B.  175
HIVON/LIVERNOIS, Joseph  80
HIX, Burden  201
    George  119, 160
HIXON, Daniel  201
HOAGLAND, Abraham  183
HOARD, Edward  192
    Levi  193
    Robert C.  217
HOBBS, Joseph  208
HOBS, James  64
HODGE, Alfred  122
    Amanda (Mallory)  122
    Benjamin  122
    Lorin  122
    Pebe (Baker)  122
    Sarah (Churchill)  122
    Sophia (English)  122
HODGES, Henry W.  219
    Schuyler  186
HODIENNE, Antoine  110
    Elizabeth (Stanbach)  110
HOFFMAN, George  85
    Henry B.  209
    Maria C. (Audrain)  117
    Nicholas  218
HOFMASTER, Nicholas  195

HOGAN, Caroline  125
    Mary  125, 208
HOGARTHY/HAGARTY, John  211
HOISINGTON, Earl D.  155
HOIT, Stephen  205
HOKINS, Obery  151
HOLBROOK, Benijah  161
    S. A.  189
HOLCOMB, Alanson R.  199
    Noah  202
HOLCRAFT, Adam  214
HOLDING, Theodore G.  162
HOLDR?, Layth  70
HOLIDAY, John  214
HOLLAND, Philanda  172
HOLLENBACK, Samuel S.  210
HOLLENBECK, David  187
HOLLEY, John  214
HOLLISTER, John B.  193
HOLMAN, Frederick  219
HOLMES, David  209
    Isaac C.  202
    John  176
    Roland R.  219
    Rosecrance  163
    Samuel  204
HOLROCK, Peter  145
HOMER, James  125
HOMIER, Toussaint  209
HONSIN, William  194
HOOD, John  216
HOOKER, Cyprian S.  163
HOPKINS, Hiram  194
    Horace  186
    Leonard  160
    Richard  204
    Sherman  184
    Socrates  182
    Tacy L. (...)  195
HOPSON, William  217
HORAN, Patrick  217
HORE, Thomas  219
HORN, Enoch  205
HORNDORF, John  210
HORNELL, George  181
HORNER, ... (...)  85
    Archibald  85
    Benjamin A.  180
HORSAN, Francis  194
HORSON, Jacob  194
HORTON, Benjamin  185
    Caleb  176
    John  184
    Samuel  176
HOSFORD, Joseph  85
HOSMER, Artemas  158
    Artemus  113, 150, 163
    Artimus  150
    Ephraim  113
    Mary (Dunn)  113
    Mercy (...)  113
    Sally (Lacy)  113

HOTCHKILL, Calvin  187
HOTTENSTEIN, Phillip  189
HOUDE, Genevieve  102
HOUGH, Ira M.  156
HOUGHTALING, Garret  165
HOULD/HOULL, Joseph  211
HOULE, Amos  158
HOULL, Hould  211
HOULTON, Sam'l  213
HOUSE, Jer.  106
HOUSTON, William  165
HOUZER, Jcob  219
HOVEY, Horace  185
HOVY, Sewel  194
HOW, Amos  155
HOWARD, Aron  194
HOWARD, Charles  105, 172
    Henry  170
    Horatio H.  181
    Hugh  76
    John  170, 202
    Ruth (...)  105
    Warren  105
HOWE, Amos  113, 205
    Anna (...)  113
    Horatio  196
    Isaac  196
    Orson  202
HOWELL, Anson  188
    James  63
    William  180
HOWL, Job  194
    Peter  213
HOXIE, Job  192
HOXSIE, Job  129
HOY, William H.  189
HUBBARD, Betsey (...)  119
    Daniel W.  211
    Diadate  183
    Diodate  104
    Edward  104
    Eli  136, 176
    George  113, 158
    Giles  189
    Letetia  196
    Manoah  119, 150
    Manoah, see Noah  137
    Monoah  160
    Noah  137
    Sarah (Mooney)  104
HUBBARDS, Manoah  160
HUBBEL, Malon  187
    Samuel  187
HUBER dit LACROIX, Jacques  7
HUBERT, ...  56
    Jacques  6, 7, 209
    Marguerite (Godet)  6
    Romania (Berthelet de Veau)  6

HUBERT dit LACROIX, Jacques  6
    Romania (Berthelet de Veau)  6

HUDSON, ... (...) 85
  Henry  88, 85, 151, 160
  John  198, 206
  John S.  209
  William  164
HUGG, David  197
  George  93
  Ira M.  165
  William  206
HUFFMAN, Joshua  126
HUGG, ...  127
  John  126
HUISINGTON, Royal  161
HULBERT, Isaiah  205
  John  213
  W. C.  122
HULL, (Gen.) ...  138
  Abigail  85
  Israel  62
  Levi J.  197
  R.  214
HULSE, Isaac  206
HUMINWAY, Josiah  190
HUMPHREY, Levi P.  174
HUNAUT, Gabl  64
HUNGERFORD, Samuel  179
HUNOT, Gabriel  55
HUNT, Ann (Mackintosh)  103
  Henry J.  88, 103
  Israel  76, 85
  Jeremiah  183, 185
  John  120, 152
  Levi  183
  Martha (Larned)  102
  S. W.  146
  Sarah G.  106
  Seymour  183
  Thomas  103
  Timothy  202
  William  198, 205
  William B.  164
HUNTER, Abbe  102
  Daniel  181
  Elisha  106, 186
  James J.  180
  John W.  106, 183
  Joseph B.  216
  Rufus  214
  William  205
HUNTLEY, Enoch  129
HUNTLY, Asa  192
HURD, Alanson M.  170
  David  199
  Ebenezer  102, 173
  George  201
  Hiram  211
  William  183
HURLBERT, William  199
HURT, Josh  64
  Wm.  64, 78
HURTEBIZE, Joseph  48

Michigan Censuses 1710-1830

HURTEBIZE, Pieriche  48
HUS-COURNOYER, Joseph  142
HUSTON, Alexander  206
HUTCHINSON, Henry  183
HUTTELSTONE, ...  112
HUXFORD, Lucy  200
HUYCH, John  188
HUYET, see Champagne  17
  Pierre  32
HUYET dit CHAMPAGNE, Pierre
  17, 23, 32
HUYET-CHAMPAGNE, see Champain
  73
  Archange  142
  Francois  111
  Monique  129
  Pierre  111
  Regina Christina  132
HYACINTE, Joseph  77
HYCAINTHE, see Reaume  22
HYDE, Elisha  216
  John  111, 158, 162
  Milton  185
HYLER, Hamson  213
HYMAN, Henry  76
HYVERNOIS, see Livernois  43
  Etienne  43, 55

INGERSOL, Delia  120
  Riley  175
INGERSOLL, Erastus  179
  Thomas  180
INGRAIM, Isaac  213
INGRAM, John  211
ININOIS, Josh  67
INNIS, Robert  61
INSLY, John  205
IOURO, Joco  131
IRISH, Joseph M.  180
  Rial  180
  Thomas  180
IRVINE, Thomas W.  210
IRWIN, Alexander J.  210
  Hannah (Rees)  103
  Robert  81, 103, 145, 210
  Samuel  210
ISBEL, James  175
IVAN, Joseph  177
IVES, Amasa  182
  William  182

JACK (negro)  88
JACKS, Joseph L.  207
JACKSON, Anson  188
  Charles  172
  Enos  174
  Jacob  188
  James  202
  John  81
  Joseph  184
  William  188, 196

JACOB, ...  66
  Angelique  140
  Catherine  143
  Estne  36
  Etiene  66
  Etienne  22, 33, 43, 66, 80,
    140, 143
  Ettienne  50
  Genevieve  139
  Jacques  80
  Jean  66, 80, 143
  John  139, 177
  Joseph  80, 143, 177
  Lewis  177
  Louis  143, 177
  Louisa  142
  Margaret (Bernard-Lajoie)
    143
  Martha (Pouget)  143
  Peter  77
  Pierre  140, 143
  Simon  80
JACOBS, Andrew  176
  David M.  174
  James  197
  John  145
JACOX, Abijah  166
  Eliza  132
  James  156
  Linus  181
JACQUES  123
  And.  31
  Andre  33
  Isaac  211
JADOST, see Jadot  22
JODOT, ...  31
  Louis  22, 32, 33
JAGOB, Ant.  31
JAICOX, see Jacox
  James  156
  Isiah  156
JAMES, Henry  89
  Horatio  195
  Mason R.  182
  Thomas  196
  Thomas P.  123
JAMESON, Louis T.  213
JANDRONS, Louis  63
  Simon  63
JANESS, ... (...)  44
JANESSE, Francois  51
JANIS  37
  Francois Nicolas  16, 33
  Nicolas  22
JANISSE, see Janis  16
JANNISSE, see Janis, Nicholas
  22
JANOT, Louis  30
JANSON-LaPALME, Charles  33
JANUARY, Seymour  213
JARAIN, Josh  72

JARROT, Francis 219
JARVAIS, Pierre 215
JARVIS, Philip 133
  Warren 180
JASSAINT, Charles 215
JASSMIN, Touissant 79
JAUNISSE, ... 32
JAVERAIS dit LADEROUTE,
    Pierre 22
JAVILLON, Felicite 48
JAYNE, William 202
JEAN, Robert 53
JEANDRON, Michael 208
JEBEAU, Stephen Gibaut 23
JEFAY, ... 24
JEFFERS, John A. 136
  Regina (Boemier) 136
  Susanne (Robertson) 136
JEFFRIES, Philander M. 174
JENAW, Catherine (...) 195
JENETTE, see Janett 17
  see LeTourneau 17
JENKINS, Baldwin 207
  Thomas 217
JENKS, Morris 182
  Orin 183
  Prudence 183
JENNINGS, Elias 202
  Ira 183
JERAUME, ... 62
JEROME, Archange 139
  J. Bte 80, 139
  Jean Bte 82
  John Bte 141
  Mary (Delienes-Belanger)
    141
JERSY(?), Henry 193
JERVAIS, ... 24
  Amable 211
JERVOIS, Louis 32
JESSAMINE, Touissant 116, 159
  Tousant 116
JEWEL, Elias 164
  Edmund 185
  Eleazer 186
  Geo. W. 203
  George 155
  Thomas 210
JEWITT, George 167
JINETICE/JEUNESSE, John 105
JIRAIX, see Javerais 22
JIVRAY, Jas. 215
JOBBIN, Josh 67
JOBIN, ... (...) 178
  Joseph 80, 138
  Louis 138
  Magdeleine 6
  Margaret (Levry-Martin) 138
JOCELIN, Charles 197
JOERLICO?. ... 23
JOHN, Fabien 191

JOHN, Joseph 150, 189
  Moses 191
JOHNDRON, Alexander 114
  Mary Louise (Hamilton) 114
JOHNS, Candis (...) 105
  Hiram 119, 160
  Jeanne (Cissne) 119
  Thomas 104, 153, 180
JOHNSON, Abbe (Hunter) 102
  Abigail 117
  Abner 155, 162
  Agathe (...) 136
  Charles 186
  David 102, 186
  Deborah 102
  Dudley 213
  Elijah 188
  Elizabeth (Disbrow) 136
  Esau 217
  George 88, 118, 160
  George M. 153, 161
  Horace 187
  James 126, 155, 166
  James G. 184
  John 147, 206
  John W. 146
  Joseph 179
  Joshua 125
  Lathrop 206
  Lemuel 206
  Lewis B. 184
  Lewis S. 210
  Nathan 165
  Oliver 136, 173
  Penfield 179
  Prime 111, 158, 167
  Robert 136
  Royal 102
  Samuel D. 172
  Sarah (Blake) 136
  Stewart 172
  Suzanne 109
  Thomas 186
  Whiting 218
  Willard 183
  William 129, 162, 213
JOHNSTON, Ephraim 213
  George 145, 210, 214
  Susan 214
  William C. 105
JOISBAINE, Antoine 215
JOLIBOIS, Margaret 115
JOLIEAU, Etienne 121
JOLLET, Antoinette (Bareillos-
    Lajoie) 102
  Louis 102
  Luke, see Louis 102
JOLLIE, Louis 146
JOLY, Pierre 88
JOMVINE, Jean B. 211
JONCAIRE, Catherine 110

JONCAIRE, Chabert 77
JONCAIRE-CHABERT, Francois
    110
  Josette (Chobere) 110
JONES, ... (...) 85
  Avery 183
  Barney 181
  Benaniah 187
  Benjamin 52
  Catherine (Annin) 104
  Charles 78, 207
  David 209
  DeGarmo 172
  D'Garmo 104
  Ebenezer 153, 165
  Ephraim
  Genevieve (Cosme) 140
  George 206
  George W. 219
  Ignace 191
  Israel/Isaac 85
  J. Bte 78
  John 182
  John M. 205
  Jonathan 207
  Levi 202
  Northrup 183
  Peter 188
  R. H. 88
  Robert 140
  Samuel 126
  Seth 166
  Richard 152
  Thomas 81
  Thomas S. 140
  William 85
  William W. 175
JONEVINE, Joseph 215
JONS, Bte 65
  Benjamin 65
  Frans 64
JOODERAN, Alexander 159
JORDAN, Joseph 145
  Thomas 76
JOREGNY, ... 21
JOSLIN, Abigail 127
  Abigail (Wilder) 127
  John 202
  Richard 153, 155
  Samuel 127
JOSTLING, Richard 165
JOUBERT, Jean Baptiste 23
JOURDAIN, Andre 80
  Joseph 211
JOURDAIN dit LaBROSSE, Domini-
    que, see LaBoise 22
JOURDAN, Pierre 178
  Thomas 219
JOVIN, Battes 145
JOY, Francis 125
JUBAIS, see Joubert 23

JUBENVIL, Phleben/Fabian 170
JUBENVILL, Antoine 171
　John B. 173
JUBENVILLE, Antoine 82
　Bte 88
JUDD, Daniel S. 186
JUDSON, Alfred 181
　Lewis 204
JUILLET dit MONTREUIL, Antoine 22
JUNETTE, Monsieur ... 133
JUSTICE, John 170
　William 206
JUTRAT, Catherine (L'Archeveque) 118
　Jean 48

KADIAN, Amiable 214
KARR, James 203
KAVENAUGH, Lawrence 206
KAY, Eleasur 172
　Hugh W. 185
KEAN, Robert 62
KEARSLEY, Jonathan 110, 171
　Margaret (Hetick) 110
KEATER, Peter 162
KEEHE, John 215
KEELER, Colman J. 136, 176
　Samuel F. 176
KEENE, William 85
KEENEY, Jonathan 170
　Salmon 177
KEHORE, Morgan 216
KEITH, Daniel 214
　Jane 119
　Jane (Dick) 119
　John 160
　William 106, 119, 150, 166
KELLAR, Peter 209
KELLER, Joseph 153, 161
KELLEY, Charles 187
　Daniel 187
KELLOG, John C. 217
KELLOGG, Benjamin 202
　Ezekiel 186
　Ira 156
KELLY, Elisha 165
　Hannah 160
　Hugh 101
　John 205
　Wm. 76
KELOGG, Charles H. 203
KELSEY, Archange (Navarre) 137
　Reuben 137
KELSO, Henry B. 211
KEMP, Jacob H. 91
　James 184
KENDALL, James 217
KENDRICK, Ann 125
KENNEDAY, Ambrose 219

KENNEDAY, Guyon 216
KENNEDY, John 183
KENNEY, Horace 205
KENT, Walker 179
KENWICH, Michael 216
KENZIE, Jacob 207
　John 207
KERBY, John 150, 164
KERCHEVAL, Benjamin B. 172
KERLEY, Michael 170
KESLER, John 193
KETCHUM, Jacob 189
KETTREDGE, Ebenezer 194
KEYES, John F. 182
KEYS, Laben 204
KICKSON, John 141
　Mary 141
　Sarah (Peck) 141
KID, David 126
　Joseph 173
KIDD, William R. 186
KIDDER, Horace 188
KIDZIE, Margret 190
KIEFER, Henry 126
　Mary (Malone) 126
KIES, Alpheus 189
KILBOURN, Abr. 160
　Abraham 118
　Anthony 117
　Joseph 117, 174
　Mehetable (...) 118
　Mehitabel 160
KILE, James 161
KILROY, John W. 185
KIMBALL, Chester 210
KIMBLE, Eben 193
KIMMELL, Henry 203
KING, Abigail 117
　Anthony 192
　Asel 194
　Benjamin 218
　John 137
　John W. 210
　Jonathan P. 209, 210
　Joseph 88
　Maria 172
　Mary 111, 157
KINGSLEY, Charles 200
　Esther 138
　James 198
　Joseph 153, 161
　Lucinda 136
　Salmon 153
KINNEY, John 85
　Lewis 216
　Marines 201
　Peter 218
KINSEY, George W. 126
KINSHALLOW, R. 214
KINZIE, John H. 211
KIRBY, Alice (...) 116

KIRBY, Ephraim 106
　Harriet 106
　John 90, 116, 120, 159
　Jno. 79
KIRCHERVILES, Benj. B. 154
KIRGAN/McKIRGAN?, John W. 54
KIRK, Jonathan 205
　William 208
KIRKENDALL, Robert 218
KIRKPATRICK, Francis 219
　James H. 216
　Richard H. 216
KITTRIDGE, Benjamin 192
　Ebenezar 132
　William 197
KITTSON, John 209
　Norman W. 209
KLINEDOB, George 198
KLINGER, Peter 203
KNAGS, George 81
　Rachell 81
KNAGGS, ... (...) 176
　... (Schley) 109
　Alexis 176
　Catherine (Douget) 141
　Catherine Visger 109
　Elizabeth 136
　George 44, 51, 85, 109, 136, 141, 177
　James 141, 154, 177
　James W. 164
　Jemima (Griffen) 141
　John 154, 164
　Josette (Labadie) 109
　Margaret 160
　Peter W. 109, 155, 157, 160
　Rachel 82
　Rachel (Schley) 136, 141
　Thomas 141
　Whitmore 109, 151, 157
　William 93
　Witmore 76
　Wittemor 66
　Wm. 66, 89
KNAP, Benona 194
　James 152
KNAPP, ... (...) 132
　Abner 187
　Bela 172, 195
　Benj. 112, 158
　Benjamin 112, 167
　Daniel 112
　Isaac 112
　James 112
　John 112, 158
　Katherine (...) 112
　Lodowick 174
　Simon 174
　Thomas 152
　Thomas L. 162
　Walter 112

KNIGHT, Ebenezer 184
   Elisha 202
   Godfrey 205
   John 207
   Nathan 185
KNOWLTON, Thomas 141, 170
KNOX, 85, 152, 167
   James 217
KNOXON, Thomas 157, 161
KOURNES, Arch. 76
KREMER, John 160
KRISLEY, Jonathan 157
KROMER, John 173
KUNSE, August 170
KYES, Sewel 191
KYLE, David 180
   Hamilton 180
   Terrance 218
   William 185
KYSER, Henry 180
KYSNE, John 205

LABADI, Chs. 78
LABADIE, see Descomps 20, 23
   see Habady 130
   ... 31
   Alexander 156
   Alexis 77, 116, 140, 174, 176
   Antoine 104, 141
   Antoine Louis 33
   Apollonia (Girardin) 130
   Cecile 141
   Chas. 158
   Charles 111
   Eleanor 104
   Elizabeth 116
   Francoise 140
   Josette 109
   Margaret 106, 139
   Mary Ann (Greffard) 130
   Mary Anne (Cicotte) 111
   Medard 178
   Medard, see Medu 144
   Medu 144
   Michel 144
   P. D. 154
   Peter D. 178
   Pierre 76, 77, 1109, 111, 140, 144, 157
   Pierre Louis 33
   Teresa 144
   Teresa (Robert) 144
   Therese (Gaillard-Loinais) 109
LABADIE-BADICHON, Antoine 132
   Victoria 132
LABADY, see Labadie, see Descomps 17
   see Descomps dit Labadie 20
   Alexander 63

LABADY, Alexis 55, 81, 89
   Alexr 64
   Antoine L. 52
   Baptiste 72
   Charles 89
   Chs. 65
   Francis 191
   Louis 48
   Medard 66, 81
   Pierre 42, 55, 56, 63, 91
   Pierre D. 89
   Pierre Descompte 43
LABARDE, Rosalie 128
LABATT, Paul 127
   Philip 128
LABATTE, Francois 212
LABAU, Francis 133
   /Lebeau, Julia 133
LABAY, Charles 124
LABE, Jean Bt. 156
LABEAU, Etienne 141
   Mary Judith (Chauvin) 141
   Rene 141
LaBEDE, Eneas 215
LaBELLAINE, Jos. C. 101
LABELLE, ... 85
   Antoine 91
   J. 215
LABERDY, Alexander 166
   Charles 166
   Mary 166
LABERRY, Piere 164
LABIDULY, Charles 156
LABLA, Joseph 132
   Mary Louis (Pilet) 132
LABLAIN, Peter 166
   Tarrais 166
LABLANCE, Lewis 156
   Peter 156
   Pierre 158
LaBOISE, see Jourdain dit LaBrosse 22
   ... 37
LABONTEE, Louis 66
LABORD, Alexander 210
   John B. 145
LaBORDE, Baptiste 60
   Jean B. 211
LABORN, John 176
LABOUCHE, Peter 123
LABOW, John Bte 166
   Vernick 166
LaBROCE, ... 24
LABROSSE, Dominic 77
   Dominique 44, 55
   Donque 64
   Dque 89
LaBUTE, see Chene dit LaButte 21
   ... 32
   Pierre 44, 51

LABUTTE, see Chene, see La Butte 16
   37
   ... 24, 25
   Pierre 14 , 33
LaCASS, Jean Bt. 175
LaCASSE, Jean Baptiste 32
LaCAUSSE, ... 30
LAC du FLAMBEAU, ... 121, 123, 125
LACELLE, Angelique 109
   Felicity 138
   J. Bte. 138
   James 139, 141
   Mary Anne 141
   Nicolas 33
   Theotiste 139
LACEY, Thomas 217
LACHANCE, Jules 209
LACHAPELLE, Antoine 212
   Antwain 146
LACIE, John Bt. 159
   Jos. 159
LaCORN, see Corneau, see Le Corneau dit Sanssoucy 14
LaCOURCE, see Rivard dit La Coursiere 21
LACOURSE, Augustus 142
   John Bte 143
   Susanne (Deloeil) 143
LACOURSIERE, Jean Bte 52
LACROIS, ... (...) 174
LaCROIX, ... 5
   Archange (Jerome) 139
   Dominique 139, 175
   Hubert 81, 139
   Jacques 6, 7
   Joseph P. 92
   Marguerite (Godet) 6
   Michel 92
   Peter 175
   Romania (Berthelet de Veau) 6
LACY, Elijah 206
   Ephraim 206
   Sally 113
LADAROOT, John 159
LADAROUT, Archange (Cardinal) 117
   John 117
LADD, Ira 211
   Nathaniel 186
LaDEBOUCHE, Louis 213
LADEROOT, Ignas 163
   John 163
   Peter 163
LADEROUT, John Baptist 160
   Peter 160
LADEROUTE 36
   see Javerais 22
   see LaDeroute 21

LADEROUTE, see Seguin 16, 17
  Baptiste 80, 88
  Bte 70
  Cajetan 32, 70
  Francois 12
  G. 30
  Gaelan? 21
  Gaetan 53
  Gajetan 36, 40
  J. 30
  Jos 36
  Joseph 21, 32, 40, 78, 90
  see SEGUIN-LADEROUTE
    Joseph 117
    Monique 117
    Pierre 117
    Teresa 117
LADEROUTTE, Josh 70
LaDONSEUR, Leon 115
LaDOUCEUR, see LaDonseur 115
  ... 48
  Archange (Tremblay) 115
  Guillaume 33
  J. Bte 115
  Joseph 33
  Leon 159
LADUC, Cecilia (Champagne) 142
  Francis 142, 159
  Hicynth 144
  J. Bte 139
  Jeremie 208
  Louis 142
  Louise (Gallard) 139
  Margaret (Trudel) 142
LADUCER, Leon 161
LADUCK, Louis 167
LaDUKE, Cecilia (Descomps-Labadie) 110
  Francis 114
  Louis 110, 157
  Rene 110
  Suzanne (Drouillard) 114
LaDURANTAYE, Marguerite 33
LAFAYETTE, Peter 166
LAFAURET/FORET, Joseph 150
LAFERTE, see Laferty 115
  Charles 150
  Louis 89
  Louis Veziere 77
  Marie 140
LAFERTY, ... (...) 154
  Catherine (Campau) 115
  Catherine (Lafoy) 110
  Joseph 110
  Louis 115
  Pierre 110
LAFEUILLADE, see Davignon 17
  see Davignon dit LaFeuillade 21
LAFFARTY, Pierre 157

LAFFERTY, Catherine 164
  Mary 160
  Peter 156, 166
LAFFONTAINE 36
LAFFONTISEY, Mary 147
LAFITTE, Jas 146
LaFLEUR, see Piquet dit LaFleur 24
  see Poupard 16
  ... 5, 25
  August C. 142
  Augustin 81
  Cha. 32
  Charles 85, 104, 139, 174
  Charles Poupard 33
  Clemence (Maupetit) 6
  Isabelle (Casse) 104
  Marguerite 6
  Mary 141
  Peter 179
  Pierre Rene 6
  Rafle 130
  Raphael 130
  Theotiste (LaForge) 130
LAFLEURE, Andre 81
LAFLURE, Joseph 171
LAFOI, Augustin 76
LAFONTAIGNE, Bernard 41
LAFONTAIN, Gabriel 139
LaFONTAINE, see Dubord 22
  ... 31
  Angelique (Ptolome) 7
  Antoine 140, 143, 144, 178
  Archange (Suzor) 143
  Catherine 143, 144
  Francois 7, 33, 77
  Fs 89
  Joseph 7
  Pierre 7
  Prudent 7
  Susanne 140
LAFORDINE 62
LAFORE, Joseph 191
LAFOREST, Cecilia 132
  Guillaume 17, 21
  J. Bte 132
  Magdeleine 130
LAFORET, William 48
LAFORGE, Angelique (Pare) 140
  Bazile 70, 191
  Felix 191
  George 151, 165
  John Simon 130
  Joseph 140
  Lewis 190
  Louis 72, 82, 130, 140
  Margaret (Campau) 130
  Terese (Tremblay) 140
  Theotiste 130
LaFORTE, Louis 159
LAFOY, ... (...) 85

LAFOY, Angelique 130
  Augustin 61, 88, 85, 110
  Augustine 54, 154
  Catherine 110
LAFRAMBOISE, ... 125
  Louis 68
  Madelaine 209
LaFRANC, Antoine 114
LAFRAY, Antoin 156
  Henry 172
LAFRENIERE, Genevieve 6
LaFRONT, Antoine 114
LAFROY, Peter 172
LAGARD, Antoine 143
LAGARDE, Jean Baptiste 12
  M. 143
  Vital 33
LAGASSY, Joachim 128
  Josette 128
LAGISSIE, Souchong 128
LAGNION, Louis 157
LAGORD, Jean 77
LAGORE, Sarah 104
LAGRANDEUR, Pierre 7
LAGRAVE, Augustin 77
LAGUTHRY, Thomas 124
LAJAUNE, J. 32
LAJENESS, Jean 44
LAJEUNESSE 36
  see Binau 22
  see Bineau 20
  ... 5
  Etienne 6
  Francois 78, 177
  Francoise 119
  Frans 68
  Jean 33
  Jean Bapt. 114
  Louis 50
  Madeleine (Frappier) 6
  Teresa 136
LAJOICE, Amable (Sanscrainte) 143
  Hyacnth 143
  Louis 143
  M. (St. Louis) 143
LAJOIE, Antoinette 102
  Basile 141
  Catherine (Bissonett) 141
  Louis 141
LAJOY, Louis 43
LAJOYE, Bazil 81
  Charle 81
  Hyacinthe 81
  Louis 51, 81
LAJUINESS, Louise (Leonard) 143
LAJUINESSE, Francois 143
  Louis 143
LaLANSETTE, Antoine 151
  Edward 151

LALIAT, John Bt.  159
LALIEVRE, Charles  88
LALONDE, Antoin  213
   John B.  214
LALOUCETTE, Antoin  214
LaMARE, see LaMARRE  22
LaMARRE, ...  32
   Charles  22, 33
LAMAY, Theophil  44
LAMB, Asa  217
   Caleb A.  181
   John  184
   Otis  192
   Wm.  196
LAMBERT, see Lembert  212
   John  101
LAMBERTSON, Conrad  188
   Elizabeth  132
LAMBSON, Arba  202
   Boaz  202
LAMEREAU, Joseph  185
LAMERON, Joseph  112
LAMIRANDE, Josh  65
LAMIRAUD, John B.  121
LAMIRONDE, Joseph  91
LAMIRONTE, Jos.  77
LAMISLEO?, ...  22
LAMKINS, Benjamin  177
   Calvin  175
   Oziel  177
LAMMON, Seth  188
LAMONION, Able  162
LAMOTH, ... (...)  42
LAMOTHE, Pierre  16
LAMORIE, Antoine  177
LAMOUNT, Roderick  218
LAMOURANDE, Jean B.  175
LAMPSON, Darius  163
   Edmund  185
LaMURA, (Frs) ...  214
LANCTOT, see Lanktaw  64
LANDERY, ...  31
LANDIS, Samuel  208
LANDNER, David  155
LANDRE, Jos.  77
LANDROCHE-SCYANIS, Marie  111
   LANDROS, Jacob  207
LANDROSH, Pierre  171
LANDRY, Claude  33
LANDRY dit ST. ANDRE, Claude  20, 33
LANE(Lucy)  104
LANE, Jacob  190
   Jasper B.  173
   John  85
LANFANS, Josh  67
LANGDOC, ...  24
LANDGON, John  154
LANGEVIN-LACROIX, Marie  143
LANGLOIS  37
   ...  5, 32, 48, 69

LANGLOIS, ... (...)  176
   Ambroise  140
   Andrew  140
   Antoine  48, 51
   Catherine  144
   Fra.  31
   Francois  33, 43
   Jacques  6
   Jean Bte  61
   Joseph  177
   Marie (Dusault)  6
   Nicholas  51
   Nicolas  21, 33, 44
   Susanne (Sordelier)  140
LANGLOISE, Ambroise  81
LANGS, John  163
LANGUEDOC  36
LANGWORTHY, James H.  219
LANKTAW, Frans  64
LANMAN, Charles J.  174
LANO, David  181
LANON, Francis  153
LANOUR, Pierre  82
LaNUT, Pierre  214
LANSING, John  210
LAPAGE, Antoine  156
   Francis  85
   John Bte.  166
LAPALME, Charles  53
LAPANSE, Hubert  212
LaPARLE, John Bapt.  111
   Marie (Landroche-Scyanis)  111
LAPARTE, John B.  172
LAPERLE, Agatha  131
   Archange  130
   Genevieve  131
   J. Bt  48
   Jeanne  117
   Joseph  53, 88, 130, 131
   Pierre  52, 73
LAPHAM, David  162
   Ethan  179
   Joseph  201
   Samuel  162
   Samuel W.  154
   Smith  202
LAPIERE, John Bapt.  163
LAPIERRE, Baptiste  85
   Bpte  67
   Bte  80
   Francois  208
   Ignace  208
LaPINE, Joseph  209
LAPIPEIN, Pierre  213
LAPLANTE, Catherine  6
   Francois  81
   Jas.  214
   Madeleine  120
LAPOINTE, Clara (Cousineau)  140

LAPOINT, Guililme  143
   J. Bte.  140, 143
   John Bte.  143
   Margaret (Cousineau)  143
   Marie J. Villers-St. Louis  143
   Nicholas  140
LAPOINTE, Basile  140
   Bte  67
   Catherine  142
   Charles  212
   Guillaume  68, 81
   J. Bte  142, 143
   Jas.  214
   Jean Bte  52, 81
   Louise  114
   Margaret  143
   Marie  212
   Nicholas  177
   William  176
LAPORTE, Jas.  215
   Joseph  157
   Pierre  213
LAPOUSEE, Antoine  161
LAPPIN, Benjamin  166
   William  164
LAPPOINT, Charles  146
   Francis  146
   Peter  147
LARABEA, Hiram  155
LARABEE, James  91
LARABEL, Veronique  144
LARABELL, Antoine  177
LARABELLE, ...  78
LARANCELL, Joseph  111
   Rosalie (Delaunay)  111
LARAWA, David  201
   Jacob  202
   Jonas  201
LARBLAIS, Thomas  79
L'ARCHEVEQUE, Catherine  48

LAREAU, James, IOURO, Jaco  131
LAREBELLE, Antoine  89
LARENTE, Joseph  51
LARIOLETTE, Francois  145
   Peter  146
LARIVIERE, Joseph  82, 88
   Julien  212
   Luc  124
LARKINS, William  172
LARNED, B. F.  152
   Benjamin F.  167
   Charles  104, 173
   Martha  102
   Sylvia (Colt)  104
LARNO, Lewis  156
LAROCH, Charles  142
LaROCHE, Charles  114
LAROCK, Bazil  212

LAROCK, Bazzel 145
  Pascal 212
LaRONDE, Francois Paschal 33
  Francois Paschal Denis 22
LaRONDE, Lozette 121
LAROQUE, see Larock 212
  see Rock 212
LAROSCHE, Charles 159
LAROSE, Henry 89
  Josephine 142
LARRIWELL, Hiram 163
LARRAWAY, Henry 184
LARWILL, Charles 164
LA, Samuel 128
LASAUT, Louis 31
LASEL, see Laselle 23
  ... 24
LASELL, Paschal 172
LASELLE, ... 16
  Antoine 55
  Bte 67
  H. 55
  J. Bte 81
  Jacq. 77
  Jacques 63, 81
  Nicolas 23
LaSERRE, Bertrand 12
LASHEPELL, Antwain 146
LASHLEY, Samuel 92
LASLEY, Samuel, see La,
  Samuel 128
  Samuel 208
  Samuel C. 208
  William 208
LASON, Daniel 200
LASSELIER, ... (...) 85
LASSELL, Jacques 82
LASSELLE, ... (...) 176
  Angelique (Godfroy) 140
  Antoine 137, 176
  Catherine (Rivard) 137
  Clara (Cosme) 140
  Francois 140, 174
  Jacques 81, 140
  Jean Bt. 176
  John Bte 137
  Margaret (Meloche) 137
  Nicolas 137
LASSEUR, Edward 209
LASSOE, Peter 146
LASUEUR, Michel 25
LATERNO, Francis 167
LATHROP, Horace 184
LATHROPE, Porter 199
LATOUR, Antne. 72
  M. 215
LATOURE, Amable 41, 54
  Robert 41
LATOURNAU, Jaque 191
LATOURNEAU, Archange 101
LATURE, John Bte 145

LATURNA, Joco 133
LATURNA, Mary Ann (Duchene) 133
LATURNO, Francois 173
LAUER, Joseph D. 205
LAUGHTON, ... (...) 43
LAUMAN, Charles J. 136
  James 136
  Marion (Griswold) 136
  Mary (Guy) 136
LAUR, Charles E. 105
LAURAIN, Frans 64
  Josh 69
LAURANGER, Alexis 81
LAURENCE, Almond 204
  Jeremiah 141, 204
  Obadiah 204
  Wolcott 136
LAURENS, Amab 114
  Antoine 114
  Francis 114
  Joseph 114
  Mary 114
  Monica (Metay) 114
LAURENT, see St. Laron 72
  Antoine 154
  John 154
  Toutsaint 154
LAUSENNETTE, see Lauson 20
  Antoine Nicolas 20, 33
  Jacques 20, 33, 40, 53, 72
  Monique 131
  Nicolus 17
  Seraphin 72
LAUZON, Catherine 132
  Louise 101
  Marie 129
  Seraphin 132
LAVADOUX, ... 61
LaVASSEUR, Louis 77
LAVENTURE, Francois 212
LAVERDU, Jose 208
LAVERGNE, Louis 144
  Marie 144
LAVERTY, Alexander 200
LaVeESTEVE, Madeleine
  Frappier) 17
  Pierre 17
LAVERGE, ... 6
  Marie (Guertin) 6
LaVERMIT, Charles 114
LAVICTORIE, Amable 77
  Louis 62
LAVIGEUR, Pierre 61
LAVIGNE, Francois 157, 209
  Mad 212
LAVINE, Augustine 214
LAVIOLET, Archange (... 178
LaVIOLETTE, ... 31
  Etienne 33, 43, 50, 81, 143
  Marie J. 143

LAVIOLLET, ... 66
LAVIVIERE, Michel 212
  Pierre 212
LAVOIE, Francois 137, 176
  Louis 178
  Marie (Gouin) 137
LAVOU, Etienne 137
LAVOYE, Francois 89
LAW, John 145
LAWE, John 211
LAWLES, Mary 122
LAWLESS, Burchett B. 219
LAWLITZ, Henry 150
LAWRENCE, David 185
  James 210
  John 141
  Nathan 185
  Parker 155
  Prosper 117, 160
  W. 106
  William 211
  Wolcott 173
LAWRY, Peter 203
LAWSON, James 192
  Josh 151, 164
  Luke 187
LAY, James H. 217
LAYTHE, ... 70
LAZELL, Thomas 189
LAZER, John 153
L'BRANCHE, Francis 213
LEAKE, David 181
LEANED, Charles 171
LEARY, J. 216
LEAS, Jacob 217
LEBARON, Leander 202
LEBARRON, Lewis 202
LeBAU, see Le Beau 17
LeBEAU, see Bau dit LeBeau 22
  ... 32
  Alexis 175
  Baptiste 91
  Ettiene 178
  Fr. 36
  Fra. 31
  Francois 22, 33
  G. 105
  J. Bte 77, 140
  Jean Baptiste 33
  Jean Bt. 209
  Jean Francois 17
  Jn Bte 36
  Josette 140
  Louise 140
  Margaret 145
  Marguerite (Morel dit La
    Durantaye) 33
  Rene 81
  Rene Francois 33
  Renez 65
LeBELLERRE, Jn 66

LEBLANC, see Labla 132
   Francois 43, 114
   J. Bte 77
   Jacques 132
   Pierre 65, 77, 91
   Pierre Francois 114
LeBLANCHE, Pierre 114
LEBOEUF, Antoine 82
LEBOFF, Augustine 146
LEBON, John Bt. 158
LEBOTT, John 170
LeBOUE/BEAU, John Bapt. 113
LeBRASH, Jean Bt. 177
LEBRUFFE, Edward 121
LEBUI, Amor 123
LECLAIR, Joseph 88
   Robert 106
LeCLAIRE, Andre 65
LeCORNEAU, ... 12
LeCORNEAU dit SANSSOUCY, ... 12
LeCOURSIER, Augustin 174
   J. Bt 48
LECROIX, Michel 123
LECUYER, Benjamin 145
LECUYER, Joseph 121
   Lozette (LaRonde) 121
   Simeon 212
LeDUC, see Persil 16
   Antoine 124
   Bapt. 30
   Francois 80
   Frans 72
   Hyacinthe 64, 178
   J. Bt 44
   J. Bte 81
   Jean Baptiste 33
   Jean Bt. 175
   John Bte 139
   Joseph 20
   Josh 72, 80
   Lambert 177
   Louis 72, 77, 89, 152, 174
   Phil 30
   Philip 33, 44, 51
   Phpe 36
LeDUC dit PERSIL, Francois 16
LeDUC-PERCIE, Louis 177
LEE, Abigail (...) 138
   Benjamin 160
   George 180
   Harvey 181
   Henry 217
   Horatio 181
   Isaac 138
   Joseph 187
   Martin 182
   Thomas 200
   Warham 179
   William 186

LEEK, Horace 201
LEET, Gideon 119
   Joseph B. 150
   Lucinda 119
   Lucindy 166
   Warren 164
LEFEBVRE, Jn Bte 68
LEFER, Augustin 110
LEFLEUR, ... (...) 42
   Andre 42
   Augustin 174
   Charles 43
   Joseph Poupar 43
   Pierre 123
LEFOY, Augustin 157
LEFRANC, Antoine 78, 91
LEGARD, A. (...) 88
   Francis 143
   Jean 85
   Marie (Langevin-Lacroix) 143
LEGOD, Jean 69
LEGRAND, ... 24
   Gabriel Christopher 22
LEIB, John 163
   John L. 151, 157
   John R. 109
   Margaret (Conner) 109
LEISTER, Jsoeph 129
   Sally (...) 129
LEITH, George 60
   James 60
leJEUNESSE, Jean Btste 159
LELAND, Nathan 200
   Zenas 200
LELIVE, Chs 63
LeLIEVRE, Charles 76
   Margaret 103
LELONGEUIL, ... 22
LEMANDRE, Josh 65
LEMARS, Joseph 121
LEMAY, A. P. 89
   Angelique 109
   Catherine 141
   J. Bte 64
   Joseph 124
   Rosalie 117
   Simon 124
   Theophil 51
   Theophile 141
   Theophile (...) 78
   Theophite 64
LEMBERT/LAMBERT, Pierre 212
LEMEN-YVON, Francois, see Lemin 101
LEMENE, Francois 88
LEMERIE, Jean B. 212
LEMERIN, Joseph 166
LEMERINE, Joseph 160
LEMERY, John 212
LEMEUR, Joseph 211

LEMIEUX, see Lemeur 211
LEMIN, Angelique (Gagnier) 101
   Francis 101
LEMMERY, Joseph 121
LEMMON, Smauel 179
   William 182
LEMMONS, Joshua 153
   Zebrina 153
LEMOIN, Jean 23, 24
LEMOINE, Francois 70
   Jeanne 6
LEMON, Francis 171
   William 200
LEMON/SIMON, Isaac 196
LeMOYNE, ... 5
LEMOYNE/DESPINS/DESPEIGNES 6
LEMOYNE, Sieur De Mounier, Alexis 7
   Alexis 6, 7
   Anne 6
   Jacques 6
   Rene 6
LEMOYNE de LONGEUIL, see De Longeuil 12
LEMURAINS, Josh 64
leNEGRE, Henry 82
LENFANS 67
   Ainee 67
LENFANT, see Lefans 67
   Benjamin 68, 81, 140, 174
   Catherine 141
   Dominique 68, 81
   Joseph 42, 55, 140, 141
   Josinne 81
   Louis 81
LENGLOIE, see Langlois 21
LENGUEDOC, see LaCote dit Languedoc 21
   ... 21, 22, 23
LENO, Pierre 191
LENOIR, Nicolas 44
LENOX, Leonard 167
LEONARD, Angelique (Couture) 143
   Angelique 143
   Angelique (Robindou) 143
   Archange 144
   Callah 136
   Catherne (Valiquet) 136
   Francis 143, 144
   Francois 81, 136
   Frans 66
   Guy H. 66
   J. Bte. 143
   Jacob 178
   James 146
   Louise 143
   Luther 211
   Mary 144
   Nicolas, see Callah 136
   Peter 186
L'EQUEA, Francis 215

LEPAGE, Andre  76
  Francois  77
LEPIERE, Michael  219
LEPINE, Marette  6
LEPORT, John Bt.  158
LERIGER-LAPLANTE, Pierre
  Louis  143
LERIVIERE, Francois  124
LERONCETTE, Antoine  120
LeROY, ...  5
  Daniel  151
LeROYE, Daniel  181
  Henry W.  181
  Levi  185
LESLEY, George  210
LESPERANCE  36, 37
  ...  22, 32
  Ane  90
  Antoine  69, 79, 154, 167
  Batist  170
  Bonadventure  6
  Chs  69
  Fra.  31
  Francois  50
  Francois Rochereau  33
  J., see Billiau dit
    Lesperance  21
  Jean Baptiste  14, 33
  Joseph  44, 51, 166
  Louis  72
  Patoca  36
  Pierre  69
  Tousant  170
LESSARD, Peter  146
  Pierre  212
LESSLEY, James  194
LESTER, Joseph  192
LETOUR, Jean B.  174
LETOURNAU, Baptiste  82
  Jn Bte  73
LETOUREAU, J. Bte  133
  Jemes, see Laturna, Joco
    133
  Pierre  52
LeTOURNEAU dit JANETTE, Jean
  Baptiste  17
LETSON, Michael  203
LETTE, Mary  106
LEVAKE, H. A.  214
  Henry A.  121
LEVASSEUR, Felicite  102
LEVEQUE, Francois  82
LEVERSEUR, Pierre  52
LEVERY, Asahel  204
LEVIGNE, Francois  209
LEVINCH, Joel  203
  Nathan  204
LEVITRE, Genevieve  139
LEVRIL, ... (...)  52
  Martin  42
LEVRY, Martin  33

LEVRY-MARTIN, Margaret  138
  Martin  138
LEWIS, Andr.  146
  Charles  202
  David C.  160
  Harvey  192
  James O.  152, 170
  John  176
  Jonathan  180
  Joseph  105
  Judah  165
  Lydia (Chilson)  138
  Robert P.  117, 159, 191
  Silas  138, 202
  Thomas  166
  Warner  217
LILYS, Henry  183
LIMARE, J.  85
LIMOGES, Margaret  112
LINCOLN, Luther  155, 165
LINDEN, Morton  165
LINGART, Robert  210
LINN, Daniel  204
LIONARD, Jos.  103
  Louise (Durocher)  103
LIONARD-CHEVALIER, Jos.  130
  Louise (Durocher)  103
LIPINE, Pierre  128
LISCOMB, Wm  146
LISLERONDE, J. Bte  81
LITSENBERGER, Nicholas  40
LITTLE, ...  79
  Jacob  214
  John  90
  Robert  195
  William  116, 150, 159,
    160, 191
LITTLEFIELD, Edmund  175
LITTLETON, ... (...)  146
LITTOIS, Frederick  204
LITZIMBURGER  52
LIMERY, John  147
LIVERNOIS  36
  see Hyvernois  43
  see Ininois  67
  Angelique (Chagnon)  7
  Etienne  63
  Etienne Benoit  20
  Francis  154
  Francois  7, 115
  Jos.  159
  Joseph  77, 91, 114, 119,
    154, 160
  Josh  63
  Monica  119
  Teresa  114
  Teresa (Meloche)  114
LIVERNOIS au GAUDET, ...  5
LIVIERGE?, Nicolas  70
LIVINGSTON, Christina  118
L'LIVERNOIS, see Livernois  20

L'LONDE, Francis  215
L'MUE, Frances  213
LOCKWOOD, David  195
  J. H.  146
  James  104, 182
  James H.  212
  Jeremiah  193
  Josiah  192
  Lebeous  194
  Townsend  193
  William  197
LOGAN, Christopher  187
LOGNIER, John B.  218
  Paul  218
LOGNON, see Longden  88
  ...  48
  ... (...)  85
  Augustin  85
  Joseph  110
  Louis  63, 85, 110, 76
  Louise Drouillard  110
LONCHE, Benjamin  209
LONG, Elias  112, 152, 158,
    167
  Richard  166
  Rupard  152
  Thomas  112, 167
LONGAN, Augustin  114
  Augustine  105
  Augn  88
LONGE, Benj.  101
LONGDON/LANGDON, Austin  76
LONGON, Augustin  159
  Austine, see Longan, Austine
    105
  Beverly  162
  John  162
LONGUEUIL  37
LONGWERE, Battes  146
LONGWELL, Sellick  205
LONION, Louis  88
LOOFBOROUGH, John  222
LOOMIS, Benjamin G.  184
  Hubble  204
  Joel  185
  Leonard  171, 214
LOONEY, Abram  218
  Jesse  219
LOOTMAN, see Barrois  20
LOOTMAN dit BARROIS, see
  Barois  23
  Francois  17
LOOTMAN-BARROIS, Marie  109
LORAIN, Charles  209
  Joseph  78, 158
LORANGER, Alexis  142, 176, 177
  Augustin  142
  Catherine (Tessier)  142
  Claude  138
  Edward  175
  Joseph  138, 174

## Index

LORANGER, Rosalie (Chabert) 138
LORANGER-MAISONVILLE, Pelagie 101
LORCE, Joseph 199
LORD, David E. 198
   Richard 199
LOREE, see Force 200
LOREIAU, Louis 209
LORENS, Amab 159
   Antoine 159
   Francis 159
   Jos. 159
   Louis 159
   Mary 159
LORIER, John B. 191
LORIMER, Peter A. 216
LORIN, Perish 128
LORRAIN, see Lauran 69
   see Laurens 114
   Francois 89
   Nicholas 53
LORRANCELLE, see Larancell 111
LORROW, Amable 162
   Antoine 160
   Joseph 162
   Louis 167
   Tousaint 167
LORROW/DARROW?, Francis 164
LORSON, Jean 31
LOSON, see Lauson 17
   see Luso 144
   Antoine 82
   Jacque 82
   Jc 36
   Nicolas 36
   Nicho 30
   Saraphin 82
LOTT, George W. 217
LOUCKS, William 162
LOUDEN, Clement 155
LOUDER, Absalom 217
LOUDON (colored) 86
LOUISENOIS, Francois 123
LOUISGNAN, see Louisenois 123
LOUISGNANT, Francois 208
LOUISIGNON, Gabriel 170
LOUISINAC, see Louisenois 123
LOUISNOIS, Pierre 123
LOUISON, Clemons 163
LOUKS, Abram 207
   Makus 207
LOUPIAN, Theodore 146
LOUW, Peter 182
LOVE, Benjamin 213
   James 200
   Robert 195
LOVEJOY, Anias 214
LOVELAND, Joseph 105
LOVELESS, John 81

LOVETT, Verni 217
LOVEWELL, Nehemiah 175
LOW, Peter 187
LOWER/LOVIDER, Clement 167
LOWRY, John 199
LOYER, Jn Bte. 212
LOZON, Francois 178
   Jacques 195
   Joseph 209
L'QUIER, Jas. 215
L'TROIS, Gabriel 214
LUBY, Abijah C. 205
LUCIER, Paul 177
LUCK?, Pither 71
LUCKET, Alexander 118
   Alexdr. 160
   John, see Alexander 117
LUDSON, George 152
LULL, David 150
LUNDY, Enoch 207
LUNTZ, Chas. 214
LUPER, James 204
LUPIEN, Theodore 146
LUPTIN, John 85
LUPTON, Joseph 219
LUSIER, Joseph 54
LUSO, Francis 144
LYAS, Nathaniel 203
LYBROOK, Henry 207
LYIONS, George 158
LYNDE, Isaac 209
LYON, David 185
   George 160
   H. 76
   Henry/Sterry? 179
   Lucine 170
   Robert 162
   Samuel 187
   Timothy 161
LYOND---, Elizabeth 171
LYONS, ... 42
   Archer 85
   E. (...) 89
   Elizabeth 105
   Elizabeth (Chene) 105
   George 54, 105, 112
   Henry 155, 163
   John 204
   Susanne (Seguin-Laderoute) 112
LYTLE, John 112
   Sarah 112

MABEE, James 202
MacDOUGAL, George 60
MACE, Antoine 121
MacGEE, Henry 91
MACINTOSH, ... 41
MACK, Almon 192
   Andrew 172
   Daniel 105

MACK, Hannah (...) 105
   Harriet 103
   John M. 181
   Stephen 88, 102
MACKINTOSH, Angus 60
   Ann 103
   James 60
MACKLIN, Robert 210
MACNAMARA, ... 41
MACOMB, see McCombs 89
   Alexander 54, 106
   Alexandrine 111
   Alexr. 43
   Caroline 118
   Caroline (McComb) 118
   Christina (Livingston) 118
   Jean 118
   John 118, 160
   John Navarre 118
   Monica (Navarre) 119
   Sarah 119
   Sarah (Dring) 119
   William 43, 54, 119, 160
MACONNNEL, Elan 154
MACONNY, Baptiste 61
MACUE, ... 122
MACUMBER, Mary 179
MADDEN, William J. 217
MADISON, Asa 172
MAGEE, Henry 109, 157
MAGNAN, Jean 6
   Marie (Moitie) 6
MAHEWE, Joseph 174
MAHONEY, Patrick 160
   Ralph 196
   T. 77
   Thomas 88, 99
MAILLET, Gabriel 33
   Gabriel/Jean Baptiste 23
   Mary 131
   Pierre 79
   Teresa 115
MAILLOU, Amable 55
   Joseph, see Mailloux 22, 51
MAILOUZ 37
   see Joseph Maillou 22
MAISON, Louis 72
   Nicholas 191
MAISONVILLE, Alexis 48, 51, 62
MAJOR, Etienne 140
   John Bte. 140
   Lewis 168
   Rose (Boemier) 140
MAKENSIE, John 157
MALCHER, ... 78
   Paul 77
MALBEUF, Augustin 69
MALET, Louis 143
   Louise 143
MALLET, ... 5

MALLET, Bte/Jean Baptiste 16
  Charlotte 103
  F./Francois 17
  Madeleine (Thunes dit
    Dufresne) Peletier 6
  Minor 155
  Pierre 6
MALLETT, Joseph 172
MALLETTE, Joseph 88
MALLORY, Amanda 122
MALLOT, Miner 202
MALONE, Mary 126
MALOUT, ... (...) 44
MANASSAW, Antwoine 215
MANAUSON, Etienne 112
MANCHET 36
MANEGAN, William F. 216
MANGAS, Daniel 188
  Jacob 189
  John 188
  Henry 189
MANN, Lewis 187
MANNASSA, Etienne 112
MANSFIELD, Miles 179
  Samuel 179
MANUEL, John 170
MAPES, Samuel 201
MAPLES, Betsy 188
  David L. A. 190
  William C. 164
MARANDA, John B. 192
MARANTET 37
MARCEBOIS, Charles 122
MARCHANG, Baptist 124
MARCHAND, Jean Bt. 209
  Louis 218
MARCHETEAU, Francois 33
MARCHETEAU dit DESNOYERS,
  Francois 23, 33
  Francois, see Denoye 22
MARCOT, ... 48
  Jean Bte. 48
  Marie (Neskech) 48
MARDEN, David 180
MARENTETTE, Archange 109
MARENTETE, Francois 44
MARETTE dit LEPINE, Magdeleine 6
MARFAERE, Bt-. 73
MARGIN, J.A. 214
MARGUERITE (colored) 86
MARIAN, Isadore 158
MARIE, Louis 179
MARIEQUARRIE, John 146
MARIN, Joseph Malgue 48
MARK, William 85
MARKAITS, Mont 71
MARKHAM, A. B. 155, 163
  Isaac 199
  Israel 207
  Lane 207

MARKHAM, Samuel 207
MARKS, Ira 131, 195
MARKWEATHER, Erastus W. 155
MARLATT, Pillip 180
MARLET, Charles 123
  Josephe (Vaillancourt) 123
MARLETTE, Magdeleine 6
MARLEY, Charles 208
MARLIE, Charlie 92
MARMON, Stephen 207
MARRS, Hugh 207
MARRY, Michael 184
MARSAC, see Marfaere 73
  36
  ... (...) 40, 53
  Baptist 133
  Baptiste 82
  Benj. 78
  Benjn 90
  Cajetan 116
  Cecile 109
  Cecilia 116
  Eulalie (Gouin) 116
  Fra. 30
  Francis 116
  Francois 16, 21, 32, 33,
    79, 117, 151
  Frs. 31
  Gagetan 151
  Gagettans/Cajetan 71
  Gashet 164
  Gazel 163
  Genevieve 112
  Goyette 159
  Gozette 116
  J. Bt. 40
  J. Bte. 112
  Jacques 71, 90
  Jean 115
  Jean Bte 53
  Latroux 79
  Marie (Saucier) 116
  Paul 40, 161
  Rene 79, 116, 151, 159
  Renne 90
  Robert 90, 117, 151, 159,
    160 Robt. 79
  Teresa 115
MARSACH, John B. 191
MARSACRE, Frans 70
  Rene 70
MARSAN, Etienne 158
MARSH, Cutting 211
  John 212
MARSHAL, James 186
MARSHALL, Cecilia (Patrenotre)
  133
  Jane 119
  Rensalear 210
  Sarah (Heath) 133
  William 133

MARSON, Etienne 112
MARSTON, John 211
MARTAN, Francois 211
MARTEL 36
MARTHER, Charles 190
MARTIN, see Martan 211
  ... 41
  ... (...) 177
  Anderson 204
  Angelica 138
  Antoine 128, 208
  Basile 143
  Bazil 176
  Budd 176
  Charles 138, 178
  Edward 183
  Elijah 141, 175
  George M. 162
  Hugh M. 85
  Hugh W. 85
  Isaac 217
  Jacob 143
  Jacques 67, 81, 142
  James 138, 143, 198
  James, see Jaboc 143
  John 62, 151, 160
  Joseph 120, 176
  L. 31
  Lent 177, 204
  Marie (Desanges-Gouin) 143
  Morgan . 210
  Patrick 190
  Robert 176
  Solomon 122
  Sophia (Auban-Lagarde) 142
  Teresa 142
  Thadeus 186
  Toussaint 178
  Tusa 142
  Veronique 143
  William 184
  Wm 146
MARVIN, Calvin 182
MARY (colored) 94
  Jean 138
MASDEN, James 216
MASON, Charles 81
  Ebenezer A. 163
  Howland 179
  John W. 122
  Jos. 158
  Nicholas 131
MASSACAN, Henry 197
MASSE, ... 5
  Francois 6

  Marguerite (Couc dit LaFleur)
    Fafard 6
  Martin 6
  Michel 6
  Therese (David) 6

# Index

MASTIC, Otis 216
MASTON, Abraham 177
MATENNA, Francois 172
MATEVA, ... 122
MATHER, Benjamin 190
MATHEWS, N. E. 205
MATHIEU, Joseph 51
MATLOCK, David 216
MATOON, Andrew 194
MATOU, Marie 7
MATTA, Maurice 123
MATTHEWS, Roswell 185
    Salmon 187
    Salmon H. 201
    Salmon J. 183
MATTIS, Elizabeth (Riopel) 105
    Raney 105
MATTOCKS, Ebenezer 154
    James 174
MAUANSAU, Stephen 152
MAUER, Henry 198
MAUET, Paschal 173
MAUGER, Elizabeth 136, 143
MAUPETIT, Clemence 6
MAURAN, see Moran 23
    ... 23
MAURIN, Isedore 52
    Isidore 151
    Louis 151
MAURICE, see Morans, Moriche 70
MAURISSEAU, see Morriseau 14
MAURRE, Laurent 70
MAXWELL, James 153, 166
    Thomas 153, 101
    Thompson 101, 162
MAY, Elizabeth 109, 138
    James 54, 61, 76, 79, 88, 85, 110, 138, 154, 157
    Margaret 106
    Pierre 82
    Richardson 127, 213
    Rose (St. Cosme) 110
MAYAT, ... 32
MAYE, Pierre 71
MAYEUX, Vincent 81
MAYEYE, George 195
MAYFIELD, Elijah 216
MAYNARD 199
MAYO, David 113, 158
    Joseph 203
    Lyman 203
MAYOTT, Catherine 218
MAYVILLE, John 206
MAZZUCHELLI, Samuel 121
McALISTER, ... 111
    ... (Connolly) 111
    Catherine (McCauley) 111
    Randel 111
McARTHUR, Alexander 170

M'CARTNEY, Robert 200
McBRIDE, Elizabeth 85
    Felix 216
McCABE, Robert A. 209
McCALISTER, William 192
McCALL, Elias 190
    Hugh 199
McCAMON, John 210
McCARLY, Edward 78
McCARTHY, David 117
    Edw. 160
    Wm. 160
McCARTNEY, Orris 219
McCARTY, Edward 64, 89, 117, 118
    John 125, 145, 211
    Johsy 103
    Maria C. (Audrain) Hoffman 117
    Mary (St. Bernard) 103
    William 118, 153, 160
    William A. 117
McCAULEY, Catherine 111
McCAULLEY, Florence 61
McCLAIN, David 88
    /McLean, Daniel 76
McCLARY, David 211
McCLEAN, David 76
McCLEARY, William 207
McCLEMENS, Jane 85
McCLOSKEY, James 102
    Suzanne (Godfroy) 102
    William 217
McCLOUD, Francis 85
McCLUNG, Alexander 182
    James 182
    John 179
McCLURE, John 209
    Thomas 88, 85
    William 196
McCOLLISTER, Col. ... 157
McCOLLAM, Ethan 192
McCOLLUM, John 199
    Lydia 196
McCOMB, William 91
McCOMBE/Macomb 78
    ... 79
McCOMBS, John 89
    William 150
McCONNELL, Alfred 217
McCONPSEY, John 205
McCORD, Carahan 196
McCORMAC, William 167
McCORMACK, Absalom 219
    John 219
McCORMICK, John 201
    Samuel 201
McCORNISTEN, Wm. 216
McCOSKRY, W. 102
McCOSKY, Felicite (Levasseur) 102

McCOY, George 207
McCRACKEN, Robert 182
McCRAE, Thomas 41, 54
McCRANEY, Thomas 217
McCROSKEY, James 85
    William 179
    Wm. 88
McCUE, John, see Macue, ... 122
McCULLOCH, Cecil 208
McCULLOM, Ashbill B. 207
McCULLOUGH, Cecilia 122
McCURDY, Carson 153
    Richard 154, 164
McDADE, Philip 217
McDONA, see McDonelld 128
McDONALD, Aquila 130
    Catherine 131
    Donnald 215
    Elizabeth 130
    Henry W. 187
    James 85, 170
    John 172
McDONEL, William 190
McDONELL, Archibald 131
    Eaneas 209
    James 61
    Michael 178
    Nancy (Carter) 131
McDONELLD, Alexander 128
    Feliz 128
McDONGLE, John K. 171
McDONNELL, Alexr 76
    J. 88
    James 76
    John 104
    Richard 154
McDOUBLE, George 197
McDOUGALL, Archange (Campau) 112
    G. 88
    Genevieve (Meny) 112
    George 81, 82, , 102, 112
    James
    Robert 79, 112
    Robert C. 158
    Robt 69
    Rt 90
McDOWELL, Richard 160
    Samuel 199
    Thomas 173
McELVEIN, Greer 205
    Jeremiah 205
    John 205
McENTERFER, Jacob 204
    Solomon 204
MceRae/McCrae, Thos. 76
McERGAN, John 42
McEINNESS, Paul 124
McFARLAND, Walter 161
McFARLANE, Issabelle 215

McFARLIN, Joseph 186
McFOSLIN, Walter 155
McGAVRY, Morass 196
McGILPIN, Matthew 205
McGONOGALL, Sally 102
McGOUNDES, George 199
McGRAW, Henry 127
   Thomas 186
McGREGOR, Capt. ... 41
   Alexander 193
   Gregor 52, 61
   John 61
   Jno. 78
McGUFFY, Neal 204
McGULPIN, David 209
   George 208
   Madeleine (Crequi) 122
   Magdeleine (Bourassa) 122
   Patrick 54, 55, 122
   William 122, 209
McHENRY, James 181, 219
McINTIRE, Alexander 197
   Timothy 197
McINTOSH, Angus 85
   Daniel 207
McINTYRE, Charles 210
McIVOR, Daniel 195
McKAY, Hugh 131
McKEE, Alexander 85
   Thomas 80
McKEEN, George 165
McKEENAN, Phillip 199
McKENZIE, John 111
McKEY, Anthony 190
   Samuel 205
McKINLEY, Alexander 217
McKINNEY, Barnard 126
   Patrick 216
   Thomas 207
McKINSTRY, Andrus 198
   Charles 103
   David C. 103, 171
   Noble 205
McKIRGAN/KIRGAN?, John W. 54
McKNIGHT, Sheldon 173
McKONKER, Wm. 160
McKONKEY, William 120
McLAREN, Robert 172
McLAUGHLIN, Joseph 181
   Wm 146
McLEAN, ... (...) 85
   Charles 186
   David 85
   Polly 85
McLEOD, ... 41
   Normand 54
McLOY, Joseph 196
McMAHON, Morton 216
McMANUS, ... (...) 175
   Honora (O'Roke) 142
   James 142

McMATH, Fleming 196
   Mary 167
   Rocky 155
McMACKIMON, James 213
McMICHAEL, William 180
McMILLAN, Alexander 205
   Ananias 103
   Mary/Polly (Willard) 103
   Polly 103
McMILLEN, Mary 171
McMURPHY, Wm. 156
McNAIR, William 188
McNEAL, Daniel 146
   Danl 88
NcNEIL, Dennis 85
McNEIR, Thomas 146
McNIFF, ... (...) 88
   Catherine 101, 170
   Eleanor 85
   Margaret 85
   Patrick 62, 76
McNULTY, Anthony 174
   John 218
McPHERSON, John 40, 41, 54
McRAY, Jos. B. 189
McTAVISH, Simon 54
McVAUGHTON, A. 214
McVAY, Elizabeth (Burbank) 117
   Henry 85, 117
   Hugh 118, 154, 160
   Mary Ann 117
   Wm. 156
   Wm. Henry 117
McVEY, Hugh 89, 167
McWILLIAMS, ... 41
   Andrew 219
MEACHAM, Jesse 202
   George 206
   Sylvester 206
MEAD, Amos 179, 187
   Samuel 180
MECHANT, Constant 122
MEDAIRA, George 217
MEDARD, Couture 80
MEDOR, Ante 77
MEDO, Baptist 132
MEEK, John 163
   William 203
MEEKER, Jonathan 219
   Nathan 203
MEEM, John 90
MELDRAM, ... 41
MELDRUM, ... 74, 82
   Colin 73
   David 191
   Francis 146
   Genevieve (Rivard) 132
   George 60, 78, 79, 90, 104, 112, 132
   James 192

MELDRUM, John 85, 112, 151, 158
   Mary Ann 104
   Sarah 163
   Sarah (Lytle) 112
   William 132, 191, 194
MELE, see Maillet 23
MELLE, Rene 77
MELLEN, Charles, see Millen, C. 106
   Eliza (Scott) 106
MELOCHE, Angelique 143
   Antoine 43, 50
   Archange 115
   Baptiste 20
   Bte 36, 69
   Catharine 103
   Catherine 112
   Elizabeth 133
   Felicite 111
   Fr 36
   Francois 20, 33, 41, 52, 115
   Francoise 115
   Frans 71
   J. Bte. 112
   Jean Baptiste 33
   Jean Bt 41
   Jean Bte 53, 111
   John 152
   Margaret 137
   Obmiser? 69
   Papiche 36
   Pierre 16, 22, 32, 33, 44, 50, 51
   Pre 36
   Simon 40, 53, 77
   Teresa 114
   Therese 111
MELCOKE, Bapt. 30
   Fra. 30
MELOSH, John 166
MELVILLE, John 206
MELVIN, James 216
MENA, Antoine 131
   Genevieve (Laperle) 131
   Joseph 131
   Mary Ann (Petit) 131
MENAGE, Louis 219
MENANCON, Etienne 77
MENARD, ... (...) 43
   Angelique 143
   Angelique (Jacob) 140
   Basille (Suzor) 144
   Catherine 102, 104, 111
   Charles 147, 212
   Clara 143
   Francis 140, 143, 144
   Francois 81, 177, 178
   Frans 67
   Genevieve 139

MENARD, Jean Marie 140, 175, 177
    John M. 140
    Joseph 66, 81, 144, 175
    Josh 66
    Louise 139
    Monique (Beauregard) 140
    Pierre 140
MENEY, Antoine 52
    Pierre 41
MENOR, Charles 147
MENSONON, Etienne 91
MENY, Antoine, see Menny, Anthony 73
    Antoine 17, 20, 32, 112, 132
    Archange 131
    Dominique 194
    Genevieve 112
    Joseph 138
    Louise 138
    Mary Ann (Petit) Mena 131
    Monique 132
    Pierre, see Minny, Piro 73
    Pierre 131
    Regina 139
    Teresa 132
MENNY, Anthony, see Meny, Antoine 73
MEPHARSON, Jean 71
MERCIER, John 88
MERLIN, Thomas 187
MERO, Antoine 138
    Felicity (Lacelle) 138
    Joseph Miron 138
MERRILL, Moses E. 209
    Peter D. 183
    Roswell T. 181
MERRIT, ... (...) 176
    Briah 170
    David 190
MERRITT, Adna 167
    Willis 188
MERSAU, Antoine 178
MERSHAW, J. B. 215
    Jas. 213
MERSHON, John 210
MERTE, ... 32
MESATTE, Abraham 78
MESNIE, see Montmeny 23
MESSENGER, Amasa 192
    Jedediah 192
MESSERSMITH, John 217
METAY, see Mettie 141
    Joseph 33, 141
    Monica 114
    Philip 63
    Rene 114, 115
    Susanne 115
METAY dti LaDOUCEUR, Joseph 33

METAYER, see Meteier 17
METCALF, George 189
METCOE?, Jacques 69
METE, Jos 36
METEE, Theophile 88
METEIER, Joseph 17
METIVIA, Joseph 196
METIVIER, Medard, see Mateva, ... 122
METLER, Dan B. 173
METNOR, Joseph 191
METTA, Morrice 123
METTE, Catherine 85
    Felise 78
    Felix 89, 85
    Feophile/Theophile 76
    Renne 89
    Theophilus 85
METTER, Theophile 157
METTEZ, Antoine 154, 164
    Catherine (Dufor) 105
    Catherine (Peltier) 103, 110
    Hubert 177
    John 172
    Joseph 105, 110
    Leon 177
    Marie (Gamelin) 103
    Pierre 63
    Rene, see Mattis, Raney 105
    Richard 177
    Theophile 103
    Theophilis 170
    Theophilus 103, 110, 163, 173
METTIE, Catherine (Lemay) 141
    Cecile (Labadie) 141
    Felix 141
    Francis 141
METTIZ, Francois 151
MEXICO, John Bapt. 113
    John Bt. 158
    John Bte 167
MICHAEL 123
    Peter 201
MICHEL, see Michel Yax 21
    Baptiste 82
MICHEL dit LORRAIN, Nicholas 53
MIDDAUGH, Samuel 181
MIDGES, John 164
MIERS, William 210
MILES, William 127
MILHOMME, see Petit 22
    ... 24
MILLARD, Daniel 187
    Eleazer 184
    Jedediah 190
    Nathaniel 184
MILLEN, C. 106

MILLER
    Abram 216
    Adam 206
    Andrew 186
    Charles 211
    Daniel 130, 193
    David 88
    Eleanson 217
    Henry 126
    Hiram 178, 192
    Ira 193
    Isaac 197, 210
    Isaac D. 162
    Jaque 191
    James 197
    James H. 178
    Jerad 195
    John 155, 162, 181, 183, 185, 204, 212
    Joe 130
    Joseph 130, 193
    Joshua 178
    Minard 198
    Morris 171
    Nathan B. 193
    Oliver W. 101, 170
    Pelagie (Loranger-Maisonville) 101
    Rachel 202
    Robert 191
    Silas 194
MILLERD, Orestus 192
MILLINGTON, Abel 197
MILLION, Benjamin 217
    Crawford 217
MILLIS, Samuel L. 187
MILLS, Augustus 199
    Chester 210
    Elihue 199
    Jesse 176
    Lorin 198
    Major D. 200
    Moody 176
    Perses 199
    Simon 199
    Sylvester 198
    William 175
MILLSAP, Bird 216
MILLSPAW, Cornelius 187
MILMAN, Alexander 115
    Ann 115
MILMINE, Alex 76
MINAWSAW, Stephen 166
MINET, Joseph 218
MINEY, see Meny 20
    Antoine 40, 53
    Joseph 195
    Lambert 194
MINI, Pierre 82
MINICLEN, Marian 215
MINICLIER, Joseph 214

MINNY, Piro, see Meny,
　　Pierre 73
MINY, see Meny 17
　Ant. 30, 36
MIRELLE, Bte Mont 69
MIRL, Beriah Wm. 152
MIRON, Antoine 81
MIRTEN, see St. Martin 23
MISSEC, Pierre 81
MITCHEL, David 122
　Timothy 189
MITCHELL, George 122
　James 91
　William 208
MOE, C. Higgins 129
　Elam 199
　John 199
　Nan 129
　Nun 129, 192
MOFFAT, John 189
MOITIE, Marie 6
MOMFORD, Joseph 93
MOMINY, Jacque 139
　Louis 139
　Margaret (Gagnier) 139
　Terese (Couture) 139
MOMMINI, Bte. 81
MOMONE, Francois 176
MOMONIE, Bartholomew 176
　Louis 177
MONCELL, Charles 208
MONDAY, Spencer 146
MONEGHAN, Patrick 216
MONET, Michel 63
MONETT, Michael 167
MONETTE, Anne (Grefard) 103
　John Bte 103
　John L. 143
　M. Josephe (Quevillon) 103
　Margaret (Sanscrainte) 143
　Marianne 85
　Michael 103
　Michel 85, 143, 151
MONFORTON, Guillaume 50
　William 44
MONIER, Louis 91
MONIQUE, Antoine 144
MONK, Ephraim 181
MONMINI, Francois 81
　Louis 81
MONMIREL, see Durand 23
MONMIRELLE, see Montmirel
　see Durand 17
MONNEY, Richard 63
MONROE, Banjamin 179
　Frederick 180

MONROE, Freedom 192
　James 106
MONSSEAU, Charles 208
MONTEITH, ... (Harris) 102
　John 102
　Sarah (Granger) 102
MONTEREVE, J. B. 211
MONTEURE, Andrew 178
MONTMENEY, Louis 50
MONTMENY, see Mominy 139
MONTMENY, Louis Jean 23, 33,
　139
　Margaret 140
MONTMINI, Louis 43
MONTMINIE, Louis Jean 68
MONTMINY, ... 31
MONTOUR, Joseph 145
MONTPLAISIR, Jock B. 218
MONTRAX, Pierre 128
MONTREUIL, see Juillet 22
　Antne 66
　Baptiste 61, 82
MONTREVILLE, Louis 177
MONTVAILLE, Louison 212
MOODY, James 219
MOON, Margaret 173
　Matthew 173
MOONY, Sarah 104
MOOR, ... (...) 133
MOORE, Alfred 165
　Daniel 216
　Francis 130
　James 81, 141
　John 217
　Laurence 130
　Laurent 82
　Louis 82
　Margaret 103
　Peter 213
　Samuel 81
　Susan 137
　Susanne (Pineau) 130
　Ursule (Belanger) 130
　William 209
MOORS, Jeremiah 171
MORACE, Joseph 90
MORAIN, George 166
　Isidore 90
　Moris 164
MORAIS, Alexander M. 181
MORAN, see Maurre 70
　see Morain 90
　see Norrain 90
　36
　... 22, 31
　Capt. ... 41

MORAN, ... (...) 41
　Antoine 40
　Archange (...) 112
　Catherine (Boyer) 113
　Catherine (Campau) 111, 116
　Cha. 30, 32
　Charles 20, 54, 90, 111,
　　113, 152
　Charles Claude 116
　Claude 33
　Claude Charles 32
　Felicite (Meloche) 111
　George 151
　Isadore 112
　Isidore 40
　Joseph 113
　Lewis M. 186
　Louis 90, 111, 116, 152,
　　158, 159
　Maurice 79
　Maurise 151
　Morice 90
　Morris 111
　Therese 111
MORAN dit GRIMARD, Charles
　21, 32
MORAND, Chs. 79
MORANS, Chs 70
　Joseph 70
　Louis 69
　Moriche 70
　Pierre 70
MORAS, see Morace 90
　Antoine 53, 78
　Monique 130
　Nicolas 130
MORASS, Antoine 191
　Frances (Chauvin) 129
　Ignace 68, 129, 191
　Joseph 139, 177
　Monique (Gouin) 139
　Nicholas 129
　Nicolas 112, 139
　Therese (Poissant-Lasaline)
　　112
　Victor 112, 158, 160
MORASSE, Antne 68
　Victor 90
MORE, Alfred 156
　Louis 176
　John B. 191
　Paul 191
　Tousainth 191
MOREHOUSE, Clairsa 113
MOREL, Marguerite 33
MOREL dit LaDURANTAVE,
　Marguerite 33

MORET, Josephine 142
MORGAN, Chauncey 155
   John 219
   W. 212
MORICEAU, Victoire 77
MORIN, ... (...) 48
   Andrew 121
   Benjamin 209
   Isadore 176
   Isidore 78
   Jean 48, 54
   Louis 176
   Philip 173
MORISEAU, Victor 43
MORISSAU, Victor 65
MORLEY, Frances 104
MORON, Morris 158
MOROSH, Jacob 213
MORRAH, Joseph 156
MORRAIN, Charles 163
   Lewis 163
MORRASS, Victor 151
MORRELL, Daniel 201
   Hugh 126
   Ira 219
   Joseph 218
MORREN, Robert 217
MORRILL, Abner 185
MORRIN, Benjamin 121
   Margaret (Bazinet) 121
MORRIS, Benjamin 171
   Catherine 101
   Charles 188
   Dolphin 208
   George 181
   Lois 165
   Samuel 207
   William 185, 207
MORRISEAU, Pierre 12
   Victor 12
MORRISEAUX, Victoire 55
MORRISON, James 217
   John 187
   Joseph 187
   Margaret 85
   Mary 104
   Orville 184
   V. (...) 91
   William M. 219
MORROW, Isadore 160
   Joseph 166
MORSE, George P. 184
   John 205
   John G. 199
   Margaret 110
MORT, Ls 73
MORTON, Betsy 203
   Doras 181
   Ebenezer 199
   Jonothan G. 198
   Samuel 207
   Thomas 214

MORY, Stephen 167
MOSES, ... 125
MOSHER, Ira D. 201
MOSLEY, Henry J. 218
   Joseph 170
MOSS, Thomas 219
MOSSAIE, Antoine 121
MOSSES, D. 215
MOTON, Catherine (Navarre) 138
   Francis 138
MOU?, Mahaly 133
MOUNIER, ... 5
MOUNTINGER, Jacob 160
MOURAND, Louis 79
MOURLAND, Jacob 207
   William 207
MOUTON, Francois 50, 177
MOWERY, A. 215
MOYER, Love 189
MUDG, Elijah 153
   Elisha 153
   John 153
MUDGE, Mich 164
MUIR, Andrew 197
MULFORD, Samuel B. 179
MULHOLLAND, Daniel 136
   Isabella (Egnew) 136
   James 201
MULHOLLEN, Daniel 177
   James 177
   John 174
MULKS, John 177
MULLAR, Pierre 128
MULLER, Peter 128
MULLET, John 162
MULLEUR, Peter 128
MUNCEY, Jesse 123, 208
   Thomas 207
MUNDY, James H. 202
MUNROE, Robert 85
MURLIN, Samuel 187
MURPHY, Andrew 218, 219
   Daniel 146
   Dennis 218
   James 218
   James L. 210
   John 190
   Michael 218
   Patrick 218
   Richard 217
   Stephen 210
   Thomas 88
MURRAY, Asahil 187
   Elijah 210
   Obediah 185
   Orlando 187
   Peter 88
   Reuben 180
MURRY, Andrew 178
   Daniel 204
MURWINE, Sheldon 188

MUSHOW, P. 146
MUSSY, Archibald Y. 156
MYE, Joseph 131
   Margaret 131
MYERLY, John 210
MYERS, Haritte 157
   Harriet 110
   Harriet (...) 110
   Henry 78, 193
   Ignace 110
   James 91
MYRES, Harriet 170

NADAULT, Antoine 81
NADAUT, Antoine 67
NADEAU, Alexis 175
   Antoine 81, 174, 175
   Charles 174
   Jacob 76
   Jean B. 175
   Joseph 174, 175
   Louise 139
   Martin 76, 175
   Monique 141
   Pierre 177
   Rene 92, 123, 208
   Theotiste 144
NADEUA, Angelique 144
   Martin 144
NADO, Jacob 85
NAGLE, James 218
NAILSON/HARRISON, Joseph 62
NALLY, Robert 215
NAMENVILLE, Joseph 208
NANLEST, see Prudhomme dit
   Nantais 21
NANTAIS, Jn Bte 72
   Joseph 66
   Julian 32
NAPER, William 190
NAPP, James 204
   Thomas 204
NAPTON, Ezekiel 210
NASH, Israel 163
   Timothy 189
   Zena 198
NASSICO, Jean Bt. 156
NAVARE, Ant. 77
   Francois 81
   Hutro 81
   Isadore 81
   Jacques 81
   Jean 81
   Pierre 77
   Robert 81
NAVARRE 36
   ... 24, 31
   ... (...) 174
   Alexis 142, 175
   Antne 63
   Antoine 178
   Archange 137

NAVARRE, Archange
    (Marentette) 109
  Augustin 175
  Basile (LaPointe) 140
  Catharine 111
  Catherine 137, 138
  Catherine (Couture) 137
  Francois 137, 140, 176,
    178
  Francoise (Labadie) 140
  Frans 66
  Genevieve (Bourdeau) 140
  I. Marie 63
  Isidor 66
  Isidore 137
  Issadore 140
  Jaque 140
  Jacques 66, 137, 174, 176
  Jean 154
  Jean Marie 142, 174
  Jean Mrie 67
  John Francis 138
  John M. 109, 157, 160
  Marie (Laferte) 140
  Marie (Lootman-Barrois)
    109
  Marie (Suzor) 140
  Marie Louis (Godet) 137
  Monica 119
  Monique (Dusault) 142
  Paul 145, 178
  Platt 145, 175
  Pierre 63, 176
  Robert 14, 16, 20, 33, 43,
    55, 56, 63, 67, 89, 109,
    111, 119, 137, 140, 175,
    176
  Robert F. 178
  Robt. 76
  Susan (Moore) 137
  Utreau 63
  Utro 137
NAVARRE-UTRAU, Francois, see
  Navarre, Utro 137
NAVRE, Ensign 63
NAWFERT, David 112
NEALE, Seely 203
NEALEY, Lewis 219
NEDDO, Alexis 145
  Antoine 136
  Archange (Couture) 136
  Charles 136
  Joseph 139, 145
  Louise (Menard) 139
  Martin 145
  Mary (Duclos) 136
  Rami 123
  Ursule (Gaillard) 139
NEILL, T. 214
NEIMAN, John F. 210
NELL (colored) 86

NELLOUR, John 77
NELSON, George 151
  Jno 77
  Jonathan 89
  Thomas 189
NEMSICA, Francis 156
NENECT, Antoin 156
NEPHEW, Alex 213
  Antoine 171
  Joseph 137, 174
  Louise (Boemier) 137
  Michel 137
NESBIT, John 205
NESKECH, Marie 48
NEVEAUX, Joseph 121
NEVEO, Joseph 121
NEVEU, see Nephew 171
  Antoine 88
NEVEU-FRANCOEUR, see Nephew
    137
  see Nevieuz 102
NEVEUX, Antone 152
NEVIEUZ, Antoine 102
  Genevieve (Houde) 102
NEVILLE, James 212
NEWBERRY, Henry 172
NEWBURY, Francis 153
NEWCOMB, Alphonso 181
NEWCOME, Sylvania 203
NEWELL, Arza 204
  Augustus B. 206
NEWFART, David 158
NEWHALL, Benjamin 194
NEWKIRK, Daniel 177
NEWMAN, Ezra 185
  James V. 179
  Nathaniel 163
  Moris 163
NEWTON, Luther 204
  Samuel 201
  Seymour 179
NICHALS, Josiah 182
NICHOLAS, Francois 219
NICHOLLS, Abner 216
  Henry 222
NICHOLS, Andrew 118, 160
  Cyril 200
  Daniel B. 192
  Elisha 192
  Jonathan 204
  John 211
  Josiah 201
  Rufus 200
  Samuel D. 180
  Tilly 197
  William 127, 193, 201
NICKERSON, Lewis 188
NICKLA, Louis 130
NICLA, Baptist 131
NIFFIN, Daniel 190
NIPIAKI, Jane 114

NISBET, William 189
NIXEN, John 199
NOAH, John P. 113, 158
NOBLE, Charles 101, 174
  Elizabeth (...) Cooper 105
  Girardus 200
  Israel 171
  Nathan 173
  Nathaniel 200
  Sally 200
  Thomas 200
NOBLES, Aaron 113
  Aron 158
NOLINE, Louis 214
  Michel 214
NORFOLK, Mary 166
NORRAIN, Louis 90
NORRIS, Benjamin 182
  George 162
  Josiah 199
  Mark 197
  Waldrom 202
NORT, Martin 217
NORTH, John 182
NORTHROP, Lewis 167
  Polly 150
NORTHRUP, Hosea 194
NORTON, Daniel T. 202
  Elias 197
  Giles 207
  Howel B. 189
  Lewis 180
  Nathan 207
  Noah 188
  Selden 205
NORWOOD, Phillemon W. 128
NOURCIER, Joseph 124
NOWLAND, Arthur 198
  Sally 85
NOXON, Mary (...) 110
  Thomas 110, 150
NOYCE, Abram 171
NOYES, James 199
NUBACK, Ebenezer 195
NUGENT, James 209, 217
NUSON, Jean Bt. 156
  Simon 156
NYE, Alvin 193
  Horatio 193
  Jefferson 193
  Marcus 192
  Nathan 193
NYES, see Mye 131

OAKES, Charles H. 209
OAKLEY, Eno 198
OBIAN, Antoine 206
OBIEN, Joseph 162
OBIN, Angelique (Brillant)
    116
  James 116

## Index

OBIN, Margaret 109, 157
  Margaret (Casse-St. Aubin) 109
O'BRIEN, Elijah 213
  James 218
O'CONNER, John 171, 189
O'DELL, Daniel 170, 188
  James 206
  Mathew G. 206
  Thomas 203
O'DIAN, Alexander 203
ODIEN, Alexis 154
ODIENNE, Alexander 110
ODIN, Antoine 166
OGDEN, James 195
OGILEY, Charles 174
OHARROW, John 189
OKEEF, George A. 171
"OLD" JACK 154
OLDS, Daniel 211
  Ezra 204
  Joseph 204
  Obd. 204
O'LEARY, Peter 218
OLMSTEAD, Gideon 197
  Jonathan 218
OLMSTED, Benjamin J. 197
  Israel H. 197
  Zacharian 185
O'MARA, John 216
ON--L, Antne 69
O'NEIL, Dennis 218
ORGE, ... 122
ORMSBY, C. N. 188
ORN, Ebenezer 219
O'RORKE, Bridget (...) 142
  Honora 142
  Patrick 142
ORR, Andrew 217
  Jacob 156, 164
  James 125
ORRY, Edward 128
ORSEN, David H. 197
ORVIS, Ruth 119
OSBAND, William A. 153
OSBURN, Israel 163
  Jesse 170, 189
  William 161
OSMER, Wheaton 196
  William 196
OSTERSTAG, Lewis 218
OSTRANDER, Alexander 181
  Solomon 189
OTIS, Asa H. 162
  Isaac 198
  Ora 162
OUABANKIKOVE, Marguerite 6
OUDAIN, Antoine 63
OUELET 37
  see Woillet 67, 89
OUILLETTE, Jean 51

OUSTERHOUT, Cornelius 200
OUSTEROUT, James 161
OVEROCHER, ... 203
OVERSTREET, William C. 218
OWEN, David W. 198
  Elizabeth 104
  James 138
  Thomas J. 172
OWENS, Alijah 192
  Wilfred 146
OWLE, Joseph 145
OWLS, William 191

PA--ENS, see Palms 23
PACKARD, Austin 202
  Benjamin H. 198
  Margaret 171
PACKER, William 201
PACKERD, William 163
PACHIN, Able 165
PADDOCK, David 181
PAEN, see Pean 14
PAGE, Curtis 189
  David 198
  Ezekiel 198
  Francis 123
  Reed 204
  Rufus 201
  William 174
PAGEE, Frances 206
PAGEOS, see Pageot 22
PAGEOT, Thomas 12
  Thomas Joseph 22, 33
PAGOT, ... 31
PAGOTTE, Thomas 43, 50
PAILES, Philo 156
PAILLE, see Baille 21
  ... 25
PAINE, Betsey 119
  Edward 119
  Joseph 217
PAJAE, Francois 123
PAJEAU 36
PAJOR, see Pageot 14
PALLIOTTE, Joseph 69
PALMER, Archange (Tremblay) 117
  George 195
  James 161
  John 88, 85, 117, 160, 164, 172
  Mary Amy (Witherell) 104
  Richard H. 219
  Thomas 104, 172
PALMERTON, Craig 184
PALMS, ... 23
PANGBURN, William 164
PANIZ, Ruby 48
PANIZE, Angelique 48
  Lizette 48
  Marianne 48

PAPINEAU, see Poppino 117
PAQUETTE, (Frs.) H. 208
  Joseph 212
  Pierre 211
PARAIN, Joachim 89
PARDEE, Willis 179
PARE, Felix 177
  George 85
  Jean Baptiste 33
  Jn Bte 37
PARENT 37
  ... 5, 32
  ... (...) 44
  Gilles 16
  Jacques 44, 51
  Joseph 6
  Julien 44, 51
  Laurance 33
  Laurence 21
  Laurent 16, 44, 51
  Magdeleine 7
  Magdeleine (Marette dit Lapine) 6
PARGE, Francois 123
PARGET, Thomas 206
PARISIAN, Jacques 125
PARK, ... 74, 82
  Alanson 182
  Calvin 184
  John 113, 158
  Joseph 183
  Myron 184
  Robert 182
  William 43, 54, 60
  Wm. 78
PARKE, Ezra S. 185
  Harvey 181
PARKER, Andrew 198
  Asa 182
  Barnaby 142
  Charles 186
  Daniel 174
  David 181
  Elisha B. 201
  Enos 180
  Geo. 200
  Harvey 182
  Parker Jacob B. 174
  Joshua 175
  Luther 137, 173
  Margaret (Price) Troutwine 101
  Oliver 101, 181
  Robert 91
  Samuel 127
  Thomas 88
  Tom (colored) 86
PARKERD, Asa 163
PARKERSON, J. 214
PARKHURST, Abel P. 202
PARKINSON, Daniel M. 217

PARKINSON, James 213
  John 165, 217
PARKS, Amos 192
  B. 146
PARLETON, Welcome J. 201
PARLOW, Samuel 165
PARNIER, Joseph 139
  Josette 139
  Josh 65
PARNIER-VADEBONCOEUR,
  Therese 109
PARO, John B. 124
PARRA, Samuel 171
PARREY, J. Bt. 48
  Jean Bte. 51, 52
PARRISH, Dawson F. 219
  Gilbert 185
  Levi 216
  Thomas 219
PARRY, Fanny 151
  Jean Bt 44
PARSONS, Chester 202
  Joseph 198
  Nehemiah P. 198
  Orrin 202
  Roswell 199
PARTLOW, William 171
PARTRIDGE, Asa 129
PASSAGE, John 170
PATE, Ebenezer 153, 167
PATTEE, John 166
PATCHEN, James 188
PATCHVIN, Paschall 158
PATEL, ... 17
PATENAUDE, Ns 90
PATERNAUDE, see Patrenctre 90
PATNAUDE, Nicholas 73
PATNODE, Nicolas 82
PATNOTRE, Louis 61
PATNOTTE, Nicholas 40, 52
  Nicolas 79
PATOKA, see Peltier 23
PATRENOTRE, Cecilia 133
  Margaret 133
  Nicolas 21, 133
PATRICK, Joshua 89
  Pierce 186
  William 183
PATTEN, Joseph 186
PATTERSON, James 203
  John 106
  Nicholas 213
  Robert 201
PATTESON, John 171
PATTINSON, Hugh 60
  Richard 60
PATTISON, Richard 85
PAUL, Jacob 200
  John 218
  Joseph 128, 209

PAUL, Josette 123
PAULING, ... 54
PAUQUETTE, Antoine 218
  Pierre 219
PAVETT, Joseph 156
PAXTON, Genevieve (Levitre) 139
  John 139, 174
  Samuel 217
  Theotiste (Lacelle) 139
  Thomas 139
PAYANT, Toussaint 209
PAYEN de NOYON, Pierre 12
PAYET, Marie 145
PAYNE, Harmon A. 187
  Henry 204
PEAN, Seigneur of Lirandiere,
  Ives-Jacues 12
PEARSALL, Michael 183
  Nathaniel 181
PEARSOLL, Clement 184
PEAS, Lymon 188
PEASE, Barney 180
PECHEY, Monica (Desaulniers) 116
  Pierre 116
PECK, Isaac 163
  Joseph H. 198
  Russel 206
  Sarah 141
PECKINS, Martin 133
PEIRCE, Warner 177
PEKOIN, Joseph 213
PELETIER, Francois 6
  Madeleine (Thunes dit Du Fresne) 6
PELKEY, Jacques 172
  Joseph 156
  Louis 171
PELLEGORE, Battes 146
  Joseph 211
PELLETIER, Alexis 72, 82
  Andre 78
  Antoine 76
  Baptiste 62, 78
  Bat. 79
  Bte 69
  Charles 80
  Chs 69
  Felix 79
  Isidore 76
  Jacques 77
  Louis 62, 76
  Phili 69
PELTEN, Hart 213
PELTIER, see Patoka 23
  Alexis 133
  Andre 48, 52, 103
  Andrew 110, 129
  Antoine 62
  Archange 103

PELTIER, Archange (Casse-St. Aubin) 129
  Bapt. 30
  Baptist 191
  Baptiste 90, 85
  Bte 36
  Catharine (Meloche) 103
  Catharine (Williams) 103
  Catherine 103, 110
  Catherine (St. Aubin) 130
  Catherine (Vallee) 109
  Charles 90, 129, 131, 191
  Ezekiel A. 173
  Felicity 119
  Felix 90, 130, 191, 196
  Isidore 85
  J. Bte 88, 109, 130
  Jacques 44, 55, 62, 89, 119
  Jean 209
  Jean Baptiste 16, 20, 33
  Jean Bt 41
  Jean Bte 53
  John 119, 160
  John B. 151
  John Bapt. 109
  John Bt. 157
  John Bte. 103, 163
  Joseph 133, 191
  Leon 190
  Lewis 164
  Loison 157
  Louis 88
  Louison 110
  M. (Pominville) 130
  Margaret (Patrenotre) 133
  Rosalie 129
  Suzanne (Facer) 109
  Therese 105
PELTON, Nathan 188
PEMBER, Jabez T. 184
PEMBERTON, Richd 89
PENDERGRASS, Richard 123
PENNINGTON, John 188
PENNOCK, Joseph 191
PENNY, James T. 170
PEPIN, Baril 64
  Bazil 81
  Francis 76
  Frans 64
  Michel 81
PERAU, Louis 151
PERCELLE, Lepton 128
PERCIE, see LeDuc-Percie 177
PERCY, Louis 82
PERE, Chene, Charles 16
PEREN, see Langlois and/or Parent 21
PERIAW, Francis 147
PERIN, David 181
  Jesse 183
  Johnathan 183

# Index

PERINIER, Joseph 53
PERKINS, George 172
  Harvey 182
  Nathan 218
  Samuel 103, 171
  William 196
PERNIER, Louis 65
  Paul 65, 81
PERRAULT, Jean B. 208
PERRAULT'S, ... 120
PERRE, Jean 31
PERRIER, Peter 156
PERRIN, Austin 163
  Ezra I. 186
PERRINE, Baptiste 82
PERRIS, Julius 208
PERRY, Chester 197
  Edmond 186
  George 186
  Grant 200
  John H. 193
  Joseph 200
  Morris 184
  Nathaniel 210
  Norman 194
  Peter 114, 158, 166
  Robert 186
  Simeon 186
  Warren 189
PERRYGORE, Battes 146
PERSALL, Clark 162
  John 162
PERSIL, see LeDuc 16
  Louis 90
PERSONS, Philip 166
PETER, J. BT 44
PETERMAULX, Francois 123
PETERS, Cassander 188
  George W. 201
  Jesse 202
  Joseph 202
  Richard 175
PETERSON, John G. 201
  Mary 201
  Richard 200
  Solomon 200
PETIET, Samuel 196
PETIS, Lewis 191
PETIT, Antoine 73, 82
  Baptiste 73, 82
  Catherine 115
  Jeanne 132
  John B. 195
  Joseph 124
  Julia 109
  Louis 73, 82, 140, 174
  Mary Ann 131
  Michael 121
  Nicholas 52
  Nicolas 131, 132
  Samuel 90
  Solomon 140

PETIT, Susanne (LaFontaine) 140
  Theodocia (Deveauz) 105
  William 105
PETIT dit MILHOMME, Francois/Jean 22
PETIT-BOISMOREL, Madeleine 7
PETRE, Francis 163
  Francois 116, 151, 159
  Veronica (Rivard) 116
PETTEE/PELTIER, ... (...) 132
PETTENGILL, Benjamin 200
PETTIBONE, Harmon 180
  John 203
  Olive 203
  Roswell 180
PETTIGREW, John 207
PHALAN, Catherine 172
  James 208
  Thomas 217
PHEARSON, Amable (Desaulniers-Lajomondiere) 111
  John 111
PHELPS, Alfred 184
  Amariah 204
  Benjamin 185
  Guy 183
  Isaiah 200
  Joseph 145
  Justin 201
  Levi 163
  Oliver W. 210
  Samuel 170
  Theodore E. 178
  William A. 217
PHERSON, John 158
PHILAMORE, Robert 111
PHILBRICK, Nathan 182
PHILEMON, Mary (Shackleton) 111
  Robert, see Philamore 111
PHILETT, Joseph 164
PHILIPS, William M. 206
PHILIS, ... 5
  Charlotte (Savarias) 7
  Jacques 7
PHILLIP, Prince 158
PHILLIPS, Archibald 186
  Chester 187
  Daniel W. 192
  David 155, 163
  Emily 113
  Isaac 179
  Jacob 183
  John 176, 198
  Jose 197
  Luther 186
  Phillip 176
  Prince 113
  Ross 179
  Veronica (Williams) 113

PHILLIPS, William 184
PHORBS/FORBS, John 167
PIASLEY, Abraham 182
PIATT, Joe 159
  Joseph 166
PICAR, Joseph 120
PICARD, see Picar 120
  Antoine 121
  Jean Bt. 208
  John B. 92
PICHET, see Pechey 116
  Basil 116
  Pierre 150
PICK, Moses 182
PICKENS, Martin 195
PICKET, Axy 114
  Samuel B. 171
PICOT, Joseph 114
  Pierre 111, 157
  Victoire (...) 111
PICOTE de BELETRE, Francois Marie 12
PICOTTE, Elizabeth (Pineau) 114
  Joseph 114
  Pierre 177

PIECHEY, Pierre 159
PIERCE, ... 128
  ... (Laframboise) 125
  Ann (Kendrick) 125
  Benjamin 125, 127
  Benjamin K. 125
  John S. 125
  Joseph 127
  Marietta O. (Puthuff) 125
  Timothy 186
PIERSON, Samuel 197
PIGEON, Aloysius 33
PIKE, ... (...) 43
  John 54, 206
  Leonard 101
PILET, Jacq. 17
  Pacques 132
  James 32
  Jean 16
  Jean Baptiste or Jacques 24
  Jeanne 130
  Joseph 24
  Mary Louisa 132
PILETTE, Jos. 32
  Joseph 33
  Mar. 30
PILLET, see Juillet dit Montreuil 22
  Jean 20
PILOTTE, Lizette 209
PINARD, Joseph 60, 77, 85
PINE, Alan 203
  Mary 203
PINEAU, Elizabeth 114

273

PINEAU, Joseph 143
  Marie 143
  Susanne 130
PINEAU-LAPERLE, Alexis 111
PININWELL, Robert 206
PINKERTON, Thomas 179
PINKNEY, Thomas 161
PINTERS, Benjamin 203
PION, ... 124
  Jean Bt. 212
PIQUET dit LAFLEUR, Charles 24
PIQUETTE, Charles 215
  Francis 214
  Jean Baptiste 85
  John Battise 214
  Tousaint 214
PIRIN, Calvin 183
  Phineas 183
PITRE, see Petre 116
  Guillme 77
  J. Bte 116
  Jean Bte 55
PITTMAN, Daniel 189
PITTRE, Denis 70
  Jn Bte 70
PITTS, John 175
PIZANNE, Paggy/Pelagie 212
PLACKETT, John 210
PLANK, Christopher 217
PLANT, Joseph 219
PLANTE, Antoine 77
PLATT, Ezra 198
PLEWIN, William 204
PLICHON, Louis 17
PLOOF, Martin 214
PLUME, George 126
PLUMLEY, John 127
PLUMMER, Avery 178
POINENNIEA, Chas. 159
POIDIN, Louis 213
POIRIER, Charles 117
  Charles Paul, see Poureia, Charles 117
  Clemence (Maupetit) 6
  Pierre Rene 6
POIRIER dit LAFLEUR, Clemence (Maupetit) 6
  Pierre Rene 6
POIRRIER, (Charles?) 68
POISON, Louis 121
POISSANT-LASALINE, Paul 112
  Therese 112
POITEVIN, see Gibaut 24
POLANDER, Joseph 218
  Josette 43
POLLOCK, Harry 154
POMANVILLE, Joseph 192
POMEREILLE, Joseph 133
POMINVILLE, see Palliotte 69
  Joachim 124

POMINVILLE, Joseph 116
  Joseph, see Pomereille, Joseph 133
  L. (...) 90
  M. 130
POMPEY (colored) 86
PONCHAT, Mary 117
POND, Augustin 208
  Peter 36
POOL, Thomas 202
POOLEY, Edward 189
POPE, Stephen 189
POPINO, Seth L. 160
POPKINS, James 201
POPPINO, Seth 117
POPPLETON, William 182
PORLIER, see Pothier 24
  Binac 42
  James 146, 212
POROSE, John Bte 166
PORTER, Daniel 201
  Elisha M. 192
  Giles 106
  Willard 180
PORYETTE, Jos. 30
POST, Jeremiah 202
POSTIER, see Pothier 24
POSTLE, George 183, 185
POTDEVIN, see Gibaut dit Poitevin 24
  36
  Pire 44
POTHIER dit CAMPAU, Michel 24
POTRAIN, John 167
POTTER 183
  D. 215
  Henry 137
  Thomas 219
POTTIER, Antoine 85
POTVAIN, Pascal 152
  Joseph 124, 190
  Pascal 112
POUCHETTE, Dominique 138
  Joseph 138
  Mary Ann (Bernard-Lajoie) 138
POUDRAIN, Paskile 167
POUGE, see Pouget 23
  ... 24
  Dominique 177
POUGET 36
  Bte 66
  Catherine 141
  Joseph 32, 50, 81, 141, 143
  Joseph Gabriel 23
  Josh 66
  Martha 143
POULIN, Francis 140
  Francois 144, 176
  Joseph 176
  Mary 140

POUPAR, Joseph 55
POUPARD, ... (...) 174
  Andre 144, 175
  Andrew 144
  Angelique (Nadeau) 144
  Ch. 76
  Charles 61, 90, 85, 104
  Felicite (Campau) 104
  Joseph 144, 175
  Simon 172
  Theotiste (Nadeau) 144
POUPARD dit LAFLEUR, Charles 16
POUPARD-LAFLEUR, Charles 104
  Isabelle (Casse) 104
POUPARRE, Andre 67
POUREIA, Charles 117
  Jeanne (Laperle) 117
POWEL, Archilbald 193
  George T. 193
POWELL, Daniel 181
  Peter 212
  Robert B. 218
POWER, Arthur 179
  James 179
  Nathan 180
  Samuel 180
POWERS, Almira Rood 110
  Alvin 175
  Henry 205
  Isaac 187
  John 188, 204
  M. 210
  Strange 146
  William 204
POWERS, M. 211
  Strange/Strange 212
POZE, see Powers 211, 212
PRADET-LAFORGE, John Simon 130
PRARIE, Julien 177
PRATER, Jonathan 207
PRATT, Edmund 201
  Elkhanna 201
  Francois 51
  Joseph 189
  Levi B. 202
  Samuel 203
PRAY, Esak 201
PREDOM, Glote 142
  Teresa (Martin) 142
PRENTICE, Augustin 176
  Ezra 193
  Joseph 176
PRENTIS, Gilbert W. 180
PRENTISS, Joseph 136
PRESCOTT, Ezra 129
PRESSON, Henry 118, 160
  Mary Ann (McVay) 117
PRESTON, see Presson 118
  Ira 192
  John 190
  Moses 136

# Index

PRESTON, William 142, 175
  William P. 219
PREVOUR, Antoine 82
PRICE, Adam 192
  George 89
  Henry 193
  John 206
  Joshua 192
  Louisa 192
  Margaret 101
  Peter 194
  Phillip 192
  Thomas H. 217
  Tobias 192
  William 184
PRICKET, Richard 211
PRICKETT, Richard 145
PRIEST, Erastus 196
PRIMER, John B. 217
PRINCE, Eric 180
  Joseph 212
PRINGLE, William 199
PRIVONLILLE, J. B. 213
PROCTOR, Benjamin 194
  John 194
PROHA, Paul 215
PROU, see Prue 141, 142
  Francis 142
PROULT, Jacques 66
PROUX, ... (...) 174
  Charles 81, 177
  Louis 174
  Pierre 43, 50
PROVENCAL, ... (...) 76
  Anne 85
  James 85
  Pierre 62, 105
PROVENCELLE, Catherine (Vallee) 105
PROVENSALLE, Louis 124
PROVINCAL, C. (...) 88
  Pierre 42
PROVINCE, Piere 145
PROVOST, Charles A. 208
  Francois 212
PROVOW, Francis 146
PRUDHOME, Francois 50
PRUDHOMME 36
  Claude 177
  Claude, see Predom, Glote 142
  Fra. 31
  Francoix Zavier 22, 33
  Jacques 81
  Pierre 50, 142
PRUDHOMME dit NATAIS, Jean Baptiste 21
PRUE, Charles 141, 143
  Teresa (Goyou) 142
  Mary Kickson 141
PTOLOME, Angelique 7

PUFFER, Abigail (Joslin) 127
  Caty (Clapp) 127
  Nathan 127
PULLAH, Francis 144
  Marie (Lavergne) 144
PULLEN, James 203
PULSIVER, Joseph 167
PULSOPHER, Joseph 152
PURDY, James 165
  William 185
PURKEY, Jacob 116, 159
PURSLEY, Daniel 64, 65
PURVIS, Wm 146
PUTHUFF, Marietta O. 125
  Mary (Smith) 128
  William 125
PUTNAM, Gen. ... 137
  Amie 200
  Huzziel 207
  Irv. H. 207
PUZO, Sidney 201

QUACKENBUSH, Adrian 200
QUERET, John 146
QUESNEL, see Quintin 21
  Jacques 22
  James 139
  Louise 139
QUESNEL dit ST. DENIS dit ST. REMY, Jacques 22
QUEVILLON, M. Josephe 103
QUEZENO, Joseph 123
QUICK, Denis 183
  Elijah 164
QUINBEE 201
QUINBY, Dennis 219
QUINTIN, ... 21

RABBAY, Antoine 172
RABERGON, Jos. 159
RACIOTE, Regis 177
RAIMON, Francs 91
RAIMOND, Batiste 72
  Josiah 89
RAINOLD, George 64
  John 64
RAMIBAULT, Charles Nicolas 23
RAMO, Francis 164
RAMON, Daniel 78
RAMSDELL, Dirl 155
  Dyer 163
RAMSDELL, Gennet 163
  Noah 165
RAMSEY, John 174
RANDALL, Alanson 198
  Isaac 190
  Sam'l 190
  Zadock 200
RANDLE, James 162
RANDOLPH, Asa 179
  Merit 179

RANDOLPH, Stephen 196
RANKIN, James 41, 51
  John 217
RANSOM, Ammerst C. 218
RAPITALE/RATILLE, Baptiste 82
RAPP, Margaret 145
RASH, Geo. 200
RATEL, see Rattail 130
  Antoine 130
  Charles 131
RATELLE, Etienne 177
RATTAIL, Archange (Laperle) 130
  Etienne 130
  John B. 131
  Mary (Valley) 131
  Paul 131
  Pelagia (Duchene) 131
RATTEL, John B. 191
  Paul 191
RAU, see Reau 22
  see Roe 139
  J. Bte. 139, 142, 143, 144
  Jean Baptiste 22
  Jn Bte 36
  Joseph, see Roe, Joseph 142
  Margaret 144
  Victoire 143
RAVENNE, ... 32
RAVENO, Jean Bt. 156
RAWSON, Amariah 196
  Luther 161
RAY, John 207, 217
  Jonas 190
  Richard 219
RAYMON, Mary 171
RAYMOND, Adam/Andrew 85
  Catherine 105
  Francis, see Reynom, Francis 117
  Henry 170
  Josia 160
  Josiah 118
  Michel 117
RAYMOND-TOULOUSE, J. Bte. 131
RAMSAY, Elizabeth (...) 105
  John 105
RANDALL, James 127
READ, Robert R. 216
  William M. 212
READING, Asa H. 198
READLION, Josiah 127
REAMES, Moses 207
REAMS, William 207
REAU, see Bau dit LeBeau 22
  Jean Bte 43, 81
REAUME, see Reome 16
  36, 37, 51
  ... 24
  Agathe 139, 140
  Angelique 143
  Batiste 66

REAUME, Bonaventure 48, 52
   Charles 51
   Claude 44
   Ettiene 179
   Hyacinthe, see Reome 16
   J. Bt. 44
   J. Bte 81, 140
   Jacente 22
   John Bte 56
   Joseph 41, 67, 81, 139, 179
   Julia 145
   Madeleine 48
   Margaret 139
   Marie 145
   Monique 139
   P. 32
   Pierre 33, 44, 51, 52
   Temus 23
REAUME dit THEMUS, Louis 21
   Pierre 33
REBURN, John 77
RECHA, Piere 164
RECHEIL, Hipolite 121
RECORD, Catherine (Boyer) 132
   Oliver 132, 195
REDMOND, Henry 216
REDWAY, Capus 194
REED, Antoine 212
   Benjamin 204
   Charles F. 170
   D. B. 189
   Don A. 189
   Gersham 189
   James 195, 212
   John 60, 82, 207, 210
   John T. 210
   Nathan 207
   Thomas 110, 157, 187
REES, Hannah 103
REEVES, Steven 187
REGALLE, Abraham 78
REGLY, John 78
REGNON, Francis 160
REGIS, "Old" ... 14
REID, Benlding 204
   Duncan 104
   Eleanor (Descomps-Labadie) 104
   John 160
   Samuel 172
   Thomas 197
RELLE, Constant 122
REMINGTON, Sylvester 173
REMOND, (Frs.) ... 78
RENAU, see Renaud 22
   Joseph 151
   Louis 40, 82
RENAUD, see Reneau 90
   see Rumeau 88
   Anne 101

RENAUD, Cecilia 120
   Charles 22, 33, 50
   Louis 53, 101
   Marie Anne Casse 101
RENAUT, ... 72
   Antoine 72
   Cha. 31
   Gabl. 72
   Louis 72, 77
RENEAU, Andrew 85
   Antoine 90, 150
   Cecile 85
   Charles 43
   Francois 90
   Garmish 85
   Henriette
   Joseph 90, 150
   Laurent 174
   Louis 79, 172
RENEF, Leonard 106
RENNO, Joseph 161
RENNOLD, Arnold 215
RENO, Adelaide (Comparet) 142
   Francois 142
   Laurent 142
   Louise 142
RENVILLE, Joseph 209
RENWICK, George 201
   John 199
REOME, Charles 146
   Pierre, see Reaume 16
   Yacinthe, see Reaume 16
REULAND, Joseph 141
REVARD, Antoine 112, 142
   Eleanor (Daudelin) 142
   Frances 111
   Isabelle (Chapoton) 111
   J. Bte 112
   Jean Bte 111
   John Bte 142
   Roalie (Saucier) 112
REVARRD, Archange (Yulon) 142
   August 142
REVAU, see Reveau 17
   Jean Louis 33
REVAU-LAJEUNESSE, Louis 136
   Teresa 136
REVAUR, Jean Bte 54
REVAURE, Antoine 56
REVEAU, Jean Louis 50
   Louis 17
REVIT, Paul 121
REVOR, Joseph 147
REX, George 210
REYNOLDS, Chancy 163
   Thomas 54
REYNOM, Francis 118
   Rosalie (Lemay) 117
REYNOR, Antoine 161
RHEAUME, L., see Reaume dit Themus 21

RHELE, John B. 123
RHEUME, Genevieve (Suzor) 141
   J. Bte. 141
   Joseph 141
RHINEHART, George 187
   John 206
RHODES, Antoine 82
   Edmond S. 142
   Hiram M. 184
   Oren 137
   Samuel 183
RICARD, see Record 132
   Alexis 132
   Gabriel 76
RICCA, Thomas 153
RICE, Abner 187, 191
   Asa 198
   Harly 192
   Ira 155, 202
   Joseph 213
   Justin 172
   Lewis 173
   Peter 133, 184
   Randal S. 170
   Randall S. 136
   Squire 201
   Zeba 183
RICH, Samuel 207
RICHARD, Gabl 89
   Gabriel 78, 85, 103, 171
RICHARDS, Charles 204
   Daniel 196
   Martin W. 186
   William 193
   William T. 219
RICHARDSON, John D. 205
   Oragin D. 181
   Peter 180
   Samuel 166
   Simeon 201
RICHAVEN, John J. 155
RICHEY, John 199
RICHIO, Margaret 213
RICKMAN, James 214
RICKMON, Samuel 127
RICHMOND, Morris 201
RICKERT, Abraham 203
RIDDY, Edward 42
RIDER, Charles 145
   David 153, 165

RIDING, Edward 61
RIDLEY, ... 54
RIGGLE, Benjamin 152
RIGGS, Hezekiah 198
   Jeremiah 185
   Joseph P. 198
   Lauren P. 186
   William G. 204
   Wm. L. 174
RILEY, George 213

## Index

RILEY, James 210
  M. 215
RIOPEL, Amable 78
  Ambroise 42, 89
  Antoine 81
  Dominque 157, 160
  Elizabeth 105
  Hyacinthe 89
  Jean Bt. 196
  John Bt. 159
  Jos. 159
  Pierre 89
  Yessich 159
RIOPELL, Ambrois 63
  Dominick 154
  John Bte. 160
  Joseph 154, 160
  Pierre 63, 77
  Touissen 65
  Toullaine 78
  Rousant 160
RIOPELLE, Ambroise 55, 110, 115
  Angela (Bondy) 115
  Antne 68
  Archange (Meloche) 115
  Colette (Guoin) 110
  Dominique 110
  Francoise (Meloche) 115
  John Bapt. 115
  Joseph 115
  Teresa Maillet 115
  Yessiah 115
RIPLEY, John F. 157
RISDON, Orange 202
RITCHY, Geo. 214
RITTER, Sarah 207
RIVARD, see Rivaure 41
  37
  ... 21, 67
  Agnes 115
  Agnes (Saucier) 120
  Antoine 66, 81, 90, 142, 152, 158, 163, 191
  Archange 164
  Archange (Saucier) 120
  Archange (Seguin) 120
  Augustus, see Revarrd, Augustus 142
  Baptiste 90
  Bte 71
  Catherine 137
  Charles 71, 90, 115, 116, 120, 132, 160, 191
  Chas. 79
  Chs 69
  Elizabeth 116
  Eustach 163
  Francis 160
  Francois 78, 90, 151
  Genevieve 132

RIVARD, Hiram 191
  J. Bte. 79, 116, 120
  James 64
  Jean 30
  Jean Baptist 79
  Jean Baptiste 32
  John B. 191
  John Bt. 159
  John Bte 166
  Joseph 147, 212
  Josephe 48
  Leon 151, 163
  Leon F. 151
  Michael 120, 132, 160
  Michel 71, 79, 90, 151, 164
  Mitchel 191
  Monica 116
  Nicholas 71, 79
  Peter 163
  Piere 164
  Pierre 80, 90, 120, 151, 160
  Pierris 70
  Simon 79
  Veronica 116
RIVARD dit LaCOURSIER, Luke Antoine 21
RIVARD-LACOURSIERE, Augustin, see Lacourse, Augustus 142
  Francis 142
RIVAURE, see Rivard 41
  Jean Bte. 41
RIVET, see Revit 121
  Teresa 123
RIVORED, (Frs.) ...
ROACH, E. B. 146
ROBATAILE, Joseph 191
ROBEAR, Elois 205
ROBB, David 81
  James 139, 175
  John 138
  Margaret 145
ROBBE, Gabriel 146
  John 204
ROBBINS, Benjamin 203
ROBEDOUX, Louison 43
ROBERT, Agat 140
  Agathe (Reaume) 140
  Agnes 141
  Angelique (Ptolome) 7
  Ant. 32
  Ante/Antoine 17
  Antne 66
  Anthony 141
  Antoine 22, 33, 51, 52, 81, 142, 144, 174
  Coleta 141
  Francois 7, 81, 140, 174
  Frans 68
  Ignace 178

ROBERT, Isaac 142, 178
  Isadore 140
  Isidor 66
  Isidore 81
  Jean 41
  Jean Bt. 175
  Joseph 7, 72, 81, 140, 175, 176, 178
  Josh 66
  Julia (Bourdeau) 140
  Louise (Dival) 140
  Marie (Godet) 140
  Monique (Chamberland) 142
  Pelagie 141
  Pierre 7, 55, 140, 176
  Pierre Nicolas 23
  Pre 36
  Prudent 7
  Robiche 73
  Susanne 145
  Suzanne 109
  Teresa 144
  Teresa (Drouillard) 142
ROBERT dit LAFONTAINE, Angelique (Ptolome) 7
  Francois 7
  Joseph 7
  Pierre 7
  Purdent 7
ROBERTJEAN, Joseph 82
  Josh 90
  Robert 82
  Rosalie 130
ROBERTJEANNES, see Robertjohn 115
ROBERTJOHN, Catherine (Petit) 115
  Joseph 115, 161
  Robert 115
ROBERTOY, Joseph 130
ROBERTS, ... 5
  George 201
  Griffith 163
  Ira 185
  John 170
  Moses 152, 204
  Samuel 200
  William 186
ROBERTSON, David 190
  Henry 195
  James 72, 129, 195
  John 85, 195
  Joseph 127
  Louise (Lauzon) 101
  Mary Ann 85
  Susanne 136
  Thomas 195
  William 61, 85, 101
  Wm. 77, 78
ROBETAILLE, Jacques 60
ROBIDEAU, Agnes (Chauvin) 142

ROBIDEAU, Archange (Bernard) 142
  Catherine (Lapointe) 142
  Etienne 142
  John Mary 140
  Joseph 142, 177
  Louis 140, 142
  Margaret 142
  Pierre 142, 176
ROBIDOU, Angelique 143
  Bonadventure 81
  Etienne 81
  Joseph 81, 142
  Louis 81
  Mary 142
ROBIDOUX, Charles 51, 67
  Etienne 44, 66, 67
  Josh 67
  Louis 51, 66, 176
ROBILLARD, Joseph 208
ROBINSON, ... (...) 85
  Abner 183
  David 188
  Edward 122
  Elijah E. 124, 211
  Elizabeth 131
  Eunice (...) 122
  Francis 208
  George 217
  James 217
  John 85
  John R. 180
  Rix 122, 209
  Seth 200
  William 172
  William D. 163
ROBISON, James 82
  William 90
ROBITALLE, Chs 69
  Joseph 130
  Josh 70
  Sophia 130
ROBSON, John 101
ROBY, Francis 193
  Hannah 172
  Hannah (...) 103
  John S. 103
  Thomas 193
ROC, Angelique 48
  Joseph 48
  Louise 48
ROCHAMBEAU, Francois 209
ROCHE, Benjamin 48
ROCHEREAU, see Sarasteau 69
  ... 69
ROCK, Augustine 146
  Augustin, see LaRoque,
    Agustin 212
ROCKWELL, John 181
ROCOUR, ... (...) 79
ROCOURT, Jean Bte. 42

RODDE, Joseph 48
  Josephe (Rivard) 48
RODE, ... 48
  Junior 69
RODEBOUGH, John 165
  Peter 165
RODENBOUGH, John 153
  Peter 153
RODIER, see Rode 69
ROE, ... (...) 178
  Antoine 177
  Bpte 67
  Dominique 139
  Genevieve (Cousineau) 142
  Genevieve (Jacob) 139
  J. Bte. 143
  Jean Bt. 177
  John 211
  John Bte 139, 143
  Joseph 142, 177
  Margaret (Lapointe) 143
ROGER, Nathan 193
ROGERS, Alexander 208
  Cary 188
  Chester 89
  Edward L. 203
  Francis 127
  Henry 127
  Parley 187
  Solomon 179
  Steamboat J. 106
  John 216
ROHAVILLE, T. 214
ROI, Louis 77
ROITEL, Catherine 140
  Joseph 140
ROLAND, Pierre 77
ROLETTE, Joseph 92, 124, 146, 212
ROLLE, ... 48
ROLLINS, Ashford 219
  George 218
ROMAIN-SANSCRAINTE, see St.
  Crant 139
  J. Bte. 139
ROMER, J. M. 215
RONDE, L. 31
  Lisle 36
ROOD, Edins 162
  Ezra 181
  Gilbert F. 110
  Gustavus B. 110, 157, 170
  Sidney G. 110
ROOP, John 176
  Joseph 176
ROOT, Amos 175
  Augustus 201
  Erastus 199
  Levi 106
  Roswell 155, 161, 186
  William 138

ROPES, Robert 216
ROQUETTE, Victor 120
ROSE, ... 5
  Denison R. 164
  Edward A. 195
  Elias 210
  J. L. 197
  Josephur 174
  Lewis 173
  Nicholas 7
  William 197
ROSEAU, Jean Bt. 174
ROSENCRANTS, Josiah 196
ROSENGRANTS, Aaron 199
ROSETER, John 173
ROSS, D. 215
  David 85
  William 215
ROSSE, Jean 32
ROSSEAU, Jean Bt. 114
  John Bte 139
  Margaret (Reaume) 139
ROTNOUR, Francis 161
  Michael 161
ROUCOURT, Jean Bte 55
ROUGH, James 88
ROUISSON, J. Bte 77
ROULA, Charles 119
  Louis 119
  Victorie (Vermet) 119
ROULAU, Chs 64
ROULEAU, see Roula 119
  see Roulo 115
  Charles 89
  Chs. 78
  Ignace 154
  J. Bte 76
  Joseph 144
ROULEAUX, Charles 154
ROULO, Charles 114, 115
  Chas. 159
  Jeanne (Chauvin) 115
  Louis 160
  Maria (Henry) 114
ROULOE, Lewis 156
ROULOUGH, Charles 162
  Louis 160
ROUNDTREE, John H. 219
ROUQUETTE, Victor, see
  Roquette 102
ROURK, Arthur 113, 152
ROUSAW, John Bte 166
  Solomon 166
ROUSE, Henry 202
  Lewis 145
  Louis 211
  Thomas 182
ROUSSAIN, Eustace 214
ROUSSEAU, Antoine 43, 50
  Augustin 209
  Jean Batille 158

# Index

ROUSSELL, Eaton 195
ROUSSON, see Rosseau 130
  J. Bte 115, 139
  Jean Bt. 179
  Jn Bte 65
ROUTURE, Antoine 70
ROUYAT, Bapt. 31
  Sim. 32
ROWAN, Wallace 216
ROWBEDO, J. B. 213
ROWE, Frederick 178
  Joseph 105
  Wm. H. 188
ROWENS, John 101
ROWLAND, ... (Springer) 101
  Catherine (McNiff) 101
  Joseph 103
  Thomas 101, 170
ROWLEY, Beckley 109
  Berkley 157
  Henry 201
ROY, Augustin 88
  Benjamin 146
  Franc./Francois 16
  Francis 219
  Marguerite (Ouabankikove) 6
  Mary 85
  Michael 50
  Micheal 44
  Pierre 6
  William 213
RUARK, see Rourk 113
  Arthur 158
RUBY, Roswell 176
RUCKER, Jane (Keith) 119
  Jane (Marshall) 119
  John 119
  John A. 119, 150, 162
  John K. 160
  John Peter 119
  Sarah (Macomb) 119
RUDD, Alexander 140
RUDES, Oren 204
RUFF, Francis 118, 153, 160, 164
  Mary/Polly (...) 117
RUGGLES, Isaac W. 181
RULAND, Israel 63
  Joseph 175
  William 174
RULO, Charles 156
  John Bte 144
  Moinique (Senecal) 144
RULOU, Charles 158
RUMEAU, Louis 88
RUMSEY, Henry 199
RUNYEN, John 180
RUPART, Frederick 60
RUPLEY, John F. 109, 162
  Margaret (Dumay) 109
  Suzanne (Johnson) 109
RUSETTE, Benjamin 120

RUSS, Isaac 132
RUSSEL, William 170
RUSSELL, ... 129
  Daniel W. 197
  Hiram 85
  John N. 197
  William 90
  Wm. 77
RUST, Clement P. 182
  Hiram 182
RUSTO, J. 150
RUTTER, G. R. 215
RYAN, Edward 90
  Laurence 218
  Samuel 210
  William 175, 209
RYLEY, John 196
RYN, Edward 159
RYND, F. 214
RYON, Abigail 171
  Abigail (Johnson) 117
  Edward 117

SABIN, Ezekiel H. 180
SACKET, Samuel 192
SACKETT, Dines 162
SACKRIDER, Thomas 188
SAGE, Ebenezer 180
SAGER, John 164
SAGUIN, see Seguir dit Laderoute 12
SAILS, Edward 196
St. ---, Francois 91
St. ABADIE, Louis 31
St. AGNE dit HOGUE, see St. Yves 7
St. AMOUR, Baptist 171
  Bte 91
  Louis 66, 209
St. ANDRE, see Landry dit St. Andre 20
  36
  Claude 33
St. ANTOINE, Charles 212
St. ARNAUD, Edward 208
St. AUBAIN, Cha. 30
  Gab. 30
  Jas. 31
  Noel 30
  Pier 30
St. AUBAN, ... 23
  Charles 21
  Gabriel 20
  Pierre 23
St. AUBIN, see St. Obin
  ... 5
  (Frs.) ... 158
  Archange 129
  Baptiste 150
  Basalique (Campau) 111
  Catherine 130
  Charles 32, 40

St. AUBIN, Chs 36
  Francis 191
  Francois 111, 151
  Frans 72
  Gab 36
  Gabriel 33, 80, 151
  J. Bte 129
  J. C. 36
  Jac. 16
  Jacques 16, 20, 33, 40, 53, 80
  Jean 6
  Jean Bte 159
  L. S. 36
  Louis 40, 53, 72, 82, 111
  Louisa (Gaultier) 6
  Margaret, see Casse 116
  Noel 20, 32, 36, 41, 53
  Pierre 32, 40, 53
St. BERNARD, see Bernard 20
  36
  ... 21, 24, 85
  Catherine (Lafontaine) 143
  G. 30
  Guilme 36
  Henry 151, 176
  Israel 143
  Joseph 142, 143, 178
  Louis 195
  Mary 103
St. CIER, Jacynth 146
St. CIRE, Hyacinth 212
St. CLAIR, William H. 160
St. COMB, Antoine 174
St. COMBE, Amable 63
St. COSME 36
  ... (...) 54
  Amable 81
  Pierre 23, 42
  Pierre Laurent 17
  Rose 109, 110
St. CRANT, Alexis 139
  Francis 138
  Marie (Bourdeau) 138
  Monique (Reaume) 139
St. CYR, Michael 218
St. DENIS, see Quesnel dit St. Denis dit St. Remy 22
St. ESTIENNE, see Guignard dit St. Etienne 22
  Jos. 32
  Joseph 33, 44
St. GEORGE, See Godfroy 17
  see Godfroy dit St. George 21
  Cecilia (Greffard) 115
  Francois 115
  Hully 167
  Louis 106
  Marie Duchene) 115
  Peter 161
  Pierre 115, 150, 159

St. GERMAIN 17
  Alolphe L. 208
  Charles 48
  Felicite (Chavignon) 48
  Magdeleine (Chevalier) 48
  Pierre 48
St. GRANT, Coleta (Robert) 141
  J. Bte 144
  John Bte 141
  Peter 144
  Veronique (Larabel) 144
St. JEAN, see Serre 22
  ... 43
  Jean Crispe 40
  Joseph 43, 55
  M. 79
St. JEAN a MARRAIS(?), M. 80
St. JOHN, Elizabeth 151
  Francis 122
  Joseph 116, 159
  M. A. 216
St. JOHNS, Francis 213
St. JOSEPH, ... 123
St. LARON, Baptiste 72
St. LORENT, Louis 150
St. LOUIS 36
  see Villers 22
  Christome 67
  Louis 33, 44, 52
  M. 143
St. MARE, see St. Martin 23
  36
  ... 23, 31
  ... (...) 42
  Alexis 128
  Jean 14
  Touissant Antoine Adhemar 20
St. OBIN, Baptiste 90
  Francis 167
  Francois 90
  Jacques 90
  John Bapt. 116
St. ONGE, ... 5
  Louis, see Orge, ... 122
  Louise Jeanne (Bailly) 6
  Marie (Guertin) Laverge 6
  Marie (Moitie) Magnan 6
  Pierre 6
St. ONGE dit CHENE, Louis Jean (Bailly) 6
  Marie (Moitie) Magnan 6
  Pierre 6
St. PIERRE, Jos. 76
St. PIERRE dit TRANCHEMONTAGNE, Pierre 12
St. REMI, ... 31
St. REMIE 23
St. REMIS, See Quensel dit St. Denis dit St. Remy 22

St. REMY, see Quesnel 22
  36
SAINTROCK, Battes 146
St. VINCENT, Jean B. 211
St. YVES, ... 5
  Joseph 7
  Pierre 7
SALES, Samuel 206
SALIAC, John Bapt. 114
  Joseph 114
  Maria Anne (Bondy) 114
SALIOT, see Saliac 114
  Archange 112
  J. Bte. 77, 139
  Jean 43
  Marie 114
  Mary 139
  Teresa 114
SALIOTTE, Jean 50
SALLIER, Archange 166
  John Bte 166
SALLIOT, Bte 65
SALONCETTE, Antoine 120
SALSBURY, Abram 154
  Levi 188
SAMBERNOR, see St. Bernard 131
  Louis 131
SAMONS, Davis 81
SANBURN, Elijah 183
SANCHAGRIN, Jean Bt. 41
  Jean Bte 54
SANCRAINT, Peter 166
SANDERS, Aimy 195
  Betsey 146
  Franklin P. 182
  Samuel 91
SANDERSON, Henry 101, 170
  Lydia (Stevens) 101
SANDS, Amos 155
  Esther 164
SANFORD, Hector 133
  Joel H. 197
SAN PIQUED, Pierre 215
SANSBERRY, Richard 133
SANSBROY, Abraham 160
SANSCHAGRIN, see Duberger 24
SANSCRAINTE, Alex 179
  Amable 143
  Francois 175
  J. Bte. 64, 138, 141, 143
  Jean Baptiste 64
  Jean Bt. 176
  Jean Bte 52
  Margaret 143
  Peter 179
SANSFACON, Andrew 130
SANSQUARTIER, ... 72
  Josh. 77
SANSSOUCY, ... 12
SARAH, Alexis 62

SARASTEAU?. Josh 69
SARGEANT, Antoine 178
  John 157, 185
  Thomas 91
SARGENT, John 109, 198
  Margaret (...) 109
  Nancy (...) 109
  Thomas 109
SARGENTS, John 214
SARRELL, ... 125
SATERTHWEIGHT, Reuben 189
SATTERLEE, Richard S. 209
  Samuel 183
SAUCER, Charles 161
  Robert 219
SAUCIER, see Socie 116
  Agnes 120
  Archange 120
  Genevieve 142
  Joseph 40, 52, 85, 112, 116, 120
  Josh 71
  Louise 112
  Marie 116
  Roalie 112
  Theotiste 116
SAULAU, ... 31
SAULE, Phillip 203
SAUNDERS, ... 54
  Harry 133
  Jesse 211
SAUTURE, Dominique 145
SAVAGE, Towner 205
SAVARIAS, Charlotte 7
SAVENYAC, Francis 111
  Genieve (Campau) 111
SAVIGNAC, see Savenyac 111
  John Bapt., see Savingac 105
  Cecile (...) 111
  Cecile (Chauvin) 105
  G. (Lebeau) 105
  J. Bte 105, 111
  John Bapt. 105
SAVINA, Peter 173
SAWTELL, Asa 181
SAXTON, Joel 181
SAYERS, George 209
SCANLON, Cornelius 173
  Jeremiah 127
SCANTLING, James 216
SCARBEAU, Charles 61
SCARRET, Peter 127
SCHIEFFELIN, Jacob 54
SCHINDLER, Therese 209
SCHLEY, ... 109
  Rachel 136, 141
SCHNALL, John J. 189
SCHOCK, Jacob 189
SCHOFIELD, Edward 138
SCHOOLCRAFT, H. R. 215
  James 216

## Index

SCHOONOVER, Peter 182
SCHRANDEL, Mary 118
SCHRIEFFELIN, Jno. 78
SCHWARTS, John E. 170
SCOFIELD, James 198
SCOT, John 172
SCOTT, David 199
    Eleasor 129
    Eleazer 192
    Eliza 106
    George 188, 217
    John 173
    Margaret 42
    Mary Ann (Meldrum) 104
    Nathan 185
    Silas 193
    Thomas 171
    William 54, 88, 193
    William McDowall 85
    Winfield 106
    Wm. 76
    Wm. McDowell 104
SCOVILL, Luther 162
SCRANTON, Evelyn 202
SCUDDER, Isaac 179
SEAR, George 130
SEARL, George 76
SEARLES, Abraham 217
SEARS, Joseph 197
    Peter 201
SECARD, Melish 124
SECK, Dorothea 131
SECORD, Isaac 199
SEEK, ... (...) 85
    Conrad 76, 88, 85, 104, 152, 172
    Mary (Morrison) 104
SEELEY, Gershom 203
    Harvey 181
    Joel 180
SEFFORD, Henry 207
SEGUIN, Archange 119, 120
    Cejetan 32
    Ignase 151
    John B. 151
    Joseph 17, 32, 120
    Julian 119
    Pierre 90, 151
SEGUIN dit LADEROUTE, see LaDeroute 21
    Cajean 32
    Francoise 14
    Joseph 16, 17, 32
SEGUIN-LADEROUTE, J. Bte. see Ladrout, John 117
    Joseph 112, 117
    Monique 117
    Pierre 117
    Susanne 112
    Teresa 117
SEGUIR, Francois 12

SEGUR, Nelson 124
SELLERS, Joseph 213
SELLIER, Pierre 208
SENECAL, Monique 144
SENESCHEL, Paul 209
SENET, see Senne 90
    Ignatius 120
    Pierre 133
    Soulange 120
SENEY, Ignace 190
SENIAT, Ignace 71
SENNE, Ignace 90
    Jean Bte 90
SEQUEY, ... 91
SERE, Joseph 62
SERRE, Joseph 90
SERRE dit St. Jean, Denis 22
SETERLEN, see Sterling 23
SERVISS, Henry 182
SESSIONS, Dunius 194
    Jeremiah 180
SETFORD, James 177
SEXTON, Earl 174
SEYMOUR, Ira 201
SEZEAU, Antoine 144
SHACKLETON, Henry 111
    Mary 111
SHADBOLT, Ludlow 185
SHADWICK, Thomas 160
SHAFER, Abraham J. 205
SHAFFER, John G. 200
SHAGGS, John 76
SHANK, Saripha 171
SHANNON, Daniel 218
SHARER, Peter 218
SHARIA, Oliver 146
SHARIFOO, Peter 146
SHARKIE, Francois, see Chartier, Francois 73
SHARP, George 61
SHATTELREAU, Dominque 144
SHATTELROE, Archange (Dusault) 144
    Joseph 144
SHATTUCK, George G. 218
SHAW, ... 127
    Caleb 81
    Freeman 81
    George M. 184
    John 65, 77, 89
    Joseph 161
    Leonard 161
    Mathew 126, 127
    Thomas 215
    William 42
SHAY, Nicholas 216
SHEARER, James 209
SHERMAN, Samuel P. 180
SHEER, Wm. A. 215
SHEHAMER, Daniel 203
SHELBY, Michael 218

SHELDON, Eliza (Whiting) 102
    John 184
    John P. 102, 184
    Thomas C. 172
    Timothy F. 163
    Timothy J. 156
SHELHOUSE, Roswell 205
SHENVAIR, Francis 147
SHEPHERD, Martin 182
    William 60
SHERMAN, ... 211
    Gardner 113, 158
    George 201
    John 216
    Oliver P. 219
    Deuel 179
    William H. 201
SHERWOOD, Catherine (...) 111
    Samuel 111, 158, 173
SHEW, Jacob 175
    James 174
    William 174
SHEYNEY/CHENE, Patrick 170
SHIELDS, Martin 207
SHILLING, Peter 200
SHILMAN, Isaac 193
SHINNABARGER, Jacob 204
SHIPLEY, John 219
SHIPPEY, Enoch 202
    Stephen 185
SHOCKLEY, Elijah 146
SHOOK, Elias 217
SHORES, Lewis 210
SHORTIER, Francis 195
SHOVAN, Tusan, see Chauvin, Touissant 73
SHOVIN, John Bt. 159
SHUART, Garret 206
    Isaac 207
    Samuel 207
SHULL, Jessie 147
SHULTZ,
    Valentine 204
SHUMWAY, Levi 188
SHURTLIFF, Louise 103
SHUSTER, Jacob 214
SIBLEY, ... (...) 85
    Caleo 209
    Henry H. 210
    Reuben 102
    Solo 76
    Solomon 85, 102, 125, 171
    William 137, 176
SILLAY, James 160
SILSBEE, John 206
SILSBY, Phineas 203
SIMARE, Jean 79
SIMBTON, Lt. 196
SIMMONS, Abigail 179
    Archange (Tremblay) Palmer 117
    Cyrenus 179

SIMMONS, David 145, 175, 179
  Gardner 155, 165
  Grafton 180
  Joshua 162
  Silas 188
  Stepehn 117
  Stephen G. 153, 160
  William 117
  William H. 161
  Zebina 162
SIMON, see Lemon 196
SIMONS, John 201
SIMPKINS, Alpheus 127
SIMPLE, Pere 54
SIMPSON, Andrew 181
  Elias 207
  John 146, 207, 212
  Joseph 150, 166
  Thomas 181, 207, 216
SIMS 201
  Isaac 203
  Phillip 203
  William 172
SIMSBURY, Richard 196
SINVINE, William 214
SIRE, see Sear 130
SIRED, Henry D. 173
SIRVE, Corlenias 213
SISSON, Holden 189
  Neron 196
  Thomas 189
SKAGG, John, see Knaggs 85
SKIDMORE, James 187
SKINNER, Isaac P. 138, 173
  John B. 217
SKYANIS, Andre 53
SLAUGHTER, James 171
SLEEPER, Josiah 194
SLOCUM, Benjamin 155, 161
SLOSS, William 172
SLUMB, Joseph 173
SLY, Jacob 181
  Silas 163
SMART, George 85
  Robert 76, 88, 85, 104, 171
SMEDLEY, Moses 113, 158
SMITH, ... 78
  A. J. 204
  Aaron 185
  Alba P. 199
  Alfonso 193
  Alva 162
  Ann 137
  Anne 106
  Arby 193
  Asa L. 198
  Benjamin 146, 211
  Benjamin H. 197
  Bernard 218
  Canada 206
  Catherine (McDonald) 131
  Daniel 190

SMITH, Daniel N. 150
  David 113, 152, 158, 167
  Denison 186
  Ebenezer 161, 185
  Ebenezer F. 180
  Eleazer 196
  Elias 200
  Ephraim K. 209
  Frederick 199
  George 187
  Gilman 119, 160
  Harry 205
  Henry 200
  Henry S. 181
  Hezekiah B. 179
  Hiram 184
  Ira 184
  Isaac 199
  Isaac L. 183
  Jacob 88, 86, 102, 106, 206
  James 175, 198, 205
  Jean Bt. 175
  Jefferson 200, 216
  Jehial 184
  Jeremiah 186
  Jesse C. 199
  Job 181
  Job C. 190
  John 189, 202, 211
  John C. 181, 210
  John F. 155
  John K. 131, 195
  John T. 166
  Jos. L. 106
  Joseph H. 162
  Laban 180
  Lewis 180
  Luke 216
  Martin 175
  Mary 128
  Moses 189
  Nelson 179
  Osman 202
  Reuben R. 194
  Richard 76, 88, 150
  Robert 190
  Robert D. 160
  Smauel 150, 154, 160, 185, 205
  Samuel M. 177
  Silas 173
  Stephen 177, 180
  Sylvester 185
  Terence 119
  Thomas 42, 62, 86, 128
  Timothy L. 206
  William 60, 161, 163, 189, 192
  Wm. 78
SMYTH, ... (...) 94
  John 170

SMYTH, Prudence (Brady) 103
  Richard 86, 103, 166
  Terrence 160
  William 153
SNAY, Peter 133
SNECALLE, Andrew 70
SNELL, William 185
SNELLING, Abba 160
SNEY, Joseph 146
SNIDER, Hiram 162
SNOW, Alanson 197
  William T. 184
SOCIE, Joseph 116
  Marie Josephe (Thibault) 116
SOCIER, Joseph 79, 151, 154
SOFACON, Catherine (Chauvin) 130
  Joseph 130
SOLANT, see Solo 42
  Gland 42
SOLAUT, Alexis 67
  Calude 56
SOLEAU, ... (...) 175
  Claude 176
  Tousaint 175
SOLIERE, Benjamin 176
SOLO, see Solant 42
  Alexis 145
  Claude 23, 33, 42
  Jean Bte 81
  Pierre 81
  Tusa 145
SOLOE, see Solo 23
SOLOMON, Ezekiel W. 210
SORCIER, Baptiste 90
  Joseph 89
SORDELLIER, Francis 44
  Francois 144
  Genevieve 144
  Margaret 142
  Susanne 140
SOROR, Pierre 62
SORTER, George 175
  Isaac 175
SOSORE, Louis 50
SOUDRIETTE, Alexis 174
  Charles 81
  Joseph 81, 145
SOUDRYET, Joseph 68
SOUDRYETTE, Frans 67
SOULIERE, Leon 176
SOULS, William 194
SOUMANDE, Antoine 50
SOURDELLET, Francois 52
SOUTHARD, John 187
SOUTHERLAND, Castle 198
  John A. 128
SOUTHTER, D. 215
SPACY, James 112
SPAFFORD, Omri 217
SPARKS, Cornelius 206
  John 106

SPAULDING, Sam'l 215
SPEER, Abram 150
   Moore 203
SPEERS, Abraham 137
SPENCE, J. 214
SPENCER, Abigail (...) 112
   E. 109
   Edward H. 186
   Gerry 170
   Joseph 76, 112, 152, 158
   Merrit, 194
   Nathaniel 112
SPENSE, Joel 213
SPERRY, Almon 189
   Anson 197
   Bazile 161
   Jemes 158
   Joseph 198
   William 197
SPINNINGS, Joseph 200
SPLAN, John 172
SPOFFORD, Abner 189
SPOOR, Adolphus 202
SPRAGE, Ara 166
SPRAGUE, Leonard 182
SPRAGUE, Mary Ann 120
   Orin 182
   Roger 185
   Silas 183
   Timothy 175
   Walter 180
SPRINGER, ... 101
SPRINGSTEEN, Cornelius 166
SPURGIN, Elijah 205
SQUIRES, Ethan 192
   James 175
   Jemima (Dilno) 129
   Luman 192
   Nathaniel 192
   Nathl 129
STACEY, ... (...) 154
   Elizabeth 105
   William 91, 105
   Wm. 160
STACY, Elizabeth 162
   Elizabeth (Thomas) 117
   William 117
STACKHOUSE, Samuel 197
STAFFANCE, ... (...) 194
   John 194
STAIMBUF, John, see Steinbeck 115
STAINBACK, John 77
STALEN, Leonard 205
STANARD, Daniel 186
STANBACH, Elizabeth 110
STANBACK, Jno. 77
STANBURGH, Jacob 161
   Joziah 161
   Samuel 161
STANLEY, Benjamin 115

STANLEY, Benjamin C. 181
   Benjn 159
   Washington 183
   William 182
STANTON, Alexandrine (Macomb) 111
   Henry 111, 158
   James 163
STARK, Cary 197
   Charles 201
   John 154
   Reubin 165
   Ruben 153
STARKS, John 118, 160, 162
STARKWEATHER, Erastus 165
   Erastus W. 155
   James 193
   William 165
   Wm. 155
STEAD, Benjamin 104
   Frances (Morley) 104
   Hannah 166
   Joseph 129
   Mary A. (...) 129
   Robert 151
   Thomas 167
STEBBINS, Samuel 218
   William 138
STEELE, Edward 180
   James 184
STEERS, William 91
   Wm. 78
STEINBACK, John 159
STEINBECK, Charlotte (Campau) 115
   John 91, 115
STEINE, George 128
STEPHENS, Asher 188
   Charles 189
   Elisha 162
   John 128
   Mabel 165
   William 194, 204
STEPHENSON, Benjamin C. 217
   Lewis 204
STERLINE, Samuel 155
STERLING, Isaac 199
   James 23
   Joseph 202
   Samuel 163
   Stephen 195
   William 41
STERN, Jabez 78
STERNS, Samuel 197
STERRS, William 160
STETSON, Turner 188
STETSTIS, Leonard 204
STEUART, Adam D. 209
STEVENS, Cyprian 171
   Daniel 215
   Ebenezer G. 180

STEVENS, Elizabeth 104
   Jacob 186
   James 209, 214
   Jesse 203
   Jno. W. 215
   Joseph 201
   Levi 210
   Lydia 101
   Noah 203
   Rufus 186
   W. 215
   Weston 196
   William T. 198
   Wm. 216
STEVINSON, Robert
STEVIS, William 154
STEWARD, Edmund 194
   Harvey 194
   Ira 165
STEWART, A. C. 204
   Adam 125
   Adam D. 101
   Ambrose 138
   Charles 86
   Daniel 195
   David 198
   Hart L. 204
   James 177, 196
   John 197
   Matthew A. 171
   Samuel A. 190
   Samuel M. 204
   Taylor 197
STICKNEY, Benjamin F. 136, 176
STILES, David 197
   Rudd 197
STILLMAN, Jared A. 202
STILLWELL, Thos. 205
STIT, Andrew 193
STITT, William 213
STOAT, David 200
STOCKING, Amos 189
STOCKTON, ... (Smith) 106
   John 129, 190
   Major 106
   Mary (Allen) 129
   Rodman 160
   Sylvester 181
STODDARD, Arlinda 199
   Luther 174
   Reuben 174
STONE, ... 86
   Aron 193
   Augustus 166
   Barnard 120
   Danford M. 202
   David 122
   Elisha 193
   Jeremiah 188
   Jonas 125
   Jonas A. 208

STONE, Samuel 174
  Warren 155, 165
  William 210
  Zelotus 193
STONER, John 101
  Mary 171
STORKEN, Jared 185
STORY, Martin 171
  William 127
STOUGHTON, Amaziah 182, 186
  Dillacene 181
  James 180
STOUT, Cornelius A. 188
  George 190
STOWELL, Ira 187
STRAM, Louis 212
STRATTON, Ruth 199
STREET, James 106
  Jos. M. 212
STREITE, John 117, 159
STRICKLAND, Joel B. 199
  John 199
STRIET, Jacob G. 195
STRINGER, John 181
STRONG, John 154, 160
  Warham 78
STROOPSINSKY, Joseph 210
STROUD, Henry 78
  Wm. 78
STROUP, Samuel 190
STUARD, Wilks L. 192
STUART, Ebenezer 179
  Ira 155
  Janitt 182
  Joseph 174
  Joseph W. 199
  Robert 209
STUBBS, Michael 199
  William 199
STUFFY, Jacob 200
STURGESS, John 119
  Thomas 183
STURGIS, Ardiloury 119
  John, see Sturges, John 119
  John 152
  Lewis B. 171
STURGISS, John 160, 204, 216
VULIVAN, Benj. 215
  Patrick 218
  Thomas 206
SUGAR, Francis 172
SUMERFIE(L)D, Ephraim 196
SUMNER, Samuel 192
SUNDERLAND, Joseph 214
SUSAN (colored) 86
SUSOR, ... 66
  Batiste 66
  Louis 66
  Louis Francois 22
SUSORD, see Susor 22
SUTCLIFF, James 137, 166

SUTFINS, Isaac 215
SUTRADDO, Joseph 215
SUTS, William 125
SUTTON, Benjamin 199
  Isaac 200
SUZAR, Jean Bt. 178
SUZOR, see Ceasore 43
  36
  Archange 143
  Bazille 144
  Dominique 144, 178
  Genevieve 141
  J. Bte 81, 144
  John Bte. 144
  Louis 81, 139, 141, 143, 144
  Louis Francois 140
  Marie 140
  Monique (Duval) 144
  Teresa (Labadie) 144
SWAIN, Aaron 202
SWAN, Avery 187
  Edward 187
  Elias S. 172
  Ziba 186
SWARTOUT, Anthony R. 203
SWEENY, Charles 76
SWEET, John 172
SWEETING, Almond 203
SWIFT, Marcus 153, 161
SWINFIN, John 127
SYKES, Abram 173
SYLVESTER, William 125, 209

TABEAU, Jean Bt. 209
TABINE, Samuel 164
TACIER, Elizabeth 138
TACLES, Alexander 193
TAEBAIER, Baptiste 147
TAFFT, James T. 161
  Sylvanus 163
TAFT, Adon 155
  James T. 155
  Job M. 155
  Seth 195
  Pitts 179
TAILLON, Bte 68, 81
TALLMADGE, Nathaniel 179
TALLMAGE, Isaac 215
TALLMAN, Nathaniel 130
TALOOSE, James 73
TALOUSE, Raymond, see Taloose, James 72
TAMISANT, Joseph 152
TAMISIR 36
TAMIZIR 36
TANGUAY, ... 7
TANNER, John 214
TARRIER, Philip 120
TAYLER, Henry 190
  Isaac 205

TAYLOR, Amos 178
  Charles B. 200
  Elias 204, 205
  Elisha 184
  George 183, 189
  Joshua B. 184
  Lemuel 184
  N. T. 192
  Obadiah 209
  Orestes 187
  Philo 163
  Robert M. 208
  Whitman 208
  William G. 136
TEBEAU, Louis 154
TEBO, Archange (Bertrand) 132
  Augustine 146
  Louis 132
TEEPLE, George B. 187
TEERE, Henry 86
TEES, ... 63
TEIPEL, Peter 155
  William 155
TELLER, ... 41
  Pierre 219
TenEYCK, Anna (...) 103
  Conrad 88, 86, 103, 153, 162
  Jeremiah 103
  Jeremiah V. R. 102
  Martha 171
TENIOR, Phillip 151
TENNY, William 180
TENY, Joseph 155
TEPLE, Peter 163
  William 163
TERDEIFF, Pier 215
TEREAWEN, Horace 171
TERHUNE, John 198
TERNIER, Philip 120
TERRILL, Lyman 163
TERRY, Charles 186
  John B. 216
  Joshua 181
  Joshua S. 181
  Nathan 186
  Robert 219
TESSERAUX 123
TESSIER, Pierre 142
TESTIEAU, Jean Candinal 21
TESSIERS, Chs. 67
TESTROE, John B. 123
TETARD, see Forville 20
  Pierre 33
TETARD dit FORTVILLE, Pierre 16, 33
THARE, Ameriah 165
  John 165
THARP, John 218
THAYER, Charles 198
  John G. 197
  Rufus 155, 179

# Index

THE, Nicolas 48
THEBAULT, Basil 159
   Francis 159
   Lambert 158
THEBE, Ignace 130
   Magdeleine (LaForest) 130
THEBEAU, Louis 42
THEBO, Ignace 191
   Jaque 191
THEMUS, Pierre 33
THERIEN, Peter J. 209
THESSERAULT, Jean B. 208
THIBALT, Bazil 195
THIBAU, Gabriel 71
THIBAUD, Joseph 76
   Louis 79
   Posper 81
THIBAUDAU, Lambert 152
THIBAUDAUT, ... 68
   J. Bte 88
THIBAULT, see Thebe 130
   Agnes (Rivard) 115
   Augustin 116
   Augustine 146
   Sugustus 211
   Bazzil 115
   Euphrosine 116
   F. 90
   Francis 115
   Genevieve 103
   Genevieve (Meny) 112
   Ignace 115, 130, 132
   James 86
   Jane 172
   Joseph 61, 88, 103
   Joseph Louis 112
   Lambert 90, 112, 163
   Louis 33, 86 103, 167
   Marie Josephe 116
   Prosper 104
THIBAUT, see Tebo 132
   Basil 71
   Francois 150
   Ignace 72, 79
   Louis 31
   Prospert 68
THIBEAU, Ignace 40, 53
   Joseph 151
   Louis 54
THIBEAULT, Francis 161
THIBOLT, Louis 196
THIRSTEN, Balkley 152
   Jason 152
THIRSTON, Blakly 204
   Sabin 204
THOMAS, Aaron 78, 91, 109, 117, 153, 160
   Alansen 160
   Alanson 118, 160
   Allen B. 197
   Archange 132

THOMAS, Aron 157, 160
   Baptist 130, 191
   Catherine (...) 119
   Cecilia (Dubay) 130
   Daniel 201
   Dominique 115, 152, 159, 171
   Eleanor (...) 117
   Elizabeth 117
   Elizabeth (Cloutier) 115
   Elizabeth (McDonald) 130
   Felix 130, 191
   George 130, 191
   Hanson 153
   Helen 78
   Henry 187
   Isaac 201
   Jacob 73, 115, 130, 132
   Jim 196
   Joel 109, 119, 153, 157, 160
   John 78, 91, 217
   John B. 192
   John C. 216
   Jonathan 201
   Levi 176
   Margaret 118
   Mary (Blay) 130
   Nancy (...) 109
   Nathan 201
   Phebe (...) 109
   Robert 130, 185, 191
   S. 214
   Sophia (...) 119
   Susanne (Deshetres) 130
   William 124, 187
THOMERSON, William 127
THOMPSON, ... 41
   A. R. 196
   Buford 201
   Daniel 154, 164
   Douglas 186
   Elizabeth 197
   Esquire 207
   Francis 125
   Isaac 193
   James 41, 54, 194
   John 202
   Linus 211
   Nancy 160
   Nathaniel 194
   Nearmyna 193
   Otis C. 185
   Thadeus 183
   Thomas 213
   Washington 186
   William 127, 181, 204, 210, 215
THORN, ... 41
   Alice 133
   Elizabeth 116

THORN, Elizabeth (Cottrell) 131
   William 82, 131
   Wm. 73
THORNTON, Sarah 179
THORP, Abner 207
   Augustus 137
   Jesse 184
   Miles 174
THRASHER, Stephen 216
THROOP, Ezra B. 192
   George 194
THOULOUSE, Jean 48, 53
THUNES, Madeleine 6
THUNES dit DuFRESNE, Madeleine 6
THUOT-DUVAL, Ignace 144
   Igance, see Tuott-Duvall, Eneas 140
   Monique 144
   Thomas 140
THUOTH, Ignace 66
THURSTON, Beckley 112, 158
   Betsey (Paine) 119
   Blakeley 112
   Daniel 192
   Jason 119, 160
   Joel 112, 119
   Miriam (...) 112
   Mariam (Blakely) 119
   Phebe (...) 112
   Russell 185
TIBBALS, Lewis 184
TIBBETS, William 206
TIBBETT, Benjamin 81
TIBBITS, Allan 155
   Allen 138
   Daniel 161
   George 180
   John 155
   William 163
   Wm. 155
TIBBITTS, Allen 165
   John 161
TIBERDO, Joseph 163, 209
TIBITS, Henry 161
TIBMAN, William C. 197
TICHENER, Caleb 165
TIERS, Mathew 186
TILTON, William 189
TINGLEY, John 191
TINGLY, Benjamin 186
TIRIOT dit CAPUCIEN, Jean Baptiste 23
TIRRIER, Philip 164
TITSWORTH, Abram 207
   Joseph 176
TITUS, Jarvis 201
   Thomas I. 209
TOBIAS, Daniel 202
TODD, John 186

TODD, Joseph 181
  Joseph J. 181
  Ransom 197
  Samuel 162, 173, 188
TOIN, Charles 124
TOLMAN, Timothy 180
TOLIGNE, Samuel 155
TOMASON, William 127
TOMASSE, Thomas 82
TOMLINSON, Charles B. 217
TOMPKINS, John Q. 105
TOMS, Ira 182
TOOKER, Hiram 203
TOPPING, Ethan 210
  Samuel T. 198
TOPPONG, Charles D. 200
TORANJEAU, Augustin 43
  Augustine 51
  J. Bt 44
TOBERT, Samuel 182
TORREY, Edward 198
  Nancy 172
TORRINGTON, James 194
TORRINGTON, Sully 192
TORRY, D. 188
  Joseph W. 173
  Oliver 180
TOUEY, Jesse 207
TOUISSANT, Judith 109
TOULOUSE, Amable, see Raymond-Toulouse 131
  Jacque 82
TOULSON, Wm. 146
TOUPIN, Louis 33
TOUPIN dit DuSAULT, Louis 21, 33
TOUPIN-DUSAULT, Francis 139
  Louise 139
TOURANGEAU 36
  ... 31
  Jean Baptiste 33
  Joseph 77
TOURANGEAUX, ... 25
  Jean Baptiste 23
  Jean Bte. 50, 51
TOUSSAINT, Pierre 215
TOUTEAU, Jean Baptiste 7
  Joseph 7
  Magdeleine (Parent) 7
TOWER, Samuel S. 185
TOWLE, Ira 163
TOWN, Ephraim 86
  Sarah 86
  Wyman A. 174
TOWNSEND, Abraham 207
  Envis 194
  Gamael 207
  John 206
  Robert 193
TRACEY, Edward 216
TRAIN, Jonathan 197

TRAMBLE, Ambroize 151
  Evangele 159
  Henry 150
  John 150
  John B. 150
  Joseph 151
  Louis 150
  Magdelaine 150
  Robert 151
  Thomas 150
  Vangille 150
TRAMBLY, Joseph 74
TRANCHE, Charles 212
TRANCHEMONTAGNE, Pierre 12
TRAVERSI, Pierre 81
TRAVERSY, Ambroise 67
TRAVERSY, Ambroise 67
  Pierre 67
TREMBLAI, Frans 72
  Louis 70
TREMBLAIE, Pere 70
TREMBLAY, see Tremble 101
  see Tremblet 21
  Ambroise 17, 115
  Archange 113, 115, 117
  Augustin 17, 52, 133
  Esther 137
  Francis 131
  Francois 52
  Joseph 53, 137, 140
  Judith 133
  Julia 132
  Louis 52, 55, 115, 117, 119
  Louis Jean, see Tremble 115
  Louis Michel 32
  Louis Michel, see Tremblet 21
  Magdeleine 131
  Marie 119
  Michel 62
  Pier. 17
  Teresa 117
  Therese 140
  Therese 109
TREMBLE, A. (...) 90
  Ambroise 40, 79
  Ambroise, see Trimble 116
  Ambrose 115
  Andress 159
  Baptis 71
  Baptiste 82
  Benoit 130
  Benoitt 190
  Catherine (Campau) 129
  Cecile (Aide-Crequi) 109
  Cecile (Marsac) 109, 116
  Euphrosine (Thibault) 116
  Evangelist 161
  Felicite (Alard) 115
  Francis 116

TREMBLE, Francis O. 131
  Francois 40, 82
  Gagetan 79
  Gageth/Cajetan 71
  Gegette 89
  Gazeton 190
  Gazette 133
  Henry 133
  Ignace 90
  John Bapt. 115
  John Bt. 159
  Joseph 40, 79, 82, 109, 116, 151, 157, 159
  Joseph Francoise 115
  Joseph L. 90
  Josh 71
  Leander 193
  Leo 129
  Leonard 79, 90
  Lewis 191, 194
  Lizette, see Tremblay 101
  Louis 79, 90, 116, 129
  Louise 40
  Louison 115, 159
  Marie (Chapoton) 129
  Medan/Medard 171
  Michael, see Mitchell 129
  Michel 70, 71, 82, 88
  Mitchell 129, 194
  Peter 190
  Pierre 90, 116, 150, 159
  Susanne (Greffard) 116
  Thomas 71, 90, 116, 159
TREMBLER, Louis 30
TREMBLET, Pierre 21
TREMBLEY, Ambrois 136
TRETON, Juliet 30
TRIMBLE, ... 41, 54
  Ardress 116
  John 213
TRIMBLEY, Jacob 210
TRIMMER, James 184
TRIPP, Seth 202
TRISKET, George 160
TROLENSHO, J. B. 213
TROWBRIDGE, Charles 152
  Stephen V. R. 183
TROMBLEE, Ambrose 164
  Augustus 163
  Henry 161
  John Bte 161
  Joseph 163
  Lewis 161
  Peter 164
  Thomas 164
TROMBLEY, Cecile (Yax) 102
  John L. 164
  Josephe (Chapoton) 102
  Louis 102, 196
  Michael 86
  Micheaux 102

## Index

TROTIER, Alexis  33
  Antne  64
TROTIER dit DesRUISSEAUX,
  Alexis  24, 33
TROTIER SIEUR de RUISSEAU,
  Alexis  12
TROTOT, ...  32
TROTTER, John  198
TROTTIER, Alexis  16
  Francois  208
  Isac  171
TROUTWINE, Margaret (Price)  101
  Nimrod  101
TROWBRIDGE, Charles C.  162
TRUAX, A. C.  88
  Abraham  119, 160, 166
  Abram C.  150
  Caleb  119
  Fytje (Van Patten)  119
  Hyram A.  152
  John  172
  Lucy Melinda (Brigham)  119
TREDEAUX, ...  5
TRUDEL,  142, 208, 209
  Louis  65
  Margaret  142
TRUDELE, Francois  91
TRUDELLE, ...  55
  Francois  78
  Micholas  77
TRUE, Daniel  198
TRUMBULL, ... (...)  86
  James  203
TRUTEAU, Etienne  7
TUBS, Benjamin  193
TUCKER, Catherine (Heyl)  129, 130
  Charles  129, 191
  Edward  132, 191
  Henry  73, 82, 130
  Isaac  187
  Jacob  130, 191
  John  130, 191
  John S.  187
  Joseph  129
  Josh  172
  Josette (Chapoton)  130
  Nancy (Edwards)  130
  Susanne  130
  William  41, 54, 72, 82, 117, 129, 130, 191
  Wm.  73, 159
TUCKEY, Francois  128
TULL, David  166
TULLER, A.  188
  Charles  212
TUNNICLIFF, Joseph  138
  Pauline (Drouillard)  138
TUOTT-DUVAL, Eneas  140
  Louise (Lebeau)  140

TUOTTE/THUOT, Francis  141
TUPER, Charles  193
TURELLE, J. B.  213
TURNER, Elijah  219
  Isaiah G.  180
  John W.  180
  Josiah P.  198
TURPIN, ...  5
  Jean Baptiste  6
  Marguerite (Fafard)  6
TUTLE, Christopher  77
TUTTLE, Christopher  86
  Daniel  118, 153, 160, 162, 165
  Enoch  120, 160
  Harvey  120, 153
  Henry  183
  Hiram  197
  Jane (...)  117
  Loyal  197
  Ralph  205
  Warren  161
TWIGGS, D. E.  211
TYE, Catherine  188
TYLER, ...  152
  Eleanor (...)  112
  Isaiah  112
  Isaih  158
  John  160, 203
  Thomas  198

UNDERWOOD, A.  189
  Asa  184
  Elias  189
  Francois  62
  Orson  197
UPDIKE, Ralph  199
UPTON, Henry  187
URINO, Antoine  159
URNO, Antoine  115
  Jos.  159
  Joseph  115
UTLEY, Ephraim  163
  Sanford  182
  William  163, 185

VADBONCOUR, Hypolithe  63
VADEBON(COEUR), Josh.  77
  Louis  77
VADEMID, Ann  86
VADNAIS, Nicholas  73
VAGNE, Nicolas  82
VAILLANCOUR, Joseph  208
VAILLANCOURT, Joseph  123
  Josephe  123
VAIRIN, John B.  218
  Joseph  218
VALANCE, Hartwin  105
VALANTINE, John  154
VALCOUR, Cecile  143
  Joseph  44, 52

VALENCOURT, Joseph  120
VALENTINE, Cornelius  183
  James  186
  John  183
  Matthias  202
VALIQUET, Catherine  136
  Pierre  68
VALIQUETTE, Francis  144
  Francois  138, 143
  John Bte  138
  Joseph  144
  Louise (Meny)  138
  Monique (Gagnier)  143, 144
  Newel  143
  Noel  178
  Noel, see Newel  143
  Pierre  177
  Toussaint  178
VALLADE, Joseph  42
VALLEE, Catherine  109
  Elizabeth (Drouillard)  105
  Jean  105
VALLEE dit VERSAILLES, Jean  25
VALLENTINE, Moses  190
VALLEY, Charles  131
  Mary  131
  Perish  61
  Pierre  61
VALLIQUETTE, Joseph  178
VALNEY, ... (...), see Vademid  86
VANALSTINE, Andw  88
VAN AMBURG, Henry  179
  Matthew  179
  Ornage K.  179
VAN ANTWERP, Francis  171
  William  184
VANATTER, Daniel  183
VAN AVERY, Peter  117, 159
VAN BUSKERK, Henry  187
VANBUSKIRK, M.  214
VANDERHOOF, Thomas  207
VANDS, Collin  192
VAN DUYN, Isaac  179
  James  179
VANEVERY, Peter  151
VAN FOSSEN, Samuel  198
  William  200
VANIER, Isidore  209
VAN LUWEN, John  155
VANMATRE, Andrew P.  217
  Lewis  217
VANNVATER, John  183
VANNATTEN, Joseph  131
VANNATTER, Henry  185
VAN ORSDAL, Abram  189
VAN PATTEN, Fytje  119
VAN RANSLEAR, Tyler  202
VANSCOTER, Thomas  200
VAN TOSLER, Mary  101

VAN VALKENBERGH, Porter 202
VANVOTENBURG, Jas. 146
VAN WAGONER, Harry 185
  Jacob 184
  Michael 154
VARICK, Bte 72
VARMET, Joseph 143
  Marie (Pineau) 143
VARMETHE, Josh 65
VARNAY, Nicholas 88
VARNIER, Antoine 191
  Charles 150
  John B. 191
  Leon 150
  Robert 150
VARNOIT, Et. 31
VARVET, Baptist 154
VASDEBONIER, Thomas 208
VASSIERE-LAFERTE, Joseph 110
  Louis 110
VAUDRIE, Mich. 31
VAUDRY 36
  Francois 22
  Michel 33
VAUGN, John 181
VAUNDREN, Micael 128
VEAU, Joseph 208
VEAUDRY, see Vaudry 22
VELAIRE, Christome 139
  Josette (Suzor) 139
VENDSTINE, Nicholas 202
VERBRINKIEN, Paul 163
VERMET, Alexis 154
  Angelique 145
  Antoine 77, 88, 119, 164
  Charles 177
  Charles L. 159
  Joseph 91, 164
  Victoire 119
VERMETTE, see LaVermit 114
  Joseph 55
  Mary (...) 178
VERMIT, Alexander 167
  John Bte 162
VERNE(T), Nicholas 71
VERNET, Antoine 117
  Catherine 117
VERNEY, ... (...) 86
  Nicolas 86
VERNIER, Baptiste 79
  Catherine (Billiau) 115
  J. Bte 90, 131
  John B. 131
  John Bapt. 115
  John Batist 170
  John Bt. 159
  Laurent 115
  Monique (Lauson) 131
VERNIER-LaDOUCEUR, see
  Vernier 115
VERSAILLE, see Vallee dit
  Versailles 25

VERTEFEUILLE, Francis 147
VESIERE, Alexis 63
  Louis 78
VESIERRE, Louis 65
VESSIERE, Louis 68, 39
VIAU, Marguerite (...) 32
VINCENT, John 218
VICKERS, Jonathan 173
VICKERY, Edward 165
  George 165
VIEAUX, Jacques 211
VIETTE, Julien 124
VIGARE, Andrew 69
VIGE, Andre 64, 77
VIGER, see Vigare 69
VIGILE, Andre 91
VILLENDINE, Moses 185
VILLER, Louis 32
VILLERE, Francois 176
VILLERS, Chrysostome 81
  Louis 17, 33
VILLERS dit St. LOUIS, Louis 22, 33
VILLERS-St. LOUIS, Chrysostum 143
  Jeanne 143
  Louis 139
  Marie J. 143
VILLET, Johan 86
VILLIOTEE, Julien 124
VILLON, Ming 146
VINCENT, Baptist 123
  Benjamin 121
  Clotide (Bourgeat) 122
  Clotide (Bourget) 123
  David 165
  J. Bte 122
  Jacques 86
  James 61
  Narcis 122
  Narcisse 123, 171
  Teresa 123
VINCES, B. K. 121
VINCINT, Benjamin 161
VINEL, Hiram 174
VINYARD, James R. 219
VISGAR 41
  Agathe (Cicotte) 109
  Joseph 154, 155, 166
VISGER, see Visgar 109
  Ann (Godfroy) 109
  Catherine 109
  Jacob 63, 89, 157
  John 63
  Joseph W. 109, 157
VISIER, Louis 42
VISSIERE, Louis 55
Vn Loovin, John 161
Vn SICKLE, John 165
VOILETTE, J. Bt 44
VOORHEIRS, Isaac 187
VOORHIES, Isaac J. 186

VOORHIES, Jacob N. 187
  James N. 203
VORN, Simpson 209
VOYER, ... (...) 86
  Ignace 30
  Joseph 54, 61, 86
  Josette (colored) 86
VOYEZ, Joseph 76
VREELAND, Hugh 199
  James 166
VRELAND, Darius C. 166
  Euas 166
  Garret 167
  Garret A. 166
VRULAND, Elias 152
  Garret 152
  Garrit 152
  Jacob 152
  James 152
  Samuel 152
VURTIFY, Francis 147

WACHTER, Christia 215
WADE, John 214
  Josiah 214
WADSWORTH, N. W. 173
WALDROM, John 182
WAISTCOAT, Elizabeth 103
WAIT, Amos 199
WAITE, Samuel 86
WAKEFIELD, Zial 162
WAKEMAN, Austen 183
WALACE, James 204
WALDON, Jabez 127
WALES, Solomon 192
WALKER, Daniel 199
  Elizabeth 152
  Elizabeth (...) 109
  John 109, 157
  Solomon 179
  Stephen H. 210
  William 175
WALLACE, James 78
  Mansfield 214
  Robert 181
  Theodore G. 120
  William 128, 217
WALLEN, Chas. 78
WALLER, Robert 219
WALLES, Austin 155
WALLING, Samuel B. 206
WALMSLEY, Joel 126
WALSH, Nicholas 216
  Paula 113
WALSWORTH, Daniel 188
WALTON, Hannah (...) 120
  Isaiah 120
  Isaih 160
WALWORTH, Benjamin 202
  John 202
  Mary 202
  William M. 202

# Index

WANSEY, Henry 203
  Jared 203
WARD, ... (...) 132
  Barret 215
  Ebenezer 176
  Eber 209
  Elihu 150, 175
  Elizabeth (Lambertson) 132
  Henry 155, 161
  Sam 132
  Samuel 195
  Simon 204
  Thomas 218
WARDEN, Clark 195
WARE, Reuben S. 217
WARFIELD, Peter 222
WARFLE, Martin 200
WARING, Daniel 189
  John 172
WARNER, Chauncey 208
  Eds 194
  Elijah 122
  Henry 200
  John 184
  Seth A. L. 182
WARNONE(?), Thomas 77
WARREN, Abel 192
  Elisha 153, 162
  Elizabeth (Stacey) 105
  Hart 150, 164
  John A. 194
  Lorenzo 182
  Lyman 121, 214
  Mary (Cadotte) 121
  Philip 105, 171
  Truman A. 121
WARRINER, P. W. 173
WARRINGTON, Levi 211
WASHINGTON, George 150, 164, 167
WASWORTH, John 190
WATERMAN, Martha 204
WATKINS, Cyrus 184
WATSON, Catherine (...) 101
  George E. 101
  J. 91
  John 78, 86, 101
  Joseph 88, 128
  Sally Mira (Witherell) 128
  Victor 171
  William 88, 86
WATTELL, Alexn 78
WATTLES, William 171
WAUGH, Freeman 187
  Sheldon 187
WAYMAN, William 219
WAYNE, Antony 86
WEARING, Wills 193
WEAVER, Elizabeth 117, 160
  Joseph 91
  Mary 160

WEAVER, William 117
WEBB, Ezekiel 179
WEBBER, Benjamin 199
WEBSTER, Calvin P. 187
  Charles 193
  Chester 187
  Ely 193
  Isaac P. 181
  Luther H. 185
  Major 192
  Milton H. 193
  Noah 194
  Price B. 193
  Roswell 193
  William C. 206
WEED, Leonard 185
WEEKS, James 198
WEESE, John 170
WELCH, ... (...) 61
  Benjamin 162
  Fanny 198
  George 86
  Henry 198
  James 118, 160, 162, 197
  John 132, 162
  Mary 132
  Polly 86
  Thomas 88, 86, 160
  William W. 207
WELCOME, Henry 209
WELDON, Samuel 188
WELLER, Obadiah 199
  Thomas 199
WELLMAN, David 178
  Zadik 158
  Zadoc 113
WELLS, ... (...) 175
  Charles 194
  Henry 153, 161
  Jonathan 166
  Lewis 141, 175
  Martha 152, 166
  Morris 175
  Nicholas 216
  Noah M. 166
  Rufus 162
  Samuel N. 192
  Seth 141
  Stephen 170
WELMAN, Joel 182
WELSH, Benjamin 155
  John 139
  John G. 153
  Pierre 124
  Thomas 219
WENDALL, Tunis S. 172
WENDELL, Abraham 208
  John J. 173
  Josiah 88
WENDLE, Abraham 151
WENTWORTH, Elijah 216

WESSON, Sewell 181
WEST, Abram 188
  Andrew 186
  Benjamin W. 184
  Elijah 136
  Francis 138
  Gordeon 190
WESTERFIELD, Aaron 217
WESTFALL, John 165
WESTON, Orin 179
  William 162
WESTROPE, Abner 219
WETMORE, Luke 199
  Oliver 197
  Oliver W. 199
WHALEN, Bazilla 195
WHEATON, Bullock 201
  Henry 173
  James 203
  Martha 171
WHEELER, Aaron 133
  Caleb 190
  Francis 146
  Isaiah 184
  James 208
  Josiah 189
  Loring 219
  Tillison 201
WHEELOCK, Rue 202
  Silas 201
WHELAN, John 203
WHETON, John 123
WHIPLE, Henry 205
WHIPPLE, Arnold 163
  Archange (Peltier) 103
  Eunice (...) 103
  Israel 163
  James 171
  John 103, 174
  Joseph 103
WHIRLSLIN, Jason 152
WHISTLER, John 211
  Sarah 103
  Wm. 146
WHITCOMB, Aaron 215
  Levi 200
WHITE, ... 42
  Caroline (Hogan) 125
  Charles 151
  D. 214
  Eber 200
  Edward 104, 180
  George 182
  James 127
  John 173, 211
  Orrin 200
  Peter 208
  Robert 125
  William 127
WHITEHEAD, Henry 206

WHITEHEAD, John 62
WHITEMAN, Henry 128
  Mary 164
WHITING, Eliza 102
  John 106
  John L. 106
  Peter H. 196
WHITMAN, Martin C. 207
WHITMORE, Leonard 176
  Luther 176
WHITNEY, Abraham 185
  Andrew G. 103
  Daniel 211
  Henry 172
  Jacob 202
  James 188
  Noah 176
WHITTEMORE, Gideon O. 181
WHITTLE, Richard 42
WHITTY, James O. 125
WICOFF, Joseph 201
WIGERT, Peter 205
WIGHT, Thadeus 187
WIGHTMAN, Abraham 153
  Hiram 153, 164
  James 153
  Madison 153
  Volney 153, 164
WILBER, John 185
  Cadle 193
WILCOX, ... 122
  Almira Rood (Powers) 110
  Asabel 119
  Ashhell 160
  Charles 110
  Chas. 157
  Elias 192
  Eliza 81
  Hiram 193
  John 182, 210
  Joseph 182
  Lafayette 213
  Lucy 190
  Lyman G. 184
  Nathan 138
  O. B. 122
  Theron 203
WILCOXEN, Nathan 155
WILCOXSON, Gideon 198
WILDER, Abigail 127
  Reuben 204
WILDS, John 205
WILEY, David 188
WILKINS, Thomas 106
WILKINSON, Binajah 204
  Carlisle 166
  Isaac 161
  James 179
  Joseph 78, 86
  St. James 76
  William 176
WILLAMY, Stephen 139

WILLARD, Abner 103, 111
  Alexander 218
  Josiah 125
  Levi 103, 111, 157, 171
  Mary/Polly 103
  Samuel 177
  William 177
WILLARDS, Levy 154
WILLCOX, Adna 166
  Almina 163
  Charles 104, 122
  Nathan 166
WILLEGUS, Elias 125
WILLET, Thomas 150
WILLETS, Thomas 115
WILLETT, Thomas 161
WILLEVENY, Elenne 86
  Maurice 86
WILLHEILM, Jacob 164
WILLIAM, Jacob 166
WILLIAMS, ... 41
  Alba 202
  Alpheus 103, 104
  Benajah 207
  Benjamin 118, 153, 165
  Benj. N. 160
  Betsy 174
  Catharine 103
  David 184
  Ebenezer 197
  Eleazer 212
  Elizabeth 86
  Ephraim S. 186
  Ferdinand 186
  Gardiner 186
  Harriet 104
  Harvey 103, 172
  Hervey, see Harvey 103
  Isaac 42, 55, 207
  James 76, 171
  Jas. 146
  John 86, 117, 153, 201
  John R. 88, 101, 102, 170
  Kera 86
  Mary (Ponchat) 117
  Nancy (...) 117
  Nathan 54
  Oliver 186
  Polly (Andress) 119
  Spencer 201
  T. 54, 215
  Thomas 41, 102, 128
  Veronica 113
  William 152, 195
WILLIAMSON, John B. 146
  Joseph 86
WILLIONE, Daniel 215
WILLITS, Eli 183
  Elijah 183
  Isaac 185
WILLITTS, Thomas 159
WILLMAN, Aaron 183

WILLMARTH, Daniel 205
WILLSON, David 206
  John 161
  Joseph 165
  Robert 207
  Thomas 137
  William 136
WILLOUGHBY, Hannah 119
WILMARTH, Hiram 179
WILSON, ... 55
  David 179
  Ebenezer 186
  Elizabeth (Meloche) 133
  George 193
  Horace 171
  Jean Henry 77
  John 170, 185, 197, 218
  Juda (Denison) 110
  Lewis 110, 157
  Margan 206
  Moses 148
  Richard 216
  Samuel 133, 196
  Stephen 184
  William 176, 197, 210
WINCHAL, Mark 194
WINCHELL, David 204
  John 204
WINCHILL, Robert F. 186
WING, A. E. 172
  Austin E. 102
  Enoch 102
  Samuel 113, 155, 158
WINSLOW, David G. 185
WISBROOK, Andrew 195
  Andrew A. 195
  John H. 196
WISE, Jesse 157
WISEWELL, Oliver 78
WISMER, Morgan L. 180
WISMETT, Charles 171
WISNER, D. K. 203
WISSWELL, James 219
WITHERALD, James 151
WITHERELL, Amy 120
  Amy (Hawkins) 109
  F. G. H. 160
  Benjamin F. H. 120, 170
  Benjamin Franklin Hawkins 120
  Casandra (Brady) 120
  Delia (Ingersol) 120
  James 104, 109, 120, 128, 157, 167
  Mary Amy 104
  Mary Ann (Sprague) 120
  Sally Mira 128
WITHY, Orison 192
WITT, James 152
WITTER, Samuel 208
WIXOM, Benjamin P. 180
  Isaac 180
  Robert 182

## Index

WOHERTY, James 216
WOILLET, Alexander 89
   Alexr. 67
WOLCOTT, Chauncey D. 180
   Nelson 180
WOLVERTON, James B. 195
WOOD, Abner 205
   Clark 189
   Daniel 181
   Elizabeth 201
   Ira 197
   Jacob 179
   James 197
   John 184, 188
   Jonathan 205
   Joseph 173, 201
   Justus 172
   Lucy 179
   Reuben 155, 165
   Sanford 193
   Thomas 202
   Vinus 193
WOOD dit BOIS, Louis 218
WOODBRIDGE, Dudley 101
   William 101, 167
   Wm. 101
WOODBURY, Nancy 136
WOODCOCK, Isaac 154
WOODELS, Joel 78
WOODEN, Peter 203
WOODFORD, Solomon 180
WOODRUFF, Benjamin 197
   Elias 162
WOODS, James 153, 164, **222**
   John 216
   Mathew 167
   Matthew 155
WOODSWORTH, Samuel 217
WOODWARD, Jacob 189
   James 170
WOODWORTH, Benj. 101
   Benjamin 170
   Constant 202
WOOL, Henry 173
WOOLMAN, Hiram 194
WOOLSEY, John W. 170
WOOLVERTON, James B. 132

WOOSTER, Hinman 184
WORDEN, Isaac B. 176
   John S. 203
WORTHING, Winthrop 187
WORTHINGTON, Timothy 125
WRATH, Samuel 200
WRIGHT, ... 42
   Alice 105
   Elijah 189
   Henry 197
   James C. **219**
   Jno. 73
   Jobe 207
   John 82
   Phineas L. 194
   Rufus 199
   William B. 207
WYBROUGH, Wm. 215
WYNECORE, Henry 215

XAINTONGE, see Gareau dit St. Onge, Pierre 6

YACK, Bte 72
   Jean 71
   Jean Baptist 79
   Michel 78
   Pierre 71, 79
   Simon 71, 79
YACKS, Mich. 30
   Michael 40
YALE, John 196
   Michel 70
YARK, Michel 70
YARNS, George 208
YAX, see Yark 70
   Ann (Hathaway) 131
   Archange 144
   Archange (Seguin) 119
   Archange (Thomas) 132
   Baptist 132
   Bridget 129
   Catherine (Herbinne) 119
   Cecile 102
   Francis 132, 191
   Gilbert 191, 195
   Hubert 191
   J. Bte 131, 132, 144

YAX, John B. 195
   Joseph 132
   Lambert 131
   Michael 119, 132
   Michel 21, 32, 52, 53
   Monique (Huyet-Champagne) 129
   Peter 129
   Pierre 52, 90, 119, 129, 132, 160
   Regina Christina (Juyet-hampagne) 132
   Simon 89
   Teresa 116
   Teresa (Meny) 132
   Victoria (Labadie-Badichon) 132
YEAGER, Henry 154
YEAR, Joseph 132
YERKES, Joseph 155
   William 179
YERKUS, John 165
   Joseph 162
YOUNG, Daniel 216
   David 184
   Emanuel M. 184
   George 164
   James 189, 196, 215
   John 183
   Joseph 153
   Peter 78
YOUNGLOVE, Alexr. 157
   Catherine (Joncaire) 110
   Exra 160
   Ezra 110, 154
   Samuel 110
YOUNGS, John 197
YOUTRA, see Jutrat, Jean 48
YUON, Angelique 101, 145
   Archange 143
   Joseph 101, 142
   Joseph, see Evon, Joseph 142
   Margaret (Sordelier) 142

ZANES, Maxwell 207
ZUCK, Christian 199

## LAC SUPERIEUR

I. Minong
Michipico[...]
I. du Montreal
R. Betchumont
des Groseliers
Anse des Sauteur
du St Esprit
Ste Kiaonam
I. S. Michel
Village des Sauteur
Maison Françoise
Anse Kinonam
OUT
I. au Parisien
SauteMarie
Village d'Outaouacs
Isle et Habitation
Iles des
de Missilimakinak
Poutouatami
Manitouali
Lacs aux
Outaouacs
LAC
Baqueville
Anse au Tonnerre
au Raisin
Noire
R. Marquet
aux Ailes
Nation
des
LAC DES
Renards
au Canot Portage S. François
ILINOIS
R. des Renards
wconsin
Melloki R.
la Grande
o mine de plomp
R. Macame
R. au Parisien Maskoutés
R. Neve
ou Nation du feu
Chicagou R.
R. a la Roche
les
Kicapou
Christal
de roche
Oiatinon
Miamis
R. des Ilinois
Ouramani R.
R. des Ilinoi
Ouabache
t S. Louis appelle
cy devant F. Crevecoeur

ILINOIS